W9-CDT-503

THE COMPLETE WRITINGS
OF THUCYDIDES

THE PELOPONNESIAN WAR

THE COMPLETE WRITINGS OF

THUCYDIDES

THE PELOPONNESIAN WAR

*The unabridged Crawley translation with
an introduction by* JOHN H. FINLEY, JR.,
*Eliot Professor of Greek Literature,
Harvard University*

THE

MODERN LIBRARY

NEW YORK

THE MODERN LIBRARY
is published by RANDOM HOUSE, INC.

BENNETT CERF • DONALD S. KLOPFER

Manufactured in the United States of America by H. Wolff

INTRODUCTION

By John H. Finley, Jr.

THOUGH the exact dates of Thucydides' birth and death are unknown, he seems to have been a comparatively young man in the eighth year of the Peloponnesian War, 424 B.C., when he was elected an Athenian general, was stationed in Thrace, there failed to prevent the capture of Amphipolis by the gifted Spartan general Brasidas, and was punished by exile. He says (V 26) that his exile lasted twenty years—which is to say, for the rest of the war—and that during this time he had opportunity to associate with both sides. He belonged to a leading Athenian family, and doubtless had means for study, interview and travel. A later tradition of unknown reliability says that he continued to live in Thrace near the coast some distance east of the modern Salonika, where he himself says (IV 105) that he operated a gold mine, presumably a reason why he was originally sent to this fringe of the Greek world. He returned to Athens after the peace of 404, but hardly survived his return by many years, since the *History* is incomplete. It stops abruptly in the twenty-first year of the war, and the Eighth Book, which lacks speeches, seems in a less finished state than the other books, imperfect in some detail as these too may be.

On these assumptions, he was born around 460 and lived perhaps a few, certainly not many, years into the fourth century. He was thus two generations younger than Aeschylus (b. 525), who saw the overthrow of the tyrants, the creation of the democracy, and the brilliant repulse of Persia. He was a generation younger than Pericles (b. circ. 493), Sophocles, Phidias, Anaxagoras and Herodotus, men who in their different ways created and reflect the noonday of Athens. Midway in age between Euripides (b. 480) and Socrates (b. 469), on the one hand, and Aristophanes (b. circ. 445), on the other, he shared these men's analytical spirit, their social temper and emphasis, and their struggle towards rational generalization. He was the child of times when habits of thought and expression were changing fast, partly because of the war but chiefly through the now accomplished change of Athens herself from a secondary state to the recognized center of trade, inquiry and the arts.

To mention some of his contemporaries is to note a curious fact about him—his obscurity in an age when obscurity was uncommon. His exile is, of course, part of the explanation; he watched from a distance while others played parts on the bright and animated stage of Athenian life. From this isolation come traits suggestive of the later exile, Dante, and the cast-off politician, Machiavelli: detachment from, yet obsession with, politics, the observer's capacity to categorize and distill, joined with the suppressed passion bred of disappointment. But unlike these men, he gained no immediate compensation of fame. It is true that Xenophon and two other historians whose works are lost continued the *History* from where he dropped it; true also that those writers of the fourth century, notably Demosthenes and Isocrates, who most respected and understood the historical achievements of Attic democracy, show his influence. But Plato and Aristotle give few signs of valuing or even of knowing the *History,* naturally so, perhaps. The admirer of Pericles obviously has little to say to one who, in the *Gorgias,* condemns shipbuilding, harbors and walls as worse than a misuse of Pericles' leadership. Nor does Thucydides' attempt to find meaning and order beneath the surface confusion of history share the spirit of Aristotle's famous judgment that history is less philosophic than poetry. Full appreciation of Thucydides waited for Sallust and Tacitus and, in general, for those who witnessed in Rome a still more violent political evolution than that which he had observed and tried to analyze in Athens.

His obscurity during and just after his own time thus reflects not only his exile but in part his subject also, which is the analysis of political power. With Athens' defeat in the Peloponnesian War and the waning of her strength, the philosophers of the fourth century found in abstract and ideal analysis a center of interest less close to the violence of history than was his. They characteristically did not admire, as he did, either the enormous and confused creativity of the great age or the democracy which was its driving force. It is on first glance astonishing that the Athenians, who invented democracy, on the whole speak so badly of it. But such views reflect the defeat and disillusion of the fourth century; earlier writers, who knew the democracy at its greatest, had not discovered political theory. Thus Aeschylus, who shared the democracy's highest triumphs, reflects them, but not critically or literally, in his great themes and symbols, and Herodotus, whose admiration for Athens is unbounded, conceives of history as a pageant and spectacle to be described for its grandeur, not as a process to be analyzed for its motive forces. Hence it is that the *History,* virtually alone of Athenian writings, records analytically the creative workings of the first democracy, and, what is more, in a sympathetic spirit and from the point of view of an observer and pupil of events, not of a moralist and censor.

As noted, his subject is the analysis of political power. He says as much at the end of the well-known passage on his method (I 22): "The lack of the fabulous may make my work dull. But I shall be satisfied if it be thought useful by those who wish to know the exact character of events now past which, human nature being what it is, will recur in similar or analogous forms. It has not been composed to court temporary applause but as a lasting possession." The first and part of the last sentence glance somewhat acridly at the kind of narrative for which Herodotus was known. The main statement expresses a cyclical view of history by which future events repeat the shapes of past events and the past accordingly becomes the guide to the future. This view gives the work its purpose and prescribes somewhat secondarily its ideal of accuracy. For only if the past is exactly known can it become a reliable guide to the future. The *History* is sometimes described as if its chief merit were to have adumbrated the positivist ideal of historical accuracy which became widespread in the nineteenth century. Certainly Thucydides goes to great pains for accuracy. For instance, since the calendars of the Greek states differed and there was no single ruling chronology, he fixed (II 2) the outbreak of the war by reference

to Athens, Sparta and Argos, and then followed an annalistic
method, further subdividing each year into a winter season of
roughly five months and a campaigning season of the remainder, towards the beginning or end of which he could then
place events with some accuracy. He is punctilious in such de-
tails as the names of generals or rulers, the size and scope of
expeditions and the history of outlying places which were
touched by the war. Yet, to repeat, this ideal of accuracy is in
the end secondary. His first purpose is to elucidate the motives, policies, decisions and acts of leadership which dictated
the course of the war, since obviously only knowledge of these
could give posterity the instruction which he feels history
should give. He writes, in effect, a manual for future states-
men, explaining what were in his opinion the errors which cost
Athens the war despite her initial advantage. As annalist he is
interested in the exact course of events. As statesman and observer of policy, he is interested in the decisions prior to these
events, and it is this interest which is the stronger.

It may appear somewhat roundabout to turn at this point
to his style. Yet style prescribes the cast and mold of a man's
thought, which can be misunderstood if something other is
sought in a work than what the style requires. The earliest
Greek prose, which Herodotus is just transcending, used short
declarative statements with little emphasis or subordination.
It has something of the lucid freshness of the early books of
the Old Testament. At farthest remove from this nascent
prose is the so-called periodic style of Plato, Isocrates and the
writers of the fourth century generally. By studious subordination of minor points to the major idea of a sentence, it
achieves impressive organic unity but commonly at the cost
of sapping the vitality of subordinate ideas. This is the style
which, adopted from Isocrates by Cicero, passed from him
into the English cadences of Gibbon and Burke. Thucydides'
prose stands somewhere between these two, the simple and the
periodic, styles. His chief devices are antithesis, comparison
and contrast. Within any given sentence, clause will be paired
with clause, subject with subject, verb with verb. This elaborately antithetical method is more characteristic, to be sure,
of the speeches than of the common narrative. But when even
the narrative mounts to emphasis or generalization, the familiar pairing and contrast of ideas return, and the antithetical

style reasserts itself. It is a hard style, because the reader is never decisively directed to one of the proffered choices, but it is intensely vivid and living, because each element in each contrast stands out with a kind of tough, uncurbed vitality. It is a style of sharp and brilliant facets, rather than of organically rounded wholes.

The reason for thus dwelling on Thucydides' style is that, as suggested, it is not something that merely marks sentences; it shapes and directs his entire thought. The *History* itself can be said to fall into a few large antitheses and is most easily grasped when these are seen. Nor is this antithetical method one which Thucydides consciously chose from alternative possibilities. The sophistic movement, which was one of the two or three dominant intellectual forces of the time and the one by which he was most deeply influenced, represented in general the attempt to substitute prose, concept and analysis for poetry, myth and symbol as the chief means of interpreting life and society. This attempt gathered the greater force because, with the immense spread of communication and growth of knowledge which the Athenian empire elicited, society itself seemed to be changing and novelty was in the air. Having inherited only the simple style of the earliest prose, the first sophists evolved the more subtle manner which Thucydides took over and himself elaborated. It was antithetical because it was created for oral presentation of arguments on either side of a question. Moreover, style could hardly leap in a generation from its early artlessness to the self-confidence and finish of the fourth century, and there necessarily intervened a period of exuberance and experiment. In his boldness Thucydides may be contrasted with his measured and disciplined successors, much as Milton's or Browne's adventurous prose is contrasted with Addison's or Johnson's. In short, as heir and pupil of the sophists, Thucydides undertook the ambitious task of elucidating the movement of political power in his time, on the assumption that this movement of power would be relevant to future times also, and in a manner well adapted by its antithetical subtlety to express the social and moral dilemmas which the sophists had first expounded and which, in the peculiar circumstances of his life, he saw yet more intensely.

A final point should be made about his intellectual inheritance. The sophistic movement, if perhaps the greatest force in his time, was not without rivals in the time itself or in effect on him. In the second book (47–53) he describes the plague which in 430 first ravaged the population herded behind the city walls to escape the Spartan invasion. After stating that he himself fell ill, he goes on to a detailed catalogue of characteristic symptoms, in the hope, he says (II 48), that he may be of use towards its detection on any recurrence. This ideal of future usefulness is evidently much the same here as for the *History* as a whole. Now medicine was currently making brilliant advances, and some of the finest works which come down under the name of Hippocrates—for example, *Airs, Waters and Places, The Sacred Disease, The Epidemics* —date from this time. These works rest on the theory that every disease has its characteristic course, usually marked by certain days of crisis; hence that painstaking observation of symptoms will enable the physician to foresee the progress and often the outcome of an illness. Thucydides was unquestionably familiar with these ideas. They are visible not only in the predictive purpose of the work, but in the technical term (*prophasis,* I 23) which he uses to designate the cause of the war, and even perhaps in the assumption that the war, like disease, had certain turning points and times of crisis, which he marks by speeches and otherwise singles out. In contrast to the sophistic movement, which stressed dialectical analysis, this scientific school espoused rigor of observation. Such movements, of course, tend not to take place in isolation, and much else in the period—for example, advances in mathematics, in astronomy and the calendar, in city planning—convey a new admiration for exactitude and even for specialism. Thucydides seems uniquely to have combined these opposite tendencies of dialectic and observation, of generalization and exactitude, and it is another mark of the intensity which his exile bred that he could thus bend to his inclusive purpose these otherwise disparate ways of thought.

To turn then to the *History,* it has been stated that in the large, as in the small, the cast of Thucydides' thought is antithetical. Two dominant lines of antithesis control the work with different force at different times. The first is the contrast of Athens to Sparta, which is canvassed in detail at the start, reaches a climax in Athens' victory at Pylos in Book Four, and dies away with the spectacle in Books Six and Seven of the squandering at Syracuse of her once great superiority. The second is the contrast of the wisely led democracy of Pericles to the corrupt democracy of his successors, a theme broached with Pericles' speeches and the estimate of him in II 65, continued with the first symptoms of mistake and mis-government in the Mytilenean debate of Book Three, gen-eralized in the fearful analysis of revolution of III 82–83, made operative in the refusal of Sparta's offers of peace after Pylos, and reaching its height in the Melian Dialogue at the end of Book Five and the Sicilian disaster of Book Seven. These pairs of contrasts are not, of course, kept strictly sepa-rate. The contrast of Athens to Sparta is that of democracy to oligarchy, which in turn implies the contrast of the Periclean to the later democracy.

The initial contrast, which dominates the first two books, is made from many sides. Athens is the new, Sparta the estab-lished power; Athens' strength is naval, Sparta's military. Naval power reflects a commercial economy; military power, an agricultural economy. The former encourages enterprise and initiative; the latter, tenacity and tradition. Hence the one rests on democratic freedom; the other, on oligarchic dis-cipline. As said, the naval, commercial, democratic polity of Athens is far the more recent. The historian regards Themis-tocles as its creator, Pericles as its perfector. Accordingly its potential strength was not widely grasped, and when Pericles accepted Sparta's late challenge to a growth of power to which she had offered only slight opposition since the Persian wars, many foresaw Athens' quick defeat. Such was not Pericles' view, and one way of regarding the *History* is to see it as, in inception at least, an argument for the correctness of Pericles' insight as against that of the crowd. The innovating character of Athens' economy is set forth in the first nineteen sections of Book One, the so-called Archaeology, in which earlier aggregations of naval power, as far back as the Cretan and Mycenaean, are surveyed and found inferior to that of Athens. A later digression (I 89–118), the so-called Pente-contaëtia or history of the Fifty Years, sketches Athens' rise since the Persian wars. Thucydides evidently regarded naval power in Greek history as the key to dominance, fumblingly held in earlier eras, but grasped with genius in his own time. His many-sided initial contrast of Athens to Sparta establishes the superiority of the naval and commercial state in its interlocking aspects of freedom, energy, spirit of innovation, wealth and leadership.

The picture of Athens' initial, though ill appreciated, strength reaches its height in the three speeches and estimate of Pericles, which in turn prepare the way for the contrast of him to his successors. The celebrated Funeral Oration (II 35–46) is probably the greatest short analysis of the strength of democracy from any time, certainly from antiquity. "We love beauty with simplicity, we pursue wisdom without softness," sums up Pericles' optimistic confidence that personal satisfaction and growth need not impair vigor or corporate responsibility. "Every man among us is, if not an initiator, at least a judge of policy," expresses the democratic faith in open discussion and decision. The last speech (II 60–64), a defense of his policy delivered under the shadow of the plague, faces in harder tones the necessity of historical growth and change. Athens' empire, he says, is represented as an act of tyranny, but the world must change and creation will be admired in every age by those who feel the will to do. The realism of this speech, if one may venture such a judgment, seems particularly congenial to Thucydides. He makes clear from the outset the inevitable conflict between local independence and the growth of an embracing political system such as the Athenian Empire, which system, however, is the prerequisite of material progress. Further, the rise of Athens upset the traditional balance of power in Greece and the agricultural economy on which it rested. He says as much when he names Sparta's fear of Athens' growing power as the essential cause of the war (I 23). He accepts this necessity of change, and, taken together, the Funeral Oration and last speech represent the rise of Athens as not only a new phase in an inevitable and endless struggle for power but as embodying also a fresh and higher, if still imperfect, vision of growth and freedom.

Space forbids discussing at length the second part of the second contrast, that of Pericles' successors to himself. The plague (from which he died) and the many hardships attend-

ant on the war set up a vicious cycle whereby popular feeling
ran high and leaders played on this feeling. The ideal of tem-
perateness and unity presented in the Funeral Oration was
not in fact confirmed, and class struggle increasingly divided
Athens and other cities. Democracy was represented by Pericles as co-operative government by all citizens, rich and poor;
now, as later in Plato and Aristotle, it comes to mean dominance by the *demos*, narrowly defined as the proletariat. A
revolution in Corcyra prompts Thucydides to a terrifying
analysis of this change (III 82–3), whereby a middle faction
ceases to exist and the state is torn apart by factions of the
extreme, each supported by help from outside. The watch-cry
of the extreme democrats in Athens was a war of conquest.
The motives were partly self-advancement by leaders, partly
fear of oligarchy abroad and even at home, partly revenge for
the invasion of Attica and partly a vision of increased public
employment in an extended empire. The mood of fear is revealed in a debate on the punishment of Mytilene (III 37–
48), an allied city which had attempted revolt. Though rela-
tively mild counsels prevailed in the end, the debate shows a
new stridency and doubt of reason, and marks in Cleon the
rise of a politician who, unlike Pericles, had no wish to repress
such emotions.

The turning point in the first ten years of war was the
Athenian victory of Pylos, a victory achieved by the Periclean
strategy of encirclement and harrying of the Peloponnesus.
Terrified by visions of revolt among her subject population
and doubtful even of her time-honored military discipline,
which had not shown to advantage at Pylos, Sparta now
offered peace (IV 17–20). Pericles, whose view of the war was
defensive, would certainly have accepted it, but Cleon refused, urging a war of conquest (IV 21). This refusal establishes the pattern of the rest of the *History*. From now on
Athens no longer represents a hopeful and creative force
whose humanity, though imperfect, far surpasses the repres-
siveness of Sparta. She herself becomes the repressor and con-
queror. Reverses followed Pylos (it is now that Thucydides
is exiled), and with the death of Cleon and of the Spartan
Brasidas, the so-called Peace of Nicias is made in 421. But
with the rise of Pericles' ward and Cleon's far more gifted suc-

cessor, the brilliant and unstable Alcibiades, the war of conquest begins openly. Its tone is set in the bitter dialogue in
which the Athenians point out to the islanders of Melos the
unenviable role of weakness in a world dominated by force
(V 85–112). In the debate in Athens preceding the Sicilian
expedition, the change is evident in the helplessness of Nicias,
the timorous heir of Periclean moderation, and the confidence
of Alcibiades. As description, the account of the slow death at
Syracuse of Athens' strength and hope is Thucydides' master-
piece and one of the masterpieces of all historical writing. But
the main lines of evaluation are already drawn. Whether the
political folly of the Athenians led to Alcibiades' dismissal
from his command or his own weaknesses were his and his
country's undoing, a mood of fear, instability and division is
equally apparent. Had the *History* gone on to the final defeat
of 405, it would certainly have shown only a continued alter-
nation by which democracy endowed Athens with strength
beyond any of her rivals, yet robbed her of that strength by
political division.

Two final points remain, the one of substance, the other of
method. As for the former, the democratic government of
Athens, even at the time of her widest power, relied on methods adapted from the town meeting. The generals, who were
annually elected, could be questioned and even deposed at
stated monthly meetings of the assembly; and this same assembly could be packed by any faction which took the trouble.
Democratic government, always less decisive and certain of
its direction than are more authoritarian controls, is seen at
its most unstable and precarious in Athens, and the wonder is
not that it erred but that it showed such deep roots of strength.

This leads to the second point, which concerns Thucydides'
method, particularly in the speeches. He says (I 22) that the
speeches follow the main tenor of what was actually said, yet
present what he judges the essential elements of each succes-
sive situation. Obviously there might in theory be room here
for the rhetorical distortion which later became the vice of
ancient historiography. But history is not a science. Even the
most careful of modern historians must in the last analysis
separate what he judges the important from the unimportant,
and in this act of choice and emphasis his insight and depth of

experience reveal themselves. Thucydides is to be judged by these criteria of depth and insight. His method is what he makes of it. In his hands it becomes a means of selecting and exposing, with utmost presentness, the outlooks and states of mind of a static and a changing society and of democracy in its strength and weakness, together with those choices by which crucial change was brought about. History is to him the interplay of decisive personalities with a more impersonal movement of events. An almost subconscious tone of tragic necessity accompanies the optimistic assumption that mistakes could have been avoided by right judgment. The claim of permanent usefulness which he made for the *History* is justified in the sense that no historical work goes farther towards distilling the general trend from the specific occurrence, with due respect for each. It thus eminently reflects the mysterious ambiguity of history itself as between the unique and the typical, the novel and the recurrent.

BIBLIOGRAPHY

C. F. Abbott, *Thucydides: A Study in Historical Reality*. London: Routledge, 1925.

J. B. Bury, *The Ancient Greek Historians*. London: Macmillan, 1909.

C. N. Cochrane, *Thucydides and the Science of History*. Oxford, 1929.

F. M. Cornford, *Thucydides Mythistoricus*. London: Arnold, 1907.

J. H. Finley, Jr., *Thucydides*. Cambridge: Harvard University Press, 1942.

A. W. Gomme, *Essays in Greek History and Literature*. Oxford: Blackwell, 1937; also the introduction to his *Historical Commentary on Thucydides*. Oxford, 1945.

G. B. Grundy, *Thucydides and the History of His Age*. London: Murray, 1911. Second edition, Oxford: Blackwell, 1948.

B. W. Henderson, *The Great War between Athens and Sparta*. London: Macmillan, 1927.

W. W. Jaeger, "Thucydides: Political Philosopher," in *Paideia*, I, Bk. 2, ch. 6, transl. by G. Highet. New York: Oxford, 1939.

R. C. Jebb, "The Speeches of Thucydides," in *Essays and Addresses*. Cambridge, 1907; also in E. Abbott, *Hellenica*. London: Longmans, 2nd ed., 1898.

W. R. M. Lamb, *Clio Enthroned*, Cambridge, 1914.

R. W. Macan, "Herodotus and Thucydides," *Cambridge Ancient History*, V, 398–419.

P. Shorey, "Implicit Ethics and Psychology of Thucydides," *Trans. Amer. Philological Assoc.*, 1893, pp. 66–88.

A. Zimmern, "Thucydides the Imperialist," in *Solon and Croesus*. Oxford, 1928.

CONTENTS

BOOK I

BOOK II

BOOK III

CONTENTS

BOOK IV

GREECE
at the beginning of the
PELOPONNESIAN WAR
431 B.C.

Athens and Allies   Sparta and Allies

THRACE

Byzantium
Selymbria
Perinthus
DORISCUS
Propontis
Calchedon
Cyzicus

MACEDONIA
Pella
Amphipolis
Thasos
Therma
CHALCIDICE
Acanthus
Samothracia
Ægospotami
Chersonese
Sestus
Lampsacus
Imbros
Abydos
PHRYGIA
Pydna
Potidæa
Olynthus
Torone
Lemnos
Hellespont
Mende
Scione

Antandrus

Macestus R.

ÆGEAN

Larissa
Peneus R.
THESSALY
Pharsalus

Methymna
Lesbos
Mitylene
Pergamum

SEA

Scyrus
Arginusæ Is.
Phocæa
Cyme
Hermus R.
Sardis

MALIS

DORIS
Delphi
Chaeronea
BŒOTIA
EUBŒA
Chalcis
Eretria

Chios
Chios
Clazomenæ

ÆTOLIA

Colophon
Ephesus
Mæander R.

ACHAIA
Patræ
Sicyon
Corinth
Thespiae
Plataea
Thebes
Decelea
ATHENS
Megara
Eleusis

Andros
Samos
Icaria
Samos

Miletus

ELIS
Olympia
ARCADIA
Mantineae
Argos
Argolis
Epidaurus
Ægina
Troezen
Hermione

Ceos
Tenos
Mykonos
Delos

Halicarnassus

Cythnus
Syrus
Paros
Siphnus

Naxos

Cos

SPORADES

Cnidus

ITHOME
MESSENIA
Pylus
Sphacteria I.
Methone
Thyrea
LACONIA
SPARTA

Amorgus
Ios
Melos
Thera

CYCLADES

Lindus

RHODES

Cythera

Carpathus

Casus

Cydonia
Cnossus
CRETE
Gortyna

N

Scale of Miles

0   50   100   200

R. W. Galvin, Cart.

THE COMPLETE WRITINGS
OF THUCYDIDES

THE PELOPONNESIAN WAR

BOOK I

CHAPTER I

THE STATE OF GREECE FROM THE EARLIEST TIMES TO THE COMMENCEMENT OF THE PELOPONNESIAN WAR

Hellas in ancient times—Origin of name 'Hellenes'—Piracy—Agamemnon's power—Character of ancient expeditions—Hellas after the Trojan war—B.C. 705-521: Rise of navies—B.C. 546-480: Tyrants as obstacles to national growth; Marathon and Salamis—B.C. 476-431: The Lacedæmonian confederacy and the Athenian empire—Historical fallacies—Sources of this history—War inevitable.

THUCYDIDES, an Athenian, wrote the history of the war between the Peloponnesians and the Athenians, beginning at the moment that it broke out, and believing that it would be a great war, and more worthy of relation than any that had preceded it. This belief was not without its grounds. The preparations of both the combatants were in every department in the last state of perfection: and he could see the rest of the Hellenic race taking sides in the quarrel; those who delayed doing so at once having it in contemplation. Indeed this was the greatest movement yet known in history, not only of the Hellenes, but of a large part of the barbarian world—I had almost said of mankind. For though the events of remote antiquity, and even those that more immediately precede the war, could not from lapse of time be clearly ascertained, yet the evidences which an inquiry carried as far back as was practicable leads me to trust, all point to the conclusion that there was nothing on a great scale, either in war or in other matters.

For instance, it is evident that the country now called Hellas had in ancient times no settled population; on the contrary, migrations were of frequent occurrence, the several tribes readily abandoning their homes under the pressure of superior numbers. Without commerce, without freedom of communication either by land or sea, cultivating no more of their territory than the exigencies of life required, destitute of capital, never planting their land (for they could not tell when an invader might not come and take it all away, and when he did come they had no walls to stop him), thinking that the necessities of daily sustenance could be supplied at one place as well as another, they cared little for shifting their habitation, and consequently neither built large cities nor attained to any other form of greatness. The richest soils were always most subject to this change of masters; such as the district now called Thessaly, Bœotia, most of the Peloponnese, Arcadia excepted, and the most fertile parts of the rest of Hellas. The goodness of the land favoured the aggrandisement of particular individuals, and thus created faction which proved a fertile source of ruin. It also invited invasion. Accordingly Attica, from the poverty of its soil enjoying from a very remote period freedom from faction, never changed its inhabitants. And here is no inconsiderable exemplification of my assertion, that the migrations were the cause of there being no correspondent growth in other parts. The most powerful victims of war or faction from the rest of Hellas took refuge with the Athenians as a safe retreat; and at an early period, becoming naturalised, swelled the already large population of the city to such a height that Attica became at last too small to hold them, and they had to send out colonies to Ionia.

There is also another circumstance that contributes not a little to my conviction of the weakness of ancient times. Before the Trojan war there is no indication of any common action in Hellas, nor indeed of the universal prevalence of the name; on the contrary, before the time of Hellen, son of Deucalion, no such appellation existed, but the country went by the names of the different tribes, in particular of the Pelasgian. It was not till Hellen and his sons grew strong in Phthiotis, and were invited as allies into the other cities, that one by one they gradually acquired from the connection the name of Hellenes; though a long time elapsed before that name could fasten itself upon all. The best proof of this is furnished by Homer. Born long after the Trojan war, he nowhere calls all of them by that name, nor indeed any of them except the followers of Achilles from Phthiotis, who were the original Hellenes: in his poems they are called Danaans,

Argives, and Achæans. He does not even use the term barbarian, probably because the Hellenes had not yet been
marked off from the rest of the world by one distinctive
appellation. It appears therefore that the several Hellenic
communities, comprising not only those who first acquired the
name, city by city, as they came to understand each other, but
also those who assumed it afterwards as the name of the whole
people, were before the Trojan war prevented by their want
of strength and the absence of mutual intercourse from displaying any collective action.

Indeed, they could not unite for this expedition till they
had gained increased familiarity with the sea. And the first
person known to us by tradition as having established a navy
is Minos. He made himself master of what is now called the
Hellenic sea, and ruled over the Cyclades, into most of which
he sent the first colonies, expelling the Carians and appointing
his own sons governors; and thus did his best to put down
piracy in those waters, a necessary step to secure the revenues
for his own use.

For in early times the Hellenes and the barbarians of the
coast and islands, as communication by sea became more
common, were tempted to turn pirates, under the conduct of
their most powerful men; the motives being to serve their own
cupidity and to support the needy. They would fall upon a
town unprotected by walls, and consisting of a mere collec-
tion of villages, and would plunder it; indeed, this came to be
the main source of their livelihood, no disgrace being yet
attached to such an achievement, but even some glory. An
illustration of this is furnished by the honour with which some
of the inhabitants of the continent still regard a successful
marauder, and by the question we find the old poets everywhere representing the people as asking of voyagers—'Are
they pirates?'—as if those who are asked the question would
have no idea of disclaiming the imputation, or their interroga-
tors of reproaching them for it. The same rapine prevailed
also by land.

And even at the present day many parts of Hellas still follow the old fashion, the Ozolian Locrians, for instance, the
Ætolians, the Acarnanians, and that region of the continent;
and the custom of carrying arms is still kept up among these

continentals, from the old piratical habits. The whole of Hellas used once to carry arms, their habitations being unprotected, and their communication with each other unsafe; indeed, to wear arms was as much a part of everyday life with them as with the barbarians. And the fact that the people in these parts of Hellas are still living in the old way points to a time when the same mode of life was once equally common to all. The Athenians were the first to lay aside their weapons, and to adopt an easier and more luxurious mode of life; indeed, it is only lately that their rich old men left off the luxury of wearing undergarments of linen, and fastening a knot of their hair with a tie of golden grasshoppers, a fashion which spread to their Ionian kindred, and long prevailed among the old men there. On the contrary a modest style of dressing, more in conformity with modern ideas, was first adopted by the Lacedæmonians, the rich doing their best to assimilate their way of life to that of the common people. They also set the example of contending naked, publicly stripping and anointing themselves with oil in their gymnastic exercises. Formerly, even in the Olympic contests, the athletes who contended wore belts across their middles; and it is but a few years since that the practice ceased. To this day among some of the barbarians, especially in Asia, when prizes for boxing and wrestling are offered, belts are worn by the combatants. And there are many other points in which a likeness might be shown between the life of the Hellenic world of old and the barbarian of to-day.

With respect to their towns, later on, at an era of increased facilities of navigation and a greater supply of capital, we find the shores becoming the site of walled towns, and the isthmuses being occupied for the purposes of commerce, and defence against a neighbour. But the old towns, on account of the great prevalence of piracy, were built away from the sea, whether on the islands or the continent, and still remain in their old sites. For the pirates used to plunder one another, and indeed all coast populations, whether seafaring or not.

The islanders, too, were great pirates. These islanders were Carians and Phœnicians, by whom most of the islands were colonised, as was proved by the following fact. During the purification of Delos by Athens in this war all the graves in the island were taken up, and it was found that above half

their inmates were Carians: they were identified by the
fashion of the arms buried with them, and by the method of
interment, which was the same as the Carians still follow. But
as soon as Minos had formed his navy, communication by sea
became easier, as he colonised most of the islands, and thus
expelled the malefactors. The coast populations now began to
apply themselves more closely to the acquisition of wealth,
and their life became more settled; some even began to build
themselves walls on the strength of their newly-acquired
riches. For the love of gain would reconcile the weaker to the
dominion of the stronger, and the possession of capital enabled
the more powerful to reduce the smaller towns to subjection.
And it was at a somewhat later stage of this development that
they went on the expedition against Troy.

What enabled Agamemnon to raise the armament was more,
in my opinion, his superiority in strength, than the oaths of
Tyndareus, which bound the Suitors to follow him. Indeed,
the account given by those Peloponnesians who have been the
recipients of the most credible tradition is this. First of all
Pelops, arriving among a needy population from Asia with
vast wealth, acquired such power that, stranger though he
was, the country was called after him; and this power fortune
saw fit materially to increase in the hands of his descendants.
Eurystheus had been killed in Attica by the Heraclids. Atreus
was his mother's brother; and to the hands of his relation,
who had left his father on account of the death of Chrysippus,
Eurystheus, when he set out on his expedition, had committed
Mycenæ and the government. As time went on and Eurystheus
did not return, Atreus complied with the wishes of the Myce-
næans, who were influenced by fear of the Heraclids,—besides,
his power seemed considerable, and he had not neglected to
court the favour of the populace,—and assumed the sceptre of
Mycenæ and the rest of the dominions of Eurystheus. And so
the power of the descendants of Pelops came to be greater
than that of the descendants of Perseus. To all this Agamemnon succeeded. He had also a navy far stronger than his contemporaries, so that, in my opinion, fear was quite as strong
an element as love in the formation of the confederate expedition. The strength of his navy is shown by the fact that his
own was the largest contingent, and that of the Arcadians was

furnished by him; this at least is what Homer says, if his testimony is deemed sufficient. Besides, in his account of the transmission of the sceptre, he calls him

'Of many an isle, and of all Argos king.'

Now Agamemnon's was a continental power; and he could not have been master of any except the adjacent islands (and these would not be many), but through the possession of a fleet.

And from this expedition we may infer the character of earlier enterprises. Now Mycenæ may have been a small place, and many of the towns of that age may appear comparatively insignificant, but no exact observer would therefore feel justified in rejecting the estimate given by the poets and by tradition of the magnitude of the armament. For I suppose if Lacedæmon were to become desolate, and the temples and the foundations of the public buildings were left, that as time went on there would be a strong disposition with posterity to refuse to accept her fame as a true exponent of her power. And yet they occupy two-fifths of Peloponnese and lead the whole, not to speak of their numerous allies without. Still, as the city is neither built in a compact form nor adorned with magnificent temples and public edifices, but composed of villages after the old fashion of Hellas, there would be an impression of inadequacy. Whereas, if Athens were to suffer the same misfortune, I suppose that any inference from the appearance presented to the eye would make her power to have been twice as great as it is. We have therefore no right to be sceptical, nor to content ourselves with an inspection of a town to the exclusion of a consideration of its power; but we may safely conclude that the armament in question surpassed all before it, as it fell short of modern efforts; if we can here also accept the testimony of Homer's poems, in which, without allowing for the exaggeration which a poet would feel himself licensed to employ, we can see that it was far from equalling ours. He has represented it as consisting of twelve hundred vessels; the Bœotian complement of each ship being a hundred and twenty men, that of the ships of Philoctetes fifty. By this, I conceive, he meant to convey the maximum and the minimum complement: at any rate he does not specify the amount of any others in his catalogue of the ships. That they were all rowers as well as warriors we see from his account of the ships of Philoctetes, in which all the men at the oar are bowmen. Now it is improbable that many supernumeraries sailed if we except the kings and high officers; especially as they had to cross the open sea with munitions of war, in ships, moreover, that had no decks, but were equipped in the old piratical fashion. So that if we strike the average of the largest and smallest ships, the number of those who sailed will appear inconsiderable, representing, as they did, the whole force of Hellas. And this was due not so much to scarcity of men as of money. Difficulty of subsistence made the invaders reduce the numbers of the army to a point at which it might live on the country during the prosecution of the war. Even after the victory they obtained on their arrival—and a victory there must have been, or the fortifications of the naval camp could never have been built—there is no indication of their whole force having been employed; on the contrary, they seem to have turned to cultivation of the Chersonese and to piracy from want of supplies. This was what really enabled the Trojans to keep the field for ten years against them; the dispersion of the enemy making them always a match for the detachment left behind. If they had brought plenty of supplies with them, and had persevered in the war without scattering for piracy and agriculture, they would have easily defeated the Trojans in the field; since they could hold their own against them with the division on service. In short, if they had stuck to the siege, the capture of Troy would have cost them less time and less trouble. But as want of money proved the weakness of earlier expeditions, so from the same cause even the one in question, more famous than its predecessors, may be pronounced on the evidence of what it effected to have been inferior to its renown and to the current opinion about it formed under the tuition of the poets.

Even after the Trojan war Hellas was still engaged in removing and settling, and thus could not attain to the quiet which must precede growth. The late return of the Hellenes from Ilium caused many revolutions, and factions ensued almost everywhere; and it was the citizens thus driven into exile who founded the cities. Sixty years after the capture of

Ilium the modern Bœotians were driven out of Arne by the Thessalians, and settled in the present Bœotia, the former Cadmeis; though there was a division of them there before, some of whom joined the expedition to Ilium. Twenty years later the Dorians and the Heraclids became masters of Peloponnese; so that much had to be done and many years had to elapse before Hellas could attain to a durable tranquillity undisturbed by removals, and could begin to send out colonies, as Athens did to Ionia and most of the islands, and the Peloponnesians to most of Italy and Sicily and some places in the rest of Hellas. All these places were founded subsequently to the war with Troy.

But as the power of Hellas grew, and the acquisition of wealth became more an object, the revenues of the states increasing, tyrannies were by their means established almost everywhere,—the old form of government being hereditary monarchy with definite prerogatives,—and Hellas began to fit out fleets and apply herself more closely to the sea. It is said that the Corinthians were the first to approach the modern style of naval architecture, and that Corinth was the first place in Hellas where galleys were built; and we have Ameinocles, a Corinthian shipwright, making four ships for the Samians. Dating from the end of this war, it is nearly three hundred years ago that Ameinocles went to Samos. Again, the earliest sea-fight in history was between the Corinthians and Corcyræans; this was about two hundred and sixty years ago, dating from the same time. Planted on an isthmus, Corinth had from time out of mind been a commercial emporium; as formerly almost all communication between the Hellenes within and without Peloponnese was carried on overland, and the Corinthian territory was the highway through which it travelled. She had consequently great money resources, as is shown by the epithet 'wealthy' bestowed by the old poets on the place, and this enabled her, when traffic by sea became more common, to procure her navy and put down piracy; and as she could offer a mart for both branches of the trade, she acquired for herself all the power which a large revenue affords. Subsequently the Ionians attained to great naval strength in the reign of Cyrus, the first king of the Persians, and of his son Cambyses, and while they were at war with the former commanded for a while the Ionian sea. Polycrates also, the tyrant of Samos, had a powerful navy in the reign of Cambyses with which he reduced many of the islands, and among them Rhenea, which he consecrated to the Delian Apollo. About this time also the Phocæans, while they were founding Marseilles, defeated the Carthaginians in a sea-fight. These were the most powerful navies. And even these, although so many generations had elapsed since the Trojan war, seem to have been principally composed of the old fifty-oars and long-boats, and to have counted few galleys among their ranks. Indeed it was only shortly before the Persian war and the death of Darius the successor of Cambyses, that the Sicilian tyrants and the Corcyræans acquired any large number of galleys. For after these there were no navies of any account in Hellas till the expedition of Xerxes; Ægina, Athens, and others may have possessed a few vessels, but they were principally fifty-oars. It was quite at the end of this period that the war with Ægina and the prospect of the barbarian invasion enabled Themistocles to persuade the Athenians to build the fleet with which they fought at Salamis; and even these vessels had not complete decks.

The navies, then, of the Hellenes during the period we have traversed were what I have described. All their insignificance did not prevent their being an element of the greatest power to those who cultivated them, alike in revenue and in dominion. They were the means by which the islands were reached and reduced, those of the smallest area falling the easiest prey. Wars by land there were none, none at least by which power was acquired; we have the usual border contests, but of distant expeditions with conquest for object we hear nothing among the Hellenes. There was no union of subject cities round a great state, no spontaneous combination of equals for confederate expeditions; what fighting there was consisted merely of local warfare between rival neighbours. The nearest approach to a coalition took place in the old war between Chalcis and Eretria; this was a quarrel in which the rest of the Hellenic name did to some extent take sides.

Various, too, were the obstacles which the national growth encountered in various localities. The power of the Ionians was advancing with rapid strides, when it came into collision with Persia, under King Cyrus, who, after having dethroned Crœsus and overrun everything between the Halys and the sea, stopped not till he had reduced the cities of the coast; the islands being only left to be subdued by Darius and the Phœnician navy. Again, wherever there were tyrants, their habit of providing simply for themselves, of looking solely to their personal comfort and family aggrandisement, made safety the great aim of their policy, and prevented anything great proceeding from them; though they would each have their affairs with their immediate neighbours. All this is only true of the mother country, for in Sicily they attained to very great power. Thus for a long time everywhere in Hellas do we find causes which make the states alike incapable of combination for great and national ends, or of any vigorous action of their own.

But at last a time came when the tyrants of Athens and the far older tyrannies of the rest of Hellas were, with the exception of those in Sicily, once and for all put down by Lacedæmon; for this city, though after the settlement of the Dorians, its present inhabitants, it suffered from factions for an unparalleled length of time, still at a very early period obtained good laws, and enjoyed a freedom from tyrants which was unbroken; it has possessed the same form of government for more than four hundred years, reckoning to the end of the late war, and has thus been in a position to arrange the affairs of the other states. Not many years after the deposition of the tyrants, the battle of Marathon was fought between the Medes and the Athenians. Ten years afterwards the barbarian returned with the armada for the subjugation of Hellas. In the face of this great danger the command of the confederate Hellenes was assumed by the Lacedæmonians in virtue of their superior power; and the Athenians having made up their minds to abandon their city, broke up their homes, threw themselves into their ships, and became a naval people. This coalition, after repulsing the barbarian, soon afterwards split into two sections, which included the Hellenes who had revolted from the king, as well as those who had aided him in the war. At the head of the one stood Athens, at the head of the other Lacedæmon, one the first naval, the other the first military power in Hellas. For a short time the league held together, till the Lacedæmonians and Athenians quarrelled, and made war upon each other with their allies, a duel into which all the Hellenes sooner or later were drawn, though some might at first remain neutral. So that the whole period from the Median war to this, with some peaceful intervals, was spent by each power in war, either with its rival, or with its own revolted allies, and consequently afforded them constant practice in military matters, and that experience which is learnt in the school of danger.

The policy of Lacedæmon was not to exact tribute from her allies, but merely to secure their subservience to her interests by establishing oligarchies among them; Athens, on the contrary, had by degrees deprived hers of their ships, and imposed instead contributions in money on all except Chios and Lesbos. Both found their resources for this war separately to exceed the sum of their strength when the alliance flourished intact.

Having now given the result of my inquiries into early times, I grant that there will be a difficulty in believing every particular detail. The way that most men deal with traditions, even traditions of their own country, is to receive them all alike as they are delivered, without applying any critical test whatever. The general Athenian public fancy that Hipparchus was tyrant when he fell by the hands of Harmodius and Aristogiton; not knowing that Hippias, the eldest of the sons of Pisistratus, was really supreme, and that Hipparchus and Thessalus were his brothers; and that Harmodius and Aristogiton suspecting, on the very day, nay at the very moment fixed on for the deed, that information had been conveyed to Hippias by their accomplices, concluded that he had been warned, and did not attack him, yet, not liking to be apprehended and risk their lives for nothing, fell upon Hipparchus near the temple of the daughters of Leos, and slew him as he was arranging the Panathenaic procession.

There are many other unfounded ideas current among the rest of the Hellenes, even on matters of contemporary history which have not been obscured by time. For instance, there is the notion that the Lacedæmonian kings have two votes each, the fact being that they have only one; and that there is a company of Pitane, there being simply no such thing. So little pains do the vulgar take in the investigation of truth, accepting readily the first story that comes to hand. On the whole, however, the conclusions I have drawn from the proofs quoted may, I believe, safely be relied on. Assuredly they will not be disturbed either by the lays of a poet displaying the exaggeration of his craft, or by the compositions of the chroniclers that are attractive at truth's expense; the subjects they treat of being out of the reach of evidence, and time having robbed most of them of historical value by enthroning them in the region of legend. Turning from these, we can rest satisfied with having proceeded upon the clearest data, and having arrived at conclusions as exact as can be expected in matters of such antiquity. To come to this war; despite the known disposition of the actors in a struggle to overrate its importance, and when it is over to return to their admiration of earlier events, yet an examination of the facts will show that it was much greater than the wars which preceded it.

With reference to the speeches in this history, some were delivered before the war began, others while it was going on; some I heard myself, others I got from various quarters; it was in all cases difficult to carry them word for word in one's memory, so my habit has been to make the speakers say what was in my opinion demanded of them by the various occasions, of course adhering as closely as possible to the general sense of what they really said. And with reference to the narrative of events, far from permitting myself to derive it from the first source that came to hand, I did not even trust my own impressions, but it rests partly on what I saw myself, partly on what others saw for me, the accuracy of the report being always tried by the most severe and detailed tests possible. My conclusions have cost me some labour from the want of coincidence between accounts of the same occurrences by different eye-witnesses, arising sometimes from imperfect memory, sometimes from undue partiality for one side or the other. The absence of romance in my history will, I fear, detract somewhat from its interest; but if it be judged useful by those inquirers who desire an exact knowledge of the past as an aid to the interpretation of the future, which in the course of human things must resemble if it does not reflect it, I shall be content. In fine, I have written my work, not as an essay which is to win the applause of the moment, but as a possession for all time.

The Median war, the greatest achievement of past times, yet found a speedy decision in two actions by sea and two by land. The Peloponnesian war was prolonged to an immense length, and long as it was it was short without parallel for the misfortunes that it brought upon Hellas. Never had so many cities been taken and laid desolate, here by the barbarians, here by the parties contending (the old inhabitants being sometimes removed to make room for others); never was there so much banishing and blood-shedding, now on the field of battle, now in the strife of action. Old stories of occurrences handed down by tradition, but scantily confirmed by experience, suddenly ceased to be incredible; there were earthquakes of unparalleled extent and violence; eclipses of the sun occurred with a frequency unrecorded in previous history; there were great droughts in sundry places and consequent famines, and that most calamitous and awfully fatal visitation, the plague. All this came upon them with the late war, which was begun by the Athenians and Peloponnesians by the dissolution of the thirty years' truce made after the conquest of Eubœa. To the question why they broke the treaty, I answer by placing first an account of their grounds of complaint and points of difference, that no one may ever have to ask the immediate cause which plunged the Hellenes into a war of such magnitude. The real cause I consider to be the one which was formally most kept out of sight. The growth of the power of Athens, and the alarm which this inspired in Lacedæmon, made war inevitable. Still it is well to give the grounds alleged by either side, which led to the dissolution of the treaty and the breaking out of the war.

CHAPTER II

CAUSES OF THE WAR—THE AFFAIR OF EPIDAMNUS—
THE AFFAIR OF POTIDÆA

*The plight of the Epidamnians—*B.C. 436: *Corinth sends aid—Corcyra
besieges Epidamnus—*B.C. 435: *War declared between Corcyra and
Corinth; defeat of Corinth—*B.C. 434-433: *Corinth prepares—
Corcyra sends embassy to Athens—Their ambassador's plea for
alliance—The Corinthian's reply—*B.C. 432: *Defensive alliance between Athens and Corcyra—Naval battle between Corinthians
and Corcyræans—Athenians join engagement—Both sides claim
victory—*B.C. 432: *Revolt of Potidæa—Defeat of Potidæans.*

THE city of Epidamnus stands on the right of the entrance
of the Ionic gulf. Its vicinity is inhabited by the Taulantians,
an Illyrian people. The place is a colony from Corcyra,
founded by Phalius, son of Eratocleides, of the family of the
Heraclids, who had according to ancient usage been summoned for the purpose from Corinth, the mother country. The
colonists were joined by some Corinthians, and others of the
Dorian race. Now, as time went on, the city of Epidamnus
became great and populous; but falling a prey to factions arising, it is said, from a war with her neighbours the barbarians,
she became much enfeebled, and lost a considerable amount
of her power. The last act before the war was the expulsion
of the nobles by the people. The exiled party joined the barbarians, and proceeded to plunder those in the city by sea and
land; and the Epidamnians finding themselves hard pressed,
sent ambassadors to Corcyra beseeching their mother country
not to allow them to perish, but to make up matters between
them and the exiles, and to rid them of the war with the barbarians. The ambassadors seated themselves in the temple of
Hera as suppliants, and made the above requests to the Corcyræans. But the Corcyræans refused to accept their supplication, and they were dismissed without having effected anything.

When the Epidamnians found that no help could be expected from Corcyra, they were in a strait what to do next. So
they sent to Delphi and inquired of the god, whether they
should deliver their city to the Corinthians, and endeavour
to obtain some assistance from their founders. The answer he

gave them was to deliver the city, and place themselves under Corinthian protection. So the Epidamnians went to Corinth, and delivered over the colony in obedience to the commands of the oracle. They showed that their founder came from Corinth, and revealed the answer of the god; and they begged them not to allow them to perish, but to assist them. This the Corinthians consented to do. Believing the colony to belong as much to themselves as to the Corcyræans, they felt it to be a kind of duty to undertake their protection. Besides, they hated the Corcyræans for their contempt of the mother country. Instead of meeting with the usual honours accorded to the parent city by every other colony at public assemblies, such as precedence at sacrifices, Corinth found herself treated with contempt by a power, which in point of wealth could stand comparison with any even of the richest communities in Hellas, which possessed great military strength, and which sometimes could not repress a pride in the high naval position of an island whose nautical renown dated from the days of its old inhabitants, the Phæacians. This was one reason of the care that they lavished on their fleet, which became very efficient; indeed they began the war with a force of a hundred and twenty galleys.

All these grievances made Corinth eager to send the promised aid to Epidamnus. Advertisement was made for volunteer settlers, and a force of Ambraciots, Leucadians, and Corinthians was despatched. They marched by land to Apollonia, a Corinthian colony, the route by sea being avoided from fear of Corcyræan interruption. When the Corcyræans heard of the arrival of the settlers and troops in Epidamnus, and the surrender of the colony to Corinth, they took fire. Instantly putting to sea with five-and-twenty ships, which were quickly followed by others, they insolently commanded the Epidamnians to receive back the banished nobles—(it must be premised that the Epidamnian exiles had come to Corcyra, and pointing to the sepulchres of their ancestors, had appealed to their kindred to restore them)—and to dismiss the Corinthian garrison and settlers. But to all this the Epidamnians turned a deaf ear. Upon this the Corcyræans commenced operations against them with a fleet of forty sail. They took with them the exiles, with a view to their restoration, and

also secured the services of the Illyrians. Sitting down before
the city, they issued a proclamation to the effect that any of
the natives that chose, and the foreigners, might depart un-
harmed, with the alternative of being treated as enemies. On
their refusal the Corcyræans proceeded to besiege the city,
which stands on an isthmus; and the Corinthians, receiving
intelligence of the investment of Epidamnus, got together an
armament and proclaimed a colony to Epidamnus, perfect
political equality being guaranteed to all who chose to go.
Any who were not prepared to sail at once, might by paying
down the sum of fifty Corinthian drachmæ have a share in
the colony without leaving Corinth. Great numbers took advantage of this proclamation, some being ready to start
directly, others paying the requisite forfeit. In case of their
passage being disputed by the Corcyræans, several cities were
asked to lend them a convoy. Megara prepared to accompany
them with eight ships, Pale in Cephallonia with four; Epidaurus furnished five, Hermione one, Trœzen two, Leucas
ten, and Ambracia eight. The Thebans and Phliasians were
asked for money, the Eleans for hulls as well; while Corinth
herself furnished thirty ships and three thousand heavy infantry.

When the Corcyræans heard of their preparations they came
to Corinth with envoys from Lacedæmon and Sicyon, whom
they persuaded to accompany them, and bade her recall the
garrison and settlers, as she had nothing to do with Epidamnus. If, however, she had any claims to make, they were willing to submit the matter to the arbitration of such of the cities
in Peloponnese as should be chosen by mutual agreement, and
that the colony should remain with the city to whom the arbi-
trators might assign it. They were also willing to refer the
matter to the oracle at Delphi. If, in defiance of their protesta-
tions, war was appealed to, they should be themselves compelled by this violence to seek friends in quarters where they
had no desire to seek them, and to make even old ties give way
to the necessity of assistance. The answer they got from
Corinth was, that if they would withdraw their fleet and the
barbarians from Epidamnus negotiation might be possible;
but, while the town was still being besieged, going before arbi-
trators was out of the question. The Corcyræans retorted that

if Corinth would withdraw her troops from Epidamnus they
would withdraw theirs, or they were ready to let both parties
remain *in statu quo,* an armistice being concluded till judgment could be given.

Turning a deaf ear to all these proposals, when their ships
were manned and their allies had come in, the Corinthians
sent a herald before them to declare war, and getting under
weigh with seventy-five ships and two thousand heavy infantry, sailed for Epidamnus to give battle to the Corcyræans.
The fleet was under the command of Aristeus, son of Pellichas,
Callicrates, son of Callias, and Timanor, son of Timanthes;
the troops under that of Archetimus, son of Eurytimus, and
Isarchidas, son of Isarchus. When they had reached Actium
in the territory of Anactorium, at the mouth of the gulf of
Ambracia, where the temple of Apollo stands, the Corcyræans
sent on a herald in a light boat to warn them not to sail against
them. Meanwhile they proceeded to man their ships, all of
which had been equipped for action, the old vessels being
undergirded to make them seaworthy. On the return of the
herald without any peaceful answer from the Corinthians, their
ships being now manned, they put out to sea to meet the
enemy with a fleet of eighty sail (forty were engaged in the
siege of Epidamnus), formed line and went into action, and
gained a decisive victory, and destroyed fifteen of the Corinthian vessels. The same day had seen Epidamnus compelled
by its besiegers to capitulate; the conditions being that the
foreigners should be sold, and the Corinthians kept as
prisoners of war, till their fate should be otherwise decided.

After the engagement the Corcyræans set up a trophy on
Leukimme, a headland of Corcyra, and slew all their captives
except the Corinthians, whom they kept as prisoners of war.
Defeated at sea, the Corinthians and their allies repaired
home, and left the Corcyræans masters of all the sea about
those parts. Sailing to Leucas, a Corinthian colony, they
ravaged their territory, and burnt Cyllene, the harbour of the
Eleans, because they had furnished ships and money to
Corinth. For almost the whole of the period that followed the
battle they remained masters of the sea, and the allies of
Corinth were harassed by Corcyræan cruisers. At last Corinth,
roused by the sufferings of her allies, sent out ships and troops

in the fall of the summer, who formed an encampment at Actium and about Chimerium, in Thesprotis, for the protection of Leucas and the rest of the friendly cities. The Corcyræans on their part formed a similar station on Leukimme. Neither party made any movement, but they remained confronting each other till the end of the summer, and winter was at hand before either of them returned home.

Corinth, exasperated by the war with the Corcyræans, spent the whole of the year after the engagement and that succeeding it in building ships, and in straining every nerve to form an efficient fleet; rowers being drawn from Peloponnese and the rest of Hellas by the inducement of large bounties. The Corcyræans, alarmed at the news of their preparations, being without a single ally in Hellas (for they had not enrolled themselves either in the Athenian or in the Lacedæmonian confederacy), decided to repair to Athens in order to enter into alliance, and to endeavour to procure support from her. Corinth also, hearing of their intentions, sent an embassy to Athens to prevent the Corcyræan navy being joined by the Athenian, and her prospect of ordering the war according to her wishes being thus impeded. An assembly was convoked, and the rival advocates appeared: the Corcyræans spoke as follows:—

'Athenians! when a people that have not rendered any important service or support to their neighbours in times past, for which they might claim to be repaid, appear before them as we now appear before you to solicit their assistance, they may fairly be required to satisfy certain preliminary conditions. They should show, first, that it is expedient or at least safe to grant their request; next, that they will retain a lasting sense of the kindness. But if they cannot clearly establish any of these points, they must not be annoyed if they meet with a rebuff. Now the Corcyræans believe that with their petition for assistance they can also give you a satisfactory answer on these points, and they have therefore despatched us hither. It has so happened that our policy as regards you, with respect to this request, turns out to be inconsistent, and as regards our interests, to be at the present crisis inexpedient. We say inconsistent, because a power which has never in the whole of her past history been willing to ally herself with any of her neighbours, is now found asking them to ally themselves with her. And we say inexpedient, because in our present war with Corinth it has left us in a position of entire isolation, and what once seemed the wise precaution of refusing to involve ourselves in alliances with other powers, lest we should also involve ourselves in risks of their choosing, has now proved to be folly and weakness. It is true that in the late naval engagement we drove back the Corinthians from our shores single-handed. But they have now got together a still larger armament from Peloponnese and the rest of Hellas; and we, seeing our utter inability to cope with them without foreign aid, and the magnitude of the danger which subjection to them implies, find it necessary to ask help from you and from every other power. And we hope to be excused if we forswear our old principle of complete political isolation, a principle which was not adopted with any sinister intention, but was rather the consequence of an error in judgment.

'Now there are many reasons why in the event of your compliance you will congratulate yourselves on this request having been made to you. First, because your assistance will be rendered to a power which, herself inoffensive, is a victim to the injustice of others. Secondly, because all that we most value is at stake in the present contest, and your welcome of us under these circumstances will be a proof of good will which will ever keep alive the gratitude you will lay up in our hearts. Thirdly, yourselves excepted, we are the greatest naval power in Hellas. Moreover, can you conceive a stroke of good fortune more rare in itself, or more disheartening to your enemies, than that the power whose adhesion you would have valued above much material and moral strength, should present herself self-invited, should deliver herself into your hands without danger and without expense, and should lastly put you in the way of gaining a high character in the eyes of the world, the gratitude of those whom you shall assist, and a great accession of strength for yourselves? You may search all history without finding many instances of a people gaining all these advantages at once, or many instances of a power that comes in quest of assistance being in a position to give to the people whose alliance she solicits as much safety and honour as she will receive. But it will be urged that it is only in the case of a war that we shall be found useful. To this we answer that if any of you imagine that that war is far off, he is grievously mistaken, and is blind to the fact that Lacedæmon regards you with jealousy and desires war, and that Corinth is powerful there,—the same, remember, that is your enemy, and is even now trying to subdue us as a preliminary to attacking you. And this she does to prevent our becoming united by a common enmity, and her having us both on her hands, and also to insure getting the start of you in one of two ways, either by crippling our power or by making its strength her own. Now it is our policy to be beforehand with her—that is, for Corcyra to make an offer of alliance and for you to accept it; in fact, we ought to form plans against her instead of waiting to defeat the plans she forms against us.

'If she asserts that for you to receive a colony of hers into alliance is not right, let her know that every colony that is well treated honours its parent state, but becomes estranged from it by injustice. For colonists are not sent forth on the understanding that they are to be the slaves of those that remain behind, but that they are to be their equals. And that Corinth was injuring us is clear. Invited to refer the dispute about Epidamnus to arbitration, they chose to prosecute their complaints by war rather than by a fair trial. And let their conduct towards us who are their kindred be a warning to you not to be misled by their deceit, nor to yield to their direct requests; concessions to adversaries only end in self-reproach, and the more strictly they are avoided the greater will be the chance of security.

'If it be urged that your reception of us will be a breach of the treaty existing between you and Lacedæmon, the answer is that we are a neutral state, and that one of the express provisions of that treaty is that it shall be competent for any Hellenic state that is neutral to join whichever side it pleases. And it is intolerable for Corinth to be allowed to obtain men for her navy not only from her allies, but also from the rest of Hellas, no small number being furnished by your own subjects; while we are to be excluded both from the alliance left open to us by treaty, and from any assistance that we might get from other quarters, and you are to be accused of political immorality if you comply with our request. On the other hand, we shall have much greater cause to complain of you, if you do not comply with it; if we, who are in peril, and are no enemies of yours, meet with a repulse at your hands, while Corinth, who is the aggressor and your enemy, not only meets with no hindrance from you, but is even allowed to draw material for war from your dependencies. This ought not to be, but you should either forbid her enlisting men in your dominions, or you should lend us too what help you may think advisable.

'But your real policy is to afford us avowed countenance and support. The advantages of this course, as we premised in the beginning of our speech, are many. We mention one that is perhaps the chief. Could there be a clearer guarantee of our good faith than is offered by the fact that the power which is at enmity with you, is also at enmity with us, and that that power is fully able to punish defection. And there is a wide difference between declining the alliance of an inland and of a maritime power. For your first endeavour should be to prevent, if possible, the existence of any naval power except your own; failing this, to secure the friendship of the strongest that does exist. And if any of you believe that what we urge is expedient, but fear to act upon this belief, lest it should lead to a breach of the treaty, you must remember that on the one hand, whatever your fears, your strength will be formidable to your antagonists; on the other, whatever the confidence you derive from refusing to receive us, your weakness will have no terrors for a strong enemy. You must also remember that your decision is for Athens no less than for Corcyra, and that you are not making the best provision for her interests, if at a time when you are anxiously scanning the horizon that you may be in readiness for the breaking out of the war which is all but upon you, you hesitate to attach to your side a place whose adhesion or estrangement is alike pregnant with the most vital consequences. For it lies conveniently for the coast-navigation in the direction of Italy and Sicily, being able to bar the passage of naval reinforcements from thence to Peloponnese, and from Peloponnese thither; and it is in other respects a most desirable station. To sum up as shortly as possible, embracing both general and particular considerations, let this show you the folly of sacri-

ficing us. Remember that there are but three considerable
naval powers in Hellas, Athens, Corcyra, and Corinth, and
that if you allow two of these three to become one, and
Corinth to secure us for herself, you will have to hold the sea
against the united fleets of Corcyra and Peloponnese. But if
you receive us, you will have our ships to reinforce you in the
struggle.'

Such were the words of the Corcyræans. After they had
finished, the Corinthians spoke as follows:—

'These Corcyræans in the speech we have just heard do not
confine themselves to the question of their reception into your
alliance. They also talk of our being guilty of injustice, and
their being the victims of an unjustifiable war. It becomes
necessary for us to touch upon both these points before we
proceed to the rest of what we have to say, that you may have
a more correct idea of the grounds of our claim, and have good
cause to reject their petition. According to them, their old
policy of refusing all offers of alliance was a policy of moderation. It was in fact adopted for bad ends, not for good; indeed
their conduct is such as to make them by no means desirous
of having allies present to witness it, or of having the shame
of asking their concurrence. Besides, their geographical situation makes them independent of others, and consequently the
decision in cases where they injure any lies not with judges
appointed by mutual agreement, but with themselves, because
while they seldom make voyages to their neighbours, they are
constantly being visited by foreign vessels which are compelled to put in to Corcyra. In short, the object that they
propose to themselves in their specious policy of complete
isolation, is not to avoid sharing in the crimes of others, but to
secure a monopoly of crime to themselves,—the license of outrage wherever they can compel, of fraud wherever they can
elude, and the enjoyment of their gains without shame. And
yet if they were the honest men they pretend to be, the less
hold that others had upon them, the stronger would be the
light in which they might have put their honesty by giving
and taking what was just.

'But such has not been their conduct either towards others
or towards us. The attitude of our colony towards us has always been one of estrangement, and is now one of hostility;

for, say they, "We were not sent out to be ill-treated." We rejoin that we did not found the colony to be insulted by them, but to be their head, and to be regarded with a proper respect. At any rate, our other colonies honour us, and we are very much beloved by our colonists; and clearly, if the majority are satisfied with us, these can have no good reason for a dissatisfaction in which they stand alone, and we are not acting improperly in making war against them, nor are we making war against them without having received signal provocation. Besides, if we were in the wrong, it would be honourable in them to give way to our wishes, and disgraceful for us to trample on their moderation; but in the pride and license of wealth they have sinned again and again against us, and never more deeply than when Epidamnus, our dependency, which they took no steps to claim in its distress, upon our coming to relieve it, was by them seized, and is now held by force of arms.

'As to their allegation that they wished the question to be first submitted to arbitration, it is obvious that a challenge coming from the party who is safe in a commanding position, cannot gain the credit due only to him who, before appealing to arms, in deeds as well as words, places himself on a level with his adversary. In their case, it was not before they laid siege to the place, but after they at length understood that we should not tamely suffer it, that they thought of the specious word arbitration. And not satisfied with their own misconduct there, they appear here now requiring you to join with them not in alliance, but in crime, and to receive them in spite of their being at enmity with us. But it was when they stood firmest, that they should have made overtures to you, and not at a time when we have been wronged, and they are in peril; nor yet at a time when you will be admitting to a share in your protection those who never admitted you to a share in their power, and will be incurring an equal amount of blame from us with those in whose offences you had no hand. No, they should have shared their power with you before they asked you to share your fortunes with them.

'So then the reality of the grievances we come to complain of and the violence and rapacity of our opponents have both been proved. But that you cannot equitably receive them, this you have still to learn. It may be true that one of the provisions of the treaty is that it shall be competent for any state, whose name was not down on the list, to join whichever side it pleases. But this agreement is not meant for those whose object in joining is the injury of other powers, but for those whose need of support does not arise from the fact of defection, and whose adhesion will not bring to the power that is mad enough to receive them war instead of peace; which will be the case with you, if you refuse to listen to us. For you cannot become their auxiliary and remain our friend; if you join in their attack, you must share the punishment which the defenders inflict on them. And yet you have the best possible right to be neutral, or failing this, you should on the contrary join us against them. Corinth is at least in treaty with you; with Corcyra you were never even in truce. But do not lay down the principle that defection is to be patronised. Did we on the defection of the Samians record our vote against you, when the rest of the Peloponnesian powers were equally divided on the question whether they should assist them? No, we told them to their face that every power has a right to punish its own allies. Why, if you make it your policy to receive and assist all offenders, you will find that just as many of your dependencies will come over to us, and the principle that you establish will press less heavily on us than on yourselves.

'This then is what Hellenic law entitles us to demand as a right. But we have also advice to offer and claims on your gratitude, which, since there is no danger of our injuring you, as we are not enemies, and since our friendship does not amount to very frequent intercourse, we say ought to be liquidated at the present juncture. When you were in want of ships of war for the war against the Æginetans, before the Persian invasion, Corinth supplied you with twenty vessels. That good turn, and the line we took on the Samian question, when we were the cause of the Peloponnesians refusing to assist them, enabled you to conquer Ægina, and to punish Samos. And we acted thus at crises when, if ever, men are wont in their efforts against their enemies to forget everything for the sake of victory, regarding him who assists them then as a friend, even if thus far he has been a foe, and him who opposes them then as a foe, even if he has thus far been a friend; indeed they allow their real interests to suffer from their absorbing preoccupation in the struggle.

'Weigh well these considerations, and let your youth learn what they are from their elders, and let them determine to do unto us as we have done unto you. And let them not acknowledge the justice of what we say, but dispute its wisdom in the contingency of war. Not only is the straightest path generally speaking the wisest; but the coming of the war which the Corcyræans have used as a bugbear to persuade you to do wrong, is still uncertain, and it is not worth while to be carried away by it into gaining the instant and declared enmity of Corinth. It were, rather, wise to try and counteract the unfavourable impression which your conduct to Megara has created. For kindness opportunely shown has a greater power of removing old grievances than the facts of the case may warrant. And do not be seduced by the prospect of a great naval alliance. Abstinence from all injustice to other first-rate powers is a greater tower of strength, than anything that can be gained by the sacrifice of permanent tranquillity for an apparent temporary advantage. It is now our turn to benefit by the principle that we laid down at Lacedæmon, that every power has a right to punish her own allies. We now claim to receive the same from you, and protest against your rewarding us for benefiting you by our vote by injuring us by yours. On the contrary, return us like for like, remembering that this is that very crisis in which he who lends aid is most a friend, and he who opposes is most a foe. And for these Corcyræans —neither receive them into alliance in our despite, nor be their abettors in crime. So do, and you will act as we have a right to expect of you, and at the same time best consult your own interests.'

Such were the words of the Corinthians.

When the Athenians had heard both out, two assemblies were held. In the first there was a manifest disposition to listen to the representations of Corinth; in the second, public feeling had changed, and an alliance with Corcyra was decided on, with certain reservations. It was to be a defensive, not an offensive alliance. It did not involve a breach of the treaty with Peloponnese: Athens could not be required to

join Corcyra in any attack upon Corinth. But each of the
contracting parties had a right to the other's assistance against
invasion. whether of his own territory, or that of an ally. For
it began now to be felt that the coming of the Peloponnesian
war was only a question of time, and no one was willing to see
a naval power of such magnitude as Corcyra sacrificed to
Corinth; though if they could let them weaken each other by
mutual conflict, it would be no bad preparation for the struggle which Athens might one day have to wage with Corinth
and the other naval powers. At the same time the island
seemed to lie conveniently on the coasting passage to Italy
and Sicily. With these views, Athens received Corcyra into
alliance, and on the departure of the Corinthians not long
afterwards, sent ten ships to their assistance. They were commanded by Lacedæmonius, the son of Cimon, Diotimus, the
son of Strombichus, and Porteas, the son of Epicles. Their instructions were to avoid collision with the Corinthian fleet
except under certain circumstances. If it sailed to Corcyra and
threatened a landing on her coast, or in any of her possessions,
they were to do their utmost to prevent it. These instructions
were prompted by an anxiety to avoid a breach of the treaty.

Meanwhile the Corinthians completed their preparations,
and sailed for Corcyra with a hundred and fifty ships. Of
these Elis furnished ten, Megara twelve, Leucas ten, Ambracia
twenty-seven, Anactorium one, and Corinth herself ninety.
Each of these contingents had its own admiral, the Corinthian
being under the command of Xenoclides, son of Euthycles,
with four colleagues. Sailing from Leucas, they made land at
the part of the continent opposite Corcyra. They anchored in
the harbour of Chimerium, in the territory of Thesprotis,
above which, at some distance from the sea, lies the city of
Ephyre, in the Elean district. By this city the Acherusian
lake pours its waters into the sea. It gets its name from the
river Acheron, which flows through Thesprotis, and falls into
the lake. There also the river Thyamis flows, forming the
boundary between Thesprotis and Kestrine; and between
these rivers rises the point of Chimerium. In this part of the
continent the Corinthians now came to anchor, and formed an
encampment. When the Corcyræans saw them coming, they
manned a hundred and ten ships. commanded by Meikiades,

Aisimides, and Eurybatus, and stationed themselves at one
of the Sybota isles; the ten Athenian ships being present. On
point Leukimme they posted their land forces, and a thousand
heavy infantry who had come from Zacynthus to their assistance. Nor were the Corinthians on the mainland without their
allies. The barbarians flocked in large numbers to their assistance, the inhabitants of this part of the continent being old
allies of theirs.

When the Corinthian preparations were completed they
took three days' provisions, and put out from Chimerium by
night, ready for action. Sailing with the dawn, they sighted
the Corcyræan fleet out at sea, and coming towards them.
When they perceived each other, both sides formed in order
of battle. On the Corcyræan right wing lay the Athenian ships,
the rest of the line being occupied by their own vessels formed
in three squadrons, each of which was commanded by one of
the three admirals. Such was the Corcyræan formation. The
Corinthian was as follows: on the right wing lay the Megarian
and Ambraciot ships, in the centre the rest of the allies in
order. But the left was composed of the best sailers in the
Corinthian navy, to encounter the Athenians and the right
wing of the Corcyræans. As soon as the signals were raised
on either side, they joined battle. Both sides had a large
number of heavy infantry on their decks, and a large number
of archers and darters, the old imperfect armament still prevailing. The sea-fight was an obstinate one, though not remarkable for its science; indeed it was more like a battle
by land. Whenever they charged each other, the multitude
and crush of the vessels made it by no means easy to get
loose; besides, their hopes of victory lay principally in the
heavy infantry on the decks, who stood and fought in order,
the ships remaining stationary. The manœuvre of breaking
the line was not tried: in short, strength and pluck had more
share in the fight than science. Everywhere tumult reigned,
the battle being one scene of confusion; meanwhile the Athenian ships, by coming up to the Corcyræans whenever they
were pressed, served to alarm the enemy, though their commanders could not join in the battle from fear of their instructions. The right wing of the Corinthians suffered most. The
Corcyræans routed it, and chased them in disorder to the

continent with twenty ships, sailed up to their camp, and burnt
the tents which they found empty, and plundered the stuff.
So in this quarter the Corinthians and their allies were defeated, and the Corcyræans were victorious. But where the
Corinthians themselves were, on the left, they gained a decided success; the scanty forces of the Corcyræans being
further weakened by the want of the twenty ships absent
on the pursuit. Seeing the Corcyræans hard pressed, the
Athenians began at length to assist them more unequivocally.
At first, it is true, they refrained from charging any ships;
but when the rout was becoming patent, and the Corinthians
were pressing on, the time at last came when every one set
to, and all distinction was laid aside, and it came to this point,
that the Corinthians and Athenians raised their hands against
each other.

After the rout, the Corinthians, instead of employing themselves in lashing fast and hauling after them the hulls of the
vessels which they had disabled, turned their attention to the
men, whom they butchered as they sailed through, not caring
so much to make prisoners. Some even of their own friends
were slain by them, by mistake, in their ignorance of the defeat
of the right wing. For the number of the ships on both sides,
and the distance to which they covered the sea, made it difficult after they had once joined, to distinguish between the
conquering and the conquered; this battle proving far greater
than any before it, any at least between Hellenes, for the
number of vessels engaged. After the Corinthians had chased
the Corcyræans to the land, they turned to the wrecks and
their dead, most of whom they succeeded in getting hold of
and conveying to Sybota, the rendezvous of the land forces
furnished by their barbarian allies. Sybota, it must be known,
is a desert harbour of Thesprotis. This task over, they mustered anew, and sailed against the Corcyræans, who on their
part advanced to meet them with all their ships that were fit
for service and remaining to them, accompanied by the Athenian vessels, fearing that they might attempt a landing in
their territory. It was by this time getting late, and the pæan
had been sung for the attack, when the Corinthians suddenly
began to back water. They had observed twenty Athenian
ships sailing up, which had been sent out afterwards to re-

inforce the ten vessels by the Athenians, who feared, as it turned out justly, the defeat of the Corcyræans and the inability of their handful of ships to protect them. These ships were thus seen by the Corinthians first. They suspected that they were from Athens, and that those which they saw were not all, but that there were more behind; they accordingly began to retire. The Corcyræans meanwhile had not sighted them, as they were advancing from a point which they could not so well see, and were wondering why the Corinthians were backing water, when some caught sight of them, and cried out that there were ships in sight ahead. Upon this they also retired; for it was now getting dark, and the retreat of the Corinthians had suspended hostilities. Thus they parted from each other, and the battle ceased with night. The Corcyræans were in their camp at Leukimme, when these twenty ships from Athens, under the command of Glaucon, the son of Leagrus, and Andocides, son of Leogoras, bore on through the corpses and the wrecks, and sailed up to the camp, not long after they were sighted. It was now night, and the Corcyræans feared that they might be hostile vessels; but they soon knew them, and the ships came to anchor.

The next day the thirty Athenian vessels put out to sea, accompanied by all the Corcyræan ships that were seaworthy, and sailed to the harbour at Sybota, where the Corinthians lay, to see if they would engage. The Corinthians put out from the land, and formed a line in the open sea, but beyond this made no further movement, having no intention of assuming the offensive. For they saw reinforcements arrived fresh from Athens, and themselves confronted by numerous difficulties, such as the necessity of guarding the prisoners whom they had on board, and the want of all means of refitting their ships in a desert place. What they were thinking more about was how their voyage home was to be effected; they feared that the Athenians might consider that the treaty was dissolved by the collision which had occurred, and forbid their departure. Accordingly they resolved to put some men on board a boat, and send them without a herald's wand to the Athenians, as an experiment. Having done so, they spoke as follows: 'You do wrong, Athenians, to begin war and break the treaty. Engaged in chastising our enemies, we find you placing

yourselves in our path in arms against us. Now if your inten,
tions are to prevent us sailing to Corcyra, or anywhere else
that we may wish, and if you are for breaking the treaty, first
take us that are here, and treat us as enemies.' Such was what
they said, and all the Corcyræan armament that were within
hearing immediately called out to take them and kill them.
But the Athenians answered as follows: 'Neither are we beginning war, Peloponnesians, nor are we breaking the treaty;
but these Corcyræans are our allies, and we are come to help
them. So if you want to sail anywhere else, we place no obstacle in your way; but if you are going to sail against Corcyra, or any of her possessions, we shall do our best to stop
you.'

Receiving this answer from the Athenians, the Corinthians
commenced preparations for their voyage home, and set up a
trophy in Sybota, on the continent; while the Corcyræans
took up the wrecks and dead that had been carried out to them
by the current, and by a wind which rose in the night and
scattered them in all directions, and set up their trophy in
Sybota, on the island, as victors. The reasons each side had
for claiming the victory were these. The Corinthians had been
victorious in the sea-fight until night; and having thus been
enabled to carry off most wrecks and dead, they were in possession of no fewer than a thousand prisoners of war, and
had sunk close upon seventy vessels. The Corcyræans had destroyed about thirty ships, and after the arrival of the Athenians had taken up the wrecks and dead on their side; they
had besides seen the Corinthians retire before them, backing
water on sight of the Athenian vessels, and upon the arrival
of the Athenians refuse to sail out against them from Sybota.
Thus both sides claimed the victory.

The Corinthians on the voyage home took Anactorium,
which stands at the mouth of the Ambracian gulf. The place
was taken by treachery, being common ground to the Corcyræans and Corinthians. After establishing Corinthian settlers
there, they retired home. Eight hundred of the Corcyræans
were slaves; these they sold; two hundred and fifty they
retained in captivity, and treated with great attention, in the
hope that they might bring over their country to Corinth on
their return; most of them being, as it happened, men of very

high position in Corcyra. In this way Corcyra maintained her
political existence in the war with Corinth, and the Athenian
vessels left the island. This was the first cause of the war that
Corinth had against the Athenians, viz. that they had fought
against them with the Corcyræans in time of treaty.

Almost immediately after this, fresh differences arose between the Athenians and Peloponnesians, and contributed
their share to the war. Corinth was forming schemes for
retaliation, and Athens suspected her hostility. The Potidæans,
who inhabit the isthmus of Pallene, being a Corinthian colony,
but tributary allies of Athens, were ordered to raze the wall
looking towards Pallene, to give hostages, to dismiss the
Corinthian magistrates, and in future not to receive the persons sent from Corinth annually to succeed them. It was
feared that they might be persuaded by Perdiccas and the
Corinthians to revolt, and might draw the rest of the allies
in the direction of Thrace to revolt with them. These precautions against the Potidæans were taken by the Athenians
immediately after the battle at Corcyra. Not only was Corinth
at length openly hostile, but Perdiccas, son of Alexander, king
of the Macedonians, had from an old friend and ally been
made an enemy. He had been made an enemy by the Athenians
entering into alliance with his brother Philip and Derdas,
who were in league against him. In his alarm he had sent to
Lacedæmon to try and involve the Athenians in a war with
the Peloponnesians, and was endeavouring to win over Corinth
in order to bring about the revolt of Potidæa. He also made
overtures to the Chalcidians in the direction of Thrace, and
to the Bottiæans, to persuade them to join in the revolt;
for he thought that if these places on the border could be made
his allies, it would be easier to carry on the war with their
co-operation. Alive to all this, and wishing to anticipate the
revolt of the cities, the Athenians acted as follows. They
were just then sending off thirty ships and a thousand heavy
infantry for his country under the command of Archestratus,
son of Lycomedes, with four colleagues. They instructed the
captains to take hostages of the Potidæans, to raze the wall,
and to be on their guard against the revolt of the neighbouring cities.

Meanwhile the Potidæans sent envoys to Athens on the

chance of persuading them to take no new steps in their matters; they also went to Lacedæmon with the Corinthians to
secure support in case of need. Failing after prolonged negotiation to obtain anything satisfactory from the Athenians;
being unable, for all they could say, to prevent the vessels
that were destined for Macedonia from also sailing against
them; and receiving from the Lacedæmonian government a
promise to invade Attica, if the Athenians should attack
Potidæs, the Potidæans, thus favoured by the moment, at
last entered into league with the Chalcidians and Bottiæans,
and revolted. And Perdiccas induced the Chalcidians to abandon and demolish their towns on the seaboard, and settling
inland at Olynthus, to make that one city a strong place:
meanwhile to those who followed his advice he gave a part of
his territory in Mygdonia round Lake Bolbe as a place of
abode while the war against the Athenians should last. They
accordingly demolished their towns, removed inland, and
prepared for war.

The thirty ships of the Athenians, arriving before the
Thracian places, found Potidæa and the rest in revolt. Their
commanders considering it to be quite impossible with their
present force to carry on war with Perdiccas, and with the
confederate towns as well, turned to Macedonia, their original
destination, and having established themselves there, carried
on war in co-operation with Philip, and the brothers of Derdas, who had invaded the country from the interior.

Meanwhile the Corinthians, with Potidæa in revolt, and the
Athenian ships on the coast of Macedonia, alarmed for the
safety of the place, and thinking its danger theirs, sent volunteers from Corinth, and mercenaries from the rest of Peloponnese, to the number of sixteen hundred heavy infantry in all,
and four hundred light troops. Aristeus, son of Adimantus,
who was always a steady friend to the Potidæans, took com
mand of the expedition, and it was principally for love of him
that most of the men from Corinth volunteered. They arrived
in Thrace forty days after the revolt of Potidæa.

The Athenians also immediately received the news of the
revolt of the cities. On being informed that Aristeus and his
reinforcements were on their way, they sent two thousand
heavy infantry of their own citizens and forty ships against

the places in revolt, under the command of Callias, son of Calliades, and four colleagues. They arrived in Macedonia first, and found the force of a thousand men that had been first sent out, just become masters of Therme and besieging Pydna. Accordingly they also joined in the investment, and besieged Pydna for a while. Subsequently they came to terms and concluded a forced alliance with Perdiccas, hastened by the calls of Potidæa, and by the arrival of Aristeus at that place. They withdrew from Macedonia, going to Berœa and thence to Strepsa, and, after a futile attempt on the latter place, they pursued by land their march to Potidæa with three thousand heavy infantry of their own citizens, besides a number of their allies, and six hundred Macedonian horsemen, the followers of Philip and Pausanias. With these sailed seventy ships along the coast. Advancing by short marches, on the third day they arrived at Gigonus, where they encamped.

Meanwhile the Potidæans and the Peloponnesians with Aristeus were encamped on the side looking towards Olynthus on the isthmus, in expectation of the Athenians, and had established their market outside the city. The allies had chosen Aristeus general of all the infantry; while the command of the cavalry was given to Perdiccas, who had at once left the alliance of the Athenians and gone back to that of the Potidæans, having deputed Iolaus as his general. The plan of Aristeus was to keep his own force on the isthmus, and await the attack of the Athenians; leaving the Chalcidians and the allies outside the isthmus, and the two hundred cavalry from Perdiccas in Olynthus to act upon the Athenian rear, on the occasion of their advancing against him; and thus to place the enemy between two fires. While Callias the Athenian general and his colleagues despatched the Macedonian horse and a few of the allies to Olynthus, to prevent any movement being made from that quarter, the Athenians themselves broke up their camp and marched against Potidæa. After they had arrived at the isthmus, and saw the enemy preparing for battle, they formed against him, and soon afterwards engaged. The wing of Aristeus, with the Corinthians and other picked troops round him, routed the wing opposed to it, and followed for a considerable distance in pursuit. But the rest of the army of the Potidæans and of the Peloponnesians was defeated by the Athenians, and took refuge within the fortifications. Returning from the pursuit, Aristeus perceived the defeat of the rest of the army. Being at a loss which of the two risks to choose, whether to go to Olynthus or to Potidæa, he at last determined to draw his men into as small a space as possible, and force his way with a run into Potidæa. Not without difficulty, through a storm of missiles, he passed along by the breakwater through the sea, and brought off most of his men safe, though a few were lost. Meanwhile the auxiliaries of the Potidæans from Olynthus, which is about seven miles off, and in sight of Potidæa, when the battle began and the signals were raised, advanced a little way to render assistance; and the Macedonian horse formed against them to prevent it. But on victory speedily declaring for the Athenians and the signals being taken down, they retired back within the wall; and the Macedonians returned to the Athenians. Thus there were no cavalry present on either side. After the battle the Athenians set up a trophy, and gave back their dead to the Potidæans under truce. The Potidæans and their allies had close upon three hundred killed; the Athenians a hundred and fifty of their own citizens, and Callias their general.

The wall on the side of the isthmus had now works at once raised against it, and manned by the Athenians. That on the side of Pallene had no works raised against it. They did not think themselves strong enough at once to keep a garrison in the isthmus, and to cross over to Pallene and raise works there; they were afraid that the Potidæans and their allies might take advantage of their division to attack them. Meanwhile the Athenians at home learning that there were no works at Pallene, sometime afterwards sent off sixteen hundred heavy infantry of their own citizens under the command of Phormio, son of Asopius. Arrived at Pallene, he fixed his head-quarters at Aphytis, and led his army against Potidæa by short marches, ravaging the country as he advanced. No one venturing to meet him in the field, he raised works against the wall on the side of Pallene. So at length Potidæa was strongly invested on either side, and from the sea by the ships co-operating in the blockade. Aristeus, seeing its investment complete, and having no hope of its salvation, except in the event of some movement from the Peloponnese, or of some

other improbable contingency, advised all except five hundred
to watch for a wind, and sail out of the place, in order that
their provisions might last the longer. He was willing to be
himself one of those who remained. Unable to persuade them,
and desirous of acting on the next alternative, and of having
things outside in the best posture possible, he eluded the
guardships of the Athenians and sailed out. Remaining among
the Chalcidians, he continued to carry on the war; in particular he laid an ambuscade near the city of the Sermylians,
and cut off many of them; he also communicated with Peloponnese, and tried to contrive some method by which help
might be brought. Meanwhile, after the completion of the
investment of Potidæa, Phormio next employed his sixteen
hundred men in ravaging Chalcidice and Bottica: some of the
towns also were taken by him.

CHAPTER III

CONGRESS OF THE PELOPONNESIAN CONFEDERACY AT
LACEDÆMON

B.C. 432: *Allies summoned to Lacedæmon—Speech of the Corinthians—
Reply of the Athenian envoys—Speech of Archidamus–Speech of
Sthenelaidas—The assembly decides for war.*

THE Athenians and Peloponnesians had these antecedent
grounds of complaint against each other: the complaint of
Corinth was that her colony of Potidæa, and Corinthian and
Peloponnesian citizens within it, were being besieged; that of
Athens against the Peloponnesians that they had incited a
town of hers, a member of her alliance and a contributor to
her revenue, to revolt, and had come and were openly fighting
against her on the side of the Potidæans. For all this, war
had not yet broken out: there was still truce for a while; for
this was a private enterprise on the part of Corinth.

But the siege of Potidæa put an end to her inaction; she
had men inside it: besides, she feared for the place. Immediately summoning the allies to Lacedæmon, she came and
loudly accused Athens of breach of the treaty and aggression
on the rights of Peloponnese. With her, the Æginetans, formally unrepresented from fear of Athens, in secret proved not
the least urgent of the advocates for war, asserting that they

had not the independence guaranteed to them by the treaty. After extending the summons to any of their allies and others who might have complaints to make of Athenian aggression, the Lacedæmonians held their ordinary assembly, and invited them to speak. There were many who came forward and made their several accusations; among them the Megarians, in a long list of grievances, called special attention to the fact of their exclusion from the ports of the Athenian empire and the market of Athens, in defiance of the treaty. Last of all the Corinthians came forward, and having let those who preceded them inflame the Lacedæmonians, now followed with a speech to this effect:—

'Lacedæmonians! the confidence which you feel in your constitution and social order, inclines you to receive any reflexions of ours on other powers with a certain scepticism. Hence springs your moderation, but hence also the rather limited knowledge which you betray in dealing with foreign politics. Time after time was our voice raised to warn you of the blows about to be dealt us by Athens, and time after time, instead of taking the trouble to ascertain the worth of our communications, you contented yourselves with suspecting the speakers of being inspired by private interest. And so, instead of calling these allies together before the blow fell, you have delayed to do so till we are smarting under it; allies among whom we have not the worst title to speak, as having the greatest complaints to make, complaints of Athenian outrage and Lacedæmonian neglect. Now if these assaults on the rights of Hellas had been made in the dark you might be unacquainted with the facts, and it would be our duty to enlighten you. As it is, long speeches are not needed where you see servitude accomplished for some of us, meditated for others—in particular for our allies—and prolonged preparations in the aggressor against the hour of war. Or what, pray, is the meaning of their reception of Corcyra by fraud, and their holding it against us by force? what of the siege of Potidæa?—places one of which lies most conveniently for any action against the Thracian towns; while the other would have contributed a very large navy to the Peloponnesians?

'For all this you are responsible. You it was who first allowed them to fortify their city after the Median war, and afterwards to erect the long walls,—you who, then and now, are always depriving of freedom not only those whom they have enslaved, but also those who have as yet been your allies. For the true author of the subjugation of a people is not so much the immediate agent, as the power which permits it having the means to prevent it; particularly if that power aspires to the glory of being the liberator of Hellas. We are at last assembled. It has not been easy to assemble, nor even now are our objects defined. We ought not to be still inquiring into the fact of our wrongs, but into the means of our defence. For the aggressors with matured plans to oppose to our indecision have cast threats aside and betaken themselves to action. And we know what are the paths by which Athenian aggression travels, and how insidious is its progress. A degree of confidence she may feel from the idea that your bluntness of perception prevents your noticing her; but it is nothing to the impulse which her advance will receive from the knowledge that you see, but do not care to interfere. You, Lacedæmonians, of all the Hellenes are alone inactive, and defend yourselves not by doing anything but by looking as if you would do something; you alone wait till the power of an enemy is becoming twice its original size, instead of crushing it in its infancy. And yet the world used to say that you were to be depended upon; but in your case, we fear, it said more than the truth. The Mede, we ourselves know, had time to come from the ends of the earth to Peloponnese, without any force of yours worthy of the name advancing to meet him. But this was a distant enemy. Well, Athens at all events is a near neighbour, and yet Athens you utterly disregard; against Athens you prefer to act on the defensive instead of on the offensive, and to make it an affair of chances by deferring the struggle till she has grown far stronger than at first. And yet you know that on the whole the rock on which the barbarian was wrecked was himself, and that if our present enemy Athens has not again and again annihilated us, we owe it more to her blunders than to your protection. Indeed, expectations from you have before now been the ruin of some, whose faith induced them to omit preparation.

'We hope that none of you will consider these words of remonstrance to be rather words of hostility; men remonstrate

with friends who are in error, accusations they reserve for
enemies who have wronged them. Besides, we consider that
we have as good a right as any one to point out a neighbour's
faults, particularly when we contemplate the great contrast
between the two national characters; a contrast of which,
as far as we can see, you have little perception, having never
yet considered what sort of antagonists you will encounter
in the Athenians, how widely, how absolutely different from
yourselves. The Athenians are addicted to innovation, and
their designs are characterised by swiftness alike in conception and execution; you have a genius for keeping what you
have got, accompanied by a total want of invention, and when
forced to act you never go far enough. Again, they are adventurous beyond their power, and daring beyond their judgment, and in danger they are sanguine; your wont is to attempt less than is justified by your power, to mistrust even
what is sanctioned by your judgment, and to fancy that from
danger there is no release. Further, there is promptitude on
their side against procrastination on yours; they are never
at home, you are never from it: for they hope by their absence
to extend their acquisitions, you fear by your advance to
endanger what you have left behind. They are swift to follow
up a success, and slow to recoil from a reverse. Their bodies
they spend ungrudgingly in their country's cause; their intel-
lect they jealously husband to be employed in her service.
A scheme unexecuted is with them a positive loss, a successful
enterprise a comparative failure. The deficiency created by
the miscarriage of an undertaking is soon filled up by fresh
hopes; for they alone are enabled to call a thing hoped for a
thing got, by the speed with which they act upon their resolutions. Thus they toil on in trouble and danger all the days of
their life, with little opportunity for enjoying, being ever
engaged in getting: their only idea of a holiday is to do what
the occasion demands, and to them laborious occupation is less
of a misfortune than the peace of a quiet life. To describe
their character in a word, one might truly say that they were
born into the world to take no rest themselves and to give
none to others.

'Such is Athens, your antagonist. And yet, Lacedæmonians,
you still delay, and fail to see that peace stays longest with

those, who are not more careful to use their power justly than
to show their determination not to submit to injustice. On the
contrary, your ideal of fair dealing is based on the principle
that if you do not injure others, you need not risk your own
fortunes in preventing others from injuring you. Now you
could scarcely have succeeded in such a policy even with a
neighbour like yourselves; but in the present instance, as we
have just shown, your habits are old-fashioned as compared
with theirs. It is the law as in art, so in politics, that improvements ever prevail; and though fixed usages may be best for
undisturbed communities, constant necessities of action must
be accompanied by the constant improvement of methods.
Thus it happens that the vast experience of Athens has carried
her further than you on the path of innovation.

'Here, at least, let your procrastination end. For the present,
assist your allies and Potidæa in particular, as you promised,
by a speedy invasion of Attica, and do not sacrifice friends
and kindred to their bitterest enemies, and drive the rest of
us in despair to some other alliance. Such a step would not be
condemned either by the gods who received our oaths, or by
the men who witnessed them. The breach of a treaty cannot
be laid to the people whom desertion compels to seek new relations, but to the power that fails to assist its confederate. But
if you will only act, we will stand by you; it would be unnatural for us to change, and never should we meet with such
a congenial ally. For these reasons choose the right course,
and endeavour not to let Peloponnese under your supremacy
degenerate from the prestige that it enjoyed under that of
your ancestors.'

Such were the words of the Corinthians. There happened
to be Athenian envoys present at Lacedæmon on other business. On hearing the speeches they thought themselves called
upon to come before the Lacedæmonians. Their intention was
not to offer a defence on any of the charges which the cities
brought against them, but to show on a comprehensive view
that it was not a matter to be hastily decided on, but one that
demanded further consideration. There was also a wish to call
attention to the great power of Athens, and to refresh the
memory of the old and enlighten the ignorance of the young,
from a notion that their words might have the effect of induc-

ing them to prefer tranquillity to war. So they came to the Lacedæmonians and said that they too, if there was no objection, wished to speak to their assembly. They replied by inviting them to come forward. The Athenians advanced, and spoke as follows:—

'The object of our mission here was not to argue with your allies, but to attend to the matters on which our State despatched us. However, the vehemence of the outcry that we hear against us has prevailed on us to come forward. It is not to combat the accusations of the cities (indeed you are not the judges before whom either we or they can plead), but to prevent your taking the wrong course on matters of great importance by yielding too readily to the persuasions of your allies. We also wish to show on a review of the whole indictment that we have a fair title to our possessions, and that our country has claims to consideration. We need not refer to remote antiquity: there we could appeal to the voice of tradition, but not to the experience of our audience. But to the Median war and contemporary history we must refer, although we are rather tired of continually bringing this subject forward. In our action during that war we ran great risk to obtain certain advantages: you had your share in the solid results, do not try to rob us of all share in the good that the glory may do us. However, the story shall be told not so much to deprecate hostility as to testify against it, and to show, if you are so ill-advised as to enter into a struggle with Athens, what sort of an antagonist she is likely to prove. We assert that at Marathon we were at the front, and faced the barbarian single-handed. That when he came the second time, unable to cope with him by land we went on board our ships with all our people, and joined in the action at Salamis. This prevented his taking the Peloponnesian states in detail, and ravaging them with his fleet; when the multitude of his vessels would have made any combination for self-defence impossible. The best proof of this was furnished by the invader himself. Defeated at sea, he considered his power to be no longer what it had been, and retired as speedily as possible with the greater part of his army.

'Such, then, was the result of the matter, and it was clearly proved that it was on the fleet of Hellas that her cause depended. Well, to this result we contributed three very useful elements, viz. the largest number of ships, the ablest commander, and the most unhesitating patriotism. Our contingent of ships was little less than two-thirds of the whole four hundred; the commander was Themistocles, through whom chiefly it was that the battle took place in the straits, the acknowledged salvation of our cause. Indeed, this was the reason of your receiving him with honours such as had never been accorded to any foreign visitor. While for daring patriotism we had no competitors. Receiving no reinforcements from behind, seeing everything in front of us already subjugated, we had the spirit, after abandoning our city, after sacrificing our property (instead of deserting the remainder of the league or depriving them of our services by dispersing), to throw ourselves into our ships and meet the danger, without a thought of resenting your neglect to assist us. We assert, therefore, that we conferred on you quite as much as we received. For you had a stake to fight for; the cities which you had left were still filled with your homes, and you had the prospect of enjoying them again; and your coming was prompted quite as much by fear for yourselves as for us; at all events, you never appeared till we had nothing left to lose. But we left behind us a city that was a city no longer, and staked our lives for a city that had an existence only in desperate hope, and so bore our full share in your deliverance and in ours. But if we had copied others, and allowed fears for our territory to make us give in our adhesion to the Mede before you came, or if we had suffered our ruin to break our spirit and prevent us embarking in our ships, your naval inferiority would have made a sea-fight unnecessary, and his objects would have been peaceably attained.

'Surely, Lacedæmonians, neither by the patriotism that we displayed at that crisis, nor by the wisdom of our counsels, do we merit our extreme unpopularity with the Hellenes, not at least unpopularity for our empire. That empire we acquired by no violent means, but because you were unwilling to prosecute to its conclusion the war against the barbarian, and because the allies attached themselves to us and spontaneously asked us to assume the command. And the nature of the case first compelled us to advance our empire to its present height;

fear being our principal motive, though honour and interest afterwards came in. And at last, when almost all hated us, when some had already revolted and had been subdued, when you had ceased to be the friends that you once were, and had become objects of suspicion and dislike, it appeared no longer safe to give up our empire; especially as all who left us would fall to you. And no one can quarrel with a people for making, in matters of tremendous risk, the best provision that it can for its interest.

'You, at all events, Lacedæmonians, have used your supremacy to settle the states in Peloponnese as is agreeable to you. And if at the period of which we were speaking you had persevered to the end of the matter, and had incurred hatred in your command, we are sure that you would have made yourselves just as galling to the allies, and would have been forced to choose between a strong government and danger to yourselves. It follows that it was not a very wonderful action, or contrary to the common practice of mankind, if we did accept an empire that was offered to us, and refused to give it up under the pressure of three of the strongest motives, fear, honour, and interest. And it was not we who set the example, for it has always been the law that the weaker should be subject to the stronger. Besides, we believed ourselves to be worthy of our position, and so you thought us till now, when calculations of interest have made you take up the cry of justice—a consideration which no one ever yet brought forward to hinder his ambition when he had a chance of gaining anything by might. And praise is due to all who, if not so superior to human nature as to refuse dominion, yet respect justice more than their position compels them to do.

'We imagine that our moderation would be best demonstrated by the conduct of others who should be placed in our position; but even our equity has very unreasonably subjected us to condemnation instead of approval. Our abatement of our rights in the contract trials with our allies, and our causing them to be decided by impartial laws at Athens, have gained us the character of being litigious. And none care to inquire why this reproach is not brought against other imperial powers, who treat their subjects with less moderation than we do; the secret being that where force can be used, law

is not needed. But our subjects are so habituated to associate
with us as equals, that any defeat whatever that clashes with
their notions of justice, whether it proceeds from a legal judgment or from the power which our empire gives us, makes
them forget to be grateful for being allowed to retain most of
their possessions, and more vexed at a part being taken, than
if we had from the first cast law aside and openly gratified
our covetousness. If we had done so, not even would they
have disputed that the weaker must give way to the stronger.
Men's indignation, it seems, is more excited by legal wrong
than by violent wrong; the first looks like being cheated by
an equal, the second like being compelled by a superior. At
all events they contrived to put up with much worse treatment than this from the Mede, yet they think our rule severe,
and this is to be expected, for the present always weighs heavy
on the conquered. This at least is certain. If you were to succeed in overthrowing us and in taking our place, you would
speedily lose the popularity with which fear of us has invested
you, if your policy of to-day is at all to tally with the sample
that you gave of it during the brief period of your command
against the Mede. Not only is your life at home regulated by
rules and institutions incompatible with those of others, but
your citizens abroad act neither on these rules nor on those
which are recognised by the rest of Hellas.

'Take time then in forming your resolution, as the matter
is of great importance; and do not be persuaded by the opinions and complaints of others to bring trouble on yourselves,
but consider the vast influence of accident in war, before you
are engaged in it. As it continues, it generally becomes an
affair of chances, chances from which neither of us is exempt,
and whose event we must risk in the dark. It is a common
mistake in going to war to begin at the wrong end, to act
first, and wait for disaster to discuss the matter. But we are
not yet by any means so misguided, nor, so far as we can see,
are you; accordingly, while it is still open to us both to choose
aright, we bid you not to dissolve the treaty, or to break your
oaths, but to have our differences settled by arbitration according to our agreement. Or else we take the gods who
heard the oaths to witness, and if you begin hostilities, what-

ever line of action you choose, we will try not to be behindhand in repelling you.'

Such were the words of the Athenians. After the Lacedæmonians had heard the complaints of the allies against the Athenians, and the observations of the latter, they made all withdraw, and consulted by themselves on the question before them. The opinions of the majority all led to the same conclusion; the Athenians were open aggressors, and war must be declared at once. But Archidamus, the Lacedæmonian king, came forward, who had the reputation of being at once a wise and a moderate man, and made the following speech:—

'I have not lived so long, Lacedæmonians, without having had the experience of many wars, and I see those among you of the same age as myself, who will not fall into the common misfortune of longing for war from inexperience or from a belief in its advantage and its safety. This, the war on which you are now debating, would be one of the greatest magnitude, on a sober consideration of the matter. In a struggle with Peloponnesians and neighbours our strength is of the same character, and it is possible to move swiftly on the different points. But a struggle with a people who live in a distant land, who have also an extraordinary familiarity with the sea, and who are in the highest state of preparation in every other department; with wealth private and public, with ships, and horses, and heavy infantry, and a population such as no one other Hellenic place can equal, and lastly a number of tributary allies—what can justify us in rashly beginning such a struggle? wherein is our trust that we should rush on it unprepared? Is it in our ships? There we are inferior; while if we are to practise and become a match for them, time must intervene. Is it in our money? There we have a far greater deficiency. We neither have it in our treasury, nor are we ready to contribute it from our private funds. Confidence might possibly be felt in our superiority in heavy infantry and population, which will enable us to invade and devastate their lands. But the Athenians have plenty of other land in their empire, and can import what they want by sea. Again, if we are to attempt an insurrection of their allies, these will have to be supported with a fleet, most of them being islanders. What then is to be our war? For unless we can either beat them at sea, or deprive them of the revenues which feed their navy, we shall meet with little but disaster. Meanwhile our honour will be pledged to keeping on, particularly if it be the opinion that we began the quarrel. For let us never be elated by the fatal hope of the war being quickly ended by the devastation of their lands. I fear rather that we may leave it as a legacy to our children; so improbable is it that the Athenian spirit will be the slave of their land, or Athenian experience be cowed by war.

'Not that I would bid you be so unfeeling as to suffer them to injure your allies, and to refrain from unmasking their intrigues; but I do bid you not to take up arms at once, but to send and remonstrate with them in a tone not too suggestive of war, nor again too suggestive of submission, and to employ the interval in perfecting our own preparations. The means will be, first, the acquisition of allies, Hellenic or barbarian it matters not, so long as they are an accession to our strength naval or pecuniary—I say Hellenic or barbarian, because the odium of such an accession to all who like us are the objects of the designs of the Athenians is taken away by the law of self-preservation—and secondly the development of our home resources. If they listen to our embassy, so much the better; but if not, after the lapse of two or three years our position will have become materially strengthened, and we can then attack them if we think proper. Perhaps by that time the sight of our preparations, backed by language equally significant, will have disposed them to submission, while their land is still untouched, and while their counsels may be directed to the retention of advantages as yet undestroyed. For the only light in which you can view their land is that of a hostage in your hands, a hostage the more valuable the better it is cultivated. This you ought to spare as long as possible, and not make them desperate, and so increase the difficulty of dealing with them. For if while still unprepared, hurried away by the complaints of our allies, we are induced to lay it waste, have a care that we do not bring deep disgrace and deep perplexity upon Peloponnese. Complaints, whether of communities or individuals, it is possible to adjust; but war undertaken by a coalition for sectional interests, whose progress there is no

means of foreseeing, does not easily admit of creditable settlement.

'And none need think it cowardice for a number of confederates to pause before they attack a single city. The
Athenians have allies as numerous as our own, and allies
that pay tribute, and war is a matter not so much of arms
as of money, which makes arms of use. And this is more than
ever true in a struggle between a continental and a maritime
power. First, then, let us provide money, and not allow ourselves to be carried away by the talk of our allies before we
have done so: as we shall have the largest share of responsibility for the consequences be they good or bad, we have also
a right to a tranquil inquiry respecting them.

'And the slowness and procrastination, the parts of our
character that are most assailed by their criticism, need not
make you blush. If we undertake the war without preparation,
we should by hastening its commencement only delay its conclusion: further, a free and a famous city has through all time
been ours. The quality which they condemn is really nothing
but a wise moderation; thanks to its possession, we alone do
not become insolent in success and give way less than others
in misfortune; we are not carried away by the pleasure of
hearing ourselves cheered on to risks which our judgment
condemns; nor, if annoyed, are we any the more convinced
by attempts to exasperate us by accusation. We are both
warlike and wise, and it is our sense of order that makes us so.
We are warlike, because self-control contains honour as a
chief constituent, and honour bravery. And we are wise, because we are educated with too little learning to despise the
laws, and with too severe a self-control to disobey them, and
are brought up not to be too knowing in useless matters,—
such as the knowledge which can give a specious criticism of
an enemy's plans in theory, but fails to assail them with equal
success in practice,—but are taught to consider that the
schemes of our enemies are not dissimilar to our own, and
that the freaks of chance are not determinable by calculation.
In practice we always base our preparations against an enemy
on the assumption that his plans are good; indeed, it is right
to rest our hopes not on a belief in his blunders, but on the
soundness of our provisions. Nor ought we to believe that there

is much difference between man and man, but to think that the superiority lies with him who is reared in the severest school. These practices, then, which our ancestors have delivered to us, and by whose maintenance we have always profited, must not be given up. And we must not be hurried into deciding in a day's brief space a question which concerns many lives and fortunes and many cities, and in which honour is deeply involved,—but we must decide calmly. This our strength peculiarly enables us to do. As for the Athenians, send to them on the matter of Potidæa, send on the matter of the alleged wrongs of the allies, particularly as they are prepared with legal satisfaction; and to proceed against one who offers arbitration as against a wrongdoer, law forbids. Meanwhile do not omit preparation for war. This decision will be the best for yourselves, the most terrible to your opponents.'

Such were the words of Archidamus. Last came forward Sthenelaidas, one of the Ephors for that year, and spoke to the Lacedæmonians as follows:—

'The long speech of the Athenians I do not pretend to understand. They said a good deal in praise of themselves, but nowhere denied that they are injuring our allies and Peloponnese. And yet if they behaved well against the Mede then, but ill towards us now, they deserve double punishment for having ceased to be good and for having become bad. We meanwhile are the same then and now, and shall not, if we are wise, disregard the wrongs of our allies, or put off till to-morrow the duty of assisting those who must suffer to-day. Others have much money and ships and horses, but we have good allies whom we must not give up to the Athenians, nor by lawsuits and words decide the matter, as it is anything but in word that we are harmed, but render instant and powerful help. And let us not be told that it is fitting for us to deliberate under injustice; long deliberation is rather fitting for those who have injustice in contemplation. Vote therefore, Lacedæmonians, for war, as the honour of Sparta demands, and neither allow the further aggrandisement of Athens, nor betray our allies to ruin, but with the gods let us advance against the aggressors.'

With these words he, as Ephor, himself put the question

to the assembly of the Lacedæmonians. He said that he could not determine which was the loudest acclamation (their mode of decision is by acclamation not by voting); the fact being that he wished to make them declare their opinion openly and thus to increase their ardour for war. Accordingly he said, 'All Lacedæmonians who are of opinion that the treaty has been broken, and that Athens is guilty, leave your seats and go there,' pointing out a certain place; 'all who are of the opposite opinion, there.' They accordingly stood up and divided; and those who held that the treaty had been broken were in a decided majority. Summoning the allies, they told them that their opinion was that Athens had been guilty of injustice, but that they wished to convoke all the allies and put it to the vote; in order that they might make war, if they decided to do so, on a common resolution. Having thus gained their point, the delegates returned home at once; the Athenian envoys a little later, when they had despatched the objects of their mission. This decision of the assembly judging that the treaty had been broken, was made in the fourteenth year of the thirty years' truce, which was entered into after the affair of Eubœa.

The Lacedæmonians voted that the treaty had been broken, and that war must be declared, not so much because they were persuaded by the arguments of the allies, as because they feared the growth of the power of the Athenians, seeing most of Hellas already subject to them.

CHAPTER IV

FROM THE END OF THE PERSIAN TO THE BEGINNING OF THE
PELOPONNESIAN WAR—THE PROGRESS FROM SUPREMACY
TO EMPIRE

B.C. 479: *How the power of Athens grew—Themistocles and the
Spartans—Fortification of Piræus—*B.C. 478: *Pausanias and the
end of Spartan supremacy—*B.C. 477: *Foundation of the Athenian
empire—*B.C. 476-466: *War against Eion, Scyros and Carystus;
revolt of Naxos—*B.C. 466-464: *Cimon's victories; revolt of Thasos
—Athens and Sparta sever relations—Megara joins Athens—Revolt of Egypt from Persia—Corinthians invade Megarid; their
defeat—*B.C. 458-457: *Building of the long walls; battle of Tanagra
—*B.C. 456-455: *Conquest of Bœotia; Athenian disaster in Egypt—*
B.C. 454-450: *Athenian expeditions to Thessaly and Cyprus—*B.C.
449-445: *Cimon's death; battle of Coronœa; loss of Bœotia—*
B.C. 445-440: *Pericles conquers Eubœa; Thirty Years' Truce—
Samos surrenders.*

THE way in which Athens came to be placed in the circumstances under which her power grew was this. After the Medes
had returned from Europe, defeated by sea and land by the
Hellenes, and after those of them who had fled with their
ships to Mycale had been destroyed, Leotychides, King of the
Lacedæmonians, the commander of the Hellenes at Mycale,
departed home with the allies from Peloponnese. But the
Athenians and the allies from Ionia and Hellespont, who had
now revolted from the king, remained and laid siege to Sestos,
which was still held by the Medes. After wintering before it,
they became masters of the place on its evacuation by the
barbarians; and after this they sailed away from Hellespont
to their respective cities. Meanwhile the Athenian people, after
the departure of the barbarian from their country, at once
proceeded to carry over their children and wives, and such
property as they had left, from the places where they had
deposited them, and prepared to rebuild their city and their
walls. For only isolated portions of the circumference had
been left standing, and most of the houses were in ruins;
though a few remained, in which the Persian grandees had
taken up their quarters.

Perceiving what they were going to do, the Lacedæmonians
sent an embassy to Athens. They would have themselves
preferred to see neither her nor any other city in possession

of a wall; though here they acted principally at the instigation
of their allies, who were alarmed at the strength of her newly
acquired navy, and the valour which she had displayed in
the war with the Medes. They begged her not only to abstain
from building walls for herself, but also to join them in
throwing down the walls that still held together of the ultra-
Peloponnesian cities. The real meaning of their advice, the
suspicion that it contained against the Athenians, was not
proclaimed; it was urged that so the barbarian, in the event
of a third invasion, would not have any strong place, such
as he now had in Thebes, for his base of operations; and that
Peloponnese would suffice for all as a base both for retreat
and offence. After the Lacedæmonians had thus spoken, they
were, on the advice of Themistocles, immediately dismissed
by the Athenians, with the answer that ambassadors should
be sent to Sparta to discuss the question. Themistocles told
the Athenians to send him off with all speed to Lacedæmon,
but not to despatch his colleagues as soon as they had selected
them, but to wait until they had raised their wall to the height
from which defence was possible. Meanwhile the whole population in the city was to labour at the wall, the Athenians,
their wives and their children, sparing no edifice, private or
public, which might be of any use to the work, but throwing
all down. After giving these instructions, and adding that he
would be responsible for all other matters there, he departed.
Arrived at Lacedæmon he did not seek an audience with the
authorities, but tried to gain time and made excuses. When
any of the government asked him why he did not appear in
the assembly, he would say that he was waiting for his colleagues, who had been detained in Athens by some engagement; however, that he expected their speedy arrival, and
wondered that they were not yet there. At first the Lacedæmonians trusted the words of Themistocles, through their
friendship for him; but when others arrived, all distinctly declaring that the work was going on and already attaining some
elevation, they did not know how to disbelieve it. Aware of
this, he told them that rumours are deceptive, and should not
be trusted; they should send some reputable persons from
Sparta to inspect, whose report might be trusted. They
despatched them accordingly. Concerning these Themistocles

secretly sent word to the Athenians to detain them as far as possible without putting them under open constraint, and not to let them go until they had themselves returned. For his colleagues had now joined him, Abronichus, son of Lysicles, and Aristides, son of Lysimachus, with the news that the wall was sufficiently advanced; and he feared that when the Lacedæmonians heard the facts, they might refuse to let them go. So the Athenians detained the envoys according to his message, and Themistocles had an audience with the Lacedæmonians, and at last openly told them that Athens was now fortified sufficiently to protect its inhabitants; that any embassy which the Lacedæmonians or their allies might wish to send to them, should in future proceed on the assumption that the people to whom they were going was able to distinguish both its own and the general interests. That when the Athenians thought fit to abandon their city and to embark in their ships, they ventured on that perilous step without consulting them; and that on the other hand, wherever they had deliberated with the Lacedæmonians, they had proved themselves to be in judgment second to none. That they now thought it fit that their city should have a wall, and that this would be more for the advantage of both the citizens of Athens and the Hellenic confederacy; for without equal military strength it was impossible to contribute equal or fair counsel to the common interest. It followed, he observed, either that all the members of the confederacy should be without walls, or that the present step should be considered a right one.

The Lacedæmonians did not betray any open signs of anger against the Athenians at what they heard. The embassy, it seems, was prompted not by a desire to obstruct, but to guide the counsels of their government: besides, Spartan feeling was at that time very friendly towards Athens on account of the patriotism which she had displayed in the struggle with the Mede. Still the defeat of their wishes could not but cause them secret annoyance. The envoys of each state departed home without complaint.

In this way the Athenians walled their city in a little while. To this day the building shows signs of the haste of its execution; the foundations are laid of stones of all kinds, and in some places not wrought or fitted, but placed just in the order in which they were brought by the different hands; and many columns, too, from tombs and sculptured stones were put in with the rest. For the bounds of the city were extended at every point of the circumference; and so they laid hands on everything without exception in their haste. Themistocles also persuaded them to finish the walls of Piræus, which had been begun before, in his year of office as archon; being influenced alike by the fineness of a locality that has three natural harbours, and by the great start which the Athenians would gain in the acquisition of power by becoming a naval people. For he first ventured to tell them to stick to the sea and forthwith began to lay the foundations of the empire. It was by his advice, too, that they built the walls of that thickness which can still be discerned round Piræus, the stones being brought up by two waggons meeting each other. Between the walls thus formed there was neither rubble nor mortar, but great stones hewn square and fitted together, cramped to each other on the outside with iron and lead. About half the height that he intended was finished. His idea was by their size and thickness to keep off the attacks of an enemy; he thought that they might be adequately defended by a small garrison of invalids, and the rest be freed for service in the fleet. For the fleet claimed most of his attention. He saw, as I think, that the approach by sea was easier for the king's army than that by land: he also thought Piræus more valuable than the upper city; indeed, he was always advising the Athenians, if a day should come when they were hard pressed by land, to go down into Piræus, and defy the world with their fleet. Thus, therefore, the Athenians completed their wall, and commenced their other buildings immediately after the retreat of the Mede.

Meanwhile Pausanias, son of Cleombrotus, was sent out from Lacedæmon as commander-in-chief of the Hellenes, with twenty ships from Peloponnese. With him sailed the Athenians with thirty ships, and a number of the other allies. They made an expedition against Cyprus and subdued most of the island, and afterwards against Byzantium, which was in the hands of the Medes, and compelled it to surrender. This event took place while the Spartans were still supreme. But the violence of Pausanias had already begun to be disagreeable to the

Hellenes, particularly to the Ionians and the newly liberated populations. These resorted to the Athenians and requested them as their kinsmen to become their leaders, and to stop any attempt at violence on the part of Pausanias. The Athenians accepted their overtures, and determined to put down any attempt of the kind and to settle everything else as their interests might seem to demand. In the meantime the Lacedæmonians recalled Pausanias for an investigation of the reports which had reached them. Manifold and grave accusations had been brought against him by Hellenes arriving in Sparta; and, to all appearance, there had been in him more of the mimicry of a despot than of the attitude of a general. As it happened, his recall came just at the time when the hatred which he had inspired had induced the allies to desert him, the soldiers from Peloponnese excepted, and to range themselves by the side of the Athenians. On his arrival at Lacedæmon, he was censured for his private acts of oppression, but was acquitted on the heaviest counts and pronounced not guilty; it must be known that the charge of Medism formed one of the principal, and to all appearance one of the best-founded articles against him. The Lacedæmonians did not, however, restore him to his command, but sent out Dorkis and certain others with a small force; who found the allies no longer inclined to concede to them the supremacy. Perceiving this they departed, and the Lacedæmonians did not send out any to succeed them. They feared for those who went out a deterioration similar to that observable in Pausanias; besides, they desired to be rid of the Median war, and were satisfied of the competency of the Athenians for the position, and of their friendship at the time towards themselves.

The Athenians having thus succeeded to the supremacy by the voluntary act of the allies through their hatred of Pausanias, fixed which cities were to contribute money against the barbarian, which ships; their professed object being to retaliate for their sufferings by ravaging the king's country. Now was the time that the office of 'Treasurers for Hellas' was first instituted by the Athenians. These officers received the tribute, as the money contributed was called. The tribute was first fixed at four hundred and sixty talents. The common treasury was at Delos, and the congresses were held in the

temple. Their supremacy commenced with independent allies
who acted on the resolutions of a common congress. It was
marked by the following undertakings in war and in administration during the interval between the Median and the present war, against the barbarian, against their own rebel allies,
and against the Peloponnesian powers which would come in
contact with them on various occasions. My excuse for relat-
ing these events, and for venturing on this digression, is that
this passage of history has been omitted by all my predecessors, who have confined themselves either to Hellenic history
before the Median war, or to the Median war itself. Hellani-
cus, it is true, did touch on these events in his Athenian
history; but he is somewhat concise and not accurate in his
dates. Besides, the history of these events contains an explanation of the growth of the Athenian empire.

First the Athenians besieged and captured Eion on the
Strymon from the Medes, and made slaves of the inhabitants,
being under the command of Cimon, son of Miltiades. Next
they enslaved Scyros the island in the Ægean, containing a
Dolopian population, and colonised it themselves. This was
followed by a war against Carystus, in which the rest of
Eubœa remained neutral, and which was ended by surrender
on conditions. After this Naxos left the confederacy, and a
war ensued, and she had to return after a siege; this was the
first instance of the engagement being broken by the subjugation of an allied city, a precedent which was followed by that
of the rest in the order which circumstances prescribed. Of
all the causes of defection, that connected with arrears of
tribute and vessels, and with failure of service, was the chief;
for the Athenians were very severe and exacting, and made
themselves offensive by applying the screw of necessity to
men who were not used to and in fact not disposed for any
continuous labour. In some other respects the Athenians were
not the old popular rulers they had been at first; and if they
had more than their fair share of service, it was correspond-
ingly easy for them to reduce any that tried to leave the
confederacy. For this the allies had themselves to blame; the
wish to get off service making most of them arrange to pay
their share of the expense in money instead of in ships, and
so to avoid having to leave their homes. Thus while Athens

was increasing her navy with the funds which they contributed, a revolt always found them without resources or
experience for war.

Next we come to the actions by land and by sea at the
river Eurymedon, between the Athenians with their allies, and
the Medes, when the Athenians won both battles on the same
day under the conduct of Cimon, son of Miltiades, and captured and destroyed the whole Phœnician fleet, consisting of
two hundred vessels. Some time afterwards occurred the defection of the Thasians, caused by disagreements about the
marts on the opposite coast of Thrace, and about the mine in
their possession. Sailing with a fleet to Thasos, the Athenians
defeated them at sea and effected a landing on the island.
About the same time they sent ten thousand settlers of their
own citizens and the allies to settle the place then called
Ennea Hodoi or Nine Ways, now Amphipolis. They succeeded in gaining possession of Ennea Hodoi from the
Edonians, but on advancing into the interior of Thrace were
cut off in Drabescus, a town of the Edonians, by the assembled
Thracians, who regarded the settlement of the place Ennea
Hodoi as an act of hostility. Meanwhile the Thasians being
defeated in the field and suffering siege, appealed to Lacedæmon, and desired her to assist them by an invasion of
Attica. Without informing Athens she promised and intended
to do so, but was prevented by the occurrence of the earthquake, accompanied by the secession of the Helots and the
Thuriats and Æthæans of the Periœci to Ithome. Most of
the Helots were the descendants of the old Messenians that
were enslaved in the famous war; and so all of them came to
be called Messenians. So the Lacedæmonians being engaged in
a war with the rebels in Ithome, the Thasians in the third
year of the siege obtained terms from the Athenians by razing
their walls, delivering up their ships, and arranging to pay the
monies demanded at once, and tribute in future; giving up
their possessions on the continent together with the mine.

The Lacedæmonians meanwhile finding the war against the
rebels in Ithome likely to last, invoked the aid of their allies,
and especially of the Athenians, who came in some force
under the command of Cimon. The reason for this pressing
summons lay in their reputed skill in siege operations; a long

siege had taught the Lacedæmonians their own deficiency in this art, else they would have taken the place by assault. The first open quarrel between the Lacedæmonians and Athenians arose out of this expedition. The Lacedæmonians, when assault failed to take the place, apprehensive of the enterprising and revolutionary character of the Athenians, and further looking upon them as of alien extraction, began to fear that if they remained, they might be tempted by the besieged in Ithome to attempt some political changes. They accordingly dismissed them alone of the allies, without declaring their suspicions, but merely saying that they had now no need of them. But the Athenians, aware that their dismissal did not proceed from the more honourable reason of the two, but from suspicions which had been conceived, went away deeply offended, and conscious of having done nothing to merit such treatment from the Lacedæmonians; and the instant that they returned home they broke off the alliance which had been made against the Mede, and allied themselves with Sparta's enemy Argos; each of the contracting parties taking the same oaths and making the same alliance with the Thessalians.

Meanwhile the rebels in Ithome, unable to prolong further a ten years' resistance, surrendered to Lacedæmon; the conditions being that they should depart from Peloponnese under safe conduct, and should never set foot in it again: any one who might hereafter be found there was to be the slave of his captor. It must be known that the Lacedæmonians had an old oracle from Delphi, to the effect that they should let go the suppliant of Zeus at Ithome. So they went forth with their children and their wives, and being received by Athens from the hatred that she now felt for the Lacedæmonians, were located at Naupactus, which she had lately taken from the Ozolian Locrians. The Athenians received another addition to their confederacy in the Megarians; who left the Lacedæmonian alliance, annoyed by a war about boundaries forced on them by Corinth. The Athenians occupied Megara and Pegæ, and built the Megarians their long walls from the city to Nisæa, in which they placed an Athenian garrison. This was the principal cause of the Corinthians conceiving such a deadly hatred against Athens.

Meanwhile Inaros, son of Psammetichus, a Libyan king of

the Libyans on the Egyptian border, having his head-quarters
at Marea, the town above Pharos, caused a revolt of almost
the whole of Egypt from King Artaxerxes, and placing himself
at its head, invited the Athenians to his assistance. Abandoning
a Cyprian expedition upon which they happened to be engaged
with two hundred ships of their own and their allies, they
arrived in Egypt and sailed from the sea into the Nile, and
making themselves masters of the river and two-thirds of
Memphis, addressed themselves to the attack of the remaining
third, which is called White Castle. Within it were Persians
and Medes who had taken refuge there, and Egyptians who
had not joined the rebellion.

Meanwhile the Athenians, making a descent from their
fleet upon Haliæ, were engaged by a force of Corinthians and
Epidaurians; and the Corinthians were victorious. Afterwards
the Athenians engaged the Peloponnesian fleet off Cecru-
phalia; and the Athenians were victorious. Subsequently war
broke out between Ægina and Athens, and there was a great
battle at sea off Ægina between the Athenians and Æginetans,
each being aided by their allies; in which victory remained
with the Athenians, who took seventy of the enemy's ships,
and landed in the country and commenced a siege under the
command of Leocrates, son of Strœbus. Upon this the Peloponnesians, desirous of aiding the Æginetans, threw into
Ægina a force of three hundred heavy infantry, who had before been serving with the Corinthians and Epidaurians.
Meanwhile the Corinthians and their allies occupied the
heights of Geraneia, and marched down into the Megarid, in
the belief that with a large force absent in Ægina and
Egypt, Athens would be unable to help the Megarians without
raising the siege of Ægina. But the Athenians, instead of
moving the army of Ægina, raised a force of the old and young
men that had been left in the city, and marched into the
Megarid under the command of Myronides. After a drawn
battle with the Corinthians, the rival hosts parted, each with
the impression that they had gained the victory. The
Athenians, however, if anything, had rather the advantage,
and on the departure of the Corinthians set up a trophy.
Urged by the taunts of the elders in their city, the Corinthians
made their preparations, and about twelve days afterwards

came and set up their trophy as victors. Sallying out from
Megara, the Athenians cut off the party that was employed in
erecting the trophy, and engaged and defeated the rest. In
the retreat of the vanquished army, a considerable division,
pressed by the pursuers and mistaking the road, dashed into
a field on some private property, with a deep trench all
round it, and no way out. Being acquainted with the place, the
Athenians hemmed their front with heavy infantry, and placing the light troops round in a circle, stoned all who had gone
in. Corinth here suffered a severe blow. The bulk of her army
continued its retreat home.

About this time the Athenians began to build the long walls
to the sea, that towards Phalerum and that towards Piræus.
Meanwhile the Phocians made an expedition against Doris,
the old home of the Lacedæmonians, containing the towns of
Bœum, Kitinium, and Erineum. They had taken one of these
towns, when the Lacedæmonians under Nicomedes, son of
Cleombrotus, commanding for King Pleistoanax, son of Pausanias, who was still a minor, came to the aid of the Dorians
with fifteen hundred heavy infantry of their own, and ten
thousand of their allies. After compelling the Phocians to
restore the town on conditions, they began their retreat. The
route by sea, across the Crissæan gulf, exposed them to the
risk of being stopped by the Athenian fleet; that across
Geraneia seemed scarcely safe, the Athenians holding Megara
and Pegæ. For the pass was a difficult one, and was always
guarded by the Athenians; and, in the present instance, the
Lacedæmonians had information that they meant to dispute
their passage. So they resolved to remain in Bœotia, and to
consider which would be the safest line of march. They had
also another reason for this resolve. Secret encouragement
had been given them by a party in Athens, who hoped to put
an end to the reign of democracy and the building of the
long walls. Meanwhile the Athenians marched against them
with their whole levy and a thousand Argives and the respective contingents of the rest of their allies. Altogether they were
fourteen thousand strong. The march was prompted by the
notion that the Lacedæmonians were at a loss how to effect
their passage, and also by suspicions of an attempt to overthrow the democracy. Some cavalry also joined the Athenians

from their Thessalian allies; but these went over to the Lacedæmonians during the battle.

The battle was fought at Tanagra in Bœotia. After heavy loss on both sides victory declared for the Lacedæmonians and their allies. After entering the Megarid and cutting down the fruit trees, the Lacedæmonians returned home across Geraneia and the isthmus. Sixty-two days after the battle the Athenians marched into Bœotia under the command of Myronides, defeated the Bœotians in battle at Œnophyta, and became masters of Bœotia and Phocis. They dismantled the walls of the Tanagræans, took a hundred of the richest men of the Opuntian Locrians as hostages, and finished their /own long walls. This was followed by the surrender of the Æginetans to Athens on conditions; they pulled down their walls, gave up their ships, and agreed to pay tribute in future. The Athenians sailed round Peloponnese under Tolmides, son of Tolmæus, burnt the arsenal of Lacedæmon, took Chalcis, a town of the Corinthians, and in a descent upon Sicyon defeated the Sicyonians in battle.

Meanwhile the Athenians in Egypt and their allies were still there, and encountered all the vicissitudes of war. First the Athenians were masters of Egypt, and the king sent Megabazus, a Persian, to Lacedæmon with money to bribe the Peloponnesians to invade Attica and so draw off the Athenians from Egypt. Finding that the matter made no progress, and that the money was only being wasted, he recalled Megabazus with the remainder of the money, and sent Megabuzus, son of Zopyrus, a Persian, with a large army to Egypt. Arriving by land he defeated the Egyptians and their allies in a battle, and drove the Hellenes out of Memphis, and at length shut them up in the island of Prosopitis, where he besieged them for a year and six months. At last, draining the canal of its waters, which he diverted into another channel, he left their ships high and dry and joined most of the island to the mainland, and then marched over on foot and captured it. Thus the enterprise of the Hellenes came to ruin after six years of war. Of all that large host a few travelling through Libya reached Cyrene in safety, but most of them perished. And thus Egypt returned to its subjection to the king, except Amyrtæus, the king in the marshes, whom they were unable to capture from the extent of the marsh; the marshmen being also the most warlike of the Egyptians. Inaros, the Libyan king, the sole author of the Egyptian revolt, was betrayed, taken, and crucified. Meanwhile a relieving squadron of fifty vessels had sailed from Athens and the rest of the confederacy for Egypt. They put in to shore at the Mendesian mouth of the Nile, in total ignorance of what had occurred. Attacked on the land side by the troops, and from the sea by the Phœnician navy, most of the ships were destroyed; the few remaining being saved by retreat. Such was the end of the great expedition of the Athenians and their allies to Egypt.

Meanwhile Orestes, son of Echecratidas, the Thessalian king, being an exile from Thessaly, persuaded the Athenians to restore him. Taking with them the Bœotians and Phocians their allies, the Athenians marched to Pharsalus in Thessaly. They became masters of the country, though only in the immediate vicinity of the camp; beyond which they could not go for fear of the Thessalian cavalry. But they failed to take the city or to attain any of the other objects of their expedition, and returned home with Orestes without having effected anything. Not long after this a thousand of the Athenians embarked in the vessels that were at Pegæ (Pegæ, it must be remembered, was now theirs), and sailed along the coast to Sicyon under the command of Pericles, son of Xanthippus. Landing in Sicyon and defeating the Sicyonians who engaged them, they immediately took with them the Achæans, and sailing across, marched against and laid siege to Œniadæ in Acarnania. Failing however to take it, they returned home.

Three years afterwards a truce was made between the Peloponnesians and Athenians for five years. Released from Hellenic war, the Athenians made an expedition to Cyprus with two hundred vessels of their own and their allies, under the command of Cimon. Sixty of these were detached to Egypt at the instance of Amyrtæus, the king in the marshes; the rest laid siege to Kitium, from which, however, they were compelled to retire by the death of Cimon and by scarcity of provisions. Sailing off Salamis in Cyprus, they fought with the Phœnicians, Cyprians, and Cilicians by land and sea, and being victorious on both elements departed home, and with them the returned squadron from Egypt. After this the

Lacedæmonians marched out on a sacred war, and becoming masters of the temple at Delphi, placed it in the hands of the Delphians. Immediately after their retreat, the Athenians marched out, became masters of the temple, and placed it in the hands of the Phocians.

Some time after this, Orchomenus, Chæronea, and some other places in Bœotia, being in the hands of the Bœotian exiles, the Athenians marched against the above-mentioned hostile places with a thousand Athenian heavy infantry and the allied contingents, under the command of Tolmides, son of Tolmæus. They took Chæronea, and made slaves of the inhabitants, and leaving a garrison, commenced their return. On their road they were attacked at Coronæa, by the Bœotian exiles from Orchomenus, with some Locrians and Eubœan exiles, and others who were of the same way of thinking, were defeated in battle, and some killed, others taken captive. The Athenians evacuated all Bœotia by a treaty providing for the recovery of the men; and the exiled Bœotians returned, and with all the rest regained their independence.

This was soon afterwards followed by the revolt of Eubœa from Athens. Pericles had already crossed over with an army of Athenians to the island, when news was brought to him that Megara had revolted, that the Peloponnesians were on the point of invading Attica, and that the Athenian garrison had been cut off by the Megarians, with the exception of a few who had taken refuge in Nisæa. The Megarians had introduced the Corinthians, Sicyonians, and Epidaurians into the town before they revolted. Meanwhile Pericles brought his army back in all haste from Eubœa. After this the Peloponnesians marched into Attica as far as Eleusis and Thrius, ravaging the country under the conduct of King Pleistoanax, the son of Pausanias, and without advancing further returned home. The Athenians then crossed over again to Eubœa under the command of Pericles, and subdued the whole of the island: all but Histiæa was settled by convention; the Histiæans they expelled from their homes, and occupied their territory themselves.

Not long after their return from Eubœa, they made a truce with the Lacedæmonians and their allies for thirty years, giving up the posts which they occupied in Peloponnese, Nisæa

Pegæ, Trœzen, and Achaia. In the sixth year of the truce,
war broke out between the Samians and Milesians about
Priene. Worsted in the war, the Milesians came to Athens with
loud complaints against the Samians. In this they were joined
by certain private persons from Samos itself, who wished to
revolutionise the government. Accordingly the Athenians
sailed to Samos with forty ships and set up a democracy;
took hostages from the Samians, fifty boys and as many men,
lodged them in Lemnos, and after leaving a garrison in the
island returned home. But some of the Samians had not remained in the island, but had fled to the continent. Making
an agreement with the most powerful of those in the city,
and an alliance with Pissuthnes, son of Hystaspes, the then
satrap of Sardis, they got together a force of seven hundred
mercenaries, and under cover of night crossed over to Samos.
Their first step was to rise on the commons, most of whom
they secured, their next to steal their hostages from Lemnos;
after which they revolted, gave up the Athenian garrison
left with them and its commanders to Pissuthnes, and instantly
prepared for an expedition against Miletus. The Byzantines
also revolted with them.

As soon as the Athenians heard the news, they sailed with
sixty ships against Samos. Sixteen of these went to Caria to
look out for the Phœnician fleet, and to Chios and Lesbos
carrying round orders for reinforcements, and so never engaged; but forty-four ships under the command of Pericles
with nine colleagues gave battle, off the island of Tragia, to
seventy Samian vessels, of which twenty were transports, as
they were sailing from Miletus. Victory remained with the
Athenians. Reinforced afterwards by forty ships from Athens,
and twenty-five Chian and Lesbian vessels, the Athenians
landed, and having the superiority by land invested the city
with three walls; it was also invested from the sea. Meanwhile
Pericles took sixty ships from the blockading squadron, and
departed in haste for Caunus and Caria, intelligence having
been brought in of the approach of the Phœnician fleet to
the aid of the Samians; indeed Stesagoras and others had left
the island with five ships to bring them. But in the meantime
the Samians made a sudden sally, and fell on the camp, which
they found unfortified. Destroying the look-out vessels, and

engaging and defeating such as were being launched to meet
them, they remained masters of their own seas for fourteen
days, and carried in and carried out what they pleased. But
on the arrival of Pericles, they were once more shut up. Fresh
reinforcements afterwards arrived—forty ships from Athens
with Thucydides, Hagnon, and Phormio; twenty with Tlepo-
lemus and Anticles, and thirty vessels from Chios and Lesbos.
After a brief attempt at fighting, the Samians, unable to hold
out, were reduced after a nine months' siege, and surrendered
on conditions; they razed their walls, gave hostages, delivered
up their ships, and arranged to pay the expenses of the war
by instalments. The Byzantines also agreed to be subject as
before.

CHAPTER V

SECOND CONGRESS AT LACEDÆMON—PREPARATIONS FOR WAR AND DIPLOMATIC SKIRMISHES—CYLON—PAUSANIAS— THEMISTOCLES

B.C. 479-432: *Advance of Athens and apathy of Sparta—Corinthians
plead for war—The allies vote for war—The story of Cylon—
The curse of Tænarus—Intrigues of Pausanias and Xerxes—Extravagance of Pausanias—Intrigues with the Helots—Death of
Pausanias—Themistocles implicated with Pausanias—Flight to
Persia—Death of Themistocles—Lacedæmonian demands—Speech
of Pericles—Athenians persuaded by Pericles.*

AFTER this, though not many years later, we at length come
to what has been already related, the affairs of Corcyra and
Potidæa, and the events that served as a pretext for the present
war. All these actions of the Hellenes against each other and
the barbarian occurred in the fifty years' interval between the
retreat of Xerxes and the beginning of the present war. During this interval the Athenians succeeded in placing their
empire on a firmer basis, and advanced their own home power
to a very great height. The Lacedæmonians, though fully
aware of it, opposed it only for a little while, but remained
inactive during most of the period, being of old slow to go
to war except under the pressure of necessity, and in the
present instance being hampered by wars at home; until the
growth of the Athenian power could be no longer ignored,
and their own confederacy became the object of its encroach-

ments. They then felt that they could endure it no longer, but that the time had come for them to throw themselves heart and soul upon the hostile power, and break it, if they could, by commencing the present war. And though the Lacedæmonians had made up their own minds on the fact of the breach of the treaty and the guilt of the Athenians, yet they sent to Delphi and inquired of the god whether it would be well with them if they went to war; and, as it is reported, received from him the answer that if they put their whole strength into the war, victory would be theirs, and the promise that he himself would be with them, whether invoked or uninvoked. Still they wished to summon their allies again, and to take their vote on the propriety of making war. After the ambassadors from the confederates had arrived and a congress had been convened, they all spoke their minds, most of them denouncing the Athenians and demanding that the war should begin. In particular the Corinthians. They had before on their own account canvassed the cities in detail to induce them to vote for the war, in the fear that it might come too late to save Potidæa; they were present also on this occasion, and came forward the last, and made the following speech:—

'Fellow allies, we can no longer accuse the Lacedæmonians of having failed in their duty: they have not only voted for war themselves, but have assembled us here for that purpose. We say their duty, for supremacy has its duties. Besides equitably administering private interests, leaders are required to show a special care for the common welfare in return for the special honours accorded to them by all in other ways. For ourselves, all who have already had dealings with the Athenians require no warning to be on their guard against them. The states more inland and out of the highway of communication should understand that if they omit to support the coast powers, the result will be to injure the transit of their produce for exportation and the reception in exchange of their imports from the sea; and they must not be careless judges of what is now said, as if it had nothing to do with them, but must expect that the sacrifice of the powers on the coast will one day be followed by the extension of the danger to the interior, and must recognise that their own interests are deeply involved in

this discussion. For these reasons they should not hesitate
to exchange peace for war. If wise men remain quiet, while
they are not injured, brave men abandon peace for war when
they are injured, returning to an understanding on a favourable opportunity: in fact, they are neither intoxicated by their
success in war, nor disposed to take an injury for the sake of
the delightful tranquillity of peace. Indeed, to falter for the
sake of such delights is, if you remain inactive, the quickest
way of losing the sweets of repose to which you cling; while to
conceive extravagant pretensions from success in war is to
forget how hollow is the confidence by which you are elated.
For if many ill-conceived plans have succeeded through the
still greater fatuity of an opponent, many more, apparently
well laid, have on the contrary ended in disgrace. The confidence with which we form our schemes is never completely
justified in their execution; speculation is carried on in safety,
but, when it comes to action, fear causes failure.

'To apply these rules to ourselves, if we are now kindling
war it is under the pressure of injury, and with adequate
grounds of complaint; and after we have chastised the Athenians we will in season desist. We have many reasons to expect
success,—first, superiority in numbers and in military experience, and secondly our general and unvarying obedience
in the execution of orders. The naval strength which they
possess shall be raised by us from our respective antecedent
resources, and from the monies at Olympia and Delphi. A loan
from these enables us to seduce their foreign sailors by the
offer of higher pay. For the power of Athens is more mercenary than national; while ours will not be exposed to the
same risk, as its strength lies more in men than in money. A
single defeat at sea is in all likelihood their ruin: should
they hold out, in that case there will be the more time for us
to exercise ourselves in naval matters; and as soon as we have
arrived at an equality in science, we need scarcely ask whether
we shall be their superiors in courage. For the advantages that
we have by nature they cannot acquire by education; while
their superiority in science must be removed by our practice.
The money required for these objects shall be provided by our
contributions: nothing indeed could be more monstrous than
the suggestion that, while their allies never tire of contributing

for their own servitude, we should refuse to spend for vengeance and self-preservation the treasure which by such refusal
we shall forfeit to Athenian rapacity, and see employed for our
own ruin.

'We have also other ways of carrying on the war, such as
revolt of their allies, the surest method of depriving them of
their revenues, which are the source of their strength, and
establishment of fortified positions in their country, and
various operations which cannot be foreseen at present. For
war of all things proceeds least upon definite rules, but draws
principally upon itself for contrivances to meet an emergency;
and in such cases the party who faces the struggle and keeps
his temper best meets with most security, and he who loses his
temper about it with correspondent disaster. Let us also reflect
that if it was merely a number of disputes of territory between
rival neighbours, it might be borne; but here we have an
enemy in Athens, that is a match for our whole coalition, and
more than a match for any of its members; so that unless as a
body and as individual nationalities and individual cities we
make an unanimous stand against her, she will easily conquer
us divided and in detail. That conquest, terrible as it may
sound, would, it must be known, have no other end than
slavery pure and simple; a word which Peloponnese cannot
even hear whispered without disgrace, or without disgrace see
so many states abused by one. Meanwhile the opinion would
be either that we were justly so used, or that we put up with it
from cowardice, and were proving degenerate sons in not even
securing for ourselves the freedom which our fathers gave to
Hellas; and in allowing the establishment in Hellas of a tyrant
state, though in individual states we think it our duty to put
down sole rulers. And we do not know how this conduct can
be held free from three of the gravest failings, want of sense,
of courage, or of vigilance. For we do not suppose that you
have taken refuge in that contempt of an enemy which has
proved so fatal in so many instances,—a feeling which from
the numbers that it has ruined has come to be called, not con-
temptuous but contemptible.

"There is, however, no advantage in reflexions on the past
further than may be of service to the present. For the future
we must provide by maintaining what the present gives us

and redoubling our efforts; it is hereditary to us to win virtue as the fruit of labour, and you must not change the habit, even though you should have a slight advantage in wealth and resources; for it is not right that what was won in want should be lost in plenty. No, we must boldly advance to the war for many reasons; the god has commanded it and promised to be with us, and the rest of Hellas will all join in the struggle, part from fear, part from interest. You will not be the first to break a treaty which the god, in advising us to go to war, judges to be violated already, but rather to support a treaty that has been outraged: indeed, treaties are broken not by resistance but by aggression.

'Your position, therefore, from whatever quarter you may view it, will amply justify you in going to war; and this step we recommend in the interests of all, bearing in mind that identity of interests is the surest of bonds whether between states or individuals. Delay not, therefore, to assist Potidæa, a Dorian city besieged by Ionians, which is quite a reversal of the order of things; nor to assert the freedom of the rest. It is impossible for us to wait any longer when waiting can only mean immediate disaster for some of us, and, if it comes to be known that we have conferred but do not venture to protect ourselves, like disaster in the near future for the rest. Delay not, fellow allies, but convinced of the necessity of the crisis and the wisdom of this counsel, vote for the war, undeterred by its immediate terrors, but looking beyond to the lasting peace by which it will be succeeded. Out of war peace gains fresh stability, but to refuse to abandon repose for war is not so sure a method of avoiding danger. We must believe that the tyrant city that has been established in Hellas has been established against all alike, with a programme of universal empire, part fulfilled, part in contemplation; let us then attack and reduce it, and win future security for ourselves and free‹ dom for the Hellenes who are now enslaved.'

Such were the words of the Corinthians. The Lacedæmonians having now heard all give their opinion, took the vote of all the allied states present in order, great and small alike; and the majority voted for war. This decided, it was still impossible for them to commence at once, from their want of preparation; but it was resolved that the means requisite were to be procured by the different states, and that there was to be no delay. And indeed, in spite of the time occupied with the necessary arrangements, less than a year elapsed before Attica was invaded, and the war openly begun.

This interval was spent in sending embassies to Athens charged with complaints, in order to obtain as good a pretext for war as possible, in the event of her paying no attention to them. The first Lacedæmonian embassy was to order the Athenians to drive out the curse of the goddess; the history of which is as follows. In former generations there was an Athenian of the name of Cylon, a victor at the Olympic games, of good birth and powerful position, who had married a daughter of Theagenes, a Megarian, at that time tyrant of Megara. Now this Cylon was inquiring at Delphi; when he was told by the god to seize the Acropolis of Athens on the grand festival of Zeus. Accordingly, procuring a force from Theagenes and persuading his friends to join him, when the Olympic festival in Peloponnese came, he seized the Acropolis, with the intention of making himself tyrant, thinking that this was the grand festival of Zeus, and also an occasion appropriate for a victor at the Olympic games. Whether the grand festival that was meant was in Attica or elsewhere was a question which he never thought of, and which the oracle did not offer to solve. For the Athenians also have a festival which is called the grand festival of Zeus Meilichios or Gracious, viz. the Diasia. It is celebrated outside the city, and the whole people sacrifice not real victims but a number of bloodless offerings peculiar to the country. However, fancying he had chosen the right time, he made the attempt. As soon as the Athenians perceived it, they flocked in, one and all, from the country, and sat down, and laid siege to the citadel. But as time went on, weary of the labour of blockade, most of them departed; the responsibility of keeping guard being left to the nine archons, with plenary powers to arrange everything according to their good judgment. It must be known that at that time most political functions were discharged by the nine archons. Meanwhile Cylon and his besieged companions were distressed for want of food and water. Accordingly Cylon and his brother made their escape; but the rest being hard pressed, and some even dying of famine, seated themselves as suppliants at the altar in the

Acropolis. The Athenians who were charged with the duty of keeping guard, when they saw them at the point of death in the temple, raised them up on the understanding that no harm should be done to them, led them out and slew them. Some who as they passed by took refuge at the altars of the awful goddesses were despatched on the spot. From this deed the men who killed them were called accursed and guilty against the goddess, they and their descendants. Accordingly these cursed ones were driven out by the Athenians, driven out again by Cleomenes of Lacedæmon and an Athenian faction; the living were driven out, and the bones of the dead were taken up; thus they were cast out. For all that, they came back afterwards, and their descendants are still in the city.

This, then, was the curse that the Lacedæmonians ordered them to drive out. They were actuated primarily, as they pretended, by a care for the honour of the gods; but they also knew that Pericles, son of Xanthippus, was connected with the curse on his mother's side, and they thought that his banishment would materially advance their designs on Athens. Not that they really hoped to succeed in procuring this; they rather thought to create a prejudice against him in the eyes of his countrymen from the feeling that the war would be partly caused by his misfortune. For being the most powerful man of his time, and the leading Athenian statesman, he opposed the Lacedæmonians in everything, and would have no concessions, but ever urged the Athenians on to war.

The Athenians retorted by ordering the Lacedæmonians to drive out the curse of Tænarus. The Lacedæmonians had once raised up some Helot suppliants from the temple of Poseidon at Tænarus, led them away and slain them; for which they believe the great earthquake at Sparta to have been a retribution. The Athenians also ordered them to drive out the curse of the goddess of the Brazen House; the history of which is as follows. After Pausanias the Lacedæmonian had been recalled by the Spartans from his command in the Hellespont (this is his first recall), and had been tried by them and acquitted, not being again sent out in a public capacity, he took a galley of Hermione on his own responsibility, without the authority of the Lacedæmonians, and arrived as a private person in the Hellespont. He came ostensibly for the Hellenic war, really

to carry on his intrigues with the king, which he had begun
before his recall, being ambitious of reigning over Hellas. The
circumstance which first enabled him to lay the king under an
obligation, and to make a beginning of the whole design was
this. Some connexions and kinsmen of the king had been taken
in Byzantium, on its capture from the Medes, when he was
first there, after the return from Cyprus. These captives he
sent off to the king without the knowledge of the rest of the
allies, the account being that they had escaped from him. He
managed this with the help of Gongylus, an Eretrian, whom
he had placed in charge of Byzantium and the prisoners. He
also gave Gongylus a letter for the king, the contents of which
were as follows, as was afterwards discovered: 'Pausanias, the
general of Sparta, anxious to do you a favour, sends you these
his prisoners of war. I propose also, with your approval, to
marry your daughter, and to make Sparta and the rest of
Hellas subject to you. I may say that I think I am able to do
this, with your co-operation. Accordingly if any of this please
you, send a safe man to the sea through whom we may in
future conduct our correspondence.'

This was all that was revealed in the writing, and Xerxes
was pleased with the letter. He sent off Artabazus, son of
Pharnaces, to the sea with orders to supersede Megabates,
the previous governor in the satrapy of Daskylion, and to
send over as quickly as possible to Pausanias at Byzantium a
letter which he entrusted to him; to show him the royal signet,
and to execute any commission which he might receive from
Pausanias on the king's matters, with all care and fidelity.
Artabazus on his arrival carried the king's orders into effect,
and sent over the letter, which contained the following answer:—'Thus saith King Xerxes to Pausanias. For the men
whom you have saved for me across sea from Byzantium, an
obligation is laid up for you in our house, recorded forever;
and with your proposals I am well pleased. Let neither night
nor day stop you from diligently performing any of your
promises to me, neither for cost of gold nor of silver let them
be hindered, nor yet for number of troops, wherever it may be
that their presence is needed; but with Artabazus, an honourable man whom I send you, boldly advance my objects and
yours, as may be most for the honour and interest of us both.'

Before held in high honour by the Hellenes as the hero of Platæa, Pausanias, after the receipt of this letter, became prouder than ever, and could no longer live in the usual style, but went out of Byzantium in a Median dress, was attended on his march through Thrace by a bodyguard of Medes and Egyptians, kept a Persian table, and was quite unable to contain his intentions, but betrayed by his conduct in trifles what his ambition looked one day to enact on a grander scale. He also made himself difficult of access, and displayed so violent a temper to every one without exception that no one could come near him. Indeed, this was the principal reason why the confederacy went over to the Athenians.

The above-mentioned conduct, coming to the ears of the Lacedæmonians, occasioned his first recall. And after his second voyage out in the ship of Hermione, without their orders, he gave proofs of similar behaviour. Besieged and expelled from Byzantium by the Athenians, he did not return to Sparta; but news came that he had settled at Colonæ in the Troad, and was intriguing with the barbarians, and that his stay there was for no good purpose; and the Ephors, now no longer hesitating, sent him a herald and a scytale with orders to accompany the herald or be declared a public enemy. Anxious above everything to avoid suspicion, and confident that he could quash the charge by means of money, he returned a second time to Sparta. At first thrown into prison by the Ephors (whose powers enable them to do this to the king), he soon compromised the matter and came out again, and offered himself for trial to any who wished to institute an inquiry concerning him.

Now the Spartans had no tangible proof against him— neither his enemies nor the nation—of that indubitable kind required for the punishment of a member of the royal family, and at that moment in high office; he being regent for his first cousin King Pleistarchus, Leonidas' son, who was still a minor. But by his contempt of the laws and imitation of the barbarians, he gave grounds for much suspicion of his being discontented with things established; all the occasions on which he had in any way departed from the regular customs were passed in review, and it was remembered that he had taken upon himself to have inscribed on the tripod at Delphi,

which was dedicated by the Hellenes as the first-fruits of the
spoil of the Medes, the following couplet:—

> 'The Mede defeated, great Pausanias raised
> This monument, that Phœbus might be praised.'

At the time the Lacedæmonians had at once erased the
couplet, and inscribed the names of the cities that had aided
in the overthrow of the barbarian and dedicated the offering.
Yet it was considered that Pausanias had here been guilty of
a grave offence, which, interpreted by the light of the attitude
which he had since assumed, gained a new significance, and
seemed to be quite in keeping with his present schemes. Besides, they were informed that he was even intriguing with the
Helots; and such indeed was the fact, for he promised them
freedom and citizenship if they would join him in insurrection,
and would help him to carry out his plans to the end. Even
now, mistrusting the evidence even of the Helots themselves,
the Ephors would not consent to take any decided step against
him; in accordance with their regular custom towards themselves, namely, to be slow in taking any irrevocable resolve in
the matter of a Spartan citizen, without indisputable proof. At
last, it is said, the person who was going to carry to Artabazus
the last letter for the king, a man of Argilus, once the favourite
and most trusty servant of Pausanias, turned informer.
Alarmed by the reflexion that none of the previous messengers
had ever returned, having counterfeited the seal, in order that,
if he found himself mistaken in his surmises, or if Pausanias
should ask to make some correction, he might not be discovered, he undid the letter, and found the postscript that
he had suspected, viz., an order to put him to death.

On being shown the letter the Ephors now felt more certain. Still, they wished to hear Pausanias commit himself with
their own ears. Accordingly the man went by appointment to
Tænarus as a suppliant, and there built himself a hut divided
into two by a partition; within which he concealed some of the
Ephors and let them hear the whole matter plainly. For
Pausanias came to him and asked him the reason of his suppliant position; and the man reproached him with the order
that he had written concerning him, and one by one declared
all the rest of the circumstances, how he who had never yet

brought him into any danger, while employed as agent between him and the king, was yet just like the mass of his
servants, to be rewarded with death. Admitting all this, and
telling him not to be angry about the matter, Pausanias gave
him the pledge of raising him up from the temple, and begged
him to set off as quickly as possible, and not to hinder the
business in hand.

The Ephors listened carefully, and then departed, taking
no action for the moment, but, having at last attained to
certainty, were preparing to arrest him in the city. It is reported that, as he was about to be arrested in the street, he
saw from the face of one of the Ephors what he was coming
for; another, too, made him a secret signal, and betrayed it to
him from kindness. Setting off with a run for the temple of
the goddess of the Brazen House, the enclosure of which was
near at hand, he succeeded in taking sanctuary before they
took him, and entering into a small chamber, which formed
part of the temple, to avoid being exposed to the weather, lay
still there. The Ephors, for the moment distanced in the pursuit, afterwards took off the roof of the chamber, and having
made sure that he was inside, shut him in, barricaded the
doors, and staying before the place, reduced him by starvation. When they found that he was on the point of expiring,
just as he was, in the chamber, they brought him out of the
temple, while the breath was still in him, and as soon as he was
brought out he died. They were going to throw him into the
Kaiadas, where they cast criminals, but finally decided to
inter him somewhere near. But the god at Delphi afterwards
ordered the Lacedæmonians to remove the tomb to the place
of his death—where he now lies in the consecrated ground, as
an inscription on a monument declares—and, as what had
been done was a curse to them, to give back two bodies instead
of one to the goddess of the Brazen House. So they had two
brazen statues made, and dedicated them as a substitute for
Pausanias. Accordingly the Athenians retorted by telling the
Lacedæmonians to drive out what the god himself had pronounced to be a curse.

To return to the Medism of Pausanias. Matter was found
in the course of the inquiry to implicate Themistocles; and
the Lacedæmonians accordingly sent envoys to the Athenians.

and required them to punish him as they had punished Pausanias. The Athenians consented to do so. But he had, as it happened, been ostracised, and, with a residence at Argos, was in the habit of visiting other parts of Peloponnese. So they sent with the Lacedæmonians, who were ready to join in the pursuit, persons with instructions to take him wherever they found him. But Themistocles got scent of their intentions, and fled from Peloponnese to Corcyra, which was under obligations towards him. But the Corcyræans alleged that they could not venture to shelter him at the cost of offending Athens and Lacedæmon, and they conveyed him over to the continent opposite. Pursued by the officers who hung on the report of his movements, at a loss where to turn, he was compelled to stop at the house of Admetus, the Molossian king, though they were not on friendly terms. Admetus happened not to be indoors, but his wife, to whom he made himself a suppliant, instructed him to take their child in his arms and sit down by the hearth. Soon afterwards Admetus came in, and Themistocles told him who he was, and begged him not to revenge on Themistocles in exile any opposition which his requests might have experienced from Themistocles at Athens. Indeed, he was now far too low for his revenge; retaliation was only honourable between equals. Besides, his opposition to the king had only affected the success of a request, not the safety of his person; if the king were to give him up to the pursuers that he mentioned, and the fate which they intended for him, he would just be consigning him to certain death.

The king listened to him and raised him up with his son, as he was sitting with him in his arms after the most effectual method of supplication, and on the arrival of the Lacedæmonians not long afterwards, refused to give him up for anything they could say, but sent him off by land to the other sea to Pydna in Alexander's dominions, as he wished to go to the Persian king. There he met with a merchantman on the point of starting for Ionia. Going on board, he was carried by a storm to the Athenian squadron which was blockading Naxos. In his alarm—he was luckily unknown to the people in the vessel—he told the master who he was and what he was flying for, and said that, if he refused to save him, he would declare that he was taking him for a bribe. Meanwhile their safety consisted in letting no one leave the ship until a favourable time for sailing should arise. If he complied with his wishes, he promised him a proper recompense. The master acted as he desired, and, after lying to for a day and a night out of the reach of the squadron, at length arrived at Ephesus.

After having rewarded him with a present of money, as soon as he received some from his friends at Athens and from his secret hoards at Argos, Themistocles started inland with one of the Coast-Persians, and sent a letter to King Artaxerxes, Xerxes' son, who had just come to the throne. Its contents were as follows: 'I, Themistocles, am come to you, who did your house more harm than any of the Hellenes, when I was compelled to defend myself against your father's invasion,—harm, however, far surpassed by the good that I did him during his retreat, which brought no danger for me but much for him. For the past, you are a good turn in my debt,'—here he mentioned the warning sent to Xerxes from Salamis to retreat, as well as his finding the bridges unbroken, which, as he falsely pretended, was due to him,—'for the present, able to do you great service, I am here, pursued by the Hellenes for my friendship for you. However, I desire a year's grace, when I shall be able to declare in person the objects of my coming.'

It is said that the king approved his intention, and told him to do as he said. He employed the interval in making what progress he could in the study of the Persian tongue, and of the customs of the country. Arrived at Court at the end of the year, he attained to very high consideration there, such as no Hellene has ever possessed before or since; partly from his splendid antecedents, partly from the hopes which he held out of effecting for him the subjugation of Hellas, but principally by the proof which experience daily gave of his capacity. For Themistocles was a man who exhibited the most indubitable signs of genius; indeed, in this particular he has a claim on our admiration quite extraordinary and unparalleled. By his own native capacity, alike unformed and unsupplemented by study, he was at once the best judge in those sudden crises which admit of little or of no deliberation, and the best prophet of the future, even to its most distant possibilities. An able

theoretical expositor of all that came within the sphere of his
practice, he was not without the power of passing an adequate
judgment in matters in which he had no experience. He could
also excellently divine the good and evil which lay hid in the
unseen future. In fine, whether we consider the extent of his
natural powers, or the slightness of his application, this extraordinary man must be allowed to have surpassed all others
in the faculty of intuitively meeting an emergency. Disease
was the real cause of his death; though there is a story of his
having ended his life by poison, on finding himself unable to
fulfil his promises to the king. However this may be, there is
a monument to him in the market-place of Asiatic Magnesia.
He was governor of the district, the king having given him
Magnesia, which brought in fifty talents a year, for bread,
Lampsacus, which was considered to be the richest wine country, for wine, and Myos for other provisions. His bones, it is
said, were conveyed home by his relatives in accordance with
his wishes, and interred in Attic ground. This was done without the knowledge of the Athenians; as it is against the law
to bury in Attica an outlaw for treason. So ends the history
of Pausanias and Themistocles, the Lacedæmonian and the
Athenian, the most famous men of their time in Hellas.

To return to the Lacedæmonians. The history of their first
embassy, the injunctions which it conveyed, and the rejoinder
which it provoked, concerning the expulsion of the accursed
persons, have been related already. It was followed by a second, which ordered Athens to raise the siege of Potidæa, and
to respect the independence of Ægina. Above all, it gave her
most distinctly to understand that war might be prevented by
the revocation of the Megara decree, excluding the Megarians
from the use of Athenian harbours and of the market of
Athens. But Athens was not inclined either to revoke the
decree, or to entertain their other proposals; she accused the
Megarians of pushing their cultivation into the consecrated
ground and the unenclosed land on the border, and of harbouring her runaway slaves. At last an embassy arrived with
the Lacedæmonian ultimatum. The ambassadors were Ramphias, Melesippus, and Agesander. Not a word was said on
any of the old subjects; there was simply this:—'Lacedæmon
wishes the peace to continue, and there is no reason why it

should not, if you would leave the Hellenes independent.' Upon this the Athenians held an assembly, and laid the matter before their consideration. It was resolved to deliberate once for all on all their demands, and to give them an answer. There were many speakers who came forward and gave their support to one side or the other, urging the necessity of war, or the revocation of the decree and the folly of allowing it to stand in the way of peace. Among them came forward Pericles, son of Xanthippus, the first man of his time at Athens, ablest alike in counsel and in action, and gave the following advice:—

'There is one principle, Athenians, which I hold to through everything, and that is the principle of no concession to the Peloponnesians. I know that the spirit which inspires men while they are being persuaded to make war, is not always retained in action; that as circumstances change, resolutions change. Yet I see that now as before the same, almost literally the same, counsel is demanded of me; and I put it to those of you, who are allowing yourselves to be persuaded, to support the national resolves even in the case of reverses, or to forfeit all credit for their wisdom in the event of success. For sometimes the course of things is as arbitrary as the plans of man; indeed this is why we usually blame chance for whatever does not happen as we expected. Now it was clear before, that Lacedæmon entertained designs against us; it is still more clear now. The treaty provides that we shall mutually submit our differences to legal settlement, and that we shall meanwhile each keep what we have. Yet the Lacedæmonians never yet made us any such offer, never yet would accept from us any such offer; on the contrary, they wish complaints to be settled by war instead of by negotiation; and in the end we find them here dropping the tone of expostulation and adopting that of command. They order us to raise the siege of Potidæa, to let Ægina be independent, to revoke the Megara decree; and they conclude with an ultimatum warning us to leave the Hellenes independent. I hope that you will none of you think that we shall be going to war for a trifle if we refuse to revoke the Megara decree, which appears in front of their complaints, and the revocation of which is to save us from war, or let any feeling of self-reproach linger in your minds, as if you went to war for slight cause. Why, this trifle contains the whole

seal and trial of your resolution. If you give way, you will
instantly have to meet some greater demand, as having been
frightened into obedience in the first instance; while a firm
refusal will make them clearly understand that they must treat
you more as equals. Make your decision therefore at once,
either to submit before you are harmed, or if we are to go to
war, as I for one think we ought, to do so without caring
whether the ostensible cause be great or small, resolved against
making concessions or consenting to a precarious tenure of
our possessions. For all claims from an equal, urged upon a
neighbour as commands, before any attempt at legal settlement, be they great or be they small, have only one meaning,
and that is slavery.

'As to the war and the resources of either party, a detailed
comparison will not show you the inferiority of Athens. Personally engaged in the cultivation of their land, without funds
either private or public, the Peloponnesians are also without
experience in long wars across sea, from the strict limit which
poverty imposes on their attacks upon each other. Powers of
this description are quite incapable of often manning a fleet
or often sending out an army: they cannot afford the absence
from their homes, the expenditure from their own funds; and
besides, they have not command of the sea. Capital, it must
be remembered, maintains a war more than forced contributions. Farmers are a class of men that are always more ready
to serve in person than in purse. Confident that the former
will survive the dangers, they are by no means so sure that the
latter will not be prematurely exhausted, especially if the war
last longer than they expect, which it very likely will. In a
single battle the Peloponnesians and their allies may be able
to defy all Hellas, but they are incapacitated from carrying
on a war against a power different in character from their
own, by the want of the single council-chamber requisite to
prompt and vigorous action, and the substitution of a diet
composed of various races, in which every state possesses an
equal vote, and each presses its own ends, a condition of things
which generally results in no action at all. The great wish of
some is to avenge themselves on some particular enemy, the
great wish of others to save their own pocket. Slow in assembling, they devote a very small fraction of the time to the

consideration of any public object, most of it to the prosecution of their own objects. Meanwhile each fancies that no
harm will come of his neglect, that it is the business of some-
body else to look after this or that for him; and so, by the
same notion being entertained by all separately, the common
cause imperceptibly decays.

'But the principal point is the hindrance that they will
experience from want of money. The slowness with which it
comes in will cause delay; but the opportunities of war wait
for no man. Again, we need not be alarmed either at the possibility of their raising fortifications in Attica, or at their navy.
It would be difficult for any system of fortifications to establish a rival city, even in time of peace, much more, surely, in
an enemy's country, with Athens just as much fortified against
it, as it against Athens; while a mere post might be able to do
some harm to the country by incursions and by the facilities
which it would afford for desertion, but can never prevent our
sailing into their country and raising fortifications there, and
making reprisals with our powerful fleet. For our naval skill
is of more use to us for service on land, than their military skill
for service at sea. Familiarity with the sea they will not find
an easy acquisition. If you who have been practising at it
ever since the Median invasion have not yet brought it to
perfection, is there any chance of anything considerable being
effected by an agricultural, unseafaring population, who will
besides be prevented from practising by the constant presence
of strong squadrons of observation from Athens? With a small
squadron they might hazard an engagement, encouraging
their ignorance by numbers; but the restraint of a strong force
will prevent their moving, and through want of practice they
will grow more clumsy, and consequently more timid. It must
be kept in mind that seamanship, just like anything else, is a
matter of art, and will not admit of being taken up occasionally
as an occupation for times of leisure; on the contrary, it is so
exacting as to leave leisure for nothing else.

'Even if they were to touch the moneys at Olympia or
Delphi, and try to seduce our foreign sailors by the temptation
of higher pay, that would only be a serious danger if we could
not still be a match for them, by embarking our own citizens
and the aliens resident among us. But in fact by this means

we are always a match for them; and, best of all, we have a larger and higher class of native coxswains and sailors among our own citizens than all the rest of Hellas. And to say nothing of the danger of such a step, none of our foreign sailors would consent to become an outlaw from his country, and to take service with them and their hopes, for the sake of a few days' high pay.

'This, I think, is a tolerably fair account of the position of the Peloponnesians; that of Athens is free from the defects that I have criticised in them, and has other advantages of its own, which they can show nothing to equal. If they march against our country we will sail against theirs, and it will then be found that the desolation of the whole of Attica is not the same as that of even a fraction of Peloponnese; for they will not be able to supply the deficiency except by a battle, while we have plenty of land both on the islands and the continent. The rule of the sea is indeed a great matter. Consider for a moment. Suppose that we were islanders: can you conceive a more impregnable position? Well, this in future should, as far as possible, be our conception of our position. Dismissing all thought of our land and houses, we must vigilantly guard the sea and the city. No irritation that we may feel for the former must provoke us to a battle with the numerical superiority of the Peloponnesians. A victory would only be succeeded by another battle against the same superiority: a reverse involves the loss of our allies, the source of our strength, who will not remain quiet a day after we become unable to march against them. We must cry not over the loss of houses and land but of men's lives; since houses and land do not gain men, but men them. And if I had thought that I could persuade you, I would have bid you go out and lay them waste with your own hands, and show the Peloponnesians that this at any rate will not make you submit.

'I have many other reasons to hope for a favourable issue, if you can consent not to combine schemes of fresh conquest with the conduct of the war, and will abstain from wilfully involving yourselves in other dangers; indeed, I am more afraid of our own blunders than of the enemy's devices. But these matters shall be explained in another speech, as events require; for the present dismiss these men with the answer that we will allow Megara the use of our market and harbours, when the Lacedæmonians suspend their alien acts in favour of us and our allies, there being nothing in the treaty to prevent either one or the other: that we will leave the cities independent, if independent we found them when we made the treaty, and when the Lacedæmonians grant to their cities an independence not involving subservience to Lacedæmonian interest, but such as each severally may desire: that we are willing to give the legal satisfaction which our agreements specify, and that we shall not commence hostilities, but shall resist those who do commence them. This is an answer agreeable at once to the rights and the dignity of Athens. It must be thoroughly understood that war is a necessity; but that the more readily we accept it, the less will be the ardour of our opponents, and that out of the greatest dangers communities and individuals acquire the greatest glory. Did not our fathers resist the Medes not only with resources far different from ours, but even when those resources had been abandoned; and more by wisdom than by fortune, more by daring than by strength, did not they beat off the barbarian and advance their affairs to their present height? We must not fall behind them, but must resist our enemies in any way and in every way, and attempt to hand down our power to our posterity unimpaired.'

Such were the words of Pericles. The Athenians, persuaded of the wisdom of his advice, voted as he desired, and answered the Lacedæmonians as he recommended, both on the separate points and in the general; they would do nothing on dictation, but were ready to have the complaints settled in a fair and impartial manner by the legal method, which the terms of the truce prescribed. So the envoys departed home, and did not return again.

These were the charges and differences existing between the rival powers before the war, arising immediately from the affair at Epidamnus and Corcyra. Still intercourse continued in spite of them, and mutual communication. It was carried on without heralds, but not without suspicion, as events were occurring which were equivalent to a breach of the treaty and matter for war.

BOOK II

CHAPTER VI

BEGINNING OF THE PELOPONNESIAN WAR—FIRST INVASION OF ATTICA—FUNERAL ORATION OF PERICLES

B.C. 431: *Hostilities begin—Theban occupation of Platœa—Massacre of the Thebans—Athens intervenes—Preparations for war—Athenian and Spartan allies—Speech of Archidamus—Archidamus advances with his army—Pericles' strategy—Athenian discontent at abandoning homes—Archidamus invades Attica—Firmness of Pericles—Invaders withdraw—Expulsion of the Æginetans—Sitalces allied with Athens—Pericles leads invasion of Megarid—Funeral of first victims—Pericles delivers eulogium.*

THE war between the Athenians and Peloponnesians and the allies on either side now really begins. For now all intercourse except through the medium of heralds ceased, and hostilities were commenced and prosecuted without intermission. The history follows the chronological order of events by summers and winters.

The thirty years' truce which was entered into after the conquest of Eubœa lasted fourteen years. In the fifteenth, in the forty-eighth year of the priestess-ship of Chrysis at Argos, in the Ephorate of Ænesias at Sparta, in the last month but two of the Archonship of Pythodorus at Athens, and six months after the battle of Potidæa, just at the beginning of spring, a Theban force a little over three hundred strong, under the command of their Bœotarchs, Pythangelus, son of Phyleides, and Diemporus, son of Onetorides, about the first watch of the night, made an armed entry into Platæa, a town of Bœotia in alliance with Athens. The gates were opened to them by a Platæan called Naucleides, who, with his party, had invited them in, meaning to put to death the citizens of the opposite party, bring over the city to Thebes, and thus obtain power for themselves. This was arranged through Eurymachus, son of Leontiades, a person of great influence at Thebes. For Platæa had always been at variance with Thebes; and the latter, foreseeing that war was at hand, wished to surprise her old enemy in time of peace, before hostilities had actually broken out. Indeed this was how they got in so easily without being observed, as no guard had been posted. After the soldiers had grounded arms in the market-place, those who had invited them in wished them to set to work at once and go to their enemies' houses. This, however, the Thebans refused to do, but determined to make a conciliatory proclamation, and if possible to come to a friendly understanding with the citizens. Their herald accordingly invited any who wished to resume their old place in the confederacy of their countrymen to ground arms with them, for they thought that in this way the city would readily join them.

On becoming aware of the presence of the Thebans within their gates, and of the sudden occupation of the town, the Platæans concluded in their alarm that more had entered than was really the case, the night preventing their seeing them. They accordingly came to terms, and accepting the proposal, made no movement; especially as the Thebans offered none of them any violence. But somehow or other, during the negotiations, they discovered the scanty numbers of the Thebans, and decided that they could easily attack and overpower them; the mass of the Platæans being averse to revolting from Athens. At all events they resolved to attempt it. Digging through the party walls of the houses, they thus managed to join each other without being seen going through the streets, in which they placed waggons without the beasts in them, to serve as a barricade, and arranged everything else as seemed convenient for the occasion. When everything had been done that circumstances permitted, they watched their opportunity and went out of their houses against the enemy. It was still night, though daybreak was at hand: in daylight it was thought that their attack would be met by men full of courage and on equal terms with their assailants, while in darkness it would fall upon panic-stricken troops, who would also be at a disadvantage from their enemy's knowledge of the locality. So they made their assault at once, and came to close quarters as quickly as they could.

The Thebans, finding themselves outwitted, immediately closed up to repel all attacks made upon them. Twice or thrice they beat back their assailants. But the men shouted and charged them, the women and slaves screamed and yelled from the houses and pelted them with stones and tiles; besides, it had been raining hard all night; and so at last their courage gave way, and they turned and fled through the town. Most of the fugitives were quite ignorant of the right ways out, and this, with the mud, and the darkness caused by the moon being in her last quarter, and the fact that their pursuers knew their way about and could easily stop their escape, proved fatal to many. The only gate open was the one by which they had entered, and this was shut by one of the Platæans driving the spike of a javelin into the bar instead of the bolt; so that even here there was no longer any means of exit. They were now chased all over the town. Some got on the wall and threw themselves over, in most cases with a fatal result. One party managed to find a deserted gate, and obtaining an axe from a woman, cut through the bar; but as they were soon observed only a few succeeded in getting out. Others were cut off in detail in different parts of the city. The most numerous and compact body rushed into a large building next to the city wall: the doors on the side of the street happened to be open, and the Thebans fancied that they were the gates of the town, and that there was a passage right through to the outside. The Platæans, seeing their enemies in a trap, now consulted whether they should set fire to the building and burn them just as they were, or whether there was anything else that they could do with them; until at length these and the rest of the Theban survivors found wandering about the town agreed to an unconditional surrender of themselves and their arms to the Platæans.

While such was the fate of the party in Platæa, the rest of the Thebans who were to have joined them with all their forces before daybreak, in case of anything miscarrying with the body that had entered, received the news of the affair on the road, and pressed forward to their succour. Now Platæa is nearly eight miles from Thebes, and their march was delayed by the rain that had fallen in the night, for the river Asopus had risen and was not easy of passage; and so, having to march in the rain, and being hindered in crossing the river, they arrived too late, and found the whole party either slain or captive. When they learned what had happened, they at once formed a design against the Platæans outside the city. As the attack had been made in time of peace, and was perfectly unexpected, there were of course men and stock in the fields; and the Thebans wished if possible to have some prisoners to exchange against their countrymen in the town, should any chance to have been taken alive. Such was their plan. But the Platæans suspected their intention almost before it was formed, and becoming alarmed for their fellow-citizens outside the town, sent a herald to the Thebans, reproaching them for their unscrupulous attempt to seize their city in time of peace, and warning them against any outrage on those outside. Should the warning be disregarded, they threatened to put to death the men they had in their hands, but added that, on the Thebans retiring from their territory, they would surrender the prisoners to their friends. This is the Theban account of the matter, and they say that they had an oath given them. The Platæans, on the other hand, do not admit any promise of an immediate surrender, but make it contingent upon subsequent negotiation: the oath they deny altogether. Be this as it may, upon the Thebans retiring from their territory without committing any injury, the Platæans hastily got in whatever they had in the country and immediately put the men to death. The prisoners were a hundred and eighty in number; Eurymachus, the person with whom the traitors had negotiated, being one.

This done, the Platæans sent a messenger to Athens, gave back the dead to the Thebans under a truce, and arranged things in the city as seemed best to meet the present emergency. The Athenians meanwhile, having had word of the affair sent them immediately after its occurrence, had instantly seized all the Bœotians in Attica, and sent a herald to the Platæans to forbid their proceeding to extremities with their Theban prisoners without instructions from Athens. The news of the men's death had of course not arrived; the first messenger having left Platæa just when the Thebans entered it, the second just after their defeat and capture; so there was no later news. Thus the Athenians sent their orders in ignorance of the facts; and the herald on his arrival found the men slain. After this the Athenians marched to Platæa and brought in provisions, and left a garrison in the place, also taking away the women and children and such of the men as were least efficient.

After the affair at Platæa the treaty had been broken by an overt act, and Athens at once prepared for war, as did also Lacedæmon and her allies. They resolved to send embassies to the king and to such other of the barbarian powers as either party could look to for assistance, and tried to ally themselves with the independent states at home. Lacedæmon, in addition to the existing marine, gave orders to the states that had declared for her in Italy and Sicily to build vessels up to a grand total of five hundred, the quota of each city being determined by its size, and also to provide a specified sum of money. Till these were ready they were to remain neutral and to admit single Athenian ships into their harbours. Athens on her part reviewed her existing confederacy, and sent embassies to the places more immediately round Peloponnese, Corcyra, Cephallenia, Acarnania, and Zacynthus; perceiving that if these could be relied on she could carry the war all round Peloponnese.

And if both sides nourished the boldest hopes and put forth their utmost strength for the war, this was only natural. Zeal is always at its height at the commencement of an undertaking; and on this particular occasion Peloponnese and Athens were both full of young men whose inexperience made them eager to take up arms, while the rest of Hellas stood straining with excitement at the conflict of its leading cities. Everywhere predictions were being recited and oracles being chanted by such persons as collect them, and this not only in the contending cities. Further, some while before this, there was an earthquake at Delos, for the first time in the memory of the Hellenes. This was said and thought to be ominous of the events impending; indeed, nothing of the kind that happened was allowed to pass without remark. The good wishes of men made greatly for the Lacedæmonians, especially as they proclaimed themselves the liberators of Hellas. No private or public effort that could help them in speech or action was omitted; each thinking that the cause suffered wherever he could not himself see to it. So general was the indignation felt against Athens, whether by those who wished to escape from her empire, or were apprehensive of being absorbed by it. Such were the preparations and such the feelings with which the contest opened.

The allies of the two belligerents were the following. These were the allies of Lacedæmon: all the Peloponnesians within the Isthmus except the Argives and Achæans, who were neu-tral; Pellene being the only Achæan city that first joined in the war, though her example was afterwards followed by the rest. Outside Peloponnese the Megarians, Locrians, Bœotians, Phocians, Ambraciots, Leucadians, and Anactorians. Of these, ships were furnished by the Corinthians, Megarians, Sycyo-nians, Pellenians, Eleans, Ambraciots, and Leucadians; and cavalry by the Bœotians, Phocians, and Locrians. The other states sent infantry. This was the Lacedæmonian confederacy. That of Athens comprised the Chians, Lesbians, Platæans, the Messenians in Naupactus, most of the Acarnanians, the Corcyræans, Zacynthians, and some tributary cities in the following countries, viz., Caria upon the sea with her Dorian neighbours, Ionia, the Hellespont, the Thracian towns, the islands lying between Peloponnese and Crete towards the east, and all the Cyclades except Melos and Thera. Of these, ships were furnished by Chios, Lesbos, and Corcyra, infantry and money by the rest. Such were the allies of either party and their resources for the war.

Immediately after the affair at Platæa, Lacedæmon sent round orders to the cities in Peloponnese and the rest of her confederacy to prepare troops and the provisions requisite for a foreign campaign, in order to invade Attica. The several states were ready at the time appointed and assembled at the Isthmus; the contingent of each city being two-thirds of its whole force. After the whole army had mustered, the Lace-dæmonian king, Archidamus, the leader of the expedition, called together the generals of all the states and the principal persons and officers, and exhorted them as follows:—

'Peloponnesians and allies, our fathers made many cam-paigns both within and without Peloponnese, and the elder men among us here are not without experience in war. Yet we have never set out with a larger force than the present;

and if our numbers and efficiency are remarkable, so also is the power of the state against which we march. We ought not then to show ourselves inferior to our ancestors, or unequal to our own reputation. For the hopes and attention of all Hellas are bent upon the present effort, and its sympathy is with the enemy of the hated Athens. Therefore, numerous as the invading army may appear to be, and certain as some may think it that our adversary will not meet us in the field, this is no sort of justification for the least negligence upon the march; but the officers and men of each particular city should always be prepared for the advent of danger in their own quarters. The course of war cannot be foreseen, and its attacks are generally dictated by the impulse of the moment; and where overweening self-confidence has despised preparation, a wise apprehension has often been able to make head against superior numbers. Not that confidence is out of place in an army of invasion, but in an enemy's country it should also be accompanied by the precautions of apprehension: troops will by this combination be best inspired for dealing a blow, and best secured against receiving one. In the present instance, the city against which we are going, far from being so impotent for defence, is on the contrary most excellently equipped at all points; so that we have every reason to expect that they will take the field against us, and that if they have not set out already before we are there, they will certainly do so when they see us in their territory wasting and destroying their property. For men are always exasperated at suffering injuries to which they are not accustomed, and on seeing them inflicted before their very eyes; and where least inclined for reflexion, rush with the greatest heat to action. The Athenians are the very people of all others to do this, as they aspire to rule the rest of the world, and are more in the habit of invading and ravaging their neighbours' territory, than of seeing their own treated in the like fashion. Considering, therefore, the power of the state against which we are marching, and the greatness of the reputation which, according to the event, we shall win or lose for our ancestors and ourselves, remember as you follow where you may be led to regard discipline and vigilance as of the first importance, and to obey with alacrity the orders transmitted to you; as nothing contributes so much to the credit and safety of an army as the union of large bodies by a single discipline.'

With this brief speech dismissing the assembly, Archidamus first sent off Melesippus, son of Diacritus, a Spartan, to Athens, in case she should be more inclined to submit on seeing the Peloponnesians actually on the march. But the Athenians did not admit him into the city or to their assembly; Pericles having already carried a motion against admitting either herald or embassy from the Lacedæmonians after they had once marched out. The herald was accordingly sent away without an audience, and ordered to be beyond the frontier that same day; in future, if those who sent him had a proposition to make they must retire to their own territory before they despatched embassies to Athens. An escort was sent with Melesippus to prevent his holding communication with any one. When he reached the frontier and was just going to be dismissed, he departed with these words: 'This day will be the beginning of great misfortunes to the Hellenes.' As soon as he arrived at the camp, and Archidamus learnt that the Athenians had still no thoughts of submitting, he at length began his march, and advanced with his army into their territory. Meanwhile the Bœotians, sending their contingent and cavalry to join the Peloponnesian expedition, went to Platæa with the remainder and laid waste the country.

While the Peloponnesians were still mustering at the Isthmus, or on the march before they invaded Attica, Pericles, son of Xanthippus, one of the ten generals of the Athenians, finding that the invasion was to take place, conceived the idea that Archidamus, who happened to be his friend, might possibly pass by his estate without ravaging it. This he might do, either from a personal wish to oblige him, or acting under instructions from Lacedæmon for the purpose of creating a prejudice against him, as had been before attempted in the demand for the expulsion of the accursed family. He accordingly took the precaution of announcing to the Athenians in the assembly that, although Archidamus was his friend, yet this friendship should not extend to the detriment of the state, and that in case the enemy should make his houses and lands an exception to the rest and not pillage them, he at once gave them up to be public property, so that they should not bring him into suspicion. He also gave the citizens some advice on their present affairs in the same strain as before. They were to prepare for the war, and to carry in their property from the country. They were not to go out to battle, but to come into the city and guard it, and get ready their fleet, in which their real strength lay. They were also to keep a tight rein on their allies—the strength of Athens being derived from the money brought in by their payments, and success in war depending principally upon conduct and capital. Here they had no reason to despond. Apart from other sources of income, an average revenue of six hundred talents of silver was drawn from the tribute of the allies; and there were still six thousand talents of coined silver in the Acropolis, out of nine thousand seven hundred that had once been there, from which the money had been taken for the porch of the Acropolis, the other public buildings, and for Potidæa. This did not include the uncoined gold and silver in public and private offerings, the sacred vessels for the processions and games, the Median spoils, and similar resources to the amount of five hundred talents. To this he added the treasures of the other temples. These were by no means inconsiderable, and might fairly be used. Nay, if they were ever absolutely driven to it, they might take even the gold ornaments of Athene herself; for the statue contained forty talents of pure gold and it was all removable. This might be used for self-preservation, and must every penny of it be restored. Such was their financial position— surely a satisfactory one. Then they had an army of thirteen thousand heavy infantry, besides sixteen thousand more in the garrisons and on home duty at Athens. This was at first the number of men on guard in the event of an invasion: it was composed of the oldest and youngest levies and the resident aliens who had heavy armour. The Phaleric wall ran for four miles, before it joined that round the city; and of this last nearly five had a guard, although part of it was left without one, viz. that between the Long Wall and the Phaleric. Then there were the Long Walls to Piræus, a distance of some four miles and a half, the outer of which was manned. Lastly, the circumference of Piræus with Munychia was nearly seven miles and a half; only half of this, however, was guarded. Pericles also showed them that they had twelve hundred horse

including mounted archers, with sixteen hundred archers un-
mounted, and three hundred galleys fit for service. Such were
the resources of Athens in the different departments when the
Peloponnesian invasion was impending and hostilities were
being commenced. Pericles also urged his usual arguments for
expecting a favourable issue to the war.

The Athenians listened to his advice, and began to carry
in their wives and children from the country, and all their
household furniture, even to the woodwork of their houses
which they took down. Their sheep and cattle they sent over
to Eubœa and the adjacent islands. But they found it hard
to move, as most of them had been always used to live in the
country.

From very early times this had been more the case with
the Athenians than with others. Under Cecrops and the first
kings, down to the reign of Theseus, Attica had always consisted of a number of independent townships, each with its
own town-hall and magistrates. Except in times of danger
the king at Athens was not consulted; in ordinary seasons
they carried on their government and settled their affairs
without his interference; sometimes even they waged war
against him, as in the case of the Eleusinians with Eumolpus
against Erechtheus. In Theseus, however, they had a king of
equal intelligence and power; and one of the chief features in
his organisation of the country was to abolish the council-
chambers and magistrates of the petty cities, and to merge
them in the single council-chamber and town-hall of the
present capital. Individuals might still enjoy their private
property just as before, but they were henceforth compelled
to have only one political centre, viz. Athens; which thus
counted all the inhabitants of Attica among her citizens, so
that when Theseus died he left a great state behind him. Indeed, from him dates the Synœcia, or Feast of Union; which
is paid for by the state, and which the Athenians still keep
in honour of the goddess. Before this the city consisted of
the present citadel and the district beneath it looking rather
towards the south. This is shown by the fact that the temples
of the other deities, besides that of Athene, are in the citadel;
and even those that are outside it are mostly situated in this
quarter of the city, as that of the Olympian Zeus, of the

Pythian Apollo, of Earth, and of Dionysus in the Marshes,
the same in whose honour the older Dionysia are to this day
celebrated in the mouth of Anthesterion not only by the Athenians but also by their Ionian descendants. There are also
other ancient temples in this quarter. The fountain too, which,
since the alteration made by the tyrants, has been called
Enneacrounos, or Nine Pipes, but which, when the spring
was open, went by the name of Callirhoe, or Fairwater, was
in those days, from being so near, used for the most important
offices. Indeed, the old fashion of using the water before
marriage and for other sacred purposes is still kept up. Again,
from their old residence in that quarter, the citadel is still
known among Athenians as the *city*.

The Athenians thus long lived scattered over Attica in
independent townships. Even after the centralisation of Theseus, old habit still prevailed; and from the early times down
to the present war most Athenians still lived in the country
with their families and households, and were consequently
not at all inclined to move now, especially as they had only
just restored their establishments after the Median invasion.
Deep was their trouble and discontent at abandoning their
houses and the hereditary temples of the ancient constitution,
and at having to change their habits of life and to bid fare-
well to what each regarded as his native city.

When they arrived at Athens, though a few had houses of
their own to go to, or could find an asylum with friends or
relatives, by far the greater number had to take up their
dwelling in the parts of the city that were not built over and
in the temples and chapels of the heroes, except the Acropolis
and the temple of the Eleusinian Demeter and such other
places as were always kept closed. The occupation of the plot
of ground lying below the citadel called the Pelasgian had been
forbidden by a curse; and there was also an ominous fragment
of a Pythian oracle which said—

> 'Leave the Pelasgian parcel desolate,
> Woe worth the day that men inhabit it!'

Yet this too was now built over in the necessity of the moment.
And in my opinion, if the oracle proved true, it was in the
opposite sense to what was expected. For the misfortunes of

the state did not arise from the unlawful occupation, but the
necessity of the occupation from the war; and though the god
did not mention this, he foresaw that it would be an evil day
for Athens in which the plot came to be inhabited. Many also
took up their quarters in the towers of the walls or wherever
else they could. For when they were all come in, the city
proved too small to hold them; though afterwards they divided
the long walls and a great part of Piræus into lots and settled
there. All this while great attention was being given to the
war; the allies were being mustered, and an armament of a
hundred ships equipped for Peloponnese. Such was the state
of preparation at Athens.

Meanwhile the army of the Peloponnesians was advancing.
The first town they came to in Attica was Œnoe, where they
were to enter the country. Sitting down before it, they prepared to assault the wall with engines and otherwise. Œnoe,
standing upon the Athenian and Bœotian border, was of
course a walled town, and was used as a fortress by the
Athenians in time of war. So the Peloponnesians prepared for
their assault, and wasted some valuable time before the place.
This delay brought the gravest censure upon Archidamus.
Even during the levying of the war he had gained credit for
weakness and Athenian sympathies by the half measures he
had advocated; and after the army had assembled he had
further injured himself in public estimation by his loitering
at the Isthmus and the slowness with which the rest of the
march had been conducted. But all this was as nothing to the
delay at Œnoe. During this interval the Athenians were carrying in their property; and it was the belief of the Peloponnesians that a quick advance would have found everything still
out, had it not been for his procrastination. Such was the feeling of the army towards Archidamus during the siege. But he,
it is said, expected that the Athenians would shrink from letting their land be wasted, and would make their submission
while it was still uninjured; and this was why he waited.

But after he had assaulted Œnoe, and every possible attempt to take it had failed, as no herald came from Athens,
he at last broke up his camp and invaded Attica. This was
about eighty days after the Theban attempt upon Platæa,
just in the middle of summer, when the corn was ripe, and

Archidamus, son of Zeuxis, King of Lacedæmon, was in command. Encamping in Eleusis and the Thriasian plain, they began their ravages, and putting to flight some Athenian horse at a place called Rheiti, or the Brooks, they then advanced, keeping Mount Ægaleus on their right, through Cropia, until they reached Acharnæ, the largest of the Athenian demes or townships. Sitting down before it, they formed a camp there, and continued their ravages for a long while.

The reason why Archidamus remained in order of battle at Acharnæ during this incursion, instead of descending into the plain, is said to have been this. He hoped that the Athenians might possibly be tempted by the multitude of their youth and the unprecedented efficiency of their service to come out to battle and attempt to stop the devastation of their lands. Accordingly, as they had not met him at Eleusis or the Thriasian plain, he tried if they could be provoked to a sally by the spectacle of a camp at Acharnæ. He thought the place itself a good position for encamping; and it seemed likely that such an important part of the state as the three thousand heavy infantry of the Acharnians would refuse to submit to the ruin of their property, and would force a battle on the rest of the citizens. On the other hand, should the Athenians not take the field during this incursion, he could then fearlessly ravage the plain in future invasions, and extend his advance up to the very walls of Athens. After the Acharians had lost their own property they would be less willing to risk themselves for that of their neighbours; and so there would be division in the Athenian counsels. These were the motives of Archidamus for remaining at Acharnæ.

In the meanwhile, as long as the army was at Eleusis and the Thriasian plain, hopes were still entertained of its not advancing any nearer. It was remembered that Pleistoanax, son of Pausanias, king of Lacedæmon, had invaded Attica with a Peloponnesian army fourteen years before, but had retreated without advancing farther than Eleusis and Thria, which indeed proved the cause of his exile from Sparta, as it was thought he had been bribed to retreat. But when they saw the army at Acharnæ, barely seven miles from Athens, they lost all patience. The territory of Athens was being ravaged before the very eyes of the Athenians, a sight which the young

men had never seen before and the old only in the Median
wars; and it was naturally thought a grievous insult, and the
determination was universal, especially among the young
men, to sally forth and stop it. Knots were formed in the
streets and engaged in hot discussion; for if the proposed sally
was warmly recommended, it was also in some cases opposed.
Oracles of the most various import were recited by the col-
lectors, and found eager listeners in one or other of the
disputants. Foremost in pressing for the sally were the Acharnians, as constituting no small part of the army of the state,
and as it was their land that was being ravaged. In short, the
whole city was in a most excited state; Pericles was the object
of general indignation; his previous counsels were totally forgotten; he was abused for not leading out the army which he
commanded, and was made responsible for the whole of the
public suffering.

He, meanwhile, seeing anger and infatuation just now in
the ascendant, and confident of his wisdom in refusing a sally,
would not call either assembly or meeting of the people, fearing the fatal results of a debate inspired by passion and not
by prudence. Accordingly, he addressed himself to the defence
of the city, and kept it as quiet as possible, though he constantly sent out cavalry to prevent raids on the lands near
the city from flying parties of the enemy. There was a trifling
affair at Phrygia between a squadron of the Athenian horse
with the Thessalians and the Bœotian cavalry; in which the
former had rather the best of it, until the heavy infantry
advanced to the support of the Bœotians, when the Thessalians and Athenians were routed and lost a few men, whose
bodies, however, were recovered the same day without a truce.
The next day the Peloponnesians set up a trophy. Ancient
alliance brought the Thessalians to the aid of Athens; those
who came being the Larisæans, Pharsalians, Cranonians,
Pyrasians, Gyrtonians, and Pheræans. The Larisæan commanders were Polymedes and Aristonus, two party leaders in
Larisa; the Pharsalian general was Menon; each of the other
cities had also its own commander.

In the meantime the Peloponnesians, as the Athenians did
not come out to engage them, broke up from Acharnæ and
ravaged some of the demes between Mount Parnes and Bri-

lessus. While they were in Attica, the Athenians sent off the hundred ships which they had been preparing round Peloponnese, with a thousand heavy infantry and four hundred archers on board, under the command of Carcinus, son of Xenotimus, Proteas, son of Epicles, and Socrates, son of Antigenes. This armament weighed anchor and started on its cruise, and the Peloponnesians, after remaining in Attica as long as their provisions lasted, retired through Bœotia by a different road to that by which they had entered. As they passed Oropus they ravaged the territory of Graea which is held by the Oropians from Athens, and reaching Peloponnese broke up to their respective cities.

After they had retired the Athenians set guards by land and sea at the points at which they intended to have regular stations during the war. They also resolved to set apart a special fund of a thousand talents from the monies in the Acropolis. This was not to be spent, but the current expenses of the war were to be otherwise provided for. If any one should move or put to the vote a proposition for using the money for any purpose whatever except that of defending the city in the event of the enemy bringing a fleet to make an attack by sea, it should be a capital offence. With this sum of money they also set aside a special fleet of one hundred galleys, the best ships of each year, with their captains. None of these was to be used except with the money and against the same peril, should such peril arise.

Meanwhile the Athenians in the hundred ships round Peloponnese, reinforced by a Corcyræan squadron of fifty vessels and some others of the allies in those parts, cruised about the coasts and ravaged the country. Among other places they landed in Laconia and made an assault upon Methone; there being no garrison in the place, and the wall being weak. But it so happened that Brasidas, son of Tellis, a Spartan, was in command of a guard for the defence of the district. Hearing of the attack, he hurried with a hundred heavy infantry to the assistance of the besieged, and dashing through the army of the Athenians, which was scattered over the country and had its attention turned to the wall, threw himself into Methone. He lost a few men in making good his entrance, but saved the place and won the thanks of Sparta by his exploit, being thus the first officer who obtained this notice during the war. The Athenians at once weighed anchor and continued their cruise. Touching at Pheia in Elis, they ravaged the country for two days and defeated a picked force of three hundred men that had come from the vale of Elis and the immediate neighbourhood to the rescue. But a stiff squall came down upon them, and not liking to face it in a place where there was no harbour, most of them got on board their ships, and doubling Point Ichthys sailed into the port of Pheia. In the meantime the Messenians, and some others who could not get on board, marched over by land and took Pheia. The fleet afterwards sailed round and picked them up and then put to sea; Pheia being evacuated, as the main army of the Eleans had now come up. The Athenians continued their cruise, and ravaged other places on the coast.

About the same time the Athenians sent thirty ships to cruise round Locris and also to guard Eubœa; Cleopompus, son of Clinias, being in command. Making descents from the fleet he ravaged certain places on the sea-coast, and captured Thronium and took hostages from it. He also defeated at Alope the Locrians that had assembled to resist him.

During the summer the Athenians also expelled the Æginetans with their wives and children from Ægina, on the ground of their having been the chief agents in bringing the war upon them. Besides, Ægina lies so near Peloponnese, that it seemed safer to send colonists of their own to hold it, and shortly afterwards the settlers were sent out. The banished Æginetans found an asylum in Thyrea, which was given to them by Lacedæmon, not only on account of her quarrel with Athens, but also because the Æginetans had laid her under obligations at the time of the earthquake and the revolt of the Helots. The territory of Thyrea is on the frontier of Argolis and Laconia, reaching down to the sea. Those of the Æginetans who did not settle here were scattered over the rest of Hellas.

The same summer, at the beginning of a new lunar month, the only time by the way at which it appears possible, the sun was eclipsed after noon. After it had assumed the form of a crescent and some of the stars had come out, it returned to its natural shape.

During the same summer Nymphodorus, son of Pythes, an Abderite, whose sister Sitalces had married, was made their *Proxenus* by the Athenians and sent for to Athens. They had hitherto considered him their enemy; but he had great influence with Sitalces, and they wished this prince to become their ally. Sitalces was the son of Teres and king of the Thracians. Teres, the father of Sitalces, was the first to establish the great kingdom of the Odrysians on a scale quite unknown to the rest of Thrace, a large portion of the Thracians being independent. This Teres is in no way related to Tereus who married Pandion's daughter Procne from Athens; nor indeed did they belong to the same part of Thrace. Tereus lived in Daulis, part of what is now called Phocis, but which at that time was inhabited by Thracians. It was in this land that the women perpetrated the outrage upon Itys; and many of the poets when they mention the nightingale call it the Daulian bird. Besides, Pandion in contracting an alliance for his daughter would consider the advantages of mutual assistance, and would naturally prefer a match at the above moderate distance to the journey of many days which separates Athens from the Odrysians. Again the names are different; and this Teres was king of the Odrysians, the first by the way who attained to any power. Sitalces, his son, was now sought as an ally by the Athenians, who desired his aid in the reduction of the Thracian towns and of Perdiccas. Coming to Athens, Nymphodorus concluded the alliance with Sitalces and made his son Sadocus an Athenian citizen, and promised to finish the war in Thrace by persuading Sitalces to send the Athenians a force of Thracian horse and targeteers. He also reconciled them with Perdiccas, and induced them to restore Therme to him; upon which Perdiccas at once joined the Athenians and Phormio in an expedition against the Chalcidians. Thus Sitalces, son of Teres, king of the Thracians, and Perdiccas, son of Alexander, king of the Macedonians, became allies of Athens.

Meanwhile the Athenians in the hundred vessels were still cruising round Peloponnese. After taking Sollium, a town belonging to Corinth, and presenting the city and territory to the Acarnanians of Palaira, they stormed Astacus, expelled its tyrant Evarchus, and gained the place for their confed-

eracy. Next they sailed to the island of Cephallenia and
brought it over without using force. Cephallenia lies off
Acarnania and Leucas, and consists of four states, the Paleans,
Cranians, Samæans, and Pronæans. Not long afterwards the
fleet returned to Athens. Towards the autumn of this year the
Athenians invaded the Megarid with their whole levy, resident
aliens included, under the command of Pericles, son of Xanthippus. The Athenians in the hundred ships round Peloponnese on their journey home had just reached Ægina, and hearing that the citizens at home were in full force at Megara,
now sailed over and joined them. This was without doubt the
largest army of Athenians ever assembled, the state being
still in the flower of her strength and yet unvisited by the
plague. Full ten thousand heavy infantry were in the field,
all Athenian citizens, besides the three thousand before Potidæa. Then the resident aliens who joined in the incursion were
at least three thousand strong; besides which there was a multitude of light troops. They ravaged the greater part of the
territory, and then retired. Other incursions into the Megarid
were afterwards made by the Athenians annually during the
war, sometimes only with cavalry, sometimes with all their
forces. This went on until the capture of Nisæa. Atalanta also,
the desert island off the Opuntian coast, was towards the end
of this summer converted into a fortified post by the Athenians, in order to prevent privateers issuing from Opus and
the rest of Locris and plundering Eubœa. Such were the events
of this summer after the return of the Peloponnesians from
Attica.

In the ensuing winter the Acarnanian Evarchus wishing to
return to Astacus, persuaded the Corinthians to sail over with
forty ships and fifteen hundred heavy infantry and restore
him; himself also hiring some mercenaries. In command of
the force were Euphamidas, son of Aristonymus, Timoxenus,
son of Timocrates, and Eumachus, son of Chrysis, who sailed
over and restored him, and after failing in an attempt on
some places on the Acarnanian coast which they were desirous
of gaining, began their voyage home. Coasting along shore
they touched at Cephallenia and made a descent on the
Cranian territory, and losing some men by the treachery of

the Cranians, who fell suddenly upon them, put to sea somewhat hurriedly and returned home.

In the same winter the Athenians gave a funeral at the
public cost to those who had first fallen in this war. It was a
custom of their ancestors, and the manner of it is as follows.
Three days before the ceremony, the bones of the dead are
laid out in a tent which has been erected; and their friends
bring to their relatives such offerings as they please. In the
funeral procession cypress coffins are borne in cars, one for
each tribe; the bones of the deceased being placed in the
coffin of their tribe. Among these is carried one empty bier
decked for the missing, that is, for those whose bodies could
not be recovered. Any citizen or stranger who pleases, joins in
the procession: and the female relatives are there to wail at the
burial. The dead are laid in the public sepulchre in the most
beautiful suburb of the city, in which those who fall in war are
always buried; with the exception of those slain at Marathon,
who for their singular and extraordinary valour were interred
on the spot where they fell. After the bodies have been laid
in the earth, a man chosen by the state, of approved wisdom
and eminent reputation, pronounces over them an appropriate
panegyric; after which all retire. Such is the manner of the
burying; and throughout the whole of the war, whenever the
occasion arose, the established custom was observed. Meanwhile these were the first that had fallen, and Pericles, son of
Xanthippus, was chosen to pronounce their eulogium. When
the proper time arrived, he advanced from the sepulchre to an
elevated platform in order to be heard by as many of the
crowd as possible, and spoke as follows:

'Most of my predecessors in this place have commended
him who made this speech part of the law, telling us that it is
well that it should be delivered at the burial of those who fall
in battle. For myself, I should have thought that the worth
which had displayed itself in deeds, would be sufficiently
rewarded by honours also shown by deeds; such as you now
see in this funeral prepared at the people's cost. And I could
have wished that the reputations of many brave men were
not to be imperilled in the mouth of a single individual, to
stand or fall according as he spoke well or ill. For it is hard to
speak properly upon a subject where it is even difficult to con-

vince your hearers that you are speaking the truth. On the one hand, the friend who is familiar with every fact of the story, may think that some point has not been set forth with that fulness which he wishes and knows it to deserve; on the other, he who is a stranger to the matter may be led by envy to suspect exaggeration if he hears anything above his own nature. For men can endure to hear others praised only so long as they can severally persuade themselves of their own ability to equal the actions recounted: when this point is passed, envy comes in and with it incredulity. However, since our ancestors have stamped this custom with their approval, it becomes my duty to obey the law and to try to satisfy your several wishes and opinions as best I may.

'I shall begin with our ancestors: it is both just and proper that they should have the honour of the first mention on an occasion like the present. They dwelt in the country without break in the succession from generation to generation, and handed it down free to the present time by their valour. And if our more remote ancestors deserve praise, much more do our own fathers, who added to their inheritance the empire which we now possess, and spared no pains to be able to leave their acquisitions to us of the present generation. Lastly, there are few parts of our dominions that have not been augmented by those of us here, who are still more or less in the vigour of life; while the mother country has been furnished by us with everything that can enable her to depend on her own resources whether for war or for peace. That part of our history which tells of the military achievements which gave us our several possessions, or of the ready valour with which either we or our fathers stemmed the tide of Hellenic or foreign aggression, is a theme too familiar to my hearers for me to dilate on, and I shall therefore pass it by. But what was the road by which we reached our position, what the form of government under which our greatness grew, what the national habits out of which it sprang; these are questions which I may try to solve before I proceed to my panegyric upon these men; since I think this to be a subject upon which on the present occasion a speaker may properly dwell, and to which the whole assemblage, whether citizens or foreigners, may listen with advantage.

'Our constitution does not copy the laws of neighbouring states; we are rather a pattern to others than imitators ourselves. Its administration favours the many instead of the few; this is why it is called a democracy. If we look to the laws, they afford equal justice to all in their private differences; if to social standing, advancement in public life falls to reputation for capacity, class considerations not being allowed to interfere with merit; nor again does poverty bar the way, if a man is able to serve the state, he is not hindered by the obscurity of his condition. The freedom which we enjoy in our government extends also to our ordinary life. There, far from exercising a jealous surveillance over each other, we do not feel called upon to be angry with our neighbour for doing what he likes, or even to indulge in those injurious looks which cannot fail to be offensive, although they inflict no positive penalty. But all this ease in our private relations does not make us lawless as citizens. Against this fear is our chief safeguard, teaching us to obey the magistrates and the laws, particularly such as regard the protection of the injured, whether they are actually on the statute book, or belong to that code which, although unwritten, yet cannot be broken without acknowledged disgrace.

'Further, we provide plenty of means for the mind to refresh itself from business. We celebrate games and sacrifices all the year round, and the elegance of our private establishments forms a daily source of pleasure and helps to banish the spleen; while the magnitude of our city draws the produce of the world into our harbour, so that to the Athenian the fruits of other countries are as familiar a luxury as those of his own.

'If we turn to our military policy, there also we differ from our antagonists. We throw open our city to the world, and never by alien acts exclude foreigners from any opportunity of learning or observing, although the eyes of an enemy may occasionally profit by our liberality; trusting less in system and policy than to the native spirit of our citizens; while in education, where our rivals from their very cradles by a painful discipline seek after manliness, at Athens we live exactly as we please, and yet are just as ready to encounter every legitimate danger. In proof of this it may be noticed that the Lacedæmonians do not invade our country alone, but bring with them all their confederates; while we Athenians advance unsupported into the territory of a neighbour, and fighting upon a foreign soil usually vanquish with ease men who are defending their homes. Our united force was never yet encountered by any enemy, because we have at once to attend to our marine and to despatch our citizens by land upon a hundred different services; so that, wherever they engage with some such fraction of our strength, a success against a detachment is magnified into a victory over the nation, and a defeat into a reverse suffered at the hands of our entire people. And yet if with habits not of labour but of ease, and courage not of art but of nature, we are still willing to encounter danger, we have the double advantage of escaping the experience of hardships in anticipation and of facing them in the hour of need as fearlessly as those who are never free from them.

'Nor are these the only points in which our city is worthy of admiration. We cultivate refinement without extravagance and knowledge without effeminacy; wealth we employ more for use than for show, and place the real disgrace of poverty not in owning to the fact but in declining the struggle against it. Our public men have, besides politics, their private affairs to attend to, and our ordinary citizens, though occupied with the pursuits of industry, are still fair judges of public matters; for, unlike any other nation, regarding him who takes no part in these duties not as unambitious but as useless, we Athenians are able to judge at all events if we cannot originate, and instead of looking on discussion as a stumbling-block in the way of action, we think it an indispensable preliminary to any wise action at all. Again, in our enterprises we present the singular spectacle of daring and deliberation, each carried to its highest point, and both united in the same persons; although usually decision is the fruit of ignorance, hesitation of reflexion. But the palm of courage will surely be adjudged most justly to those, who best know the difference between hardship and pleasure and yet are never tempted to shrink from danger. In generosity we are equally singular, acquiring our friends by conferring not by receiving favours. Yet, of course, the doer of the favour is the firmer friend of the two, in order by continued kindness to keep the recipient in his debt; while the debtor feels less keenly from the very consciousness that the return he makes will be a payment, not a free gift. And it is only the Athenians who, fearless of consequences, confer their benefits not from calculations of expediency, but in the confidence of liberality.

'In short, I say that as a city we are the school of Hellas; while I doubt if the world can produce a man, who where he has only himself to depend upon, is equal to so many emergencies, and graced by so happy a versatility as the Athenian. And that this is no mere boast thrown out for the occasion, but plain matter of fact, the power of the state acquired by these habits proves. For Athens alone of her contemporaries is found when tested to be greater than her reputation, and alone gives no occasion to her assailants to blush at the antagonist by whom they have been worsted, or to her subjects to question her title by merit to rule. Rather, the admiration of the present and succeeding ages will be ours, since we have not left our power without witness, but have shown it by mighty proofs; and far from needing a Homer for our panegyrist, or other of his craft whose verses might charm for the moment only for the impression which they gave to melt at the touch of fact, we have forced every sea and land to be the highway of our daring, and everywhere, whether for evil or for good, have left imperishable monuments behind us. Such is the Athens for which these men, in the assertion of their resolve not to lose her, nobly fought and died; and well may every one of their survivors be ready to suffer in her cause.

'Indeed if I have dwelt at some length upon the character of our country, it has been to show that our stake in the struggle is not the same as theirs who have no such blessings to lose, and also that the panegyric of the men over whom I am now speaking might be by definite proofs established. That panegyric is now in a great measure complete; for the Athens that I have celebrated is only what the heroism of these and their like have made her, men whose fame, unlike that of most Hellenes, will be found to be only commensurate with their deserts. And if a test of worth be wanted, it is to be found in their closing scene, and this not only in the cases in which it set the final seal upon their merit, but also in those in which it gave the first intimation of their having any. For there is justice in the claim that steadfastness in his country's battles should be as a cloak to cover a man's other imperfections; since the good action has blotted out the bad, and his merit as a citizen more than outweighed his demerits as an individual. But none of these allowed either wealth with its prospect of future enjoyment to unnerve his spirit, or poverty with its hope of a day of freedom and riches to tempt him to shrink from danger. No, holding that vengeance upon their enemies was more to be desired than any personal blessings, and reckoning this to be the most glorious of hazards, they joyfully determined to accept the risk, to make sure of their vengeance and to let their wishes wait; and while committing to hope the uncertainty of final success, in the business before them they thought fit to act boldly and trust in themselves. Thus choosing to die resisting, rather than to live submitting, they fled only from dishonour, but met danger face to face, and after one brief moment, while at the summit of their fortune, escaped, not from their fear, but from their glory.

'So died these men as became Athenians. You, their survivors, must determine to have as unaltering a resolution in the field, though you may pray that it may have a happier issue. And not contented with ideas derived only from words of the advantages which are bound up with the defence of your country, though these would furnish a valuable text to a speaker even before an audience so alive to them as the present, you must yourselves realise the power of Athens, and feed your eyes upon her from day to day, till love of her fills your hearts; and then when all her greatness shall break upon you, you must reflect that it was by courage, sense of duty, and a keen feeling of honour in action that men were enabled to win all this, and that no personal failure in an enterprise could make them consent to deprive their country of their valour, but they laid it at her feet as the most glorious contribution that they could offer. For this offering of their lives made in common by them all they each of them individually received that renown which never grows old, and for a sepulchre, not so much that in which their bones have been deposited, but that noblest of shrines wherein their glory is laid up to be eternally remembered upon every occasion on which deed or story shall fall for its commemoration. For heroes have the whole earth for their tomb; and in lands far from their

own, where the column with its epitaph declares it, there is
enshrined in every breast a record unwritten with no tablet
to preserve it, except that of the heart. These take as your
model, and judging happiness to be the fruit of freedom and
freedom of valour, never decline the dangers of war. For it is
not the miserable that would most justly be unsparing of their
lives; these have nothing to hope for: it is rather they to
whom continued life may bring reverses as yet unknown, and
to whom a fall, if it came, would be most tremendous in its
consequences. And surely, to a man of spirit, the degradation
of cowardice must be immeasurably more grievous than the
unfelt death which strikes him in the midst of his strength and
patriotism!

'Comfort, therefore, not condolence, is what I have to offer
to the parents of the dead who may be here. Numberless are
the chances to which, as they know, the life of man is subject;
but fortunate indeed are they who draw for their lot a death
so glorious as that which has caused your mourning, and to
whom life has been so exactly measured as to terminate in the
happiness in which it has been passed. Still I know that this is
a hard saying, especially when those are in question of whom
you will constantly be reminded by seeing in the homes of
others blessings of which once you also boasted: for grief is
felt not so much for the want of what we have never known,
as for the loss of that to which we have been long accustomed.
Yet you who are still of an age to beget children must bear up
in the hope of having others in their stead; not only will they
help you to forget those whom you have lost, but will be to the
state at once a reinforcement and a security; for never can a
fair or just policy be expected of the citizen who does not, like
his fellows, bring to the decision the interests and apprehensions of a father. While those of you who have passed your
prime must congratulate yourselves with the thought that the
best part of your life was fortunate, and that the brief span
that remains will be cheered by the fame of the departed. For
it is only the love of honour that never grows old; and honour
it is, not gain, as some would have it, that rejoices the heart
of age and helplessness.

'Turning to the sons or brothers of the dead, I see an
arduous struggle before you. When a man is gone, all are wont

to praise him, and should your merit be ever so transcendent, you will still find it difficult not merely to overtake, but even to approach their renown. The living have envy to contend with, while those who are no longer in our path are honoured with a goodwill into which rivalry does not enter. On the other hand, if I must say anything on the subject of female excellence to those of you who will now be in widowhood. it will be all comprised in this brief exhortation. Great will be your glory in not falling short of your natural character; and greatest will be hers who is least talked of among the men whether for good or for bad.

'My task is now finished. I have performed it to the best of my ability, and in words, at least, the requirements of the law are now satisfied. If deeds be in question, those who are here interred have received part of their honours already, and for the rest, their children will be brought up till manhood at the public expense: the state thus offers a valuable prize, as the garland of victory in this race of valour, for the reward both of those who have fallen and their survivors. And where the rewards for merit are greatest, there are found the best citizens.

'And now that you have brought to a close your lamentations for your relatives, you may depart.'

CHAPTER VII

SECOND YEAR OF THE WAR—THE PLAGUE OF ATHENS—POSITION AND POLICY OF PERICLES—FALL OF POTIDÆA

B.C. 430: *Outbreak of the plague—Description of symptoms—Demoralization a consequence of the plague—Peloponnesians ravage coast—Plague overtakes invaders—Pericles blamed—He defends himself—Fined first, then restored to full power—Peloponnesian envoys detained by Sitalces and put to death by Athenians—Ambraciots attack Amphilochian Argos—Fall of Potidæa.*

SUCH was the funeral that took place during this winter, with which the first year of the war came to an end. In the first days of summer the Lacedæmonians and their allies, with two-thirds of their forces as before, invaded Attica, under the command of Archidamus, son of Zeuxidamus, king of Lacedæmon, and sat down and laid waste the country. Not many days after their arrival in Attica the plague first began to show itself among the Athenians. It was said that it had broken out in many places previously in the neighbourhood of Lemnos and elsewhere; but a pestilence of such extent and mortality was nowhere remembered. Neither were the physicians at first of any service, ignorant as they were of the proper way to treat it, but they died themselves the most thickly, as they visited the sick most often; nor did any human art succeed any better. Supplications in the temples, divinations, and so forth were found equally futile, till the overwhelming nature of the disaster at last put a stop to them altogether.

It first began, it is said, in the parts of Ethiopia above Egypt, and thence descended into Egypt and Libya and into most of the king's country. Suddenly falling upon Athens, it first attacked the population in Piræus,—which was the occasion of their saying that the Peloponnesians had poisoned the reservoirs, there being as yet no wells there—and afterwards appeared in the upper city, when the deaths became much more frequent. All speculation as to its origin and its causes, if causes can be found adequate to produce so great a disturbance, I leave to other writers, whether lay or professional; for myself, I shall simply set down its nature, and explain the symptoms by which perhaps it may be recognised by the student, if it should ever break out again. This I can the better do, as I had the disease myself, and watched its operation in the case of others.

That year then is admitted to have been otherwise unprecedentedly free from sickness; and such few cases as occurred, all determined in this. As a rule, however, there was no ostensible cause; but people in good health were all of a sudden attacked by violent heats in the head, and redness and inflammation in the eyes, the inward parts, such as the throat or tongue, becoming bloody and emitting an unnatural and fetid breath. These symptoms were followed by sneezing and hoarseness, after which the pain soon reached the chest, and produced a hard cough. When it fixed in the stomach, it upset it; and discharges of bile of every kind named by physicians ensued, accompanied by very great distress. In most cases also an ineffectual retching followed, producing violent spasms, which in some cases ceased soon after, in others much later. Externally the body was not very hot to the touch, nor pale in its appearance, but reddish, livid, and breaking out into small pustules and ulcers. But internally it burned so that the patient could not bear to have on him clothing or linen even of the very lightest description; or indeed to be otherwise than stark naked. What they would have liked best would have been to throw themselves into cold water; as indeed was done by some of the neglected sick, who plunged into the rain-tanks in their agonies of unquench-able thirst; though it made no difference whether they drank little or much. Besides this, the miserable feeling of not being able to rest or sleep never ceased to torment them. The body meanwhile did not waste away so long as the distemper was at its height, but held out to a marvel against its ravages; so that when they succumbed, as in most cases, on the seventh or eighth day to the internal inflammation, they had still some strength in them. But if they passed this stage, and the disease descended further into the bowels, inducing a violent ulceration there accompanied by severe diarrhœa, this brought on a weakness which was generally fatal. For the disorder first settled in the head, ran its course from thence through the whole of the body, and even where it did not prove mortal, it still left its mark on the extremities; for it settled in the privy parts, the fingers and the toes, and many escaped with the loss of these, some too with that of their eyes. Others again were seized with an entire loss of memory on their first recovery, and did not know either themselves or their friends.

But while the nature of the distemper was such as to baffle all description, and its attacks almost too grievous for human nature to endure, it was still in the following circumstance that its difference from all ordinary disorders was most clearly shown. All the birds and beasts that prey upon human bodies, either abstained from touching them (though there were many lying unburied), or died after tasting them. In proof of this, it was noticed that birds of this kind actually disappeared; they were not about the bodies, or indeed to be seen at all. But of course the effects which I have mentioned could best be studied in a domestic animal like the dog.

Such then, if we pass over the varieties of particular cases, which were many and peculiar, were the general features of the distemper. Meanwhile the town enjoyed an immunity from all the ordinary disorders; or if any case occurred, it ended in this. Some died in neglect, others in the midst of every attention. No remedy was found that could be used as a specific; for what did good in one case, did harm in another. Strong and weak constitutions proved equally incapable of resistance, all alike being swept away, although dieted with the utmost precaution. By far the most terrible feature in the malady was the dejection which ensued when any one felt himself sickening, for the despair into which they instantly fell took away their power of resistance, and left them a much easier prey to the disorder; besides which, there was the awful spectacle of men dying like sheep, through having caught the infection in nursing each other. This caused the greatest mortality. On the one hand, if they were afraid to visit each other, they perished from neglect; indeed many houses were emptied of their inmates for want of a nurse: on the other, if they ventured to do so, death was the consequence. This was especially the case with such as made any pretensions to goodness: honour made them unsparing of themselves in their attendance in their friends' houses, where even the members of the family were at last worn out by the moans of the dying, and succumbed to the force of the disaster. Yet it was with those who had recovered from the disease that the sick and the dying found most compassion. These knew what it was from experience, and had now no fear for themselves; for the same man was never attacked twice—never at least fatally. And such persons not only received the congratulations of others, but themselves also, in the elation of the moment, half entertained the vain hope that they were for the future safe from any disease whatsoever.

An aggravation of the existing calamity was the influx from the country into the city, and this was especially felt by the new arrivals. As there were no houses to receive them, they had to be lodged at the hot season of the year in stifling cabins, where the mortality raged without restraint. The bodies of dying men lay one upon another, and half-dead creatures reeled about the streets and gathered round all the fountains in their longing for water. The sacred places also in which they

had quartered themselves were full of corpses of persons that
had died there, just as they were; for as the disaster passed
all bounds, men, not knowing what was to become of them,
became utterly careless of everything, whether sacred or pro-
fane. All the burial rites before in use were entirely upset,
and they buried the bodies as best they could. Many from
want of the proper appliances, through so many of their
friends having died already, had recourse to the most shame-
less sepultures: sometimes getting the start of those who had
raised a pile, they threw their own dead body upon the
stranger's pyre and ignited it; sometimes they tossed the
corpse which they were carrying on the top of another that
was burning, and so went off.

Nor was this the only form of lawless extravagance which
owed its origin to the plague. Men now coolly ventured on
what they had formerly done in a corner, and not just as
they pleased, seeing the rapid transitions produced by persons
in prosperity suddenly dying and those who before had nothing succeeding to their property. So they resolved to spend.
quickly and enjoy themselves, regarding their lives and riches
as alike things of a day. Perseverance in what men called
honour was popular with none, it was so uncertain whether
they would be spared to attain the object; but it was settled
that present enjoyment, and all that contributed to it, was
both honourable and useful. Fear of gods or law of man there
was none to restrain them. As for the first, they judged it to
be just the same whether they worshipped them or not, as
they saw all alike perishing; and for the last, no one expected
to live to be brought to trial for his offences, but each felt that
a far severer sentence had been already passed upon them all
and hung ever over their heads, and before this fell it was only
reasonable to enjoy life a little.

Such was the nature of the calamity, and heavily did it
weigh on the Athenians; death raging within the city and
devastation without. Among other things which they remembered in their distress was, very naturally, the following verse
which the old men said had long ago been uttered:

'A Dorian war shall come and with it death.'

So a dispute arose as to whether dearth and not death had

not been the word in the verse; but at the present juncture, it was of course decided in favour of the latter; for the people made their recollection fit in with their sufferings. I fancy, however, that if another Dorian war should ever afterwards come upon us, and a dearth should happen to accompany it, the verse will probably be read accordingly. The oracle also which had been given to the Lacedæmonians was now remembered by those who knew of it. When the God was asked whether they should go to war, he answered that if they put their might into it, victory would be theirs, and that he would himself be with them. With this oracle events were supposed to tally. For the plague broke out so soon as the Peloponnesians invaded Attica, and never entering Peloponnese (not at least to an extent worth noticing), committed its worst ravages at Athens, and next to Athens, at the most populous of the other towns. Such was the history of the plague.

After ravaging the plain the Peloponnesians advanced into the Paralian region as far as Laurium, where the Athenian silver mines are, and first laid waste the side looking towards Peloponnese, next that which faces Eubœa and Andros. But Pericles, who was still general, held the same opinion as in the former invasion, and would not let the Athenians march out against them.

However while they were still in the plain, and had not yet entered the Paralian land, he had prepared an armament of a hundred ships for Peloponnese, and when all was ready put out to sea. On board the ships he took four thousand Athenian heavy infantry, and three hundred cavalry in horse transports, then for the first time made out of old galleys; fifty Chian and Lesbian vessels also joining in the expedition. When this Athenian armament put out to sea, they left the Peloponnesians in Attica in the Paralian region. Arriving at Epidaurus in Peloponnese they ravaged most of the territory, and even had hopes of taking the town by an assault: in this however they were not successful. Putting out from Epidaurus, they laid waste the territory of Troezen, Halieis, and Hermione, all towns on the coast of Peloponnese, and thence sailing to Prasiai, a maritime town in Laconia, ravaged part of its territory, and took and sacked the place itself; after which they

returned home, but found the Peloponnesians gone and no
longer in Attica.

During the whole time that the Peloponnesians were in
Attica and the Athenians on the expedition in their ships,
men kept dying of the plague both in the armament and in
Athens. Indeed it was actually asserted that the departure
of the Peloponnesians was hastened by fear of the disorder;
as they heard from deserters that it was in the city, and also
could see the burials going on. Yet in this invasion they remained longer than in any other, and ravaged the whole
country, for they were about forty days in Attica.

The same summer Hagnon, son of Nicias, and Cleopompus,
son of Clinias, the colleagues of Pericles, took the armament
of which he had lately made use, and went off upon an expedition against the Chalcidians in the direction of Thrace and
Potidæa, which was still under siege. As soon as they arrived,
they brought up their engines against Potidæa and tried every
means of taking it, but did not succeed either in capturing the
city or in doing anything else worthy of their preparations.
For the plague attacked them here also, and committed such
havoc as to cripple them completely, even the previously
healthy soldiers of the former expedition catching the infection from Hagnon's troops; while Phormio and the sixteen
hundred men whom he commanded only escaped by being no
longer in the neighbourhood of the Chalcidians. The end of
it was that Hagnon returned with his ships to Athens, having
lost one thousand and fifty out of four thousand heavy infantry in about forty days; though the soldiers stationed there
before remained in the country and carried on the siege of
Potidæa.

After the second invasion of the Peloponnesians a change
came over the spirit of the Athenians. Their land had now
been twice laid waste; and war and pestilence at once pressed
heavy upon them. They began to find fault with Pericles, as
the author of the war and the cause of all their misfortunes,
and became eager to come to terms with Lacedæmon, and
actually sent ambassadors thither, who did not however succeed in their mission. Their despair was now complete and
all vented itself upon Pericles. When he saw them exasperated
at the present turn of affairs and acting exactly as he had

anticipated, he called an assembly, being (it must be remembered) still general, with the double object of restoring confidence and of leading them from these angry feelings to a
calmer and more hopeful state of mind. He accordingly came
forward and spoke as follows:

'I was not unprepared for the indignation of which I have
been the object, as I know its causes; and I have called an
assembly for the purpose of reminding you upon certain
points, and of protesting against your being unreasonably irritated with me, or cowed by your sufferings. I am of opinion
that national greatness is more for the advantage of private
citizens, than any individual well-being coupled with public
humiliation. A man may be personally ever so well off, and
yet if his country be ruined he must be ruined with it; whereas
a flourishing commonwealth always affords chances of salvation to unfortunate individuals. Since then a state can support
the misfortunes of private citizens, while they cannot support
hers, it is surely the duty of every one to be forward in her
defence, and not like you to be so confounded with your
domestic afflictions as to give up all thoughts of the common
safety, and to blame me for having counselled war and yourselves for having voted it. And yet if you are angry with me,
it is with one who, as I believe, is second to no man either
in knowledge of the proper policy, or in the ability to expound
it, and who is moreover not only a patriot but an honest one.
A man possessing that knowledge without that faculty of
exposition might as well have no idea at all on the matter:
if he had both these gifts, but no love for his country, he would
be but a cold advocate for her interests; while were his
patriotism not proof against bribery, everything would go
for a price. So that if you thought that I was even moderately
distinguished for these qualities when you took my advice
and went to war, there is certainly no reason now why I should
be charged with having done wrong.

'For those of course who have a free choice in the matter
and whose fortunes are not at stake, war is the greatest of
follies. But if the only choice was between submission with
loss of independence, and danger with the hope of preserving
that independence,—in such a case it is he who will not accept
the risk that deserves blame, not he who will. I am the same

man and do not alter, it is you who change, since in fact you took my advice while unhurt, and waited for misfortune to repent of it; and the apparent error of my policy lies in the infirmity of your resolution, since the suffering that it entails is being felt by every one among you, while its advantage is still remote and obscure to all, and a great and sudden reverse having befallen you, your mind is too much depressed to persevere in your resolves. For before what is sudden, unexpected, and least within calculation the spirit quails; and putting all else aside, the plague has certainly been an emergency of this kind. Born, however, as you are, citizens of a great state, and brought up, as you have been, with habits equal to your birth, you should be ready to face the greatest disasters and still to keep unimpaired the lustre of your name. For the judgment of mankind is as relentless to the weakness that falls short of a recognised renown, as it is jealous of the arrogance that aspires higher than its due. Cease then to grieve for your private afflictions, and address yourselves instead to the safety of the commonwealth.

'If you shrink before the exertions which the war makes necessary, and fear that after all they may not have a happy result, you know the reasons by which I have often demonstrated to you the groundlessness of your apprehension. If those are not enough, I will now reveal an advantage arising from the greatness of your dominion, which I think has never yet suggested itself to you, which I never mentioned in my previous speeches, and which has so bold a sound that I should scarce adventure it now, were it not for the unnatural depression which I see around me. You perhaps think that your empire extends only over your allies; I will declare to you the truth. The visible field of action has two parts, land and sea. In the whole of one of these you are completely supreme, not merely as far as you use it at present, but also to what further extent you may think fit: in fine, your naval resources are such that your vessels may go where they please, without the king or any other nation on earth being able to stop them. So that although you may think it a great privation to lose the use of your land and houses, still you must see that this power is something widely different; and instead of fretting on their account, you should really regard them in the light of the gardens and other accessories that embellish a great fortune, and as, in comparison, of little moment. You should know too that liberty preserved by your efforts will easily recover for us what we have lost, while, the knee once bowed, even what you have will pass from you. Your fathers receiving these possessions not from others, but from themselves, did not let slip what their labour had acquired, but delivered them safe to you; and in this respect at least you must prove yourselves their equals, remembering that to lose what one has got is more disgraceful than to be baulked in getting, and you must confront your enemies not merely with spirit but with disdain. Confidence indeed a blissful ignorance can impart, ay, even to a coward's breast, but disdain is the privilege of those who, like us, have been assured by reflexion of their superiority to their adversary. And where the chances are the same, knowledge fortifies courage by the contempt which is its consequence, its trust being placed, not in hope, which is the prop of the desperate, but in a judgment grounded upon existing resources, whose anticipations are more to be depended upon.

'Again, your country has a right to your services in sustaining the glories of her position. These are a common source of pride to you all, and you cannot decline the burdens of empire and still expect to share its honours. You should remember also that what you are fighting against is not merely slavery as an exchange for independence, but also loss of empire and danger from the animosities incurred in its exercise. Besides, to recede is no longer possible, if indeed any of you in the alarm of the moment has become enamoured of the honesty of such an unambitious part. For what you hold is, to speak somewhat plainly, a tyranny; to take it perhaps was wrong, but to let it go is unsafe. And men of these retiring views, making converts of others, would quickly ruin a state; indeed the result would be the same if they could live independent by themselves; for the retiring and unambitious are never secure without vigorous protectors at their side; in fine, such qualities are useless to an imperial city, though they may help a dependency to an unmolested servitude.

'But you must not be seduced by citizens like these nor be angry with me,—who, if I voted for war, only did as you did yourselves,—in spite of the enemy having invaded your country and done what you could be certain that he would do, if you refused to comply with his demands; and although besides what we counted for, the plague has come upon us—the only point indeed at which our calculation has been at fault. It is this, I know, that has had a large share in making me more unpopular than I should otherwise have been,—quite undeservedly, unless you are also prepared to give me the credit of any success with which chance may present you. Besides, the hand of Heaven must be borne with resignation, that of the enemy with fortitude; this was the old way at Athens, and do not you prevent it being so still. Remember, too, that if your country has the greatest name in all the world, it is because she never bent before disaster; because she has expended more life and effort in war than any other city, and has won for herself a power greater than any hitherto known, the memory of which will descend to the latest posterity; even if now, in obedience to the general law of decay, we should ever be forced to yield, still it will be remembered that we held rule over more Hellenes than any other Hellenic state, that we sustained the greatest wars against their united or separate powers, and inhabited a city unrivalled by any other in resources or magnitude. These glories may incur the censure of the slow and unambitious; but in the breast of energy they will awake emulation, and in those who must remain without them an envious regret. Hatred and unpopularity at the moment have fallen to the lot of all who have aspired to rule others; but where odium must be incurred, true wisdom incurs it for the highest objects. Hatred also is short-lived; but that which makes the splendour of the present and the glory of the future remains for ever unforgotten. Make your decision, therefore, for glory then and honour now, and attain both objects by instant and zealous effort: do not send heralds to Lacedæmon, and do not betray any sign of being oppressed by your present sufferings, since they whose minds are least sensitive to calamity, and whose hands are most quick to meet it, are the greatest men and the greatest communities.'

Such were the arguments by which Pericles tried to cure the Athenians of their anger against him and to divert their thoughts from their immediate afflictions. As a community he succeeded in convincing them; they not only gave up all idea of sending to Lacedæmon, but applied themselves with increased energy to the war; still as private individuals they could not help smarting under their sufferings, the common people having been deprived of the little that they ever possessed, while the higher orders had lost fine properties with costly establishments and buildings in the country, and, worst of all, had war instead of peace. In fact, the public feeling against him did not subside until he had been fined. Not long afterwards, however, according to the way of the multitude, they again elected him general and committed all their affairs to his hands, having now become less sensitive to their private and domestic afflictions, and understanding that he was the best man of all for the public necessities. For as long as he was at the head of the state during the peace, he pursued a moderate and conservative policy; and in his time its greatness was at its height. When the war broke out, here also he seems to have rightly gauged the power of his country. He outlived its commencement two years and six months, and the correctness of his previsions respecting it became better known by his death. He told them to wait quietly, to pay attention to their marine, to attempt no new conquests, and to expose the city to no hazards during the war, and doing this, promised them a favourable result. What they did was the very contrary, allowing private ambitions and private interests, in matters apparently quite foreign to the war, to lead them into projects unjust both to themselves and to their allies—projects whose success would only conduce to the honour and advantage of private persons, and whose failure entailed certain disaster on the country in the war. The causes of this are not far to seek. Pericles indeed, by his rank, ability, and known integrity, was enabled to exercise an independent control over the multitude—in short, to lead them instead of being led by them; for as he never sought power by improper means, he was never compelled to flatter them, but, on the contrary, enjoyed so high an estimation that he could afford to anger them by contradiction. Whenever he saw them unseasonably and insolently elated, he would with a word reduce them to alarm; on the other hand, if they fell victims to a panic, he could at once restore them to confidence. In

short, what was nominally a democracy became in his hands
government by the first citizen. With his successors it was
different. More on a level with one another, and each grasping
at supremacy, they ended by committing even the conduct
of state affairs to the whims of the multitude. This, as might
have been expected in a great and sovereign state, produced a
host of blunders, and amongst them the Sicilian expedition;
though this failed not so much through a miscalculation of
the power of those against whom it was sent, as through a
fault in the senders in not taking the best measures afterwards to assist those who had gone out, but choosing rather
to occupy themselves with private cabals for the leadership
of the commons, by which they not only paralysed operations
in the field, but also first introduced civil discord at home. Yet
after losing most of their fleet besides other forces in Sicily,
and with faction already dominant in the city, they could
still for three years make head against their original adversaries, joined not only by the Sicilians, but also by their own
allies nearly all in revolt, and at last by the king's son, Cyrus,
who furnished the funds for the Peloponnesian navy. Nor did
they finally succumb till they fell the victims of their own
intestine disorders. So superfluously abundant were the resources from which the genius of Pericles foresaw an easy
triumph in the war over the unaided forces of the Peloponnesians.

During the same summer the Lacedæmonians and their
allies made an expedition with a hundred ships against
Zacynthus, an island lying off the coast of Elis, peopled by a
colony of Achæans from Peloponnese, and in alliance with
Athens. There were a thousand Lacedæmonian heavy infantry
on board, and Cnemus, a Spartan, as admiral. They made a
descent from their ships, and ravaged most of the country;
but as the inhabitants would not submit, they sailed back
home.

At the end of the same summer the Corinthian Aristeus,
Aneristus, Nicolaus, and Pratodamus, envoys from Lace-
dæmon, Timagoras, a Tegean, and a private individual named
Pollis from Argos, on their way to Asia to persuade the king
to supply funds and join in the war, came to Sitalces, son of
Teres in Thrace, with the idea of inducing him, if possible, to

forsake the alliance of Athens and to march on Potidæa then besieged by an Athenian force, and also of getting conveyed by his means to their destination across the Hellespont to Pharnabazus, who was to send them up the country to the king. But there chanced to be with Sitalces some Athenian ambassadors, Learchus, son of Callimachus, and Ameiniades, son of Philemon, who persuaded Sitalces' son, Sadocus, the new Athenian citizen, to put the men into their hands and thus prevent their crossing over to the king and doing their part to injure the country of his choice. He accordingly had them seized, as they were travelling through Thrace to the vessel in which they were to cross the Hellespont, by a party whom he had sent on with Learchus and Ameiniades, and gave orders for their delivery to the Athenian ambassadors, by whom they were brought to Athens. On their arrival, the Athenians, afraid that Aristeus, who had been notably the prime mover in the previous affairs of Potidæa and their Thracian possessions, might live to do them still more mischief if he escaped, slew them all the same day, without giving them a trial or hearing the defence which they wished to offer, and cast their bodies into a pit; thinking themselves justified in using in retaliation the same mode of warfare which the Lacedæmonians had begun, when they slew and cast into pits all the Athenian and allied traders whom they caught on board the merchantmen round Peloponnese. Indeed, at the outset of the war, the Lacedæmonians butchered as enemies all whom they took on the sea, whether allies of Athens or neutrals.

About the same time towards the close of the summer, the Ambraciot forces, with a number of barbarians that they had raised, marched against the Amphilochian Argos and the rest of that country. The origin of their enmity against the Argives was this. This Argos and the rest of Amphilochia were colonised by Amphilochus, son of Amphiaraus. Dissatisfied with the state of affairs at home on his return thither after the Trojan war, he built this city in the Ambracian gulf, and named it Argos after his own country. This was the largest town in Amphilochia, and its inhabitants the most powerful. Under the pressure of misfortune many generations afterwards, they called in the Ambraciots, their neighbours on the

Amphilochian border, to join their colony; and it was by this union with the Ambraciots that they learnt their present Hellenic speech, the rest of the Amphilochians being barbarians. After a time the Ambraciots expelled the Argives and held the city themselves. Upon this the Amphilochians gave themselves over to the Acarnanians; and the two together called the Athenians, who sent them Phormio as general and thirty ships; upon whose arrival they took Argos by storm, and made slaves of the Ambraciots; and the Amphilochians and Acarnanians inhabited the town in common. After this began the alliance between the Athenians and Acarnanians. The enmity of the Ambraciots against the Argives thus commenced with the enslavement of their citizens; and afterwards during the war they collected this armament among themselves and the Chaonians, and other of the neighbouring barbarians. Arrived before Argos, they became masters of the country; but not being successful in their attacks upon the town, returned home and dispersed among their different peoples.

Such were the events of the summer. The ensuing winter the Athenians sent twenty ships round Peloponnese, under the command of Phormio, who stationed himself at Naupactus and kept watch against any one sailing in or out of Corinth and the Crissæan gulf. Six others went to Caria and Lycia under Melesander, to collect tribute in those parts, and also to prevent the Peloponnesian privateers from taking up their station in those waters and molesting the passage of the merchantmen from Phaselis and Phœnicia and the adjoining continent. However, Melesander, going up the country into Lycia with a force of Athenians from the ships and the allies, was defeated and killed in battle, with the loss of a number of his troops.

The same winter the Potidæans at length found themselves no longer able to hold out against their besiegers. The inroads of the Peloponnesians into Attica had not had the desired effect of making the Athenians raise the siege. Provisions there were none left; and so far had distress for food gone in Potidæa that, besides a number of other horrors, instances had even occurred of the people having eaten one another. So in this extremity they at last made proposals for capitulating to the Athenian generals in command against them, Xenophon, son of Euripides, Hestiodorus, son of Aristocleides, and Phanomachus, son of Callimachus. The generals accepted their proposals, seeing the sufferings of the army in so exposed a position; besides which the state had already spent two thousand talents upon the siege. The terms of the capitulation were as follows: a free passage out for themselves, their children, wives and auxiliaries, with one garment apiece, the women with two, and a fixed sum of money for their journey. Under this treaty they went out to Chalcidice and other places, according as was in their power. The Athenians, however, blamed the generals for granting terms without instructions from home, being of opinion that the place would have had to surrender at discretion. They afterwards sent settlers of their own to Potidæa, and colonised it. Such were the events of the winter, and so ended the second year of this war of which Thucydides was the historian.

CHAPTER VIII

THIRD YEAR OF THE WAR—INVESTMENT OF PLATÆA—NAVAL VICTORIES OF PHORMIO—THRACIAN IRRUPTION INTO MACEDONIA UNDER SITALCES

B.C. 429: *Platæans appeal to Archidamus—Platæa abides by Athenian alliance—Archidamus begins siege—Building of defences—Attempt to burn town foiled—Blockade begun—Athenian force defeated by Chalcidians—Expedition against Acarnania—Stratians repel attack—Phormio's strategy—Athenian naval victory—Preparations for renewal of battle—First advantages for Peloponnesians—Athenians gain decisive victory—Plan of surprise attack upon Piræus—Peloponnesians repelled from Salamis—Sitalces' expedition against Perdiccas—Phormio in Acarnania.*

THE next summer the Peloponnesians and their allies, instead of invading Attica, marched against Platæa, under the command of Archidamus, son of Zeuxidamus, king of the Lacedæmonians. He had encamped his army and was about to lay waste the country, when the Platæans hastened to send envoys to him, and spoke as follows: 'Archidamus and Lacedæmonians, in invading the Platæan territory, you do what is wrong in itself, and worthy neither of yourselves nor of the fathers who begot you. Pausanias, son of Cleombrotus, your countryman, after freeing Hellas from the Medes with the help of those Hellenes who were willing to undertake the risk of the battle fought near our city, offered sacrifice to Zeus the Liberator in the market-place of Platæa, and calling all the allies together restored to the Platæans their city and territory, and declared it independent and inviolate against aggression or conquest. Should any such be attempted, the allies present were to help according to their power. Your fathers rewarded us thus for the courage and patriotism that we displayed at that perilous epoch; but you do just the contrary, coming with our bitterest enemies, the Thebans, to enslave us. We appeal, therefore, to the gods to whom the oaths were then made, to the gods of your ancestors, and lastly to those of our country, and call upon you to refrain from violating our territory or transgressing the oaths, and to let us live independent, as Pausanias decreed.'

The Platæans had got thus far when they were cut short by Archidamus saying, 'There is justice, Platæans, in what you say, if you act up to your words. According to the grant of Pausanias, continue to be independent yourselves, and join in freeing those of your fellow-countrymen who, after sharing in the perils of that period, joined in the oaths to you, and are now subject to the Athenians; for it is to free them and the rest that all this provision and war has been made. I could wish that you would share our labours and abide by the oaths yourselves; if this is impossible, do what we have already required of you—remain neutral, enjoying your own; join neither side, but receive both as friends, neither as allies for the war. With this we shall be satisfied.' Such were the words of Archidamus. The Platæans, after hearing what he had to say, went into the city and acquainted the people with what had passed, and presently returned for answer that it was impossible for them to do what he proposed without consulting the Athenians, with whom their children and wives now were; besides which they had their fears for the town. After his departure, what was to prevent the Athenians from coming and taking it out of their hands, or the Thebans, who would be included in the oaths, from taking advantage of the proposed neutrality to make a second attempt to seize the city? Upon these points he tried to reassure them by saying: 'You have only to deliver over the city and houses to us Lacedæmonians, to point out the boundaries of your land, the number of your fruit-trees, and whatever else can be numerically stated, and yourselves to withdraw wherever you like as long as the war shall last. When it is over we will restore to you whatever we received, and in the interim hold it in trust and keep it in cultivation, paying you a sufficient allowance.'

When they had heard what he had to say, they re-entered the city, and after consulting with the people said that they wished first to acquaint the Athenians with this proposal, and in the event of their approving to accede to it; in the meantime they asked him to grant them a truce and not to lay waste their territory. He accordingly granted a truce for the number of days requisite for the journey, and meanwhile abstained from ravaging their territory. The Platæan envoys went to Athens, and consulted with the Athenians, and returned with the following message to those in the city: 'The Athenians say, Platæans, that they never hitherto, since we became their allies, on any occasion abandoned us to an enemy, nor will they now neglect us, but will help us according to their ability; and they adjure you by the oaths which your fathers swore, to keep the alliance unaltered.'

On the delivery of this message by the envoys, the Platæans resolved not to be unfaithful to the Athenians but to endure, if it must be, seeing their lands laid waste and any other trials that might come to them, and not to send out again, but to answer from the wall that it was impossible for them to do as the Lacedæmonians proposed. As soon as he had received this answer, King Archidamus proceeded first to make a solemn appeal to the gods and heroes of the country in words following:—'Ye gods and heroes of the Platæan territory, be my witnesses that not as aggressors originally, nor until these had first departed from the common oath, did we invade this land, in which our fathers offered you their prayers before defeating the Medes, and which you made auspicious to the Hellenic arms; nor shall we be aggressors in the measures to which we may now resort, since we have made many fair proposals but have not been successful. Graciously accord that those who were the first to offend may be punished for it, and that vengeance may be attained by those who would righteously inflict it.'

After this appeal to the gods Archidamus put his army in motion. First he enclosed the town with a palisade formed of the fruit-trees which they cut down, to prevent further egress from Platæa; next day they threw up a mound against the city, hoping that the largeness of the force employed would insure the speedy reduction of the place. They accordingly cut down timber from Cithæron, and built it up on either side, laying it like lattice-work to serve as a wall to keep the mound from spreading abroad, and carried to it wood and stones and earth and whatever other material might help to complete it. They continued to work at the mound for seventy days and nights without intermission, being divided into relief parties to allow of some being employed in carrying while others took sleep and refreshment; the Lacedæmonian officer attached to each contingent keeping the men to the work. But the Platæans observing the progress of the mound, constructed a wall of wood and fixed it upon that part of the city wall against which the mound was being erected, and built up bricks inside it which they took from the neighbouring houses. The timbers served to bind the building together, and to prevent its becoming weak as it advanced in height; it had also a covering of skins and hides, which protected the woodwork against the attacks of burning missiles and allowed the men to work in safety. Thus the wall was raised to a great height, and the mound opposite made no less rapid progress. The Platæans also thought of another expedient; they pulled out part of the wall upon which the mound abutted, and carried the earth into the city.

Discovering this the Peloponnesians twisted up clay in wattles of reed and threw it into the breach formed in the mound, in order to give it consistency and prevent its being carried away like the soil. Stopped in this way the Platæans changed their mode of operation, and digging a mine from the town calculated their way under the mound, and began to carry off its material as before. This went on for a long while without the enemy outside finding it out, so that for all they threw on the top their mound made no progress in proportion, being carried away from beneath and constantly settling down in the vacuum. But the Platæans fearing that even thus they might not be able to hold out against the superior numbers of the enemy, had yet another invention. They stopped working at the large building in front of the mound, and starting at either end of it inside from the old low wall, built a new one in the form of a crescent running in towards the town; in order that in the event of the great wall being taken this might remain, and the enemy have to throw up a fresh mound against it, and as they advanced within might not only have their trouble over again, but also be exposed to missiles on their flanks. While raising the mound the Peloponnesians also brought up engines against the city, one of which was brought up upon the mound against the great building and shook down a good piece of it, to the no small alarm of the Platæans. Others were advanced against different parts of the wall but were lassoed and broken by the Platæans; who also hung up great beams by long iron chains from either extremity of two poles laid on the wall and projecting over it, and drew them up at an angle whenever any point was threatened by the engine, and loosing their hold let the beam go with its chains slack, so that it fell with a run and snapped off the nose of the battering ram.

After this the Peloponnesians, finding that their engines effected nothing, and that their mound was met by the counter-work, concluded that their present means of offence were unequal to the taking of the city, and prepared for its circum-vallation. First, however, they determined to try the effects of fire and see whether they could not, with the help of a wind, burn the town as it was not a large one; indeed they thought of every possible expedient by which the place might be reduced without the expense of a blockade. They accordingly brought faggots of brushwood and threw them from the mound, first into the space between it and the wall; and this soon becoming full from the number of hands at work, they next heaped the faggots up as far into the town as they could reach from the top, and then lighted the wood by setting fire to it with sulphur and pitch. The consequence was a fire greater than any one had ever yet seen produced by human agency, though it could not of course be compared to the spontaneous conflagrations sometimes known to occur through

the wind rubbing the branches of a mountain forest together.
And this fire was not only remarkable for its magnitude, but
was also, at the end of so many perils, within an ace of proving
fatal to the Platæans; a great part of the town became entirely
inaccessible, and had a wind blown upon it, in accordance
with the hopes of the enemy, nothing could have saved them.
As it was, there is also a story of heavy rain and thunder
having come on by which the fire was put out and the danger
averted.

Failing in this last attempt the Peloponnesians left a portion
of their forces on the spot, dismissing the rest, and built a wall
of circumvallation round the town, dividing the ground among
the various cities present; a ditch being made within and
without the lines, from which they got their bricks. All being
finished by about the rising of Arcturus, they left men enough
to man half the wall, the rest being manned by the Bœotians,
and drawing off their army dispersed to their several cities.
The Platæans had before sent off their wives and children and
oldest men and the mass of the noncombatants to Athens; so
that the number of the besieged left in the place comprised
four hundred of their own citizens, eighty Athenians, and a
hundred and ten women to bake their bread. This was the
sum total at the commencement of the siege, and there was
no one else within the walls, bond or free. Such were the
arrangements made for the blockade of Platæa.

The same summer and simultaneously with the expedition
against Platæa, the Athenians marched with two thousand
heavy infantry and two hundred horse against the Chalcidians
in the direction of Thrace and the Bottiæans, just as the corn
was getting ripe, under the command of Xenophon, son of
Euripides, with two colleagues. Arriving before Spartolus in
Bottiæa, they destroyed the corn and had some hopes of the
city coming over through the intrigues of a faction within.
But those of a different way of thinking had sent to Olynthus;
and a garrison of heavy infantry and other troops arrived
accordingly. These issuing from Spartolus were engaged by
the Athenians in front of the town: the Chalcidian heavy
infantry, and some auxiliaries with them, were beaten and
retreated into Spartolus; but the Chalcidian horse and light
troops defeated the horse and light troops of the Athenians

The Chalcidians had already a few targeteers from Crusis, and presently after the battle were joined by some others from Olynthus; upon seeing whom the light troops from Spartolus, emboldened by this accession and by their previous success, with the help of the Chalcidian horse and the reinforcement just arrived again attacked the Athenians, who retired upon the two divisions which they had left with their baggage. Whenever the Athenians advanced, their adversary gave way, pressing them with missiles the instant they began to retire. The Chalcidian horse also, riding up and charging them just as they pleased, at last caused a panic amongst them and routed and pursued them to a great distance. The Athenians took refuge in Potidæa, and afterwards recovered their dead under truce, and returned to Athens with the remnant of their army; four hundred and thirty men and all the generals having fallen. The Chalcidians and Bottiæans set up a trophy, took up their dead, and dispersed to their several cities.

The same summer, not long after this, the Ambraciots and Chaonians, being desirous of reducing the whole of Acarnania and detaching it from Athens, persuaded the Lacedæmonians to equip a fleet from their confederacy and send a thousand heavy infantry to Acarnania, representing that if a combined movement were made by land and sea, the coast Acarnanians would be unable to march, and the conquest of Zacynthus and Cephallenia easily following on the possession of Acarnania, the cruise round Peloponnese would be no longer so convenient for the Athenians. Besides which there was a hope of taking Naupactus. The Lacedæmonians accordingly at once sent off a few vessels with Cnemus, who was still high admiral, and the heavy infantry on board; and sent round orders for the fleet to equip as quickly as possible and sail to Leucas. The Corinthians were the most forward in the business; the Ambraciots being a colony of theirs. While the ships from Corinth, Sicyon and the neighbourhood were getting ready, and those from Leucas, Anactorium and Ambracia, which had arrived before, were waiting for them at Leucas, Cnemus and his thousand heavy infantry had run into the gulf, giving the slip to Phormio, the commander of the Athenian squadron stationed off Naupactus, and began at once to prepare for the land expedition. The Hellenic troops with him consisted of the Ambraciots, Leucadians, and Anactorians, and the thousand Peloponnesians with whom he came; the barbarian of a thousand Chaonians, who, belonging to a nation that has no king, were led by Photys and Nicanor, the two members of the royal family to whom the chieftainship for that year had been confided. With the Chaonians came also some Thesprotians, like them without a king, some Molossians and Atintanians led by Sabylinthus, the guardian of king Tharyps who was still a minor, and some Paravæans, under their King Orœdus, accompanied by a thousand Orestians, subjects of King Antiochus and placed by him under the command of Orœdus. There were also a thousand Macedonians sent by Perdiccas without the knowledge of the Athenians, but they arrived too late. With this force Cnemus set out, without waiting for the fleet from Corinth. Passing through the territory of Amphilochian Argos, and sacking the open village of Limnæa, they advanced to Stratus the Acarnanian capital; this once taken, the rest of the country, they felt convinced would speedily follow.

The Acarnanians, finding themselves invaded by a large army by land, and from the sea threatened by a hostile fleet, made no combined attempt at resistance, but remained to defend their homes, and sent for help to Phormio, who replied that when a fleet was on the point of sailing from Corinth, it was impossible for him to leave Naupactus unprotected. The Peloponnesians meanwhile and their allies advanced upon Stratus in three divisions, with the intention of encamping near it and attempting the wall by force if they failed to succeed by negotiation. The order of march was as follows: the centre was occupied by the Chaonians and the rest of the barbarians, with the Leucadians and Anactorians and their followers on the right, and Cnemus with the Peloponnesians and Ambraciots on the left; each division being a long way off from, and sometimes even out of sight of, the others. The Hellenes advanced in good order, keeping a look-out till they encamped in a good position; but the Chaonians, filled with self-confidence, and having the highest character for courage among the tribes of that part of the continent, without waiting to occupy their camp, rushed on with the rest of the barbarians, in the idea that they should take the town by assault and obtain the sole glory of the enterprise. While they were coming on, the Stratians, becoming aware how things stood, and thinking that the defeat of this division would considerably dishearten the Hellenes behind it, occupied the environs of the town with ambuscades, and as soon as they approached engaged them at close quarters from the city and the ambuscades. A panic seizing the Chaonians, great numbers of them were slain; and as soon as they were seen to give way the rest of the barbarians turned and fled. Owing to the distance by which their allies had preceded them, neither of the Hellenic divisions knew anything of the battle, but fancied they were hastening on to encamp. However, when the flying barbarians broke in upon them, they opened their ranks to receive them, brought their divisions together, and stopped quiet where they were for the day; the Stratians not offering to engage them, as the rest of the Acarnanians had not yet arrived, but contenting themselves with slinging at them from a distance, which distressed them greatly, as there was no stirring without their armour. The Acarnanians would seem to excel in this mode of warfare.

As soon as night fell, Cnemus hastily drew off his army to the river Anapus, about nine miles from Stratus, recovering his dead next day under truce, and being there joined by the friendly Œniadæ, fell back upon their city before the enemy's reinforcements came up. From hence each returned home; and the Stratians set up a trophy for the battle with the barbarians.

Meanwhile the fleet from Corinth and the rest of the confederates in the Crissæan gulf, which was to have co-operated with Cnemus and prevented the coast Acarnanians from joining their countrymen in the interior, was disabled from doing so by being compelled about the same time as the battle at Stratus to fight with Phormio and the twenty Athenian vessels stationed at Naupactus. For they were watched, as they coasted along out of the gulf, by Phormio, who wished to attack in the open sea. But the Corinthians and allies had started for Acarnania without any idea of fighting at sea, and with vessels more like transports for carrying soldiers; besides which, they never dreamed of the twenty Athenian ships venturing to engage their forty-seven. However, while they were coasting along their own shore, there were the Athenians

sailing along in line with them; and when they tried to cross
over from Patræ in Achæa to the mainland on the other side,
on their way to Acarnania, they saw them again coming out
from Chalcis and the river Evenus to meet them. They
slipped from their moorings in the night, but were observed,
and were at length compelled to fight in mid passage. Each
state that contributed to the armament had its own general;
the Corinthian commanders were Machaon, Isocrates, and
Agatharchidas. The Peloponnesians ranged their vessels in as
large a circle as possible without leaving an opening, with the
prows outside and the sterns in; and placed within all the
small craft in company, and their five best sailers to issue out
at a moment's notice and strengthen any point threatened by
the enemy.

The Athenians, formed in line, sailed round and round them,
and forced them to contract their circle, by continually brush-
ing past and making as though they would attack at once,
having been previously cautioned by Phormio not to do so
till he gave the signal. His hope was that the Peloponnesians
would not retain their order like a force on shore, but that
the ships would fall foul of one another and the small craft
cause confusion; and if the wind should blow from the gulf
(in expectation of which he kept sailing round them, and
which usually rose towards morning), they would not, he
felt sure, remain steady an instant. He also thought that it
rested with him to attack when he pleased, as his ships were
better sailers, and that an attack timed by the coming of the
wind would tell best. When the wind came down, the enemy's
ships were now in a narrow space, and what with the wind
and the small craft dashing against them, at once fell into
confusion: ship fell foul of ship, while the crews were pushing
them off with poles, and by their shouting, swearing and strug-
gling with one another, made captains' orders and boatswains'
cries alike inaudible, and through being unable for want of
practice to clear their oars in the rough water, prevented the
vessels from obeying their helmsmen properly. At this moment
Phormio gave the signal, and the Athenians attacked. Sinking
first one of the admirals, they then disabled all they came
across, so that no one thought of resistance for the confusion,
but fled for Patræ and Dyme in Achæa. The Athenians gave

chase and captured twelve ships, and taking most of the men
out of them sailed to Molycrium, and after setting up a trophy
on the promontory of Rhium and dedicating a ship to Poseidon, returned to Naupactus. As for the Peloponnesians, they
at once sailed with their remaining ships along the coast from
Dyme and Patræ to Cyllene, the Eleian arsenal; where
Cnemus and the ships from Leucas that were to have joined
them, also arrived after the battle of Stratus.

The Lacedæmonians now sent to the fleet to Cnemus three
commissioners, Timocrates, Brasidas, and Lycophron, with
orders to prepare to engage again with better fortune, and
not to be driven from the sea by a few vessels; for they
could not at all account for their discomfiture, the less so as
it was their first attempt at sea; and they fancied that it was
not that their marine was so inferior, but that there had been
misconduct somewhere, not considering the long experience
of the Athenians as compared with the little practice which
they had had themselves. The commissioners were accordingly
sent in anger. As soon as they arrived they set to work with
Cnemus to order ships from the different states, and to put
those which they already had in fighting order. Meanwhile
Phormio sent word to Athens of their preparations and his
own victory, and desired as many ships as possible to be
speedily sent to him, as he stood in daily expectation of a
battle. Twenty were accordingly sent, but instructions were
given to their commander to go first to Crete. For Nicias, a
Cretan of Gortys, who was *Proxenus* of the Athenians, had
persuaded them to sail against Cydonia, promising to procure
the reduction of that hostile town; his real wish being to
oblige the Polichnitans, neighbours of the Cydonians. He
accordingly went with the ships to Crete, and, accompanied by
the Polichnitans, laid waste the lands of the Cydonians; and,
what with adverse winds and stress of weather, wasted no
little time there.

While the Athenians were thus detained in Crete, the Peloponnesians in Cyllene got ready for battle, and coasted along
to Panormus in Achæa, where their land army had come to
support them. Phormio also coasted along to Molycrian
Rhium, and anchored outside it with twenty ships, the same
as he had fought with before. This Rhium was friendly to the

Athenians. The other, in Peloponnese, lies opposite to it; the sea between them is about three-quarters of a mile broad, and forms the mouth of the Crissæan gulf. At this, the Achæan Rhium, not far off Panormus, where their army lay, the Peloponnesians now cast anchor with seventy-seven ships, when they saw the Athenians do so. For six or seven days they remained opposite each other, practising and preparing for the battle; the one resolved not to sail out of the Rhia into the open sea, for fear of the disaster which had already happened to them, the other not to sail into the straits, thinking it advantageous to the enemy to fight in the narrows. At last Cnemus and Brasidas and the rest of the Peloponnesian commanders, being desirous of bringing on a battle as soon as possible, before reinforcements should arrive from Athens, and noticing that the men were most of them cowed by the previous defeat and out of heart for the business, first called them together and encouraged them as follows:—

'Peloponnesians, the late engagement which may have made some of you afraid of the one now in prospect, really gives no just ground for apprehension. Preparation for it, as you know, there was little enough; and the object of our voyage was not so much to fight at sea as an expedition by land. Besides this, the chances of war were largely against us; and perhaps also inexperience had something to do with our failure in our first naval action. It was not, therefore, cowardice that produced our defeat, nor ought the determination which force has not quelled, but which still has a word to say with its adversary, to lose its edge from the result of an accident; but admitting the possibility of a chance miscarriage, we should know that brave hearts must be always brave, and while they remain so can never put forward inexperience as an excuse for misconduct. Nor are you so behind the enemy in experience as you are ahead of him in courage; and although the science of your opponents would, if valour accompanied it, have also the presence of mind to carry out at an emergency the lesson it has learnt, yet a faint heart will make all art powerless in the face of danger. For fear takes away presence of mind, and without valour art is useless. Against their superior experience set your superior daring, and against the fear induced by defeat the fact of your having been then unprepared; remember, too, that you have always the advantage of superior numbers, and of engaging off your own coast, supported by your heavy infantry; and as a rule, numbers and equipment give victory. At no point, therefore, is defeat likely; and as for our previous mistakes, the very fact of their occurrence will teach us better for the future. Steersmen and sailors may, therefore, confidently attend to their several duties, none quitting the station assigned to them: as for ourselves, we promise to prepare for the engagement at least as well as your previous commanders, and to give no excuse for any one misconducting himself. Should any insist on doing so, he shall meet with the punishment he deserves, while the brave shall be honoured with the appropriate rewards of valour.'

The Peloponnesian commanders encouraged their men after this fashion. Phormio, meanwhile, being himself not without fears for the courage of his men, and noticing that they were forming in groups among themselves and were alarmed at the odds against them, desired to call them together and give them confidence and counsel in the present emergency. He had before continually told them, and had accustomed their minds to the idea, that there was no numerical superiority that they could not face; and the men themselves had long been persuaded that Athenians need never retire before any quantity of Peloponnesian vessels. At the moment, however, he saw that they were dispirited by the sight before them, and wishing to refresh their confidence, called them together and spoke as follows:—

'I see, my men, that you are frightened by the number of the enemy, and I have accordingly called you together, not liking you to be afraid of what is not really terrible. In the first place, the Peloponnesians, already defeated, and not even themselves thinking that they are a match for us, have not ventured to meet us on equal terms, but have equipped this multitude of ships against us. Next, as to that upon which they most rely, the courage which they suppose constitutional to them, their confidence here only arises from the success which their experience in land service usually gives them, and which they fancy will do the same for them at sea. But this advantage will in all justice belong to us on this element, if to them on that; as they are not superior to us in courage, but we are each of us more confident, according to our experience in our particular department. Besides, as the Lacedæmonians use their supremacy over the allies to promote their own glory, they are most of them being brought into danger against their will, or they would never, after such a decided defeat, have ventured upon a fresh engagement. You need not, therefore, be afraid of their dash. You, on the contrary, inspire a much greater and better founded alarm, both because of your late victory and also of their belief that we should not face them unless about to do something worthy of a success so signal. An adversary numerically superior, like the one before us, comes into action trusting more to strength than to resolution; while he who voluntarily confronts tremendous odds must have very great internal resources to draw upon. For these reasons the Peloponnesians fear our irrational audacity more than they would ever have done a more commensurate preparation. Besides, many armaments have before now succumbed to an inferior through want of skill or sometimes of courage; neither of which defects certainly are ours. As to the battle, it shall not be, if I can help it, in the strait, nor will I sail in there at all; seeing that in a contest between a number of clumsily managed vessels and a small, fast, well-handled squadron, want of sea room is an undoubted disadvantage. One cannot run down an enemy properly without having a sight of him a good way off, nor can one retire at need when pressed; one can neither break the line nor return upon his rear, the proper tactics for a fast sailer; but the naval action necessarily becomes a land one, in which numbers must decide the matter. For all this I will provide as far as can be. Do you stay at your posts by your ships, and be sharp at catching the word of command, the more so as we are observing one another from so short a distance; and in action think order and silence all important—qualities useful in war generally, and in naval engagements in particular—; and behave before the enemy in a manner worthy of your past exploits. The issues you will fight for are great—to destroy the naval hopes of the Peloponnesians or to bring nearer to the Athenians their fears for the sea. And I may once more remind you that you have defeated most of them already; and beaten men do not face a danger twice with the same determination.'

Such was the exhortation of Phormio. The Peloponnesians finding that the Athenians did not sail into the gulf and the narrows, in order to lead them in whether they wished it or not, put out at dawn, and forming four abreast, sailed inside the gulf in the direction of their own country, the right wing leading as they had lain at anchor. In this wing were placed twenty of their best sailers; so that in the event of Phormio thinking that their object was Naupactus, and coasting along thither to save the place, the Athenians might not be able to escape their onset by getting outside their wing, but might be cut off by the vessels in question. As they expected, Phormio, in alarm for the place at that moment emptied of its garrison, as soon as he saw them put out, reluctantly and hurriedly embarked and sailed along shore; the Messenian land forces moving along also to support him. The Peloponnesians seeing him coasting along with his ships in single file, and by this inside the gulf and close in shore as they so much wished, at one signal tacked suddenly and bore down in line at their best speed on the Athenians, hoping to cut off the whole squadron. The eleven leading vessels, however, escaped the Peloponnesian wing and its sudden movement, and reached the more open water; but the rest were overtaken as they tried to run through, driven ashore and disabled; such of the crews being slain as had not swum out of them. Some of the ships the Peloponnesians lashed to their own, and towed off empty; one they took with the men in it; others were just being towed off, when they were saved by the Messenians dashing into the sea with their armour and fighting from the decks that they had boarded.

Thus far victory was with the Peloponnesians, and the Athenian fleet destroyed; the twenty ships in the right wing being meanwhile in chase of the eleven Athenian vessels that had escaped their sudden movement and reached the more open water. These, with the exception of one ship, all outsailed them and got safe into Naupactus, and forming close in shore opposite the temple of Apollo, with their prows facing the enemy, prepared to defend themselves in case the Peloponnesians should sail in shore against them. After a while the Peloponnesians came up, chanting the pæan for their victory as they sailed on; the single Athenian ship remaining being chased by a Leucadian far ahead of the rest. But there happened to be a merchantman lying at anchor in the roadstead, which the Athenian ship found time to sail round, and struck the Leucadian in chase amidships and sank her. An exploit so sudden and unexpected produced a panic among the Peloponnesians; and having fallen out of order in the excitement of victory, some of them dropped their oars and stopped their way in order to let the main body come up —an unsafe thing to do considering how near they were to the enemy's prows; while others ran aground in the shallows, in their ignorance of the localities.

Elated at this incident, the Athenians at one word gave a cheer, and dashed at the enemy, who, embarrassed by his mistakes and the disorder in which he found himself, only stood for an instant, and then fled for Panormus, whence he had put out. The Athenians following on his heels took the six vessels nearest them, and recovered those of their own which had been disabled close in shore and taken in tow at the beginning of the action; they killed some of the crews and took some prisoners. On board the Leucadian which went down off the merchantman, was the Lacedæmonian Timocrates, who killed himself when the ship was sunk, and was cast up in the harbour of Naupactus. The Athenians on their return set up a trophy on the spot from which they had put out and turned the day, and picking up the wrecks and dead that were on their shore, gave back to the enemy their dead under truce. The Peloponnesians also set up a trophy as victors for the defeat inflicted upon the ships they had disabled in shore, and dedicated the vessel which they had taken at Achæan Rhium, side by side with the trophy. After this, apprehensive of the reinforcement expected from Athens, all except the Leucadians sailed into the Crissæan gulf for Corinth. Not long after their retreat, the twenty Athenian ships, which were to have joined Phormio before the battle, arrived at Naupactus.

Thus the summer ended. Winter was now at hand; but before dispersing the fleet, which had retired to Corinth and the Crissæan gulf, Cnemus, Brasidas, and the other Peloponnesian captains allowed themselves to be persuaded by the Megarians to make an attempt upon Piræus, the port of Athens, which from her decided superiority at sea had been

naturally left unguarded and open. Their plan was as follows:—The men were each to take their oar, cushion, and
rowlock thong, and going overland from Corinth to the sea
on the Athenian side, to get to Megara as quickly as they
could, and launching forty vessels, which happened to be
in the docks at Nisæa, to sail at once to Piræus. There was
no fleet on the look-out in the harbour, and no one had the
least idea of the enemy attempting a surprise; while an open
attack would, it was thought, never be deliberately ventured
on, or, if in contemplation, would be speedily known at
Athens. Their plan formed, the next step was to put it in execution. Arriving by night and launching the vessels from
Nisæa, they sailed, not to Piræus as they had originally intended, being afraid of the risk, besides which there was some
talk of a wind having stopped them, but to the point of Salamis
that looks towards Megara; where there was a fort and a
squadron of three ships to prevent anything sailing in or out
of Megara. This fort they assaulted, and towed off the galleys
empty, and surprising the inhabitants began to lay waste the
rest of the island.

Meanwhile fire signals were raised to alarm Athens, and
a panic ensued there as serious as any that occurred during
the war. The idea in the city was that the enemy had already
sailed into Piræus: in Piræus it was thought that they had
taken Salamis and might at any moment arrive in the port;
as indeed might easily have been done if their hearts had been
a little firmer: certainly no wind would have prevented them.
As soon as day broke the Athenians assembled in full force,
launched their ships, and embarking in haste and uproar went
with the fleet to Salamis, while their soldiery mounted guard
in Piræus. The Peloponnesians, on becoming aware of the
coming relief, after they had overrun most of Salamis, hastily
sailed off with their plunder and captives and the three ships
from Fort Budorum to Nisæa; the state of their ships also
causing them some anxiety, as it was a long while since they
had been launched, and they were not water-tight. Arrived
at Megara, they returned back on foot to Corinth. The
Athenians finding them no longer at Salamis, sailed back
themselves; and after this made arrangements for guarding

Piræus more diligently in future, by closing the harbours, and by other suitable precautions.

About the same time, at the beginning of this winter, Sitalces, son of Teres, the Odrysian king of Thrace, made an expedition against Perdiccas, son of Alexander, king of Macedonia, and the Chalcidians in the neighbourhood of Thrace; his object being to enforce one promise and fulfil another. On the one hand Perdiccas had made him a promise, when hard pressed at the commencement of the war, upon condition that Sitalces should reconcile the Athenians to him and not attempt to restore his brother and enemy, the pretender Philip, but had not offered to fulfil his engagement; on the other he, Sitalces, on entering into alliance with the Athenians, had agreed to put an end to the Chalcidian war in Thrace. These were the two objects of his invasion. With him he brought Amyntas, the son of Philip, whom he destined for the throne of Macedonia, and some Athenian envoys then at his court on this business, and Hagnon as general; for the Athenians were to join him against the Chalcidians with a fleet and as many soldiers as they could get together.

Beginning with the Odrysians, he first called out the Thracian tribes subject to him between Mounts Hæmus and Rhodope and the Euxine and Hellespont; next the Getæ beyond Hæmus, and the other hordes settled south of the Danube in the neighbourhood of the Euxine, who, like the Getæ, border on the Scythians and are armed in the same manner, being all mounted archers. Besides these he summoned many of the Hill Thracian independent swordsmen, called Dii and mostly inhabiting Mount Rhodope, some of whom came as mercenaries, others as volunteers; also the Agrianes and Lææans, and the rest of the Pæonian tribes in his empire, at the confines of which these lay, extending up to the Lææan Pæonians and the river Strymon, which flows from Mount Scombrus through the country of the Agrianes and Lææans; there the empire of Sitalces ends and the territory of the independent Pæonians begins. Bordering on the Triballi, also independent, were the Treres and Tilatæans, who dwell to the north of Mount Scombrus and extend towards the setting sun as far as the river Oskius. This river rises in the same mountains as the Nestus and Hebrus, a wild and extensive range connected with Rhodope.

The empire of the Odrysians extended along the seaboard from Abdera to the mouth of the Danube in the Euxine. The navigation of this coast by the shortest route takes a merchantman four days and four nights with a wind astern the whole way: by land an active man, travelling by the shortest road, can get from Abdera to the Danube in eleven days. Such was the length of its coast line. Inland from Byzantium to the Laeaeans and the Strymon, the farthest limit of its extension into the interior, it is a journey of thirteen days for an active man. The tribute from all the barbarian districts and the Hellenic cities, taking what they brought in under Seuthes, the successor of Sitalces, who raised it to its greatest height, amounted to about four hundred talents in gold and silver. There were also presents in gold and silver to a no less amount, besides stuff, plain and embroidered, and other articles, made not only for the king, but also for the Odrysian lords and nobles. For there was here established a custom opposite to that prevailing in the Persian kingdom, namely, of taking rather than giving; more disgrace being attached to not giving when asked than to asking and being refused; and although this prevailed elsewhere in Thrace, it was practised most extensively among the powerful Odrysians, it being impossible to get anything done without a present. It was thus a very powerful kingdom; in revenue and general prosperity surpassing all in Europe between the Ionian gulf and the Euxine, and in numbers and military resources coming decidedly next to the Scythians, with whom indeed no people in Europe can bear comparison, there not being even in Asia any nation singly a match for them if unanimous, though of course they are not on a level with other races in general intelligence and the arts of civilised life.

It was the master of this empire that now prepared to take the field. When everything was ready, he set out on his march for Macedonia, first through his own dominions, next over the desolate range of Cercine that divides the Sintians and Paeonians, crossing by a road which he had made by felling the timber on a former campaign against the latter people. Passing over these mountains, with the Paeonians on his right and the

Sintians and Mædians on the left, he finally arrived at
Doberus, in Pæonia, losing none of his army on the march,
except perhaps by sickness, but receiving some augmentations,
many of the independent Thracians volunteering to join him
in the hope of plunder; so that the whole is said to have formed
a grand total of a hundred and fifty thousand. Most of this
was infantry, though there was about a third cavalry, furnished principally by the Odrysians themselves and next to
them by the Getæ. The most warlike of the infantry were the
independent swordsmen who came down from Rhodope; the
rest of the mixed multitude that followed him being chiefly
formidable by their numbers.

Assembling in Doberus, they prepared for descending from
the heights upon Lower Macedonia, where the dominions of
Perdiccas lay; for the Lyncestæ, Elimiots, and other tribes
more inland, though Macedonians by blood and allies and
dependents of their kindred, still have their own separate governments. The country on the sea coast, now called Macedonia, was first acquired by Alexander, the father of Perdiccas,
and his ancestors, originally Temenids from Argos. This was
effected by the expulsion from Pieria of the Pierians, who
afterwards inhabited Phagres and other places under Mount
Pangæus, beyond the Strymon (indeed the country between
Pangæus and the sea is still called the Pierian gulf); of the
Bottiæans, at present neighbours of the Chalcidians, from
Bottia, and by the acquisition in Pæonia of a narrow strip
along the river Axius extending to Pella and the sea; the district of Mygdonia, between the Axius and the Strymon, being
also added by the expulsion of the Edonians. From Eordia
also were driven the Eordians, most of whom perished, though
a few of them still live round Physca, and the Almopians from
Almopia. These Macedonians also conquered places belonging
to the other tribes, which are still theirs—Anthemus, Crestonia, Bisaltia, and much of Macedonia proper. The whole is
now called Macedonia, and at the time of the invasion of
Sitalces, Perdiccas, Alexander's son, was the reigning king.

These Macedonians, unable to take the field against so
numerous an invader, shut themselves up in such strong places
and fortresses as the country possessed. Of these there was
no great number, most of those now found in the country

having been erected subsequently by Archelaus, the son of
Perdiccas, on his accession, who also cut straight roads, and
otherwise put the kingdom on a better footing as regards
horses, heavy infantry, and other war material than had been
done by all the eight kings that preceded him. Advancing from
Doberus, the Thracian host first invaded what had been once
Philip's government, and took Idomene by assault, Gortynia,
Atalanta, and some other places by negotiation, these last
coming over for love of Philip's son, Amyntas, then with
Sitalces. Laying siege to Europus, and failing to take it, he
next advanced into the rest of Macedonia to the left of Pella
and Cyrrhus, not proceeding beyond this into Bottia and
Pieria, but staying to lay waste Mygdonia, Crestonia, and
Anthemus. The Macedonians never even thought of meeting
him with infantry; but the Thracian host was, as opportunity
offered, attacked by handfuls of their horse, which had been
reinforced from their allies in the interior. Armed with cuiras-
ses, and excellent horsemen, wherever these charged they overthrew all before them, but ran considerable risk in entangling
themselves in the masses of the enemy, and so finally desisted
from these efforts, deciding that they were not strong enough
to venture against numbers so superior.

Meanwhile Sitacles opened negotiations with Perdiccas on
the objects of his expedition; and finding that the Athenians,
not believing that he would come, did not appear with their
fleet, though they sent presents and envoys, despatched a large
part of his army against the Chalcidians and Bottiæans, and
shutting them up inside their walls laid waste their country.
While he remained in these parts, the people farther south,
such as the Thessalians, and the Hellenes as far as Thermopylæ, all feared that the army might advance against them,
and prepared accordingly. These fears were shared by the
Thracians beyond the Strymon to the north, who inhabited the
plains, such as the Panæans, the Odomanti, the Droi and
the Dersæans, all of whom are independent. It was even matter
of conversation among the Hellenes who were enemies of
Athens whether he might not be invited by his ally to advance
also against them. Meanwhile he held Chalcidice and Bottice
and Macedonia, and was ravaging them all; but finding that
he was not succeeding in any of the objects of his invasion, and

that his army was without provisions and was suffering from
the severity of the season, he listened to the advice of Seuthes,
son of Sparadocus, his nephew and highest officer, and decided
to retreat without delay. This Seuthes had been secretly gained
by Perdiccas by the promise of his sister in marriage with a
rich dowry. In accordance with this advice, and after a stay
of thirty days in all, eight of which were spent in Chalcidice,
he retired home as quickly as he could; and Perdiccas afterwards gave his sister Stratonice to Seuthes as he had promised.
Such was the history of the expedition of Sitalces.

In the course of this winter, after the dispersion of the
Peloponnesian fleet, the Athenians in Naupactus, under
Phormio, coasted along to Astacus, and disembarked, and
marched into the interior of Acarnania with four hundred
Athenian heavy infantry and four hundred Messenians. After
expelling some suspected persons from Stratus, Coronta, and
other places, and restoring Cynes, son of Theolytus, to
Coronta, they returned to their ships, deciding that it was
impossible in the winter season to march against Œniadæ, a
place which, unlike the rest of Acarnania, had been always
hostile to them; for the river Achelous flowing from Mount
Pindus through Dolopia and the country of the Agræans and
Amphilochians and the plain of Acarnania, past the town of
Stratus in the upper part of its course, forms lakes where it
falls into the sea round Œniadæ, and thus makes it impracticable for an army in winter by reason of the water. Opposite
to Œniadæ lie most of the islands called Echinades, so close to
the mouths of the Achelous that that powerful stream is constantly forming deposits against them, and has already
joined some of the islands to the continent, and seems likely
in no long while to do the same with the rest. For the current
is strong, deep, and turbid, and the islands are so thick together that they serve to imprison the alluvial deposit and
prevent its dispersing, lying, as they do, not in one line, but
irregularly, so as to leave no direct passage for the water into
the open sea. The islands in question are uninhabited and of
no great size. There is also a story that Alcmæon, son of Am-
phiraus, during his wanderings after the murder of his mother
was bidden by Apollo to inhabit this spot, through an oracle
which intimated that he would have no release from his terrors

until he should find a country to dwell in which had not been seen by the sun, or existed as land at the time he slew his mother; all else being to him polluted ground. Perplexed at this, the story goes on to say, he at last observed this deposit of the Achelous, and considered that a place sufficient to support life upon, might have been thrown up during the long interval that had elapsed since the death of his mother and the beginning of his wanderings. Settling, therefore, in the district round Œniadæ, he founded a dominion, and left the country its name from his son Acarnan. Such is the story we have received concerning Alcmæon.

The Athenians and Phormio putting back from Acarnania and arriving at Naupactus, sailed home to Athens in the spring, taking with them the ships that they had captured, and such of the prisoners made in the late actions as were freemen; who were exchanged, man for man. And so ended this winter, and the third year of this war, of which Thucydides was the historian.

BOOK III

CHAPTER IX

B.C. 428: *Invasion of Attica—Revolt of Lesbos—Athenian expedition—
Phormio's son in Acarnania—Mitylenian's speech at Olympiad—
Lesbos joins Peloponnesian league—Total of Athenian ships—Mitylene blockaded—Platæans scale the wall and escape—Salæthus on
mission to Mitylene—*B.C. 427: *Capitulation of Mitylenians—Speech
of Teutiaplus—Cruelty of Alcidas—Paches arrives at Mitylene—
Cleon's speech—Speech of Diodotus—Diodotus' counsel prevails.*

THE next summer, just as the corn was getting ripe, the
Peloponnesians and their allies invaded Attica under the command of Archidamus, son of Zeuxidamus, king of the
Lacedæmonians, and sat down and ravaged the land; the
Athenian horse as usual attacking them, wherever it was
practicable, and preventing the mass of the light troops from
advancing from their camp and wasting the parts near the
city. After staying the time for which they had taken provisions, the invaders retired and dispersed to their several
cities.

Immediately after the invasion of the Peloponnesians all
Lesbos, except Methymna, revolted from the Athenians. The
Lesbians had wished to revolt even before the war, but the
Lacedæmonians would not receive them; and yet now when
they did revolt, they were compelled to do so sooner than they
had intended. While they were waiting until the moles for
their harbours and the ships and walls that they had in building should be finished, and for the arrival of archers and corn
and other things that they were engaged in fetching from the
Pontus, the Tenedians, with whom they were at enmity, and
the Methymnians, and some factious persons in Mitylene
itself, who were *Proxeni* of Athens, informed the Athenians
that the Mitylenians were forcibly uniting the island under

their sovereignty, and that the preparations about which they were so active, were all concerted with the Bœotians their kindred and the Lacedæmonians with a view to a revolt, and that unless they were immediately prevented, Athens would lose Lesbos.

However, the Athenians, distressed by the plague, and by the war that had recently broken out and was now raging, thought it a serious matter to add Lesbos with its fleet and untouched resources to the list of their enemies; and at first would not believe the charge, giving too much weight to their wish that it might not be true. But when an embassy which they sent had failed to persuade the Mitylenians to give up the union and preparations complained of, they became alarmed, and resolved to strike the first blow. They accordingly suddenly sent off forty ships that had been got ready to sail round Peloponnese, under the command of Cleippides, son of Deinias, and two others; word having been brought them of a festival in honour of the Malean Apollo outside the town, which is kept by the whole people of Mitylene, and at which, if haste were made, they might hope to take them by surprise. If this plan succeeded, well and good; if not, they were to order the Mitylenians to deliver up their ships and to pull down their walls, and if they did not obey, to declare war. The ships accordingly set out; the ten galleys, forming the contingent of the Mitylenians present with the fleet according to the terms of the alliance, being detained by the Athenians, and their crews placed in custody. However, the Mitylenians were informed of the expedition by a man who crossed from Athens to Eubœa, and going overland to Geræstus, sailed from thence by a merchantman which he found on the point of putting to sea, and so arrived at Mitylene the third day after leaving Athens. The Mitylenians accordingly refrained from going out to the temple at Malea, and moreover barricaded and kept guard round the half-finished parts of their walls and harbours.

When the Athenians sailed in not long after and saw how things stood, the generals delivered their orders, and upon the Mitylenians refusing to obey, commenced hostilities. The Mitylenians, thus compelled to go to war without notice and unprepared, at first sailed out with their fleet and made some

show of fighting, a little in front of the harbour; but being
driven back by the Athenian ships, immediately offered to
treat with the commanders, wishing, if possible, to get the
ships away for the present upon any tolerable terms. The
Athenian commanders accepted their offers, being themselves
fearful that they might not be able to cope with the whole of
Lesbos; and an armistice having been concluded, the Mitylenians sent to Athens one of the informers, already repentant
of his conduct, and others with him, to try to persuade the
Athenians of the innocence of their intentions and to get the
fleet recalled. In the meantime, having no great hope of a
favourable answer from Athens, they also sent off a galley
with envoys to Lacedæmon, unobserved by the Athenian
fleet which was anchored at Malea to the north of the town.

While these envoys, reaching Lacedæmon after a difficult
journey across the open sea, were negotiating for succours
being sent them, the ambassadors from Athens returned without having effected anything; and hostilities were at once
begun by the Mitylenians and the rest of Lesbos, with the
exception of the Methymnians, who came to the aid of the
Athenians with the Imbrians and Lemnians and some few of
the other allies. The Mitylenians made a sortie with all their
forces against the Athenian camp; and a battle ensued, in
which they gained some slight advantage, but retired notwithstanding, not feeling sufficient confidence in themselves to
spend the night upon the field. After this they kept quiet,
wishing to wait for the chance of reinforcements arriving from
Peloponnese before making a second venture, being encouraged by the arrival of Meleas, a Laconian, and Hermæondas,
a Theban, who had been sent off before the insurrection but
had been unable to reach Lesbos before the Athenian expedition, and who now stole in in a galley after the battle, and
advised them to send another galley and envoys back with
them, which the Mitylenians accordingly did.

Meanwhile the Athenians, greatly encouraged by the inaction of the Mitylenians, summoned allies to their aid, who
came in all the quicker from seeing so little vigour displayed
by the Lesbians, and bringing round their ships to a new
station to the south of the town, fortified two camps, one on
each side of the city, and instituted a blockade of both the

harbours. The sea was thus closed against the Mitylenians, who however commanded the whole country, with the rest of the Lesbians who had now joined them; the Athenians only holding a limited area round their camps, and using Malea more as the station for their ships and their market.

While the war went on in this way at Mitylene, the Athenians, about the same time in this summer, also sent thirty ships to Peloponnese under Osopius, son of Phormio; the Acarnanians insisting that the commander sent should be some son or relative of Phormio. As the ships coasted along shore they ravaged the seaboard of Laconia; after which Asopius sent most of the fleet home, and himself went on with twelve vessels to Naupactus, and afterwards raising the whole Acarnanian population made an expedition against Œniadæ, the fleet sailing along the Achelous, while the army laid waste the country. The inhabitants, however, showing no signs of submitting, he dismissed the land forces and himself sailed to Leucas, and making a descent upon Nericus was cut off during his retreat, and most of his troops with him, by the people in those parts aided by some coast-guards; after which the Athenians sailed away, recovering their dead from the Leucadians under truce.

Meanwhile the envoys of the Mitylenians sent out in the first ship were told by the Lacedæmonians to come to Olympia, in order that the rest of the allies might hear them and decide upon their matter, and so they journeyed thither. It was the Olympiad in which the Rhodian Dorieus gained his second victory, and the envoys having been introduced to make their speech after the festival, spoke as follows.

'Lacedæmonians and allies, the rule established among the Hellenes is not unknown to us. Those who revolt in war and forsake their former confederacy are favourably regarded by those who receive them, in so far as they are of use to them, but otherwise are thought less well of, through being considered traitors to their former friends. Nor is this an unfair way of judging, where the rebels and the power from whom they secede are at one in policy and sympathy, and a match for each other in resources and power, and where no reasonable ground exists for the rebellion. But with us and the Athenians this was not the case; and no one need think the worse of us

for revolting from them in danger, after having been honoured by them in time of peace.

'Justice and honesty will be the first topics of our speech,
especially as we are asking for alliance; because we know
that there can never be any solid friendship between individuals, or union between communities that is worth the name,
unless the parties be persuaded of each other's honesty, and
be generally congenial the one to the other; since from difference in feeling springs also difference in conduct. Between
ourselves and the Athenians alliance began, when you withdrew from the Median war and they remained to finish the
business. But we did not become allies of the Athenians for
the subjugation of the Hellenes, but allies of the Hellenes for
their liberation from the Mede; and as long as the Athenians
led us fairly we followed them loyally; but when we saw
them relax their hostility to the Mede, to try to compass the
subjection of the allies, then our apprehensions began. Unable, however, to unite and defend themselves, on account of
the number of confederates that had votes, all the allies were
enslaved, except ourselves and the Chians, who continued to
send our contingents as independent and nominally free.
Trust in Athens as a leader, however, we could no longer feel,
judging by the examples already given; it being unlikely that
she would reduce our fellow-confederates, and not do the
same by us who were left, if ever she had the power.

'Had we all been still independent, we could have had more
faith in their not attempting any change; but the greater
number being their subjects, while they were treating us as
equals, they would naturally chafe under this solitary instance
of independence as contrasted with the submission of the
majority; particularly as they daily grew more powerful, and
we more destitute. Now the only sure basis of an alliance is
for each party to be equally afraid of the other: he who would
like to encroach is then deterred by the reflexion that he will
not have odds in his favour. Again, if we were left independent,
it was only because they thought they saw their way to empire
more clearly by specious language and by the paths of policy
than by those of force. Not only were we useful as evidence
that powers who had votes, like themselves, would not, surely,
join them in their expeditions, against their will, without the

party attacked being in the wrong; but the same system also enabled them to lead the stronger states against the weaker first, and so to leave the former to the last, stripped of their natural allies, and less capable of resistance. But if they had begun with us, while all the states still had their resources under their own control, and there was a centre to rally round, the work of subjugation would have been found less easy. Besides this, our navy gave them some apprehension: it was always possible that it might unite with you or with some other power, and become dangerous to Athens. The court which we paid to their commons and its leaders for the time being, also helped us to maintain our independence. However, we did not expect to be able to do so much longer, if this war had not broken out, from the examples that we had had of their conduct to the rest.

'How then could we put our trust in such friendship or freedom as we had here? We accepted each other against our inclination; fear made them court us in war, and us them in peace; sympathy, the ordinary basis of confidence, had its place supplied by terror, fear having more share than friendship in detaining us in the alliance; and the first party that should be encouraged by the hope of impunity was certain to break faith with the other. So that to condemn us for being the first to break off, because they delay the blow that we dread, instead of ourselves delaying to know for certain whether it will be dealt or not, is to take a false view of the case. For if we were equally able with them to meet their plots and imitate their delay, we should be their equals and should be under no necessity of being their subjects; but the liberty of offence being always theirs, that of defence ought clearly to be ours.

'Such, Lacedæmonians and allies, are the grounds and the reasons of our revolt; clear enough to convince our hearers of the fairness of our conduct, and sufficient to alarm ourselves, and to make us turn to some means of safety. This we wished to do long ago, when we sent to you on the subject while the peace yet lasted, but were baulked by your refusing to receive us; and now, upon the Bœotians inviting us, we at once responded to the call, and decided upon a twofold revolt, from the Hellenes and from the Athenians, not to aid the latter in harming the former, but to join in their liberation, and not to allow the Athenians in the end to destroy us, but to act in time against them. Our revolt, however, has taken place prematurely and without preparation—a fact which makes it all the more incumbent on you to receive us into alliance and to send us speedy relief, in order to show that you support your friends, and at the same time do harm to your enemies. You have an opportunity such as you never had before. Disease and expenditure have wasted the Athenians: their ships are either cruising round your coasts, or engaged in blockading us; and it is not probable that they will have any to spare, if you invade them a second time this summer by sea and land; but they will either offer no resistance to your vessels, or withdraw from both our shores. Nor must it be thought that this is a case of putting yourselves into danger for a country which is not yours. Lesbos may appear far off, but when help is wanted she will be found near enough. It is not in Attica that the war will be decided, as some imagine, but in the countries by which Attica is supported; and the Athenian revenue is drawn from the allies, and will become still larger if they reduce us; as not only will no other state revolt, but our resources will be added to theirs, and we shall be treated worse than those that were enslaved before. But if you will frankly support us, you will add to your side a state that has a large navy, which is your great want; you will smooth the way to the overthrow of the Athenians by depriving them of their allies, who will be greatly encouraged to come over; and you will free yourselves from the imputation made against you, of not supporting insurrection. In short, only show yourselves as liberators, and you may count upon having the advantage in the war.

'Respect, therefore, the hopes placed in you by the Hellenes, and that Olympian Zeus, in whose temple we stand as very suppliants; become the allies and defenders of the Mitylenians, and do not sacrifice us, who put our lives upon the hazard, in a cause in which general good will result to all from our success, and still more general harm if we fail through your refusing to help us; but be the men that the Hellenes think you, and our fears desire.'

Such were the words of the Mitylenians. After hearing them

out, the Lacedæmonians and confederates granted what they urged, and took the Lesbians into alliance, and deciding in favour of the invasion of Attica, told the allies present to march as quickly as possible to the Isthmus with two-thirds of their forces; and arriving there first themselves, got ready hauling machines to carry their ships across from Corinth to the sea on the side of Athens, in order to make their attack by sea and land at once. However, the zeal which they displayed was not imitated by the rest of the confederates, who came in but slowly, being engaged in harvesting their corn and sick of making expeditions.

Meanwhile the Athenians, aware that the preparations of the enemy were due to his conviction of their weakness, and wishing to show him that he was mistaken, and that they were able, without moving the Lesbian fleet, to repel with ease that with which they were menaced from Peloponnese, manned a hundred ships by embarking the citizens of Athens, except the knights and Pentecosiomedimni, and the resident aliens; and putting out to the Isthmus, displayed their power, and made descents upon Peloponnese wherever they pleased. A disappointment so signal made the Lacedæmonians think that the Lesbians had not spoken the truth; and embarrassed by the non-appearance of the confederates, coupled with the news that the thirty ships round Peloponnese were ravaging the lands near Sparta, they went back home. Afterwards, however, they got ready a fleet to send to Lesbos, and ordering a total of forty ships from the different cities in the league, appointed Alcidas to command the expedition in his capacity of high admiral. Meanwhile the Athenians in the hundred ships, upon seeing the Lacedæmonians go home, went home likewise.

If at the time that this fleet was at sea, Athens had almost the largest number of first-rate ships in commission that she ever possessed at any one moment, she had as many or even more when the war began. At that time one hundred guarded Attica, Euboea, and Salamis; a hundred more were cruising round Peloponnese, besides those employed at Potidæa and in other places; making a grand total of two hundred and fifty vessels employed on active service in a single summer. It was this, with Potidæa, that most exhausted her revenues—

Potidæa being blockaded by a force of heavy infantry (each drawing two drachmæ a day, one for himself and another for his servant), which amounted to three thousand at first, and was kept at this number down to the end of the siege; besides sixteen hundred with Phormio who went away before it was over; and the ships being all paid at the same rate. In this way her money was wasted at first; and this was the largest number of ships ever manned by her.

About the same time that the Lacedæmonians were at the Isthmus, the Mitylenians marched by land with their mercenaries against Methymna, which they thought to gain by treachery. After assaulting the town, and not meeting with the success that they anticipated, they withdrew to Antissa, Pyrrha, and Eresus; and taking measures for the better security of these towns and strengthening their walls, hastily returned home. After their departure the Methymnians marched against Antissa, but were defeated in a sortie by the Antissians and their mercenaries, and retreated in haste after losing many of their number. Word of this reaching Athens, and the Athenians learning that the Mitylenians were masters of the country and their own soldiers unable to hold them in check, they sent out about the beginning of autumn Paches, son of Epicurus, to take the command, and a thousand Athenian heavy infantry; who worked their own passage, and arriving at Mitylene, built a single wall all round it, forts being erected at some of the strongest points. Mitylene was thus blockaded strictly on both sides, by land and by sea; and winter now drew near.

The Athenians needing money for the siege, although they had for the first time raised a contribution of two hundred talents from their own citizens, now sent out twelve ships to levy subsidies from their allies, with Lysicles and four others in command. After cruising to different places and laying them under contribution, Lysicles went up the country from Myus, in Caria, across the plain of the Meander, as far as the hill of Sandius; and being attacked by the Carians and the people of Anaia, was slain with many of his soldiers.

The same winter the Platæans, who were still being besieged by the Peloponnesians and Bœotians, distressed by the failure of their provisions, and seeing no hope of relief from

Athens, nor any other means of safety, formed a scheme with the Athenians besieged with them for escaping, if possible, by forcing their way over the enemy's walls; the attempt having been suggested by Theænetus, son of Tolmides, a soothsayer, and Eupompides, son of Daïmachus one of their generals. At first all were to join: afterwards, half hung back, thinking the risk great; about two hundred and twenty, how-- ever, voluntarily persevered in the attempt, which was carried out in the following way. Ladders were made to match the height of the enemy's wall, which they measured by the layers of bricks, the side turned towards them not being thoroughly whitewashed. These were counted by many persons at once; and though some might miss the right calculation, most would hit upon it, particularly as they counted over and over again, and were no great way from the wall, but could see it easily enough for their purpose. The length required for the ladders was thus obtained, being calculated from the breadth of the brick.

Now the wall of the Peloponnesians was constructed as fol- lows. It consisted of two lines drawn round the place, one against the Platæans, the other against any attack on the outside from Athens, about sixteen feet apart. The inter- mediate space of sixteen feet was occupied by huts portioned out among the soldiers on guard, and built in one block, so as to give the appearance of a single thick wall with battle- ments on either side. At intervals of every ten battlements were towers of considerable size, and the same breadth as the wall, reaching right across from its inner to its outer face, with no means of passing except through the middle. Accordingly on stormy and wet nights the battlements were deserted, and guard kept from the towers, which were not far apart and roofed in above.

Such being the structure of the wall by which the Platæans were blockaded, when their preparations were completed, they waited for a stormy night of wind and rain and without any moon, and then set out, guided by the authors of the enterprise. Crossing first the ditch that ran round the town, they next gained the wall of the enemy unperceived by the sentinels, who did not see them in the darkness, or hear them, as the wind drowned with its roar the noise of their approach;

besides which they kept a good way off from each other, that
they might not be betrayed by the clash of their weapons.
They were also lightly equipped, and had only the left foot
shod to preserve them from slipping in the mire. They came up
to the battlements at one of the intermediate spaces where
they knew them to be unguarded: those who carried the ladders went first and planted them; next twelve light-armed
soldiers with only a dagger and a breastplate mounted, led by
Ammias, son of Corœbus, who was the first on the wall; his
followers getting up after him and going six to each of the
towers. After these came another party of light troops armed
with spears, whose shields, that they might advance the easier,
were carried by men behind, who were to hand them to them
when they found themselves in presence of the enemy. After
a good many had mounted they were discovered by the sentinels in the towers, by the noise made by a tile which was
knocked down by one of the Platæans as he was laying
hold of the battlements. The alarm was instantly given, and
the troops rushed to the wall, not knowing the nature of the
danger, owing to the dark night and stormy weather; the
Platæans in the town having also chosen that moment to
make a sortie against the wall of the Peloponnesians upon the
side opposite to that on which their men were getting over,
in order to divert the attention of the besiegers. Accordingly
they remained distracted at their several posts, without any
venturing to stir to give help from his own station, and at a
loss to guess what was going on. Meanwhile the three hundred
set aside for service on emergencies went outside the wall in
the direction of the alarm. Fire-signals of an attack were also
raised towards Thebes; but the Platæans in the town at once
displayed a number of others, prepared beforehand for this
very purpose, in order to render the enemy's signals unin-
telligible, and to prevent his friends getting a true idea of
what was passing and coming to his aid, before their comrades
who had gone out should have made good their escape and be
in safety.

Meanwhile the first of the scaling-party that had got up,
after carrying both the towers and putting the sentinels to
the sword, posted themselves inside to prevent any one coming
through against them; and rearing ladders from the wall, sent

several men up on the towers, and from their summit and
base kept in check all of the enemy that came up, with their
missiles, while their main body planted a number of ladders
against the wall, and knocking down the battlements, passed
over between the towers; each as soon as he had got over
taking up his station at the edge of the ditch, and plying from
thence with arrows and darts any who came along the wall to
stop the passage of his comrades. When all were over, the
party on the towers came down, the last of them not without
difficulty, and proceeded to the ditch, just as the three hundred came up carrying torches. The Platæans, standing on the
edge of the ditch in the dark, had a good view of their opponents, and discharged their arrows and darts upon the unarmed parts of their bodies, while they themselves could not
be so well seen in the obscurity for the torches; and thus even
the last of them got over the ditch, though not without effort
and difficulty; as ice had formed in it, not strong enough to
walk upon, but of that watery kind which generally comes
with a wind more east than north, and the snow which this
wind had caused to fall during the night, had made the water
in the ditch rise, so that they could scarcely breast it as they
crossed. However, it was mainly the violence of the storm
that enabled them to effect their escape at all.

Starting from the ditch, the Platæans went all together
along the road leading to Thebes, keeping the chapel of the
hero Androcrates upon their right; considering that the last
road which the Peloponnesians would suspect them of having
taken would be that towards their enemies' country. Indeed
they could see them pursuing with torches upon the Athens
road towards Cithæron and Druos-kephalai or Oakheads.
After going for rather more than half a mile upon the road
to Thebes, the Platæans turned off and took that leading to
the mountain, to Erythræ and Hysiæ, and reaching the hills,
made good their escape to Athens, two hundred and twelve
men in all; some of their number having turned back into
the town before getting over the wall, and one archer having
been taken prisoner at the outer ditch. Meanwhile the Peloponnesians gave up the pursuit and returned to their posts;
and the Platæans in the town, knowing nothing of what had
passed, and informed by those who had turned back that not

a man had escaped, sent out a herald as soon as it was day
to make a truce for the recovery of the dead bodies, and then
learning the truth, desisted. In this way the Platæan party
got over and were saved.

Towards the close of the same winter, Salæthus, a Lacedæmonian, was sent out in a galley from Lacedæmon to
Mitylene. Going by sea to Pyrrha, and from thence overland,
he passed along the bed of a torrent, where the line of circumvallation was passable, and thus entering unperceived into
Mitylene, told the magistrates that Attica would certainly be
invaded, and the forty ships destined to relieve them arrive,
and that he had been sent on to announce this and to super-
intend matters generally. The Mitylenians upon this took
courage, and laid aside the idea of treating with the Athenians;
and now this winter ended, and with it ended the fourth year
of the war of which Thucydides was the historian.

The next summer the Peloponnesians sent off the forty-two
ships for Mitylene, under Alcidas, their high admiral, and
themselves and their allies invaded Attica, their object being
to distract the Athenians by a double movement, and thus to
make it less easy for them to act against the fleet sailing to
Mitylene. The commander in this invasion was Cleomenes,
in the place of King Pausanias, son of Pleistoanax, his nephew,
who was still a minor. Not content with laying waste whatever
had shot up in the parts which they had before devastated, the
invaders now extended their ravages to lands passed over in
their previous incursions; so that this invasion was more
severely felt by the Athenians than any except the second;
the enemy staying on and on until they had overrun most of
the country, in the expectation of hearing from Lesbos of
something having been achieved by their fleet, which they
thought must now have got over. However, as they did not
obtain any of the results expected, and their provisions began
to run short, they retreated and dispersed to their different
cities.

In the meantime the Mitylenians, finding their provisions
failing, while the fleet from Peloponnese was loitering on the
way instead of appearing at Mitylene, were compelled to come
to terms with the Athenians in the following manner. Salæthus
having himself ceased to expect the fleet to arrive, now armed

the commons with heavy armour, which they had not before possessed, with the intention of making a sortie against the Athenians. The commons, however, no sooner found themselves possessed of arms than they refused any longer to obey their officers; and forming in knots together, told the authorities to bring out in public the provisions and divide them amongst them all, or they would themselves come to terms with the Athenians and deliver up the city.

The government, aware of their inability to prevent this, and of the danger they would be in, if left out of the capitulation, publicly agreed with Paches and the army to surrender Mitylene at discretion and to admit the troops into the town; upon the understanding that the Mitylenians should be allowed to send an embassy to Athens to plead their cause, and that Paches should not imprison, make slaves of, or put to death any of the citizens until its return. Such were the terms of the capitulation; in spite of which the chief authors of the negotiation with Lacedæmon were so completely overcome by terror when the army entered, that they went and seated themselves by the altars, from which they were raised up by Paches under promise that he would do them no wrong, and lodged by him in Tenedos, until he should learn the pleasure of the Athenians concerning them. Paches also sent some galleys and seized Antissa, and took such other military measures as he thought advisable.

Meanwhile the Peloponnesians in the forty ships, who ought to have made all haste to relieve Mitylene, lost time in coming round Peloponnese itself, and proceeding leisurely on the remainder of the voyage, made Delos without having been seen by the Athenians at Athens, and from thence arriving at Icarus and Myconus, there first heard of the fall of Mitylene. Wishing to know the truth, they put into Embatum, in the Erythræid, about seven days after the capture of the town. Here they learned the truth, and began to consider what they were to do; and Teutiaplus, an Elean, addressed them as follows:—

'Alcidas and Peloponnesians who share with me the command of this armament, my advice is to sail just as we are to Mitylene, before we have been heard of. We may expect to find the Athenians as much off their guard as men generally

are who have just taken a city: this will certainly be so by
sea, where they have no idea of any enemy attacking them,
and where our strength, as it happens, mainly lies; while even
their land forces are probably scattered about the houses in
the carelessness of victory. If therefore we were to fall upon
them suddenly and in the night, I have hopes, with the help
of the well-wishers that we may have left inside the town,
that we shall become masters of the place. Let us not shrink
from the risk, but let us remember that this is just the occasion for one of the baseless panics common in war; and that
to be able to guard against these in one's own case, and to
detect the moment when an attack will find an enemy at this
disadvantage, is what makes a successful general.'

These words of Teutiaplus failing to move Alcidas, some
of the Ionian exiles and the Lesbians with the expedition
began to urge him, since this seemed too dangerous, to seize
one of the Ionian cities or the Æolic town of Cyme, to use
as a base for effecting the revolt of Ionia. This was by no
means a hopeless enterprise, as their coming was welcome
everywhere; their object would be by this move to deprive
Athens of her chief source of revenue, and at the same time
to saddle her with expense, if she chose to blockade them;
and they would probably induce Pissuthnes to join them in
the war. However, Alcidas gave this proposal as bad a reception as the other, being eager, since he had come too late for
Mitylene, to find himself back in Peloponnese as soon as
possible.

Accordingly he put out from Embatum and proceeded along
shore; and touching at the Teian town, Myonnesus, there
butchered most of the prisoners that he had taken on his
passage. Upon his coming to anchor at Ephesus, envoys came
to him from the Samians at Anaia, and told him that he was
not going the right way to free Hellas in massacring men
who had never raised a hand against him, and who were not
enemies of his, but allies of Athens against their will, and that
if he did not stop he would turn many more friends into
enemies than enemies into friends. Alcidas agreed to this, and
let go all the Chians still in his hands and some of the others
that he had taken; the inhabitants, instead of flying at the
sight of his vessels, rather coming up to them, taking them

for Athenian, having no sort of expectation that while the Athenians commanded the sea Peloponnesian ships would venture over to Ionia.

From Ephesus Alcidas set sail in haste and fled. He had been seen by the Salaminian and Paralian galleys, which happened to be sailing from Athens, while still at anchor off Clarus; and fearing pursuit he now made across the open sea, fully determined to touch nowhere, if he could help it, until he got to Peloponnese. Meanwhile news of him had come in to Paches from the Erythræid, and indeed from all quarters. As Ionia was unfortified great fears were felt that the Peloponnesians coasting along shore, even if they did not intend to stay, might make descents in passing and plunder the towns; and now the Paralian and Salaminian, having seen him at Clarus, themselves brought intelligence of the fact. Paches accordingly gave hot chase, and continued the pursuit as far as the isle of Patmos, and then finding that Alcidas had got on too far to be overtaken, came back again. Meanwhile he thought it fortunate that, as he had not fallen in with them out at sea, he had not overtaken them anywhere where they would have been forced to encamp, and so give him the trouble of blockading them.

On his return along shore he touched, among other places, at Notium, the port of Colophon, where the Colophonians had settled after the capture of the upper town by Itamenes and the barbarians, who had been called in by certain individuals in a party quarrel. The capture of the town took place about the time of the second Peloponnesian invasion of Attica. However, the refugees, after settling at Notium, again split up into factions, one of which called in Arcadian and barbarian mercenaries from Pissuthnes, and entrenching these in a quarter apart, formed a new community with the Median party of the Colophonians who joined them from the upper town. Their opponents had retired into exile, and now called in Paches, who invited Hippias, the commander of the Arcadians in the fortified quarter, to a parley, upon condition that, if they could not agree, he was to be put back safe and sound in the fortification. However, upon his coming out to him, he put him into custody, though not in chains, and attacked suddenly and took by surprise the fortification, and putting the Arca-

dians and the barbarians found in it to the sword, afterwards
took Hippias into it as he had promised, and, as soon as he
was inside, seized him and shot him down. Paches then gave
up Notium to the Colophonians not of the Median party; and
settlers were afterwards sent out from Athens, and the place
colonised according to Athenian laws, after collecting all the
Colophonians found in any of the cities.

Arrived at Mitylene, Paches reduced Pyrrha and Eresus;
and finding the Lacedæmonian, Salæthus, in hiding in the
town, sent him off to Athens, together with the Mitylenians
that he had placed in Tenedos, and any other persons that he
thought concerned in the revolt. He also sent back the greater
part of his forces, remaining with the rest to settle Mitylene
and the rest of Lesbos as he thought best.

Upon the arrival of the prisoners with Salæthus, the Athenians at once put the latter to death, although he offered,
among other things, to procure the withdrawal of the Peloponnesians from Platæa, which was still under siege; and after
deliberating as to what they should do with the former, in the
fury of the moment determined to put to death not only the
prisoners at Athens, but the whole adult male population of
Mitylene, and to make slaves of the women and children. It
was remarked that Mitylene had revolted without being, like
the rest, subjected to the empire; and what above all swelled
the wrath of the Athenians was the fact of the Peloponnesian
fleet having ventured over to Ionia to her support, a fact which
was held to argue a long-meditated rebellion. They accordingly sent a galley to communicate the decree to Paches, commanding him to lose no time in despatching the Mitylenians.
The morrow brought repentance with it and reflexion on the
horrid cruelty of a decree, which condemned a whole city to
the fate merited only by the guilty. This was no sooner perceived by the Mitylenian ambassadors at Athens and their
Athenian supporters, than they moved the authorities to put
the question again to the vote; which they the more easily
consented to do, as they themselves plainly saw that most of
the citizens wished some one to give them an opportunity for
reconsidering the matter. An assembly was therefore at once
called, and after much expression of opinion upon both sides,
Cleon, son of Cleænetus, the same who had carried the former

motion of putting the Mitylenians to death, the most violent man at Athens, and at that time by far the most powerful with the commons, came forward again and spoke as follows:—

'I have often before now been convinced that a democracy is incapable of empire, and never more so than by your present change of mind in the matter of Mitylene. Fears or plots being unknown to you in your daily relations with each other, you feel just the same with regard to your allies, and never reflect that the mistakes into which you may be led by listening to their appeals, or by giving way to your own compassion, are full of danger to yourselves, and bring you no thanks for your weakness from your allies; entirely forgetting that your empire is a despotism and your subjects disaffected conspirators, whose obedience is insured not by your suicidal concessions, but by the superiority given you by your own strength and not their loyalty. The most alarming feature in the case is the constant change of measures with which we appear to be threatened, and our seeming ignorance of the fact that bad laws which are never changed are better for a city than good ones that have no authority; that unlearned loyalty is more serviceable than quick-witted insubordination; and that ordinary men usually manage public affairs better than their more gifted fellows. The latter are always wanting to appear wiser than the laws, and to overrule every proposition brought forward, thinking that they cannot show their wit in more important matters, and by such behaviour too often ruin their country; while those who mistrust their own cleverness are content to be less learned than the laws, and less able to pick holes in the speech of a good speaker; and being fair judges rather than rival athletes, generally conduct affairs successfully. These we ought to imitate, instead of being led on by cleverness and intellectual rivalry to advise your people against our real opinions.

'For myself, I adhere to my former opinion, and wonder at those who have proposed to reopen the case of the Mitylenians, and who are thus causing a delay which is all in favour of the guilty, by making the sufferer proceed against the offender with the edge of his anger blunted; although where vengeance follows most closely upon the wrong, it best equals it and most amply requites it. I wonder also who will

be the man who will maintain the contrary, and will pretend
to show that the crimes of the Mitylenians are of service to
us, and our misfortunes injurious to the allies. Such a man
must plainly either have such confidence in his rhetoric as
to adventure to prove that what has been once for all decided
is still undetermined, or be bribed to try to delude us by
elaborate sophisms. In such contests the state gives the rewards to others, and takes the dangers for herself. The persons
to blame are you who are so foolish as to institute these
contests; who go to see an oration as you would to see a sight,
take your facts on hearsay, judge of the practicability of a
project by the wit of its advocates, and trust for the truth as
to past events not to the fact which you saw more than to
the clever strictures which you heard; the easy victims of new-
fangled arguments, unwilling to follow received conclusions;
slaves to every new paradox, despisers of the commonplace;
the first wish of every man being that he could speak himself
the next to rival those who can speak by seeming to be quite
up with their ideas by applauding every hit almost before it
is made, and by being as quick in catching an argument as
you are slow in foreseeing its consequences; asking, if I may
so say, for something different from the conditions under
which we live, and yet comprehending inadequately those
very conditions; very slaves to the pleasure of the ear, and
more like the audience of a rhetorician than the council of
a city.

'In order to keep you from this, I proceed to show that no
one state has ever injured you as much as Mitylene. I can
make allowance for those who revolt because they cannot bear
our empire, or who have been forced to do so by the enemy.
But for those who possessed an island with fortifications; who
could fear our enemies only by sea, and there had their own
force of galleys to protect them; who were independent and
held in the highest honour by you—to act as these have done,
this is not revolt—revolt implies oppression; it is deliberate
and wanton aggression; an attempt to ruin us by siding with
our bitterest enemies; a worse offence than a war undertaken
on their own account in the acquisition of power. The fate of
those of their neighbours who had already rebelled and had
been subdued, was no lesson to them; their own prosperity

could not dissuade them from affronting danger; but blindly confident in the future, and full of hopes beyond their power though not beyond their ambition, they declared war and made their decision to prefer might to right, their attack being determined not by provocation but by the moment which seemed propitious. The truth is that great good fortune coming suddenly and unexpectedly tends to make a people insolent: in most cases it is safer for mankind to have success in reason than out of reason; and it is easier for them, one may say, to stave off adversity than to preserve prosperity. Our mistake has been to distinguish the Mitylenians as we have done: had they been long ago treated like the rest, they never would have so far forgotten themselves, human nature being as surely made arrogant by consideration, as it is awed by firmness. Let them now therefore be punished as their crime requires, and do not, while you condemn the aristocracy, absolve the people. This is certain, that all attacked you without distinction, although they might have come over to us, and been now again in possession of their city. But no, they thought it safer to throw in their lot with the aristocracy and so joined their rebellion! Consider therefore! if you subject to the same punishment the ally who is forced to rebel by the enemy, and him who does so by his own free choice, which of them, think you, is there that will not rebel upon the slightest pretext; when the reward of success is freedom, and the penalty of failure nothing so very terrible? We meanwhile shall have to risk our money and our lives against one state after another; and if successful, shall receive a ruined town from which we can no longer draw the revenue upon which our strength depends; while if unsuccessful, we shall have an enemy the more upon our hands, and shall spend the time that might be employed in combating our existing foes in warring with our own allies.

'No hope, therefore, that rhetoric may instil or money purchase, of the mercy due to human infirmity must be held out to the Mitylenians. Their offence was not involuntary, but of malice and deliberate; and mercy is only for unwilling offenders. I therefore now as before persist against your reversing your first decision, or giving way to the three failings most fatal to empire—pity, sentiment, and indulgence. Compassion is due to those who can reciprocate the feeling, not to those who will never pity us in return, but are our natural and necessary foes: the orators who charm us with sentiment may find other less important arenas for their talents, in the place of one where the city pays a heavy penalty for a momentary pleasure, themselves receiving fine acknowledgments for their fine phrases; while indulgence should be shown towards those who will be our friends in future, instead of towards men who will remain just what they were, and as much our enemies as before. To sum up shortly, I say that, if you follow my advice you will do what is just towards the Mitylenians, and at the same time expedient; while by a different decision you will not oblige them so much as pass sentence upon yourselves. For if they were right in rebelling, you must be wrong in ruling. However, if, right or wrong, you determine to rule, you must carry out your principle and punish the Mitylenians as your interest requires; or else you must give up your empire and cultivate honesty without danger. Make up your minds, therefore, to give them like for like; and do not let the victims who escaped the plot be more insensible than the conspirators who hatched it; but reflect what they would have done if victorious over you, especially as they were the aggressors. It is they who wrong their neighbour without a cause, that pursue their victim to the death, on account of the danger which they foresee in letting their enemy survive; since the object of a wanton wrong is more dangerous, if he escape, than an enemy who has not this to complain of. Do not, therefore, be traitors to yourselves, but recall as nearly as possible the moment of suffering and the supreme importance which you then attached to their reduction; and now pay them back in their turn, without yielding to present weakness or forgetting the peril that once hung over you. Punish them as they deserve, and teach your other allies by a striking example that the penalty of rebellion is death. Let them once understand this and you will not have so often to neglect your enemies while you are fighting with your own confederates.'

Such were the words of Cleon. After him Diodotus, son of Eucrates, who had also in the previous assembly spoken

most strongly against putting the Mitylenians to death, came
forward and spoke as follows:—

'I do not blame the persons who have reopened the case
of the Mitylenians, nor do I approve the protests which we
have heard against important questions being frequently de-
bated. I think the two things most opposed to good counsel
are haste and passion; haste usually goes hand in hand with
folly, passion with coarseness and narrowness of mind. As for
the argument that speech ought not to be the exponent of
action, the man who uses it must be either senseless or interested: senseless if he believes it possible to treat of the uncertain future through any other medium; interested if wishing
to carry a disgraceful measure and doubting his ability to
speak well in a bad cause, he thinks to frighten opponents and
hearers by well-aimed calumny. What is still more intolerable
is to accuse a speaker of making a display in order to be paid
for it. If ignorance only were imputed, an unsuccessful speaker
might retire with a reputation for honesty, if not for wisdom;
while the charge of dishonesty makes him suspected, if successful, and thought, if defeated, not only a fool but a rogue.
The city is no gainer by such a system, since fear deprives it
of its advisers; although in truth, if our speakers are to make
such assertions, it would be better for the country if they could
not speak at all, as we should then make fewer blunders. The
good citizen ought to triumph not by frightening his opponents
but by beating them fairly in argument; and a wise city without over-distinguishing its best advisers, will nevertheless not
deprive them of their due, and far from punishing an unlucky
counsellor will not even regard him as disgraced. In this way
successful orators would be least tempted to sacrifice their
convictions to popularity, in the hope of still higher honours,
and unsuccessful speakers to resort to the same popular arts
in order to win over the multitude.

'This is not our way; and, besides, the moment that a man
is suspected of giving advice, however good, from corrupt
motives, we feel such a grudge against him for the gain which
after all we are not certain he will receive, that we deprive the
city of its certain benefit. Plain good advice has thus come to
be no less suspected than bad; and the advocate of the most
monstrous measures is not more obliged to use deceit to gain

the people, than the best counsellor is to lie in order to be believed. The city and the city only, owing to these refinements, can never be served openly and without disguise; he who does serve it openly being always suspected of serving himself in some secret way in return. Still, considering the magnitude of the interests involved, and the position of affairs, we orators must make it our business to look a little further than you who judge offhand; especially as we, your advisers, are responsible, while you, our audience, are not so. For if those who gave the advice, and those who took it, suffered equally, you would judge more calmly; as it is, you visit the disasters into which the whim of the moment may have led you, upon the single person of your adviser, not upon yourselves, his numerous companions in error.

'However, I have not come forward either to oppose or to accuse in the matter of Mitylene; indeed, the question before us as sensible men is not their guilt, but our interests. Though I prove them ever so guilty, I shall not, therefore, advise their death, unless it be expedient; nor though they should have claims to indulgence, shall I recommend it, unless it be clearly for the good of the country. I consider that we are deliberating for the future more than for the present; and where Cleon is so positive as to the useful deterrent effects that will follow from making rebellion capital, I who consider the interests of the future quite as much as he, as positively maintain the contrary. And I require you not to reject my useful considerations for his specious ones: his speech may have the attraction of seeming the more just in your present temper against Mitylene; but we are not in a court of justice, but in a political assembly; and the question is not justice, but how to make the Mitylenians useful to Athens.

'Now of course communities have enacted the penalty of death for many offences far lighter than this: still hope leads men to venture, and no one ever yet put himself in peril without the inward conviction that he would succeed in his design. Again, was there ever city rebelling that did not believe that it possessed either in itself or in its alliances resources adequate to the enterprise? All, states and individuals, are alike prone to err, and there is no law that will prevent them; or why should men have exhausted the list of punishments in search of enactments to protect them from evil-doers? It is probable that in early times the penalties for the greatest offences were less severe, and that, as these were disregarded, the penalty of death has been by degrees in most cases arrived at, which is itself disregarded in like manner. Either then some means of terror more terrible than this must be discovered, or it must be owned that this restraint is useless; and that as long as poverty gives men the courage of necessity, or plenty fills them with the ambition which belongs to insolence and pride, and the other conditions of life remain each under the thraldom of some fatal and master passion, so long will the impulse never be wanting to drive men into danger. Hope also and cupidity, the one leading and the other following, the one conceiving the attempt, the other suggesting the facility of succeeding, cause the widest ruin, and, although invisible agents, are far stronger than the dangers that are seen. Fortune, too, powerfully helps the delusion, and by the unexpected aid that she sometimes lends, tempts men to venture with inferior means; and this is especially the case with communities, because the stakes played for are the highest, freedom or empire, and, when all are acting together, each man irrationally magnifies his own capacity. In fine, it is impossible to prevent, and only great simplicity can hope to prevent, human nature doing what it has once set its mind upon, by force of law or by any other deterrent force whatsoever.

'We must not, therefore, commit ourselves to a false policy through a belief in the efficacy of the punishment of death, or exclude rebels from the hope of repentance and an early atonement of their error. Consider a moment! At present, if a city that has already revolted perceive that it cannot succeed, it will come to terms while it is still able to refund expenses, and pay tribute afterwards. In the other case, what city think you would not prepare better than is now done, and hold out to the last against its besiegers, if it is all one whether it surrender late or soon? And how can it be otherwise than hurtful to us to be put to the expense of a siege, because surrender is out of the question; and if we take the city, to receive a ruined town from which we can no longer draw the revenue which forms our real strength against the enemy? We must not,

therefore, sit as strict judges of the offenders to our own prejudice, but rather see how by moderate chastisements we may
be enabled to benefit in future by the revenue-producing
powers of our dependencies; and we must make up our minds
to look for our protection not to legal terrors but to careful
administration. At present we do exactly the opposite. When
a free community, held in subjection by force, rises, as is only
natural, and asserts its independence, it is no sooner reduced
than we fancy ourselves obliged to punish it severely; although
the right course with freemen is not to chastise them rigorously when they do rise, but rigorously to watch them before
they rise, and to prevent their ever entertaining the idea, and,
the insurrection suppressed, to make as few responsible for
it as possible.

'Only consider what a blunder you would commit in doing
as Cleon recommends. As things are at present, in all the cities
the people is your friend, and either does not revolt with the
oligarchy, or, if forced to do so, becomes at once the enemy
of the insurgents; so that in the war with the hostile city you
have the masses on your side. But if you butcher the people
of Mitylene, who had nothing to do with the revolt, and who,
as soon as they got arms, of their own motion surrendered
the town, first you will commit the crime of killing your benefactors; and next you will play directly into the hands of the
higher classes, who when they induce their cities to rise, will
immediately have the people on their side, through your having announced in advance the same punishment for those who
are guilty and for those who are not. On the contrary, even if
they were guilty, you ought to seem not to notice it, in order
to avoid alienating the only class still friendly to us. In short,
I consider it far more useful for the preservation of our empire
voluntarily to put up with injustice, than to put to death, however justly, those whom it is our interest to keep alive. As for
Cleon's idea that in punishment the claims of justice and expediency can both be satisfied, facts do not confirm the possibility of such a combination.

'Confess, therefore, that this is the wisest course, and without conceding too much either to pity or to indulgence, by
neither of which motives do I any more than Cleon wish you
to be influenced, upon the plain merits of the case before you,

be persuaded by me to try calmly those of the Mitylenians whom Paches sent off as guilty, and to leave the rest undisturbed. This is at once best for the future, and most terrible to your enemies at the present moment; inasmuch as good policy against an adversary is superior to the blind attacks of brute force.'

Such were the words of Diodotus. The two opinions thus expressed were the ones that most directly contradicted each other; and the Athenians, notwithstanding their change of feeling, now proceeded to a division, in which the show of hands was almost equal, although the motion of Diodotus carried the day. Another galley was at once sent off in haste, for fear that the first might reach Lesbos in the interval, and the city be found destroyed; the first ship having about a day and a night's start. Wine and barley-cakes were provided for the vessel by the Mitylenian ambassadors, and great promises made if they arrived in time; which caused the men to use such diligence upon the voyage that they took their meals of barley-cakes kneaded with oil and wine as they rowed, and only slept by turns while the others were at the oar. Luckily they met with no contrary wind, and the first ship making no haste upon so horrid an errand, while the second pressed on in the manner described, the first arrived so little before them, that Paches had only just had time to read the decree, and to prepare to execute the sentence, when the second put into port and prevented the massacre. The danger of Mitylene had indeed been great.

The other party whom Paches had sent off as the prime movers in the rebellion, were upon Cleon's motion put to death by the Athenians, the number being rather more than a thousand. The Athenians also demolished the walls of the Mitylenians, and took possession of their ships. Afterwards tribute was not imposed upon the Lesbians; but all their land, except that of the Methymnians, was divided into three thousand allotments, three hundred of which were reserved as sacred for the gods, and the rest assigned by lot to Athenian shareholders, who were sent out to the island. With these the Lesbians agreed to pay a rent of two minæ a year for each allotment, and cultivated the land themselves. The Athenians also took possession of the towns on the continent belonging

to the Mitylenians, which thus became for the future subject
to Athens. Such were the events that took place at Lesbos.

CHAPTER X

FIFTH YEAR OF THE WAR—TRIAL AND EXECUTION OF THE
PLATÆANS—CORCYRÆAN REVOLUTION

B.C. 427: *Nicias invades Minos—Surrender of Platæa—Speech of the
Platæans—Speech of the Thebans—Extinction of Platæa—The
Corcyræan revolution—Commons victorious—Reign of terror in
Corcyra—Demoralization of all values—Excesses in Corcyra—
Athenian squadron sails for Sicily.*

ᴅᴜʀɪɴɢ the same summer, after the reduction of Lesbos, the
Athenians under Nicias, son of Niceratus, made an expedition against the island of Minos, which lies off Megara and
was used as a fortified post by the Megarians, who had built
a tower upon it. Nicias wished to enable the Athenians to
maintain their blockade from this nearer station instead of
from Budorum and Salamis; to stop the Peloponnesian galleys
and privateers sailing out unobserved from the island, as they
had been in the habit of doing; and at the same time prevent
anything from coming into Megara. Accordingly, after taking
two towers projecting on the side of Nisæa, by engines from
the sea, and clearing the entrance into the channel between
the island and the shore, he next proceeded to cut off all communication by building a wall on the mainland at the point
where a bridge across a morass enabled succours to be thrown
into the island, which was not far off from the continent. A
few days sufficing to accomplish this, he afterwards raised
some works in the island also, and leaving a garrison there,
departed with his forces.

About the same time in this summer, the Platæans being
now without provisions, and unable to support the siege, surrendered to the Peloponnesians in the following manner. An
assault had been made upon the wall, which the Platæans
were unable to repel. The Lacedæmonian commander, perceiving their weakness, wished to avoid taking the place by
storm; his instructions from Lacedæmon having been so conceived, in order that if at any future time peace should be
made with Athens, and they should agree each to restore the

places that they had taken in the war, Platæa might be held to have come over voluntarily, and not be included in the list. He accordingly sent a herald to them to ask if they were willing voluntarily to surrender the town to the Lacedæmonians, and accept them as their judges, upon the understanding that the guilty should be punished, but no one without form of law. The Platæans were now in the last state of weakness, and the herald had no sooner delivered his message than they surrendered the town. The Peloponnesians fed them for some days until the judges from Lacedæmon, who were five in number, arrived. Upon their arrival no charge was preferred; they simply called up the Platæans, and asked them whether they had done the Lacedæmonians and allies any service in the war then raging. The Platæans asked leave to speak at greater length, and deputed two of their number to represent them; Astymachus, son of Asopolaus, and Lacon, son of Aeimnestus, *Proxenus* of the Lacedæmonians, who came forward and spoke as follows:—

'Lacedæmonians, when we surrendered our city we trusted in you, and looked forward to a trial more agreeable to the forms of law than the present, to which we had no idea of being subjected; the judges also in whose hands we consented to place ourselves were you, and you only (from whom we thought we were most likely to obtain justice), and not other persons, as is now the case. As matters stand, we are afraid that we have been doubly deceived. We have good reason to suspect, not only that the issue to be tried is the most terrible of all, but that you will not prove impartial; if we may argue from the fact that no accusation was first brought forward for us to answer, but we had ourselves to ask leave to speak, and from the question being put so shortly, that a true answer to it tells against us, while a false one can be contradicted. In this dilemma, our safest, and indeed our only course, seems to be to say something at all risks: placed as we are, we could scarcely be silent without being tormented by the damning thought that speaking might have saved us. Another difficulty that we have to encounter is the difficulty of convincing you. Were we unknown to each other we might profit by bringing forward new matter with which you were unacquainted: as it is, we can tell you nothing that you do not know already, and

we fear, not that you have condemned us in your own minds
of having failed in our duty towards you, and make this our
crime, but that to please a third party we have to submit to
a trial the result of which is already decided. Nevertheless, we
will place before you what we can justly urge, not only on the
question of the quarrel which the Thebans have against us,
but also as addressing you and the rest of the Hellenes; and
we will remind you of our good services, and endeavour to
prevail with you.

'To your short question, whether we have done the
Lacedæmonians and allies any service in this war, we say, if
you ask us as enemies, that to refrain from serving you was
not to do you injury; if as friends, that you are more in fault
for having marched against us. During the peace, and against
the Mede, we acted well: we have not now been the first to
break the peace, and we were the only Bœotians who then
joined in defending against the Mede the liberty of Hellas.
Although an inland people, we were present at the action at
Artemisium; in the battle that took place in our territory we
fought by the side of yourselves and Pausanias; and in all the
other Hellenic exploits of the time we took a part quite out of
proportion to our strength. Besides, you, as Lacedæmonians,
ought not to forget that at the time of the great panic at Sparta,
after the earthquake, caused by the secession of the Helots
to Ithome, we sent the third part of our citizens to assist you.

'On these great and historical occasions such was the part
that we chose, although afterwards we became your enemies.
For this you were to blame. When we asked for your alliance
against our Theban oppressors, you rejected our petition, and
told us to go to the Athenians who were our neighbours, as
you lived too far off. In the war we never have done to you,
and never should have done to you, anything unreasonable.
If we refused to desert the Athenians when you asked us, we
did no wrong; they had helped us against the Thebans when
you drew back, and we could no longer give them up with
honour; especially as we had obtained their alliance and had
been admitted to their citizenship at our own request, and
after receiving benefits at their hands; but it was plainly our
duty loyally to obey their orders. Besides, the faults that either

of you may commit in your supremacy must be laid, not upon the followers, but on the chiefs that lead them astray.

'With regard to the Thebans, they have wronged us repeatedly, and their last aggression, which has been the means of bringing us into our present position, is within your own knowledge. In seizing our city in time of peace, and what is more at a holy time in the month, they justly encountered our vengeance, in accordance with the universal law which sanctions resistance to an invader; and it cannot now be right that we should suffer on their account. By taking your own immediate interest and their animosity as the test of justice, you will prove yourselves to be rather waiters on expediency than judges of right; although if they seem useful to you now, we and the rest of the Hellenes gave you much more valuable help at a time of greater need. Now you are the assailants, and others fear you; but at the crisis to which we allude, when the barbarian threatened all with slavery, the Thebans were on his side. It is just, therefore, to put our patriotism then against our error now, if error there has been; and you will find the merit outweighing the fault, and displayed at a juncture when there were few Hellenes who would set their valour against the strength of Xerxes, and when greater praise was theirs who preferred the dangerous path of honour to the safe course of consulting their own interest with respect to the invasion. To these few we belonged, and highly were we honoured for it; and yet we now fear to perish by having again acted on the same principles, and chosen to act well with Athens sooner than wisely with Sparta. Yet in justice the same cases should be decided in the same way, and policy should not mean anything else than lasting gratitude for the service of a good ally combined with a proper attention to one's own immediate interest.

'Consider also that at present the Hellenes generally regard you as a pattern of worth and honour; and if you pass an unjust sentence upon us in this which is no obscure cause, but one in which you, the judges, are as illustrious as we, the prisoners, are blameless, take care that displeasure be not felt at an unworthy decision in the matter of honourable men made by men yet more honourable than they, and at the consecration in the national temples of spoils taken from the

Platæans, the benefactors of Hellas. Shocking indeed will it seem for Lacedæmonians to destroy Platæa, and for the city whose name your fathers inscribed upon the tripod at Delphi for its good service, to be by you blotted out from the map of Hellas, to please the Thebans. To such a depth of misfortune have we fallen, that while the Medes' success had been our ruin, Thebans now supplant us in your once fond regards; and we have been subjected to two dangers, the greatest of any— that of dying of starvation then, if we had not surrendered our town, and now of being tried for our lives. So that we Platæans, after exertions beyond our power in the cause of the Hellenes, are rejected by all, forsaken and unassisted; helped by none of our allies, and reduced to doubt the stability of our only hope, yourselves.

'Still, in the name of the gods who once presided over our confederacy, and of our own good service in the Hellenic cause, we adjure you to relent; to recall the decision which we fear that the Thebans may have obtained from you; to ask back the gift that you have given them, that they disgrace not you by slaying us; to gain a pure instead of a guilty gratitude, and not to gratify others to be yourselves rewarded with shame. Our lives may be quickly taken, but it will be a heavy task to wipe away the infamy of the deed; as we are no enemies whom you might justly punish, but friends forced into taking arms against you. To grant us our lives would be, therefore, a righteous judgment; if you consider also that we are prisoners who surrendered of their own accord, stretching out our hands for quarter, whose slaughter Hellenic law forbids, and who besides were always your benefactors. Look at the sepulchres of your fathers, slain by the Medes and buried in our country, whom year by year we honoured with garments and all other dues, and the first fruits of all that our land produced in their season, as friends from a friendly country and allies to our old companions in arms! Should you not decide aright, your conduct would be the very opposite to ours. Consider only: Pausanias buried them thinking that he was laying them in friendly ground and among men as friendly; but you, if you kill us and make the Platæan territory Theban, will leave your fathers and kinsmen in a hostile soil and among their murderers, deprived of the honours which they now enjoy. What is more, you will enslave the land in which the freedom of the Hellenes was won, make desolate the temples of the gods to whom they prayed before they over-came the Medes, and take away your ancestral sacrifices from those who founded and instituted them.

'It were not to your glory, Lacedæmonians, either to offend in this way against the common law of the Hellenes and against your own ancestors, or to kill us your benefactors to gratify another's hatred without having been wronged your-selves: it were more so to spare us and to yield to the im-pressions of a reasonable compassion; reflecting not merely on the awful fate in store for us, but also on the character of the sufferers, and on the impossibility of predicting how soon misfortune may fall even upon those who deserve it not. We, as we have a right to do and as our need impels us, entreat you, calling aloud upon the gods at whose common altar all the Hellenes worship, to hear our request, to be not unmindful of the oaths which your fathers swore, and which we now plead—we supplicate you by the tombs of your fathers, and appeal to those that are gone to save us from falling into the hands of the Thebans and their dearest friends from being given up to their most detested foes. We also remind you of that day on which we did the most glorious deeds, by your fathers' sides, we who now on this are like to suffer the most dreadful fate. Finally, to do what is necessary and yet most difficult for men in our situation—that is, to make an end of speaking, since with that ending the peril of our lives draws near—in conclusion we say that we did not surrender our city to the Thebans (to that we would have preferred inglorious starvation), but trusted in and capitulated to you; and it would be just, if we fail to persuade you, to put us back in the same position and let us take the chance that falls to us. And at the same time we adjure you not to give us up,—your sup-pliants, Lacedæmonians, out of your hands and faith, Platæans foremost of the Hellenic patriots, to Thebans, our most hated enemies,—but to be our saviours, and not, while you free the rest of the Hellenes, to bring us to destruction.'

Such were the words of the Platæans. The Thebans, afraid that the Lacedæmonians might be moved by what they had heard, came forward and said that they too desired to address

them, since the Platæans had, against their wish, been allowed
to speak at length instead of being confined to a simple answer
to the question. Leave being granted, the Thebans spoke as
follows:—

'We should never have asked to make this speech if the
Platæans on their side had contented themselves with shortly
answering the question, and had not turned round and made
charges against us, coupled with a long defence of themselves
upon matters outside the present inquiry and not even the
subject of accusation, and with praise of what no one finds
fault with. However, since they have done so, we must answer
their charges and refute their self-praise, in order that neither
our bad name nor their good may help them, but that you
may hear the real truth on both points, and so decide.

'The origin of our quarrel was this. We settled Platæa some
time after the rest of Bœotia, together with other places out
of which we had driven the mixed population. The Platæans
not choosing to recognise our supremacy, as had been first
arranged, but separating themselves from the rest of the
Bœotians, and proving traitors to their nationality, we used
compulsion; upon which they went over to the Athenians, and
with them did as much harm, for which we retaliated.

'Next, when the barbarian invaded Hellas, they say that
they were the only Bœotians who did not Medise; and this
is where they most glorify themselves and abuse us. We say
that if they did not Medise, it was because the Athenians did
not do so either; just as afterwards when the Athenians attacked the Hellenes they, the Platæans, were again the only
Bœotians who Atticised. And yet consider the forms of our
respective governments when we so acted. Our city at that
juncture had neither an oligarchical constitution in which all
the nobles enjoyed equal rights nor a democracy, but that
which is most opposed to law and good government and nearest
a tyranny—the rule of a close cabal. These, hoping to
strengthen their individual power by the success of the Mede,
kept down by force the people, and brought him into the town.
The city as a whole was not its own mistress when it so acted,
and ought not to be reproached for the errors that it committed while deprived of its constitution. Examine only how
we acted after the departure of the Mede and the recovery

of the constitution; when the Athenians attacked the rest of Hellas and endeavoured to subjugate our country, of the greater part of which faction had already made them masters. Did not we fight and conquer at Coronea and liberate Bœotia, and do we not now actively contribute to the liberation of the rest, providing horses to the cause and a force unequalled by that of any other state in the confederacy?

'Let this suffice to excuse us for our Medism. We will now endeavour to show that you have injured the Hellenes more than we, and are more deserving of condign punishment. It was in defence against us, say you, that you became allies and citizens of Athens. If so, you ought only to have called in the Athenians against us, instead of joining them in attacking others: it was open to you to do this if you ever felt that they were leading you where you did not wish to follow, as Lacedæmon was already your ally against the Mede, as you so much insist; and this was surely sufficient to keep us off, and above all to allow you to deliberate in security. Nevertheless, of your own choice and without compulsion you chose to throw your lot in with Athens. And you say that it had been base for you to betray your benefactors; but it was surely far baser and more iniquitous to sacrifice the whole body of the Hellenes, your fellow-confederates, who were liberating Hellas, than the Athenians only, who were enslaving it. The return that you made them was therefore neither equal nor honourable, since you called them in, as you say, because you were being oppressed yourselves, and then became their accomplices in oppressing others; although baseness rather consists in not returning like for like than in not returning what is justly due but must be unjustly paid.

'Meanwhile, after thus plainly showing that it was not for the sake of the Hellenes that you alone then did not Medise, but because the Athenians did not do so either, and you wished to side with them and to be against the rest; you now claim the benefit of good deeds done to please your neighbours. This cannot be admitted: you chose the Athenians, and with them you must stand or fall. Nor can you plead the league then made and claim that it should now protect you. You abandoned that league, and offended against it by helping instead of hindering the subjugation of the Æginetans and others of

its members, and that not under compulsion, but while in en·
joyment of the same institutions that you enjoy to the present
hour, and no one forcing you as in our case. Lastly, an invitation was addressed to you before you were blockaded to be
neutral and join neither party: this you did not accept. Who
then merit the detestation of the Hellenes more justly than
you, you who sought their ruin under the mask of honour?
The former virtues that you allege you now show not to be
proper to your character; the real bent of your nature has
been at length damningly proved: when the Athenians took
the path of injustice you followed them.

'Of our unwilling Medism and your wilful Atticising this
then is our explanation. The last wrong of which you complain
consists in our having, as you say, lawlessly invaded your town
in time of peace and festival. Here again we cannot think that
we were more in fault than yourselves. If of our own proper
motion we made an armed attack upon your city and ravaged
your territory, we are guilty; but if the first men among you
in estate and family, wishing to put an end to the foreign connexion and to restore you to the common Bœotian country, of
their own free will invited us, wherein is our crime? Where
wrong is done, those who lead, as you say, are more to blame
than those who follow. Not that, in our judgment, wrong was
done either by them or by us. Citizens like yourselves, and with
more at stake than you, they opened their own walls and intro·
duced us into their own city, not as foes but as friends, to pre·
vent the bad among you from becoming worse; to give honest
men their due; to reform principles without attacking persons,
since you were not to be banished from your city, but brought
home to your kindred, nor to be made enemies to any, but
friends alike to all.

'That our intention was not hostile is proved by our behaviour. We did no harm to any one, but publicly invited
those who wished to live under a national, Bœotian government to come over to us; which at first you gladly did, and
made an agreement with us and remained tranquil, until you
became aware of the smallness of our numbers. Now it is possible that there may have been something not quite fair in
our entering without the consent of your commons. At any
rate you did not repay us in kind. Instead of refraining, as we

had done, from violence, and inducing us to retire by negotiation, you fell upon us in violation of your agreement, and slew some of us in fight, of which we do not so much complain, for in that there was a certain justice; but others who held out their hands and received quarter, and whose lives you subsequently promised us, you lawlessly butchered. If this was not abominable, what is? And after these three crimes committed one after the other—the violation of your agreement, the murder of the men afterwards, and the lying breach of your promise not to kill them, if we refrained from injuring your property in the country—you still affirm that we are the criminals and yourselves pretend to escape justice. Not so, if these your judges decide aright, but you will be punished for all together.

'Such, Lacedæmonians, are the facts. We have gone into them at some length both on your account and on our own, that you may feel that you will justly condemn the prisoners, and we, that we have given an additional sanction to our vengeance. We would also prevent you from being melted by hearing of their past virtues, if any such they had: these may be fairly appealed to by the victims of injustice, but only aggravate the guilt of criminals, since they offend against their better nature. Nor let them gain anything by crying and wailing, by calling upon your fathers' tombs and their own desolate condition. Against this we point to the far more dreadful fate of our youth, butchered at their hands; the fathers of whom either fell at Coronea, bringing Bœotia over to you, or seated, forlorn old men by desolate hearths, with far more reason implore your justice upon the prisoners. The pity which they appeal to is rather due to men who suffer unworthily; those who suffer justly as they do, are on the contrary subjects for triumph. For their present desolate condition they have themselves to blame, since they wilfully rejected the better alliance. Their lawless act was not provoked by any action of ours; hate, not justice, inspired their decision; and even now the satisfaction which they afford us is not adequate; they will suffer by a legal sentence, not as they pretend as suppliants asking for quarter in battle, but as prisoners who have surrendered upon agreement to take their trial. Vindicate, therefore, Lacedæmonians, the Hellenic law which they have broken; and to us, the victims of its violation, grant the re-ward merited by our zeal. Nor let us be supplanted in your favour by their harangues, but offer an example to the Hellenes, that the contests to which you invite them are of deeds, not words: good deeds can be shortly stated, but where wrong is done a wealth of language is needed to veil its deformity. However, if leading powers were to do what you are now doing, and putting one short question all alike were to decide accordingly, men would be less tempted to seek fine phrases to cover bad actions.'

Such were the words of the Thebans. The Lacedæmonian judges decided that the question, whether they had received any service from the Platæans in the war, was a fair one for them to put; as they had always invited them to be neutral, agreeably to the original covenant of Pausanias after the defeat of the Mede, and had again definitely offered them the same conditions before the blockade. This offer having been refused, they were now, they conceived, by the loyalty of their intention released from their covenant; and having, as they considered, suffered evil at the hands of the Platæans, they brought them in again one by one and asked each of them the same question, that is to say, whether they had done the Lacedæmonians and allies any service in the war; and upon their saying that they had not, took them out and slew them all without exception. The number of Platæans thus massacred was not less than two hundred, with twenty-five Athenians who had shared in the siege. The women were taken as slaves. The city the Thebans gave for about a year to some political emigrants from Megara, and to the surviving Platæans of their own party to inhabit, and afterwards razed it to the ground from the very foundations, and built on to the precinct of Hera an inn two hundred feet square, with rooms all round above and below, making use for this purpose of the roofs and doors of the Platæans: of the rest of the materials in the wall, the brass and the iron, they made couches which they dedicated to Hera, for whom they also built a stone chapel of a hundred feet square. The land they confiscated and let out on a ten-years' lease to Theban occupiers. The adverse attitude of the Lacedæmonians in the whole Platæan affair was mainly adopted to please the Thebans, who were thought to be useful in the war at that moment raging. Such was the end of Platæa, in the ninety-third year after she became the ally of Athens.

Meanwhile, the forty ships of the Peloponnesians that had gone to the relief of the Lesbians, and which we left flying across the open sea, pursued by the Athenians, were caught in a storm off Crete, and scattering from thence made their way to Peloponnese, where they found at Cyllene thirteen Leucadian and Ambraciot galleys, with Brasidas, son of Tellis, lately arrived as counsellor to Alcidas; the Lacedæmonians, upon the failure of the Lesbian expedition, having resolved to strengthen their fleet and sail to Corcyra, where a revolution had broken out, so as to arrive there before the twelve Athenian ships at Naupactus could be reinforced from Athens. Brasidas and Alcidas began to prepare accordingly.

The Corcyræan revolution began with the return of the prisoners taken in the sea-fights off Epidamnus. These the Corinthians had released, nominally upon the security of eight hundred talents given by their *Proxeni*, but in reality upon their engagement to bring over Corcyra to Corinth. These men proceeded to canvass each of the citizens, and to intrigue with the view of detaching the city from Athens. Upon the arrival of an Athenian and a Corinthian vessel, with envoys on board, a conference was held in which the Corcyræans voted to remain allies of the Athenians according to their agreement, but to be friends of the Peloponnesians as they had been formerly. Meanwhile, the returned prisoners brought Peithias, a volunteer *Proxenus* of the Athenians and leader of the commons, to trial, upon the charge of enslaving Corcyra to Athens. He, being acquitted, retorted by accusing five of the richest of their number of cutting stakes in the ground sacred to Zeus and Alcinous; the legal penalty being a stater for each stake. Upon their conviction, the amount of the penalty being very large, they seated themselves as suppliants in the temples, to be allowed to pay it by instalments; but Peithias, who was one of the senate, prevailed upon that body to enforce the law; upon which the accused, rendered desperate by the law, and also learning that Peithias had the intention, while still a member of the senate, to persuade the people to conclude a defensive and offensive alliance with

Athens, banded together armed with daggers, and suddenly bursting into the senate killed Peithias and sixty others, senators and private persons; some few only of the party of Peithias taking refuge in the Athenian galley, which had not yet departed.

After this outrage, the conspirators summoned the Corcyræans to an assembly, and said that this would turn out for the best, and would save them from being enslaved by Athens: for the future, they moved to receive neither party unless they came peacefully in a single ship, treating any larger number as enemies. This motion made, they compelled it to be adopted, and instantly sent off envoys to Athens to justify what had been done and to dissuade the refugees there from any hostile proceedings which might lead to a reaction.

Upon the arrival of the embassy the Athenians arrested the envoys and all who listened to them, as revolutionists, and lodged them in Ægina. Meanwhile a Corinthian galley arriving in the island with Lacedæmonian envoys, the dominant Corcyræan party attacked the commons and defeated them in battle. Night coming on, the commons took refuge in the Acropolis and the higher parts of the city, and concentrated themselves there, having also possession of the Hyllaic harbour; their adversaries occupying the market-place, where most of them lived, and the harbour adjoining, looking towards the mainland.

The next day passed in skirmishes of little importance, each party sending into the country to offer freedom to the slaves and to invite them to join them. The mass of the slaves answered the appeal of the commons; their antagonists being reinforced by eight hundred mercenaries from the continent.

After a day's interval hostilities recommenced, victory remaining with the commons, who had the advantage in numbers and position, the women also valiantly assisting them, pelting with tiles from the houses, and supporting the mêlée with a fortitude beyond their sex. Towards dusk, the oligarchs in full rout, fearing that the victorious commons might assault and carry the arsenal and put them to the sword, fired the houses round the market-place and the lodging-houses, in order to bar their advance; sparing neither their own, nor those of their neighbours; by which much stuff of the merchants was consumed and the city risked total destruction, if a wind had come to help the flame by blowing on it. Hostilities now ceasing, both sides kept quiet, passing the night on guard, while the Corinthian ship stole out to sea upon the victory of the commons, and most of the mercenaries passed over secretly to the continent.

The next day the Athenian general, Nicostratus, son of Diitrephes, came up from Naupactus with twelve ships and five hundred Messenian heavy infantry. He at once endeavoured to bring about a settlement, and persuaded the two parties to agree together to bring to trial ten of the ringleaders, who presently fled, while the rest were to live in peace, making terms with each other, and entering into a defensive and offensive alliance with the Athenians. This arranged, he was about to sail away, when the leaders of the commons induced him to leave them five of his ships to make their adversaries less disposed to move, while they manned and sent with him an equal number of their own. He had no sooner consented, than they began to enroll their enemies for the ships; and these fearing that they might be sent off to Athens, seated themselves as suppliants in the temple of the Dioscuri. An attempt on the part of Nicostratus to reassure them and to persuade them to rise proving unsuccessful, the commons armed upon this pretext, alleging the refusal of their adversaries to sail with them as a proof of the hollowness of their intentions, and took their arms out of their houses, and would have dispatched some whom they fell in with, if Nicostratus had not prevented it. The rest of the party seeing what was going on, seated themselves as suppliants in the temple of Hera, being not less than four hundred in number; until the commons, fearing that they might adopt some desperate resolution, induced them to rise, and conveyed them over to the island in front of the temple, where provisions were sent across to them.

At this stage in the revolution, on the fourth or fifth day after the removal of the men to the island, the Peloponnesian ships arrived from Cyllene where they had been stationed since their return from Ionia, fifty-three in number, still under the command of Alcidas, but with Brasidas also on board as his adviser; and dropping anchor at Sybota, a harbour on the mainland, at daybreak made sail for Corcyra.

The Corcyræans in great confusion and alarm at the state of things in the city and at the approach of the invader, at once proceeded to equip sixty vessels, which they sent out, as fast as they were manned, against the enemy, in spite of the Athenians recommending them to let them sail out first, and to follow themselves afterwards with all their ships together. Upon their vessels coming up to the enemy in this straggling fashion, two immediately deserted: in others the crews were fighting among themselves, and there was no order in anything that was done; so that the Peloponnesians seeing their confusion, placed twenty ships to oppose the Corcyræans, and ranged the rest against the twelve Athenian ships, amongst which were the two vessels *Salaminia* and *Paralus*.

While the Corcyræans, attacking without judgment and in small detachments, were already crippled by their own misconduct, the Athenians, afraid of the numbers of the enemy and of being surrounded, did not venture to attack the main body or even the centre of the division opposed to them, but fell upon its wing and sank one vessel; after which the Peloponnesians formed in a circle, and the Athenians rowed round them and tried to throw them into disorder. Perceiving this, the division opposed to the Corcyræans fearing a repetition of the disaster of Naupactus, came to support their friends, and the whole fleet now bore down, united, upon the Athenians, who retired before it, backing water, retiring as leisurely as possible in order to give the Corcyræans time to escape, while the enemy was thus kept occupied. Such was the character of this sea-fight, which lasted until sunset.

The Corcyræans now feared that the enemy would follow up their victory and sail against the town and rescue the men in the island, or strike some other blow equally decisive, and accordingly carried the men over again to the temple of Hera, and kept guard over the city. The Peloponnesians, however, although victorious in the sea-fight, did not venture to attack the town, but took the thirteen Corcyræan vessels which they had captured, and with them sailed back to the continent from whence they had put out. The next day equally they refrained from attacking the city, although the disorder and panic were at their height, and though Brasidas, it is said, urged Alcidas, his superior officer, to do so, but they landed upon the promontory of Leukimme and laid waste the country.

Meanwhile the commons in Corcyra, being still in great fear of the fleet attacking them, came to a parley with the suppliants and their friends, in order to save the town; and prevailed upon some of them to go on board the ships, of which they still manned thirty, against the expected attack. But the Peloponnesians after ravaging the country until midday sailed away, and towards nightfall were informed by beacon signals of the approach of sixty Athenian vessels from Leucas, under the command of Eurymedon, son of Thucles; which had been sent off by the Athenians upon the news of the revolution and of the fleet with Alcidas being about to sail for Corcyra.

The Peloponnesians accordingly at once set off in haste by night for home, coasting along shore; and hauling their ships across the Isthmus of Leucas, in order not to be seen doubling it, so departed. The Corcyræans, made aware of the approach of the Athenian fleet and of the departure of the enemy, brought the Messenians from outside the walls into the town, and ordered the fleet which they had manned to sail round into the Hyllaic harbour; and while it was so doing, slew such of their enemies as they laid hands on, dispatching afterwards as they landed them, those whom they had persuaded to go on board the ships. Next they went to the sanctuary of Hera and persuaded about fifty men to take their trial, and condemned them all to death. The mass of the suppliants who had refused to do so, on seeing what was taking place, slew each other there in the consecrated ground; while some hanged themselves upon the trees, and others destroyed themselves as they were severally able. During seven days that Eurymedon stayed with his sixty ships, the Corcyræans were engaged in butchering those of their fellow-citizens whom they regarded as their enemies: and although the crime imputed was that of attempting to put down the democracy, some were slain also for private hatred, others by their debtors because of the monies owed to them. Death thus raged in every shape; and, as usually happens at such times, there was no length to which violence did not go; sons were killed by their fathers, and suppliants dragged from the altar or slain upon it; while some were even walled up in the temple of Dionysus and died there.

So bloody was the march of the revolution, and the impression which it made was the greater as it was one of the first to occur. Later on, one may say, the whole Hellenic world was convulsed; struggles being everywhere made by the popular chiefs to bring in the Athenians, and by the oligarchs to introduce the Lacedæmonians. In peace there would have been neither the pretext nor the wish to make such an invitation; but in war, with an alliance always at the command of either faction for the hurt of their adversaries and their own corresponding advantage, opportunities for bringing in the foreigner were never wanting to the revolutionary parties. The sufferings which revolution entailed upon the cities were many and terrible, such as have occurred and always will occur, as long as the nature of mankind remains the same; though in a severer or milder form, and varying in their symptoms, according to the variety of the particular cases. In peace and prosperity states and individuals have better sentiments, because they do not find themselves suddenly confronted with imperious necessities; but war takes away the easy supply of daily wants, and so proves a rough master, that brings most men's characters to a level with their fortunes. Revolution thus ran its course from city to city, and the places which it arrived at last, from having heard what had been done before, carried to a still greater excess the refinement of their inventions, as manifested in the cunning of their enterprises and the atrocity of their reprisals. Words had to change their ordinary meaning and to take that which was now given them Reckless audacity came to be considered the courage of a loyal ally; prudent hesitation, specious cowardice; moderation was held to be a cloak for unmanliness; ability to see all sides of a question inaptness to act on any. Frantic violence became the attribute of manliness; cautious plotting, a justifiable means of self-defence. The advocate of extreme measures was always trustworthy; his opponent a man to be suspected. To succeed in a plot was to have a shrewd head, to divine a plot a still shrewder; but to try to provide against having to do either was to break up your party and to be afraid of your adversaries. In fine, to forestall an intending criminal, or to suggest the idea of a crime where it was wanting, was equally commended, until even blood became a weaker tie than party, from the superior readiness of those united by the latter to dare everything without reserve; for such associations had not in view the blessings derivable from established institutions but were formed by ambition for their overthrow; and the confidence of their members in each other rested less on any religious sanction than upon complicity in crime. The fair proposals of an adversary were met with jealous precautions by the stronger of the two, and not with a generous confidence. Revenge also was held of more account than self-preservation. Oaths of reconciliation, being only proffered on either side to meet an immediate difficulty, only held good so long as no other weapon was at hand; but when opportunity offered, he who first ventured to seize it and to take his enemy off his guard, thought this perfidious vengeance sweeter than an open one, since, considerations of safety apart, success by treachery won him the palm of superior intelligence. Indeed it is generally the case that men are readier to call rogues clever than simpletons honest, and are as ashamed of being the second as they are proud of being the first. The cause of all these evils was the lust for power arising from greed and ambition; and from these passions proceeded the violence of parties once engaged in contention. The leaders in the cities, each provided with the fairest professions, on the one side with the cry of political equality of the people, on the other of a moderate aristocracy, sought prizes for themselves in those public interests which they pretended to cherish, and, recoiling from no means in their struggles for ascendancy, engaged in the direct excesses; in their acts of vengeance they went to even greater lengths, not stopping at what justice or the good of the state demanded, but making the party caprice of the moment their only standard, and invoking with equal readiness the condemnation of an unjust verdict or the authority of the strong arm to glut the animosities of the hour. Thus religion was in honour with neither party; but the use of fair phrases to arrive at guilty ends was in high reputation. Meanwhile the moderate part of the citizens perished between the two, either for not joining in the quarrel, or because envy would not suffer them to escape.

Thus every form of iniquity took root in the Hellenic countries by reason of the troubles. The ancient simplicity into which honour so largely entered was laughed down and disappeared; and society became divided into camps in which no man trusted his fellow. To put an end to this, there was neither promise to be depended upon, nor oath that could command respect; but all parties dwelling rather in their calculation upon the hopelessness of a permanent state of things, were more intent upon self-defence than capable of confidence. In this contest the blunter wits were most successful. Apprehensive of their own deficiencies and of the cleverness of their antagonists, they feared to be worsted in debate and to be surprised by the combinations of their more versatile opponents, and so at once boldly had recourse to action: while their adversaries, arrogantly thinking that they should know in time, and that it was unnecessary to secure by action what policy afforded, often fell victims to their want of precaution.

Meanwhile Corcyra gave the first example of most of the crimes alluded to; of the reprisals exacted by the governed who had never experienced equitable treatment or indeed aught but insolence from their rulers—when their hour came; of the iniquitous resolves of those who desired to get rid of their accustomed poverty, and ardently coveted their neighbours' goods; and lastly, of the savage and pitiless excesses into which men who had begun the struggle not in a class but in a party spirit, were hurried by their ungovernable passions. In the confusion into which life was now thrown in the cities, human nature, always rebelling against the law and now its master, gladly showed itself ungoverned in passion, above respect for justice, and the enemy of all superiority; since revenge would not have been set above religion, and gain above justice, had it not been for the fatal power of envy. Indeed men too often take upon themselves in the prosecution of their revenge to set the example of doing away with those general laws to which all alike can look for salvation in adversity, instead of allowing them to subsist against the day of danger when their aid may be required.

While the revolutionary passions thus for the first time displayed themselves in the factions of Corcyra, Eurymedon
and the Athenian fleet sailed away; after which some five
hundred Corcyræan exiles who had succeeded in escaping,
took some forts on the mainland, and becoming masters of
the Corcyræan territory over the water, made this their base
to plunder their countrymen in the island, and did so much
damage as to cause a severe famine in the town. They also
sent envoys to Lacedæmon and Corinth to negotiate their
restoration; but meeting with no success, afterwards got
together boats and mercenaries and crossed over to the island,
being about six hundred in all; and burning their boats so
as to have no hope except in becoming masters of the country,
went up to Mount Istone, and fortifying themselves there,
began to annoy those in the city and obtained command of
the country.

At the close of the same summer the Athenians sent twenty
ships under the command of Laches, son of Melanopus, and
Charœades, son of Euphiletus, to Sicily, where the Syracusans
and Leontines were at war. The Syracusans had for allies all
the Dorian cities except Camarina—these had been included
in the Lacedæmonian confederacy from the commencement
of the war, though they had not taken any active part in it—
the Leontines had Camarina and the Chalcidian cities. In
Italy the Locrians were for the Syracusans, the Rhegians for
their Leontine kinsmen. The allies of the Leontines now sent
to Athens and appealed to their ancient alliance and to their
Ionian origin, to persuade the Athenians to send them a fleet,
as the Syracusans were blockading them by land and sea. The
Athenians sent it upon the plea of their common descent, but
in reality to prevent the exportation of Silician corn to Peloponnese and to test the possibility of bringing Sicily into
subjection. Accordingly they established themselves at
Rhegium in Italy, and from thence carried on the war in
concert with their allies.

CHAPTER XI

SIXTH YEAR OF THE WAR——CAMPAIGNS OF DEMOSTHENES IN
WESTERN GREECE——RUIN OF AMBRACIA

B.C. 427: *Plague returns to Athens*—B.C. 426: *Earthquakes and floods*—
*Athenian fleet to Melos and Tanagra—Lacedæmonians colonize
Heraclea—Demosthenes' expedition against the Ætolians—Disaster
follows—Campaign against Naupactus—Purification of Delos—
The Delian games—Eurylochus at Olpæ—Demosthenes victorious
—Rout of Ambraciot forces—Treaty between Acarnanians and
Ambraciots—Another Athenian fleet to Sicily—Eruption of Mount
Etna.*

SUMMER was now over. The winter following, the plague a
second time attacked the Athenians; for although it had never
entirely left them, still there had been a notable abatement in
its ravages. The second visit lasted no less than a year, the
first having lasted two; and nothing distressed the Athenians
and reduced their power more than this. No less than four
thousand four hundred heavy infantry in the ranks died of it,
and three hundred cavalry, besides a number of the multitude
that was never ascertained. At the same time took place the
numerous earthquakes in Athens, Eubœa, and Bœotia, particularly at Orchomenus in the last-named country.

The same winter the Athenians in Sicily and the Rhegians,
with thirty ships, made an expedition against the islands of
Æolus; it being impossible to invade them in summer, owing
to the want of water. These islands are occupied by the Lipa-
ræans, a Cnidian colony, who live in one of them of no great
size called Lipara; and from this as their headquarters cultivate the rest, Didyme, Strongyle, and Hiera. In Hiera the
people in those parts believe that Hephæstus has his forge,
from the quantity of flame which they see it send out by night,
and of smoke by day. These islands lie off the coast of the
Sicels and Messinese, and were allies of the Syracusans. The
Athenians laid waste their land, and as the inhabitants did not
submit, sailed back to Rhegium. Thus the winter ended, and
with it ended the fifth year of this war, of which Thucydides
was the historian.

The next summer the Peloponnesians and their allies set out
to invade Attica under the command of Agis, son of Archidamus, and went as far as the Isthmus, but numerous earth-

quakes occurring, turned back again without the invasion
taking place. About the same time that these earthquakes
were so common, the sea at Orobiæ, in Eubœa, retiring from
the then line of coast, returned in a huge wave and invaded a
great part of the town, and retreated leaving some of it still
under water; so that what was once land is now sea; such
of the inhabitants perishing as could not run up to the higher
ground in time. A similar inundation also occurred at Atalanta,
the island off the Opuntian-Locrian coast, carrying away part
of the Athenian fort and wrecking one of two ships which
were drawn up on the beach. At Peparethus also the sea retreated a little, without however any inundation following;
and an earthquake threw down part of the wall, the town-
hall, and a few other buildings. The cause, in my opinion, of
this phenomenon must be sought in the earthquake. At the
point where its shock has been the most violent the sea is
driven back, and suddenly recoiling with redoubled force,
causes the inundation. Without an earthquake I do not see
how such an accident could happen.

During the same summer different operations were carried
on by the different belligerents in Sicily; by the Siceliots themselves against each other, and by the Athenians and their
allies: I shall however confine myself to the actions in which
the Athenians took part, choosing the most important. The
death of the Athenian general Charœades, killed by the Syracusans in battle, left Laches in the sole command of the fleet,
which he now directed in concert with the allies against Mylæ,
a place belonging to the Messinese. Two Messinese battalions
in garrison at Mylæ laid an ambush for the party landing from
the ships, but were routed with great slaughter by the Athenians and their allies, who thereupon assaulted the fortification
and compelled them to surrender the Acropolis and to march
with them upon Messina. This town afterwards also submitted
upon the approach of the Athenians and their allies, and gave
hostages and all other securities required.

The same summer the Athenians sent thirty ships round
Peloponnese under Demosthenes, son of Alcisthenes, and
Procles, son of Theodorus, and sixty others, with two thousand
heavy infantry, against Melos, under Nicias, son of Niceratus;
wishing to reduce the Melians, who, although islanders,

refused to be subjects of Athens or even to join her confederacy. The devastation of their land not procuring their
submission, the fleet, weighing from Melos, sailed to Oropus
in the territory of Græa, and landing at nightfall, the heavy
infantry started at once from the ships by land for Tanagra
in Bœotia, where they were met by the whole levy from
Athens, agreeably to a concerted signal, under the command
of Hipponicus, son of Callias, and Eurymedon, son of Thucles.
They encamped, and passing that day in ravaging the Tana-
græan territory, remained there for the night; and next day,
after defeating those of the Tanagræans who sallied out
against them and some Thebans who had come up to help the
Tanagræans, took some arms, set up a trophy, and retired,
the troops to the city and the others to the ships. Nicias with
his sixty ships coasted along shore and ravaged the Locrian
seaboard, and so returned home.

About this time the Lacedæmonians founded their colony
of Heraclea in Trachis, their object being the following. The
Malians form in all three tribes, the Paralians, the Hiereans,
and the Trachinians. The last of these having suffered severely
in a war with their neighbours the Œtæans, at first intended to
give themselves up to Athens; but afterwards fearing not to
find in her the security that they sought, sent to Lacedæmon, having chosen Tisamenus for their ambassador. In
this embassy joined also the Dorians from the mother country
of the Lacedæmonians, with the same request, as they themselves also suffered from the same enemy. After hearing them,
the Lacedæmonians determined to send out the colony, wishing to assist the Trachinians and Dorians, and also because
they thought that the proposed town would lie conveniently
for the purposes of the war against the Athenians. A fleet
might be got ready there against Eubœa, with the advantage
of a short passage to the island; and the town would also be
useful as a station on the road to Thrace. In short, everything
made the Lacedæmonians eager to found the place. After first
consulting the god at Delphi and receiving a favourable answer, they sent off the colonists, Spartans and Periœci, inviting
also any of the rest of the Hellenes who might wish to accompany them, except Ionians, Achæans, and certain other nationalities; three Lacedæmonians leading as founders of the

colony, Leon, Alcidas, and Damagon. The settlement effected, they fortified anew the city, now called Heraclea, distant about four miles and a half from Thermopylæ and two miles and a quarter from the sea, and commenced building docks, closing the side towards Thermopylæ just by the pass itself, in order that they might be easily defended.

The foundation of this town, evidently meant to annoy Eubœa (the passage across to Cenæum in that island being a short one), at first caused some alarm at Athens, which the event however did nothing to justify, the town never giving them any trouble. The reason of this was as follows. The Thessalians, who were sovereign in those parts, and whose territory was menaced by its foundation, were afraid that it might prove a very powerful neighbour, and accordingly continually harassed and made war upon the new settlers, until they at last wore them out in spite of their originally considerable numbers, people flocking from all quarters to a place founded by the Lacedæmonians, and thus thought secure of prosperity. On the other hand the Lacedæmonians themselves, in the persons of their governors, did their full share towards ruining its prosperity and reducing its population, as they frightened away the greater part of the inhabitants by governing harshly and in some cases not fairly, and thus made it easier for their neighbours to prevail against them.

The same summer, about the same time that the Athenians were detained at Melos, their fellow-citizens in the thirty ships cruising round Peloponnese, after cutting off some guards in an ambush at Ellomenus in Leucadia, subsequently went against Leucas itself with a large armament, having been reinforced by the whole levy of the Acarnanians except Œniadæ, and by the Zacynthians and Cephallenians and fifteen ships from Corcyra. While the Leucadians witnessed the devastation of their land, without and within the isthmus upon which the town of Leucas and the temple of Apollo stand, without making any movement on account of the overwhelming numbers of the enemy, the Acarnanians urged Demosthenes, the Athenian general, to build a wall so as to cut off the town from the continent, a measure which they were convinced would secure its capture and rid them once and for all of a most troublesome enemy.

Demosthenes however had in the meanwhile been persuaded by the Messenians that it was a fine opportunity for him, having so large an army assembled, to attack the Ætolians, who were not only the enemies of Naupactus, but whose reduction would further make it easy to gain the rest of that part of the continent for the Athenians. The Ætolian nation, although numerous and warlike, yet dwelt in unwalled villages scattered far apart, and had nothing but light armour, and might, according to the Messenians, be subdued without much difficulty before succours could arrive. The plan which they recommended was to attack first the Apodotians, next the Ophionians, and after these the Eurytanians, who are the largest tribe in Ætolia, and speak, as is said, a language exceedingly difficult to understand, and eat their flesh raw. These once subdued, the rest would easily come in.

To this plan Demosthenes consented, not only to please the Messenians, but also in the belief that by adding the Ætolians to his other continental allies he would be able, without aid from home, to march against the Bœotians by way of Ozolian Locris to Kytinium in Doris, keeping Parnassus on his right until he descended to the Phocians, whom he could force to join him if their ancient friendship for Athens did not, as he anticipated, at once decide them to do so. Arrived in Phocis he was already upon the frontier of Bœotia. He accordingly weighed from Leucas, against the wish of the Acarnanians, and with his whole armament sailed along the coast to Sollium, where he communicated to them his intention; and upon their refusing to agree to it on account of the non-investment of Leucas, himself with the rest of the forces, the Cephallenians, the Messenians, and Zacynthians, and three hundred Athenian marines from his own ships (the fifteen Corcyræan vessels having departed), started on his expedition against the Ætolians. His base he established at Œneon in Locris, as the Ozolian Locrians were allies of Athens and were to meet him with all their forces in the interior. Being neighbours of the Ætolians and armed in the same way, it was thought that they would be of great service upon the expedition, from their acquaintance with the localities and the warfare of the inhabitants.

After bivouacking with the army in the precinct of Nemean

Zeus, in which the poet Hesiod is said to have been killed by
the people of the country, according to an oracle which had
foretold that he should die in Nemea, Demosthenes set out at
daybreak to invade Ætolia. The first day he took Potidania,
the next Krokyle, and the third Tichium, where he halted and
sent back the booty to Eupalium in Locris, having determined
to pursue his conquests as far as the Ophionians, and in the
event of their refusing to submit, to return to Naupactus and
make them the objects of a second expedition. Meanwhile the
Ætolians had been aware of his design from the moment of
its formation, and as soon as the army invaded their country
came up in great force with all their tribes; even the most
remote Ophionians, the Bomiensians, and Calliensians, who
extend towards the Malian Gulf, being among the number.

The Messenians, however, adhered to their original advice.
Assuring Demosthenes that the Ætolians were an easy conquest, they urged him to push on as rapidly as possible, and
to try to take the villages as fast as he came up to them,
without waiting until the whole nation should be in arms
against him. Led on by his advisers and trusting in his fortune, as he had met with no opposition, without waiting for
his Locrian reinforcements, who were to have supplied him
with the light-armed darters in which he was most deficient,
he advanced and stormed Ægitium, the inhabitants flying
before him and posting themselves upon the hills above the
town, which stood on high ground about nine miles from the
sea. Meanwhile the Ætolians had gathered to the rescue, and
now attacked the Athenians and their allies, running down
from the hills on every side and darting their javelins, falling
back when the Athenian army advanced, and coming on as it
retired; and for a long while the battle was of this character,
alternate advance and retreat, in both which operations the
Athenians had the worst.

Still as long as their archers had arrows left and were able
to use them, they held out, the light-armed Ætolians retiring
before the arrows; but after the captain of the archers had
been killed and his men scattered, the soldiers, wearied out
with the constant repetition of the same exertions and hard
pressed by the Ætolians with their javelins, at last turned and
fled, and falling into pathless gullies and places that they

were unacquainted with, thus perished, the Messenian
Chromon, their guide, having also unfortunately been killed.
A great many were overtaken in the pursuit by the swift-
footed and light-armed Ætolians, and fell beneath their javelins; the greater number however missed their road and rushed
into the wood, which had no ways out, and which was soon
fired and burnt round them by the enemy. Indeed the Athenian
army fell victims to death in every form, and suffered all the
vicissitudes of flight; the survivors escaped with difficulty to
the sea and Œneon in Locris, whence they had set out. Many
of the allies were killed, and about one hundred and twenty
Athenian heavy infantry, not a man less, and all in the prime
of life. These were by far the best men in the city of Athens
that fell during this war. Among the slain was also Procles,
the colleague of Demosthenes. Meanwhile the Athenians took
up their dead under truce from the Ætolians, and retired to
Naupactus, and from thence went in their ships to Athens;
Demosthenes staying behind in Naupactus and in the neighbourhood, being afraid to face the Athenians after the disaster.

About the same time the Athenians on the coast of Sicily
sailed to Locris, and in a descent which they made from the
ships defeated the Locrians who came against them, and took
a fort upon the river Halex.

The same summer the Ætolians, who before the Athenian
expedition had sent an embassy to Corinth and Lacedæmon,
composed of Tolophus, an Ophionian, Boriades, an Euryta-
nian, and Tisander, an Apodotian, obtained that an army
should be sent them against Naupactus, which had invited
the Athenian invasion. The Lacedæmonians accordingly sent
off towards autumn three thousand heavy infantry of the
allies, five hundred of whom were from Heraclea, the newly-
founded city in Trachis, under the command of Eurylochus,
a Spartan, accompanied by Macarius and Menedaïus, also
Spartans.

The army having assembled at Delphi, Eurylochus sent a
herald to the Ozolian Locrians; the road to Naupactus lying
through their territory, and he having besides conceived the
idea of detaching them from Athens. His chief abettors in
Locris were the Amphissians, who were alarmed at the hostility of the Phocians. These first gave hostages themselves,

and induced the rest to do the same for fear of the invading
army; first, their neighbours the Myonians, who held the
most difficult of the passes, and after them the Ipnians, Mes-
sapians, Tritæans, Chalæans, Tolophonians, Hessians, and
Œanthians, all of whom joined in the expedition; the Olpæans
contenting themselves with giving hostages, without accompanying the invasion; and the Hyæans refusing to do either,
until the capture of Polis, one of their villages.

His preparations completed, Eurylochus lodged the hostages in Kytinium, in Doris, and advanced upon Naupactus
through the country of the Locrians, taking upon his way
Œneon and Eupalium, two of their towns that refused to join
him. Arrived in the Naupactian territory, and having been
now joined by the Ætolians, the army laid waste the land
and took the suburb of the town, which was unfortified; and
after this Molycrium also, a Corinthian colony subject to
Athens. Meanwhile the Athenian Demosthenes, who since the
affair in Ætolia had remained near Naupactus, having had
notice of the army and fearing for the town, went and persuaded the Acarnanians, although not without difficulty because of his departure from Leucas, to go to the relief of
Naupactus. They accordingly sent with him on board his
ships a thousand heavy infantry, who threw themselves into
the place and saved it; the extent of its wall and the small
number of its defenders otherwise placing it in the greatest
danger. Meanwhile Eurylochus and his companions, finding
that this force had entered and that it was impossible to
storm the town, withdrew, not to Peloponnese, but to the
country once called Æolis and now Calydon and Pleuron, and
to the places in that neighbourhood and Proschium in Ætolia;
the Ambraciots having come and urged them to combine with
them in attacking Amphilochian Argos and the rest of Amphilochia and Acarnania; affirming that the conquest of these
countries would bring all the continent into alliance with
Lacedæmon. To this Eurylochus consented, and dismissing
the Ætolians, now remained quiet with his army in those parts,
until the time should come for the Ambraciots to take the
field, and for him to join them before Argos.

Summer was now over. The winter ensuing, the Athenians
in Sicily with their Hellenic allies, and such of the Sicel sub-

jects or allies of Syracuse as had revolted from her and joined their army, marched against the Sicel town Inessa, the Acropolis of which was held by the Syracusans, and after attacking it without being able to take it, retired. In the retreat, the allies retreating after the Athenians were attacked by the Syracusans from the fort, and a large part of their army routed with great slaughter. After this, Laches and the Athenians from the ships made some descents in Locris, and defeating the Locrians, who came against them with Proxenus, son of Capaton, upon the river Caïcinus, took some arms and departed.

The same winter the Athenians purified Delos, in compliance, it appears, with a certain oracle. It had been purified before by Pisistratus the tyrant; not indeed the whole island, but as much of it as could be seen from the temple. All of it was, however, now purified in the following way. All the sepulchres of those that had died in Delos were taken up, and for the future it was commanded that no one should be allowed either to die or to give birth to a child in the island; but that they should be carried over to Rhenea, which is so near to Delos that Polycrates, tyrant of Samos, having added Rhenea to his other island conquests during his period of naval ascendancy, dedicated it to the Delian Apollo by binding it to Delos with a chain.

The Athenians, after the purification, celebrated, for the first time, the quinquennial festival of the Delian games. Once upon a time, indeed, there was a great assemblage of the Ionians and the neighbouring islanders at Delos, who used to come to the festival, as the Ionians now do to that of Ephesus, and athletic and poetical contests took place there, and the cities brought choirs of dancers. Nothing can be clearer on this point than the following verses of Homer, taken from a hymn to Apollo:—

> Phœbus, where'er thou strayest, far or near,
> Delos was still of all thy haunts most dear.
> Thither the robed Ionians take their way
> With wife and child to keep thy holiday,
> Invoke thy favour on each manly game,
> And dance and sing in honour of thy name.

That there was also a poetical contest in which the Ionians went to contend, again is shown by the following, taken from the same hymn. After celebrating the Delian dance of the women, he ends his song of praise with these verses, in which he also alludes to himself:—

> Well, may Apollo keep you all! and so,
> Sweethearts, good-bye—yet tell me not I go
> Out from your hearts; and if in after hours
> Some other wanderer in this world of ours
> Touch at your shores, and ask your maidens here
> Who sings the songs the sweetest to your ear,
> Think of me then, and answer with a smile,
> " A blind old man of Scio's rocky isle."

Homer thus attests that there was anciently a great assembly and festival at Delos. In later times, although the islanders and the Athenians continued to send the choirs of dancers with sacrifices, the contests and most of the ceremonies were abolished, probably through adversity, until the Athenians celebrated the games upon this occasion with the novelty of horse-races.

The same winter the Ambraciots, as they had promised Eurylochus when they retained his army, marched out against Amphilochian Argos with three thousand heavy infantry, and invading the Argive territory occupied Olpæ, a stronghold on a hill near the sea, which had been formerly fortified by the Acarnanians and used as the place of assizes for their nation, and which is about two miles and three-quarters from the city of Argos upon the sea-coast. Meanwhile the Acarnanians went with a part of their forces to the relief of Argos, and with the rest encamped in Amphilochia at the place called Crenæ, or the Wells, to watch for Eurylochus and his Peloponnesians, and to prevent their passing through and effecting their junction with the Ambraciots; while they also sent for Demosthenes, the commander of the Ætolian expedition, to be their leader, and for the twenty Athenian ships that were cruising off Peloponnese under the command of Aristotle, son of Timocrates, and Hierophon, son of Antimnestus. On their part, the Ambraciots at Olpæ sent a messenger to their own city, to beg them to come with their whole levy to their assistance, fearing that the army of Eurylochus might not be able to pass through the Acarnanians, and that they might themselves be obliged to fight single-handed, or be unable to retreat, if they wished it, without danger.

Meanwhile Eurylochus and his Peloponnesians, learning that the Ambraciots at Olpæ had arrived, set out from Proschium with all haste to join them, and crossing the Achelous advanced through Acarnania, which they found deserted by its population, who had gone to the relief of Argos; keeping on their right the city of the Stratians and its garrison, and on their left the rest of Acarnania. Traversing the territory of the Stratians, they advanced through Phytia, next, skirting Medeon, through Limnæa; after which they left Acarnania behind them and entered a friendly country, that of the Agræans. From thence they reached and crossed Mount Thyamus, which belongs to the Agræans, and descended into the Argive territory after nightfall, and passing between the city of Argos and the Acarnanian posts at Crenæ, joined the Ambraciots at Olpæ.

Uniting here at daybreak, they sat down at the place called Metropolis, and encamped. Not long afterwards the Athenians in the twenty ships came into the Ambracian Gulf to support the Argives, with Demosthenes and two hundred Messenian heavy infantry, and sixty Athenian archers. While the fleet off Olpæ blockaded the hill from the sea, the Acarnanians and a few of the Amphilochians, most of whom were kept back by force by the Ambraciots, had already arrived at Argos, and were preparing to give battle to the enemy, having chosen Demosthenes to command the whole of the allied army in concert with their own generals. Demosthenes led them near to Olpæ and encamped, a great ravine separating the two armies. During five days they remained inactive; on the sixth both sides formed in order of battle. The army of the Peloponnesians was the largest and outflanked their opponents; and Demosthenes fearing that his right might be surrounded, placed in ambush in a hollow way overgrown with bushes some four hundred heavy infantry and light troops, who were to rise up at the moment of the onset behind the projecting left wing of the enemy, and to take them in the rear. When both sides were ready they joined battle; Demosthenes being on the right wing with the Messenians and a few Athenians, while the rest of the line was made up of the different divisions of

the Acarnanians, and of the Amphilochian darters. The Peloponnesians and Ambraciots were drawn up pell-mell together,
with the exception of the Mantineans, who were massed on
the left, without however reaching to the extremity of the
wing, where Eurylochus and his men confronted the Messenians and Demosthenes.

The Peloponnesians were now well engaged and with their
outflanking wing were upon the point of turning their enemy's
right; when the Acarnanians from the ambuscade set upon
them from behind, and broke them at the first attack, without
their staying to resist; while the panic into which they fell
caused the flight of most of their army, terrified beyond measure at seeing the division of Eurylochus and their best troops
cut to pieces. Most of the work was done by Demosthenes
and his Messenians, who were posted in this part of the field.
Meanwhile the Ambraciots (who are the best soldiers in
those countries) and the troops upon the right wing, defeated
the division opposed to them and pursued it to Argos. Returning from the pursuit, they found their main body defeated; and hard pressed by the Acarnanians, with difficulty
made good their passage to Olpæ, suffering heavy loss on the
way, as they dashed on without discipline or order, the Mantineans excepted, who kept their ranks best of any in the army
during the retreat.

The battle did not end until the evening. The next day
Menedaïus, who on the death of Eurylochus and Macarius
had succeeded to the sole command, being at a loss after so
signal a defeat how to stay and sustain a siege, cut off as he
was by land and by the Athenian fleet by sea, and equally so
how to retreat in safety, opened a parley with Demosthenes
and the Acarnanian generals for a truce and permission to
retreat, and at the same time for the recovery of the dead.
The dead they gave back to him, and setting up a trophy took
up their own also to the number of about three hundred. The
retreat demanded they refused publicly to the army; but
permission to depart without delay was secretly granted to the
Mantineans and to Menedaïus and the other commanders
and principal men of the Peloponnesians by Demosthenes and
his Acarnanian colleagues; who desired to strip the Ambraciots and the mercenary host of foreigners of their supporters;

and, above all, to discredit the Lacedæmonians and Peloponnesians with the Hellenes in those parts, as traitors and self-
seekers.

While the enemy was taking up his dead and hastily burying
them as he could, and those who obtained permission were
secretly planning their retreat, word was brought to Demosthenes and the Acarnanians that the Ambraciots from the
city, in compliance with the first message from Olpæ, were
on the march with their whole levy through Amphilochia to
join their countrymen at Olpæ, knowing nothing of what had
occurred. Demosthenes prepared to march with his army
against them, and meanwhile sent on at once a strong division
to beset the roads and occupy the strong positions. In the
meantime the Mantineans and others included in the agreement went out under the pretence of gathering herbs and fire-
wood, and stole off by twos and threes, picking on the way
the things which they professed to have come out for, until
they had gone some distance from Olpæ, when they quickened
their pace. The Ambraciots and such of the rest as had accompanied them in larger parties, seeing them going on, pushed
on in their turn, and began running in order to catch them
up. The Acarnanians at first thought that all alike were
departing without permission, and began to pursue the Peloponnesians; and believing that they were being betrayed,
even threw a dart or two at some of their generals who tried
to stop them and told them that leave had been given. Eventually, however, they let pass the Mantineans and Peloponnesians, and slew only the Ambraciots, there being much
dispute and difficulty in distinguishing whether a man was an
Ambraciot or a Peloponnesian. The number thus slain was
about two hundred; the rest escaped into the bordering territory of Agræa, and found refuge with Salynthius, the friendly
king of the Agræans.

Meanwhile the Ambraciots from the city arrived at Idomene. Idomene consists of two lofty hills, the highest of which
the troops sent on by Demosthenes succeeded in occupying
after nightfall, unobserved by the Ambraciots, who had meanwhile ascended the smaller and bivouacked upon it. After
supper Demosthenes set out with the rest of the army, as
soon as it was evening; himself with half his force making

for the pass, and the remainder going by the Amphilochian hills. At dawn he fell upon the Ambraciots while they were still abed, ignorant of what had passed, and fully thinking that it was their own countrymen,—Demosthenes having purposely put the Messenians in front with orders to address them in the Doric dialect, and thus to inspire confidence in the sentinels, who would not be able to see them, as it was still night. In this way he routed their army as soon as he attacked it, slaying most of them where they were, the rest breaking away in flight over the hills. The roads, however, were already occupied, and while the Amphilochians knew their own country, the Ambraciots were ignorant of it and could not tell which way to turn, and had also heavy armour as against a light-armed enemy, and so fell into ravines and into the ambushes which had been set for them, and perished there. In their manifold efforts to escape some even turned to the sea, which was not far off, and seeing the Athenian ships coasting along shore just while the action was going on, swam off to them, thinking it better in the panic they were in, to perish, if perish they must, by the hands of the Athenians, than by those of the barbarous and detested Amphilochians. Of the large Ambraciot force destroyed in this manner, a few only reached the city in safety; while the Acarnanians, after stripping the dead and setting up a trophy, returned to Argos.

The next day arrived a herald from the Ambraciots who had fled from Olpæ to the Agræans, to ask leave to take up the dead that had fallen after the first engagement, when they left the camp with the Mantineans and their companions, without, like them, having had permission to do so. At the sight of the arms of the Ambraciots from the city, the herald was astonished at their number, knowing nothing of the disaster and fancying that they were those of his own party. Some one asked him what he was so astonished at, and how many of them had been killed, fancying in his turn that this was the herald from the troops at Idomene. He replied, 'About two hundred;' upon which his interrogator took him up, saying, 'Why, the arms you see here are of more than a thousand.' The herald replied, 'Then they are not the arms of those who fought with us?' The other answered, 'Yes, they are, if at least you fought at Idomene yesterday.' 'But we fought with no one yesterday; but the day before in the retreat.' 'However that may be, we fought yesterday with those who came to reinforce you from the city of the Ambraciots.' When the herald heard this and knew that the reinforcement from the city had been destroyed, he broke into wailing, and stunned at the magnitude of the present evils, went away at once without having performed his errand, or again asking for the dead bodies. Indeed, this was by far the greatest disaster that befell any one Hellenic city in an equal number of days during this war; and I have not set down the number of the dead, because the amount stated seems so out of proportion to the size of the city as to be incredible. In any case I know that if the Acarnanians and Amphilochians had wished to take Ambracia as the Athenians and Demosthenes advised, they would have done so without striking a blow; as it was, they feared that if the Athenians had it they would be worse neighbours to them than the present.

After this the Acarnanians allotted a third of the spoils to the Athenians, and divided the rest among their own different towns. The share of the Athenians was captured on the voyage home; the arms now deposited in the Attic temples are three hundred panoplies, which the Acarnanians set apart for Demosthenes, and which he brought to Athens in person, his return to his country after the Ætolian disaster being rendered less hazardous by this exploit. The Athenians in the twenty ships also went off to Naupactus. The Acarnanians and Amphilochians, after the departure of Demosthenes and the Athenians, granted the Ambraciots and Peloponnesians who had taken refuge with Salynthius and the Agræans a free retreat from Œniadæ, to which place they had removed from the country of Salynthius, and for the future concluded with the Ambraciots a treaty and alliance for one hundred years, upon the terms following. It was to be a defensive, not an offensive alliance; the Ambraciots could not be required to march with the Acarnanians against the Peloponnesians, nor the Acarnanians with the Ambraciots against the Athenians; for the rest the Ambraciots were to give up the places and hostages that they held of the Amphilochians, and not to give help to Anactorium, which was at enmity with the Acarnanians. With this arrangement they put an end to the war.

After this the Corinthians sent a garrison of their own citizens to Ambracia, composed of three hundred heavy infantry, under the command of Xenocleides, son of Euthycles, who reached their destination after a difficult journey across the continent. Such was the history of the affair of Ambracia.

The same winter the Athenians in Sicily made a descent from their ships upon the territory of Himera, in concert with the Sicels, who had invaded its borders from the interior, and also sailed to the islands of Æolus. Upon their return to Rhegium they found the Athenian general, Pythodorus, son of Isolochus, come to supersede Laches in the command of the fleet. The allies in Sicily had sailed to Athens and induced the Athenians to send out more vessels to their assistance, pointing out that the Syracusans who already commanded their land were making efforts to get together a navy, to avoid being any longer excluded from the sea by a few vessels. The Athenians proceeded to man forty ships to send to them, thinking that the war in Sicily would thus be the sooner ended, and also wishing to exercise their navy. One of the generals, Pythodorus, was accordingly sent out with a few ships; Sophocles, son of Sostratides, and Eurymedon, son of Thucles, being destined to follow with the main body. Meanwhile Pythodorus had taken the command of Laches' ships, and towards the end of winter sailed against the Locrian fort, which Laches had formerly taken, and returned after being defeated in battle by the Locrians.

In the first days of this spring, the stream of fire issued from Etna, as on former occasions, and destroyed some land of the Catanians, who live upon Mount Etna, which is the largest mountain in Sicily. Fifty years, it is said, had elapsed since the last eruption, there having been three in all since the Hellenes have inhabited Sicily. Such were the events of this winter; and with it ended the sixth year of this war, of which Thucydides was the historian.

BOOK IV

CHAPTER XII

SEVENTH YEAR OF THE WAR—OCCUPATION OF PYLOS—SURRENDER OF THE SPARTAN ARMY IN SPHACTERIA

B.C. 425: *Messina revolts from Athenians—Athenian fleet at Pylos—Garrison fortified—Demosthenes exhorts his troops—Brasidas leads assault—Lacedæmonian disaster at Pylos—Terms of armistice—Speech of Lacedæmonian envoys—Failure of mission ends armistice at Pylos—Syracusans and Athenians in naval engagement—Messinese defeated—Blockade of Sphacteria—Cleon's boast—Burning of the wood—Demosthenes' tactics—Retreat of the Lacedæmonians—Parley and surrender—Cleon's boast fulfilled.*

NEXT summer, about the time of the corn's coming into ear, ten Syracusan and as many Locrian vessels sailed to Messina, in Sicily, and occupied the town upon the invitation of the inhabitants; and Messina revolted from the Athenians. The Syracusans contrived this chiefly because they saw that the place afforded an approach to Sicily, and feared that the Athenians might hereafter use it as a base for attacking them with a larger force; the Locrians because they wished to carry on hostilities from both sides of the Strait and to reduce their enemies, the people of Rhegium. Meanwhile, the Locrians had invaded the Rhegian territory with all their forces, to prevent their succouring Messina, and also at the instance of some exiles from Rhegium who were with them; the long factions by which that town had been torn rendering it for the moment incapable of resistance, and thus furnishing an additional temptation to the invaders. After devastating the country the Locrian land forces retired, their ships remaining to guard Messina, while others were being manned for the same destination to carry on the war from thence.

About the same time in the spring, before the corn was ripe, the Peloponnesians and their allies invaded Attica under

Agis, the son of Archidamus, king of the Lacedæmonians, and sat down and laid waste the country. Meanwhile the Athenians sent off the forty ships which they had been preparing to Sicily, with the remaining generals Eurymedon and Sophocles; their colleague Pythodorus having already preceded them thither. These had also instructions as they sailed by to look to the Corcyræans in the town, who were being plundered by the exiles in the mountain. To support these exiles sixty Peloponnesian vessels had lately sailed, it being thought that the famine raging in the city would make it easy for them to reduce it. Demosthenes also, who had remained without employment since his return from Acarnania, applied and obtained permission to use the fleet, if he wished it, upon the coast of Peloponnese.

Off Laconia they heard that the Peloponnesian ships were already at Corcyra, upon which Eurymedon and Sophocles wished to hasten to the island, but Demosthenes required them first to touch at Pylos and do what was wanted there, before continuing their voyage. While they were making objections, a squall chanced to come on and carried the fleet into Pylos. Demosthenes at once urged them to fortify the place, it being for this that he had come on the voyage, and made them observe there was plenty of stone and timber on the spot, and that the place was strong by nature, and together with much of the country round unoccupied; Pylos, or Coryphasium, as the Lacedæmonians call it, being about forty-five miles distant from Sparta, and situated in the old country of the Messenians. The commanders told him that there was no lack of desert headlands in Peloponnese if he wished to put the city to expense by occupying them. He, however, thought that this place was distinguished from others of the kind by having a harbour close by; while the Messenians, the old natives of the country, speaking the same dialect as the Lacedæmonians, could do them the greatest mischief by their incursions from it, and would at the same time be a trusty garrison.

After speaking to the captains of companies on the subject, and failing to persuade either the generals or the soldiers, he remained inactive with the rest from stress of weather; until the soldiers themselves wanting occupation were seized

with a sudden impulse to go round and fortify the place.
Accordingly they set to work in earnest, and having no iron
tools, picked up stones, and put them together as they happened to fit, and where mortar was needed, carried it on their
backs for want of hods, stooping down to make it stay on,
and clasping their hands together behind to prevent it falling
off; sparing no effort to be able to complete the most vulnerable points before the arrival of the Lacedæmonians, most
of the place being sufficiently strong by nature without further fortification.

Meanwhile the Lacedæmonians were celebrating a festival,
and also at first made light of the news, in the idea that whenever they chose to take the field the place would be immediately evacuated by the enemy or easily taken by force; the
absence of their army before Athens having also something
to do with their delay. The Athenians fortified the place on
the land side, and where it most required it, in six days, and
leaving Demosthenes with five ships to garrison it, with the
main body of the fleet hastened on their voyage to Corcyra
and Sicily.

As soon as the Peloponnesians in Attica heard of the occupation of Pylos, they hurried back home; the Lacedæmonians
and their king Agis thinking that the matter touched them
nearly. Besides having made their invasion early in the season,
and while the corn was still green, most of their troops were
short of provisions: the weather also was unusually bad for
the time of year, and greatly distressed their army. Many
reasons thus combined to hasten their departure and to make
this invasion a very short one; indeed they only stayed fifteen
days in Attica.

About the same time the Athenian general Simonides getting together a few Athenians from the garrisons, and a number of the allies in those parts, took Eion in Thrace, a
Mendæan colony and hostile to Athens, by treachery, but had
no sooner done so than the Chalcidians and Bottiæans came
up and beat him out of it, with the loss of many of his soldiers.

On the return of the Peloponnesians from Attica the Spartans themselves and the nearest of the Periœci at once set
out for Pylos, the other Lacedæmonians following more slowly
as they had just come in from another campaign. Word was

also sent round Peloponnese to come up as quickly as possible to Pylos; while the sixty Peloponnesian ships were sent for from Corcyra and being dragged by their crews across the isthmus of Leucas, passed unperceived by the Athenian squadron at Zacynthus, and reached Pylos, where the land forces had arrived before them. Before the Peloponnesian fleet sailed in, Demosthenes found time to send out unobserved two ships to inform Eurymedon and the Athenians on board the fleet at Zacynthus of the danger of Pylos and to summon them to his assistance. While the ships hastened on their voyage in obedience to the orders of Demosthenes, the Lacedæmonians prepared to assault the fort by land and sea, hoping to capture with ease a work constructed in haste, and held by a feeble garrison. Meanwhile, as they expected the Athenian ships to arrive from Zacynthus, they intended, if they failed to take the place before, to block up the entrance of the harbour to prevent their being able to anchor inside it. For the island of Sphacteria, stretching along in a line close in front of the harbour, at once makes it safe and narrows its entrances, leaving a passage for two ships on the side nearest Pylos and the Athenian fortifications, and for eight or nine on that next the rest of the mainland: for the rest, the island was entirely covered with wood, and without paths through not being inhabited, and about one mile and five furlongs in length. The inlets the Lacedæmonians meant to close with a line of ships placed close together, with their prows turned towards the sea, and, meanwhile, fearing that the enemy might make use of the island to operate against them, carried over some heavy infantry thither, stationing others along the coast. By this means the island and the continent would be alike hostile to the Athenians, as they would be unable to land on either; and the shore of Pylos itself outside the inlet towards the open sea having no harbour, and, therefore, presenting no point which they could use as a base to relieve their countrymen, they, the Lacedæmonians, without sea-fight or risk would in all probability become masters of the place, occupied, as it had been on the spur of the moment, and unfurnished with provisions. This being determined, they carried over to the island the heavy infantry, drafted by lot from all the companies. Some others had crossed over before in relief parties, but these last who were left there were four hundred and twenty in number, with their Helot attendants, commanded by Epitadas, son of Molobrus.

Meanwhile Demosthenes, seeing the Lacedæmonians about to attack him by sea and land at once, himself was not idle. He drew up under the fortification and enclosed in a stockade the galleys remaining to him of those which had been left him, arming the sailors taken out of them with poor shields made most of them of osier, it being impossible to procure arms in such a desert place, and even these having been obtained from a thirty-oared Messenian privateer and a boat belonging to some Messenians who happened to have come to them. Among these Messenians were forty heavy infantry, whom he made use of with the rest. Posting most of his men, unarmed and armed, upon the best fortified and strong points of the place towards the interior, with orders to repel any attack of the land forces, he picked sixty heavy infantry and a few archers from his whole force, and with these went outside the wall down to the sea, where he thought that the enemy would most likely attempt to land. Although the ground was difficult and rocky, looking towards the open sea, the fact that this was the weakest part of the wall would, he thought, encourage their ardour, as the Athenians, confident in their naval superiority, had here paid little attention to their defences, and the enemy if he could force a landing might feel secure of taking the place. At this point, accordingly, going down to the water's edge, he posted his heavy infantry to prevent, if possible, a landing, and encouraged them in the following terms:—

'Soldiers and comrades in this adventure, I hope that none of you in our present strait will think to show his wit by exactly calculating all the perils that encompass us, but that you will rather hasten to close with the enemy, without staying to count the odds, seeing in this your best chance of safety. In emergencies like ours calculation is out of place; the sooner the danger is faced the better. To my mind also most of the chances are for us, if we will only stand fast and not throw away our advantages, overawed by the numbers of the enemy. One of the points in our favour is the awkwardness of the landing. This, however, only helps us if we stand our ground. If we give way it will be practicable enough, in spite of its

natural difficulty, without a defender; and the enemy will
instantly become more formidable from the difficulty he will
have in retreating, supposing that we succeed in repulsing
him, which we shall find it easier to do, while he is on board
his ships, than after he has landed and meets us on equal
terms. As to his numbers, these need not too much alarm you.
Large as they may be he can only engage in small detachments, from the impossibility of bringing to. Besides, the
numerical superiority that we have to meet is not that of an
army on land with everything else equal, but of troops on
board ship, upon an element where many favourable accidents
are required to act with effect. I therefore consider that his
difficulties may be fairly set against our numerical deficiencies,
and at the same time I charge you, as Athenians who know
by experience what landing from ships on a hostile territory
means, and how impossible it is to drive back an enemy determined enough to stand his ground and not to be frightened
away by the surf and the terrors of the ships sailing in, to
stand fast in the present emergency, beat back the enemy at
the water's edge, and save yourselves and the place.'

Thus encouraged by Demosthenes, the Athenians felt more
confident, and went down to meet the enemy, posting themselves along the edge of the sea. The Lacedæmonians now put
themselves in movement and simultaneously assaulted the
fortification with their land forces and with their ships, forty-
three in number, under their admiral, Thrasymelidas, son of
Cratesicles, a Spartan, who made his attack just where Demosthenes expected. The Athenians had thus to defend themselves
on both sides, from the land and from the sea; the enemy
rowing up in small detachments, the one relieving the other—
it being impossible for many to bring to at once—and showing
great ardour and cheering each other on, in the endeavour to
force a passage and to take the fortification. He who most
distinguished himself was Brasidas. Captain of a galley, and
seeing that the captains and steersmen, impressed by the
difficulty of the position, hung back even where a landing
might have seemed possible, for fear of wrecking their vessels,
he shouted out to them, that they must never allow the enemy
to fortify himself in their country for the sake of saving
timber, but must shiver their vessels and force a landing; and

bade the allies, instead of hesitating in such a moment to sacrifice their ships for Lacedæmon in return for her many benefits,
to run them boldly aground, land in one way or another, and
make themselves masters of the place and its garrison.

Not content with this exhortation, he forced his own steers-
man to run his ship ashore, and stepping on to the gangway,
was endeavouring to land, when he was cut down by the
Athenians, and after receiving many wounds fainted away.
Falling into the bows, his shield slipped off his arm into the
sea, and being thrown ashore was picked up by the Athenians,
and afterwards used for the trophy which they set up for this
attack. The rest also did their best, but were not able to land,
owing to the difficulty of the ground and the unflinching
tenacity of the Athenians. It was a strange reversal of the
order of things for Athenians to be fighting from the land,
and from Laconian land too, against Lacedæmonians coming
from the sea; while Lacedæmonians were trying to land from
shipboard in their own country, now become hostile, to attack
Athenians, although the former were chiefly famous at the
time as an inland people and superior by land, the latter as a
maritime people with a navy that had no equal.

After continuing their attacks during that day and most
of the next, the Peloponnesians desisted, and the day after
sent some of their ships to Asine for timber to make engines,
hoping to take by their aid, in spite of its height, the wall
opposite the harbour, where the landing was easiest. At this
moment the Athenian fleet from Zacynthus arrived, now numbering fifty sail, having been reinforced by some of the ships
on guard at Naupactus and by four Chian vessels. Seeing the
coast and the island both crowded with heavy infantry, and
the hostile ships in harbour showing no signs of sailing out,
at a loss where to anchor, they sailed for the moment to the
desert island of Prote, not far off, where they passed the night.
The next day they got under weigh in readiness to engage in
the open sea if the enemy chose to put out to meet them,
being determined in the event of his not doing so to sail in
and attack him. The Lacedæmonians did not put out to sea,
and having omitted to close the inlets as they had intended
remained quiet on shore, engaged in manning their ships and

getting ready, in the case of any one sailing in, to fight in the
harbour, which is a fairly large one.

Perceiving this, the Athenians advanced against them by
each inlet, and falling on the enemy's fleet, most of which
was by this time afloat and in line, at once put it to flight,
and giving chase as far as the short distance allowed, disabled
a good many vessels, and took five, one with its crew on
board; dashing in at the rest that had taken refuge on shore,
and battering some that were still being manned, before they
could put out, and lashing on to their own ships and towing
off empty others whose crews had fled. At this sight the
Lacedæmonians, maddened by a disaster which cut off their
men on the island, rushed to the rescue, and going into the
sea with their heavy armour, laid hold of the ships and tried
to drag them back, each man thinking that success depended
on his individual exertions. Great was the mêlée, and quite
in contradiction to the naval tactics usual to the two combatants; the Lacedæmonians in their excitement and dismay
being actually engaged in a sea-fight on land, while the victorious Athenians, in their eagerness to push their success as
far as possible, were carrying on a land-fight from their ships.
After great exertions and numerous wounds on both sides they
separated, the Lacedæmonians saving their empty ships, except those first taken; and both parties returning to their
camp, the Athenians set up a trophy, gave back the dead,
secured the wrecks, and at once began to cruise round and
jealously watch the island, with its intercepted garrison, while
the Peloponnesians on the mainland, whose contingents had
now all come up, stayed where they were before Pylos.

When the news of what had happened at Pylos reached
Sparta, the disaster was thought so serious that the Lacedæmonians resolved that the authorities should go down to
the camp, and decide on the spot what was best to be done.
There seeing that it was impossible to help their men, and
not wishing to risk their being reduced by hunger or overpowered by numbers, they determined, with the consent of
the Athenian generals, to conclude an armistice at Pylos and
send envoys to Athens to obtain a convention, and to endeavour to get back their men as quickly as possible.

The generals accepting their offers, an armistice was concluded upon the terms following:—

That the Lacedæmonians should bring to Pylos and deliver up to the Athenians the ships that had fought in the late engagement, and all in Laconia that were vessels of war, and should make no attack on the fortification either by land or by sea.

That the Athenians should allow the Lacedæmonians on the mainland to send to the men in the island a certain fixed quantity of corn ready kneaded, that is to say, two quarts of barley meal, one pint of wine, and a piece of meat for each man, and half the same quantity for a servant.

That this allowance should be sent in under the eyes of the Athenians, and that no boat should sail to the island except openly.

That the Athenians should continue to guard the island the same as before, without however landing upon it, and should refrain from attacking the Peloponnesian troops either by land or by sea.

That if either party should infringe any of these terms in the slightest particular, the armistice should be at once void.

That the armistice should hold good until the return of the Lacedæmonian envoys from Athens—the Athenians sending them thither in a galley and bringing them back again—and upon the arrival of the envoys should be at an end, and the ships be restored by the Athenians in the same state as they received them.

Such were the terms of the armistice, and the ships were delivered over to the number of sixty, and the envoys sent off accordingly. Arrived at Athens they spoke as follows:—

'Athenians, the Lacedæmonians sent us to try to find some way of settling the affair of our men on the island, that shall be at once satisfactory to your interests, and as consistent with our dignity in our misfortune as circumstances permit. We can venture to speak at some length without any departure from the habit of our country. Men of few words where many are not wanted, we can be less brief when there is a matter of importance to be illustrated and an end to be served by its illustration. Meanwhile we beg you to take what we may say, not in a hostile spirit, nor as if we thought you ignorant and wished to lecture you, but rather as a suggestion on the best course to be taken, addressed to intelligent judges. You can now, if you choose, employ your present success to advantage, so as to keep what you have got and gain honour and reputation besides, and you can avoid the mistake of those who meet with an extraordinary piece of good fortune, and are led on by hope to grasp continually at something further, through having already succeeded without expecting it. While those who have known most vicissitudes of good and bad, have also justly least faith in their prosperity; and to teach your city and ours this lesson experience has not been wanting.

'To be convinced of this you have only to look at our present misfortune. What power in Hellas stood higher than we did? and yet we are come to you, although we formerly thought ourselves more able to grant what we are now here to ask. Nevertheless, we have not been brought to this by any decay in our power, or through having our heads turned by aggrandisement; no, our resources are what they have always been, and our error has been an error of judgment, to which all are equally liable. Accordingly the prosperity which your city now enjoys, and the accession that it has lately received, must not make you fancy that fortune will be always with you. Indeed sensible men are prudent enough to treat their gains as precarious, just as they would also keep a clear head in adversity, and think that war, so far from staying within the limit to which a combatant may wish to confine it, will run the course that its chances prescribe; and thus, not being puffed up by confidence in military success, they are less likely to come to grief, and most ready to make peace, if they can, while their fortune lasts. This, Athenians, you have a good opportunity to do now with us, and thus to escape the possible disasters which may follow upon your refusal, and the consequent imputation of having owed to accident even your present advantages, when you might have left behind you a reputation for power and wisdom which nothing could endanger.

'The Lacedæmonians accordingly invite you to make a treaty and to end the war, and offer peace and alliance and the most friendly and intimate relations in every way and on every occasion between us; and in return ask for the men on the island, thinking it better for both parties not to stand out to

the end, on the chance of some favourable accident enabling
the men to force their way out, or of their being compelled
to succumb under the pressure of blockade. Indeed if great
enmities are ever to be really settled, we think it will be, not
by the system of revenge and military success, and by forcing
an opponent to swear to a treaty to his disadvantage, but when
the more fortunate combatant waives these his privileges, to
be guided by gentler feelings, conquers his rival in generosity,
and accords peace on more moderate conditions than he expected. From that moment, instead of the debt of revenge
which violence must entail, his adversary owes a debt of generosity to be paid in kind, and is inclined by honour to stand
to his agreement. And men oftener act in this manner towards
their greatest enemies than where the quarrel is of less importance; they are also by nature as glad to give way to those
who first yield to them, as they are apt to be provoked by
arrogance to risks condemned by their own judgment.

'To apply this to ourselves: if peace was ever desirable for
both parties, it is surely so at the present moment, before anything irremediable befall us and force us to hate you eternally,
personally as well as politically, and you to miss the advantages that we now offer you. While the issue is still in
doubt, and you have reputation and our friendship in prospect, and we the compromise of our misfortune before anything fatal occur, let us be reconciled, and for ourselves choose
peace instead of war, and grant to the rest of the Hellenes a
remission from their sufferings, for which be sure they will
think they have chiefly you to thank. The war that they labour
under they know not which began, but the peace that con-
cludes it, as it depends on your decision, will by their gratitude
be laid to your door. By such a decision you can become firm
friends with the Lacedæmonians at their own invitation, which
you do not force from them, but oblige them by accepting.
And from this friendship consider the advantages that are
likely to follow: when Attica and Sparta are at one, the rest
of Hellas, be sure, will remain in respectful inferiority before
its heads.'

Such were the words of the Lacedæmonians, their idea being that the Athenians, already desirous of a truce and only
kept back by their opposition, would joyfully accept a peace

freely offered, and give back the men. The Athenians, however, having the men on the island, thought that the treaty
would be ready for them whenever they chose to make it, and
grasped at something further. Foremost to encourage them
in this policy was Cleon, son of Cleænetus, a popular leader
of the time and very powerful with the multitude, who persuaded them to answer as follows: First, the men in the island
must surrender themselves and their arms and be brought to
Athens. Next, the Lacedæmonians must restore Nisæa, Pegae,
Trœzen, and Achaia, all places acquired not by arms, but by
the previous convention, under which they had been ceded by
Athens herself at a moment of disaster, when a truce was more
necessary to her than at present. This done they might take
back their men, and make a truce for as long as both parties
might agree.

To this answer the envoys made no reply, but asked that
commissioners might be chosen with whom they might confer
on each point, and quietly talk the matter over and try to
come to some agreement. Hereupon Cleon violently assailed
them, saying that he knew from the first that they had no right
intentions, and that it was clear enough now by their refusing
to speak before the people, and wanting to confer in secret
with a committee of two or three. No! if they meant anything
honest let them say it out before all. The Lacedæmonians,
however, seeing that whatever concessions they might be prepared to make in their misfortune, it was impossible for them
to speak before the multitude and lose credit with their allies
for a negotiation which might after all miscarry, and on the
other hand, that the Athenians would never grant what they
asked upon moderate terms, returned from Athens without
having effected anything.

Their arrival at once put an end to the armistice at Pylos,
and the Lacedæmonians asked back their ships according to
the convention. The Athenians, however, alleged an attack on
the fort in contravention of the truce, and other grievances
seemingly not worth mentioning, and refused to give them
back, insisting upon the clause by which the slightest infringe-
ment made the armistice void. The Lacedæmonians, after
denying the contravension and protesting against their bad
faith in the matter of the ships, went away and earnestly ad-

dressed themselves to the war. Hostilities were now carried on at Pylos upon both sides with vigour. The Athenians cruised round the island all day with two ships going different ways; and by night, except on the seaward side in windy weather, anchored round it with their whole fleet, which having been reinforced by twenty ships from Athens come to aid in the blockade, now numbered seventy sail; while the Peloponnesians remained encamped on the continent, making attacks on the fort, and on the look-out for any opportunity which might offer itself for the deliverance of their men.

Meanwhile the Syracusans and their allies in Sicily had brought up to the squadron guarding Messina the reinforcement which we left them preparing, and carried on the war from thence, incited chiefly by the Locrians from hatred of the Rhegians, whose territory they had invaded with all their forces. The Syracusans also wished to try their fortune at sea, seeing that the Athenians had only a few ships actually at Rhegium, and hearing that the main fleet destined to join them was engaged in blockading the island. A naval victory, they thought, would enable them to blockade Rhegium by sea and land, and easily to reduce it; a success which would at once place their affairs upon a solid basis, the promontory of Rhegium in Italy and Messina in Sicily being so near each other that it would be impossible for the Athenians to cruise against them and command the strait. The strait in question consists of the sea between Rhegium and Messina, at the point where Sicily approaches nearest to the continent, and is the Charybdis through which the story makes Ulysses sail; and the narrowness of the passage and the strength of the current that pours in from the vast Tyrrhenian and Sicilian mains, have rightly given it a bad reputation.

In this strait the Syracusans and their allies were compelled to engage, late in the day, about the passage of a boat, putting out with rather more than thirty ships against sixteen Athenian and eight Rhegian vessels. Defeated by the Athenians they hastily set off, each for himself, to their own stations at Messina and Rhegium, with the loss of one ship; night coming on before the battle was finished. After this the Locrians retired from the Rhegian territory, and the ships of the Syracusans and their allies united and came to anchor at Cape Pelorus, in

the territory of Messina, where their land forces joined them.
Here the Athenians and Rhegians sailed up, and seeing the
ships unmanned, made an attack, in which they in their turn
lost one vessel, which was caught by a grappling iron, the crew
saving themselves by swimming. After this the Syracusans got
on board their ships, and while they were being towed along
shore to Messina, were again attacked by the Athenians, but
suddenly got out to sea and became the assailants, and caused
them to lose another vessel. After thus holding their own in
the voyage along shore and in the engagement as above
described, the Syracusans sailed on into the harbour of
Messina.

Meanwhile the Athenians, having received warning that
Camarina was about to be betrayed to the Syracusans by
Archias and his party, sailed thither; and the Messinese took
this opportunity to attack by sea and land with all their
forces their Chalcidian neighbour, Naxos. The first day they
forced the Naxians to keep their walls, and laid waste their
country; the next they sailed round with their ships, and laid
waste their land on the river Akesines, while their land forces
menaced the city. Meanwhile the Sicels came down from the
high country in great numbers, to aid against the Messinese;
and the Naxians, elated at the sight, and animated by a belief
that the Leontines and their other Hellenic allies were coming
to their support, suddenly sallied out from the town, and attacked and routed the Messinese, killing more than a thousand
of them; while the remainder suffered severely in their retreat
home, being attacked by the barbarians on the road, and most
of them cut off. The ships put in to Messina, and afterwards
dispersed for their different homes. The Leontines and their
allies, with the Athenians, upon this at once turned their arms
against the now weakened Messina, and attacked, the
Athenians with their ships on the side of the harbour, and the
land forces on that of the town. The Messinese, however, sallying out with Demoteles and some Locrians who had been left
to garrison the city after the disaster, suddenly attacked and
routed most of the Leontine army, killing a great number;
upon seeing which the Athenians landed from their ships, and
falling on the Messinese in disorder chased them back into the
town, and setting up a trophy retired to Rhegium. After this

the Hellenes in Sicily continued to make war on each other by land, without the Athenians.

Meanwhile the Athenians at Pylos were still besieging the Lacedæmonians in the island, the Peloponnesian forces on the continent remaining where they were. The blockade was very laborious for the Athenians from want of food and water; there was no spring except one in the citadel of Pylos itself, and that not a large one, and most of them were obliged to grub up the shingle on the sea beach and drink such water as they could find. They also suffered from want of room, being encamped in a narrow space; and as there was no anchorage for the ships, some took their meals on shore in their turn, while the others were anchored out at sea. But their greatest discouragement arose from the unexpectedly long time which it took to reduce a body of men shut up in a desert island, with only brackish water to drink, a matter which they had imagined would take them only a few days. The fact was, that the Lacedæmonians had made advertisement for volunteers to carry into the island ground corn, wine, cheese, and any other food useful in a siege; high prices being offered, and freedom promised to any of the Helots who should succeed in doing so. The Helots accordingly were most forward to engage in this risky traffic, putting off from this or that part of Peloponnese, and running in by night on the seaward side of the island. They were best pleased, however, when they could catch a wind to carry them in. It was more easy to elude the look-out of the galleys, when it blew from the seaward, as it became impossible for them to anchor round the island; while the Helots had their boats rated at their value in money, and ran them ashore, without caring how they landed, being sure to find the soldiers waiting for them at the landing-places. But all who risked it in fair weather were taken. Divers also swam in under water from the harbour, dragging by a cord in skins poppy-seed mixed with honey, and bruised linseed; these at first escaped notice, but afterwards a look-out was kept for them. In short, both sides tried every possible contrivance, the one to throw in provisions, and the other to prevent their introduction.

At Athens, meanwhile, the news that the army was in great distress, and that corn found its way in to the men in the

island caused no small perplexity; and the Athenians began
to fear that winter might come on and find them still engaged
in the blockade. They saw that the convoying of provisions
round Peloponnese would be then impossible. The country
offered no resources in itself, and even in summer they could
not send round enough. The blockade of a place without harbours could no longer be kept up; and the men would either
escape by the siege being abandoned, or would watch for bad
weather and sail out in the boats that brought in their corn.
What caused still more alarm was the attitude of the Lacedæmonians, who must, it was thought by the Athenians, feel
themselves on strong ground not to send them any more envoys; and they began to repent having rejected the treaty.
Cleon, perceiving the disfavour with which he was regarded
for having stood in the way of the convention, now said that
their informants did not speak the truth; and upon the messengers recommending them, if they did not believe them, to
send some commissioners to see, Cleon himself and Theagenes
were chosen by the Athenians as commissioners. Aware that
he would now be obliged either to say what had been already
said by the men whom he was slandering, or be proved a liar
if he said the contrary, he told the Athenians, whom he saw
to be not altogether disinclined for a fresh expedition, that
instead of sending commissioners and wasting their time and
opportunities, if they believed what was told them, they ought
to sail against the men. And pointing at Nicias, son of Niceratus, then general, whom he hated, he tauntingly said that it
would be easy, if they had men for generals, to sail with a
force and take those in the island, and that if he had himself
been in command, he would have done it.

Nicias, seeing the Athenians murmuring against Cleon for
not sailing now if it seemed to him so easy, and further seeing
himself the object of attack, told him that for all that the
generals cared, he might take what force he chose and make
the attempt. At first Cleon fancied that this resignation was
merely a figure of speech, and was ready to go, but finding
that it was seriously meant, he drew back, and said that Nicias,
not he, was general, being now frightened, and having never
supposed that Nicias would go so far as to retire in his favour.
Nicias, however, repeated his offer, and resigned the com-

mand against Pylos, and called the Athenians to witness that
he did so. And as the multitude is wont to do, the more Cleon
shrank from the expedition and tried to back out of what
he had said, the more they encouraged Nicias to hand
over his command, and clamoured at Cleon to go. At last, not
knowing how to get out of his words, he undertook the expedition, and came forward and said that he was not afraid of
the Lacedæmonians, but would sail without taking any one
from the city with him, except the Lemnians and Imbrians
that were at Athens, with some targeteers that had come up
from Ænus, and four hundred archers from other quarters.
With these and the soldiers at Pylos, he would within twenty
days either bring the Lacedæmonians alive, or kill them on
the spot. The Athenians could not help laughing at his fatuity,
while sensible men comforted themselves with the reflexion
that they must gain in either circumstance; either they would
be rid of Cleon, which they rather hoped, or if disappointed
in this expectation, would reduce the Lacedæmonians.

After he had settled everything in the assembly, and the
Athenians had voted him the command of the expedition, he
chose as his colleague Demosthenes, one of the generals at
Pylos, and pushed forward the preparations for his voyage.
His choice fell upon Demosthenes because he heard that he
was contemplating a descent on the island; the soldiers distressed by the difficulties of the position, and rather besieged
than besiegers, being eager to fight it out, while the firing of
the island had increased the confidence of the general. He had
been at first afraid, because the island having never been inhabited was almost entirely covered with wood and without
paths, thinking this to be in the enemy's favour, as he might
land with a large force, and yet might suffer loss by an attack
from an unseen position. The mistakes and forces of the enemy
the wood would in a great measure conceal from him, while
every blunder of his own troops would be at once detected,
and they would be thus able to fall upon him unexpectedly
just where they pleased, the attack being always in their
power. If, on the other hand, he should force them to engage
in the thicket, the smaller number who knew the country
would, he thought, have the advantage over the larger who
were ignorant of it, while his own army might be cut off im-

perceptibly, in spite of its numbers, as the men would not be able to see where to succour each other.

The Ætolian disaster, which had been mainly caused by the wood, had not a little to do with these reflexions. Meanwhile, one of the soldiers who were compelled by want of room to land on the extremities of the island and take their dinners, with outposts fixed to prevent a surprise, set fire to a little of the wood without meaning to do so; and as it came on to blow soon afterwards, almost the whole was consumed before they were aware of it. Demosthenes was now able for the first time to see how numerous the Lacedæmonians really were, having up to this moment been under the impression that they took in provisions for a smaller number; he also saw that the Athenians thought success important and were anxious about it, and that it was now easier to land on the island, and accordingly got ready for the attempt, sent for troops from the allies in the neighbourhood, and pushed forward his other preparations. At this moment Cleon arrived at Pylos with the troops which he had asked for, having sent on word to say that he was coming. The first step taken by the two generals after their meeting was to send a herald to the camp on the mainland, to ask if they were disposed to avoid all risk and to order the men on the island to surrender themselves and their arms, to be kept in gentle custody until some general convention should be concluded.

On the rejection of this proposition the generals let one day pass, and the next embarking all their heavy infantry on board a few ships, put out by night, and a little before dawn landed on both sides of the island from the open sea and from the harbour, being about eight hundred strong, and advanced with a run against the first post in the island. The enemy had distributed his force as follows:—In this first post there were about thirty heavy infantry; the centre and most level part, where the water was, was held by the main body, and by Epitadas their commander; while a small party guarded the very end of the island, towards Pylos, which was precipitous on the sea-side and very difficult to attack from the land, and where there was also a sort of old fort of stones rudely put together, which they thought might be useful to them, in case they should be forced to retreat. Such was their disposition.

The advanced post thus attacked by the Athenians was at once put to the sword, the men being scarcely out of bed and still arming, the landing having taken them by surprise, as they fancied the ships were only sailing as usual to their stations for the night. As soon as day broke, the rest of the army landed, that is to say, all the crews of rather more than seventy ships, except the lowest rank of oars, with the arms they carried, eight hundred archers, and as many targeteers, the Messenian reinforcements, and all the other troops on duty round Pylos, except the garrison on the fort. The tactics of Demosthenes had divided them into companies of two hundred, more or less, and made them occupy the highest points in order to paralyse the enemy by surrounding him on every side and thus leaving him without any tangible adversary, exposed to the cross-fire of their host; plied by those in his rear if he attacked in front, and by those on one flank if he moved against those on the other. In short, wherever he went he would have the assailants behind him, and these light-armed assailants, the most awkward of all; arrows, darts, stones, and slings making them formidable at a distance, and there being no means of getting at them at close quarters, as they could conquer flying, and the moment their pursuer turned they were upon him. Such was the idea that inspired Demosthenes in his conception of the descent, and presided over its execution.

Meanwhile the main body of the troops in the island (that under Epitadas), seeing their outpost cut off and an army advancing against them, serried their ranks and pressed forward to close with the Athenian heavy infantry in front of them, the light troops being upon their flanks and rear. However, they were not able to engage or to profit by their superior skill, the light troops keeping them in check on either side with their missiles, and the heavy infantry remaining stationary instead of advancing to meet them; and although they routed the light troops wherever they ran up and approached too closely, yet they retreated fighting, being lightly equipped, and easily getting the start in their flight, from the difficult and rugged nature of the ground, in an island hitherto desert, over which the Lacedæmonians could not pursue them with their heavy armour.

After this skirmishing had lasted some little while, the Lacedæmonians became unable to dash out with the same rapidity as before upon the points attacked, and the light troops, finding that they now fought with less vigour, became more confident. They could see with their own eyes that they were many times more numerous than the enemy; they were now more familiar with his aspect and found him less terrible, the result not having justified the apprehensions which they had suffered, when they first landed in slavish dismay at the idea of attacking Lacedæmonians; and accordingly their fear changing to disdain, they now rushed all together with loud shouts upon them, and pelted them with stones, darts, and arrows, whichever came first to hand. The shouting accompanying their onset confounded the Lacedæmonians, unaccustomed to this mode of fighting; dust rose from the newly-burnt wood, and it was impossible to see in front of one with the arrows and stones flying through clouds of dust from the hands of numerous assailants. The Lacedæmonians had now to sustain a rude conflict; their caps would not keep out the arrows, darts had broken off in the armour of the wounded, while they themselves were helpless for offence, being prevented from using their eyes to see what was before them, and unable to hear the words of command for the hubbub raised by the enemy; danger encompassed them on every side, and there was no hope of any means of defence or safety.

At last, after many had been already wounded in the confined space in which they were fighting, they formed in close order and retired on the fort at the end of the island, which was not far off, and to their friends who held it. The moment they gave way, the light troops became bolder and pressed upon them, shouting louder than ever, and killed as many as they came up with in their retreat, but most of the Lacedæmonians made good their escape to the fort, and with the garrison in it ranged themselves all along its whole extent to repulse the enemy wherever it was assailable. The Athenians pursuing, unable to surround and hem them in, owing to the strength of the ground, attacked them in front and tried to storm the position. For a long time, indeed for most of the day, both sides held out against all the torments of the battle, thirst, and sun, the one endeavouring to drive the enemy from the high ground, the other to maintain himself upon it, it being now more easy for the Lacedæmonians to defend themselves than before, as they could not be surrounded upon the flanks.

The struggle began to seem endless, when the commander of the Messenians came to Cleon and Demosthenes, and told them that they were losing their labour: but that if they would give him some archers and light troops to go round on the enemy's rear by a way he would undertake to find, he thought he could force the approach. Upon receiving what he asked for, he started from a point out of sight in order not to be seen by the enemy, and creeping on wherever the precipices of the island permitted, and where the Lacedæmonians, trusting to the strength of the ground, kept no guard, succeeded after the greatest difficulty in getting round without their seeing him, and suddenly appeared on the high ground in their rear, to the dismay of the surprised enemy and the still greater joy of his expectant friends. The Lacedæmonians thus placed between two fires, and in the same dilemma, to compare small things with great, as at Thermopylæ, where the defenders were cut off through the Persians getting round by the path, being now attacked in front and behind, began to give way, and overcome by the odds against them and exhausted from want of food, retreated.

The Athenians were already masters of the approaches when Cleon and Demosthenes perceiving that, if the enemy gave way a single step further, they would be destroyed by their soldiery, put a stop to the battle and held their men back; wishing to take the Lacedæmonians alive to Athens, and hoping that their stubbornness might relax on hearing the offer of terms, and that they might surrender and yield to the present overwhelming danger. Proclamation was accordingly made, to know if they would surrender themselves and their arms to the Athenians to be dealt with at their discretion.

The Lacedæmonians hearing this offer, most of them low·· ered their shields and waved their hands to show that they accepted it. Hostilities now ceased, and a parley was held between Cleon and Demosthenes and Styphon, son of Pharax, on the other side; since Epitadas, the first of the previous commanders, had been killed, and Hippagretas, the next in command, left for dead among the slain, though still alive, and thus the command had devolved upon Styphon according to the law, in case of anything happening to his superiors. Styphon and his companions said they wished to send a herald to the Lacedæmonians on the mainland, to know what they were to do. The Athenians would not let any of them go, but themselves called for heralds from the mainland, and after questions had been carried backwards and forwards two or three times, the last man that passed over from the Lace-dæmonians on the continent brought this message: 'The Lace-dæmonians bid you to decide for yourselves so long as you do nothing dishonourable;' upon which after consulting to-gether they surrendered themselves and their arms. The Athe-nians, after guarding them that day and night, the next morning set up a trophy in the island, and got ready to sail, giving their prisoners in batches to be guarded by the captains of the galleys; and the Lacedæmonians sent a herald and took up their dead. The number of the killed and prisoners taken in the island was as follows: four hundred and twenty heavy infantry had passed over; three hundred all but eight were taken alive to Athens; the rest were killed. About a hundred and twenty of the prisoners were Spartans. The Athenian loss was small, the battle not having been fought at close quarters.

The blockade in all, counting from the fight at sea to the battle in the island, had lasted seventy-two days. For twenty of these, during the absence of the envoys sent to treat for peace, the men had provisions given them, for the rest they were fed by the smugglers. Corn and other victual was found in the island; the commander Epitadas having kept the men upon half rations. The Athenians and Peloponnesians now each withdrew their forces from Pylos, and went home, and crazy as Cleon's promise was, he fulfilled it, by bringing the men to Athens within the twenty days as he had pledged him-self to do.

Nothing that happened in the war surprised the Hellenes so much as this. It was the opinion that no force or famine could make the Lacedæmonians give up their arms, but that they would fight on as they could, and die with them in their hands: indeed people could scarcely believe that those who had surrendered were of the same stuff as the fallen; and an

Athenian ally, who some time after insultingly asked one of
the prisoners from the island if those that had fallen were
men of honour, received for answer that the *atraktos*—that
is, the arrow—would be worth a great deal if it could tell men
of honour from the rest; in allusion to the fact that the killed
were those whom the stones and the arrows happened to hit.

Upon the arrival of the men the Athenians determined to
keep them in prison until the peace, and if the Peloponnesians
invaded their country in the interval, to bring them out and
put them to death. Meanwhile the defence of Pylos was not
forgotten; the Messenians from Naupactus sent to their old
country, to which Pylos formerly belonged, some of the like-
liest of their number, and began a series of incursions into
Laconia, which their common dialect rendered most destruc-
tive. The Lacedæmonians, hitherto without experience of incursions or a warfare of the kind, finding the Helots deserting,
and fearing the march of revolution in their country, began to
be seriously uneasy, and in spite of their unwillingness to
betray this to the Athenians began to send envoys to Athens,
and tried to recover Pylos and the prisoners. The Athenians,
however, kept grasping at more, and dismissed envoy after
envoy without their having effected anything. Such was the
history of the affair of Pylos.

CHAPTER XIII

SEVENTH AND EIGHTH YEARS OF THE WAR—END OF CORCY-
RÆAN REVOLUTION—PEACE OF GELA—CAPTURE OF NISÆA

B.C. 425: *Expedition against Corinth—Corinthians routed—Massacre
by Corcyræans*—B.C. 424: *Nicias commands expedition against
Cythera—Lacedæmonians in despair—Capture of Thyrea—Speech
of Hemocrates at Congress of Gela—Peace in Sicily—Betrayal of
Megara—Nisæa capitulates—Brasidas intervenes—Brasidas and
Athenians withdraw—Oligarchical revolution in Megara.*

THE same summer, directly after these events, the Athenians
made an expedition against the territory of Corinth with
eighty ships and two thousand Athenian heavy infantry, and
two hundred cavalry on board horse transports, accompanied
by the Milesians, Andrians, and Carystians from the allies,
under the command of Nicias, son of Niceratus, with two

colleagues. Putting out to sea they made land at daybreak between Chersonese and Rheitus, at the beach of the country underneath the Solygian hill, upon which the Dorians in old times established themselves and carried on war against the Æolian inhabitants of Corinth, and where a village now stands called Solygia. The beach where the fleet came to is about a mile and a half from the village, seven miles from Corinth, and two and a quarter from the Isthmus. The Corinthians had heard from Argos of the coming of the Athenian armament, and had all come up to the Isthmus long before, with the exception of those who lived beyond it, and also of five hundred who were away in garrison in Ambracia and Leucadia; and they were there in full force watching for the Athenians to land. These last, however, gave them the slip by coming in the dark; and being informed by signals of the fact, the Corinthians left half their number at Cenchreæ, in case the Athenians should go against Crommyon, and marched in all haste to the rescue.

Battus, one of the two generals present at the action, went with a company to defend the village of Solygia, which was unfortified; Lycophron remaining to give battle with the rest. The Corinthians first attacked the right wing of the Athenians, which had just landed in front of Chersonese, and afterwards the rest of the army. The battle was an obstinate one, and fought throughout hand to hand. The right wing of the Athenians and Carystians, who had been placed at the end of the line, received and with some difficulty repulsed the Corinthians, who thereupon retreated to a wall upon the rising ground behind, and throwing down the stones upon them, came on again singing the pæan, and being received by the Athenians, were again engaged at close quarters. At this moment a Corinthian company having come to the relief of the left wing, routed and pursued the Athenian right to the sea, whence they were in their turn driven back by the Athenians and Carystians from the ships. Meanwhile the rest of the army on either side fought on tenaciously, especially the right wing of the Corinthians, where Lycophron sustained the attack of the Athenian left, which it was feared might attempt the village of Solygia.

After holding on for a long while without either giving way, the Athenians aided by their horse, of which the enemy had none, at length routed the Corinthians, who retired to the hill and halting remained quiet there, without coming down again. It was in this rout of the right wing that they had the most killed, Lycophron their general being among the number. The rest of the army, broken and put to flight in this way without being seriously pursued or hurried, retired to the high ground and there took up its position. The Athenians, finding that the enemy no longer offered to engage them, stripped his dead and took up their own and immediately set up a trophy. Meanwhile, the half of the Corinthians left at Cenchreæ to guard against the Athenians sailing on Crommyon, although unable to see the battle for Mount Oneion, found out what was going on by the dust, and hurried up to the rescue; as did also the older Corinthians from the town, upon discovering what had occurred. The Athenians seeing them all coming against them, and thinking that they were reinforcements arriving from the neighbouring Peloponnesians, withdrew in haste to their ships with their spoils and their own dead, except two that they left behind, not being able to find them, and going on board crossed over to the islands opposite, and from thence sent a herald, and took up under truce the bodies which they had left behind. Two hundred and twelve Corinthians fell in the battle, and rather less than fifty Athenians.

Weighing from the islands, the Athenians sailed the same day to Crommyon in the Corinthian territory, about thirteen miles from the city, and coming to anchor laid waste the country, and passed the night there. The next day, after first coasting along to the territory of Epidaurus and making a descent there, they came to Methana between Epidaurus and Trœzen, and drew a wall across and fortified the isthmus of the peninsula, and left a post there from which incursions were henceforth made upon the country of Trœzen, Haliœ, and Epidaurus. After walling off this spot the fleet sailed off home.

While these events were going on, Eurymedon and Soph- ocles had put to sea with the Athenian fleet from Pylos on their way to Sicily, and arriving at Corcyra, joined the townsmen in an expedition against the party established on Mount Istone, who had crossed over, as I have mentioned after the revolution, and become masters of the country, to the great hurt of the inhabitants. Their stronghold having been taken by an attack, the garrison took refuge in a body upon some high ground and there capitulated, agreeing to give up their mercenary auxiliaries, lay down their arms, and commit themselves to the discretion of the Athenian people. The generals carried them across under truce to the island of Ptychia, to be kept in custody until they could be sent to Athens, upon the understanding that if any were caught running away, all would lose the benefit of the treaty. Meanwhile the leaders of the Corcyræan commons, afraid that the Athenians might spare the lives of the prisoners, had recourse to the following stratagem. They gained over some few men on the island by secretly sending friends with instructions to provide them with a boat, and to tell them, as if for their own sakes, that they had best escape as quickly as possible, as the Athenian generals were going to give them up to the Corcyræan people.

These representations succeeding, it was so arranged that the men were caught sailing out in the boat that was provided, and the treaty became void accordingly, and the whole body were given up to the Corcyræans. For this result the Athenian generals were in a great measure responsible; their evident disinclination to sail for Sicily, and thus to leave to others the honour of conducting the men to Athens, encouraged the intriguers in their design and seemed to affirm the truth of their representations. The prisoners thus handed over were shut up by the Corcyræans in a large building, and afterwards taken out by twenties and led past two lines of heavy infantry, one on each side, being bound together, and beaten and stabbed by the men in the lines whenever any saw pass a personal enemy; while men carrying whips went by their side and hastened on the road those that walked too slowly.

As many as sixty men were taken out and killed in this way without the knowledge of their friends in the building, who fancied they were merely being moved from one prison to another. At last, however, some one opened their eyes to the truth, upon which they called upon the Athenians to kill them themselves, if such was their pleasure, and refused any longer to go out of the building, and said they would do all they could to prevent any one coming in. The Corcyræans, not liking themselves to force a passage by the doors, got up on the top of the building, and breaking through the roof, threw down the tiles and let fly arrows at them, from which the prisoners sheltered themselves as well as they could. Most of their number, meanwhile, were engaged in dispatching themselves by thrusting into their throats the arrows shot by the enemy, and hanging themselves with the cords taken from some beds, that happened to be there, and with strips made from their clothing; adopting, in short, every possible means of self-destruction, and also falling victims to the missiles of their enemies on the roof. Night came on while these horrors were enacting, and most of it had passed before they were concluded. When it was day the Corcyræans threw them in layers upon waggons and carried them out of the city. All the women taken in the stronghold were sold as slaves. In this way the Corcyræans of the mountain were destroyed by the commons; and so after terrible excesses the party strife came to an end, at least as far as the period of this war is concerned, for of one party there was practically nothing left. Meanwhile the Athenians sailed off to Sicily, their primary destination, and carried on the war with their allies there.

At the close of the summer, the Athenians at Naupactus and the Acarnanians made an expedition against Anactorium, the Corinthian town lying at the mouth of the Ambracian gulf, and took it by treachery; and the Acarnanians themselves sending settlers from all parts of Acarnania occupied the place.

Summer was now over. During the winter ensuing Aristides, son of Archippus, one of the commanders of the Athenian ships sent to collect money from the allies, arrested at Eion on the Strymon Artaphernes, a Persian, on his way from the king to Lacedæmon. He was conducted to Athens, where the Athenians got his despatches translated from the Assyrian character and read them. With numerous references to other subjects, they in substance told the Lacedæmonians that the king did not know what they wanted, as of the many ambassadors they had sent him no two ever told the same story; if however they were prepared to speak plainly they might send him some envoys with this Persian. The Athenians afterwards sent back Artaphernes in a galley to Ephesus, and ambassadors with him, who heard there of the death of King Artaxerxes, son of Xerxes, which took place about that time, and so returned home.

The same winter the Chians pulled down their new wall at the command of the Athenians, who suspected them of meditating an insurrection, after first however obtaining pledges from the Athenians, and security as far as this was possible for their continuing to treat them as before. Thus the winter ended, and with it ended the seventh year of this war of which Thucydides is the historian.

In the first days of the next summer there was an eclipse of the sun at the time of new moon, and in the early part of the same month an earthquake. Meanwhile, the Mitylenian and other Lesbian exiles set out, for the most part from the continent, with mercenaries hired in Peloponnese, and others levied on the spot, and took Rhœteum, but restored it without injury on the receipt of two thousand Phocæan staters. After this they marched against Antandrus and took the town by treachery, their plan being to free Antandrus and the rest of the Actæan towns, formerly owned by Mitylene but now held by the Athenians. Once fortified there, they would have every facility for shipbuilding from the vicinity of Ida and the consequent abundance of timber, and plenty of other supplies, and might from this base easily ravage Lesbos, which was not far off, and make themselves masters of the Æolian towns on the continent.

While these were the schemes of the exiles, the Athenians in the same summer made an expedition with sixty ships, two thousand heavy infantry, a few cavalry, and some allied troops from Miletus and other parts, against Cythera, under the command of Nicias, son of Niceratus, Nicostratus, son of Diotrephes, and Autocles, son of Tolmæus. Cythera is an island lying off Laconia, opposite Malea; the inhabitants are Lacedæmonians of the class of the Periœci; and an officer called the Judge of Cythera went over to the place annually from Sparta. A garrison of heavy infantry was also regularly sent there, and great attention paid to the island, as it was the landing-place for the merchantmen from Egypt and Libya, and at the same time secured Laconia from the attacks of privateers from the sea, at the only point where it is assailable, as the whole coast rises abruptly towards the Sicilian and Cretan seas.

Coming to land here with their armament, the Athenians with ten ships and two thousand Milesian heavy infantry took the town of Scandea, on the sea; and with the rest of their forces landing on the side of the island looking towards Malea, went against the lower town of Cythera, where they found all the inhabitants encamped. A battle ensuing, the Cytherians held their ground for some little while, and then turned and fled into the upper town, where they soon afterwards capitulated to Nicias and his colleagues, agreeing to leave their fate to the decision of the Athenians, their lives only being safe. A correspondence had previously been going on between Nicias and certain of the inhabitants, which caused the surrender to be effected more speedily, and upon terms more advantageous, present and future, for the Cytherians; who would otherwise have been expelled by the Athenians on account of their being Lacedæmonians and their island being so near to Laconia. After the capitulation, the Athenians occupied the town of Scandea near the harbour, and appointing a garrison for Cythera, sailed to Asine, Helus, and most of the places on the sea, and making descents and passing the night on shore at such spots as were convenient, continued ravaging the country for about seven days.

The Lacedæmonians seeing the Athenians masters of Cythera, and expecting descents of the kind upon their coasts, nowhere opposed them in force, but sent garrisons here and there through the country, consisting of as many heavy infantry as the points menaced seemed to require, and generally stood very much upon the defensive. After the severe and unexpected blow that had befallen them in the island, the occupation of Pylos and Cythera, and the apparition on every side of a war whose rapidity defied precaution, they lived in constant fear of internal revolution, and now took the unusual step of raising four hundred horse and a force of archers, and became more timid than ever in military matters, finding themselves involved in a maritime struggle, which their organisation had never contemplated, and that against Athenians with whom an enterprise unattempted was always looked upon

as a success sacrificed. Besides this, their late numerous reverses of fortune, coming close one upon another without
any reason, had thoroughly unnerved them, and they were
always afraid of a second disaster like that on the island, and
thus scarcely dared to take the field, but fancied that they
could not stir without a blunder, for being new to the experience of adversity they had lost all confidence in themselves.

Accordingly they now allowed the Athenians to ravage their
seaboard, without making any movement, the garrisons in
whose neighbourhood the descents were made always thinking
their numbers insufficient, and sharing the general feeling.
A single garrison which ventured to resist, near Cotyrta and
Aphrodisia, struck terror by its charge into the scattered mob
of light troops, but retreated, upon being received by the
heavy infantry, with the loss of a few men and some arms,
for which the Athenians set up a trophy, and then sailed off
to Cythera. From thence they sailed round to the Limeran
Epidaurus, ravaged part of the country, and so came to Thyrea
in the Cynurian territory, upon the Argive and Laconian border. This district had been given by its Lacedæmonian owners
to the expelled Æginetans to inhabit, in return for their good
offices at the time of the earthquake and the rising of the
Helots; and also because, although subjects of Athens, they
had always sided with Lacedæmon.

While the Athenians were still at sea, the Æginetans evacuated a fort which they were building upon the coast, and retreated into the upper town where they lived, rather more
than a mile from the sea. One of the Lacedæmonian district
garrisons which was helping them in the work, refused to enter
here with them at their entreaty, thinking it dangerous to shut
themselves up within the wall, and retiring to the high ground
remained quiet, not considering themselves a match for the
enemy. Meanwhile the Athenians landed, and instantly advanced with all their forces and took Thyrea. The town they
burnt, pillaging what was in it; the Æginetans who were not
slain in action they took with them to Athens, with Tantalus,
son of Patrocles, their Lacedæmonian commander, who had
been wounded and taken prisoner. They also took with them
a few men from Cythera whom they thought it safest to
remove. These the Athenians determined to lodge in the

islands: the rest of the Cytherians were to retain their lands and pay four talents' tribute; the Æginetans captured to be all put to death, on account of the old inveterate feud; and Tantalus to share the imprisonment of the Lacedæmonians taken on the island.

The same summer, the inhabitants of Camarina and Gela in Sicily first made an armistice with each other, after which embassies from all the other Sicilian cities assembled at Gela to try to bring about a pacification. After many expressions of opinion on one side and the other, according to the griefs and pretensions of the different parties complaining, Hermocrates, son of Hermon, a Syracusan, the most influential man among them, addressed the following words to the assembly:—

'If I now address you, Sicilians, it is not because my city is the least in Sicily or the greatest sufferer by the war, but in order to state publicly what appears to me to be the best policy for the whole island. That war is an evil is a proposition so familiar to every one that it would be tedious to develop it. No one is forced to engage in it by ignorance, or kept out of it by fear, if he fancies there is anything to be gained by it. To the former the gain appears greater than the danger, while the latter would rather stand the risk than put up with any immediate sacrifice. But if both should happen to have chosen the wrong moment for acting in this way, advice to make peace would not be unserviceable; and this, if we did but see it, is just what we stand most in need of at the present juncture.

'I suppose that no one will dispute that we went to war at first, in order to serve our own several interests, that we are now, in view of the same interests, debating how we can make peace; and that if we separate without having as we think our rights, we shall go to war again. And yet, as men of sense, we ought to see that our separate interests are not alone at stake in the present congress: there is also the question whether we have still time to save Sicily, the whole of which in my opinion is menaced by Athenian ambition; and we ought to find in the name of that people more imperious arguments for peace than any which I can advance, when we see the first power in Hellas watching our mistakes with the few ships that she has at present in our waters, and under the fair name of alliance speciously seeking to turn to account the natural hostility that exists between us. If we go to war, and call in to help us a people that are ready enough to carry their arms even where they are not invited; and if we injure ourselves at our own expense, and at the same time serve as the pioneers of their dominion, we may expect when they see us worn out, that they will one day come with a larger armament, and seek to bring all of us into subjection.

'And yet as sensible men, if we call in allies and court danger, it should be in order to enrich our different countries with new acquisitions, and not to ruin what they possess already; and we should understand that the intestine discords which are so fatal to communities generally, will be equally so to Sicily, if we, its inhabitants, absorbed in our local quarrels, neglect the common enemy. These considerations should reconcile individual with individual, and city with city, and unite us in a common effort to save the whole of Sicily. Nor should any one imagine that the Dorians only are enemies of Athens, while the Chalcidian race is secured by its Ionian blood; the attack in question is not inspired by hatred of one of two nationalities, but by a desire for the good things in Sicily, the common property of us all. This is proved by the Athenian reception of the Chalcidian invitation: an ally who has never given them any assistance whatever, at once receives from them almost more than the treaty entitles him to. That the Athenians should cherish this ambition and practise this policy is very excusable; and I do not blame those who wish to rule, but those who are over ready to serve. It is just as much in men's nature to rule those who submit to them, as it is to resist those who molest them; one is not less invariable than the other. Meanwhile all who see these dangers and refuse to provide for them properly, or who have come here without having made up their minds that our first duty is to unite to get rid of the common peril, are mistaken. The quickest way to be rid of it is to make peace with each other; since the Athenians menace us not from their own country, but from that of those who invited them here. In this way instead of war issuing in war, peace quietly ends our quarrels; and the guests who come hither under fair pretences for bad ends, will have good reason for going away without having attained them.

'So far as regards the Athenians such are the great advantages proved inherent in a wise policy. Independently of this, in the face of the universal consent that peace is the first of blessings, how can we refuse to make it amongst ourselves; or do you not think that the good which you have, and the ills that you complain of, would be better preserved and cured by quiet than by war; that peace has its honours and splendours of a less perilous kind, not to mention the numerous other blessings that one might dilate on, with the not less numerous miseries of war? These considerations should teach you not to disregard my words, but rather to look in them every one for his own safety. If there be any here who feels certain either by right or might to effect his object, let not this surprise be to him too severe a disappointment. Let him remember that many before now have tried to chastise a wrongdoer, and failing to punish their enemy have not even saved themselves; while many who have trusted in force to gain an advantage, instead of gaining anything more, have been doomed to lose what they had. Vengeance is not necessarily successful because wrong has been done, or strength sure because it is confident; but the incalculable element in the future exercises the widest influence, and is the most treacherous, and yet in fact the most useful of all things, as it frightens us all equally, and thus makes us consider before attacking each other.

'Let us therefore now allow the undefined fear of this unknown future, and the immediate terror of the Athenians' presence to produce their natural impression, and let us consider any failure to carry out the programmes that we may each have sketched out for ourselves as sufficiently accounted for by these obstacles, and send away the intruder from the country; and if everlasting peace be impossible between us, let us at all events make a treaty for as long a term as possible, and put off our private differences to another day. In fine, let us recognise that the adoption of my advice will leave us each citizens of a free state, and as such arbiters of our own destiny, able to return good or bad offices with equal effect; while its rejection will make us dependent on others, and thus not only impotent to repel an insult, but on the most favourable supposition, friends to our direst enemies, and at feud with our natural friends.

'For myself, though, as I said at first, the representative of a great city, and able to think less of defending myself than of attacking others, I am prepared to concede something in prevision of these dangers. I am not inclined to ruin myself for the sake of hurting my enemies, or so blinded by animosity as to think myself equally master of my own plans and of fortune which I cannot command; but I am ready to give up anything in reason. I call upon the rest of you to imitate my conduct of your own free will, without being forced to do so by the enemy. There is no disgrace in connexions giving way to one another, a Dorian to a Dorian, or a Chalcidian to his brethren; above and beyond this we are neighbours, live in the same country, are girt by the same sea, and go by the same name of Sicilians. We shall go to war again, I suppose, when the time comes, and again make peace among ourselves by means of future congresses; but the foreign invader, if we are wise, will always find us united against him, since the hurt of one is the danger of all; and we shall never, in future, invite into the island either allies or mediators. By so acting we shall at the present moment do for Sicily a double service, ridding her at once of the Athenians, and of civil war, and in future shall live in freedom at home, and be less menaced from abroad.'

Such were the words of Hermocrates. The Sicilians took his advice, and came to an understanding among themselves to end the war, each keeping what they had—the Camarinæans taking Morgantina at a price fixed to be paid to the Syracusans —and the allies of the Athenians called the officers in command, and told them that they were going to make peace and that they would be included in the treaty. The generals assenting, the peace was concluded, and the Athenian fleet afterwards sailed away from Sicily. Upon their arrival at Athens, the Athenians banished Pythodorus and Sophocles, and fined Eurymedon for having taken bribes to depart when they might have subdued Sicily. So thoroughly had the present prosperity persuaded the citizens that nothing could withstand them, and that they could achieve what was possible and impracticable alike, with means ample or inadequate it mattered not. The secret of this was their general extraordinary success, which made them confuse their strength with their hopes.

The same summer the Megarians in the city, pressed by the hostilities of the Athenians, who invaded their country twice every year with all their forces, and harassed by the incursions of their own exiles at Pegæ, who had been expelled in a revolution by the popular party, began to ask each other whether it would not be better to receive back their exiles, and free the town from one of its two scourges. The friends of the emigrants perceiving the agitation, now more openly than before demanded the adoption of this proposition; and the leaders of the commons, seeing that the sufferings of the times had tired out the constancy of their supporters, entered in their alarm into correspondence with the Athenian generals, Hippocrates, son of Ariphron, and Demosthenes, son of Alcisthenes, and resolved to betray the town, thinking this less dangerous to themselves than the return of the party which they had banished. It was accordingly arranged that the Athenians should first take the long walls extending for nearly a mile from the city to the port of Nisæa, to prevent the Peloponnesians coming to the rescue from that place, where they formed the sole garrison to secure the fidelity of Megara; and that after this the attempt should be made to put into their hands the upper town, which it was thought would then come over with less difficulty.

The Athenians, after plans had been arranged between themselves and their correspondents both as to words and actions, sailed by night to Minoa, the island off Megara, with six hundred heavy infantry under the command of Hippocrates, and took post in a quarry not far off, out of which bricks used to be taken for the walls; while Demosthenes, the other commander, with a detachment of Platæan light troops and another of Peripoli, placed himself in ambush in the precinct of Enyalius, which was still nearer. No one knew of it, except those whose business it was to know that night. A little before daybreak, the traitors in Megara began to act. Every night for a long time back, under pretence of marauding, in order to have a means of opening the gates, they had been used, with the consent of the officer in command, to carry by night a sculling boat upon a cart along the ditch to the sea, and so to sail out, bringing it back again before day upon the cart, and taking it within the wall through the gates, in order, as they pretended, to baffle the Athenian blockade at Minoa, there being no boat to be seen in the harbour. On the present occasion the cart was already at the gates, which had been opened in the usual way for the boat, when the Athenians, with whom this had been concerted, saw it, and ran at the top of their speed from the ambush in order to reach the gates before they were shut again, and while the cart was still there to prevent their being closed; their Megarian accomplices at the same moment killing the guard at the gates. The first to run in was Demosthenes with his Platæans and Peripoli, just where the trophy now stands; and he was no sooner within the gates than the Platæans engaged and defeated the nearest party of Peloponnesians who had taken the alarm and come to the rescue, and secured the gates for the approaching Athenian heavy infantry.

After this, each of the Athenians as fast as they entered went against the wall. A few of the Peloponnesian garrison stood their ground at first, and tried to repel the assault, and some of them were killed; but the main body took fright and fled; the night attack and the sight of the Megarian traitors in arms against them making them think that all Megara had gone over to the enemy. It so happened also that the Athenian herald of his own idea called out and invited any of the Megarians that wished, to join the Athenian ranks; and this was no sooner heard by the garrison than they gave way, and, convinced that they were the victims of a concerted attack, took refuge in Nisæa. By daybreak, the walls being now taken and the Megarians in the city in great agitation, the persons who had negotiated with the Athenians, supported by the rest of the popular party which was privy to the plot, said that they ought to open the gates and march out to battle. It had been concerted between them that the Athenians should rush in, the moment that the gates were opened, while the conspirators were to be distinguished from the rest by being anointed with oil, and so to avoid being hurt. They could open the gates with more security, as four thousand Athenian heavy infantry from Eleusis, and six hundred horse, had marched all night, according to agreement, and were now close at hand. The conspira-

tors were all ready anointed and at their posts by the gates,
when one of their accomplices denounced the plot to the opposite party, who gathered together and came in a body, and
roundly said that they must not march out—a thing they had
never yet ventured on even when in greater force than at
present—or wantonly compromise the safety of the town, and
that if what they said was not attended to, the battle would
have to be fought in Megara. For the rest, they gave no signs
of their knowledge of the intrigue, but stoutly maintained that
their advice was the best, and meanwhile kept close by and
watched the gates, making it impossible for the conspirators
to effect their purpose.

The Athenian generals seeing that some obstacle had arisen,
and that the capture of the town by force was no longer practicable, at once proceeded to invest Nisæa, thinking that if
they could take it before relief arrived, the surrender of
Megara would soon follow. Iron, stone-masons, and everything
else required quickly coming up from Athens, the Athenians
started from the wall which they occupied, and from this
point built a cross wall looking towards Megara down to the
sea on either side of Nisæa; the ditch and the walls being
divided among the army, stones and bricks taken from the
suburb, and the fruit-trees and timber cut down to make a
palisade wherever this seemed necessary; the houses also in
the suburb with the addition of battlements sometimes entering into the fortification. The whole of this day the work continued, and by the afternoon of the next the wall was all but
completed, when the garrison in Nisæa, alarmed by the absolute want of provisions, which they used to take in for the day
from the upper town, not anticipating any speedy relief from
the Peloponnesians, and supposing Megara to be hostile,
capitulated to the Athenians on condition that they should
give up their arms, and should each be ransomed for a stipulated sum; their Lacedæmonian commander, and any others
of his countrymen in the place, being left to the discretion of
the Athenians. On these conditions they surrendered and came
out, and the Athenians broke down the long walls at their
point of junction with Megara, took possession of Nisæa, and
went on with their other preparations.

Just at this time the Lacedæmonian Brasidas, son of Tellis,

happened to be in the neighbourhood of Sicyon and Corinth, getting ready an army for Thrace. As soon as he heard of the capture of the walls, fearing for the Peloponnesians in Nisæa and the safety of Megara, he sent to the Bœotians to meet him as quickly as possible at Tripodiscus, a village so called of the Megarid, under Mount Geraneia, and went himself, with two thousand seven hundred Corinthian heavy infantry, four hundred Phliasians, six hundred Sicyonians, and such troops of his own as he had already levied, expecting to find Nisæa not yet taken. Hearing of its fall (he had marched out by night to Tripodiscus), he took three hundred picked men from the army, without waiting till his coming should be known, and came up to Megara unobserved by the Athenians, who were down by the sea, ostensibly, and really if possible, to attempt Nisæa, but above all to get into Megara and secure the town. He accordingly invited the townspeople to admit his party, saying that he had hopes of recovering Nisæa.

However, one of the Megarian factions feared that he might expel them and restore the exiles; the other that the commons, apprehensive of this very danger, might set upon them, and the city be thus destroyed by a battle within its gates under the eyes of the ambushed Athenians. He was accordingly refused admittance, both parties electing to remain quiet and await the event; each expecting a battle between the Athenians and the relieving army, and thinking it safer to see their friends victorious before declaring in their favour.

Unable to carry his point, Brasidas went back to the rest of the army. At daybreak the Bœotians joined him. Having determined to relieve Megara, whose danger they considered their own, even before hearing from Brasidas, they were already in full force at Platæa, when his messenger arrived to add spurs to their resolution; and they at once sent on to him two thousand two hundred heavy infantry, and six hundred horse, returning home with the main body. The whole army thus assembled numbered six thousand heavy infantry. The Athenian heavy infantry were drawn up by Nisæa and the sea; but the light troops being scattered over the plain were attacked by the Bœotian horse and driven to the sea, being taken entirely by surprise, as on previous occasions no relief had ever come to the Megarians from any quarter. Here the

Bœotians were in their turn charged and engaged by the Athenian horse, and a cavalry action ensued which lasted a long
time, and in which both parties claimed the victory. The
Athenians killed and stripped the leader of the Bœotian horse
and some few of his comrades who had charged right up to
Nisæa, and remaining masters of the bodies gave them back
under truce, and set up a trophy; but regarding the action as
a whole the forces separated without either side having gained
a decisive advantage, the Bœotians returning to their army
and the Athenians to Nisæa.

After this Brasidas and the army came nearer to the sea
and to Megara, and taking up a convenient position, remained
quiet in order of battle, expecting to be attacked by the Athenians and knowing that the Megarians were waiting to see
which would be the victor. This attitude seemed to present two
advantages. Without taking the offensive or willingly provok-
ing the hazards of a battle, they openly showed their readiness
to fight, and thus without bearing the burden of the day would
fairly reap its honours; while at the same time they effectually
served their interests at Megara. For if they had failed to show
themselves, they would not have had a chance, but would
have certainly been considered vanquished, and have lost
the town. As it was, the Athenians might possibly not be inclined to accept their challenge, and their object would be
attained without fighting. And so it turned out. The Athenians
formed outside the long walls, and the enemy not attacking,
there remained motionless; their generals having decided that
the risk was too unequal. In fact most of their objects had
been already attained; and they would have to begin a battle
against superior numbers, and if victorious could only gain
Megara, while a defeat would destroy the flower of their heavy
soldiery. For the enemy it was different; as even the states
actually represented in his army risked each only a part of
its entire force, he might well be more audacious. Accordingly
after waiting for some time without either side attacking, the
Athenians withdrew to Nisæa, and the Peloponnesians after
them to the point from which they had set out. The friends of
the Megarian exiles now threw aside their hesitation, and
opened the gates to Brasidas and the commanders from the
different states—looking upon him as the victor and upon the

Athenians as having declined the battle—and receiving them into the town proceeded to discuss matters with them; the party in correspondence with the Athenians being paralysed by the turn things had taken.

Afterwards Brasidas let the allies go home, and himself went back to Corinth, to prepare for his expedition to Thrace, his original destination. The Athenians also returning home, the Megarians in the city most implicated in the Athenian negotiation, knowing that they had been detected, presently disappeared; while the rest conferred with the friends of the exiles, and restored the party at Pegæ, after binding them under solemn oaths to take no vengeance for the past, and only to consult the real interests of the town. However, as soon as they were in office, they held a review of the heavy infantry, and separating the battalions, picked out about a hundred of their enemies, and of those who were thought to be most involved in the correspondence with the Athenians, brought them before the people, and compelling the vote to be given openly, had them condemned and executed, and established a close oligarchy in the town—a revolution which lasted a very long while, although effected by a very few partisans.

CHAPTER XIV

EIGHTH AND NINTH YEARS OF THE WAR—INVASION OF BŒOTIA—FALL OF AMPHIPOLIS—BRILLIANT SUCCESSES OF BRASIDAS

B.C. 424: *Democratic conspiracy in Bœotia—Brasidas marches through Thessaly—Spartan massacre of Helots—Brasidas' speech at Acanthus—Revolt of Acanthus—Fortification of Delium—Pagondas urges Bœotians to attack Athenians—Hippocrates exhorts his soldiers—Defeat of the Athenians—Truce denied Athenians—Recovery of Delium—Brasidas at Amphipolis—Thucydides delayed; Amphipolis lost—Alarm in Athens—Brasidas enters Torone—His address to the inhabitants—Capture of Lecythus—B.C. 423: Terms of Spartan-Athenian armistice—Brasidas at Scione—Revolt of Mende—Campaign against Arrhabœus—Speech of Brasidas—Retreat of Brasidas—Athenians recover Mende.*

THE same summer the Mitylenians were about to fortify Antandrus, as they had intended, when Demodocus and Aristides, the commanders of the Athenian squadron engaged in levying subsidies, heard on the Hellespont of what was being done to the place (Lamachus their colleague having sailed with ten ships into the Pontus) and conceived fears of its becoming a second Anaia,—the place in which the Samian exiles had established themselves to annoy Samos, helping the Peloponnesians by sending pilots to their navy, and keeping the city in agitation and receiving all its outlaws. They accordingly got together a force from the allies and set sail, defeated in battle the troops that met them from Antandrus, and retook the place. Not long after, Lamachus, who had sailed into the Pontus, lost his ships at anchor in the river Calex, in the territory of Heraclea, rain having fallen in the interior and the flood coming suddenly down upon them; and himself and his troops passed by land through the Bithynian Thracians on the Asiatic side, and arrived at Chalcedon, the Megarian colony at the mouth of the Pontus.

The same summer the Athenian general, Demosthenes, arrived at Naupactus with forty ships immediately after the return from the Megarid. Hippocrates and himself had had overtures made to them by certain men in the cities in Bœotia, who wished to change the constitution and introduce a democracy as at Athens; Ptœodorus, a Theban exile, being the chief mover in this intrigue. The seaport town of Siphæ, in the bay of Crisæ, in the Thespian territory, was to be betrayed to them by one party; Chæronea (a dependency of what was formerly called the Minyan, now the Bœotian, Orchomenus), to be put into their hands by another from that town, whose exiles were very active in the business, hiring men in Peloponnese. Some Phocians also were in the plot, Chæronea being the frontier town of Bœotia and close to Phanotis in Phocis. Meanwhile the Athenians were to seize Delium, the sanctuary of Apollo, in the territory of Tanagra looking towards Eubœa; and all these events were to take place simultaneously upon a day appointed, in order that the Bœotians might be unable to unite to oppose them at Delium, being everywhere detained by disturbances at home. Should the enterprise succeed, and Delium be fortified, its authors confidently expected that even if no revolution should immediately follow in Bœotia, yet with these places in their hands, and the country being harassed by incursions, and a refuge in each instance near for the partisans engaged in them, things would not remain as they were, but that the rebels being supported by the Athenians and the forces of the oligarchs divided, it would be possible after a while to settle matters according to their wishes.

Such was the plot in contemplation. Hippocrates with a force raised at home awaited the proper moment to take the field against the Bœotians; while he sent on Demosthenes with the forty ships above mentioned to Naupactus, to raise in those parts an army of Acarnanians and of the other allies, and sail and receive Siphæ from the conspirators; a day having been agreed on for the simultaneous execution of both these operations. Demosthenes on his arrival found Œniadæ already compelled by the united Acarnanians to join the Athenian confederacy, and himself raising all the allies in those countries marched against and subdued Salynthius and the Agræans; after which he devoted himself to the preparations necessary to enable him to be at Siphæ by the time appointed.

About the same time in the summer, Brasidas set out on his march for the Thracian places with seventeen hundred heavy infantry, and arriving at Heraclea in Trachis, from thence sent on a messenger to his friends at Pharsalus, to ask them to conduct himself and his army through the country. Accordingly there came to Melitia in Achaia Panærus, Dorus, Hippolochidas, Torylaus, and Strophacus, the Chalcidian *Proxenus,* under whose escort he resumed his march, being accompanied also by other Thessalians, among whom was Niconidas from Larissa, a friend of Perdiccas. It was never very easy to traverse Thessaly without an escort; and throughout all Hellas for an armed force to pass without leave through a neighbour's country, was a delicate step to take. Besides this the Thessalian people had always sympathised with the Athenians. Indeed if instead of the customary close oligarchy there had been a constitutional government in Thessaly, he would never have been able to proceed; since even as it was, he was met on his march at the river Enipeus by certain of the opposite party who forbade his further progress, and complained of his making the attempt without the consent of the nation. To this his escort answered that they had no intention of taking him through against their will; they were only friends in attendance on an unexpected visitor. Brasidas himself added that he came as a friend to Thessaly and its inhabitants; his arms not being directed against them but against the Athenians, with whom he was at war, and that although he knew of no quarrel between the Thessalians and Lacedæmonians to prevent the two nations having access to each other's territory, he neither would nor could proceed against their wishes; he could only beg them not to stop him. With this answer they went away, and he took the advice of his escort, and pushed on without halting, before a greater force might gather to prevent him. Thus in the day that he set out from Melitia he performed the whole distance to Pharsalus, and encamped on the river Apidanus; and so to Phacium, and from thence to Perrhæbia. Here his Thessalian escort went back, and the Perrhæbians, who are subjects of Thessaly, set him down at Dium in the dominions of Perdiccas, a Macedonian town under Mount Olympus, looking towards Thessaly.

In this way Brasidas hurried through Thessaly before any one could be got ready to stop him, and reached Perdiccas and Chalcidice. The departure of the army from Peloponnese had been procured by the Thracian towns in revolt against Athens and by Perdiccas, alarmed at the successes of the Athenians. The Chalcidians thought that they would be the first objects of an Athenian expedition, not that the neighbouring towns which had not yet revolted did not also secretly join in the invitation; and Perdiccas also had his apprehensions on account of his old quarrels with the Athenians, although not openly at war with them, and above all wished to reduce Arrhabæus king of the Lyncestians. It had been less difficult for them to get an army to leave Peloponnese, because of the ill fortune of the Lacedæmonians at the present moment. The attacks of the Athenians upon Peloponnese, and in particular upon Laconia, might, it was hoped, be diverted most effectually by annoying them in return, and by sending an army to their allies, especially as they were willing to maintain it and asked for it to aid them in revolting. The Lacedæmonians were also glad to have an excuse for sending some of the Helots out of the country, for fear that the present aspect of affairs and the occupation of Pylos might encourage them to move. Indeed fear of their numbers and obstinacy even persuaded the Lacedæmonians to the action which I shall now relate, their policy at all times having been governed by the necessity of taking precautions against them. The Helots were invited by a proclamation to pick out those of their number who claimed to have most distinguished themselves against the enemy, in order that they might receive their freedom; the object being to test them, as it was thought that the first to claim their freedom would be the most high-spirited and the most apt to rebel. As many as two thousand were selected accordingly, who crowned themselves and went round the temples, rejoicing in their new freedom. The Spartans, however, soon afterwards did away with them, and no one ever knew how each of them perished. The Spartans now therefore gladly sent seven hundred as heavy infantry with Brasidas, who recruited the rest of his force by means of money in Peloponnese.

Brasidas himself was sent out by the Lacedæmonians mainly at his own desire, although the Chalcidians also were eager to have a man so thorough as he had shown himself whenever there was anything to be done at Sparta, and whose after-service abroad proved of the utmost use to his country. At the present moment his just and moderate conduct towards the towns generally succeeded in procuring their revolt, besides the places which he managed to take by treachery; and thus when the Lacedæmonians desired to treat, as they ultimately did, they had places to offer in exchange, and the burden of war meanwhile shifted from Peloponnese. Later on in the war, after the events in Sicily, the present valour and conduct of Brasidas, known by experience to some, by hearsay to others, was what mainly created in the allies of Athens a feeling for the Lacedæmonians. He was the first who went out and showed himself so good a man at all points as to leave behind him the conviction that the rest were like him.

Meanwhile his arrival in the Thracian country no sooner became known to the Athenians than they declared war against Perdiccas, whom they regarded as the author of the expedition, and kept a closer watch on their allies in that quarter.

Upon the arrival of Brasidas and his army, Perdiccas immediately started with them and with his own forces against

Arrhabæus, son of Bromerus king of the Lyncestian Macedonians, his neighbour, with whom he had a quarrel and whom
he wished to subdue. However, when he arrived with his army
and Brasidas at the pass leading into Lyncus, Brasidas told
him that before commencing hostilities he wished to go and
try to persuade Arrhabæus to become the ally of Lacedæmon,
this latter having already made overtures intimating his
willingness to make Brasidas arbitrator between them, and
the Chalcidian envoys accompanying him having warned him
not to remove the apprehensions of Perdiccas, in order to
insure his greater zeal in their cause. Besides, the envoys of
Perdiccas had talked at Lacedæmon about his bringing many
of the places round him into alliance with them; and thus
Brasidas thought he might take a larger view of the question
of Arrhabæus. Perdiccas however retorted that he had not
brought him with him to arbitrate in their quarrel, but to put
down the enemies whom he might point out to him; and that
while he, Perdiccas, maintained half his army it was a breach
of faith for Brasidas to parley with Arrhabæus. Nevertheless
Brasidas disregarded the wishes of Perdiccas and held the
parley in spite of him, and suffered himself to be persuaded
to lead off the army without invading the country of Arrhabæus; after which Perdiccas, holding that faith had not been
kept with him, contributed only a third instead of half of the
support of the army.

The same summer, without loss of time, Brasidas marched
with the Chalcidians against Acanthus, a colony of the Andrians, a little before vintage. The inhabitants were divided
into two parties on the question of receiving him; those who
had joined the Chalcidians in inviting him, and the popular
party. However, fear for their fruit, which was still out, enabled Brasidas to persuade the multitude to admit him alone,
and to hear what he had to say before making a decision; and
he was admitted accordingly and appeared before the people,
and not being a bad speaker for a Lacedæmonian, addressed
them as follows:—

'Acanthians, the Lacedæmonians have sent out me and my
army to make good the reason that we gave for the war when
we began it, viz. that we were going to war with the Athenians
in order to free Hellas. Our delay in coming has been caused

by mistaken expectations as to the war at home, which led us to hope, by our own unassisted efforts and without your risking anything, to effect the speedy downfall of the Athenians; and you must not blame us for this, as we are now come the moment that we were able, prepared with your aid to do our best to subdue them. Meanwhile I am astonished at finding your gates shut against me, and at not meeting with a better welcome. We Lacedæmonians thought of you as allies eager to have us, to whom we should come in spirit even before we were with you in body; and in this expectation undertook all the risks of a march of many days through a strange country, so far did our zeal carry us. It will be a terrible thing if after this you have other intentions, and mean to stand in the way of your own and Hellenic freedom. It is not merely that you oppose me yourselves; but wherever I may go people will be less inclined to join me, on the score that you, to whom I first came—an important town like Acanthus, and prudent men like the Acanthians—refused to admit me. I shall have nothing to prove that the reason which I advance is the true one; it will be said either that there is something unfair in the freedom which I offer, or that I am here in insufficient force and unable to protect you against an attack from Athens. Yet when I went with the army which I now have to the relief of Nisæa, the Athenians did not venture to engage me although in greater force than I; and it is not likely they will ever send across sea against you an army as numerous as they had at Nisæa. And for myself, I have come here not to hurt but to free the Hellenes, witness the solemn oaths by which I have bound my government that the allies that I may bring over shall be independent; and besides my object in coming is not by force or fraud to obtain your alliance, but to offer you mine to help you against your Athenian masters. I protest, therefore, against any suspicions of my intentions after the guarantees which I offer, and equally so against doubts of my ability to protect you, and I invite you to join me without hesitation.

'Some of you may hang back because they have private enemies, and fear that I may put the city into the hands of a party: none need be more tranquil than they. I am not come here to help this party or that; and I do not consider that

I should be bringing you freedom in any real sense, if I should disregard your constitution, and enslave the many to the few or the few to the many. This would be heavier than a foreign yoke; and we Lacedæmonians instead of being thanked for our pains, should get neither honour nor glory, but contrari-wise reproaches. The charges which strengthen our hands in the war against the Athenians would on our own showing be merited by ourselves, and more hateful in us than in those who make no pretensions to honesty; as it is more disgraceful for persons of character to take what they covet by fair-seeming fraud than by open force; the one aggression having for its justification the might which fortune gives, the other being simply a piece of clever roguery. A matter which concerns us thus nearly we naturally look to most jealously; and over and above the oaths that I have mentioned, what stronger assur-ance can you have, when you see that our words, compared with the actual facts, produce the necessary conviction that it is our interest to act as we say?

'If to these considerations of mine you put in the plea of inability, and claim that your friendly feeling should save you from being hurt by your refusal; if you say that freedom, in your opinion, is not without its dangers, and that it is right to offer it to those who can accept it, but not to force it on any against their will, then I shall take the gods and heroes of your country to witness that I came for your good and was rejected, and shall do my best to compel you by laying waste your land. I shall do so without scruple, being justified by the necessity which constrains me, first, to prevent the Lace-dæmonians from being damaged by you, their friends, in the event of your non-adhesion, through the monies that you pay to the Athenians; and secondly, to prevent the Hellenes from being hindered by you in shaking off their servitude. Other-wise indeed we should have no right to act as we propose; except in the name of some public interest, what call should we Lacedæmonians have to free those who do not wish it? Empire we do not aspire to: it is what we are labouring to put down; and we should wrong the greater number if we allowed you to stand in the way of the independence that we offer to all. Endeavour, therefore, to decide wisely, and strive to begin the work of liberation for the Hellenes, and lay up for yourselves endless renown, while you escape private loss, and cover your commonwealth with glory.'

Such were the words of Brasidas. The Acanthians, after much had been said on both sides of the question, gave their votes in secret, and the majority, influenced by the seductive arguments of Brasidas and by fear for their fruit, decided to revolt from Athens; not however admitting the army until they had taken his personal security for the oaths sworn by his government before they sent him out, assuring the independence of the allies whom he might bring over. Not long after, Stagirus, a colony of the Andrians, followed their example and revolted.

Such were the events of this summer. It was in the first days of the winter following that the places in Bœotia were to be put into the hands of Athenian generals, Hippocrates and Demosthenes, the latter of whom was to go with his ships to Siphæ, the former to Delium. A mistake, however, was made in the days on which they were each to start; and Demosthenes sailing first to Siphæ, with the Acarnanians and many of the allies from those parts on board, failed to effect anything, through the plot having been betrayed by Nicomachus, a Phocian from Phanotis, who told the Lacedæmonians, and they the Bœotians. Succours accordingly flocked in from all parts of Bœotia, Hippocrates not being yet there to make his diversion, and Siphæ and Chæronea were promptly secured, and the conspirators, informed of the mistake, did not venture on any movement in the towns.

Meanwhile Hippocrates made a levy in mass of the citizens, resident aliens, and foreigners in Athens, and arrived at his destination after the Bœotians had already come back from Siphæ, and encamping his army began to fortify Delium, the sanctuary of Apollo, in the following manner. A trench was dug all round the temple and the consecrated ground, and the earth thrown up from the excavation was made to do duty as a wall, in which stakes were also planted, the vines round the sanctuary being cut down and thrown in, together with stones and bricks pulled down from the houses near; every means, in short, being used to run up the rampart. Wooden towers were also erected where they were wanted, and where there was no part of the temple buildings left standing. as on the side where the gallery once existing had fallen in. The work was begun on the third day after leaving home, and continued during the fourth, and till dinner-time on the fifth, when most of it being now finished the army removed from Delium about a mile and a quarter on its way home. From this point most of the light troops went straight on, while the heavy infantry halted and remained where they were; Hippocrates having stayed behind at Delium to arrange the posts, and to give directions for the completion of such part of the outworks as had been left unfinished.

During the days thus employed the Bœotians were mustering at Tanagra, and by the time that they had come in from all the towns, found the Athenians already on their way home. The rest of the eleven Bœotarchs were against giving battle, as the enemy was no longer in Bœotia, the Athenians being just over the Oropian border, when they halted; but Pagondas, son of Æolidas, one of the Bœotarchs of Thebes (Arianthides, son of Lysimachidas, being the other), and then commander-in-chief, thought it best to hazard a battle. He accordingly called the men to him, company after company, to prevent their all leaving their arms at once, and urged them to attack the Athenians, and stand the issue of a battle, speaking as follows:—

'Bœotians, the idea that we ought not to give battle to the Athenians unless we came up with them in Bœotia, is one which should never have entered into the head of any of us, your generals. It was to annoy Bœotia that they crossed the frontier and built a fort in our country; and they are therefore, I imagine, our enemies wherever we may come up with them, and from wheresoever they may have come to act as enemies do. And if any one has taken up with the idea in question for reasons of safety, it is high time for him to change his mind. The party attacked, whose own country is in danger, can scarcely discuss what is prudent with the calmness of men who are in full enjoyment of what they have got, and are thinking of attacking a neighbour in order to get more. It is your national habit, in your country or out of it, to oppose the same resistance to a foreign invader; and when that invader is Athenian, and lives upon your frontier besides, it is doubly imperative to do so. As between neighbours gen-

erally, freedom means simply a determination to hold one's
own; and with neighbours like these, who are trying to enslave
near and far alike, there is nothing for it but to fight it out
to the last. Look at the condition of the Euboeans and of most
of the rest of Hellas, and be convinced that others have to
fight with their neighbours for this frontier or that, but that
for us conquest means one frontier for the whole country,
about which no dispute can be made, for they will simply come
and take by force what we have. So much more have we to
fear from this neighbour than from another. Besides, people
who, like the Athenians in the present instance, are tempted
by pride of strength to attack their neighbours, usually march
most confidently against those who keep still, and only defend
themselves in their own country, but think twice before they
grapple with those who meet them outside their frontier and
strike the first blow if opportunity offers. The Athenians have
shown us this themselves; the defeat which we inflicted upon
them at Coronea, at the time when our quarrels had allowed
them to occupy the country, has given great security to
Boeotia until the present day. Remembering this, the old must
equal their ancient exploits, and the young, the sons of the
heroes of that time, must endeavour not to disgrace their
native valour; and trusting in the help of the god whose
temple has been sacrilegiously fortified, and in the victims
which in our sacrifices have proved propitious, we must march
against the enemy, and teach him that he must go and get
what he wants by attacking some one who will not resist him,
but that men whose glory it is to be always ready to give
battle for the liberty of their own country, and never unjustly
to enslave that of others, will not let him go without a struggle.'

By these argument Pagondas persuaded the Boeotians to
attack the Athenians, and quickly breaking up his camp led
his army forward, it being now late in the day. On nearing
the enemy, he halted in a position where a hill intervening
prevented the two armies from seeing each other, and then
formed and prepared for action. Meanwhile Hippocrates at
Delium, informed of the approach of the Boeotians, sent orders
to his troops to throw themselves into line, and himself joined
them not long afterwards, leaving about three hundred horse
behind him at Delium, at once to guard the place in case of

attack, and to watch their opportunity and fall upon the
Bœotians during the battle. The Bœotians placed a detachment to deal with these, and when everything was arranged
to their satisfaction appeared over the hill, and halted in the
order which they had determined on, to the number of seven
thousand heavy infantry, more than ten thousand light troops,
one thousand horse, and five hundred targeteers. On their
right were the Thebans and those of their province, in the
centre the Haliartians, Coronæans, Copæans, and the other
people around the lake, and on the left the Thespians, Tanagræans, and Orchomenians, the cavalry and the light troops
being at the extremity of each wing. The Thebans formed
twenty-five shields deep, the rest as they pleased. Such was
the strength and disposition of the Bœotian army.

On the side of the Athenians, the heavy infantry throughout the whole army formed eight deep, being in numbers equal
to the enemy, with the cavalry upon the two wings. Light
troops regularly armed there were none in the army, nor had
there ever been any at Athens. Those who had joined in the
invasion, though many times more numerous than those of
the enemy, had mostly followed unarmed, as part of the levy
in mass of the citizens and foreigners at Athens, and having
started first on their way home were not present in any number. The armies being now in line and upon the point of engaging, Hippocrates, the general, passed along the Athenian
ranks, and encouraged them as follows:—

'Athenians, I shall only say a few words to you, but brave
men require no more, and they are addressed more to your
understanding than to your courage. None of you must fancy
that we are going out of our way to run this risk in the country
of another. Fought in their territory the battle will be for ours:
if we conquer, the Peloponnesians will never invade your country without the Bœotian horse, and in one battle you will win
Bœotia and in a manner free Attica. Advance to meet them
then like citizens of a country in which you all glory as the
first in Hellas, and like sons of the fathers who beat them at
Œnophyta with Myronides and thus gained possession of
Bœotia.'

Hippocrates had got half through the army with his exhortation, when the Bœotians, after a few more hasty words

from Pagondas, struck up the pæan, and came against them
from the hill; the Athenians advancing to meet them, and
closing at a run. The extreme wing of neither army came into
action, one like the other being stopped by the water-courses
in the way; the rest engaged with the utmost obstinacy, shield
against shield. The Bœotian left, as far as the centre, was
worsted by the Athenians. The Thespians in that part of the
field suffered most severely. The troops alongside them having given way, they were surrounded in a narrow space and
cut down fighting hand to hand; some of the Athenians also
fell into confusion in surrounding the enemy and mistook
and so killed each other. In this part of the field the Bœotians
were beaten, and retreated upon the troops still fighting; but
the right, where the Thebans were, got the better of the
Athenians and shoved them further and further back, though
gradually at first. It so happened also that Pagondas, seeing
the distress of his left, had sent two squadrons of horse, where
they could not be seen, round the hill, and their sudden
appearance struck a panic into the victorious wing of the
Athenians, who thought that it was another army coming
against them. At length in both parts of the field, disturbed
by this panic, and with their line broken by the advancing
Thebans, the whole Athenian army took to flight. Some made
for Delium and the sea, some for Oropus, others for Mount
Parnes, or wherever they had hopes of safety, pursued and cut
down by the Bœotians, and in particular by the cavalry, composed partly of Bœotians and partly of Locrians, who had
come up just as the rout began. Night however coming on to
interrupt the pursuit, the mass of the fugitives escaped more
easily than they would otherwise have done. The next day the
troops at Oropus and Delium returned home by sea, after
leaving a garrison in the latter place, which they continued to
hold notwithstanding the defeat.

The Bœotians set up a trophy, took up their own dead, and
stripped those of the enemy, and leaving a guard over them
retired to Tanagra, there to take measures for attacking
Delium. Meanwhile a herald came from the Athenians to ask
for the dead, but was met and turned back by a Bœotian herald, who told him that he would effect nothing until the return
of himself the Bœotian herald, and who then went on to the

Athenians, and told them on the part of the Bœotians that they had done wrong in transgressing the law of the Hellenes. Of what use was the universal custom protecting the temples in an invaded country, if the Athenians were to fortify Delium and live there, acting exactly as if they were on unconsecrated ground, and drawing and using for their purposes the water which they, the Bœotians, never touched except for sacred uses? Accordingly for the god as well as for themselves, in the name of the deities concerned, and of Apollo, the Bœotians invited them first to evacuate the temple, if they wished to take up the dead that belonged to them.

After these words from the herald, the Athenians sent their own herald to the Bœotians to say that they had not done any wrong to the temple, and for the future would do it no more harm than they could help; not having occupied it originally in any such design, but to defend themselves from it against those who were really wronging them. The law of the Hellenes was that conquest of a country, whether more or less extensive, carried with it possession of the temples in that country, with the obligation to keep up the usual cere-monies, at least as far as possible. The Bœotians and most other people who had turned out the owners of a country, and put themselves in their places by force, now held as of right the temples which they originally entered as usurpers. If the Athenians could have conquered more of Bœotia this would have been the case with them: as things stood, the piece of it which they had got they should treat as their own, and not quit unless obliged. The water they had disturbed under the impulsion of a necessity which they had not wan-tonly incurred, having been forced to use it in defending themselves against the Bœotians who had first invaded Attica. Besides, anything done under the pressure of war and danger might reasonably claim indulgence even in the eye of the god; or why, pray, were the altars the asylum for involuntary offences? Transgression also was a term applied to presump-tuous offenders, not to the victims of adverse circumstances. In short, which were most impious—the Bœotians who wished to barter dead bodies for holy places, or the Athenians who refused to give up holy places to obtain what was theirs by right? The condition of evacuating Bœotia must therefore be

withdrawn. They were no longer in Bœotia. They stood where
they stood by the right of the sword. All that the Bœotians
had to do was to tell them to take up their dead under a truce
according to the national custom.

The Bœotians replied that if they were in Bœotia, they must
evacuate that country before taking up their dead; if they
were in their own territory, they could do as they pleased:
for they knew that, although the Oropid where the bodies as
it chanced were lying (the battle having been fought on the
borders) was subject to Athens, yet the Athenians could not
get them without their leave. Besides, why should they grant
a truce for Athenian ground? And what could be fairer than
to tell them to evacuate Bœotia if they wished to get what
they asked? The Athenian herald accordingly returned with
this answer, without having accomplished his object.

Meanwhile the Bœotians at once sent for darters and
slingers from the Malian gulf, and with two thousand Corinthian heavy infantry who had joined them after the battle,
the Peloponnesian garrison which had evacuated Nisæa, and
some Megarians with them, marched against Delium, and
attacked the fort, and after divers efforts finally succeeded
in taking it by an engine of the following description. They
sawed in two and scooped out a great beam from end to end,
and fitting it nicely together again like a pipe, hung by chains
a cauldron at one extremity, with which communicated an
iron tube projecting from the beam, which was itself in great
part plated with iron. This they brought up from a distance
upon carts to the part of the wall principally composed of
vines and timber, and when it was near, inserted huge bellows
into their end of the beam and blew with them. The blast
passing closely confined into the cauldron, which was filled
with lighted coals, sulphur and pitch, made a great blaze, and
set fire to the wall, which soon became untenable for its defenders, who left it and fled; and in this way the fort was
taken. Of the garrison some were killed and two hundred
made prisoners; most of the rest got on board their ships and
returned home.

Soon after the fall of Delium, which took place seventeen
days after the battle, the Athenian herald, without knowing
what had happened, came again for the dead, which were now

restored by the Bœotians, who no longer answered as at first.
Not quite five hundred Bœotians fell in the battle, and nearly
one thousand Athenians, including Hippocrates the general,
besides a great number of light troops and camp followers.

Soon after this battle Demosthenes, after the failure of his
voyage to Siphæ and of the plot on the town, availed himself
of the Acarnanian and Agræan troops and of the four hundred Athenian heavy infantry which he had on board, to make
a descent on the Sicyonian coast. Before however all his
ships had come to shore, the Sicyonians came up and routed
and chased to their ships those that had landed, killing
some and taking others prisoners; after which they set up a
trophy, and gave back the dead under truce.

About the same time with the affair of Delium took place
the death of Sitalces, king of the Odrysians, who was defeated
in battle, in a campaign against the Triballi; Seuthes, son
of Sparadocus, his nephew, succeeding to the kingdom of the
Odrysians, and of the rest of Thrace ruled by Sitalces.

The same winter Brasidas, with his allies in the Thracian
places, marched against Amphipolis, the Athenian colony on
the river Strymon. A settlement upon the spot on which the
city now stands, was before attempted by Aristagoras, the
Milesian (when he fled from king Darius), who was however
dislodged by the Edonians; and thirty-two years later by the
Athenians, who sent thither ten thousand settlers of their own
citizens, and whoever else chose to go. These were cut off
at Drabescus by the Thrasians. Twenty-nine years after, the
Athenians returned (Hagnon, son of Nicias, being sent out
as leader of the colony) and drove out the Edonians, and
founded a town on the spot, formerly called Ennea-hodoi or
Nine Ways. The base from which they started was Eion, their
commercial seaport at the mouth of the river, not more than
three miles from the present town, which Hagnon named
Amphipolis, because the Strymon flows round it on two sides,
and he built it so as to be conspicuous from the sea and land
alike, running a long wall across from river to river, to complete the circumference.

Brasidas now marched against this town, starting from
Arne in Chalcidice. Arriving about dusk at Aulon and Bromis-
cus, where the lake of Bolbe runs into the sea, he supped there,

and went on during the night. The weather was stormy and it was snowing a little, which encouraged him to hurry on, in order, if possible, to take every one at Amphipolis by surprise, except the party who were to betray it. The plot was carried on by some natives of Argilus, an Andrian colony, residing in Amphipolis, where they had also other accomplices gained over by Perdiccas or the Chalcidians. But the most active in the matter were the inhabitants of Argilus itself, which is close by, who had always been suspected by the Athenians, and had had designs on the place. These men now saw their opportunity arrive with Brasidas, and having for some time been in correspondence with their countrymen in Amphipolis for the betrayal of the town, at once received him into Argilus, and revolted from the Athenians, and that same night took him on to the bridge over the river; where he found only a small guard to oppose him, the town being at some distance from the passage, and the walls not reaching down to it as at present. This guard he easily drove in, partly through there being treason in their ranks, partly from the stormy state of the weather and the suddenness of his attack, and so got across the bridge, and immediately became master of all the property outside; the Amphipolitans having houses all over the quarter.

The passage of Brasidas was a complete surprise to the people in the town; and the capture of many of those outside, and the flight of the rest within the wall, combined to produce great confusion among the citizens; especially as they did not trust one another. It is even said that if Brasidas, instead of stopping to pillage, had advanced straight against the town, he would probably have taken it. In fact, however, he established himself where he was and overran the country outside, and for the present remained inactive, vainly awaiting a demonstration on the part of his friends within. Meanwhile the party opposed to the traitors proved numerous enough to prevent the gates being immediately thrown open, and in concert with Eucles, the general, who had come from Athens to defend the place, sent to the other commander in Thrace, Thucydides, son of Olorus, the author of this history, who was at the isle of Thasos, a Parian colony, half a day's sail from Amphipolis, to tell him to come to their relief. On receipt of this message he at once set sail with seven ships which he had with him, in order, if possible, to reach Amphipolis in time to prevent its capitulation, or in any case to save Eion.

Meanwhile Brasidas, afraid of succours arriving by sea from Thasos, and learning that Thucydides possessed the right of working the gold mines in that part of Thrace, and had thus great influence with the inhabitants of the continent, hastened to gain the town, if possible, before the people of Amphipolis should be encouraged by his arrival to hope that he could save them by getting together a force of allies from the sea and from Thrace, and so refuse to surrender. He accordingly offered moderate terms, proclaiming that any of the Amphipolitans and Athenians who chose, might continue to enjoy their property with full rights of citizenship; while those who did not wish to stay had five days to depart, taking their property with them.

The bulk of the inhabitants, upon hearing this, began to change their minds, especially as only a small number of the citizens were Athenians, the majority having come from different quarters, and many of the prisoners outside had relations within the walls. They found the proclamation a fair one in comparison of what their fear had suggested; the Athenians being glad to go out, as they thought they ran more risk than the rest, and further, did not expect any speedy relief, and the multitude generally being content at being left in possession of their civic rights, and at such an unexpected reprieve from danger. The partisans of Brasidas now openly advocated this course, seeing that the feeling of the people had changed, and that they no longer gave ear to the Athenian general present; and thus the surrender was made and Brasidas was admitted by them on the terms of his proclamation. In this way they gave up the city, and late in the same day Thucydides and his ships entered the harbour of Eion, Brasidas having just got hold of Amphipolis, and having been within a night of taking Eion: had the ships been less prompt in relieving it, in the morning it would have been his.

After this Thucydides put all in order at Eion to secure it against any present or future attack of Brasidas, and received such as had elected to come there from the interior according to the terms agreed on. Meanwhile Brasidas suddenly sailed

with a number of boats down the river to Eion to see if he
could not seize the point running out from the wall, and so
command the entrance; at the same time he attempted it by
land, but was beaten off on both sides and had to content
himself with arranging matters at Amphipolis and in the
neighbourhood. Myrcinus, an Edonian town, also came over
to him; the Edonian king Pittacus having been killed by the
sons of Goaxis and his own wife Brauro; and Galepsus and
Œsime, which are Thasian colonies, not long after followed
its example. Perdiccas too came up immediately after the
capture and joined in these arrangements.

The news that Amphipolis was in the hands of the enemy
caused great alarm at Athens. Not only was the town valuable
for the timber it afforded for shipbuilding, and the money
that it brought in; but also, although the escort of the Thessalians gave the Lacedæmonians a means of reaching the allies of Athens as far as the Strymon, yet as long as they were
not masters of the bridge but were watched on the side of
Eion by the Athenian galleys, and on the land side impeded
by a large and extensive lake formed by the waters of the
river, it was impossible for them to go any further. Now, on
the contrary, the path seemed open. There was also the fear
of the allies revolting, owing to the moderation displayed by
Brasidas in all his conduct, and to the declarations which he
was everywhere making that he was sent out to free Hellas.
The towns subject to the Athenians, hearing of the capture
of Amphipolis and of the terms accorded to it, and of the
gentleness of Brasidas, felt most strongly encouraged to
change their condition, and sent secret messages to him,
begging him to come on to them; each wishing to be the first
to revolt. Indeed there seemed to be no danger in so doing;
their mistake in their estimate of the Athenian power was as
great as that power afterwards turned out to be, and their
judgment was based more upon blind wishing than upon any
sound prevision; for it is a habit of mankind to entrust to
careless hope what they long for, and to use sovereign reason
to thrust aside what they do not fancy. Besides the late severe
blow which the Athenians had met with in Bœotia, joined to
the seductive, though untrue, statements of Brasidas, about
the Athenians not having ventured to engage his single army

at Nisæa, made the allies confident, and caused them to believe that no Athenian force would be sent against them.
Above all the wish to do what was agreeable at the moment,
and the likelihood that they should find the Lacedæmonians
full of zeal at starting, made them eager to venture. Observing this, the Athenians sent garrisons to the different towns, as
far as was possible at such short notice and in winter; while
Brasidas sent despatches to Lacedæmon asking for reinforcements, and himself made preparations for building galleys in
the Strymon. The Lacedæmonians however did not send him
any, partly through envy on the part of their chief men, partly
because they were more bent on recovering the prisoners of
the island and ending the war.

The same winter the Megarians took and razed to the
foundations the long walls which had been occupied by the
Athenians; and Brasidas after the capture of Amphipolis
marched with his allies against Acte, a promontory running
out from the king's dike with an inward curve, and ending in
Athos, a lofty mountain looking towards the Ægean sea. In
it are various towns, Sane, an Andrian colony, close to the
canal, and facing the sea in the direction of Eubœa; the others
being Thyssus, Cleone, Acrothoi, Olophyxus, and Dium, inhabited by mixed barbarian races speaking the two languages.
There is also a small Chalcidian element; but the greater number are Tyrrheno-Pelasgians once settled in Lemnos and
Athens, and Bisaltians, Crestonians, and Edonians; the towns
being all small ones. Most of these came over to Brasidas;
but Sane and Dium held out and saw their land ravaged by
him and his army.

Upon their not submitting, he at once marched against
Torone in Chalcidice, which was held by an Athenian garrison, having been invited by a few persons who were prepared
to hand over the town. Arriving in the dark a little before
daybreak, he sat down with his army near the temple of the
Dioscuri, rather more than a quarter of a mile from the city.
The rest of the town of Torone and the Athenians in garrison
did not perceive his approach; but his partisans knowing that
he was coming (a few of them had secretly gone out to meet
him), were on the watch for his arrival, and were no sooner
aware of it than they took in to them seven light-armed men

with daggers, who alone of twenty men ordered on this service dared to enter, commanded by Lysistratus an Olynthian. These passed through the sea wall, and without being seen went up and put to the sword the garrison of the highest post in the town, which stands on a hill, and broke open the postern on the side of Canastræum.

Brasidas meanwhile came a little nearer and then halted with his main body, sending on one hundred targeteers to be ready to rush in first, the moment that a gate should be thrown open and the beacon lighted as agreed. After some time passed in waiting and wondering at the delay, the targeteers by degrees got up close to the town. The Toronæans inside at work with the party that had entered, had by this time broken down the postern and opened the gates leading to the market-place by cutting through the bar, and first brought some men round and let them in by the postern, in order to strike a panic into the surprised townsmen by suddenly attacking them from behind and on both sides at once; after which they raised the fire-signal as had been agreed, and took in by the market gates the rest of the targeteers.

Brasidas seeing the signal told the troops to rise, and dashed forward amid the loud hurrahs of his men, which carried dismay among the astonished townspeople. Some burst in straight by the gate, others over some square pieces of timber placed against the wall (which had fallen down and was being rebuilt) to draw up stones; Brasidas and the greater number making straight uphill for the higher part of the town, in order to take it from top to bottom, and once for all, while the rest of the multitude spread in all directions.

The capture of the town was effected before the great body of the Toronæans had recovered from their surprise and confusion; but the conspirators and the citizens of their party at once joined the invaders. About fifty of the Athenian heavy infantry happened to be sleeping in the market-place when the alarm reached them. A few of these were killed fighting; the rest escaped, some by land, others to the two ships on the station, and took refuge in Lecythus, a fort garrisoned by their own men in the corner of the town running out into the sea and cut off by a narrow isthmus; where they were joined by the Toronæans of their party.

Day now arrived, and the town being secured, Brasidas made a proclamation to the Toronæans who had taken refuge with the Athenians, to come out, as many as chose, to their homes without fearing for their rights or persons, and sent a herald to invite the Athenians to accept a truce, and to evacuate Lecythus with their property, as being Chalcidian ground. The Athenians refused this offer, but asked for a truce for a day to take up their dead. Brasidas granted it for two days, which he employed in fortifying the houses near, and the Athenians in doing the same to their positions. Meanwhile he called a meeting of the Toronæans, and said very much what he had said at Acanthus, namely, that they must not look upon those who had negotiated with him for the capture of the town as bad men or as traitors, as they had not acted as they had done from corrupt motives or in order to enslave the city, but for the good and freedom of Torone; nor again must those who had not shared in the enterprise fancy that they would not equally reap its fruits, as he had not come to destroy either city or individual. This was the reason of his proclamation to those that had fled for refuge to the Athenians: he thought none the worse of them for their friendship for the Athenians; he believed that they had only to make trial of the Lacedæmonians to like them as well, or even much better, as acting much more justly: it was for want of such a trial that they were now afraid of them. Meanwhile he warned all of them to prepare to be staunch allies, and for being held responsible for all faults in future: for the past, they had not wronged the Lacedæmonians but had been wronged by others who were too strong for them, and any opposition that they might have offered him could be excused.

Having encouraged them with this address, as soon as the truce expired he made his attack upon Lecythus; the Athenians defending themselves from a poor wall and from some houses with parapets. One day they beat him off; the next the enemy were preparing to bring up an engine against them from which they meant to throw fire upon the wooden defences, and the troops were already coming up to the point where they fancied they could best bring up the engine, and where the place was most assailable; meanwhile the Athenians put a wooden tower upon a house opposite, and carried up a quantity of jars and casks of water and big stones, and a large number of men also climbed up. The house thus laden too heavily suddenly broke down with a loud crash; at which the men who were near and saw it were more vexed than frightened; but those not so near, and still more those furthest off thought that the place was already taken at that point, and fled in haste to the sea and the ships.

Brasidas, perceiving that they were deserting the parapet, and seeing what was going on, dashed forward with his troops, and immediately took the fort, and put to the sword all whom he found in it. In this way the place was evacuated by the Athenians, who went across in their boats and ships to Pallene. Now there is a temple of Athene in Lecythus, and Brasidas had proclaimed in the moment of making the assault, that he would give thirty silver minæ to the man first on the wall. Being now of opinion that the capture was scarcely due to human means, he gave the thirty minæ to the goddess for her temple, and razed and cleared Lecythus, and made the whole of it consecrated ground. The rest of the winter he spent in settling the places in his hands, and in making designs upon the rest; and with the expiration of the winter the eighth year of this war ended.

In the spring of the summer following, the Lacedæmonians and Athenians made an armistice for a year; the Athenians thinking that they would thus have full leisure to take their precautions before Brasidas could procure the revolt of any more of their towns, and might also, if it suited them, conclude a general peace; the Lacedæmonians divining the actual fears of the Athenians, and thinking that after once tasting a respite from trouble and misery they would be more disposed to consent to a reconciliation, and to give back the prisoners, and make a treaty for the longer period. The great idea of the Lacedæmonians was to get back their men while Brasidas' good fortune lasted: further successes might make the struggle a less unequal one in Chalcidice, but would leave them still deprived of their men, and even in Chalcidice not more than a match for the Athenians and by no means certain of victory. An armistice was accordingly concluded by Lacedæmon and her allies upon the terms following:—

I. *As to the temple and oracle of the Pythian Apollo, we*

*are agreed that whosoever will shall have access to it, without
fraud or fear, according to the usages of his forefathers. The
Lacedæmonians and the allies present agree to this, and
promise to send heralds to the Bœotians and Phocians, and
to do their best to persuade them to agree likewise.*

*2. As to the treasure of the god, we agree to exert ourselves
to detect all malversators, truly and honestly following the
customs of our forefathers, we and you and all others willing
to do so, all following the customs of our forefathers. As to
these points the Lacedæmonians and the other allies are agreed
as has been said.*

*3. As to what follows, the Lacedæmonians and the other
allies agree, if the Athenians conclude a treaty, to remain, each
of us in our own territory, retaining our respective acquisitions; the garrison in Coryphasium keeping within Buphras
and Tomeus; that in Cythera attempting no communication
with the Peloponnesian confederacy, neither we with them,
nor they with us; that in Nisæa and Minoa not crossing the
road leading from the gates of the temple of Nisus to that of
Poseidon and from thence straight to the bridge at Minoa;
the Megarians and the allies being equally bound not to cross
this road, and the Athenians retaining the island they have
taken, without any communication on either side; as to
Troezen, each side retaining what it has, and as was arranged
with the Athenians.*

*4. As to the use of the sea, so far as refers to their own coast
and to that of their confederacy, that the Lacedæmonians and
their allies may voyage upon it in any vessel rowed by oars
and of not more than five hundred talents' tonnage, not a
vessel of war.*

*5. That all heralds and embassies, with as many attend-
ants as they please, for concluding the war and adjusting
claims, shall have free passage, going and coming, to Peloponnese or Athens by land and by sea.*

*6. That during the truce, deserters whether bond or free
shall be received neither by you, nor by us.*

*7. Further, that satisfaction shall be given by you to us
and by us to you according to the public law of our several
countries, all disputes being settled by law without recourse
to hostilities.*

The Lacedæmonians and allies agree to these articles: but if you have anything fairer or juster to suggest, come to Lacedæmon and let us know; whatever shall be just will meet with no objection either from the Lacedæmonians or from the allies. Only let those who come come with full powers, as you desire us. The truce shall be for one year.

Approved by the people

The tribe of Acamantis had the prytany, Phœnippus was secretary, Niciades chairman. Laches moved, in the name of the good luck of the Athenians, that they should conclude the armistice upon the terms agreed upon by the Lacedæmonians and the allies. It was agreed accordingly in the popular assembly, that the armistice should be for one year, beginning that very day, the fourteenth of the month of Elaphebolion; during which time ambassadors and heralds should go and come between the two countries to discuss the bases of a pacification. That the generals and prytanes should call an assembly of the people, in which the Athenians should first consult on the peace, and on the mode in which the embassy for putting an end to the war should be admitted. That the embassy now present should at once take the engagement before the people to keep well and truly this truce for one year.

On these terms the Lacedæmonians concluded with the Athenians and their allies on the twelfth day of the Spartan month Gerastius; the allies also taking the oaths. Those who concluded and poured the libation were Taurus, son of Echetimides, Athenæus, son of Pericleidas, and Philocharidas, son of Eryxilaidas, Lacedæmonians; Æneas, son of Ocytus, and Euphamidas, son of Aristonymus, Corinthians; Damotimus, son of Naucrates, and Onasimus, son of Megacles, Sicyonians; Nicasus, son of Cecalus, and Menecrates, son of Amphidorus, Megarians; and Amphias, son of Eupaidas, an Epidaurian; and the Athenian generals Nicostratus, son of Diitrephes, Nicias, son of Niceratus, and Autocles, son of Tolmæus. Such was the armistice, and during the whole of it conferences went on on the subject of a pacification.

In the days in which they were going backwards and forwards to these conferences, Scione, a town in Pallene, revolted from Athens, and went over to Brasidas. The Scionæans say that they are Pallenians from Peloponnese, and that their

first founders on their voyage from Troy were carried in to
this spot by the storm which the Achæans were caught in,
and there settled. The Scionæans had no sooner revolted than
Brasidas crossed over by night to Scione, with a friendly
galley ahead and himself in a small boat some way behind;
his idea being that if he fell in with a vessel larger than the
boat he would have the galley to defend him, while a ship
that was a match for the galley, would probably neglect the
small vessel to attack the large one, and thus leave him time to
escape. His passage effected, he called a meeting of the
Scionæans and spoke to the same effect as at Acanthus and
Torone, adding that they merited the utmost commendation
in that, in spite of Pallene within the isthmus being cut off
by the Athenian occupation of Potidæa and of their own
practically insular position, they had of their own free will
gone forward to meet their liberty instead of timorously waiting until they had been by force compelled to their own manifest good. This was a sign that they would valiantly undergo
any trial, however great; and if he should order affairs as he
intended, he should count them among the truest and sincerest
friends of the Lacedæmonians, and would in every other way
honour them.

The Scionæans were elated by his language, and even those
who had at first disapproved of what was being done catching
the general confidence, they determined on a vigorous conduct
of the war, and welcomed Brasidas with all possible honours,
publicly crowning him with a crown of gold as the liberator
of Hellas; while private persons crowded round him and
decked him with garlands as though he had been an athlete.
Meanwhile Brasidas left them a small garrison for the present
and crossed back again, and not long afterwards sent over a
larger force, intending with the help of the Scionæans to attempt Mende and Potidæa before the Athenians should arrive; Scione, he felt, being too like an island for them not to
relieve it. He had besides intelligence in the above towns about
their betrayal.

In the midst of his designs upon the towns in question, a
galley arrived with the commissioners carrying round the news
of the armistice, Aristonymus for the Athenians and Athenæus for the Lacedæmonians. The troops now crossed back to

Torone, and the commissioners gave Brasidas notice of the convention. All the Lacedæmonian allies in Thrace accepted what had been done; and Aristonymus made no difficulty about the rest, but finding, on counting the days, that the Scionæans had revolted after the date of the convention, refused to include them in it. To this Brasidas earnestly objected, asserting that the revolt took place before, and would not give up the town. Upon Aristonymus reporting the case to Athens, the people at once prepared to send an expedition to Scione. Upon this, envoys arrived from Lacedæmon, alleging that this would be a breach of the truce, and laying claim to the town upon the faith of the assertion of Brasidas, and meanwhile offering to submit the question to arbitration. Arbitration, however, was what the Athenians did not choose to risk; being determined to send troops at once to the place, and furious at the idea of even the islanders now daring to revolt, in a vain reliance upon the power of the Lacedæmonians by land. Besides the facts of the revolt were rather as the Athenians contended, the Scionæans having revolted two days after the convention. Cleon accordingly succeeded in carrying a decree to reduce and put to death the Scionæans; and the Athenians employed the leisure which they now enjoyed in preparing for the expedition.

Meanwhile Mende revolted, a town in Pallene and a colony of the Eretrians, and was received without scruple by Brasidas, in spite of its having evidently come over during the armistice, on account of certain infringements of the truce alleged by him against the Athenians. This audacity of Mende was partly caused by seeing Brasidas forward in the matter and by the conclusions drawn from his refusal to betray Scione; and besides, the conspirators in Mende were few, and, as I have already intimated, had carried on their practices too long not to fear detection for themselves, and not to wish to force the inclination of the multitude. This news made the Athenians more furious than ever, and they at once prepared against both towns. Brasidas expecting their arrival conveyed away to Olynthus in Chalcidice the women and children of the Scionæans and Mendæans, and sent over to them five hundred Peloponnesian heavy infantry and three hundred Chalcidian targeteers, all under the command of Polydamidas.

Leaving these two towns to prepare together against the speedy arrival of the Athenians, Brasidas and Perdiccas started on a second joint expedition into Lyncus against Arrhabæus; the latter with the forces of his Macedonian subjects, and a corps of heavy infantry composed of Hellenes domiciled in the country; the former with the Pelopon· nesians whom he still had with him and the Chalcidians, Acanthians, and the rest in such force as they were able. In all there were about three thousand Hellenic heavy infantry, accompanied by all the Macedonian cavalry with the Chalcidians, near one thousand strong, besides an immense crowd of barbarians. On entering the country of Arrhabæus, they found the Lyncestians encamped awaiting them, and themselves took up a position opposite. The infantry on either side were upon a hill, with a plain between them, into which the horse of both armies first galloped down, and engaged a cavalry action. After this the Lyncestian heavy infantry advanced from their hill to join their cavalry and offered battle; upon which Brasidas and Perdiccas also came down to meet them, and engaged and routed them with heavy loss; the survivors taking refuge upon the heights and there remaining inactive. The victors now set up a trophy and waited two or three days for the Illyrian mercenaries who were to join Perdiccas. Perdiccas then wished to go on and attack the villages of Arrhabæus, and to sit still no longer; but Brasidas, afraid that the Athenians might sail up during his absence, and of something happening to Mende, and seeing besides that the Illyrians did not appear, far from seconding this wish was anxious to return.

While they were thus disputing, the news arrived that the Illyrians had actually betrayed Perdiccas and had joined Arrhabæus; and the fear inspired by their warlike character made both parties now think it best to retreat. However, owing to the dispute, nothing had been settled as to when they should start; and night coming on, the Macedonians and the barbarian crowd took fright in a moment in one of those mysterious panics to which great armies are liable; and persuaded that an army many times more numerous than that which had really arrived was advancing and all but upon them, suddenly broke and fled in the direction of home, and thus com-

pelled Perdiccas, who at first did not perceive what had
occurred, to depart without seeing Brasidas, the two armies
being encamped at a considerable distance from each other.
At daybreak Brasidas, perceiving that the Macedonians had
gone on, and that the Illyrians and Arrhabæus were on the
point of attacking him, formed his heavy infantry into a
square, with the light troops in the centre, and himself also
prepared to retreat. Posting his youngest soldiers to dash out
wherever the enemy should attack them, he himself with three
hundred picked men in the rear intended to face about during
the retreat and beat off the most forward of their assailants.
Meanwhile, before the enemy approached, he sought to sustain the courage of his soldiers with the following hasty
exhortation:—

'Peloponnesians, if I did not suspect you of being dismayed
at being left alone to sustain the attack of a numerous and
barbarian enemy, I should just have said a few words to you
as usual without further explanation. As it is, in the face of
the desertion of our friends and the numbers of the enemy, I
have some advice and information to offer, which, brief as
they must be, will, I hope, suffice for the more important
points. The bravery that you habitually display in war does
not depend on your having allies at your side in this or that
encounter, but on your native courage; nor have numbers
any terrors for citizens of states like yours, in which the many
do not rule the few, but rather the few the many, owing their
position to nothing else than to superiority in the field. Inexperience now makes you afraid of barbarians; and yet the
trial of strength which you had with the Macedonians among
them, and my own judgment, confirmed by what I hear from
others, should be enough to satisfy you that they will not
prove formidable. Where an enemy seems strong but is really
weak, a true knowledge of the facts makes his adversary the
bolder, just as a serious antagonist is encountered most confidently by those who do not know him. Thus the present
enemy might terrify an inexperienced imagination, they are
formidable in outward bulk, their loud yelling is unbearable,
and the brandishing of their weapons in the air has a threaten-
ing appearance. But when it comes to real fighting with an
opponent who stands his ground, they are not what they

seemed; they have no regular order that they should be ashamed of deserting their positions when hard pressed; flight and attack are with them equally honourable, and afford no test of courage; their independent mode of fighting never leaving any one who wants to run away without a fair excuse for so doing. In short, they think frightening you at a secure distance a surer game than meeting you hand to hand; otherwise they would have done the one and not the other. You can thus plainly see that the terrors with which they were at first invested are in fact trifling enough, though to the eye and ear very prominent. Stand your ground therefore when they advance, and again wait your opportunity to retire in good order, and you will reach a place of safety all the sooner, and will know for ever afterwards that rabble such as these, to those who sustain their first attack, do but show off their courage by threats of the terrible things that they are going to do, at a distance, but with those who give way to them are quick enough to display their heroism in pursuit when they can do so without danger.'

With this brief address Brasidas began to lead off his army. Seeing this, the barbarians came on with much shouting and hubbub, thinking that he was flying and that they would overtake him and cut him off. But wherever they charged they found the young men ready to dash out against them, while Brasidas with his picked company sustained their onset. Thus the Peloponnesians withstood the first attack, to the surprise of the enemy, and afterwards received and repulsed them as fast as they came on, retiring as soon as their opponents became quiet. The main body of the barbarians ceased therefore to molest the Hellenes with Brasidas in the open country, and leaving behind a certain number to harass their march, the rest went on after the flying Macedonians, slaying those with whom they came up, and so arrived in time to occupy the narrow pass between two hills that leads into the country of Arrhabæus. They knew that this was the only way by which Brasidas could retreat, and now proceeded to surround him just as he entered the most impracticable part of the road, in order to cut him off.

Brasidas, perceiving their intention, told his three hundred to run on without order, each as quickly as he could, to the

hill which seemed easiest to take, and to try to dislodge the
barbarians already there, before they should be joined by
the main body closing round him. These attacked and overpowered the party upon the hill, and the main army of the
Hellenes now advanced with less difficulty towards it; the
barbarians being terrified at seeing their men on that side
driven from the height, and no longer following the main
body, who, they considered, had gained the frontier and made
good their escape. The heights once gained, Brasidas now
proceeded more securely, and the same day arrived at Arnisa,
the first town in the dominions of Perdiccas. The soldiers,
enraged at the desertion of the Macedonians, vented their
rage on all their yokes of oxen which they found on the road,
and on any baggage which had tumbled off (as might easily
happen in the panic of a night retreat), by unyoking and
cutting down the cattle and taking the baggage for themselves.
From this moment Perdiccas began to regard Brasidas as an
enemy and to feel against the Peloponnesians a hatred which
could not be congenial to the adversary of the Athenians.
However, he departed from his natural interests and made it
his endeavour to come to terms with the latter and to get rid
of the former.

On his return from Macedonia to Torone, Brasidas found
the Athenians already masters of Mende, and remained quiet
where he was, thinking it now out of his power to cross over
into Pallene and assist the Mendæans, but he kept good
watch over Torone. For about the same time as the campaign
in Lyncus, the Athenians sailed upon the expedition which
we left them preparing against Mende and Scione, with fifty
ships, ten of which were Chians, one thousand Athenian heavy
infantry and six hundred archers, one hundred Thracian mercenaries and some targeteers drawn from their allies in the
neighbourhood, under the command of Nicias, son of Niceratus, and Nicostratus, son of Diitrephes. Weighing from Potidæa, the fleet came to land opposite the temple of Poseidon,
and proceeded against Mende; the men of which town, reinforced by three hundred Scionæans, with their Peloponnesian auxiliaries, seven hundred heavy infantry in all, under
Polydamidas, they found encamped upon a strong hill outside
the city. These Nicias, with one hundred and twenty light-

armed Methonæans, sixty picked men from the Athenian
heavy infantry, and all the archers, tried to reach by a path
running up the hill, but received a wound and found himself
unable to force the position; while Nicostratus, with all the
rest of the army, advancing upon the hill, which was naturally
difficult, by a different approach further off, was thrown into
utter disorder; and the whole Athenian army narrowly escaped
being defeated. For that day, as the Mendæans and their allies
showed no signs of yielding, the Athenians retreated and encamped, and the Mendæans at nightfall returned into the
town.

The next day the Athenians sailed round to the Scione side
and took the suburb, and all day plundered the country,
without any one coming out against them, partly because of
intestine disturbances in the town; and the following night
the three hundred Scionæans returned home. On the morrow
Nicias advanced with half the army to the frontier of Scione
and laid waste the country; while Nicostratus with the remainder sat down before the town near the upper gate on the
road to Potidæa. The arms of the Mendæans and of their
Peloponnesian auxiliaries within the wall happened to be
piled in that quarter, where Polydamidas accordingly began
to draw them up for battle, encouraging the Mendæans to
make a sortie. At this moment one of the popular party
answered him factiously that they would not go out and did
not want a war, and for thus answering was dragged by the
arm and knocked about by Polydamidas. Hereupon the infuriated commons at once seized their arms and rushed at
the Peloponnesians and at their allies of the opposite faction.
The troops thus assaulted were at once routed, partly from
the suddenness of the conflict and partly through fear of the
gates being opened to the Athenians, with whom they imagined
that the attack had been concerted. As many as were not
killed on the spot took refuge in the citadel, which they had
held from the first; and the whole Athenian army, Nicias having by this time returned and being close to the city, now
burst into Mende, which had opened its gates without any
convention, and sacked it just as if they had taken it by
storm, the generals even finding some difficulty in restraining
them from also massacring the inhabitants. After this the

Athenians told the Mendæans that they might retain their civil rights, and themselves judge the supposed authors of the revolt; and cut off the party in the citadel by a wall built down to the sea on either side, appointing troops to maintain the blockade. Having thus secured Mende, they proceeded against Scione.

The Scionæans and Peloponnesians marched out against them, occupying a strong hill in front of the town, which had to be captured by the enemy before they could invest the place. The Athenians stormed the hill, defeated and dislodged its occupants, and having encamped and set up a trophy, prepared for the work of circumvallation. Not long after they had begun their operations, the auxiliaries besieged in the citadel of Mende forced the guard by the sea side and arrived by night at Scione, into which most of them succeeded in entering, passing through the besieging army.

While the investment of Scione was in progress, Perdiccas sent a herald to the Athenian generals and made peace with the Athenians, through spite against Brasidas for the retreat from Lyncus, from which moment indeed he had begun to negotiate. The Lacedæmonian Ischagoras was just then upon the point of starting with an army overland to join Brasidas; and Perdiccas, being now required by Nicias to give some proof of the sincerity of his reconciliation to the Athenians, and being himself no longer disposed to let the Peloponnesians into his country, put in motion his friends in Thessaly, with whose chief men he always took care to have relations, and so effectually stopped the army and its preparation that they did not even try the Thessalians. Ischagoras himself, however, with Ameinias and Aristeus, succeeded in reaching Brasidas; they had been commissioned by the Lacedæmonians to inspect the state of affairs, and brought out from Sparta (in violation of all precedent) some of their young men to put in command of the towns, to guard against their being entrusted to the persons upon the spot. Brasidas accordingly placed Clearidas, son of Cleonymus, in Amphipolis, and Pasitelidas, son of Hegesander, in Torone.

The same summer the Thebans dismantled the wall of the Thespians on the charge of Atticism, having always wished to do so, and now finding it an easy matter, as the flower of the Thespian youth had perished in the battle with the Athenians. The same summer also the temple of Hera at Argos was burnt down, through Chrysis, the priestess, placing a lighted torch near the garlands and then falling asleep, so that they all caught fire and were in a blaze before she observed it. Chrysis that very night fled to Phlius for fear of the Argives, who, agreeably to the law in such a case, appointed another priestess named Phaeinis. Chrysis at the time of her flight had been priestess for eight years of the present war and half the ninth. At the close of the summer the investment of Scione was completed, and the Athenians, leaving a detachment to maintain the blockade, returned with the rest of their army.

During the winter following the Athenians and Lacedæmonians were kept quiet by the armistice; but the Mantineans and Tegeans, and their respective allies, fought a battle at Laodicium, in the Oresthid. The victory remained doubtful, as each side routed one of the wings opposed to them, and both set up trophies and sent spoils to Delphi. After heavy loss on both sides the battle was undecided, and night interrupted the action; yet the Tegeans passed the night on the field and set up a trophy at once, while the Mantineans withdrew to Bucolion and set up theirs afterwards.

At the close of the same winter, in fact almost in spring, Brasidas made an attempt upon Potidæa. He arrived by night, and succeeded in planting a ladder against the wall without being discovered, the ladder being planted just in the interval between the passing round of the bell and the return of the man who brought it back. Upon the garrison, however, taking the alarm immediately afterwards, before his men came up, he quickly led off his troops, without waiting until it was day. So ended the winter and the ninth year of this war of which Thucydides is the historian.

BOOK V

CHAPTER XV

TENTH YEAR OF THE WAR—DEATH OF CLEON AND BRASIDAS —PEACE OF NICIAS

B.C. 422: *End of the armistice—Cleon's foray into Chalcidice—At Eion—Brasidas' strategy—His speech—Defeat of the Athenians— Death of Cleon and Brasidas in battle—General desire for peace— Treaty concluded; its terms—B.C. 421: Method of reckoning time—Terms of alliance.*

THE next summer the truce for a year ended, after lasting until the Pythian games. During the armistice the Athenians expelled the Delians from Delos, concluding that they must have been polluted by some old offence at the time of their consecration, and that this had been the omission in the previous purification of the island, which, as I have related, had been thought to have been duly accomplished by the removal of the graves of the dead. The Delians had Atramyttium in Asia given them by Pharnaces, and settled there as they removed from Delos.

Meanwhile Cleon prevailed on the Athenians to let him set sail at the expiration of the armistice for the towns in the direction of Thrace with twelve hundred heavy infantry and three hundred horse from Athens, a larger force of the allies, and thirty ships. First touching at the still besieged Scione, and taking some heavy infantry from the army there, he next sailed into Cophosa harbour in the territory of Torone, which is not far from the town. From thence, having learnt from deserters that Brasidas was not in Torone, and that its garrison was not strong enough to give him battle, he advanced with his army against the town, sending ten ships to sail round into the harbour. He first came to the fortification lately thrown up in front of the town by Brasidas in order to take in the suburb, to do which he had pulled down part of the original wall and made it all one city. To this point Pasitelidas, the Lacedæmonian commander, with such garrison as there was in the place, hurried to repel the Athenian assault; but finding himself hard pressed, and seeing the ships that had been sent round sailing into the harbour, Pasitelidas began to be afraid that they might get up to the city before its defenders were there, and the fortification being also carried, he might be taken prisoner, and so abandoned the outwork and ran into the town. But the Athenians from the ships had already taken Torone, and their land forces following at his heels burst in with him with a rush over the part of the old wall that had been pulled down, killing some of the Peloponnesians and Toronæans in the mêlée, and making prisoners of the rest, and Pasitelidas their commander amongst them. Brasidas meanwhile had advanced to relieve Torone, and had only about four miles more to go when he heard of its fall on the road, and turned back again. Cleon and the Athenians set up two trophies, one by the harbour, the other by the fortification, and making slaves of the wives and children of the Toronæans, sent the men with the Peloponnesians and any Chalcidians that were there, to the number of seven hundred, to Athens; whence, however, they all came home afterwards, the Peloponnesians on the conclusion of peace, and the rest by being exchanged against other prisoners with the Olynthians. About the same time Panactum, a fortress on the Athenian border, was taken by treachery by the Bœotians. Meanwhile Cleon, after placing a garrison in Torone, weighed anchor and sailed round Athos on his way to Amphipolis.

About the same time Phæax, son of Erasistratus, set sail with two colleagues as ambassador from Athens to Italy and Sicily. The Leontines, upon the departure of the Athenians from Sicily after the pacification, had placed a number of new citizens upon the roll, and the commons had a design for redividing the land; but the upper classes, aware of their intention, called in the Syracusans and expelled the commons. These last were scattered in various directions; but the upper classes came to an agreement with the Syracusans, abandoned and laid waste their city, and went and lived at Syracuse, where they were made citizens. Afterwards some of them were dissatisfied, and leaving Syracuse occupied Phocææ, a quar-

ter of the town of Leontini, and Bricinniæ, a strong place in
the Leontine country, and being there joined by most of the
exiled commons carried on war from the fortifications. The
Athenians hearing this, sent Phæax to see if they could not
by some means so convince their allies there and the rest
of the Sicilians of the ambitious designs of Syracuse, as to
induce them to form a general coalition against her, and thus
save the commons of Leontini. Arrived in Sicily, Phæax succeeded at Camarina and Agrigentum, but meeting with a
repulse at Gela did not go on to the rest, as he saw that he
should not succeed with them, but returned through the
country of the Sicels to Catana, and after visiting Bricinniæ
as he passed, and encouraging its inhabitants, sailed back to
Athens.

During his voyage along the coast to and from Sicily, he
treated with some cities in Italy on the subject of friendship
with Athens, and also fell in with some Locrian settlers exiled
from Messina, who had been sent thither when the Locrians
were called in by one of the factions that divided Messina
after the pacification of Sicily, and Messina came for a time
into the hands of the Locrians. These being met by Phæax
on their return home received no injury at his hands, as the
Locrians had agreed with him for a treaty with Athens. They
were the only people of the allies who, when the reconciliation
between the Sicilians took place, had not made peace with
her; nor indeed would they have done so now, if they had
not been pressed by a war with the Hipponians and Med-
mæans who lived on their border, and were colonists of theirs.
Phæax meanwhile proceeded on his voyage, and at length
arrived at Athens.

Cleon, whom we left on his voyage from Torone to Amphipolis, made Eion his base, and after an unsuccessful assault
upon the Andrian colony of Stagirus, took Galepsus, a colony
of Thasos, by storm. He now sent envoys to Perdiccas to
command his attendance with an army, as provided by the
alliance; and others to Thrace, to Polles, king of the Odoman-
tians, who was to bring as many Thracian mercenaries as
possible; and himself remained inactive in Eion, awaiting
their arrival. Informed of this, Brasidas on his part took up
a position of observation upon Cerdylium, a place situated

in the Argilian country on high ground across the river, not far from Amphipolis, and commanding a view on all sides, and thus made it impossible for Cleon's army to move without his seeing it; for he fully expected that Cleon, despising the scanty numbers of his opponent, would march against Amphipolis with the force that he had got with him. At the same time Brasidas made his preparations, calling to his standard fifteen hundred Thracian mercenaries, and all the Edonians, horse and targeteers; he also had a thousand Myrcinian and Chalcidian targeteers, besides those in Amphipolis, and a force of heavy infantry numbering altogether about two thousand, and three hundred Hellenic horse. Fifteen hundred of these he had with him upon Cerdylium; the rest were stationed with Clearidas in Amphipolis.

After remaining quiet for some time, Cleon was at length obliged to do as Brasidas expected. His soldiers, tired of their inactivity, began also seriously to reflect on the weakness and incompetence of their commander and the skill and valour that would be opposed to him, and on their own original unwillingness to accompany him. These murmurs coming to the ears of Cleon, he resolved not to disgust the army by keeping it in the same place, and broke up his camp and advanced. The temper of the general was what it had been at Pylos, his success on that occasion having given him confidence in his capacity. He never dreamed of any one coming out to fight him, but said that he was rather going up to view the place; and if he waited for his reinforcements it was not in order to make victory secure in case he should be compelled to engage, but to be enabled to surround and storm the city. He accordingly came and posted his army upon a strong hill in front of Amphipolis, and proceeded to examine the lake formed by the Strymon, and how the town lay on the side of Thrace. He thought to retire at pleasure without fighting, as there was no one to be seen upon the wall or coming out of the gates, all of which were shut. Indeed, it seemed a mistake not to have brought down engines with him; he could then have taken the town, there being no one to defend it.

As soon as Brasidas saw the Athenians in motion he descended himself from Cerdylium and entered Amphipolis. He did not venture to go out in regular order against the Athenians: he mistrusted his strength, and thought it inadequate to the attempt; not in numbers—these were not so unequal—but in quality, the flower of the Athenian army being in the field, with the best of the Lemnians and Imbrians. He therefore prepared to assail them by stratagem. By showing the enemy the number of his troops, and the shifts which he had been put to to arm them, he thought that he should have less chance of beating him than by not letting him have a sight of them, and thus learn how good a right he had to despise them. He accordingly picked out a hundred and fifty heavy infantry, and putting the rest under Clearidas determined to attack suddenly before the Athenians retired; thinking that he should not have again such a chance of catching them alone, if their reinforcements were once allowed to come up; and so calling all his soldiers together in order to encourage them and explain his intention, spoke as follows:—

'Peloponnesians, the character of the country from which we have come, one which has always owed its freedom to valour, and the fact that you are Dorians and the enemy you are about to fight Ionians, whom you are accustomed to beat, are things that do not need further comment. But the plan of attack that I propose to pursue, this it is as well to explain, in order that the fact of our adventuring with a part instead of with the whole of our forces may not damp your courage by the apparent disadvantage at which it places you. I imagine it is the poor opinion that he has of us, and the fact that he has no idea of any one coming out to engage him, that has made the enemy march up to the place and carelessly look about him as he is doing, without noticing us. But the most successful soldier will always be the man who most happily detects a blunder like this, and who carefully consulting his own means makes his attack not so much by open and regular approaches, as by seizing the opportunity of the moment; and these stratagems, which do the greatest service to our friends by most completely deceiving our enemies, have the most brilliant name in war. Therefore, while their careless confidence continues, and they are still thinking, as in my judgment they are now doing, more of retreat than of maintaining their position, while their spirit is slack and not high-strung with expectation, I with the men under my command will, if possible, take them by surprise and fall with a run upon their centre; and do you, Clearidas, afterwards, when you see me already upon them, and, as is likely, dealing terror among them, take with you the Amphipolitans, and the rest of the allies, and suddenly open the gates and dash at them, and hasten to engage as quickly as you can. That is our best chance of establishing a panic among them, as a fresh assailant has always more terrors for an enemy than the one he is immediately engaged with. Show yourself a brave man, as a Spartan should; and do you, allies, follow him like men, and remember that zeal, honour, and obedience mark the good soldier, and that this day will make you either free men and allies of Lacedæmon, or slaves of Athens; even if you escape without personal loss of liberty or life, your bondage will be on harsher terms than before, and you will also hinder the liberation of the rest of the Hellenes. No cowardice then on your part, seeing the greatness of the issues at stake, and I will show that what I preach to others I can practise myself.'

After this brief speech Brasidas himself prepared for the sally, and placed the rest with Clearidas at the Thracian gates to support him as had been agreed. Meanwhile he had been seen coming down from Cerdylium and then in the city, which is overlooked from the outside, sacrificing near the temple of Athene; in short, all his movements had been observed, and word was brought to Cleon, who had at the moment gone on to look about him, that the whole of the enemy's force could be seen in the town, and that the feet of horses and men in great numbers were visible under the gates, as if a sally were intended. Upon hearing this he went up to look, and having done so, being unwilling to venture upon the decisive step of a battle before his reinforcements came up, and fancying that he would have time to retire, bid the retreat be sounded and sent orders to the men to effect it by moving on the left wing in the direction of Eion, which was indeed the only way practicable. This however not being quick enough for him, he joined the retreat in person and made the right wing wheel round, thus turning its unarmed side to the enemy. It was then that Brasidas seeing the Athenian force in motion and his opportunity come, said to the men with him and the rest, ''Those fellows will never stand before us, one can see that by the way their spears and heads are going. Troops which do as they do seldom stand a charge. Quick, some one, and open the gates I spoke of, and let us be out and at them with no fears for the result.' Accordingly issuing out by the palisade gate and by the first in the long wall then existing, he ran at the top of his speed along the straight road, where the trophy now stands as you go by the steepest part of the hill, and fell upon and routed the centre of the Athenians, panic-stricken by their own disorder and astounded at his audacity. At the same moment Clearidas in execution of his orders issued out from the Thracian gates to support him, and also attacked the enemy. The result was that the Athenians, suddenly and unexpectedly attacked on both sides, fell into confusion; and their left towards Eion, which had already got on some distance, at once broke and fled. Just as it was in full retreat and Brasidas was passing on to attack the right, he received a wound; but his fall was not perceived by the Athenians, as he was taken up by those near him and carried off the field. The Athenian right made a better stand, and though Cleon, who from the first had no thought of fighting, at once fled and was overtaken and slain by a Myrcinian targeteer, his infantry forming in close order upon the hill twice or thrice repulsed the attacks of Clearidas, and did not finally give way until they were surrounded and routed by the missiles of the Myrcinian and Chalcidian horse and the targeteers. Thus the Athenian army was all now in flight; and such as escaped being killed in the battle by the Chalcidian horse and the targeteers, dispersed among the hills, and with difficulty made their way to Eion. The men who had taken up and rescued Brasidas, brought him into the town with the breath still in him: he lived to hear of the victory of his troops, and not long after expired. The rest of the army returning with Clearidas from the pursuit stripped the dead and set up a trophy.

After this all the allies attended in arms and buried Brasidas at the public expense in the city, in front of what is now the market-place, and the Amphipolitans having enclosed his tomb, ever afterwards sacrifice to him as a hero and have given to him the honour of games and annual offerings. They constituted him the founder of their colony, and pulled down

the Hagnonic erections and obliterated everything that could
be interpreted as a memorial of his having founded the place;
for they considered that Brasidas had been their preserver,
and courting as they did the alliance of Lacedæmon for fear
of Athens, in their present hostile relations with the latter
they could no longer with the same advantage or satisfaction
pay Hagnon his honours. They also gave the Athenians back
their dead. About six hundred of the latter had fallen and
only seven of the enemy, owing to there having been no regular
engagement, but the affair of accident and panic that I have
described. After taking up their dead the Athenians sailed off
home, while Clearidas and his troops remained to arrange
matters at Amphipolis.

About the same time three Lacedæmonians—Ramphias,
Autocharidas, and Epicydidas—led a reinforcement of nine
hundred heavy infantry to the towns in the direction of
Thrace, and arriving at Heraclea in Trachis reformed matters
there as seemed good to them. While they delayed there, this
battle took place and so the summer ended.

With the beginning of the winter following Ramphias and
his companions penetrated as far as Pierium in Thessaly; but
as the Thessalians opposed their further advance, and Brasidas whom they came to reinforce was dead, they turned back
home, thinking that the moment had gone by, the Athenians
being defeated and gone, and themselves not equal to the
execution of Brasidas' designs. The main cause however of
their return was because they knew that when they set out,
Lacedæmonian opinion was really in favour of peace.

Indeed it so happened that directly after the battle of
Amphipolis and the retreat of Ramphias from Thessaly, both
sides ceased to prosecute the war and turned their attention
to peace. Athens had suffered severely at Delium, and again
shortly afterwards at Amphipolis, and had no longer that
confidence in her strength which had made her before refuse
to treat, in the belief of ultimate victory which her success at
the moment had inspired; besides, she was afraid of her allies
being tempted by her reverses to rebel more generally, and
repented having let go the splendid opportunity for peace
which the affair of Pylos had offered. Lacedæmon, on the
other hand, found the event of the war falsify her notion

that a few years would suffice for the overthrow of the power of the Athenians by the devastation of their land. She had suffered on the island a disaster hitherto unknown at Sparta; she saw her country plundered from Pylos and Cythera; the Helots were deserting, and she was in constant apprehension that those who remained in Peloponnese would rely upon those outside and take advantage of the situation to renew their old attempts at revolution. Besides this, as chance would have it, her thirty years' truce with the Argives was upon the point of expiring; and they refused to renew it unless Cynuria were restored to them; so that it seemed impossible to fight Argos and Athens at once. She also suspected some of the cities in Peloponnese of intending to go over to the enemy, as was indeed the case.

These considerations made both sides disposed for an accommodation; the Lacedæmonians being probably the most eager, as they ardently desired to recover the men taken upon the island, the Spartans among whom belonged to the first families and were accordingly related to the governing body in Lacedæmon. Negotiations had been begun directly after their capture, but the Athenians in their hour of triumph would not consent to any reasonable terms; though after their defeat at Delium Lacedæmon, knowing that they would be now more inclined to listen, at once concluded the armistice for a year, during which they were to confer together and see if a longer period could not be agreed upon.

Now, however, after the Athenian defeat at Amphipolis, and the death of Cleon and Brasidas, who had been the two principal opponents of peace on either side—the latter from the success and honour which war gave him, the former because he thought that, if tranquillity were restored, his crimes would be more open to detection and his slanders less credited —the foremost candidates for power in either city, Pleistoanax, son of Pausanias, king of Lacedæmon, and Nicias, son of Niceratus, the most fortunate general of his time, each desired peace more ardently than ever. Nicias, while still happy and honoured, wished to secure his good fortune, to obtain a present release from trouble for himself and his countrymen, and hand down to posterity a name as an ever-successful statesman, and thought the way to do this was to

keep out of danger and commit himself as little as possible to
fortune, and that peace alone made this keeping out of danger
possible. Pleistoanax, again, was assailed by his enemies for
his restoration, and regularly held up by them to the prejudice
of his countrymen, upon every reverse that befell them, as
though his unjust restoration were the cause; the accusation
being that he and his brother Aristocles had bribed the proph-
etess of Delphi to tell the Lacedæmonian deputations which
successively arrived at the temple to bring home the seed of
the demigod son of Zeus from abroad, else they would have
to plough with a silver share. In this way, it was insisted, in
time he had induced the Lacedæmonians in the nineteenth
year of his exile to Lycæum (whither he had gone when banished on suspicion of having been bribed to retreat from
Attica, and had built half his house within the consecrated
precinct of Zeus for fear of the Lacedæmonians), to restore
him with the same dances and sacrifices with which they had
instituted their kings upon the first settlement of Lacedæmon.
The smart of this accusation, and the reflexion that in peace
no disaster could occur, and that when Lacedæmon had recovered her men there would be nothing for his enemies to take
hold of (whereas, while war lasted the highest station must
always bear the scandal of everything that went wrong), made
him ardently desire a settlement. Accordingly this winter
was employed in conferences; and as spring rapidly approached, the Lacedæmonians sent round orders to the cities
to prepare for a fortified occupation of Attica, and held this
as a sword over the heads of the Athenians to induce them
to listen to their overtures; and at last, after many claims had
been urged on either side at the conferences, a peace was
agreed on upon the following basis. Each party was to restore
its conquests, but Athens was to keep Nisæa; her demand for
Platæa being met by the Thebans asserting that they had
acquired the place not by force or treachery, but by the
voluntary adhesion upon agreement of its citizens; and the
same, according to the Athenian account, being the history
of her acquisition of Nisæa. This arranged, the Lacedæmonians summoned their allies, and all voting for peace except
the Bœotians, Corinthians, Eleans, and Megarians, who did
not approve of these proceedings, they concluded the treaty

and made peace, each of the contracting parties swearing to
the following articles:—

*The Athenians and Lacedæmonians and their allies made a
treaty, and swear to it, city by city, as follows:*

1. *Touching the national temples, there shall be a free passage by land and by sea to all who wish it, to sacrifice, travel,
consult, and attend the oracle or games, according to the customs of their countries.*

2. *The temple and shrine of Apollo at Delphi and the Delphians shall be governed by their own laws, taxed by their
own state, and judged by their own judges, the land and the
people, according to the custom of their country.*

3. *The treaty shall be binding for fifty years upon the
Athenians and the allies of the Athenians, and upon the
Lacedæmonians and the allies of the Lacedæmonians, without
fraud or hurt by land or by sea.*

4. *It shall not be lawful to take up arms, with intent to
do hurt, either for the Lacedæmonians and their allies against
the Athenians and their allies, or for the Athenians and their
allies against the Lacedæmonians and their allies, in any way
or means whatsoever. But should any difference arise between
them they are to have recourse to law and oaths, according
as may be agreed between the parties.*

5. *The Lacedæmonians and their allies shall give back
Amphipolis to the Athenians. Nevertheless, in the case of cities
given up by the Lacedæmonians to the Athenians, the inhabitants shall be allowed to go where they please and to take
their property with them; and the cities shall be independent,
paying only the tribute of Aristides. And it shall not be lawful
for the Athenians or their allies to carry on war against them
after the treaty has been concluded, so long as the tribute is
paid. The cities referred to are Argilus, Stagirus, Acanthus,
Scolus, Olynthus, and Spartolus. These cities shall be neutral,
allies neither of the Lacedæmonians nor of the Athenians; but
if the cities consent, it shall be lawful for the Athenians to
make them their allies, provided always that the cities wish it.
The Mecybernæans, Sanæans and Singæans shall inhabit their
own cities, as also the Olynthians and Acanthians; but the
Lacedæmonians and their allies shall give back Panactum to
the Athenians*

6. *The Athenians shall give back Coryphasium, Cythera, Methana, Pteleum, and Atalanta to the Lacedæmonians, and also all Lacedæmonians that are in the prison at Athens or elsewhere in the Athenian dominions, and shall let go the Peloponnesians besieged in Scione, and all others in Scione that are allies of the Lacedæmonians, and all whom Brasidas sent in there, and any others of the allies of the Lacedæmonians that may be in the prison at Athens or elsewhere in the Athenian dominions.*

7. *The Lacedæmonians and their allies shall in like manner give back any of the Athenians or their allies that they may have in their hands.*

8. *In the case of Scione, Torone, and Sermylium, and any other cities that the Athenians may have, the Athenians may adopt such measures as they please.*

9. *The Athenians shall take an oath to the Lacedæmonians and their allies, city by city. Every man shall swear by the most binding oath of his country, seventeen from each city. The oath shall be as follows:—'I will abide by this agreement and treaty honestly and without deceit.' In the same way an oath shall be taken by the Lacedæmonians and their allies to the Athenians; and the oath shall be renewed annually by both parties. Pillars shall be erected at Olympia, Pythia, the Isthmus, at Athens in the Acropolis, and at Lacedæmon in the temple at Amyclæ.*

10. *If anything be forgotten, whatever it be, and on whatever point, it shall be consistent with their oath for both parties the Athenians and Lacedæmonians to alter it, according to their discretion.*

The treaty begins from the Ephoralty of Pleistolas in Lacedæmon, on the 27th day of the month of Artemisium, and from the Archonship of Alcæus at Athens, on the 25th day of the month of Elaphebolion. Those who took the oath and poured the libations for the Lacedæmonians were Pleistoanax, Agis, Pleistolas, Damagetus, Chionis, Metagenes, Acanthus, Daithus, Ischagoras, Philocharidas, Zeuxidas, Antippus, Tellis, Alcinadas, Empedias, Menas, and Laphilus; for the Athenians, Lampon, Isthmionicus, Nicias, Laches, Euthydemus, Procles, Pythodorus, Hagnon, Myrtilus, Thrasycles, The-

agenes, Aristocrates, Iolcius, Timocrates, Leon, Lamachus and Demosthenes.

This treaty was made in the spring, just at the end of winter, directly after the city festival of Dionysus, just ten years, with the difference of a few days, from the first invasion of Attica and the commencement of this war. This must be calculated by the seasons rather than by trusting to the enumeration of the names of the several magistrates or offices of honour that are used to mark past events. Accuracy is impossible where an event may have occurred in the beginning, or middle, or at any period in their tenure of office. But by computing by summers and winters, the method adopted in this history, it will be found that, each of these amounting to half a year, there were ten summers and as many winters contained in this first war.

Meanwhile the Lacedæmonians, to whose lot it fell to begin the work of restitution, immediately set free all the prisoners of war in their possession, and sent Ischagoras, Menas, and Philocharidas as envoys to the towns in the direction of Thrace, to order Clearidas to hand over Amphipolis to the Athenians, and the rest of their allies each to accept the treaty as it affected them. They, however, did not like its terms, and refused to accept it; Clearidas also, willing to oblige the Chalcidians, would not hand over the town, averring his inability to do so against their will. Meanwhile he hastened in person to Lacedæmon with envoys from the place, to defend his disobedience against the possible accusations of Ischagoras and his companions, and also to see whether it was too late for the agreement to be altered; and on finding the Lacedæmonians were bound, quickly set out back again with instructions from them to hand over the place, if possible, or at all events to bring out the Peloponnesians that were in it.

The allies happened to be present in person at Lacedæmon, and those who had not accepted the treaty were now asked by the Lacedæmonians to adopt it. This, however, they refused to do, for the same reasons as before, unless a fairer one than the present were agreed upon; and remaining firm in their determination were dismissed by the Lacedæmonians, who now decided on forming an alliance with the Athenians,

thinking that Argos, who had refused the application of
Ampelidas and Lichas for a renewal of the treaty, would
without Athens be no longer formidable, and that the rest
of the Peloponnese would be most likely to keep quiet, if the
coveted alliance of Athens were shut against them. Accordingly, after conference with the Athenian ambassadors, an
alliance was agreed upon and oaths were exchanged, upon
the terms following:—

1. *The Lacedæmonians shall be allies of the Athenians for
fifty years.*

2. *Should any enemy invade the territory of Lacedæmon
and injure the Lacedæmonians, the Athenians shall help them
in such way as they most effectively can, according to their
power. But if the invader be gone after plundering the country, that city shall be the enemy of Lacedæmon and Athens,
and shall be chastised by both, and one shall not make peace
without the other. This to be honestly, loyally, and without
fraud.*

3. *Should any enemy invade the territory of Athens and
injure the Athenians, the Lacedæmonians shall help them in
such way as they most effectively can, according to their power.
But if the invader be gone after plundering the country, that
city shall be the enemy of Lacedæmon and Athens, and shall
be chastised by both, and one shall not make peace without
the other. This to be honestly, loyally, and without fraud.*

4. *Should the slave population rise, the Athenians shall
help the Lacedæmonians with all their might, according to
their power.*

5. *This treaty shall be sworn to by the same persons on
either side that swore to the other. It shall be renewed annually
by the Lacedæmonians going to Athens for the Dionysia, and
the Athenians to Lacedæmon for the Hyacinthia, and a pillar
shall be set up by either party; at Lacedæmon near the statue
of Apollo at Amyclæ, and at Athens on the Acropolis near the
statue of Athens. Should the Lacedæmonians and Athenians
see fit to add to or take away from the alliance in any particular, it shall be consistent with their oaths for both parties to
do so, according to their discretion.*

*Those who took the oath for the Lacedæmonians were
Pleistoanax, Agis, Pleistolas, Damagetus, Chionis, Metagenes,*

Acanthus, Daithus, Ischagoras, Philocharidas, Zeuxidas,
Antippus, Alcinadas, Tellis, Empedias, Menas, and Laphilus;
for the Athenians, Lampon, Isthmionicus, Laches, Nicias,
Euthydemus, Procles, Pythodorus, Hagnon, Myrtilus, Thra-
sycles, Theagenes, Aristocrates, Iolcius, Timocrates, Leon,
Lamachus, and Demosthenes.

This alliance was made not long after the treaty; and
the Athenians gave back the men from the island to the
Lacedæmonians, and the summer of the eleventh year began.
This completes the history of the first war, which occupied
the whole of the ten years previously.

CHAPTER XVI

FEELING AGAINST SPARTA IN PELOPONNESE—LEAGUE OF THE MANTINEANS, ELEANS, ARGIVES, AND ATHENIANS— BATTLE OF MANTINEA AND BREAKING UP OF THE LEAGUE

B.C. 421: *Dissatisfaction with treaty; its breach—Personal history of*
Thucydides—The Argive confederacy—Spartans march into
Arcadia—Mutual suspicions about treaty—Manœuvres of Bœo-
*tarchs—*B.C. 420: *Argos negotiates for Spartan alliance—Alcibiades*
turns Argos against Spartans—Alcibiades deceives envoys—Athe-
nians form alliance with Argives; its terms—Lacedæmonians
*excluded from Olympic games—*B.C. 419: *Alcibiades invades*
*Peloponnese—Argives plunder Epidaurus—*B.C. 418: *Agis takes*
field against Argos—Agis persuaded to withdraw army—Orcho-
menos capitulates—Agis' advance and retreat—Lacedæmonians
rout enemy—Peace terms—Lacedæmonian-Argive treaty of alliance
*—*B.C. 417: *Revolution at Argos—Athenians blockade Macedonia.*

AFTER the treaty and the alliance between the Lacedæmonians and Athenians, concluded after the ten years' war, in
the Ephorate of Pleistolas at Lacedæmon, and the Archonship
of Alcæus at Athens, the states which had accepted them were
at peace; but the Corinthians and some of the cities in
Peloponnese trying to disturb the settlement, a fresh agitation was instantly commenced by the allies against Lacedæmon. Further, the Lacedæmonians, as time went on, became
suspected by the Athenians through their not performing
some of the provisions in the treaty; and though for six years
and ten months they abstained from invasion of each other's
territory, yet abroad an unstable armistice did not prevent
either party doing the other the most effectual injury, until

they were finally obliged to break the treaty made after the ten years' war and to have recourse to open hostilities.

The history of this period has been also written by the same Thucydides, an Athenian, in the chronological order of events by summers and winters, to the time when the Lacedæmonians and their allies put an end to the Athenian empire, and took the Long Walls and Piræus. The war had then lasted for twenty-seven years in all. Only a mistaken judgment can object to including the interval of treaty in the war. Looked at by the light of facts it cannot, it will be found, be rationally considered a state of peace, where neither party either gave or got back all that they had agreed, apart from the violations of it which occurred on both sides in the Mantinean and Epidaurian wars and other instances, and the fact that the allies in the direction of Thrace were in as open hostility as ever, while the Bœotians had only a truce renewed every ten days. So that the first ten years' war, the treacherous armistice that followed it, and the subsequent war will, calculating by the seasons, be found to make up the number of years which I have mentioned, with the difference of a few days, and to afford an instance of faith in oracles being for once justified by the event. I certainly all along remember from the beginning to the end of the war its being commonly declared that it would last thrice nine years. I lived through the whole of it, being of an age to comprehend events, and giving my attention to them in order to know the exact truth about them. It was also my fate to be an exile from my country for twenty years after my command at Amphipolis; and being present with both parties, and more especially with the Peloponnesians by reason of my exile, I had leisure to observe affairs somewhat particularly. I will accordingly now relate the differences that arose after the ten years' war, the breach of the treaty, and the hostilities that followed.

After the conclusion of the fifty years' truce and of the subsequent alliance, the embassies from Peloponnese which had been summoned for this business returned from Lacedæmon. The rest went straight home, but the Corinthians first turned aside to Argos and opened negotiations with some of the men in office there, pointing out that Lacedæmon could have no good end in view, but only the subjugation of Peloponnese, or she would never have entered into treaty and alliance with the once detested Athenians, and that the duty of consulting for the safety of Peloponnese had now fallen upon Argos, who should immediately pass a decree inviting any Hellenic state that chose, such state being independent and accustomed to meet fellow-powers upon the fair and equal ground of law and justice, to make a defensive alliance with the Argives; appointing a few individuals with plenipotentiary powers, instead of making the people the medium of negotiation, in order that, in the case of an applicant being rejected, the fact of his overtures might not be made public. They said that many would come over from hatred of the Lacedæmonians. After this explanation of their views the Corinthians returned home.

The persons with whom they had communicated reported the proposal to their government and people, and the Argives passed the decree and chose twelve men to negotiate an alliance for any Hellenic state that wished it, except Athens and Lacedæmon, neither of which should be able to join without reference to the Argive people. Argos came in to the plan the more readily because she saw that war with Lacedæmon was inevitable, the truce being on the point of expiring; and also because she hoped to gain the supremacy of Peloponnese. For at this time Lacedæmon had sunk very low in public estimation because of her disasters, while the Argives were in a most flourishing condition, having taken no part in the Attic war, but having on the contrary profited largely by their neutrality. The Argives accordingly prepared to receive into alliance any of the Hellenes that desired it.

The Mantineans and their allies were the first to come over through fear of the Lacedæmonians. Having taken advantage of the war against Athens to reduce a large part of Arcadia into subjection, they thought that Lacedæmon would not leave them undisturbed in their conquests, now that she had leisure to interfere, and consequently gladly turned to a powerful city like Argos, the historical enemy of the Lacedæmonians, and a sister democracy. Upon the defection of Mantinea the rest of Peloponnese at once began to agitate the propriety of following her example, conceiving that the Mantineans would not have changed sides without good rea-

son; besides which they were angry with Lacedæmon among
other reasons for having inserted in the treaty with Athens
that it should be consistent with their oaths for both parties,
Lacedæmonians and Athenians, to add to or take away from
it according to their discretion. It was this clause that was the
real origin of the panic in Peloponnese, by exciting suspicions
of a Lacedæmonian and Athenian combination against their
liberties: any alteration should properly have been made
conditional upon the consent of the whole body of the allies.
With these apprehensions there was a very general desire in
each state to place itself in alliance with Argos.

In the meantime the Lacedæmonians perceiving the agitation going on in Peloponnese, and that Corinth was the author
of it and was herself about to enter into alliance with the
Argives, sent ambassadors thither in the hope of preventing
what was in contemplation. They accused her of having
brought it all about, and told her that she could not desert
Lacedæmon and become the ally of Argos, without adding
violation of her oaths to the crime which she had already committed in not accepting the treaty with Athens, when it had
been expressly agreed that the decision of the majority of the
allies should be binding, unless the gods or heroes stood in the
way. Corinth in her answer, delivered before those of her
allies who had like her refused to accept the treaty, and whom
she had previously invited to attend, refrained from openly
stating the injuries she complained of, such as the non-recovery
of Sollium or Anactorium from the Athenians, or any other
point in which she thought she had been prejudiced, but took
shelter under the pretext that she could not give up her
Thracian allies, to whom her separate individual security had
been given, when they first rebelled with Potidæa, as well as
upon subsequent occasions. She denied, therefore, that she
committed any violation of her oaths to the allies in not entering into the treaty with Athens; having sworn upon the faith
of the gods to her Thracian friends, she could not honestly give
them up. Besides, the expression was, 'unless the gods or
heroes stand in the way.' Now here, as it appeared to her, the
gods stood in the way. This was what she said on the subject
of her former oaths. As to the Argive alliance she would confer with her friends, and do whatever was right. The Lacedæ-

monian envoys returning home, some Argive ambassadors who happened to be in Corinth pressed her to conclude the alliance without further delay, but were told to attend at the next congress to be held at Corinth.

Immediately afterwards an Elean embassy arrived, and first making an alliance with Corinth went on from thence to Argos, according to their instructions, and became allies of the Argives, their country being just then at enmity with Lacedæmon and Lepreum. Some time back there had been a war between the Lepreans and some of the Arcadians; and the Eleans being called in by the former with the offer of half their lands, had put an end to the war, and leaving the land in the hands of its Leprean occupiers had imposed upon them the tribute of a talent to the Olympian Zeus. Till the Attic war this tribute was paid by the Lepreans, who then took the war as an excuse for no longer doing so, and upon the Eleans using force appealed to Lacedæmon. The case was thus submitted to her arbitrament; but the Eleans, suspecting the fairness of the tribunal, renounced the reference and laid waste the Leprean territory. The Lacedæmonians nevertheless decided that the Lepreans were independent and the Eleans aggressors, and as the latter did not abide by the arbitration, sent a garrison of heavy infantry into Lepreum. Upon this the Eleans, holding that Lacedæmon had received one of their rebel subjects, put forward the convention providing that each confederate should come out of the Attic war in possession of what he had when he went into it, and considering that justice had not been done them went over to the Argives, and now made the alliance through their ambassadors, who had been instructed for that purpose. Immediately after them the Corinthians and the Thracian Chalcidians became allies of Argos. Meanwhile the Bœotians and Megarians, who acted together, remained quiet, being left to do as they pleased by Lacedæmon, and thinking that the Argive democracy would not suit so well with their aristocratic government as the Lacedæmonian constitution.

About the same time in this summer Athens succeeded in reducing Scione, put the adult males to death, and making slaves of the women and children, gave the land for the Platæans to live in. She also brought back the Delians to

Delos, moved by her misfortunes in the field and by the commands of the god at Delphi. Meanwhile the Phocians and Locrians commenced hostilities. The Corinthians and Argives being now in alliance, went to Tegea to bring about its defection from Lacedæmon, seeing that if so considerable a state could be persuaded to join, all Peloponnese would be with them. But when the Tegeans said that they would do nothing against Lacedæmon, the hitherto zealous Corinthians relaxed their activity, and began to fear that none of the rest would now come over. Still they went to the Bœotians and tried to persuade them to alliance and a common action generally with Argos and themselves, and also begged them to go with them to Athens and obtain for them a ten days' truce similar to that made between the Athenians and Bœotians not long after the fifty years' treaty, and in the event of the Athenians refusing, to throw up the armistice, and not make any truce in future without Corinth. These were the requests of the Corinthians. The Bœotians stopped them on the subject of the Argive alliance, but went with them to Athens, where however they failed to obtain the ten days' truce; the Athenian answer being, that the Corinthians had truce already, as being allies of Lacedæmon. Nevertheless the Bœotians did not throw up their ten days' truce, in spite of the prayers and reproaches of the Corinthians for their breach of faith; and these last had to content themselves with a *de facto* armistice with Athens.

The same summer the Lacedæmonians marched into Arcadia with their whole levy under Pleistoanax, son of Pausanias, king of Lacedæmon, against the Parrhasians, who were subjects of Mantinea, and a faction of whom had invited their aid. They also meant to demolish, if possible, the fort of Cypsela which the Mantineans had built and garrisoned in the Parrhasian territory, to annoy the district of Sciritis in Laconia. The Lacedæmonians accordingly laid waste the Parrhasian country, and the Mantineans, placing their town in the hands of an Argive garrison, addressed themselves to the defence of their confederacy, but being unable to save Cypsela or the Parrhasian towns went back to Mantinea. Meanwhile the Lacedæmonians made the Parrhasians independent, razed the fortress and returned home.

The same summer the soldiers from Thrace who had gone

out with Brasidas came back, having been brought from thence after the treaty by Clearidas; and the Lacedæmonians decreed that the Helots who had fought with Brasidas should be free and allowed to live where they liked, and not long afterwards settled them with the Neodamodes at Lepreum, which is situated on the Laconian and Elean border; Lacedæmon being at this time at enmity with Elis. Those however of the Spartans who had been taken prisoners on the island and had surrendered their arms might, it was feared, suppose that they were to be subjected to some degradation in consequence of their misfortune, and so make some attempt at revolution, if left in possession of their franchise. These were therefore at once disfranchised, although some of them were in office at the time, and thus placed under a disability to take office, or buy and sell anything. After some time, however, the franchise was restored to them.

The same summer the Dians took Thyssus, a town on Acte by Athos in alliance with Athens. During the whole of this summer intercourse between the Athenians and Peloponnesians continued, although each party began to suspect the other directly after the treaty, because of the places specified in it not being restored. Lacedæmon, to whose lot it had fallen to begin by restoring Amphipolis and the other towns, had not done so. She had equally failed to get the treaty accepted by her Thracian allies, or by the Bœotians or the Corinthians; although she was continually promising to unite with Athens in compelling their compliance, if it were longer refused. She also kept fixing a time at which those who still refused to come in were to be declared enemies to both parties, but took care not to bind herself by any written agreement. Meanwhile the Athenians, seeing none of these professions performed in fact, began to suspect the honesty of her intentions, and consequently not only refused to comply with her demands for Pylos, but also repented having given up the prisoners from the island, and kept tight hold of the other places, until Lacedæmon's part of the treaty should be fulfilled. Lacedæmon, on the other hand, said she had done what she could, having given up the Athenian prisoners of war in her possession, evacuated Thrace, and performed everything else in her power. Amphipolis it was out of her ability to restore;

but she would endeavour to bring the Bœotians and Corinthians in to the treaty, to recover Panatcum, and send home
all the Athenian prisoners of war in Bœotia. Meanwhile she
required that Pylos should be restored, or at all events that
the Messenians and Helots should be withdrawn, as her troops
had been from Thrace, and the place garrisoned, if necessary,
by the Athenians themselves. After a number of different conferences held during the summer she succeeded in persuading
Athens to withdraw from Pylos the Messenians and the rest
of the Helots and deserters from Laconia, who were accordingly settled by her at Cranii in Cephallenia. Thus during
this summer there was peace and intercourse between the two
peoples.

Next winter, however, the Ephors under whom the treaty
had been made were no longer in office, and some of their successors were directly opposed to it. Embassies now arrived
from the Lacedæmonian confederacy, and the Athenians,
Bœotians, and Corinthians also presented themselves at
Lacedæmon, and after much discussion and no agreement between them, separated for their several homes; when Cleobulus and Xenares, the two Ephors who were the most anxious
to break off the treaty, took advantage of this opportunity to
communicate privately with the Bœotians and Corinthians,
and advising them to act as much as possible together, instructed the former first to enter into alliance with Argos,
and then try and bring themselves and the Argives into alliance
with Lacedæmon. The Bœotians would so be least likely to
be compelled to come in to the Attic treaty; and the Lacedæmonians would prefer gaining the friendship and alliance of
Argos even at the price of the hostility of Athens and the
rupture of the treaty. The Bœotians knew that an honourable
friendship with Agros had been long the desire of Lacedæmon;
for the Lacedæmonians believed that this would considerably facilitate the conduct of the war outside Peloponn-
nese. Meanwhile they begged the Bœotians to place Panactum
in her hands in order that she might, if possible, obtain Pylos
in exchange for it, and so be more in a position to resume hostilities with Athens.

After receiving these instructions for their governments
from Xenares and Cleobulus and their other friends at

Lacedæmon, the Bœotians and Corinthians departed. On their way home they were joined by two persons high in office at Argos who had waited for them on the road, and who now sounded them upon the possibility of the Bœotians joining the Corinthians, Eleans, and Mantineans in becoming the allies of Argos, in the idea that if this could be effected they would be able, thus united, to make peace or war as they pleased either against Lacedæmon or any other power. The Bœotian envoys were pleased at thus hearing themselves accidentally asked to do what their friends at Lacedæmon had told them; and the two Argives perceiving that their proposal was agreeable, departed with a promise to send ambassadors to the Bœotians. On their arrival the Bœotians reported to the Bœotarchs what had been said to them at Lacedæmon and also by the Argives who had met them, and the Bœotarchs, pleased with the idea, embraced it with the more eagerness from the lucky coincidence of Argos soliciting the very thing wanted by their friends at Lacedæmon. Shortly afterwards ambassadors appeared from Argos with the proposals indicated; and the Bœotarchs approved of the terms and dismissed the ambassadors with a promise to send envoys to Argos to negotiate the alliance.

In the meantime it was decided by the Bœotarchs, the Corinthians, the Megarians, and the envoys from Thrace first to interchange oaths together to give help to each other whenever it was required and not to make war or peace except in common; after which the Bœotians and Megarians, who acted together, should make the alliance with Argos. But before the oaths were taken the Bœotarchs communicated these proposals to the four councils of the Bœotians, in whom the supreme power resides, and advised them to interchange oaths with all such cities as should be willing to enter into a defensive league with the Bœotians. But the members of the Bœotian councils refused their assent to the proposal, being afraid of offending Lacedæmon by entering into a league with the deserter Corinth; the Bœotarchs not having acquainted them with what had passed at Lacedæmon and with the advice given by Cleobulus and Xenares and the Bœotian partisans there, namely, that they should become allies of Corinth and Argos as a preliminary to a junction with Lacedæmon; fancying that, even if they should say nothing about this, the councils would not vote against what had been decided and advised by the Bœotarchs. This difficulty arising, the Corinthians and the envoys from Thrace departed without anything having been concluded; and the Bœotarchs, who had previously intended after carrying this to try and effect the alliance with Argos, now omitted to bring the Argive question before the councils, or to send to Argos the envoys whom they had promised; and a general coldness and delay ensued in the matter.

In this same winter Mecyberna was assaulted and taken by the Olynthians, having an Athenian garrison inside it.

All this while negotiations had been going on between the Athenians and Lacedæmonians about the conquests still retained by each, and Lacedæmon, hoping that if Athens were to get back Panactum from the Bœotians she might herself recover Pylos, now sent an embassy to the Bœotians, and begged them to place Panactum and their Athenian prisoners in her hands, in order that she might exchange them for Pylos. This the Bœotians refused to do, unless Lacedæmon made a separate alliance with them as she had done with Athens. Lacedæmon knew that this would be a breach of faith to Athens, as it had been agreed that neither of them should make peace or war without the other; yet wishing to obtain Panactum which she hoped to exchange for Pylos, and the party who pressed for the dissolution of the treaty strongly affecting the Bœotian connexion, she at length concluded the alliance just as winter gave way to spring; and Panactum was instantly razed. And so the eleventh year of the war ended.

In the first days of the summer following, the Argives, seeing that the promised ambassadors from Bœotia did not arrive, and that Panactum was being demolished, and that a separate alliance had been concluded between the Bœotians and Lacedæmonians, began to be afraid that Argos might be left alone, and all the confederacy go over to Lacedæmon. They fancied that the Bœotians had been persuaded by the Lacedæmonians to raze Panactum and to enter into the treaty with the Athenians, and that Athens was privy to this arrangement, and even her alliance, therefore, no longer open to them —a resource which they had always counted upon, by reason of the dissensions existing, in the event of the non-continuance of their treaty with Lacedæmon. In this strait the Argives, afraid that, as the result of refusing to renew the treaty with Lacedæmon and aspiring to the supremacy in Peloponnese, they would have the Lacedæmonians, Tegeans, Bœotians, and Athenians on their hands all at once, now hastily sent off Eustrophus and Æson, who seemed the persons most likely to be acceptable, as envoys to Lacedæmon, with the view of making as good a treaty as they could with the Lacedæmonians, upon such terms as could be got, and being left in peace.

Having reached Lacedæmon, their ambassadors proceeded to negotiate the terms of the proposed treaty. What the Argives first demanded was that they might be allowed to refer to the arbitration of some state or private person the question of the Cynurian land, a piece of frontier-territory about which they have always been disputing, and which contains the towns of Thyrea and Anthene, and is occupied by the Lacedæmonians. The Lacedæmonians at first said that they could not allow this point to be discussed, but were ready to conclude upon the old terms. Eventually, however, the Argive ambassadors succeeded in obtaining from them this concession:—For the present there was to be a truce for fifty years, but it should be competent for either party, there being neither plague nor war in Lacedæmon or Argos, to give a formal challenge and decide the question of this territory by battle, as on a former occasion, when both sides claimed the victory; pursuit not being allowed beyond the frontier of Argos or Lacedæmon. The Lacedæmonians at first thought this mere folly; but at last, anxious at any cost to have the friendship of Argos, they agreed to the terms demanded, and reduced them to writing. However, before any of this should become binding, the ambassadors were to return to Argos and communicate with their people, and in the event of their approval, to come at the Feast of the Hyacinthia and take the oaths.

The envoys returned accordingly. In the meantime, while the Argives were engaged in these negotiations, the Lacedæmonian ambassadors, Andromedes, Phædimus, and Antimenidas, who were to receive the prisoners from the Bœotians and restore them and Panactum to the Athenians, found that the Bœotians had themselves razed Panactum, upon the plea that oaths had been anciently exchanged between their people and the Athenians, after a dispute on the subject, to the effect that neither should inhabit the place, but that they should graze it in common. As for the Athenian prisoners of war in the hands of the Bœotians, these were delivered over to Andromedes and his colleagues, and by them conveyed to Athens and given back. The envoys at the same time announced the razing of Panactum, which to them seemed as good as its restitution, as it would no longer lodge an enemy of Athens. This announcement was received with great indignation by the Athenians, who thought that the Lacedæmonians had played them false, both in the matter of the demolition of Panactum, which ought to have been restored to them standing, and in having, as they now heard, made a separate alliance with the Bœotians, in spite of their previous promise to join Athens in compelling the adhesion of those who refused to accede to the treaty. The Athenians also considered the other points in which Lacedæmon had failed in her compact, and thinking that they had been overreached, gave an angry answer to the ambassadors and sent them away.

The breach between the Lacedæmonians and Athenians having gone thus far, the party at Athens, also, who wished to cancel the treaty, immediately put themselves in motion. Foremost amongst these was Alcibiades, son of Clinias, a man yet young in years for any other Hellenic city, but distinguished by the splendour of his ancestry. Alcibiades thought the Argive alliance really preferable, not that personal pique had not also a great deal to do with his opposition; he being offended with the Lacedæmonians for having negotiated the treaty through Nicias and Laches, and having overlooked him on account of his youth, and also for not having shown him the respect due to the ancient connexion of his family with them as their *Proxeni,* which, renounced by his grandfather, he had lately himself thought to renew by his attentions to their prisoners taken in the island. Being thus, as he thought, slighted on all hands, he had in the first instance spoken against the treaty, saying that the Lacedæmonians were not to be trusted, but that they only treated, in order to be enabled by this means to crush Argos, and afterwards to attack Athens alone; and now, immediately upon the above breach occurring, he sent privately to the Argives, telling them to come as quickly as possible to Athens, accompanied by the Mantineans and Eleans, with proposals of alliance; as the moment was propitious and he himself would do all he could to help them.

Upon receiving this message and discovering that the Athenians, far from being privy to the Bœotian alliance, were involved in a serious quarrel with the Lacedæmonians, the Argives paid no further attention to the embassy which they had just sent to Lacedæmon on the subject of the treaty, and began to incline rather towards the Athenians, reflecting that, in the event of war, they would thus have on their side a city that was not only an ancient ally of Argos, but a sister democracy and very powerful at sea. They accordingly at once sent ambassadors to Athens to treat for an alliance, accompanied by others from Elis and Mantinea.

At the same time arrived in haste from Lacedæmon an embassy consisting of persons reputed well disposed towards the Athenians—Philocharidas, Leon, and Endius, for fear that the Athenians in their irritation might conclude alliance with the Argives, and also to ask back Pylos in exchange for Panactum, and in defence of the alliance with the Bœotians to plead that it had not been made to hurt the Athenians. Upon the envoys speaking in the senate upon these points, and stating that they had come with full powers to settle all others at issue between them, Alcibiades became afraid that if they were to repeat these statements to the popular assembly, they might gain the multitude, and the Argive alliance might be rejected, and accordingly had recourse to the following stratagem. He persuaded the Lacedæmonians by a solemn assurance that if they would say nothing of their full powers in the assembly, he would give back Pylos to them (himself, the present opponent of its restitution, engaging to obtain this from the Athenians), and would settle the other points at issue. His plan was to detach them from Nicias and to disgrace them before the people, as being without sincerity in their intentions, or even common consistency in their language, and so to get the Argives, Eleans, and Mantineans taken into alliance. This plan proved successful. When the envoys appeared before the people, and upon the question being put to them, did not say as they had said in the senate, that they had come with full powers, the Athenians lost all patience, and carried away by Alcibiades, who thundered more loudly than ever against the Lacedæmonians, were ready instantly to introduce the Argives and their companions and to take them into alliance. An earthquake, however, occurring, before anything definite had been done, this assembly was adjourned.

In the assembly held the next day, Nicias, in spite of the Lacedæmonians having been deceived themselves, and having allowed him to be deceived also in not admitting that they had come with full powers, still maintained that it was best to be friends with the Lacedæmonians, and, letting the Argive proposals stand over, to send once more to Lacedæmon and learn her intentions. The adjournment of the war could only increase their own prestige and injure that of their rivals; the excellent state of their affairs making it their interest to preserve this prosperity as long as possible, while those of Lacedæmon were so desperate that the sooner she could try her fortune again the better. He succeeded accordingly in persuading them to send ambassadors, himself being among the number, to invite the Lacedæmonians, if they were really sincere, to restore Panactum intact with Amphipolis, and to abandon their alliance with the Bœotians (unless they consented to accede to the treaty), agreeably to the stipulation which forbade either party to treat without the other. The ambassadors were also directed to say that the Athenians, had they wished to play false, might already have made alliance with the Argives, who were indeed come to Athens for that very purpose, and went off furnished with instructions as to any other complaints that the Athenians had to make. Having reached Lacedæmon they communicated their instructions, and concluded by telling the Lacedæmonians that unless they gave up their alliance with the Bœotians, in the event of their not acceding to the treaty, the Athenians for their part would ally themselves with the Argives and their friends. The Lacedæmonians, however, refused to give up the Bœotian alliance— the party of Xenares the Ephor, and such as shared their view, carrying the day upon this point—but renewed the oaths

at the request of Nicias, who feared to return without having
accomplished anything and to be disgraced; as was indeed
his fate, he being held the author of the treaty with Lacedæmon. When he returned, and the Athenians heard that nothing
had been done at Lacedæmon, they flew into a passion, and
deciding that faith had not been kept with them, took advantage of the presence of the Argives and their allies, who
had been introduced by Alcibiades, and made a treaty and
alliance with them upon the terms following:—

*The Athenians, Argives, Mantineans, and Eleans, acting
for themselves and the allies in their respective empires, made
a treaty for a hundred years, to be without fraud or hurt by
land and by sea.*

1. *It shall not be lawful to carry on war, either for the
Argives, Eleans, Mantineans, and their allies, against the
Athenians, or the allies in the Athenian empire; or for the
Athenians and their allies against the Argives, Eleans,
Mantineans, or their allies, in any way or means whatsoever.*

*The Athenians, Argives, Eleans, and Mantineans shall be
allies for a hundred years upon the terms following:—*

2. *If an enemy invade the country of the Athenians, the
Argives, Eleans, and Mantineans shall go to the relief of
Athens, according as the Athenians may require by message,
in such way as they most effectually can, to the best of their
power. But if the invader be gone after plundering the territory, the offending state shall be the enemy of the Argives,
Mantineans, Eleans, and Atheniens, and war shall be made
against it by all these cities; and no one of the cities shall be
able to make peace with that state, except all the above cities
agree to do so.*

3. *Likewise the Athenians shall go to the relief of Argos,
Mantinea, and Elis, if an enemy invade the country of Elis,
Mantinea, or Argos, according as the above cities may require
by message, in such way as they most effectually can, to the
best of their power. But if the invader be gone after plundering the territory, the state offending shall be the enemy of the
Athenians, Argives, Mantineans, and Eleans, and war shall
be made against it by all these cities, and peace may not be
made with that state except all the above cities agree to it.*

4. *No armed force shall be allowed to pass for hostile pur-*

poses through the country of the powers contracting, or of the allies in their respective empires, or to go by sea, except all the cities—that is to say, Athens, Argos, Mantinea, and Elis —vote for such passage.

5. *The relieving troops shall be maintained by the city sending them for thirty days from their arrival in the city that has required them, and upon their return in the same way; if their services be desired for a longer period the city that sent for them shall maintain them, at the rate of three Æginetan obols per day for a heavy-armed soldier, archer, or light soldier, and an Æginetan drachma for a trooper.*

6. *The city sending for the troops shall have the command when the war is in its own country; but in case of the cities resolving upon a joint expedition the command shall be equally divided among all the cities.*

7. *The treaty shall be sworn to by the Athenians for themselves and their allies, by the Argives, Mantineans, Eleans, and their allies, by each state individually. Each shall swear the oath most binding in his country over full-grown victims; the oath being as follows:*

'I WILL STAND BY THE ALLIANCE AND ITS ARTICLES, JUSTLY, INNOCENTLY, AND SINCERELY, AND I WILL NOT TRANSGRESS THE SAME IN ANY WAY OR MEANS WHATSOEVER.'

The oath shall be taken at Athens by the Senate and the magistrates, the Prytanes administering it; at Argos by the Senate, the Eighty, and the Artynæ, the Eighty administering it; at Mantinea by the Demiurgi, the Senate, and the other magistrates, the Theori and Polemarchs administering it; at Elis by the Demiurgi, the magistrates, and the Six Hundred, the Demiurgi and the Thesmophylaces administering it. The oaths shall be renewed by the Athenians going to Elis, Mantinea, and Argos thirty days before the Olympic games; by the Argives, Mantineans, and Eleans going to Athens ten days before the great feast of the Panathenæa. The articles of the treaty, the oaths, and the alliance shall be inscribed on a stone pillar by the Athenians in the citadel, by the Argives in the market-place, in the temple of Apollo; by the Mantineans in the temple of Zeus, in the market-place; and a brazen pillar shall be erected jointly by them at the Olympic games now at hand. Should the above cities see good to make any addition to these articles, whatever all the above cities shall agree upon, after consulting together, shall be binding.

Although the treaty and alliances were thus concluded, still the treaty between the Lacedæmonians and Athenians was not renounced by either party. Meanwhile Corinth, although the ally of the Argives, did not accede to the new treaty, any more than she had done to the alliance, defensive and offensive, formed before this between the Eleans, Argives, and Mantineans, when she declared herself content with the first alliance, which was defensive only, and which bound them to help each other, but not to join in attacking any. The Corinthians thus stood aloof from their allies, and again turned their thoughts towards Lacedæmon.

At the Olympic games which were held this summer, and in which the Arcadian Androsthenes was victor the first time in the wrestling and boxing, the Lacedæmonians were excluded from the temple by the Eleans, and thus prevented from sacrificing or contending, for having refused to pay the fine specified in the Olympic law imposed upon them by the Eleans, who alleged that they had attacked Fort Phyrcus, and sent heavy infantry of theirs into Lepreum during the Olympic truce. The amount of the fine was two thousand minæ, two for each heavy-armed soldier, as the law prescribes. The Lacedæmonians sent envoys, and pleaded that the imposition was unjust; saying that the truce had not yet been proclaimed at Lacedæmon when the heavy infantry were sent off. But the Eleans affirmed that the armistice with them had already begun (they proclaim it first among themselves), and that the aggression of the Lacedæmonians had taken them by surprise while they were living quietly as in time of peace, and not expecting anything. Upon this the Lacedæmonians submitted, that if the Eleans really believed that they had committed an aggression, it was useless after that to proclaim the truce at Lacedæmon; but they had proclaimed it notwithstanding, as believing nothing of the kind, and from that moment the Lacedæmonians had made no attack upon their country. Nevertheless the Eleans adhered to what they had said, that nothing would persuade them that an aggression had not been committed; if, however, the Lacedæmonians would restore Lepreum, they would give up their own share of the money and pay that of the god for them.

As this proposal was not accepted, the Eleans tried a second. Instead of restoring Lepreum, if this was objected to, the Lacedæmonians should ascend the altar of the Olympian Zeus, as they were so anxious to have access to the temple, and swear before the Hellenes that they would surely pay the fine at a later day. This being also refused, the Lacedæmonians were excluded from the temple, the sacrifice, and the games, and sacrificed at home; the Lepreans being the only other Hellenes who did not attend. Still the Eleans were afraid of the Lacedæmonians sacrificing by force, and kept guard with a heavy-armed company of their young men; being also joined by a thousand Argives, the same number of Mantineans, and by some Athenian cavalry who stayed at Harpina during the feast. Great fears were felt in the assembly of the Lacedæmonians coming in arms, especially after Lichas, son of Arcesilaus, a Lacedæmonian, had been scourged on the course by the umpires; because, upon his horses being the winners, and the Bœotian people being proclaimed the victor on account of his having no right to enter, he came forward on the course and crowned the charioteer, in order to show that the chariot was his. After this incident all were more afraid than ever, and firmly looked for a disturbance: the Lacedæmonians, however, kept quiet, and let the feast pass by, as we have seen. After the Olympic games, the Argives and the allies repaired to Corinth to invite her to come over to them. There they found some Lacedæmonian envoys; and a long discussion ensued, which after all ended in nothing, as an earthquake occurred, and they dispersed to their different homes.

Summer was now over. The winter following a battle took place between the Heracleots in Trachinia and the Ænianians, Dolopians, Malians, and certain of the Thessalians, all tribes bordering on and hostile to the town, which directly menaced their country. Accordingly, after having opposed and harassed it from its very foundation by every means in their power, they now in this battle defeated the Heracleots, Xenares, son of Cnidis, their Lacedæmonian commander, being among the slain. Thus the winter ended and the twelfth year of this

war ended also. After the battle Heraclea was so terribly reduced that in the first days of the summer following the
Bœotians occupied the place and sent away the Lacedæmonian Agesippidas for misgovernment, fearing that the town
might be taken by the Athenians while the Lacedæmonians
were distracted with the affairs of Peloponnese. The Lacedæmonians, nevertheless, were offended with them for what they
had done.

The same summer Alcibiades, son of Clinias, now one of
the generals at Athens, in concert with the Argives and the
allies, went into Peloponnese with a few Athenian heavy infantry and archers, and some of the allies in those parts whom
he took up as he passed, and with this army marched here
and there through Peloponnese, and settled various matters
connected with the alliance, and among other things induced
the Patrians to carry their walls down to the sea, intending
himself also to build a fort near the Achæan Rhium. However,
the Corinthians and Sicyonians, and all others who would
have suffered by its being built, came up and hindered him.

The same summer war broke out between the Epidaurians
and Argives. The pretext was that the Epidaurians did not
send an offering for their pasture-land to Apollo Pythæus,
as they were bound to do, the Argives having the chief manage-
ment of the temple; but, apart from this pretext, Alcibiades
and the Argives were determined, if possible, to gain possession of Epidaurus, and thus to insure the neutrality of
Corinth and give the Athenians a shorter passage for their
reinforcement from Ægina than if they had to sail round
Scyllæum. The Argives accordingly prepared to invade Epidaurus by themselves, to exact the offering.

About the same time the Lacedæmonians marched out
with all their people to Leuctra upon their frontier, opposite
to Mount Lycæum, under the command of Agis, son of Archidamus, without any one knowing their destination, not
even the cities that sent the contingents. The sacrifices, however, for crossing the frontier not proving propitious, the
Lacedæmonians returned home themselves, and sent word to
the allies to be ready to march after the month ensuing, which
happened to be the month of Carneus, a holy time for the
Dorians. Upon the retreat of the Lacedæmonians the Argives

marched out on the last day but three of the month before
Carneus, and keeping this as the day during the whole time
that they were out, invaded and plundered Epidaurus. The
Epidaurians summoned their allies to their aid, some of whom
pleaded the month as an excuse; others came as far as the
frontier of Epidaurus and there remained inactive.

While the Argives were in Epidaurus embassies from the
cities assembled at Mantinea, upon the invitation of the
Athenians. The conference having begun, the Corinthian
Euphamidas said that their actions did not agree with their
words; while they were sitting deliberating about peace, the
Epidaurians and their allies and the Argives were arrayed
against each other in arms; deputies from each party should
first go and separate the armies, and then the talk about peace,
might be resumed. In compliance with this suggestion they
went and brought back the Argives from Epidaurus, and afterwards reassembled, but without succeeding any better in coming to a conclusion; and the Argives a second time invaded
Epidaurus and plundered the country. The Lacedæmonians
also marched out to Caryæ; but the frontier sacrifices again
proving unfavorable, they went back again, and the Argives,
after ravaging about a third of the Epidaurian territory, returned home. Meanwhile a thousand Athenian heavy infantry
had come to their aid under the command of Alcibiades, but
finding that the Lacedæmonian expedition was at an end, and
that they were no longer wanted, went back again.

So passed the summer. The next winter the Lacedæmonians
managed to elude the vigilance of the Athenians, and sent in
a garrison of three hundred men to Epidaurus, under the command of Agesippidas. Upon this the Argives went to the
Athenians and complained of their having allowed an enemy
to pass by sea, in spite of the clause in the treaty by which
the allies were not to allow an enemy to pass through their
country. Unless, therefore, they now put the Messenians and
Helots in Pylos to annoy the Lacedæmonians, they, the Argives, should consider that faith had not been kept with them.
The Athenians were persuaded by Alcibiades to inscribe at
the bottom of the Laconian pillar that the Lacedæmonians
had not kept their oaths, and to convey the Helots at Cranii to
Pylos to plunder the country; but for the rest they remained

quiet as before. During this winter hostilities went on between the Argives and Epidaurians, without any pitched battle taking place, but only forays and ambuscades, in which the losses were small and fell now on one side and now on the other. At the close of the winter, towards the beginning of spring, the Argives went with scaling-ladders to Epidaurus, expecting to find it left unguarded on account of the war and to be able to take it by assault, but returned unsuccessful. And the winter ended, and with it the thirteenth year of the war ended also.

In the middle of the next summer the Lacedæmonians, seeing the Epidaurians, their allies, in distress, and the rest of Peloponnese either in revolt or disaffected, concluded that it was high time for them to interfere if they wished to stop the progress of the evil, and accordingly with their full force, the Helots included, took the field against Argos, under the command of Agis, son of Archidamus, king of the Lacedæmonians. The Tegeans and the other Arcadian allies of Lacedæmon joined in the expedition. The allies from the rest of Peloponnese and from outside mustered at Phlius; the Bœotians with five thousand heavy infantry and as many light troops, and five hundred horse and the same number of dismounted troopers; the Corinthians with two thousand heavy infantry; the rest more or less as might happen; and the Phliasians with all their forces, the army being in their country.

The preparations of the Lacedæmonians from the first had been known to the Argives, who did not, however, take the field until the enemy was on his road to join the rest at Phlius. Reinforced by the Mantineans with their allies, and by three thousand Elean heavy infantry, they advanced and fell in with the Lacedæmonians at Methydrium in Arcadia. Each party took up its position upon a hill, and the Argives prepared to engage the Lacedæmonians while they were alone; but Agis eluded them by breaking up his camp in the night, and proceeded to join the rest of the allies at Phlius. The Argives discovering this at daybreak, marched first to Argos and then to the Nemean road, by which they expected the Lacedæmonians and their allies would come down. However, Agis, instead of taking this road as they expected, gave the

Lacedæmonians, Arcadians, and Epidaurians their orders, and went along another difficult road, and descended into the plain of Argos. The Corinthians, Pellenians, and Phliasians marched by another steep road; while the Bœotians, Megarians, and Sicyonians had instructions to come down by the Nemean road where the Argives were posted, in order that if the enemy advanced into the plain against the troops of Agis, they might fall upon his rear with their cavalry. These dispositions concluded, Agis invaded the plain and began to ravage Saminthus and other places.

Discovering this, the Argives came up from Nemea, day having now dawned. On their way they fell in with the troops of the Phliasians and Corinthians, and killed a few of the Phliasians, and had perhaps a few more of their own men killed by the Corinthians. Meanwhile the Bœotians, Megarians, and Sicyonians, advancing upon Nemea according to their instructions, found the Argives no longer there, as they had gone down on seeing their property ravaged, and were now forming for battle, the Lacedæmonians imitating their example. The Argives were now completely surrounded; from the plain the Lacedæmonians and their allies shut them off from their city; above them were the Corinthians, Phliasians, and Pellenians; and on the side of Nemea the Bœotians, Sicyonians, and Megarians. Meanwhile their army was without cavalry, the Athenians alone among the allies not having yet arrived. Now the bulk of the Argives and their allies did not see the danger of their position, but thought that they could not have a fairer field, having intercepted the Lacedæmonians in their own country and close to the city. Two men, however, in the Argive army, Thrasylus, one of the five generals, and Alciphron, the Lacedæmonian *Proxenus,* just as the armies were upon the point of engaging, went and held a parley with Agis and urged him not to bring on a battle, as the Argives were ready to refer to fair and equal arbitration whatever complaints the Lacedæmonians might have against them, and to make a treaty and live in peace in future.

The Argives who made these statements did so upon their own authority, not by order of the people, and Agis on his accepted their proposals, and without himself either consulting the majority, simply communicated the matter to a single individual, one of the high officers accompanying the expedition, and granted the Argives a truce for four months, in which to fulfil their promises; after which he immediately led off the army without giving any explanation to any of the other allies. The Lacedæmonians and allies followed their general out of respect for the law, but amongst themselves loudly blamed Agis for going away from so fair a field (the enemy being hemmed in on every side by infantry and cavalry) without having done anything worthy of their strength. Indeed this was by far the finest Hellenic army ever yet brought together; and it should have been seen while it was still united at Nemea, with the Lacedæmonians in full force, the Arcadians, Bœotians, Corinthians, Sicyonians, Pellenians, Phliasians and Megarians, and all these the flower of their respective populations, thinking themselves a match not merely for the Argive confederacy, but for another such added to it. The army thus retired blaming Agis, and returned every man to his home. The Argives however blamed still more loudly the persons who had concluded the truce without consulting the people, themselves thinking that they had let escape with the Lacedæmonians an opportunity such as they should never see again; as the struggle would have been under the walls of their city, and by the side of many and brave allies. On their return accordingly they began to stone Thrasylus in the bed of the Charadrus, where they try all military causes before entering the city. Thrasylus fled to the altar, and so saved his life; his property however they confiscated.

After this arrived a thousand Athenian heavy infantry and three hundred horse, under the command of Laches and Nicostratus; whom the Argives, being nevertheless loth to break the truce with the Lacedæmonians, begged to depart, and refused to bring before the people, to whom they had a communication to make, until compelled to do so by the entreaties of the Mantineans and Eleans, who were still at Argos. The Athenians, by the mouth of Alcibiades their ambassador there present, told the Argives and the allies that they had no right to make a truce at all without the consent of their fellow-confederates, and now that the Athenians had arrived so opportunely the war ought to be resumed. These argu-

ments proving successful with the allies, they immediately
marched upon Orchomenos, all except the Argives, who, although they had consented like the rest, stayed behind at
first, but eventually joined the others. They now all sate
down and besieged Orchomenos, and made assaults upon it;
one of their reasons for desiring to gain this place being that
hostages from Arcadia had been lodged there by the Lacedæmonians. The Orchomenians, alarmed at the weakness of their
wall and the numbers of the enemy, and at the risk they ran
of perishing before relief arrived, capitulated upon condition
of joining the league, of giving hostages of their own to the
Mantineans, and giving up those lodged with them by the
Lacedæmonians. Orchomenos thus secured, the allies now
consulted as to which of the remaining places they should
attack next. The Eleans were urgent for Lepreum; the Mantineans for Tegea; and the Argives and Athenians giving their
support to the Mantineans, the Eleans went home in a rage
at their not having voted for Lepreum; while the rest of the
allies made ready at Mantinea for going against Tegea, which
a party inside had arranged to put into their hands.

Meanwhile the Lacedæmonians, upon their return from
Argos after concluding the four months' truce, vehemently
blamed Agis for not having subdued Argos, after an opportunity such as they thought they had never had before; for
it was no easy matter to bring so many and so good allies together. But when the news arrived of the capture of Orchomenos, they became more angry than ever, and, departing
from all precedent, in the heat of the moment had almost
decided to raze his house, and to fine him ten thousand
drachmæ. Agis however entreated them to do none of these
things, promising to atone for his fault by good service in the
field, failing which they might then do to him whatever they
pleased; and they accordingly abstained from razing his house
or fining him as they had threatened to do, and now made a
law, hitherto unknown at Lacedæmon, attaching to him ten
Spartans as counsellors, without whose consent he should
have no power to lead an army out of the city.

At this juncture arrived word from their friends in Tegea
that unless they speedily appeared, Tegea would go over from
them to the Argives and their allies, if it had not gone over

already. Upon this news a force marched out from Lacedæmon, of the Spartans and Helots and all their people, and that
instantly and upon a scale never before witnessed. Advancing
to Orestheum in Mænalia, they directed the Arcadians in
their league to follow close after them to Tegea, and going
on themselves as far as Orestheum, from thence sent back
the sixth part of the Spartans, consisting of the oldest and
youngest men, to guard their homes, and with the rest of their
army arrived at Tegea; where their Arcadian allies soon after
joined them. Meanwhile they sent to Corinth, to the Bœotians,
the Phocians, and Locrians, with orders to come up as quickly
as possible to Mantinea. These had but short notice; and it
was not easy except all together, and after waiting for each
other, to pass through the enemy's country, which lay right
across and blocked up the line of communication. Nevertheless they made what haste they could. Meanwhile the Lacedæmonians with the Arcadian allies that had joined them,
entered the territory of Mantinea, and encamping near the
temple of Heracles began to plunder the country.

Here they were seen by the Argives and their allies, who
immediately took up a strong and difficult position, and formed
in order of battle. The Lacedæmonians at once advanced
against them, and came on within a stone's throw or javelin's
cast, when one of the older men, seeing the enemy's position
to be a strong one, hallooed to Agis that he was minded to
cure one evil with another; meaning that he wished to make
amends for his retreat, which had been so much blamed, from
Argos, by his present untimely precipitation. Meanwhile Agis,
whether in consequence of this halloo or of some sudden new
idea of his own, quickly led back his army without engaging,
and entering the Tegean territory, began to turn off into
that of Mantinea the water about which the Mantineans and
Tegeans are always fighting, on account of the extensive damage it does to whichever of the two countries it falls into.
His object in this was to make the Argives and their allies
come down from the hill, to resist the diversion of the water,
as they would be sure to do when they knew of it, and thus to
fight the battle in the plain. He accordingly stayed that day
where he was, engaged in turning off the water. The Argives
and their allies were at first amazed at the sudden retreat of

the enemy after advancing so near, and did not know what
to make of it; but when he had gone away and disappeared,
without their having stirred to pursue him, they began anew
to find fault with their generals, who had not only let the
Lacedæmonians get off before, when they were so happily intercepted before Argos, but who now again allowed them to
run away, without any one pursuing them, and to escape at
their leisure while the Argive army was leisurely betrayed.
The generals, half-stunned for the moment, afterwards led
them down from the hill, and went forward and encamped
in the plain, with the intention of attacking the enemy.

The next day the Argives and their allies formed in the
order in which they meant to fight, if they chanced to encounter the enemy; and the Lacedæmonians returning from
the water to their old encampment by the temple of Heracles,
suddenly saw their adversaries close in front of them, all in
complete order, and advanced from the hill. A shock like that
of the present moment the Lacedæmonians do not ever remember to have experienced: there was scant time for preparation, as they instantly and hastily fell into their ranks, Agis,
their king, directing everything, agreeably to the law. For
when a king is in the field all commands proceed from him:
he gives the word to the Polemarchs; they to the Lochages;
these to the Pentecostyes; these again to the Enomotarchs,
and these last to the Enomoties. In short all orders required
pass in the same way and quickly reach the troops; as almost
the whole Lacedæmonian army, save for a small part, consists of officers under officers, and the care of what is to be
done falls upon many.

In this battle the left wing was composed of the Sciritæ,
who in a Lacedæmonian army have always that post to themselves alone; next to these were the soldiers of Brasidas from
Thrace, and the Neodamodes with them; then came the
Lacedæmonians themselves, company after company, with the
Arcadians of Heræa at their side. After these were the Mæna-
lians, and on the right wing the Tegeans with a few of the
Lacedæmonians at the extremity; their cavalry being posted
upon the two wings. Such was the Lacedæmonian formation.
That of their opponents was as follows:—On the right were
the Mantineans, the action taking place in their country:

next to them the allies from Arcadia; after whom came the
thousand picked men of the Argives, to whom the state had
given a long course of military training at the public expense;
next to them the rest of the Argives, and after them their
allies, the Cleonæans and Orneans, and lastly the Athenians
on the extreme left, and their own cavalry with them.

Such were the order and the forces of the two combatants.
The Lacedæmonian army looked the largest; though as to
putting down the numbers of either host, or of the contingents
composing it, I could not do so with any accuracy. Owing
to the secrecy of their government the number of the Lacedæmonians was not known, and men are so apt to brag about
the forces of their country that the estimate of their opponents was not trusted. The following calculation, however,
makes it possible to estimate the numbers of the Lacedæmonians present upon this occasion. There were seven companies in the field without counting the Sciritæ, who numbered
six hundred men: in each company there were four Pentecostyes, and in the Pentecosty four Enomoties. The first rank
of the Enomoty was composed of four soldiers: as to the
depth, although they had not been all drawn up alike, but
as each captain chose, they were generally ranged eight deep;
the first rank along the whole line, exclusive of the Sciritæ,
consisted of four hundred and forty-eight men.

The armies being now on the eve of engaging, each contingent received some words of encouragement from its own
commander. The Mantineans were reminded that they were
going to fight for their country and to avoid returning to the
experience of servitude after having tasted that of empire;
the Argives, that they would contend for their ancient supremacy, to regain their once equal share of Peloponnese of which
they had been so long deprived, and to punish an enemy and
a neighbour for a thousand wrongs; the Athenians, of the
glory of gaining the honours of the day with so many and
brave allies in arms, and that a victory over the Lacedæmonians in Peloponnese would cement and extend their empire, and would besides preserve Attica from all invasions in
future. These were the incitements addressed to the Argives
and their allies. The Lacedæmonians meanwhile, man to man,
and with their war-songs in the ranks, exhorted each brave

comrade to remember what he had learnt before; well aware
that the long training of action was of more saving virtue
than any brief verbal exhortation, though never so well delivered.

After this they joined battle, the Argives and their allies
advancing with haste and fury, the Lacedæmonians slowly
and to the music of many flute-players—a standing institution
in their army, that has nothing to do with religion, but is
meant to make them advance evenly, stepping in time, without breaking their order, as large armies are apt to do in the
moment of engaging.

Just before the battle joined, King Agis resolved upon the
following manœuvre. All armies are alike in this: on going
into action they get forced out rather on their right wing,
and one and the other overlap with this their adversary's
left; because fear makes each man do his best to shelter his
unarmed side with the shield of the man next him on the
right, thinking that the closer the shields are locked together
the better will he be protected. The man primarily responsible
for this is the first upon the right wing, who is always striv-
ing to withdraw from the enemy his unarmed side; and the
same apprehension makes the rest follow him. On the present
occasion the Mantineans reached with their wing far beyond
the Sciritæ, and the Lacedæmonians and Tegeans still farther
beyond the Athenians, as their army was the largest. Agis,
afraid of his left being surrounded, and thinking that the
Mantineans outflanked it too far, ordered the Sciritæ and
Brasideans to move out from their place in the ranks and
make the line even with the Mantineans, and told the Polemarchs Hipponoidas and Aristocles to fill up the gap thus
formed, by throwing themselves into it with two companies
taken from the right wing; thinking that his right would still
be strong enough and to spare, and that the line fronting the
Mantineans would gain in solidity.

However, as he gave these orders in the moment of the
onset, and at short notice, it so happened that Aristocles and
Hipponoidas would not move over, for which offence they
were afterwards banished from Sparta, as having been guilty
of cowardice; and the enemy meanwhile closed before the
Sciritæ (whom Agis on seeing that the two companies did

not move over ordered to return to their place) had time to fill up the breach in question. Now it was, however, that the Lacedæmonians, utterly worsted in respect of skill, showed themselves as superior in point of courage. As soon as they came to close quarters with the enemy, the Mantinean right broke their Sciritæ and Brasideans, and bursting in with their allies and the thousand picked Argives into the unclosed breach in their line cut up and surrounded the Lacedæmonians, and drove them in full rout to the waggons, slaying some of the older men on guard there. But the Lacedæmonians, worsted in this part of the field, with the rest of their army, and especially the centre, where the three hundred knights, as they are called, fought round King Agis, fell on the older men of the Argives and the five companies so named, and on the Cleonæans, the Orneans, and the Athenians next them, and instantly routed them; the greater number not even waiting to strike a blow, but giving way the moment that they came on, some even being trodden under foot, in their fear of being overtaken by their assailants.

The army of the Argives and their allies having given way in this quarter was now completely cut in two, and the Lacedæmonian and Tegean right simultaneously closing round the Athenians with the troops that outflanked them, these last found themselves placed between two fires, being surrounded on one side and already defeated on the other. Indeed they would have suffered more severely than any other part of the army, but for the services of the cavalry which they had with them. Agis also on perceiving the distress of his left opposed to the Mantineans and the thousand Argives, ordered all the army to advance to the support of the defeated wing; and while this took place, as the enemy moved past and slanted away from them, the Athenians escaped at their leisure, and with them the beaten Argive division. Meanwhile the Mantineans and their allies and the picked body of the Argives ceased to press the enemy, and seeing their friends defeated and the Lacedæmonians in full advance upon them, took to flight. Many of the Mantineans perished; but the bulk of the picked body of the Argives made good their escape. The flight and retreat, however, were neither hurried nor long; the Lacedæmonians fighting long and stubbornly until the rout of their enemy, but that once effected, pursuing for a short time and not far.

Such was the battle, as nearly as possible as I have described it; the greatest that had occurred for a very long while among the Hellenes, and joined by the most considerable states. The Lacedæmonians took up a position in front of the enemy's dead, and immediately set up a trophy and stripped the slain; they took up their own dead and carried them back to Tegea, where they buried them, and restored those of the enemy under truce. The Argives, Orneans, and Cleonæans had seven hundred killed; the Mantineans two hundred, and the Athenians and Æginetans also two hundred, with both their generals. On the side of the Lacedæmonians, the allies did not suffer any loss worth speaking of: as to the Lacedæmonians themselves it was difficult to learn the truth; it is said, however, that there were slain about three hundred of them.

While the battle was impending, Pleistoanax, the other king, set out with a reinforcement composed of the oldest and youngest men, and got as far as Tegea, where he heard of the victory and went back again. The Lacedæmonians also sent and turned back the allies from Corinth and from beyond the Isthmus, and returning themselves dismissed their allies, and kept the Carnean holidays, which happened to be at that time. The imputations cast upon them by the Hellenes at the time, whether of cowardice on account of the disaster in the island, or of mismanagement and slowness generally, were all wiped out by this single action: fortune, it was thought, might have humbled them, but the men themselves were the same as ever.

The day before this battle, the Epidaurians with all their forces invaded the deserted Argive territory, and cut off many of the guards left there in the absence of the Argive army. After the battle three thousand Elean heavy infantry arriving to aid the Mantineans, and a reinforcement of one thousand Athenians, all these allies marched at once against Epidaurus, while the Lacedæmonians were keeping the Carnea, and dividing the work among them began to build a wall round the city. The rest left off; but the Athenians finished at once the part assigned to them round Cape Heræum; and having all joined in leaving a garrison in the fortification in question, they returned to their respective cities.

Summer now came to an end. In the first days of the next winter, when the Carnean holidays were over, the Lacedæmonians took the field, and arriving at Tegea sent on to Argos proposals of accommodation. They had before had a party in the town desirous of overthrowing the democracy; and after the battle that had been fought, these were now far more in a position to persuade the people to listen to terms. Their plan was first to make a treaty with the Lacedæmonians, to be followed by an alliance, and after this to fall upon the commons. Lichas, son of Arcesilaus, the Argive *Proxenus,* accordingly arrived at Argos with two proposals from Lacedæmon, to regulate the conditions of war or peace, according as they preferred the one or the other. After much discussion, Alcibiades happening to be in the town, the Lacedæmonian party who now ventured to act openly, persuaded the Argives to accept the proposal for an accommodation; which ran as follows:—

The assembly of the Lacedæmonians agrees to treat with the Argives upon the terms following—

1. *The Argives shall restore to the Orchomenians their children, and to the Mœnalians their men, and shall restore the men they have in Mantinea to the Lacedæmonians.*

2. *They shall evacuate Epidaurus, and raze the fortification there. If the Athenians refuse to withdraw from Epidaurus, they shall be declared enemies of the Argives and of the Lacedæmonians, and of the allies of the Lacedæmonians and the allies of the Argives.*

3. *If the Lacedæmonians have any children in their custody, they shall restore them every one to his city.*

4. *As to the offering to the god, the Argives, if they wish, shall impose an oath upon the Epidaurians, but, if not, they shall swear it themselves.*

5. *All the cities in Peloponnese, both small and great, shall be independent according to the customs of their country.*

6. *If any of the powers outside Peloponnese invade Peloponnesian territory, the parties contracting shall unite to repel them, on such terms as they may agree upon, as being most fair for the Peloponnesians.*

7. *All allies of the Lacedæmonians outside Peloponnese shall be on the same footing as the Lacedæmonians, and the allies of the Argives shall be on the same footing as the Argives, being left in enjoyment of their own possessions.*

8. *This treaty shall be shown to the allies, and shall be concluded, if they approve: if the allies think fit, they may send the treaty to be considered at home.*

The Argives began by accepting this proposal, and the Lacedæmonian army returned home from Tegea. After this intercourse was renewed between them, and not long afterwards the same party contrived that the Argives should give up the league with the Mantineans, Eleans, and Athenians, and should make a treaty and alliance with the Lacedæmonians; which was consequently done upon the terms following:—

The Lacedæmonians and Argives agree to a treaty and alliance for fifty years upon the terms following:—

1. *All disputes shall be decided by fair and impartial arbitration, agreeably to the customs of the two countries.*

2. *The rest of the cities in Peloponnese may be included in this treaty and alliance, as independent and sovereign, in full enjoyment of what they possess; all disputes being decided by fair and impartial arbitration, agreeably to the customs of the said cities.*

3. *All allies of the Lacedæmonians outside Peloponnese shall be upon the same footing as the Lacedæmonians themselves, and the allies of the Argives shall be upon the same footing as the Argives themselves, continuing to enjoy what they possess.*

4. *If it shall be anywhere necessary to make an expedition in common, the Lacedæmonians and Argives shall consult upon it and decide, as may be most fair for the allies.*

5. *If any of the cities, whether inside or outside Peloponnese, have a question whether of frontiers or otherwise, it must be settled; but if one allied city should have a quarrel with another allied city, it must be referred to some third city thought impartial by both parties. Private citizens shall have their disputes decided according to the laws of their several countries.*

The treaty and above alliance concluded, each party at

once released everything whether acquired by war or otherwise, and thenceforth acting in common voted to receive neither herald nor embassy from the Athenians unless they evacuated their forts and withdrew from Peloponnese, and also to make neither peace nor war with any, except jointly. Zeal was not wanting: both parties sent envoys to the Thracian places and to Perdiccas, and persuaded the latter to join their league. Still he did not at once break off from Athens, although minded to do so upon seeing the way shown him by Argos, the original home of his family. They also renewed their old oaths with the Chalcidians and took new ones: the Argives, besides, sent ambassadors to the Athenians, bidding them evacuate the fort at Epidaurus. The Athenians, seeing their own men outnumbered by the rest of the garrison, sent Demosthenes to bring them out. This general, under colour of a gymnastic contest which he arranged on his arrival, got the rest of the garrison out of the place, and shut the gates behind them. Afterwards the Athenians renewed their treaty with the Epidaurians, and by themselves gave up the fortress.

After the defection of Argos from the league, the Mantineans, though they held out at first, in the end finding themselves powerless without the Argives, themselves too came to terms with Lacedæmon, and gave up their sovereignty over the towns. The Lacedæmonians and Argives, each a thousand strong, now took the field together, and the former first went by themselves to Sicyon and made the government there more oligarchical than before, and then both, uniting, put down the democracy at Argos and set up an oligarchy favourable to Lacedæmon. These events occurred at the close of the winter, just before spring; and the fourteenth year of the war ended. The next summer the people of Dium, in Athos, revolted from the Athenians to the Chalcidians, and the Lacedæmonians settled affairs in Achæa in a way more agreeable to the interests of their country. Meanwhile the popular party at Argos little by little gathered new consistency and courage, and waited for the moment of the Gymnopædic festival at Lacedæmon, and then fell upon the oligarchs. After a fight in the city victory declared for the commons, who slew some of their opponents and banished others. The Lacedæmonians for a long while let the messages of their friends at Argos remain without effect. At last they put off the Gymnopædiæ and marched to their succour, but learning at Tegea the defeat of the oligarchs, refused to go any further in spite of the entreaties of those who had escaped, and returned home and kept the festival. Later on, envoys arrived with messages from the Argives in the town and from the exiles, when the allies were also at Sparta; and after much had been said on both sides, the Lacedæmonians decided that the party in the town had done wrong, and resolved to march against Argos, but kept delaying and putting off the matter. Meanwhile the commons at Argos, in fear of the Lacedæmonians, began again to court the Athenian alliance, which they were convinced would be of the greatest service to them; and accordingly proceeded to build long walls to the sea, in order that in case of a blockade by land, with the help of the Athenians they might have the advantage of importing what they wanted by sea. Some of the cities in Peloponnese were also privy to the building of these walls; and the Argives with all their people, women and slaves not excepted, addressed themselves to the work, while carpenters and masons came to them from Athens.

Summer was now over. The winter following the Lacedæmonians, hearing of the walls that were building, marched against Argos with their allies, the Corinthians excepted, being also not without intelligence in the city itself; Agis, son of Archidamus, their king, was in command. The intelligence which they counted upon within the town came to nothing; they however took and razed the walls which were being built, and after capturing the Argive town Hysiæ and killing all the freemen that fell into their hands, went back and dispersed every man to his city. After this the Argives marched into Phlius and plundered it for harbouring their exiles, most of whom had settled there, and so returned home. The same winter the Athenians blockaded Macedonia, on the score of the league entered into by Perdiccas with the Argives and Lacedæmonians, and also of his breach of his engagements on the occasion of the expedition prepared by Athens against the Chalcidians in the direction of Thrace and against Amphipolis, under the command of Nicias, son of Niceratus.

which had to be broken up mainly because of his desertion. He was therefore proclaimed an enemy. And thus the winter ended, and the fifteenth year of the war ended with it.

CHAPTER XVII

SIXTEENTH YEAR OF THE WAR—THE MELIAN CONFERENCE— FATE OF MELOS

B.C. 416: *Athenian expedition to Melos—Discussion of envoys—Melians refuse to submit—Siege of Melos—Melians massacred and made slaves.*

THE next summer Alcibiades sailed with twenty ships to Argos and seized the suspected persons still left of the Lacedæmonian faction to the number of three hundred, whom the Athenians forthwith lodged in the neighbouring islands of their empire. The Athenians also made an expedition against the isle of Melos with thirty ships of their own, six Chian, and two Lesbian vessels, sixteen hundred heavy infantry, three hundred archers, and twenty mounted archers from Athens, and about fifteen hundred heavy infantry from the allies and the islanders. The Melians are a colony of Lacedæmon that would not submit to the Athenians like the other islanders, and at first remained neutral and took no part in the struggle, but afterwards upon the Athenians using violence and plundering their territory, assumed an attitude of open hostility. Cleomedes, son of Lycomedes, and Tisias, son of Tisimachus, the generals, encamping in their territory with the above armament, before doing any harm to their land, sent envoys to negotiate. These the Melians did not bring before the people, but bade them state the object of their mission to the magistrates and the few; upon which the Athenian envoys spoke as follows:—

Athenians.—'Since the negotiations are not to go on before the people, in order that we may not be able to speak straight on without interruption, and deceive the ears of the multitude by seductive arguments which would pass without refutation (for we know that this is the meaning of our being brought before the few), what if you who sit there were to pursue a method more cautious still! Make no set speech yourselves, but take us up at whatever you do not like, and settle that before going any farther. And first tell us if this proposition of ours suits you.'

The Melian commissioners answered:—

Melians.—'To the fairness of quietly instructing each other as you propose there is nothing to object; but your military preparations are too far advanced to agree with what you say, as we see you are come to be judges in your own cause, and that all we can reasonably expect from this negotiation is war, if we prove to have right on our side and refuse to submit, and in the contrary case, slavery.'

Athenians—'If you have met to reason about presentiments of the future, or for anything else than to consult for the safety of your state upon the facts that you see before you, we will give over; otherwise we will go on.'

Melians.—'It is natural and excusable for men in our position to turn more ways than one both in thought and utterance. However, the question in this conference is, as you say, the safety of our country; and the discussion, if you please, can proceed in the way which you propose.'

Athenians.—'For ourselves, we shall not trouble you with specious pretences—either of how we have a right to our empire because we overthrew the Mede, or are now attacking you because of wrong that you have done us—and make a long speech which would not be believed; and in return we hope that you, instead of thinking to influence us by saying that you did not join the Lacedæmonians, although their colonists, or that you have done us no wrong, will aim at what is feasible, holding in view the real sentiments of us both: since you know as well as we do that right, as the world goes, is only in question between equals in power, while the strong do what they can and the weak suffer what they must.'

Melians.—'As we think, at any rate, it is expedient—we speak as we are obliged, since you enjoin us to let right alone and talk only of interest—that you should not destroy what is our common protection, the privilege of being allowed in danger to invoke what is fair and right, and even to profit by arguments not strictly valid if they can be got to pass current. And you are as much interested in this as any, as your fall would be a signal for the heaviest vengeance and an example for the world to meditate upon.'

Athenians.—'The end of our empire, if end it should, does not frighten us: a rival empire like Lacedæmon, even if Lacedæmon was our real antagonist, is not so terrible to the vanquished as subjects who by themselves attack and over-power their rulers. This, however, is a risk that we are content to take. We will now proceed to show you that we are come here in the interest of our empire, and that we shall say what we are now going to say, for the preservation of your country; as we would fain exercise that empire over you without trouble, and see you preserved for the good of us both.'

Melians.—'And how, pray, could it turn out as good for us to serve as for you to rule?'

Athenians.—'Because you would have the advantage of submitting before suffering the worst, and we should gain by not destroying you.'

Melians.—'So that you would not consent to our being neutral, friends instead of enemies, but allies of neither side.'

Athenians.—'No; for your hostility cannot so much hurt us as your friendship will be an argument to our subjects of our weakness, and your enmity of our power.'

Melians.—'Is that your subjects' idea of equity, to put those who have nothing to do with you in the same category with peoples that are most of them your own colonists, and some conquered rebels?'

Athenians.—'As far as right goes they think one has as much of it as the other, and that if any maintain their independence it is because they are strong, and that if we do not molest them it is because we are afraid; so that besides extending our empire we should gain in security by your subjection; the fact that you are islanders and weaker than others rendering it all the more important that you should not succeed in baffling the masters of the sea.'

Melians.—'But do you consider that there is no security in the policy which we indicate? For here again if you debar us from talking about justice and invite us to obey your interest, we also must explain ours, and try to persuade you, if the two happen to coincide. How can you avoid making enemies of all existing neutrals who shall look at our case and conclude from it that one day or another you will attack them? And what is this but to make greater the enemies that

you have already, and to force others to become so who would
otherwise have never thought of it?'

Athenians.—'Why, the fact is that continentals generally
give us but little alarm; the liberty which they enjoy will
long prevent their taking precautions against us; it is rather
islanders like yourselves, outside our empire, and subjects
smarting under the yoke, who would be the most likely to
take a rash step and lead themselves and us into obvious
danger.'

Melians.—'Well then, if you risk so much to retain your
empire, and your subjects to get rid of it, it were surely
great baseness and cowardice in us who are still free not to
try everything that can be tried, before submitting to your
yoke.'

Athenians.—'Not if you are well advised, the contest not
being an equal one, with honour as the prize and shame as
the penalty, but a question of self-preservation and of not
resisting those who are far stronger than you are.'

Melians.—'But we know that the fortune of war is sometimes more impartial than the disproportion of numbers
might lead one to suppose; to submit is to give ourselves over
to despair, while action still preserves for us a hope that we
may stand erect.'

Athenians.—'Hope, danger's comforter, may be indulged
in by those who have abundant resources, if not without loss
at all events without ruin; but its nature is to be extravagant,
and those who go so far as to put their all upon the venture
see it in its true colours only when they are ruined; but so
long as the discovery would enable them to guard against it,
it is never found wanting. Let not this be the case with you,
who are weak and hang on a single turn of the scale; nor be
like the vulgar, who, abandoning such security as human
means may still afford, when visible hopes fail them in extremity, turn to invisible, to prophecies and oracles, and other
such inventions that delude men with hopes to their destruction.'

Melians.—'You may be sure that we are as well aware
as you of the difficulty of contending against your power and
fortune, unless the terms be equal. But we trust that the
gods may grant us fortune as good as yours, since we are

just men fighting against unjust, and that what we want in power will be made up by the alliance of the Lacedæmonians, who are bound, if only for very shame, to come to the aid of their kindred. Our confidence, therefore, after all is not so utterly irrational.'

Athenians.—'When you speak of the favour of the gods, we may as fairly hope for that as yourselves; neither our pretensions nor our conduct being in any way contrary to what men believe of the gods, or practise among themselves. Of the gods we believe, and of men we know, that by a necessary law of their nature they rule wherever they can. And it is not as if we were the first to make this law, or to act upon it when made: we found it existing before us, and shall leave it to exist for ever after us; all we do is to make use of it, knowing that you and everybody else, having the same power as we have, would do the same as we do. Thus, as far as the gods are concerned, we have no fear and no reason to fear that we shall be at a disadvantage. But when we come to your notion about the Lacedæmonians, which leads you to believe that shame will make them help you, here we bless your simplicity but do not envy your folly. The Lacedæmonians, when their own interests or their country's laws are in question, are the worthiest men alive; of their conduct towards others much might be said, but no clearer idea of it could be given than by shortly saying that of all the men we know they are most conspicuous in considering what is agreeable honourable, and what is expedient just. Such a way of thinking does not promise much for the safety which you now unreasonably count upon.'

Melians.—'But it is for this very reason that we now trust to their respect for expediency to prevent them from betraying the Melians, their colonists, and thereby losing the confidence of their friends in Hellas and helping their enemies.'

Athenians.—'Then you do not adopt the view that expediency goes with security, while justice and honour cannot be followed without danger; and danger the Lacedæmonians generally court as little as possible.'

Melians.—'But we believe that they would be more likely to face even danger for our sake, and with more confidence

than for others, as our nearness to Peloponnese makes it easier
for them to act, and our common blood insures our fidelity.'

Athenians.—'Yes, but what an intending ally trusts to, is
not the goodwill of those who ask his aid, but a decided superiority of power for action; and the Lacedæmonians look
to this even more than others. At least, such is their distrust
of their home resources that it is only with numerous allies
that they attack a neighbour; now is it likely that while we
are masters of the sea they will cross over to an island?'

Melians.—'But they would have others to send. The
Cretan sea is a wide one, and it is more difficult for those who
command it to intercept others, than for those who wish to
elude them to do so safely. And should the Lacedæmonians
miscarry in this, they would fall upon your land, and upon
those left of your allies whom Brasidas did not reach; and
instead of places which are not yours, you will have to fight
for your own country and your own confederacy.'

Athenians.—'Some diversion of the kind you speak of
you may one day experience, only to learn, as others have
done, that the Athenians never once yet withdrew from a
siege for fear of any. But we are struck by the fact, that after
saying you would consult for the safety of your country, in
all this discussion you have mentioned nothing which men
might trust in and think to be saved by. Your strongest arguments depend upon hope and the future, and your actual resources are too scanty, as compared with those arrayed against
you, for you to come out victorious. You will therefore show
great blindness of judgment, unless, after allowing us to retire, you can find some counsel more prudent than this. You
will surely not be caught by that idea of disgrace, which in
dangers that are disgraceful, and at the same time too plain
to be mistaken, proves so fatal to mankind; since in too many
cases the very men that have their eyes perfectly open to
what they are rushing into, let the thing called disgrace, by
the mere influence of a seductive name, lead them on to a
point at which they become so enslaved by the phrase as in
fact to fall wilfully into hopeless disaster, and incur disgrace
more disgraceful as the companion of error, than when it
comes as the result of misfortune. This, if you are well advised, you will guard against; and you will not think it dis-

honourable to submit to the greatest city in Hellas, when it makes you the moderate offer of becoming its tributary ally, without ceasing to enjoy the country that belongs to you; nor when you have the choice given you between war and security, will you be so blinded as to choose the worse. And it is certain that those who do not yield to their equals, who keep terms with their superiors, and are moderate towards their inferiors, on the whole succeed best. Think over the matter, therefore, after our withdrawal, and reflect once and again that it is for your country that you are consulting, that you have not more than one, and that upon this one deliberation depends its prosperity or ruin.'

The Athenians now withdrew from the conference; and the Melians, left to themselves, came to a decision corresponding with what they had maintained in the discussion, and answered, 'Our resolution, Athenians, is the same as it was at first. We will not in a moment deprive of freedom a city that has been inhabited these seven hundred years; but we put our trust in the fortune by which the gods have preserved it until now, and in the help of men, that is, of the Lacedæmonians; and so we will try and save ourselves. Meanwhile we invite you to allow us to be friends to you and foes to neither party, and to retire from our country after making such a treaty as shall seem fit to us both.'

Such was the answer of the Melians. The Athenians now departing from the conference said, 'Well, you alone, as it seems to us, judging from these resolutions, regard what is future as more certain than what is before your eyes, and what is out of sight, in your eagerness, as already coming to pass; and as you have staked most on, and trusted most in, the Lacedæmonians, your fortune, and your hopes, so will you be most completely deceived.'

The Athenian envoys now returned to the army; and the Melians showing no signs of yielding, the generals at once betook themselves to hostilities, and drew a line of circumvallation round the Melians, dividing the work among the different states. Subsequently the Athenians returned with most of their army, leaving behind them a certain number of their own citizens and of the allies to keep guard by land and sea. The force thus left stayed on and besieged the place.

About the same time the Argives invaded the territory of Phlius and lost eighty men cut off in an ambush by the Phliasians and Argive exiles. Meanwhile the Athenians at Pylos took so much plunder from the Lacedæmonians that the latter, although they still refrained from breaking off the treaty and going to war with Athens, yet proclaimed that any of their people that chose might plunder the Athenians. The Corinthians also commenced hostilities with the Athenians for private quarrels of their own; but the rest of the Peloponnesians stayed quiet. Meanwhile the Melians attacked by night and took the part of the Athenian lines over against the market, and killed some of the men, and brought in corn and all else that they could find useful to them, and so returned and kept quiet, while the Athenians took measures to keep better guard in future.

Summer was now over. The next winter the Lacedæmonians intended to invade the Argive territory, but arriving at the frontier found the sacrifices for crossing unfavourable, and went back again. This intention of theirs gave the Argives suspicions of certain of their fellow-citizens, some of whom they arrested; others, however, escaped them. About the same time the Melians again took another part of the Athenian lines which were but feebly garrisoned. Reinforcements afterwards arriving from Athens in consequence, under the command of Philocrates, son of Demeas, the siege was now pressed vigorously; and some treachery taking place inside, the Melians surrendered at discretion to the Athenians, who put to death all the grown men whom they took, and sold the women and children for slaves, and subsequently sent out five hundred colonists and inhabited the place themselves.

BOOK VI

CHAPTER XVIII

SEVENTEENTH YEAR OF THE WAR—THE SICILIAN CAMPAIGN
—AFFAIR OF THE HERMÆ—DEPARTURE OF THE EXPEDITION

B.C. 416: *Invasion of Sicily—Peoples and cities of Sicily—Argument
of the Egestæans—Lacedæmonians march on the Argives—B.C. 415:
Envoys return from Egesta—Nicias' counsel—Characterization of
Alcibiades—His own defense—Nicias replies—Enthusiasm for ex-
pedition—Elaborate preparations—Charges against Alcibiades—
Departure for Sicily.*

THE same winter the Athenians resolved to sail again to
Sicily, with a greater armament than that under Laches and
Eurymedon, and, if possible, to conquer the island; most of
them being ignorant of its size and of the number of its inhabitants, Hellenic and barbarian, and of the fact that they
were undertaking a war not much inferior to that against the
Peloponnesians. For the voyage round Sicily in a merchantman is not far short of eight days; and yet, large as the
island is, there are only two miles of sea to prevent its being
mainland.

It was settled originally as follows, and the peoples that
occupied it are these. The earliest inhabitants spoken of in
any part of the country are the Cyclopes and Læstrygones;
but I cannot tell of what race they were, or whence they
came or whither they went, and must leave my readers to
what the poets have said of them and to what may be generally known concerning them. The Sicanians appear to have
been the next settlers, although they pretend to have been
the first of all and aborigines; but the facts show that they
were Iberians, driven by the Ligurians from the river Sicanus
in Iberia. It was from them that the island, before called
Trinacaria, took its name of Sicania, and to the present day
they inhabit the west of Sicily. On the fall of Ilium, some

of the Trojans escaped from the Achæans, came in ships to
Sicily, and settled next to the Sicanians under the general
name of Elymi; their towns being called Eryx and Egesta.
With them settled some of the Phocians carried on their way
from Troy by a storm, first to Libya, and afterwards from
thence to Sicily. The Sicels crossed over to Sicily from their
first home Italy, flying from the Opicans, as tradition says and
as seems not unlikely, upon rafts, having watched till the wind
set down the strait to effect the passage; although perhaps
they may have sailed over in some other way. Even at the
present day there are still Sicels in Italy; and the country
got its name of Italy from Italus, a king of the Sicels, so
called. These went with a great host to Sicily, defeated the
Sicanians in battle and forced them to remove to the south and
west of the island, which thus came to be called Sicily
instead of Sicania, and after they crossed over continued to
enjoy the richest parts of the country for near three hundred
years before any Hellenes came to Sicily; indeed they still
hold the centre and north of the island. There were also
Phœnicians living all round Sicily, who had occupied promon-
tories upon the sea coasts and the islets adjacent for the purpose of trading with the Sicels. But when the Hellenes began
to arrive in considerable numbers by sea, the Phœnicians
abandoned most of their stations, and drawing together took
up their abode in Motye, Soloeis, and Panormus, near the
Elymi, partly because they confided in their alliance, and also
because these are the nearest points, for the voyage between
Carthage and Sicily.

These were the barbarians in Sicily, settled as I have said.
Of the Hellenes, the first to arrive were Chalcidians from Eubœa with Thucles, their founder. They founded Naxos and
built the altar to Apollo Archegetes, which now stands outside the town, and upon which the deputies for the games
sacrifice before sailing from Sicily. Syracuse was founded the
year afterwards by Archias, one of the Heraclids from Corinth,
who began by driving out the Sicels from the island upon which
the inner city now stands, though it is no longer surrounded
by water: in process of time the outer town also was taken
within the walls and became populous. Meanwhile Thucles
and the Chalcidians set out from Naxos in the fifth year after

the foundation of Syracuse, and drove out the Sicels by
arms and founded Leontini and afterwards Catana; the Catanians themselves choosing Evarchus as their founder.

About the same time Lamis arrived in Sicily with a colony
from Megara, and after founding a place called Trotilus beyond the river Pantacyas, and afterwards leaving it and for
a short while joining the Chalcidians at Leontini, was driven
out by them and founded Thapsus. After his death his companions were driven out of Thapsus, and founded a place
called the Hyblæan Megara; Hyblon, a Sicel king, having
given up the place and inviting them thither. Here they lived
two hundred and forty-five years; after which they were expelled from the city and the country by the Syracusan tyrant
Gelo. Before their expulsion, however, a hundred years after
they had settled there, they sent out Pamillus and founded
Selinus; he having come from their mother country Megara
to join them in its foundation. Gela was founded by Anti-
phemus from Rhodes and Entimus from Crete, who joined
in leading a colony thither, in the forty-fifth year after the
foundation of Syracuse. The town took its name from the
river Gelas, the place where the citadel now stands, and
which was first fortified, being called Lindii. The institutions
which they adopted were Dorian. Near one hundred and eight
years after the foundation of Gela, the Geloans founded Acra-
gas (Agrigentum), so called from the river of that name, and
made Aristonous and Pystilus their founders; giving their
own institutions to the colony. Zancle was originally founded
by pirates from Cuma, the Chalcidian town in the country
of the Opicans: afterwards, however, large numbers came
from Chalcis and the rest of Eubœa, and helped to people
the place; the founders being Perieres and Cratæmenes from
Cuma and Chalcis respectively. It first had the name of Zancle
given it by the Sicels, because the place is shaped like a sickle,
which the Sicels call *Zanclon;* but upon the original settlers
being afterwards expelled by some Samians and other Ionians
who landed in Sicily flying from the Medes, and the Samians
in their turn not long afterwards by Anaxilas, tyrant of Rhegium, the town was by him colonised with a mixed population,
and its name changed to Messina, after his old country.

Himera was founded from Zancle by Euclides, Simus, and

Sacon, most of those who went to the colony being Chalcidians; though they were joined by some exiles from Syracuse,
defeated in a civil war, called the Myletidæ. The language
was a mixture of Chalcidian and Doric, but the institutions
which prevailed were the Chalcidian. Acræ and Casmenæ were
founded by the Syracusans; Acræ seventy years after Syracuse, Casmenæ nearly twenty after Acræ. Camarina was first
founded by the Syracusans, close upon a hundred and thirty-
five years after the building of Syracuse; its founders being
Daxon and Menecolus. But the Camarinæans being expelled
by arms by the Syracusans for having revolted, Hippocrates,
tyrant of Gela, some time later receiving their land in ransom
for some Syracusan prisoners, resettled Camarina, himself
acting as its founder. Lastly, it was again depopulated by
Gelo, and settled once more for the third time by the Geloans.

Such is the list of the peoples, Hellenic and barbarian, inhabiting Sicily, and such the magnitude of the island which
the Athenians were now bent upon invading; being ambitious in real truth of conquering the whole, although they had
also the specious design of succouring their kindred and other
allies in the island. But they were especially incited by envoys
from Egesta, who had come to Athens and invoked their aid
more urgently than ever. The Egestæans had gone to war with
their neighbours the Selinuntines upon questions of marriage
and disputed territory, and the Selinuntines had procured the
alliance of the Syracusans, and pressed Egesta hard by land
and sea. The Egestæans now reminded the Athenians of the
alliance made in the time of Laches, during the former Leontine war, and begged them to send a fleet to their aid, and
among a number of other considerations urged as a capital
argument, that if the Syracusans were allowed to go unpun-
ished for their depopulation of Leontini, to ruin the allies still
left to Athens in Sicily, and to get the whole power of the
island into their hands, there would be a danger of their one
day coming with a large force, as Dorians, to the aid of their
Dorian brethren, and as colonists, to the aid of the Peloponnesians who had sent them out, and joining these in pulling
down the Athenian empire. The Athenians would, therefore,
do well to unite with the allies still left to them, and to make
a stand against the Syracusans; especially as they, the Eges-

tæans, were prepared to furnish money sufficient for the war. The Athenians, hearing these arguments constantly repeated in their assemblies by the Egestæans and their supporters, voted first to send envoys to Egesta, to see if there was really the money that they talked of in the treasury and temples, and at the same time to ascertain in what posture was the war with the Selinuntines.

The envoys of the Athenians were accordingly despatched to Sicily. The same winter the Lacedæmonians and their allies, the Corinthians excepted, marched into the Argive territory, and ravaged a small part of the land, and took some yokes of oxen and carried off some corn. They also settled the Argive exiles at Orneæ, and left them a few soldiers taken from the rest of the army; and after making a truce for a certain while, according to which neither Orneatæ nor Argives were to injure each other's territory, returned home with the army. Not long afterwards the Athenians came with thirty ships and six hundred heavy infantry, and the Argives joining them with all their forces, marched out and besieged the men in Orneæ for one day; but the garrison escaped by night, the besiegers having bivouacked some way off. The next day the Argives, discovering it, razed Orneæ to the ground, and went back again; after which the Athenians went home in their ships. Meanwhile the Athenians took by sea to Methone on the Macedonian border some cavalry of their own and the Macedonian exiles that were at Athens, and plundered the country of Perdiccas. Upon this the Lacedæmonians sent to the Thracian Chalcidians, who had a truce with Athens from one ten days to another, urging them to join Perdiccas in the war, which they refused to do. And the winter ended, and with it ended the sixteenth year of this war of which Thucydides is the historian.

Early in the spring of the following summer the Athenian envoys arrived from Sicily, and the Egestæans with them, bringing sixty talents of uncoined silver, as a month's pay for sixty ships, which they were to ask to have sent them. The Athenians held an assembly, and after hearing from the Egestæans and their own envoys a report, as attractive as it was untrue, upon the state of affairs generally, and in particular as to the money, of which, it was said, there was abundance in

the temples and the treasury, voted to send sixty ships to
Sicily, under the command of Alcibiades, son of Clinias,
Nicias, son of Niceratus, and Lamachus, son of Xenophanes,
who were appointed with full powers; they were to help the
Egestæans against the Selinuntines, to restore Leontini upon
gaining any advantage in the war, and to order all other matters in Sicily as they should deem best for the interests of
Athens. Five days after this a second assembly was held, to
consider the speediest means of equipping the ships, and to
vote whatever else might be required by the generals for the
expedition; and Nicias, who had been chosen to the command
against his will, and who thought that the state was not well
advised, but upon a slight and specious pretext was aspiring
to the conquest of the whole of Sicily, a great matter to
achieve, came forward in the hope of diverting the Athenians
from the enterprise, and gave them the following counsel:—

'Although this assembly was convened to consider the
preparations to be made for sailing to Sicily, I think, notwithstanding, that we have still this question to examine,
whether it be better to send out the ships at all, and that we
ought not to give so little consideration to a matter of such
moment, or let ourselves be persuaded by foreigners into
undertaking a war with which we have nothing to do. And
yet, individually, I gain in honour by such a course, and fear
as little as other men for my person—not that I think a man
need be any the worse citizen for taking some thought for
his person and estate; on the contrary, such a man would for
his own sake desire the prosperity of his country more than
others—nevertheless, as I have never spoken against my convictions to gain honour, I shall not begin to do so now, but
shall say what I think best. Against your character any words
of mine would be weak enough; if I were to advise your keeping what you have got and not risking what is actually yours
for advantages which are dubious in themselves, and which
you may or may not attain. I will, therefore, content myself
with showing that your ardour is out of season, and your ambition not easy of accomplishment.

'I affirm, then, that you leave many enemies behind you
here to go yonder and bring more back with you. You imagine,
perhaps, that the treaty which you have made can be trusted;

a treaty that will continue to exist nominally, as long as you keep quiet—for nominal it has become, owing to the practices of certain men here and at Sparta—but which in the event of a serious reverse in any quarter would not delay our enemies a moment in attacking us; first, because the convention was forced upon them by disaster and was less honourable to them than to us; and secondly, because in this very convention there are many points that are still disputed. Again, some of the most powerful states have never yet accepted the arrangement at all. Some of these are at open war with us; others (as the Lacedæmonians do not yet move) are restrained by truces renewed every ten days, and it is only too probable that if they found our power divided, as we are hurrying to divide it, they would attack us vigorously with the Siceliots, whose alliance they would have in the past valued as they would that of few others. A man ought, therefore, to consider these points, and not to think of running risks with a country placed so critically, or of grasping at another empire before we have secured the one we have already; for in fact the Thracian Chalcidians have been all these years in revolt from us without being yet subdued, and others on the continents yield us but a doubtful obedience. Meanwhile the Egestæans, our allies, have been wronged, and we run to help them, while the rebels who have so long wronged us still wait for punishment.

'And yet the latter, if brought under, might be kept under; while the Sicilians, even if conquered, are too far off and too numerous to be ruled without difficulty. Now it is folly to go against men who could not be kept under even if conquered, while failure would leave us in a very different position from that which we occupied before the enterprise. The Siceliots, again, to take them as they are at present, in the event of a Syracusan conquest (the favourite bugbear of the Egestæans), would to my thinking be even less dangerous to us than before. At present they might possibly come here as separate states for love of Lacedæmon; in the other case one empire would scarcely attack another; for after joining the Peloponnesians to overthrow ours, they could only expect to see the same hands overthrow their own in the same way. The Hellenes in Sicily would fear us most if we never went there at all, and next to this, if after displaying our power we went away again as soon as possible. We all know that that which is farthest off and the reputation of which can least be tested, is the object of admiration; at the least reverse they would at once begin to look down upon us, and would join our enemies here against us. You have yourselves experienced this with regard to the Lacedæmonians and their allies, whom your unexpected success, as compared with what you feared at first, has made you suddenly despise, tempting you further to aspire to the conquest of Sicily. Instead, however, of being puffed up by the misfortunes of your adversaries, you ought to think of breaking their spirit before giving yourselves up to confidence, and to understand that the one thought awakened in the Lacedæmonians by their disgrace is how they may even now, if possible, overthrow us and repair their dishonour; inasmuch as military reputation is their oldest and chiefest study. Our struggle, therefore, if we are wise, will not be for the barbarian Egestæans in Sicily, but how to defend ourselves most effectually against the oligarchical machinations of Lacedæmon.

'We should also remember that we are but now enjoying some respite from a great pestilence and from war, to the no small benefit of our estates and persons, and that it is right to employ these at home on our own behalf, instead of using them on behalf of these exiles whose interest it is to lie as fairly as they can, who do nothing but talk themselves and leave the danger to others, and who if they succeed will show no proper gratitude, and if they fail will drag down their friends with them. And if there be any man here, overjoyed at being chosen to command, who urges you to make the expedition, merely for ends of his own—especially if he be still too young to command—who seeks to be admired for his stud of horses, but on account of its heavy expenses hopes for some profit from his appointment, do not allow such an one to maintain his private splendour at his country's risk, but remember that such persons injure the public fortune while they squander their own, and that this is a matter of importance, and not for a young man to decide or hastily to take in hand.

'When I see such persons now sitting here at the side of

that same individual and summoned by him, alarm seizes me; and I, in my turn, summon any of the older men that may have such a person sitting next him, not to let himself be shamed down, for fear of being thought a coward if he do not vote for war, but, remembering how rarely success is got by wishing and how often by forecast, to leave to them the mad dream of conquest, and as a true lover of his country, now threatened by the greatest danger in its history, to hold up his hand on the other side; to vote that the Siceliots be left in the limits now existing between us, limits of which no one can complain (the Ionian sea for the coasting voyage, and the Sicilian across the open main), to enjoy their own possessions and to settle their own quarrels; that the Eges tæans, for their part, be told to end by themselves with the Selinuntines the war which they began without consulting the Athenians; and that for the future we do not enter into alliance, as we have been used to do, with people whom we must help in their need, and who can never help us in ours.

'And you, Prytanis, if you think it your duty to care for the commonwealth, and if you wish to show yourself a good citizen, put the question to the vote, and take a second time the opinions of the Athenians. If you are afraid to move the question again, consider that a violation of the law cannot carry any prejudice with so many abettors, that you will be the physician of your misguided city, and that the virtue of men in office is briefly this, to do their country as much good as they can, or in any case no harm that they can avoid.'

Such were the words of Nicias. Most of the Athenians that came forward spoke in favour of the expedition, and of not annulling what had been voted, although some spoke on the other side. By far the warmest advocate of the expedition was, however, Alcibiades, son of Clinias, who wished to thwart Nicias both as his political opponent and also because of the attack he had made upon him in his speech, and who was, besides, exceedingly ambitious of a command by which he hoped to reduce Sicily and Carthage, and personally to gain in wealth and reputation by means of his successes. For the position he held among the citizens led him to indulge his tastes beyond what his real means would bear, both in keeping horses and in the rest of his expenditure; and this later on had not a little to do with the ruin of the Athenian state. Alarmed at the greatness of his license in his own life and habits, and of the ambition which he showed in all things soever that he undertook, the mass of the people set him down as a pretender to the tyranny, and became his enemies; and although publicly his conduct of the war was as good as could be desired, individually, his habits gave offence to every one, and caused them to commit affairs to other hands, and thus before long to ruin the city. Meanwhile he now came forward and gave the following advice to the Athenians:—

'Athenians, I have a better right to command than others— I must begin with this as Nicias has attacked me—and at the same time I believe myself to be worthy of it. The things for which I am abused, bring fame to my ancestors and to myself, and to the country profit besides. The Hellenes, after expecting to see our city ruined by the war, concluded it to be even greater than it really is, by reason of the magnificence with which I represented it at the Olympic games, when I sent into the lists seven chariots, a number never before entered by any private person, and won the first prize, and was second and fourth, and took care to have everything else in a style worthy of my victory. Custom regards such displays as honourable, and they cannot be made without leaving behind them an impression of power. Again, any splendour that I may have exhibited at home in providing choruses or otherwise, is naturally envied by my fellow-citizens, but in the eyes of foreigners has an air of strength as in the other instance. And this is no useless folly, when a man at his own private cost benefits not himself only, but his city: nor is it unfair that he who prides himself on his position should refuse to be upon an equality with the rest. He who is badly off has his misfortunes all to himself, and as we do not see men courted in adversity, on the like principle a man ought to accept the insolence of prosperity; or else, let him first mete out equal measure to all, and then demand to have it meted out to him. What I know is that persons of this kind and all others that have attained to any distinction, although they may be unpopular in their lifetime in their relations with their fellow-men and especially with their equals, leave to posterity the desire of claiming connexion with them even without any ground, and are vaunted by the country to which they belonged, not as strangers or ill-doers, but as fellow-countrymen and heroes. Such are my aspirations, and however I am abused for them in private, the question is whether any one manages public affairs better than I do. Having united the most powerful states of Peloponnese, without great danger or expense to you, I compelled the Lacedæmonians to stake their all upon the issue of a single day at Mantinea; and although victorious in the battle, they have never since fully recovered confidence.

'Thus did my youth and so-called monstrous folly find fitting arguments to deal with the power of the Peloponnesians, and by its ardour win their confidence and prevail. And do not be afraid of my youth now, but while I am still in its flower, and Nicias appears fortunate, avail yourselves to the utmost of the services of us both. Neither rescind your resolution to sail to Sicily, on the ground that you would be going to attack a great power. The cities in Sicily are peopled by motley rabbles, and easily change their institutions and adopt new ones in their stead; and consequently the inhabitants, being without any feeling of patriotism, are not provided with arms for their persons, and have not regularly established themselves on the land; every man thinks that either by fair words or by party strife he can obtain something at the public expense, and then in the event of a catastrophe settle in some other country, and makes his preparations accordingly. From a mob like this you need not look for either unanimity in counsel or concert in action; but they will probably one by one come in as they get a fair offer, especially if they are torn by civil strife as we are told. Moreover, the Siceliots have not so many heavy infantry as they boast; just as the Hellenes generally did not prove so numerous as each state reckoned itself, but Hellas greatly over-estimated their numbers, and has hardly had an adequate force of heavy infantry throughout this war. The states in Sicily, therefore, from all that I can hear, will be found as I say, and I have not pointed out all our advantages, for we shall have the help of many barbarians, who from their hatred of the Syracusans will join us in attacking them; nor will the powers at home prove any hindrance, if you judge rightly. Our fathers with these very adversaries, which it is said we shall now leave behind us when we sail, and the Mede as their enemy as well, were able to win the empire, depending solely on their superiority at sea. The Peloponnesians had never so little hope against us at present; and let them be ever so sanguine, although strong enough to invade our country even if we stay at home, they can never hurt us with their navy, as we leave one of our own behind us that is a match for them.

'In this state of things what reason can we give to ourselves for holding back, or what excuse can we offer to our allies in Sicily for not helping them? They are our confederates, and we are bound to assist them, without objecting that they have not assisted us. We did not take them into alliance to have them to help us in Hellas, but that they might so annoy our enemies in Sicily as to prevent them from coming over here and attacking us. It is thus that empire has been won, both by us and by all others that have held it, by a constant readiness to support all, whether barbarians or Hellenes, that invite assistance; since if all were to keep quiet or to pick and choose whom they ought to assist, we should make but few new conquests, and should imperil those we have already won. Men do not rest content with parrying the attacks of a superior, but often strike the first blow to prevent the attack being made. And we cannot fix the exact point at which our empire shall stop; we have reached a position in which we must not be content with retaining but must scheme to extend it, for, if we cease to rule others, we are in danger of being ruled ourselves. Nor can you look at inaction from the same point of view as others, unless you are prepared to change your habits and make them like theirs.

'Be convinced then that we shall augment our power at home by this adventure abroad, and let us make the expedition, and so humble the pride of the Peloponnesians by sailing off to Sicily, and letting them see how little we care for the peace that we are now enjoying; and at the same time we shall either become masters, as we very easily may, of the whole of Hellas through the accession of the Sicilian Hellenes, or in any case ruin the Syracusans, to the no small advantage of ourselves and our allies. The faculty of staying if successful, or of returning, will be secured to us by our navy, as we shall be superior at sea to all the Siceliots put together. And do not let the do-nothing policy which Nicias advocates, or his setting of the young against the old, turn you from your purpose, but in the good old fashion by which our fathers, old and young together, by their united counsels brought our affairs to their present height, do you endeavour still to advance them; understanding that neither youth nor old age can do anything the one without the other, but that levity, sobriety, and deliberate judgment are strongest when united, and that, by sinking into inaction, the city, like everything else, will wear itself out, and its skill in everything decay; while each fresh struggle will give it fresh experience, and make it more used to defend itself not in word but in deed. In short, my conviction is that a city not inactive by nature could not choose a quicker way to ruin itself than by suddenly adopting such a policy, and that the safest rule of life is to take one's character and institutions for better and for worse, and to live up to them as closely as one can.'

Such were the words of Alcibiades. After hearing him and the Egestæans and some Leontine exiles, who came forward reminding them of their oaths and imploring their assistance, the Athenians became more eager for the expedition than before. Nicias, perceiving that it would be now useless to try to deter them by the old line of argument, but thinking that he might perhaps alter their resolution by the extravagance of his estimates, came forward a second time and spoke as follows:—

'I see, Athenians, that you are thoroughly bent upon the expedition, and therefore hope that all will turn out as we wish, and proceed to give you my opinion at the present juncture. From all that I hear we are going against cities that are great and not subject to one another, or in need of change, so as to be glad to pass from enforced servitude to an easier condition, or in the least likely to accept our rule in exchange for freedom; and, to take only the Hellenic towns, they are very numerous for one island. Besides Naxos and Catana, which I expect to join us from their connexion with Leontini, there are seven others armed at all points just like our own power, particularly Selinus and Syracuse, the chief objects of our expedition. These are full of heavy infantry, archers, and darters, have galleys in abundance and crowds

to man them; they have also money, partly in the hands of
private persons, partly in the temples at Selinus, and at
Syracuse first-fruits from some of the barbarians as well. But
their chief advantage over us lies in the number of their
horses, and in the fact that they grow their corn at home
instead of importing it.

'Against a power of this kind it will not do to have merely
a weak naval armament, but we shall want also a large land
army to sail with us, if we are to do anything worthy of our
ambition, and are not to be shut out from the country by a
numerous cavalry; especially if the cities should take alarm
and combine, and we should be left without friends (except
the Egestæans) to furnish us with horse to defend ourselves
with. It would be disgraceful to have to retire under compulsion, or to send back for reinforcements, owing to want
of reflexion at first: we must therefore start from home with
a competent force, seeing that we are going to sail far from
our country, and upon an expedition not like any which you
may have undertaken in the quality of allies, among your
subject states here in Hellas, where any additional supplies
needed were easily drawn from the friendly territory; but we
are cutting ourselves off, and going to a land entirely strange,
from which during four months in winter it is not even easy
for a messenger to get to Athens.

'I think, therefore, that we ought to take great numbers
of heavy infantry, both from Athens and from our allies, and
not merely from our subjects, but also any we may be able
to get for love or for money in Peloponnese, and great numbers
also of archers and slingers, to make head against the Sicilian
horse. Meanwhile we must have an overwhelming superiority
at sea, to enable us the more easily to carry in what we want;
and we must take our own corn in merchant vessels, that is to
say, wheat and parched barley, and bakers from the mills
compelled to serve for pay in the proper proportion; in order
that in case of our being weather-bound the armament may
not want provisions, as it is not every city that will be able
to entertain numbers like ours. We must also provide ourselves
with everything else as far as we can, so as not to be dependent
upon others; and above all we must take with us from home
as much money as possible, as the sums talked of as ready

at Egesta are readier, you may be sure, in talk than in any other way.

'Indeed, even if we leave Athens with a force not only equal to that of the enemy except in the number of heavy infantry in the field, but even at all points superior to him, we shall still find it difficult to conquer Sicily or save ourselves. We must not disguise from ourselves that we go to found a city among strangers and enemies, and that he who undertakes such an enterprise should be prepared to become master of the country the first day he lands, or failing in this to find everything hostile to him. Fearing this, and knowing that we shall have need of much good counsel and more good fortune—a hard matter for mortal men to aspire to—I wish as far as may be to make myself independent of fortune before sailing, and when I do sail, to be as safe as a strong force can make me. This I believe to be surest for the country at large, and safest for us who are to go on the expedition. If any one thinks differently I resign to him my command.'

With this Nicias concluded, thinking that he should either disgust the Athenians by the magnitude of the undertaking, or, if obliged to sail on the expedition, would thus do so in the safest way possible. The Athenians, however, far from having their taste for the voyage taken away by the burdensomeness of the preparations, became more eager for it than ever; and just the contrary took place of what Nicias had thought, as it was held that he had given good advice, and that the expedition would be the safest in the world. All alike fell in love with the enterprise. The older men thought that they would either subdue the places against which they were to sail, or at all events, with so large a force, meet with no disaster; those in the prime of life felt a longing for foreign sights and spectacles, and had no doubt that they should come safe home again; while the idea of the common people and the soldiery was to earn wages at the moment, and make conquests that would supply a never-ending fund of pay for the future. With this enthusiasm of the majority, the few that liked it not, feared to appear unpatriotic by holding up their hands against it, and so kept quiet.

At last one of the Athenians came forward and called upon Nicias and told him that he ought not to make excuses or put them off, but say at once before them all what forces the Athenians should vote him. Upon this he said, not without reluctance, that he would advise upon that matter more at leisure with his colleagues; as far however as he could see at present, they must sail with at least one hundred galleys—the Athenians providing as many transports as they might determine, and sending for others from the allies—not less than five thousand heavy infantry in all, Athenian and allied, and if possible more; and the rest of the armament in proportion; archers from home and from Crete, and slingers, and whatever else might seem desirable, being got ready by the generals and taken with them.

Upon hearing this the Athenians at once voted that the generals should have full powers in the matter of the numbers of the army and of the expedition generally, to do as they judged best for the interests of Athens. After this the preparations began; messages being sent to the allies and the rolls drawn up at home. And as the city had just recovered from the plague and the long war, and a number of young men had grown up and capital had accumulated by reason of the truce, everything was the more easily provided.

In the midst of these preparations all the stone Hermæ in the city of Athens, that is to say the customary square figures, so common in the doorways of private houses and temples, had in one night most of them their faces mutilated. No one knew who had done it, but large public rewards were offered to find the authors; and it was further voted that any one who knew of any other act of impiety having been committed should come and give information without fear of consequences, whether he were citizen, alien, or slave. The matter was taken up the more seriously, as it was thought to be ominous for the expedition, and part of a conspiracy to bring about a revolution and to upset the democracy.

Information was given accordingly by some resident aliens and body servants, not about the Hermæ but about some previous mutilations of other images perpetrated by young men in a drunken frolic, and of mock celebrations of the mysteries, averred to take place in private houses. Alcibiades being implicated in this charge, it was taken hold of by those who could least endure him, because he stood in the way of their obtaining the undisturbed direction of the people, and who thought that if he were once removed the first place would be theirs. These accordingly magnified the manner and loudly proclaimed that the affair of the mysteries and the mutilation of the Hermæ were part and parcel of a scheme to overthrow the democracy, and that nothing of all this had been done without Alcibiades; the proofs alleged being the general and undemocratic license of his life and habits.

Alcibiades repelled on the spot the charges in question, and also before going on the expedition, the preparations for which were now complete, offered to stand his trial, that it might be seen whether he was guilty of the acts imputed to him; desiring to be punished if found guilty, but, if acquitted, to take the command. Meanwhile he protested against their receiving slanders against him in his absence, and begged them rather to put him to death at once if he were guilty, and pointed out the imprudence of sending him out at the head of so large an army, with so serious a charge still undecided. But his enemies feared that he would have the army for him if he were tried immediately, and that the people might relent in favour of the man whom they already caressed as the cause of the Argives and some of the Mantineans joining in the expedition, and did their utmost to get this proposition rejected, putting forward other orators who said that he ought at present to sail and not delay the departure of the army, and be tried on his return within a fixed number of days; their plan being to have him sent for and brought home for trial upon some graver charge, which they would the more easily get up in his absence. Accordingly it was decreed that he should sail.

After this the departure for Sicily took place, it being now about midsummer. Most of the allies, with the corn transports and the smaller craft and the rest of the expedition, had already received orders to muster at Corcyra, to cross the Ionian sea from thence in a body to the Iapygian promontory. But the Athenians themselves, and such of their allies as happened to be with them, went down to Piræus upon a day appointed at daybreak, and began to man the ships for putting out to sea. With them also went down the whole population, one may say, of the city, both citizens and foreigners; the

inhabitants of the country each escorting those that belonged
to them, their friends, their relatives, or their sons, with hope
and lamentation upon their way, as they thought of the conquests which they hoped to make, or of the friends whom they
might never see again, considering the long voyage which they
were going to make from their country. Indeed, at this moment, when they were now upon the point of parting from one
another, the danger came more home to them than when they
voted for the expedition; although the strength of the armament, and the profuse provision which they remarked in every
department, was a sight that could not but comfort them. As
for the foreigners and the rest of the crowd, they simply went
to see a sight worth looking at and passing all belief.

Indeed this armament that first sailed out was by far the
most costly and splendid Hellenic force that had ever been
sent out by a single city up to that time. In mere number of
ships and heavy infantry that against Epidaurus under Pericles, and the same when going against Potidæa under Hagnon,
was not inferior; containing as it did four thousand Athenian
heavy infantry, three hundred horse, and one hundred galleys
accompanied by fifty Lesbian and Chian vessels and many
allies besides. But these were sent upon a short voyage and
with a scanty equipment. The present expedition was formed
in contemplation of a long term of service by land and sea
alike, and was furnished with ships and troops so as to be
ready for either as required. The fleet had been elaborately
equipped at great cost to the captains and the state; the
treasury giving a drachma a day to each seaman, and providing empty ships, sixty men of war and forty transports, and
manning these with the best crews obtainable; while the
captains gave a bounty in addition to the pay from the treasury to the *thranitæ* and crews generally, besides spending
lavishly upon figure-heads and equipments, and one and all
making the utmost exertions to enable their own ships to excel
in beauty and fast sailing. Meanwhile the land forces had
been picked from the best muster-rolls, and vied with each
other in paying great attention to their arms and personal
accoutrements. From this resulted not only a rivalry among
themselves in their different departments, but an idea among
the rest of the Hellenes that it was more a display of power

and resources than an armament against an enemy. For if any one had counted up the public expenditure of the state, and the private outlay of individuals—that is to say, the sums which the state had already spent upon the expedition and was sending out in the hands of the generals, and those which individuals had expended upon their personal outfit, or as captains of galleys had laid out and were still to lay out upon their vessels; and if he had added to this the journey money which each was likely to have provided himself with, independently of the pay from the treasury, for a voyage of such length, and what the soldiers or traders took with them for the purpose of exchange—it would have been found that many talents in all were being taken out of the city. Indeed the expedition became not less famous for its wonderful boldness and for the splendour of its appearance, than for its overwhelming strength as compared with the peoples against whom it was directed, and for the fact that this was the longest passage from home hitherto attempted, and the most ambitious in its objects considering the resources of those who undertook it.

The ships being now manned, and everything put on board with which they meant to sail, the trumpet commanded silence, and the prayers customary before putting out to sea were offered, not in each ship by itself, but by all together to the voice of a herald; and bowls of wine were mixed through all the armament, and libations made by the soldiers and their officers in gold and silver goblets. In their prayers joined also the crowds on shore, the citizens and all others that wished them well. The hymn sung and the libations finished, they put out to sea, and first sailing out in column then raced each other as far as Ægina, and so hastened to reach Corcyra, where the rest of the allied forces were also assembling.

CHAPTER XIX

SEVENTEENTH YEAR OF THE WAR—PARTIES AT SYRACUSE—
STORY OF HARMODIUS AND ARISTOGITON—DISGRACE OF
ALCIBIADES

B.C. 415: *Hermocrates warns Syracusans—Athenagros replies—Progress
of Athenian fleet—Syracusans prepare—The Egestœan stratagem
—Three generals disagree—Athenian foray from Catana—Recall
of Alcibiades—Harmodius and Aristogiton—Public hostility against
Alcibiades—He escapes and is sentenced to death by default.*

MEANWHILE at Syracuse news came in from many quarters
of the expedition, but for a long while met with no credence
whatever. Indeed, an assembly was held in which speeches,
as will be seen, were delivered by different orators, believing
or contradicting the report of the Athenian expedition; among
whom Hermocrates, son of Hermon, came forward, being
persuaded that he knew the truth of the matter, and gave the
following counsel:—

'Although I shall perhaps be no better believed than others
have been when I speak upon the reality of the expedition,
and although I know that those who either make or repeat
statements thought not worthy of belief not only gain no
converts, but are thought fools for their pains, I shall certainly
not be frightened into holding my tongue when the state is
in danger, and when I am persuaded that I can speak with
more authority on the matter than other persons. Much as
you wonder at it, the Athenians nevertheless have set out
against us with a large force, naval and military, professedly
to help the Egestæans and to restore Leontini, but really to
conquer Sicily, and above all our city, which once gained,
the rest, they think, will easily follow. Make up your minds,
therefore, to see them speedily here, and see how you can best
repel them with the means under your hands, and do not be
taken off your guard through despising the news, or neglect
the common weal through disbelieving it. Meanwhile those
who believe me need not be dismayed at the force or daring
of the enemy. They will not be able to do us more hurt than
we shall do them; nor is the greatness of their armament
altogether without advantage to us. Indeed, the greater it is
the better, with regard to the rest of the Siceliots, whom dis-

may will make more ready to join us; and if we defeat or drive them away, disappointed of the objects of their ambition (for I do not fear for a moment that they will get what they want), it will be a most glorious exploit for us, and in my judgment by no means an unlikely one. Few indeed have been the large armaments, either Hellenic or barbarian, that have gone far from home and been successful. They cannot be more numerous than the people of the country and their neighbours, all of whom fear leagues together; and if they miscarry for want of supplies in a foreign land, to those against whom their plans were laid none the less they leave renown, although they may themselves have been the main cause of their own discomfort. Thus these very Athenians rose by the defeat of the Mede, in a great measure due to accidental causes, from the mere fact that Athens had been the object of his attack; and this may very well be the case with us also.

'Let us, therefore, confidently begin preparations here; let us send and confirm some of the Sicels, and obtain the friendship and alliance of others, and despatch envoys to the rest of Sicily to show that the danger is common to all, and to Italy to get them to become our allies, or at all events to refuse to receive the Athenians. I also think that it would be best to send to Carthage as well; they are by no means there without apprehension, but it is their constant fear that the Athenians may one day attack their city, and they may perhaps think that they might themselves suffer by letting Sicily be sacrificed, and be willing to help us secretly if not openly, in one way if not in another. They are the best able to do so, if they will, of any of the present day, as they possess most gold and silver, by which war, like everything else, flourishes. Let us also send to Lacedæmon and Corinth, and ask them to come here and help us as soon as possible, and to keep alive the war in Hellas. But the true thing of all others, in my opinion, to do at the present moment, is what you, with your constitutional love of quiet, will be slow to see, and what I must nevertheless mention. If we Siceliots, all together, or at least as many as possible besides ourselves, would only launch the whole of our actual navy with two months' provisions and meet the Athenians at Tarentum and the Iapygian

promontory, and show them that before fighting for Sicily
they must first fight for their passage across the Ionian sea,
we should strike dismay into their army, and set them on
thinking that we have a base for our defensive—for Tarentum
is ready to receive us—while they have a wide sea to cross
with all their armament, which could with difficulty keep its
order through so long a voyage, and would be easy for us to
attack as it came on slowly and in small detachments. On the
other hand, if they were to lighten their vessels, and draw
together their fast sailers and with these attack us, we could
either fall upon them when they were wearied with rowing,
or if we did not choose to do so, we could retire to Tarentum;
while they, having crossed with few provisions just to give
battle, would be hard put to it in desolate places, and would
either have to remain and be blockaded, or to try to sail along
the coast, abandoning the rest of their armament, and being
further discouraged by not knowing for certain whether the
cities would receive them. In my opinion this consideration
alone would be sufficient to deter them from putting out from
Corcyra; and what with deliberating and reconnoitring our
numbers and whereabouts, they would let the season go on
until winter was upon them, or, confounded by so unexpected
a circumstance, would break up the expedition, especially as
their most experienced general has, as I hear, taken the
command against his will, and would grasp at the first excuse
offered by any serious demonstration of ours. We should also
be reported, I am certain, as more numerous than we really
are, and men's minds are affected by what they hear, and
besides the first to attack, or to show that they mean to defend
themselves against an attack, inspire greater fear because men
see that they are ready for the emergency. This would just be
the case with the Athenians at present. They are now attacking us in the belief that we shall not resist, having a right to
judge us severely because we did not help the Lacedæmonians
in crushing them; but if they were to see us showing a courage
for which they are not prepared, they would be more dismayed by the surprise than they could ever be by our actual
power. I could wish to persuade you to show this courage;
but if this cannot be, at all events lose not a moment in pre
paring generally for the war; and remember all of you that

contempt for an assailant is best shown by bravery in action, but that for the present the best course is to accept the preparations which fear inspires as giving the surest promise of safety, and to act as if the danger was real. That the Athenians are coming to attack us, and are already upon the voyage, and all but here—this is what I am sure of.'

Thus far spoke Hermocrates. Meanwhile the people of Syracuse were at great strife among themselves; some contending that the Athenians had no idea of coming and that there was no truth in what he said; some asking if they did come what harm they could do that would not be repaid them tenfold in return; while others made light of the whole affair and turned it into ridicule. In short, there were few that believed Hermocrates and feared for the future. Meanwhile Athenagoras, the leader of the people and very powerful at that time with the masses, came forward and spoke as follows:—

'For the Athenians, he who does not wish that they may be as misguided as they are supposed to be, and that they may come here to become our subjects, is either a coward or a traitor to his country; while as for those who carry such tidings and fill you with so much alarm, I wonder less at their audacity than at their folly if they flatter themselves that we do not see through them. The fact is that they have their private reasons to be afraid, and wish to throw the city into consternation to have their own terrors cast into the shade by the public alarm. In short, this is what these reports are worth; they do not arise of themselves, but are concocted by men who are always causing agitation here in Sicily. However, if you are well advised, you will not be guided in your calculation of probabilities by what these persons tell you, but by what shrewd men and of large experience, as I esteem the Athenians to be, would be likely to do. Now it is not likely that they would leave the Peloponnesians behind them, and before they have well ended the war in Hellas wantonly come in quest of a new war quite as arduous, in Sicily; indeed, in my judgment, they are only too glad that we do not go and attack them, being so many and so great cities as we are.

'However, if they should come as is reported, I consider Sicily better able to go through with the war than Peloponnese, as being at all points better prepared, and our city by itself far more than a match for this pretended army of invasion, even were it twice as large again. I know that they will not have horses with them, or get any here, except a few perhaps from the Egestæans; or be able to bring a force of heavy infantry equal in number to our own, in ships which will already have enough to do to come all this distance, however lightly laden, not to speak of the transport of the other stores required against a city of this magnitude, which will be no slight quantity. In fact, so strong is my opinion upon the subject, that I do not well see how they could avoid annihilation if they brought with them another city as large as Syracuse, and settled down and carried on war from our frontier; much less can they hope to succeed with all Sicily hostile to them, as all Sicily will be, and with only a camp pitched from the ships, and composed of tents and bare necessaries, from which they would not be able to stir far for fear of our cavalry.

'But the Athenians see this as I tell you, and as I have reason to know are looking after their possessions at home, while persons here invent stories that neither are true nor ever will be. Nor is this the first time that I see these persons, when they cannot resort to deeds, trying by such stories and by others even more abominable to frighten your people and get into their hands the government: it is what I see always. And I cannot help fearing that trying so often they may one day succeed, and that we, as long as we do not feel the smart, may prove too weak for the task of prevention, or, when the offenders are known, of pursuit. The result is that our city is rarely at rest, but is subject to constant troubles and to contests as frequent against herself as against the enemy, not to speak of occasional tyrannies and infamous cabals. However, I will try, if you will support me, to let nothing of this happen in our time, by gaining you, the many, and by chastising the authors of such machinations, not merely when they are caught in the act—a difficult feat to accomplish—but also for what they have the wish though not the power to do; as is necessary to punish an enemy not only for what he does, but also beforehand for what he intends to do, if the first to relax precaution would not be also the first to suffer. I shall also re-

prove, watch, and on occasion warn the few—the most effectual way, in my opinion, of turning them from their evil
courses. And after all, as I have often asked—What would
you have, young men? Would you hold office at once? The
law forbids it, a law enacted rather because you are not competent than to disgrace you when competent. Meanwhile you
would not be on a legal equality with the many! But how can
it be right that citizens of the same state should be held unworthy of the same privileges?

'It will be said, perhaps, that democracy is neither wise nor
equitable, but that the holders of property are also the best
fitted to rule. I say, on the contrary, first, that the word *demos,*
or people, includes the whole state, oligarchy only a part;
next, that if the best guardians of property are the rich, and
the best counsellors the wise, none can hear and decide so
well as the many; and that all these talents, severally and
collectively, have their just place in a democracy. But an
oligarchy gives the many their share of the danger, and not
content with the largest part takes and keeps the whole of the
profit; and this is what the powerful and young among you
aspire to, but in a great city cannot possibly obtain.

'But even now, foolish men, most senseless of all the Hellenes that I know, if you have no sense of the wickedness of
your designs, or most criminal if you have that sense and still
dare to pursue them,—even now, if it is not a case for repentance, you may still learn wisdom, and thus advance the
interest of the country, the common interest of us all. Reflect
that in the country's prosperity the men of merit in your ranks
will have a share and a larger share than the great mass of
your fellow-countrymen, but that if you have other designs
you run a risk of being deprived of all; and desist from reports
like these, as the people know your object and will not put up
with it. If the Athenians arrive, this city will repulse them in
a manner worthy of itself; we have, moreover, generals who
will see to this matter. And if nothing of this be true, as I incline to believe, the city will not be thrown into a panic by
your intelligence, or impose upon itself a self-chosen servitude
by choosing you for its rulers; the city itself will look into the
matter, and will judge your words as if they were acts, and
instead of allowing itself to be deprived of its liberty by listen-

ing to you, will strive to preserve that liberty, by taking care
to have always at hand the means of making itself respected.'

Such were the words of Athenagoras. One of the generals
now stood up and stopped any other speakers coming forward,
adding these words of his own with reference to the matter in
hand:—'It is not well for speakers to utter calumnies against
one another, or for their hearers to entertain them; we ought
rather to look to the intelligence that we have received, and
see how each man by himself and the city as a whole may best
prepare to repel the invaders. Even if there be no need, there
is no harm in the state being furnished with horses and arms
and all other insignia of war; and we will undertake to see to
and order this, and to send round to the cities to reconnoitre
and do all else that may appear desirable. Part of this we have
seen to already, and whatever we discover shall be laid before
you.' After these words from the general, the Syracusans departed from the assembly.

In the meantime the Athenians with all their allies had now
arrived at Corcyra. Here the generals began by again review-
ing the armament, and made arrangements as to the order in
which they were to anchor and encamp, and dividing the whole
fleet into three divisions, allotted one to each of their number,
to avoid sailing all together and being thus embarrassed for
water, harbourage, or provisions at the stations which they
might touch at, and at the same time to be generally better
ordered and easier to handle, by each squadron having its own
commander. Next they sent on three ships to Italy and Sicily
to find out which of the cities would receive them, with instructions to meet them on the way and let them know before
they put in to land.

After this the Athenians weighed from Corcyra, and proceeded to cross to Sicily with an armament now consisting of
one hundred and thirty-four galleys in all (besides two
Rhodian fifty-oars` of which one hundred were Athenian
vessels—sixty men-of-war, and forty troopships—and the remainder from Chios and the other allies; five thousand and
one hundred heavy infantry in all, that is to say, fifteen hundred Athenian citizens from the rolls at Athens and seven hundred *Thetes* shipped as marines, and the rest allied troops,
some of them Athenian subjects, and besides these five hun-

dred Argives, and two hundred and fifty Mantineans serving
for hire; four hundred and eighty archers in all, eighty of
whom were Cretans, seven hundred slingers from Rhodes, one
hundred and twenty light-armed exiles from Megara, and one
horse-transport carrying thirty horses.

Such was the strength of the first armament that sailed over
for the war. The supplies for this force were carried by thirty
ships of burden laden with corn, which conveyed the bakers,
stone-masons and carpenters, and the tools for raising fortifications, accompanied by one hundred boats, like the former
pressed into the service, besides many other boats and ships
of burden which followed the armament voluntarily for
purposes of trade; all of which now left Corcyra and struck
across the Ionian sea together. The whole force making land
at the Iapygian promontory and Tarentum, with more or less
good fortune, coasted along the shores of Italy, the cities shutting their markets and gates against them, and according them
nothing but water and liberty to anchor, and Tarentum and
Locri not even that, until they arrived at Rhegium, the extreme
point of Italy. Here at length they reunited, and not gaining
admission within the walls pitched a camp outside the city in
the precinct of Artemis, where a market was also provided
for them, and drew their ships on shore and kept quiet. Meanwhile they opened negotiations with the Rhegians, and called
upon them as Chalcidians to assist their Leontine kinsmen; to
which the Rhegians replied that they would not side with either
party, but should await the decision of the rest of the Italiots,
and do as they did. Upon this the Athenians now began to
consider what would be the best action to take in the affairs
of Sicily, and meanwhile waited for the ships sent on to come
back from Egesta, in order to know whether there was really
there the money mentioned by the messengers at Athens.

In the meantime came in from all quarters to the Syracusans, as well as from their own officers sent to reconnoitre,
the positive tidings that the fleet was at Rhegium; upon which
they laid aside their incredulity and threw themselves heart
and soul into the work of preparation. Guards or envoys, as
the case might be, were sent round to the Sicels, garrisons put
into the posts of the Peripoli in the country, horses and arms
reviewed in the city to see that nothing was wanting, and all

other steps taken to prepare for a war which might be upon them at any moment.

Meanwhile the three ships that had been sent on came from Egesta to the Athenians at Rhegium, with the news that so far from there being the sums promised, all that could be produced was thirty talents. The generals were not a little disheartened at being thus disappointed at the outset, and by the refusal to join in the expedition of the Rhegians, the people they had first tried to gain and had had most reason to count upon, from their relationship to the Leontines and constant friendship for Athens. If Nicias was prepared for the news from Egesta, his two colleagues were taken completely by surprise. The Egestæans had had recourse to the following stratagem, when the first envoys from Athens came to inspect their resources. They took the envoys in question to the temple of Aphrodite at Eryx and showed them the treasures deposited there; bowls, wine-ladles, censers, and a large number of other pieces of plate, which from being in silver gave an impression of wealth quite out of proportion to their really small value. They also privately entertained the ships' crews, and collected all the cups of gold and silver that they could find in Egesta itself or could borrow in the neighbouring Phœnician and Hellenic towns, and each brought them to the banquets as their own; and as all used pretty nearly the same, and everywhere a great quantity of plate was shown, the effect was most dazzling upon the Athenian sailors, and made them talk loudly of the riches they had seen when they got back to Athens. The dupes in question—who had in their turn persuaded the rest —when the news got abroad that there was not the money supposed at Egesta, were much blamed by the soldiers.

Meanwhile the generals consulted upon what was to be done. The opinion of Nicias was to sail with all the armament to Selinus, the main object of the expedition, and if the Egestæans could provide money for the whole force, to advise accordingly; but if they could not, to require them to supply provisions for the sixty ships that they had asked for, to stay and settle matters between them and the Selinuntines either by force or by agreement, and then to coast past the other cities, and after displaying the power of Athens and proving their zeal for their friends and allies, to sail home again (unless they should have some sudden and unexpected opportunity of serving the Leontines, or of bringing over some of the other cities), and not to endanger the state by wasting its home resources.

Alcibiades said that a great expedition like the present must not disgrace itself by going away without having done anything; heralds must be sent to all the cities except Selinus and Syracuse, and efforts be made to make some of the Sicels revolt from the Syracusans, and to obtain the friendship of others, in order to have corn and troops; and first of all to gain the Messinese, who lay right in the passage and entrance to Sicily, and would afford an excellent harbour and base for the army. Thus, after bringing over the towns and knowing who would be their allies in the war, they might at length attack Syracuse and Selinus; unless the latter came to terms with Egesta and the former ceased to oppose the restoration of Leontini.

Lamachus, on the other hand, said that they ought to sail straight to Syracuse, and fight their battle at once under the walls of the town while the people were still unprepared, and the panic at its height. Every armament was most terrible at first; if it allowed time to run on without showing itself, men's courage revived, and they saw it appear at last almost with indifference. By attacking suddenly, while Syracuse still trembled at their coming, they would have the best chance of gaining a victory for themselves and of striking a complete panic into the enemy by the aspect of their numbers—which would never appear so considerable as at present—by the anticipation of coming disaster, and above all by the immediate danger of the engagement. They might also count upon surprising many in the fields outside, incredulous of their coming; and at the moment that the enemy was carrying in his property the army would not want for booty if it sat down in force before the city. The rest of the Siceliots would thus be immediately less disposed to enter into alliance with the Syracusans, and would join the Athenians, without waiting to see which were the strongest. They must make Megara their naval station as a place to retreat to and a base from which to attack: it was an uninhabited place at no great distance from Syracuse either by land or by sea.

After speaking to this effect, Lamachus nevertheless gave

his support to the opinion of Alcibiades. After this Alcibiades sailed in his own vessel across to Messina with proposals of alliance, but met with no success, the inhabitants answering that they could not receive him within their walls, though they would provide him with a market outside. Upon this he sailed back to Rhegium. Immediately upon his return the generals manned and victualled sixty ships out of the whole fleet and coasted along to Naxos, leaving the rest of the armament behind them at Rhegium with one of their number. Received by the Naxians, they then coasted on to Catana, and being refused admittance by the inhabitants, there being a Syracusan party in the town, went on to the river Terias. Here they bivouacked, and the next day sailed in single file to Syracuse with all their ships except ten which they sent on in front to sail into the great harbour and see if there was any fleet launched, and to proclaim by herald from shipboard that the Athenians were come to restore the Leontines to their country, as being their allies and kinsmen, and that such of them, therefore, as were in Syracuse should leave it without fear and join their friends and benefactors the Athenians. After making this proclamation and reconnoitring the city and the harbours, and the features of the country which they would have to make their base of operations in the war, they sailed back to Catana.

An assembly being held here, the inhabitants refused to receive the armament, but invited the generals to come in and say what they desired; and while Alcibiades was speaking and the citizens were intent on the assembly, the soldiers broke down an ill-walled-up postern-gate without being observed, and getting inside the town, flocked into the market-place. The Syracusan party in the town no sooner saw the army inside than they became frightened and withdrew, not being at all numerous; while the rest voted for an alliance with the Athenians and invited them to fetch the rest of their forces from Rhegium. After this the Athenians sailed to Rhegium, and put off, this time with all the armament, for Catana, and fell to work at their camp immediately upon their arrival.

Meanwhile word was brought them from Camarina that if they went there the town would go over to them, and also that the Syracusans were manning a fleet. The Athenians accordingly sailed along shore with all their armament, first to Syracuse, where they found no fleet manning, and so always along the coast to Camarina, where they brought to at the beach, and sent a herald to the people, who, however, refused to receive them, saying that their oaths bound them to receive the Athenians only with a single vessel, unless they themselves sent for more. Disappointed here, the Athenians now sailed back again, and after landing and plundering on Syracusan territory and losing some stragglers from their light infantry through the coming up of the Syracusan horse, so got back to Catana.

There they found the Salaminia come from Athens for Alcibiades, with orders for him to sail home to answer the charges which the state brought against him, and for certain others of the soldiers who with him were accused of sacrilege in the matter of the mysteries and of the Hermæ. For the Athenians, after the departure of the expedition, had continued as active as ever in investigating the facts of the mysteries and of the Hermæ, and, instead of testing the informers, in their suspicious temper welcomed all indifferently, arresting and imprisoning the best citizens upon the evidence of rascals, and preferring to sift the matter to the bottom sooner than to let an accused person of good character pass unquestioned, owing to the rascality of the informer. The commons had heard how oppressive the tyranny of Pisistratus and his sons had become before it ended, and further that that tyranny had been put down at last, not by themselves and Harmodius, but by the Lacedæmonians, and so were always in fear and took everything suspiciously.

Indeed, the daring action of Aristogiton and Harmodius was undertaken in consequence of a love affair, which I shall relate at some length, to show that the Athenians are not more accurate than the rest of the world in their accounts of their own tyrants and of the facts of their own history. Pisistratus dying at an advanced age in possession of the tyranny, was succeeded by his eldest son, Hippias, and not Hipparchus, as is vulgarly believed. Harmodius was then in the flower of youthful beauty, and Aristogiton, a citizen in the middle rank of life, was his lover and possessed him. Solicited without success by Hipparchus, son of Pisistratus, Harmodius told Aristogiton, and the enraged lover, afraid that the powerful Hipparchus might take Harmodius by force, immediately formed a design, such as his condition in life permitted, for overthrowing the tyranny. In the meantime Hipparchus, after a second solicitation of Harmodius, attended with no better success, unwilling to use violence, arranged to insult him in some covert way. Indeed, generally their government was not grievous to the multitude, or in any way odious in practice; and these tyrants cultivated wisdom and virtue as much as any, and without exacting from the Athenians more than a twentieth of their income, splendidly adorned their city, and carried on their wars, and provided sacrifices for the temples. For the rest, the city was left in full enjoyment of its existing laws, except that care was always taken to have the offices in the hands of some one of the family. Among those of them that held the yearly archonship at Athens was Pisistratus, son of the tyrant Hippias, and named after his grandfather, who dedicated during his term of office the altar to the twelve gods in the market-place, and that of Apollo in the Pythian precinct. The Athenian people afterwards built on to and lengthened the altar in the market-place, and obliterated the inscription; but that in the Pythian precinct can still be seen, though in faded letters, and is to the following effect:—

> Pisistratus, the son of Hippias,
> Set up this record of his archonship
> In precinct of Apollo Pythias.

That Hippias was the eldest son and succeeded to the government, is what I positively assert as a fact upon which I have had more exact accounts than others, and may be also ascertained by the following circumstance. He is the only one of the legitimate brothers that appears to have had children; as the altar shows, and the pillar placed in the Athenian Acropolis, commemorating the crime of the tyrants, which mentions no child of Thessalus or of Hipparchus, but five of Hippias, which he had by Myrrhine, daughter of Callias, son of Hyperechides; and naturally the eldest would have married first. Again, his name comes first on the pillar after that of his father, and this too is quite natural, as he was the eldest after him, and the reigning tyrant. Nor can I ever believe that Hippias would have obtained the tyranny so easily, if Hipparchus had been in power when he was killed, and he, Hippias, had had to establish himself upon the same day; but he had no doubt been long accustomed to over-awe the citizens, and to be obeyed by his mercenaries, and thus not only conquered, but conquered with ease, without experiencing any of the embarrassment of a younger brother unused to the exercise of authority. It was the sad fate which made Hipparchus famous that got him also the credit with posterity of having been tyrant.

To return to Harmodius; Hipparchus having been repulsed in his solicitations insulted him as he had resolved, by first inviting a sister of his, a young girl, to come and bear a basket in a certain procession, and then rejecting her, on the plea that she had never been invited at all owing to her unworthiness. If Harmodius was indignant at this, Aristogiton for his sake now became more exasperated than ever; and having arranged everything with those who were to join them in the enterprise, they only waited for the great feast of the Panathenæa, the sole day upon which the citizens forming part of the procession could meet together in arms without suspicion. Aristogiton and Harmodius were to begin, but were to be supported immediately by their accomplices against the bodyguard. The conspirators were not many, for better security, besides which they hoped that those not in the plot would be carried away by the example of a few daring spirits, and use the arms in their hands to recover their liberty.

At last the festival arrived; and Hippias with his bodyguard was outside the city in the Ceramicus, arranging how the different parts of the procession were to proceed. Harmodius and Aristogiton had already their daggers and were getting ready to act, when seeing one of their accomplices talking familiarly with Hippias, who was easy of access to every one, they took fright, and concluded that they were discovered and on the point of being taken; and eager if possible to be revenged first upon the man who had wronged them and for whom they had undertaken all this risk, they rushed, as they were, within the gates, and meeting with Hipparchus by the Leocorium recklessly fell upon him at once, infuriated, Aristogiton by love, and Harmodius by insult, and smote him and slew him. Aristogiton escaped the guards at the moment, through the crowd running up, but was afterwards taken and dispatched in no merciful way: Harmodius was killed on the spot.

When the news was brought to Hippias in the Ceramicus, he at once proceeded not to the scene of action, but to the armed men in the procession, before they, being some dis-tance away, knew anything of the matter, and composing his features for the occasion, so as not to betray himself, pointed to a certain spot, and bade them repair thither without their arms. They withdrew accordingly, fancying he had something to say; upon which he told the mercenaries to remove the arms, and there and then picked out the men he thought guilty and all found with daggers, the shield and spear being the usual weapons for a procession.

In this way offended love first led Harmodius and Aristogi-ton to conspire, and the alarm of the moment to commit the rash action recounted. After this the tyranny pressed harder on the Athenians, and Hippias, now grown more fearful, put to death many of the citizens, and at the same time began to turn his eyes abroad for a refuge in case of revolution. Thus, al-though an Athenian, he gave his daughter, Archedice, to a Lampsacene, Æantides, son of the tyrant of Lampsacus, seeing that they had great influence with Darius. And there is her tomb in Lampsacus with this inscription:—

> Archedice lies buried in this earth,
> Hippias her sire, and Athens gave her birth;
> Unto her bosom pride was never known,
> Though daughter, wife, and sister to the throne.

Hippias, after reigning three years longer over the Athenians, was deposed in the fourth by the Lacedæmonians and the banished Alcmæonidæ, and went with a safe conduct to Sigeum, and to Æantides at Lampsacus, and from thence to King Darius; from whose court he set out twenty years after, in his old age, and came with the Medes to Marathon.

With these events in their minds, and recalling everything they knew by hearsay on the subject, the Athenian people grew difficult of humour and suspicious of the persons charged in the affair of the mysteries, and persuaded that all that had taken place was part of an oligarchical and monarchical conspiracy. In the state of irritation thus produced, many persons of consideration had been already thrown into prison, and far from showing any signs of abating, public feeling grew daily more savage, and more arrests were made; until at last one of those in custody, thought to be the most guilty of all, was induced by a fellow-prisoner to make a revelation, whether true or not is a matter on which there are two opinions, no one having been able, either then or since, to say for certain who did the deed. However this may be, the other found arguments to persuade him, that even if he had not done it, he ought to save himself by gaining a promise of impunity, and free the state of its present suspicions; as he would be surer of safety if he confessed after promise of impunity than if he denied and were brought to trial. He accordingly made a revelation, affecting himself and others in the affair of the Hermæ; and the Athenian people, glad at last, as they supposed, to get at the truth, and furious until then at not being able to discover those who had conspired against the commons, at once let go the informer and all the rest whom he had not denounced, and bringing the accused to trial executed as many as were apprehended, and condemned to death such as had fled and set a price upon their heads. In this it was, after all, not clear whether the sufferers had been punished unjustly, while in any case the rest of the city received immediate and manifest relief.

To return to Alcibiades: public feeling was very hostile to him, being worked on by the same enemies who had attacked him before he went out; and now that the Athenians fancied that they had got at the truth of the matter of the Hermæ, they believed more firmly than ever that the affair of the mysteries also, in which he was implicated, had been contrived by him in the same intention and was connected with the plot against the democracy. Meanwhile it so happened that, just at the time of this agitation, a small force of Lacedæmonians had advanced as far as the Isthmus, in pursuance of some scheme with the Bœotians. It was now thought that this had come by appointment, at his instigation, and not on account of the Bœotians, and that if the citizens had not acted on the information received, and forestalled them by arresting the prisoners, the city would have been betrayed. The citizens went so far as to sleep one night armed in the temple of Theseus

within the walls. The friends also of Alcibiades at Argos were
just at this time suspected of a design to attack the commons;
and the Argive hostages deposited in the islands were given up
by the Athenians to the Argive people to be put to death upon
that account: in short, everywhere something was found to
create suspicion against Alcibiades. It was therefore decided to
bring him to trial and execute him, and the Salaminia was sent
to Sicily for him and the others named in the information,
with instructions to order him to come and answer the charges
against him, but not to arrest him, because they wished to
avoid causing any agitation in the army or among the enemy
in Sicily, and above all to retain the services of the Mantineans
and Argives, who, it was thought, had been induced to join by
his influence. Alcibiades, with his own ship and his fellow-
accused, accordingly sailed off with the Salaminia from Sicily,
as though to return to Athens, and went with her as far as
Thurii, and there they left the ship and disappeared, being
afraid to go home for trial with such a prejudice existing
against them. The crew of the Salaminia stayed some time
looking for Alcibiades and his companions, and at length, as
they were nowhere to be found, set sail and departed.
Alcibiades, now an outlaw, crossed in a boat not long after
from Thurii to Peloponnese; and the Athenians passed
sentence of death by default upon him and those in his
company.

CHAPTER XX

SEVENTEENTH AND EIGHTEENTH YEARS OF THE WAR—INAC-
TION OF THE ATHENIAN ARMY—ALCIBIADES AT SPARTA—
INVESTMENT OF SYRACUSE

B.C. 415: *Courage revived in Syracuse—Plan of the Athenian generals—
Athenians land at Syracuse—Disposition for battle—Nicias
addresses his army—The battle—First victory for Athenians—
Hermocrates' counsel—Athenians at Naxos—Syracusans renew
preparations—Hermocrates speaks at Camarina—Euphemus replies—Camarina decides to remain neutral—Lacedæmonians urged
to alliance—Speech of Alcibiades—His advice followed—B.C. 414:
Athenians resume activity—Battle at Epipolæ—Athenians victorious—Gylippus in Italy—Athenian fleet relieves Argives.*

THE Athenian generals left in Sicily now divided the armament into two parts, and each taking one by lot, sailed with

the whole for Selinus and Egesta, wishing to know whether the Egestæans would give the money, and to look into the question of Selinus and ascertain the state of the quarrel between her and Egesta. Coasting along Sicily, with the shore on their left, on the side towards the Tyrrhene Gulf, they touched at Himera, the only Hellenic city in that part of the island, and being refused admission resumed their voyage. On their way they took Hyccara, a petty Sicanian seaport, nevertheless at war with Egesta, and making slaves of the inhabitants gave up the town to the Egestæans, some of whose horse had joined them; after which the army proceeded through the territory of the Sicels until it reached Catana, while the fleet sailed along the coast with the slaves on board. Meanwhile Nicias sailed straight from Hyccara along the coast and went to Egesta, and after transacting his other business and receiving thirty talents, rejoined the forces. They now sold their slaves for the sum of one hundred and twenty talents, and sailed round to their Sicel allies to urge them to send troops; and meanwhile went with half their own force to the hostile town of Hybla in the territory of Gela, but did not succeed in taking it.

Summer was now over. The winter following, the Athenians at once began to prepare for moving on Syracuse, and the Syracusans on their side for marching against them. From the moment when the Athenians failed to attack them instantly as they at first feared and expected, every day that passed did something to revive their courage; and when they saw them sailing far away from them on the other side of Sicily, and going to Hybla only to fail in their attempts to storm it, they thought less of them than ever, and called upon their generals, as the multitude is apt to do in its moments of confidence, to lead them to Catana, since the enemy would not come to them. Parties also of the Syracusan horse employed in reconnoitring constantly rode up to the Athenian armament, and among other insults asked them whether they had not really come to settle with the Syracusans in a foreign country rather than to resettle the Leontines in their own.

Aware of this, the Athenian generals determined to draw them out in mass as far as possible from the city, and themselves in the meantime to sail by night along shore, and take

up at their leisure a convenient position. This they knew they
could not so well do, if they had to disembark from their ships
in front of a force prepared for them, or to go by land openly.
The numerous cavalry of the Syracusans (a force which they
were themselves without), would then be able to do the
greatest mischief to their light troops and the crowd that followed them; but this plan would enable them to take up a
position in which the horse could do them no hurt worth speaking of, some Syracusan exiles with the army having told them
of the spot near the Olympieum, which they afterwards occupied. In pursuance of their idea, the generals imagined the
following stratagem. They sent to Syracuse a man devoted to
them, and by the Syracusan generals thought to be no less in
their interest; he was a native of Catana, and said he came
from persons in that place, whose names the Syracusan generals were acquainted with, and whom they knew to be among
the members of their party still left in the city. He told them
that the Athenians passed the night in the town, at some distance from their arms, and that if the Syracusans would name
a day and come with all their people at daybreak to attack the
armament, they, their friends, would close the gates upon the
troops in the city, and set fire to the vessels, while the Syracusans would easily take the camp by an attack upon the
stockade. In this they would be aided by many of the
Catanians, who were already prepared to act, and from whom
he himself came.

The generals of the Syracusans, who did not want confidence, and who had intended even without this to march on
Catana, believed the man without any sufficient inquiry, fixed
at once a day upon which they would be there, and dismissed
him, and the Selinuntines and others of their allies having
now arrived, gave orders for all the Syracusans to march out
in mass. Their preparations completed, and the time fixed
for their arrival being at hand, they set out for Catana, and
passed the night upon the river Symæthus, in the Leontine territory. Meanwhile the Athenians no sooner knew of their
approach than they took all their forces and such of the Sicels
or others as had joined them, put them on board their ships
and boats, and sailed by night to Syracuse. Thus, when morning broke the Athenians were landing opposite the Olympieum

ready to seize their camping ground, and the Syracusan horse
having ridden up first to Catana and found that all the armament had put to sea, turned back and told the infantry, and
then all turned back together, and went to the relief of the
city.

In the meantime, as the march before the Syracusans was
a long one, the Athenians quietly sate down their army in a
convenient position, where they could begin an engagement
when they pleased, and where the Syracusan cavalry would
have least opportunity of annoying them, either before or
during the action, being fenced off on one side by walls,
houses, trees, and by a marsh, and on the other by cliffs. They
also felled the neighbouring trees and carried them down to
the sea, and formed a palisade alongside of their ships, and
with stones which they picked up and wood hastily raised a
fort at Daskon, the most vulnerable point of their position,
and broke down the bridge over the Anapus. These preparations were allowed to go on without any interruption from the
city, the first hostile force to appear being the Syracusan cavalry, followed afterwards by all the foot together. At first they
came close up to the Athenian army, and then, finding that
they did not offer to engage, crossed the Helorine road and
encamped for the night.

The next day the Athenians and their allies prepared for
battle, their dispositions being as follows:—Their right wing
was occupied by the Argives and Mantineans, the centre by
the Athenians, and the rest of the field by the other allies.
Half their army was drawn up eight deep in advance, half close
to their tents in a hollow square, formed also eight deep, which
had orders to look out and be ready to go to the support of the
troops hardest pressed. The camp followers were placed inside
this reserve. The Syracusans, meanwhile, formed their heavy
infantry sixteen deep, consisting of the mass-levy of their own
people, and such allies as had joined them, the strongest contingent being that of the Selinuntines; next to them the cavalry of the Geloans, numbering two hundred in all, with about
twenty horse and fifty archers from Camarina. The cavalry
was posted on their right, full twelve hundred strong, and
next to it the darters. As the Athenians were about to begin
the attack, Nicias went along the lines, and addressed these

words of encouragement to the army and the nations composing it:——

'Soldiers, a long exhortation is little needed by men like ourselves, who are here to fight in the same battle, the force itself being, to my thinking, more fit to inspire confidence than a fine speech with a weak army. Where we have Argives, Mantineans, Athenians, and the first of the islanders in the ranks together, it were strange indeed, with so many and so brave companions in arms, if we did not feel confident of victory; especially when we have mass-levies opposed to our picked troops, and what is more, Siceliots, who may disdain us but will not stand against us, their skill not being at all commensurate to their rashness. You may also remember that we are far from home and have no friendly land near, except what your own swords shall win you; and here I put before you a motive just the reverse of that which the enemy are appealing to; their cry being that they shall fight for their country, mine that we shall fight for a country that is not ours, where we must conquer or hardly get away, as we shall have their horse upon us in great numbers. Remember, therefore, your renown, and go boldly against the enemy, thinking the present strait and necessity more terrible than they.'

After this address Nicias at once led on the army. The Syracusans were not at that moment expecting an immediate engagement, and some had even gone away to the town, which was close by; these now ran up as hard as they could, and though behind time, took their places here or there in the main body as fast as they joined it. Want of zeal or daring was certainly not the fault of the Syracusans, either in this or the other battles, but although not inferior in courage, so far as their military science might carry them, when this failed them they were compelled to give up their resolution also. On the present occasion, although they had not supposed that the Athenians would begin the attack, and although constrained to stand upon their defence at short notice, they at once took up their arms and advanced to meet them. First, the stone-throwers, slingers, and archers of either army began skirmishing, and routed or were routed by one another, as might be expected between light troops; next, soothsayers brought forward the usual victims, and trumpeters urged on the heavy infantry to the charge; and thus they advanced, the Syracusans to fight for their country, and each individual for his safety that day and liberty hereafter; in the enemy's army, the Athenians to make another's country theirs and to save their own from suffering by their defeat; the Argives and independent allies to help them in getting what they came for, and to earn by victory another sight of the country they had left behind; while the subject allies owed most of their ardour to the desire of self-preservation, which they could only hope for if victorious; next to which, as a secondary motive, came the chance of serving on easier terms, after helping the Athenians to a fresh conquest.

The armies now came to close quarters, and for a long while fought without either giving ground. Meanwhile there occurred some claps of thunder with lightning and heavy rain, which did not fail to add to the fears of the party fighting for the first time, and very little acquainted with war; while to their more experienced adversaries these phenomena appeared to be produced by the time of year, and much more alarm was felt at the continued resistance of the enemy. At last the Argives drove in the Syracusan left, and after them the Athenians routed the troops opposed to them, and the Syracusan army was thus cut in two and betook itself to flight. The Athenians did not pursue far, being held in check by the numerous and undefeated Syracusan horse, who attacked and drove back any of their heavy infantry whom they saw pursuing in advance of the rest; in spite of which the victors followed so far as was safe in a body, and then went back and set up a trophy. Meanwhile the Syracusans rallied at the Helorine road, where they reformed as well as they could under the circumstances, and even sent a garrison of their own citizens to the Olympieum, fearing that the Athenians might lay hands on some of the treasures there. The rest returned to the town.

The Athenians, however did not go to the temple, but collected their dead and laid them upon a pyre, and passed the night upon the field. The next day they gave the enemy back their dead under truce, to the number of about two hundred and sixty, Syracusans and allies, and gathered together the bones of their own, some fifty, Athenians and allies, and taking the spoils of the enemy, sailed back to Catana. It was now winter; and it did not seem possible for the moment to carry on the war before Syracuse, until horse should have been sent for from Athens and levied among the allies in Sicily—to do away with their utter inferiority in cavalry—and money should have been collected in the country and received from Athens, and until some of the cities, which they hoped would be now more disposed to listen to them after the battle, should have been brought over, and corn and all other necessaries provided, for a campaign in the spring against Syracuse.

With this intention they sailed off to Naxos and Catana for the winter. Meanwhile the Syracusans burned their dead, and then held an assembly, in which Hermocrates, son of Hermon, a man who with a general ability of the first order had given proofs of military capacity and brilliant courage in the war, came forward and encouraged them, and told them not to let what had occurred make them give way, since their spirit had not been conquered, but their want of discipline had done the mischief. Still they had not been beaten by so much as might have been expected, especially as they were, one might say, novices in the art of war, an army of artisans opposed to the most practised soldiers in Hellas. What had also done great mischief was the number of the generals (there were fifteen of them) and the quantity of orders given, combined with the disorder and insubordination of the troops. But if they were to have a few skilful generals, and used this winter in preparing their heavy infantry, finding arms for such as had not got any, so as to make them as numerous as possible, and forcing them to attend to their training generally, they would have every chance of beating their adversaries, courage being already theirs and discipline in the field having thus been added to it. Indeed, both these qualities would improve, since danger would exercise them in discipline, while their courage would be led to surpass itself by the confidence which skill inspires. The generals should be few and elected with full powers, and an oath should be taken to leave them entire discretion in their command: if they adopted this plan, their secrets would be better kept, all preparations would be properly made, and there would be no room for excuses.

The Syracusans heard him, and voted everything as he advised, and elected three generals, Hermocrates himself,

Heraclides, son of Lysimachus, and Sicanus, son of Execestes. They also sent envoys to Corinth and Lacedæmon to procure a force of allies to join them, and to induce the Lacedæmonians for their sakes openly to address themselves in real earnest to the war against the Athenians, that they might either have to leave Sicily or be less able to send reinforcements to their army there.

The Athenian forces at Catana now at once sailed against Messina, in the expectation of its being betrayed to them. The intrigue, however, after all came to nothing: Alcibiades, who was in the secret, when he left his command upon the summons from home, foreseeing that he would be outlawed, gave information of the plot to the friends of the Syracusans in Messina, who had at once put to death its authors, and now rose in arms against the opposite faction with those of their way of thinking, and succeeded in preventing the admission of the Athenians. The latter waited for thirteen days, and then, as they were exposed to the weather and without provisions, and met with no success, went back to Naxos, where they made places for their ships to lie in, erected a palisade round their camp, and retired into winter quarters; meanwhile they sent a galley to Athens for money and cavalry to join them in the spring. During the winter the Syracusans built a wall on to the city, so as to take in the statue of Apollo Temenites, all along the side looking towards Epipolæ, to make the task of circumvallation longer and more difficult, in case of their being defeated, and also erected a fort at Megara and another in the Olympieum, and stuck palisades along the sea wherever there was a landing place. Meanwhile, as they knew that the Athenians were wintering at Naxos, they marched with all their people to Catana, and ravaged the land and set fire to the tents and encampment of the Athenians, and so returned home. Learning also that the Athenians were sending an embassy to Camarina, on the strength of the alliance concluded in the time of Laches, to gain, if possible, that city, they sent another from Syracuse to oppose them. They had a shrewd suspicion that the Camarinæans had not sent what they did send for the first battle very willingly; and they now feared that they would refuse to assist them at all in future, after seeing the success of the

Athenians in the action, and would join the latter on the
strength of their old friendship. Hermocrates, with some
others, accordingly arrived at Camarina from Syracuse, and
Euphemus and others from the Athenians; and an assembly
of the Camarinæans having been convened, Hermocrates
spoke as follows, in the hope of prejudicing them against the
Athenians:—

'Camarinæans, we did not come on this embassy because
we were afraid of your being frightened by the actual forces
of the Athenians, but rather of your being gained by what
they would say to you before you heard anything from us.
They are come to Sicily with the pretext that you know, and
the intention which we all suspect, in my opinion less to
restore the Leontines to their homes than to oust us from
ours; as it is out of all reason that they should restore in
Sicily the cities that they lay waste in Hellas, or should cherish
the Leontine Chalcidians because of their Ionian blood, and
keep in servitude the Eubœan Chalcidians, of whom the
Leontines are a colony. No; but the same policy which has
proved so successful in Hellas is now being tried in Sicily.
After being chosen as the leaders of the Ionians and of the
other allies of Athenian origin, to punish the Mede, the
Athenians accused some of failure in military service, some
of fighting against each other, and others, as the case might
be, upon any colourable pretext that could be found, until
they thus subdued them all. In fine, in the struggle against
the Medes, the Athenians did not fight for the liberty of the
Hellenes, or the Hellenes for their own liberty, but the former
to make their countrymen serve them instead of him, the latter to change one master for another, wiser indeed than the
first, but wiser for evil.

'But we are not now come to declare to an audience familiar
with them the misdeeds of a state so open to accusation as
is the Athenian, but much rather to blame ourselves, who,
with the warnings we possess in the Hellenes in those parts
that have been enslaved through not supporting each other,
and seeing the same sophisms being now tried upon ourselves
—such as restorations of Leontine kinsfolk and support of
Egestæan allies—do not stand together and resolutely show
them that here are no Ionians, or Hellespontines, or islanders,

who change continually, but always serve a master, sometimes the Mede and sometimes some other, but free Dorians from independent Peloponnese, dwelling in Sicily. Or, are we waiting until we be taken in detail, one city after another; knowing as we do that in no other way can we be conquered, and seeing that they turn to this plan, so as to divide some of us by words, to draw some by the bait of an alliance into open war with each other, and to ruin others by such flattery as different circumstances may render acceptable? And do we fancy when destruction first overtakes a distant fellow-countryman that the danger will not come to each of us also, or that he who suffers before us will suffer in himself alone?

'As for the Camarinæan, who says that it is the Syracusan, not he, that is the enemy of the Athenian, and who thinks it hard to have to encounter risk in behalf of my country, I would have him bear in mind that he will fight in my country, not more for mine than for his own, and by so much the more safely in that he will enter on the struggle not alone, after the way has been cleared by my ruin, but with me as his ally; and that the object of the Athenian is not so much to punish the enmity of the Syracusan as to use me as a blind to secure the friendship of the Camarinæan. As for him who envies or even fears us (and envied and feared great powers must always be), and who on this account wishes Syracuse to be humbled to teach us a lesson, but would still have her survive in the interest of his own security, the wish that he indulges is not humanly possible. A man can control his own desires, but he cannot likewise control circumstances; and in the event of his calculations proving mistaken, he may live to bewail his own misfortune, and wish to be again envying my prosperity. An idle wish, if he now sacrifice us and refuse to take his share of perils which are the same, in reality though not in name, for him as for us; what is nominally the preservation of our power being really his own salvation. It was to be expected that you, of all people in the world, Camarinæans, being our immediate neighbours and the next in danger, would have foreseen this, and instead of supporting us in the lukewarm way that you are now doing, would rather come to us of your own accord, and be now offering at Syracuse the aid which you would have asked for at Camarina, if to Camarina

the Athenians had first come, to encourage us to resist the
invader. Neither you, however, nor the rest have as yet be-
stirred yourselves in this direction.

'Fear perhaps will make you study to do right both by
us and by the invaders, and plead that you have an alliance
with the Athenians. But you made that alliance, not against
your friends, but against the enemies that might attack you,
and to help the Athenians when they were wronged by others,
not when as now they are wronging their neighbours. Even
the Rhegians, Chalcidians though they be, refuse to help to
restore the Chalcidian Leontines; and it would be strange if,
while they suspect the gist of this fine pretence and are wise
without reason, you, with every reason on your side, should
yet choose to assist your natural enemies, and should join
with their direst foes in undoing those whom nature has made
your own kinsfolk. This is not to do right; but you should
help us without fear of their armament, which has no terrors
if we hold together, but only if we let them succeed in their
endeavours to separate us; since even after attacking us by
ourselves and being victorious in battle, they had to go off
without effecting their purpose.

'United, therefore, we have no cause to despair, but rather
new encouragement to league together; especially as succours
will come to us from the Peloponnesians, in military matters
the undoubted superiors of the Athenians. And you need not
think that your prudent policy of taking sides with neither,
because allies of both, is either safe for you or fair to us.
Practically it is not as fair as it pretends to be. If the vanquished be defeated, and the victor conquer, through your
refusing to join, what is the effect of your abstention but to
leave the former to perish unaided, and to allow the latter to
offend unhindered? And yet it were more honourable to join
those who are not only the injured party, but your own kindred, and by so doing to defend the common interests of
Sicily and save your friends the Athenians from doing wrong.

'In conclusion, we Syracusans say that it is useless for us to
demonstrate either to you or to the rest what you know already as well as we do; but we entreat, and if our entreaty
fail, we protest that we are menaced by our eternal enemies
the Ionians, and are betrayed by you our fellow Dorians.

If the Athenians reduce us, they will owe their victory to your decision, but in their own name will reap the honour, and will receive as the prize of their triumph the very men who enabled them to gain it. On the other hand, if we are the conquerors, you will have to pay for having been the cause of our danger. Consider, therefore; and now make your choice between the security which present servitude offers and the prospect of conquering with us and so escaping disgraceful submission to an Athenian master and avoiding the lasting enmity of Syracuse.'

Such were the words of Hermocrates; after whom Euphemus, the Athenian ambassador, spoke as follows:—

'Although we came here only to renew the former alliance, the attack of the Syracusans compels us to speak of our empire and of the good right we have to it. The best proof of this the speaker himself furnished, when he called the Ionians eternal enemies of the Dorians. It is the fact; and the Peloponnesian Dorians being our superiors in numbers and next neighbours, we Ionians looked out for the best means of escaping their domination. After the Median war we had a fleet, and so got rid of the empire and supremacy of the Lacedæmonians, who had no right to give orders to us more than we to them, except that of being the strongest at that moment; and being appointed leaders of the king's former subjects, we continue to be so, thinking that we are least likely to fall under the dominion of the Peloponnesians, if we have a force to defend ourselves with, and in strict truth having done nothing unfair in reducing to subjection the Ionians and islanders, the kinsfolk whom the Syracusans say we have enslaved. They, our kinsfolk, came against their mother country, that is to say against us, together with the Mede, and instead of having the courage to revolt and sacrifice their property as we did when we abandoned our city, chose to be slaves themselves, and to try to make us so.

'We, therefore, deserve to rule because we placed the largest fleet and an unflinching patriotism at the service of the Hellenes, and because these, our subjects, did us mischief by their ready subservience to the Medes; and, desert apart, we seek to strengthen ourselves against the Peloponnesians. We make no fine professions of having a right to rule because we over-

threw the barbarian single-handed, or because we risked what
we did risk for the freedom of the subjects in question any
more than for that of all, and for our own: no one can be
quarrelled with for providing for his proper safety. If we are
now here in Sicily, it is equally in the interest of our security,
with which we perceive that your interest also coincides. We
prove this from the conduct which the Syracusans cast against
us and which you somewhat too timorously suspect; knowing
that those whom fear has made suspicious, may be carried
away by the charm of eloquence for the moment, but when
they come to act follow their interests.

'Now, as we have said, fear makes us hold our empire in
Hellas, and fear makes us now come, with the help of our
friends, to order safely matters in Sicily, and not to enslave
any but rather to prevent any from being enslaved. Meanwhile, let no one imagine that we are interesting ourselves
in you without your having anything to do with us, seeing
that if you are preserved and able to make head against the
Syracusans, they will be less likely to harm us by sending
troops to the Peloponnesians. In this way you have everything
to do with us, and on this account it is perfectly reasonable
for us to restore the Leontines, and to make them, not subjects like their kinsmen in Eubœa, but as powerful as possible,
to help us by annoying the Syracusans from their frontier.
In Hellas we are alone a match for our enemies; and as for
the assertion that it is out of all reason that we should free
the Sicilian, while we enslave the Chalcidian, the fact is that
the latter is useful to us by being without arms and contributing money only; while the former, the Leontines and
our other friends, cannot be too independent.

'Besides, for tyrants and imperial cities nothing is unreasonable if expedient, no one a kinsman unless sure; but
friendship or enmity is everywhere an affair of time and circumstance. Here, in Sicily, our interest is not to weaken our
friends, but by means of their strength to cripple our enemies.
Why doubt this? In Hellas we treat our allies as we find them
useful. The Chians and Methymnians govern themselves and
furnish ships; most of the rest have harder terms and pay
tribute in money; while others, although islanders and easy
for us to take, are free altogether, because they occupy con-

venient positions round Peloponnese. In our settlement of the states here in Sicily, we should, therefore, naturally be guided by our interest, and by fear, as we say, of the Syracusans. Their ambition is to rule you, their object to use the suspicions that we excite to unite you, and then, when we have gone away without effecting anything, by force or through your isolation, to become the masters of Sicily. And masters they must become, if you unite with them; as a force of that magnitude would be no longer easy for us to deal with united, and they would be more than a match for you as soon as we were away.

'Any other view of the case is condemned by the facts. When you first asked us over, the fear which you held out was that of danger to Athens if we let you come under the dominion of Syracuse; and it is not right now to mistrust the very same argument by which you claimed to convince us, or to give way to suspicion because we are come with a larger force against the power of that city. Those whom you should really distrust are the Syracusans. We are not able to stay here without you, and if we proved perfidious enough to bring you into subjection, we should be unable to keep you in bondage, owing to the length of the voyage and the difficulty of guarding large, and in a military sense continental, towns: they, the Syracusans, live close to you, not in a camp, but in a city greater than the force we have with us, plot always against you, never let slip an opportunity once offered, as they have shown in the case of the Leontines and others, and now have the face, just as if you were fools, to invite you to aid them against the power that hinders this, and that has thus far maintained Sicily independent. We, as against them, invite you to a much more real safety, when we beg you not to betray that common safety which we each have in the other, and to reflect that they, even without allies, will, by their numbers, have always the way open to you, while you will not often have the opportunity of defending yourselves with such numerous auxiliaries; if, through your suspicions, you once let these go away unsuccessful or defeated, you will wish to see if only a handful of them back again, when the day is past in which their presence could do anything for you.

'But we hope, Camarinæans, that the calumnies of the Syracusans will not be allowed to succeed either with you or with the rest: we have told you the whole truth upon the things we are suspected of, and will now briefly recapitulate, in the hope of convincing you. We assert that we are rulers in Hellas in order not to be subjects; liberators in Sicily that we may not be harmed by the Sicilians; that we are compelled to interfere in many things, because we have many things to guard against; and that now, as before, we are come as allies to those of you who suffer wrong in this island, not without invitation but upon invitation. Accordingly, instead of making yourselves judges or censors of our conduct, and trying to turn us, which it were now difficult to do, so far as there is anything in our interfering policy or in our character, that chimes in with your interest, this take and make use of; and be sure that far from being injurious to all alike, to most of the Hellenes that policy is even beneficial. Thanks to it, all men in all places, even where we are not, who either apprehend or meditate aggression, from the near prospect before them, in the one case, of obtaining our intervention in their favour, in the other, of our arrival making the venture dangerous, find themselves constrained, respectively, to be moderate against their will, and to be preserved without trouble of their own. Do not you reject this security that is open to all who desire it, and is now offered to you; but do like others, and instead of being always on the defensive against the Syracusans, unite with us, and in your turn at last threaten them.'

Such were the words of Euphemus. What the Camarinæans felt was this. Sympathising with the Athenians, except in so far as they might be afraid of their subjugating Sicily, they had always been at enmity with their neighbour Syracuse. From the very fact, however, that they were their neighbours, they feared the Syracusans most of the two, and being apprehensive of their conquering even without them, both sent them in the first instance the few horsemen mentioned, and for the future determined to support them most in fact, although as sparingly as possible; but for the moment in order not to seem to slight the Athenians, especially as they had been successful in the engagement, to answer both alike

Agreeably to this resolution they answered that as both the contending parties happened to be allies of theirs, they thought it most consistent with their oaths, at present, to side with neither; with which answer the ambassadors of either party departed.

In the meantime, while Syracuse pursued her preparations for war, the Athenians were encamped at Naxos, and tried by negotiation to gain as many of the Sicels as possible. Those more in the low lands, and subjects of Syracuse, mostly held aloof; but the peoples of the interior who had never been otherwise than independent, with few exceptions, at once joined the Athenians, and brought down corn to the army, and in some cases even money. The Athenians marched against those who refused to join, and forced some of them to do so; in the case of others they were stopped by the Syracusans sending garrisons and reinforcements. Meanwhile the Athenians moved their winter quarters from Naxos to Catana, and reconstructed the camp burnt by the Syracusans, and stayed there the rest of the winter. They also sent a galley to Carthage, with proffers of friendship, on the chance of obtaining assistance, and another to Tyrrhenia; some of the cities there having spontaneously offered to join them in the war. They also sent round to the Sicels and to Egesta, desiring them to send them as many horses as possible, and meanwhile prepared bricks, iron, and all other things necessary for the work of circumvallation, intending by the spring to begin hostilities.

In the meantime the Syracusan envoys despatched to Corinth and Lacedæmon tried as they passed along the coast to persuade the Italiots to interfere with the proceedings of the Athenians, which threatened Italy quite as much as Syracuse, and having arrived at Corinth made a speech calling on the Corinthians to assist them on the ground of their common origin. The Corinthians voted at once to aid them heart and soul themselves, and then sent on envoys with them to Lacedæmon, to help them to persuade her also to prosecute the war with the Athenians more openly at home and to send succours to Sicily. The envoys from Corinth having reached Lacedæmon found there Alcibiades with his fellow-refugees, who had at once crossed over in a trading vessel from Thurii, first to Cyllene in Elis, and afterwards from thence to Lacedæmon; upon the Lacedæmonians' own invitation, after first obtaining a safe conduct, as he feared them for the part he had taken in the affair of Mantinea. The result was that the Corinthians, Syracusans, and Alcibiades, pressing all the same request in the assembly of the Lacedæmonians, succeeded in persuading them; but as the Ephors and the authorities, although resolved to send envoys to Syracuse to prevent their surrendering to the Athenians, showed no disposition to send them any assistance, Alcibiades now came forward and inflamed and stirred the Lacedæmonians by speaking as follows:—

'I am forced first to speak to you of the prejudice with which I am regarded, in order that suspicion may not make you disinclined to listen to me upon public matters. The connexion with you as your *Proxeni,* which the ancestors of our family by reason of some discontent renounced, I personally tried to renew by my good offices towards you, in particular upon the occasion of the disaster at Pylos. But although I maintained this friendly attitude, you yet chose to negotiate the peace with the Athenians through my enemies, and thus to strengthen them and to discredit me. You had therefore no right to complain if I turned to the Mantineans and Argives, and seized other occasions of thwarting and injuring you; and the time has now come when those among you, who in the bitterness of the moment may have been then unfairly angry with me, should look at the matter in its true light, and take a different view. Those again who judged me unfavourably, because I leaned rather to the side of the commons, must not think that their dislike is any better founded. We have always been hostile to tyrants, and all who oppose arbitrary power are called commons; hence we continued to act as leaders of the multitude; besides which, as democracy was the government of the city, it was necessary in most things to conform to established conditions. However, we endeavoured to be more moderate than the licentious temper of the times; and while there were others, formerly as now, who tried to lead the multitude astray, the same who banished me, our party was that of the whole people, our creed being to do our part in preserving the form of government under which the city enjoyed the utmost greatness and freedom, and which we had found existing. As for democracy, the men of sense among us knew what it was, and I perhaps as well as any, as I have the more cause to complain of it; but there is nothing new to be said of a patent absurdity—meanwhile we did not think it safe to alter it under the pressure of your hostility.

'So much then for the prejudices with which I am regarded: I now can call your attention to the questions you must consider, and upon which superior knowledge perhaps permits me to speak. We sailed to Sicily first to conquer, if possible, the Siceliots, and after them the Italiots also, and finally to assail the empire and city of Carthage. In the event of all or most of these schemes succeeding, we were then to attack Peloponnese, bringing with us the entire force of the Hellenes lately acquired in those parts, and taking a number of barbarians into our pay, such as the Iberians and others in those countries, confessedly the most warlike known, and building numerous galleys in addition to those which we had already, timber being plentiful in Italy; and with this fleet blockading Peloponnese from the sea and assailing it with our armies by land, taking some of the cities by storm, drawing works of circumvallation round others, we hoped without difficulty to effect its reduction, and after this to rule the whole of the Hellenic name. Money and corn meanwhile for the better execution of these plans were to be supplied in sufficient quantities by the newly acquired places in those countries, independently of our revenues here at home.

'You have thus heard the history of the present expedition from the man who most exactly knows what our objects were; and the remaining generals will, if they can, carry these out just the same. But that the states in Sicily must succumb if you do not help them, I will now show. Although the Siceliots, with all their inexperience, might even now be saved if their forces were united, the Syracusans alone, beaten already in one battle with all their people and blockaded from the sea, will be unable to withstand the Athenian armament that is now there. But if Syracuse falls, all Sicily falls also, and Italy immediately afterwards; and the danger which I just now spoke of from that quarter will before long be upon you.

None need therefore fancy that Sicily only is in question; Peloponnese will be so also, unless you speedily do as I tell you, and send on board ship to Syracuse troops that shall be able to row their ships themselves, and serve as heavy infantry the moment that they land; and what I consider even more important than the troops, a Spartan as commanding officer to discipline the forces already on foot and to compel recusants to serve. The friends that you have already will thus become more confident, and the waverers will be encouraged to join you. Meanwhile you must carry on the war here more openly, that the Syracusans seeing that you do not forget them, may put heart into their resistance, and that the Athenians may be less able to reinforce their armament. You must fortify Decelea in Attica, the blow of which the Athenians are always most afraid and the only one that they think they have not experienced in the present war; the surest method of harming an enemy being to find out what he most fears, and to choose this means of attacking him, since every one naturally knows best his own weak points and fears accordingly. The fortification in question, while it benefits you, will create difficulties for your adversaries, of which I shall pass over many, and shall only mention the chief. Whatever property there is in the country will most of it become yours, either by capture or surrender; and the Athenians will at once be deprived of their revenues from the silver mines at Laurium, of their present gains from their land and from the law courts, and above all of the revenue from their allies, which will be paid less regularly, as they lose their awe of Athens, and see you addressing yourselves with vigour to the war. The zeal and speed with which all this shall be done depends, Lacedæmonians, upon yourselves; as to its possibility, I am quite confident, and I have little fear of being mistaken.

'Meanwhile I hope that none of you will think any the worse of me if after having hitherto passed as a lover of my country, I now actively join its worst enemies in attacking it, or will suspect what I say as the fruit of an outlaw's enthusiasm. I am an outlaw from the iniquity of those who drove me forth, not, if you will be guided by me, from your service: my worst enemies are not you who only harmed your foes, but they who forced their friends to become enemies; and love of country is what I do not feel when I am wronged, but what I felt when secure in my rights as a citizen. Indeed I do not consider that I am now attacking a country that is still mine; I am rather trying to recover one that is mine no longer; and the true lover of his country is not he who consents to lose it unjustly rather than attack it, but he who longs for it so much that he will go all lengths to recover it. For myself, therefore, Lacedæmonians, I beg you to use me without scruple for danger and trouble of every kind, and to remember the argument in every one's mouth, that if I did you great harm as an enemy, I could likewise do you good service as a friend, inasmuch as I know the plans of the Athenians, while I only guessed yours. For yourselves I entreat you to believe that your most capital interests are now under deliberation; and I urge you to send without hesitation the expeditions to Sicily and Attica; by the presence of a small part of your forces you will save important cities in that island, and you will destroy the power of Athens both present and prospective; after this you will dwell in security and enjoy the supremacy over all Hellas, resting not on force but upon consent and affection.'

Such were the words of Alcibiades. The Lacedæmonians, who had themselves before intended to march against Athens, but were still waiting and looking about them, at once became much more in earnest when they received this particular information from Alcibiades, and considered that they had heard it from the man who best knew the truth of the matter. Accordingly they now turned their attention to the fortifying of Decelea and sending immediate aid to the Sicilians; and naming Gylippus, son of Cleandridas, to the command of the Syracusans, bade him consult with that people and with the Corinthians and arrange for succours reaching the island, in the best and speediest way possible under the circumstances. Gylippus desired the Corinthians to send him at once two ships to Asine, and to prepare the rest that they intended to send, and to have them ready to sail at the proper time. Having settled this, the envoys departed from Lacedæmon.

In the meantime arrived the Athenian galley from Sicily sent by the generals for money and cavalry; and the Athenians, after hearing what they wanted, voted to send the supplies for the armament and the cavalry. And the winter ended, and with it ended the seventeenth year of the present war of which Thucydides is the historian.

The next summer, at the very beginning of the season, the Athenians in Sicily put out from Catana, and sailed along shore to Megara in Sicily, from which, as I have mentioned above, the Syracusans expelled the inhabitants in the time of their tyrant Gelo, themselves occupying the territory. Here the Athenians landed and laid waste the country, and after an unsuccessful attack upon a fort of the Syracusans, went on with the fleet and army to the river Terias, and advancing inland laid waste the plain and set fire to the corn; and after killing some of a small Syracusan party which they encountered, and setting up a trophy, went back again to their ships. They now sailed to Catana and took in provisions there, and going with their whole force against Centoripa, a town of the Sicels, acquired it by capitulation, and departed, after also burning the corn of the Inessæans and Hybleans. Upon their return to Catana they found the horsemen arrived from Athens, to the number of two hundred and fifty (with their equipments, but without their horses which were to be procured upon the spot), and thirty mounted archers and three hundred talents of silver.

The same spring the Lacedæmonians marched against Argos, and went as far as Cleonæ, when an earthquake occurred and caused them to return. After this the Argives invaded the Thyreatid, which is on their border, and took much booty from the Lacedæmonians, which was sold for no less than twenty-five talents. The same summer, not long after, the Thespian commons made an attack upon the party in office, which was not successful, but succours arrived from Thebes, and some were caught, while others took refuge at Athens.

The same summer the Syracusans learned that the Athenians had been joined by their cavalry, and were on the point of marching against them; and seeing that without becoming masters of Epipolæ, a precipitous spot situated exactly over the town, the Athenians could not, even if victorious in battle, easily invest them, they determined to guard its approaches, in order that the enemy might not ascend unobserved by this,

the sole way by which ascent was possible, as the remainder
is lofty ground, and falls right down to the city, and can all
be seen from inside; and as it lies above the rest the place is
called by the Syracusans Epipolæ or Overtown. They accordingly went out in mass at daybreak into the meadow along
the river Anapus, their new generals, Hermocrates and his
colleagues, having just come into office, and held a review
of their heavy infantry, from whom they first selected a
picked body of six hundred, under the command of Diomilus,
an exile from Andros, to guard Epipolæ, and to be ready to
muster at a moment's notice to help wherever help should be
required.

Meanwhile the Athenians, the very same morning, were
holding a review, having already made land unobserved with
all the armament from Catana, opposite a place called Leon,
not much more than half a mile from Epipolæ, where they
disembarked their army, bringing the fleet to anchor at
Thapsus, a peninsula running out into the sea, with a narrow
isthmus, and not far from the city of Syracuse either by land
or water. While the naval force of the Athenians threw a
stockade across the isthmus and remained quiet at Thapsus,
the land army immediately went on at a run to Epipolæ, and
succeeded in getting up by Euryelus before the Syracusans
perceived them, or could come up from the meadow and the
review. Diomilus with his six hundred and the rest advanced
as quickly as they could, but they had nearly three miles to
go from the meadow before reaching them. Attacking in this
way in considerable disorder, the Syracusans were defeated
in battle at Epipolæ and retired to the town, with a loss of
about three hundred killed, and Diomilus among the number.
After this the Athenians set up a trophy and restored to the
Syracusans their dead under truce, and next day descended to
Syracuse itself; and no one coming out to meet them, re-
ascended and built a fort at Labdalum, upon the edge of the
cliffs of Epipolæ, looking towards Megara, to serve as a magazine for their baggage and money, whenever they advanced
to give battle or to work at the lines.

Not long afterwards three hundred cavalry came to them
from Egesta, and about a hundred from the Sicels, Naxians,
and others; and thus, with the two hundred and fifty from

Athens, for whom they had got horses from the Egestæans and Catanians, besides others that they bought, they now mustered six hundred and fifty cavalry in all. After posting a garrison in Labdalum, they advanced to Syca, where they sate down and quickly built the Circle or centre of their wall of circumvallation. The Syracusans, appalled at the rapidity with which the work advanced, determined to go out against them and give battle and interrupt it; and the two armies were already in battle array, when the Syracusan generals observed that their troops found such difficulty in getting into line, and were in such disorder, that they led them back into the town, except part of the cavalry. These remained and hindered the Athenians from carrying stones or dispersing to any great distance, until a tribe of the Athenian heavy in-fantry, with all the cavalry, charged and routed the Syracusan horse with some loss; after which they set up a trophy for the cavalry action.

The next day the Athenians began building the wall to the north of the Circle, at the same time collecting stone and timber, which they kept laying down towards Trogilus along the shortest line for their works from the great harbour to the sea; while the Syracusans, guided by their generals, and above all by Hermocrates, instead of risking any more general engagements, determined to build a counterwork in the direc-tion in which the Athenians were going to carry their wall. If this could be completed in time the enemy's lines would be cut; and meanwhile, if he were to attempt to interrupt them by an attack, they would send a part of their forces against him, and would secure the approaches beforehand with their stockade, while the Athenians would have to leave off working with their whole force in order to attend to them. They accordingly sallied forth and began to build, starting from their city, running a cross wall below the Athenian Circle, cutting down the olives and erecting wooden towers. As the Athenian fleet had not yet sailed round into the great harbour, the Syracusans still commanded the sea-coast, and the Athenians brought their provisions by land from Thapsus.

The Syracusans now thought the stockades and stonework of their counter-wall sufficiently far advanced; and as the Athenians, afraid of being divided and so fighting at a dis-

advantage, and intent upon their own wall, did not come out
to interrupt them, they left one tribe to guard the new work
and went back into the city. Meanwhile the Athenians destroyed their pipes of drinking-water carried underground
into the city; and watching until the rest of the Syracusans
were in their tents at midday, and some even gone away into
the city, and those in the stockade keeping but indifferent
guard, appointed three hundred picked men of their own, and
some men picked from the light troops and armed for the
purpose, to run suddenly as fast as they could to the counter-
work, while the rest of the army advanced in two divisions,
the one with one of the generals to the city in case of a sortie,
the other with the other general to the stockade by the postern
gate. The three hundred attacked and took the stockade,
abandoned by its garrison, who took refuge in the outworks
round the statue of Apollo Temenites. Here the pursuers burst
in with them, and after getting in were beaten out by the
Syracusans, and some few of the Argives and Athenians slain;
after which the whole army retired, and having demolished
the counterwork and pulled up the stockade, carried away the
stakes to their own lines, and set up a trophy.

The next day the Athenians from the Circle proceeded to
fortify the cliff above the marsh which on this side of Epipolæ
looks towards the great harbour; this being also the shortest
line for their work to go down across the plain and the marsh
to the harbour. Meanwhile the Syracusans marched out and
began a second stockade, starting from the city, across the
middle of the marsh, digging a trench alongside to make it
impossible for the Athenians to carry their wall down to the
sea. As soon as the Athenians had finished their work at the
cliff they again attacked the stockade and ditch of the Syracusans. Ordering the fleet to sail round from Thapsus into
the great harbour of Syracuse, they descended at about dawn
from Epipolæ into the plain, and laying doors and planks
over the marsh where it was muddy and firmest, crossed over
on these, and by daybreak took the ditch and the stockade,
except a small portion which they captured afterwards. A
battle now ensued, in which the Athenians were victorious, the
right wing of the Syracusans flying to the town and the left to
the river. The three hundred picked Athenians, wishing to

cut off their passage, pressed on at a run to the bridge, when
the alarmed Syracusans, who had with them most of their
cavalry, closed and routed them, hurling them back upon the
Athenian right wing, the first tribe of which was thrown into
a panic by the shock. Seeing this, Lamachus came to their aid
from the Athenian left with a few archers and with the Argives, and crossing a ditch, was left alone with a few that had
crossed with him, and was killed with five or six of his men.
These the Syracusans managed immediately to snatch up in
haste and get across the river into a place of security, themselves retreating as the rest of the Athenian army now came
up.

Meanwhile those who had at first fled for refuge to the
city, seeing the turn affairs were taking, now rallied from the
town and formed against the Athenians in front of them,
sending also a part of their number to the Circle on Epipolæ,
which they hoped to take while denuded of its defenders.
These took and destroyed the Athenian outwork of a thousand
feet, the Circle itself being saved by Nicias, who happened
to have been left in it through illness, and who now ordered
the servants to set fire to the engines and timber thrown down
before the wall; want of men, as he was aware, rendering all
other means of escape impossible. This step was justified by
the result, the Syracusans not coming any further on account of the fire, but retreating. Meanwhile succours were
coming up from the Athenians below, who had put to flight
the troops opposed to them; and the fleet also, according to
orders, was sailing from Thapsus into the great harbour. Seeing this, the troops on the heights retired in haste, and the
whole army of the Syracusans re-entered the city, thinking
that with their present force they would no longer be able to
hinder the wall reaching the sea.

After this the Athenians set up a trophy and restored to
the Syracusans their dead under truce, receiving in return
Lamachus and those who had fallen with him. The whole of
their forces, naval and military, being now with them, they
began from Epipolæ and the cliffs and enclosed the Syracusans
with a double wall down to the sea. Provisions were now
brought in for the armament from all parts of Italy; and
many of the Sicels, who had hitherto been looking to see how

things went, came as allies to the Athenians: there also arrived three ships of fifty oars from Tyrrhenia. Meanwhile
everything else progressed favourably for their hopes. The
Syracusans began to despair of finding safety in arms, no relief having reached them from Peloponnese, and were now
proposing terms of capitulation among themselves and to
Nicias, who after the death of Lamachus was left sole commander. No decision was come to, but as was natural with
men in difficulties and besieged more straitly than before,
there was much discussion with Nicias and still more in the
town. Their present misfortunes had also made them suspicious of one another; and the blame of their disasters was
thrown upon the ill-fortune or treachery of the generals under
whose command they had happened; and these were deposed
and others, Heraclides, Eucles, and Tellias, elected in their
stead.

Meanwhile the Lacedæmonian, Gylippus, and the ships
from Corinth were now off Leucas, intent upon going with all
haste to the relief of Sicily. The reports that reached them
being of an alarming kind, and all agreeing in the falsehood
that Syracuse was already completely invested, Gylippus
abandoned all hope of Sicily, and wishing to save Italy,
rapidly crossed the Ionian Sea to Tarentum with the Corinthian, Pythen, two Laconian and two Corinthian vessels, leaving the Corinthians to follow him after manning, in addition
to their own ten, two Leucadian and two Ambraciot ships.
From Tarentum Gylippus first went on an embassy to Thurii,
and claimed anew the rights of citizenship which his father
had enjoyed; failing to bring over the townspeople, he weighed
anchor and coasted along Italy. Opposite the Terinæan gulf
he was caught by the wind which blows violently and steadily
from the north in that quarter, and was carried out to sea;
and after experiencing very rough weather, remade Tarentum,
where he hauled ashore and refitted such of his ships as had
suffered most from the tempest. Nicias heard of his approach,
but, like the Thurians, despised the scanty number of his
ships, and set down piracy as the only probable object of
the voyage, and so took no precautions for the present.

About the same time in this summer, the Lacedæmonians
invaded Argos with their allies, and laid waste most of the

country. The Athenians went with thirty ships to the relief of the Argives, thus breaking their treaty with the Lacedæmonians in the most overt manner. Up to this time incursions from Pylos, descents on the coasts of the rest of Peloponnese, instead of on the Laconian, had been the extent of their cooperation with the Argives and Mantineans; and although the Argives had often begged them to land, if only for a moment, with their heavy infantry in Laconia, lay waste ever so little of it with them, and depart, they had always refused to do so. Now, however, under the command of Pythodorus, Læspodius, and Demaratus, they landed at Epidaurus, Limera, Prasiæ, and other places, and plundered the country; and thus furnished the Lacedæmonians with a better pretext for hostilities against Athens. After the Athenians had retired from Argos with their fleet, and the Lacedæmonians also, the Argives made an incursion into the Phliasid, and returned home after ravaging their land and killing some of the inhabitants.

BOOK VII

CHAPTER XXI

EIGHTEENTH AND NINETEENTH YEARS OF THE WAR—ARRIVAL OF GYLIPPUS AT SYRACUSE—FORTIFICATION OF DECELEA —SUCCESSES OF THE SYRACUSANS

B.C. 414: *Gylippus at Himera; at Epipolæ—Capture of Labdalum— Defensive measures taken by Nicias—Athenian lines broken —Nicias' letter to the Athenians—Reinforcements sent—Lacedæ- monians hasten preparations—*B.C. 413: *Invasion of Attica— Syracusans plan naval attack—Capture of Plemmyrium—Demos- thenes sails for Sicily—Athenian difficulties—Massacre in Mycales- sus—Demosthenes and Eurymedon—New allies for Syracusans— Battle in Gulf of Corinth—New naval tactics—Athenians deceived and defeated.*

AFTER refitting their ships, Gylippus and Pythen coasted along from Tarentum to Epizephyrian Locris. They now re- ceived the more correct information that Syracuse was not yet completely invested, but that it was still possible for an army arriving by Epipolæ to effect an entrance; and they consulted, accordingly, whether they should keep Sicily on their right and risk sailing in by sea, or leaving it on their left, should first sail to Himera, and taking with them the Himeræans and any others that might agree to join them. go to Syracuse by land. Finally they determined to sail for Himera, especially as the four Athenian ships which Nicias had at length sent off, on hearing that they were at Locris, had not yet arrived at Rhegium. Accordingly, before these reached their post, the Peloponnesians crossed the strait, and after touching at Rhegium and Messina, came to Himera. Arrived there, they persuaded the Himeræans to join in the war, and not only to go with them themselves but to provide arms for the seamen from their vessels which they had drawn ashore at Himera; and they sent and appointed a place for the

Selinuntines to meet them with all their forces. A few troops
were also promised by the Geloans and some of the Sicels,
who were now ready to join them with much greater alacrity,
owing to the recent death of Archonidas, a powerful Sicel
king in that neighbourhood and friendly to Athens, and owing
also to the vigour shown by Gylippus in coming from Lacedæmon. Gylippus now took with him about seven hundred of
his sailors and marines, that number only having arms, a
thousand heavy infantry and light troops from Himera with
a body of a hundred horse, some light troops and cavalry
from Selinus, a few Geloans, and Sicels numbering a thousand
in all, and set out on his march for Syracuse.

Meanwhile the Corinthian fleet from Leucas made all haste
to arrive; and one of their commanders, Gongylus, starting
last with a single ship, was the first to reach Syracuse, a little
before Gylippus. Gongylus found the Syracusans on the point
of holding an assembly to consider whether they should not
put an end to the war. This he prevented, and reassured them
by telling them that more vessels were still to arrive, and that
Gylippus, son of Cleandridas, had been despatched by the
Lacedæmonians to take the command. Upon this the Syracusans took courage, and immediately marched out with all
their forces to meet Gylippus, who they found was now close
at hand. Meanwhile Gylippus, after taking Ietæ, a fort of
the Sicels, on his way, formed his army in order of battle,
and so arrived at Epipolæ, and ascending by Euryelus, as the
Athenians had done at first, now advanced with the Syracusans against the Athenian lines. His arrival chanced at a
critical moment. The Athenians had already finished a double
wall of six or seven furlongs to the great harbour, with the
exception of a small portion next to the sea, which they were
still engaged upon; and in the remainder of the circle towards
Trogilus on the other sea, stones had been laid ready for
building for the greater part of the distance, and some points
had been left half finished, while others were entirely completed. The danger of Syracuse had indeed been great.

Meanwhile the Athenians, recovering from the confusion
into which they had been at first thrown by the sudden approach of Gylippus and the Syracusans, formed in order of
battle. Gylippus halted at a short distance off and sent on a

herald to tell them that if they would evacuate Sicily with
bag and baggage within five days' time, he was willing to make
a truce accordingly. The Athenians treated this proposition
with contempt, and dismissed the herald without an answer. After this both sides began to prepare for action. Gylippus, observing that the Syracusans were in disorder and did
not easily fall into line, drew off his troops more into the open
ground, while Nicias did not lead on the Athenians but lay still
by his own wall. When Gylippus saw that they did not come
on, he led off his army to the citadel of the quarter of Apollo
Temenites, and passed the night there. On the following day
he led out the main body of his army, and drawing them up
in order of battle before the walls of the Athenians to prevent
their going to the relief of any other quarter, despatched a
strong force against Fort Labdalum and took it, and put all
whom he found in it to the sword, the place not being within
sight of the Athenians. On the same day an Athenian galley
that lay moored off the harbour was captured by the Syracusans.

After this the Syracusans and their allies began to carry a
single wall, starting from the city, in a slanting direction up
Epipolæ, in order that the Athenians, unless they could hinder
the work, might be no longer able to invest them. Meanwhile
the Athenians, having now finished their wall down to the sea,
had come up to the heights; and part of their wall being weak,
Gylippus drew out his army by night and attacked it. However, the Athenians who happened to be bivouacking outside
took the alarm and came out to meet him, upon seeing which he
quickly led his men back again. The Athenians now built their
wall higher, and in future kept guard at this point themselves,
disposing their confederates along the remainder of the works,
at the stations assigned to them. Nicias also determined to
fortify Plemmyrium, a promontory over against the city,
which juts out and narrows the mouth of the great harbour.
He thought that the fortification of this place would make it
easier to bring in supplies, as they would be able to carry on
their blockade from a less distance, near to the port occupied
by the Syracusans; instead of being obliged, upon every
movement of the enemy's navy, to put out against them from
the bottom of the great harbour. Besides this, he now began

to pay more attention to the war by sea, seeing that the coming of Gylippus had diminished their hopes by land. Accordingly, he conveyed over his ships and some troops, and built
three forts in which he placed most of his baggage, and moored
there for the future the larger craft and men-of-war. This was
the first and chief occasion of the losses which the crews experienced. The water which they used was scarce and had to
be fetched from far, and the sailors could not go out for fire-
wood without being cut off by the Syracusan horse, who were
masters of the country; a third of the enemy's cavalry being
stationed at the little town of Olympieum, to prevent plundering incursions on the part of the Athenians at Plemmyrium.
Meanwhile Nicias learned that the rest of the Corinthian fleet
was approaching, and sent twenty ships to watch for them,
with orders to be on the look-out for them about Locris and
Rhegium and the approach to Sicily.

Gylippus, meanwhile, went on with the wall across Epipolæ,
using the stones which the Athenians had laid down for their
own wall, and at the same time constantly led out the Syracusans and their allies, and formed them in order of battle in
front of the lines, the Athenians forming against him. At last
he thought that the moment was come, and began the attack;
and a hand-to-hand fight ensued between the lines, where the
Syracusan cavalry could be of no use; and the Syracusans and
their allies were defeated and took up their dead under truce,
while the Athenians erected a trophy. After this Gylippus
called the soldiers together, and said that the fault was not
theirs but his; he had kept their lines too much within the
works, and had thus deprived them of the services of their
cavalry and darters. He would now, therefore, lead them on
a second time. He begged them to remember that in material
force they would be fully a match for their opponents, while,
with respect to moral advantages, it were intolerable if
Peloponnesians and Dorians should not feel confident of overcoming Ionians and islanders with the motley rabble that accompanied them, and of driving them out of the country.

After this he embraced the first opportunity that offered
of again leading them against the enemy. Now Nicias and the
Athenians were of opinion that even if the Syracusans should
not wish to offer battle, it was necessary for them to prevent

the building of the cross wall, as it already almost overlapped the extreme point of their own, and if it went any further it would from that moment make no difference whether they fought ever so many successful actions, or never fought at all. They accordingly came out to meet the Syracusans. Gylippus led out his heavy infantry further from the fortifications than on the former occasion, and so joined battle; posting his horse and darters upon the flank of the Athenians in the open space, where the works of the two walls terminated. During the engagement the cavalry attacked and routed the left wing of the Athenians, which was opposed to them; and the rest of the Athenian army was in consequence defeated by the Syracusans and driven headlong within their lines. The night following the Syracusans carried their wall up to the Athenian works and passed them, thus putting it out of their power any longer to stop them, and depriving them, even if victorious in the field, of all chance of investing the city for the future.

After this the remaining twelve vessels of the Corinthians, Ambraciots, and Leucadians sailed into the harbour under the command of Erasinides, a Corinthian, having eluded the Athenian ships on guard, and helped the Syracusans in completing the remainder of the cross wall. Meanwhile Gylippus went into the rest of Sicily to raise land and naval forces, and also to bring over any of the cities that either were lukewarm in the cause or had hitherto kept out of the war altogether. Syracusan and Corinthian envoys were also despatched to Lacedæmon and Corinth to get a fresh force sent over, in any way that might offer, either in merchant vessels or transports, or in any other manner likely to prove successful, as the Athenians too were sending for reinforcements; while the Syracusans proceeded to man a fleet and to exercise, meaning to try their fortune in this way also, and generally became exceedingly confident.

Nicias perceiving this, and seeing the strength of the enemy and his own difficulties daily increasing, himself also sent to Athens. He had before sent frequent reports of events as they occurred, and felt it especially incumbent upon him to do so now, as he thought that they were in a critical position, and that unless speedily recalled or strongly reinforced from home, they had no hope of safety. He feared, however, that the mes-

sengers, either through inability to speak, or through failure
of memory, or from a wish to please the multitude, might not
report the truth, and so thought it best to write a letter, to
insure that the Athenians should know his own opinion without its being lost in transmission, and be able to decide upon
the real facts of the case. His emissaries, accordingly, departed
with the letter and the requisite verbal instructions; and he
attended to the affairs of the army, making it his aim now
to keep on the defensive and to avoid any unnecessary danger.

At the close of the same summer the Athenian general
Euetion marched in concert with Perdiccas with a large body
of Thracians against Amphipolis, and failing to take it brought
some galleys round into the Strymon, and blockaded the town
from the river, having his base at Himeræum.

Summer was now over. The winter ensuing, the persons sent
by Nicias, reaching Athens, gave the verbal messages which
had been entrusted to them, and answered any questions that
were asked them, and delivered the letter. The clerk of the
city now came forward and read out to the Athenians the letter,
which was as follows:—

'Our past operations, Athenians, have been made known to
you by many other letters; it is now time for you to become
equally familiar with our present condition, and to take your
measures accordingly. We had defeated in most of our engagements with them the Syracusans, against whom we were sent,
and we had built the works which we now occupy, when
Gylippus arrived from Lacedæmon with an army obtained
from Peloponnese and from some of the cities in Sicily. In our
first battle with him we were victorious; in the battle on the
following day we were overpowered by a multitude of cavalry
and darters, and compelled to retire within our lines. We have
now, therefore, been forced by the numbers of those opposed
to us to discontinue the work of circumvallation, and to remain inactive; being unable to make use even of all the force
we have, since a large portion of our heavy infantry is absorbed in the defence of our lines. Meanwhile the enemy have
carried a single wall past our lines, thus making it impossible
for us to invest them in future, until this cross wall be attacked
by a strong force and captured. So that the besieger in name
has become, at least from the land side, the besieged in reality;

as we are prevented by their cavalry from even going for any distance into the country.

'Besides this, an embassy has been despatched to Peloponnese to procure reinforcements, and Gylippus has gone to the cities in Sicily, partly in the hope of inducing those that are at present neutral to join him in the war, partly of bringing from his allies additional contingents for the land forces and material for the navy. For I understand that they contemplate a combined attack, upon our lines with their land forces and with their fleet by sea. You must none of you be surprised that I say by sea also. They have discovered that the length of the time we have now been in commission has rotted our ships and wasted our crews, and that with the entireness of our crews and the soundness of our ships the pristine efficiency of our navy has departed. For it is impossible for us to haul our ships ashore and careen them, because, the enemy's vessels being as many or more than our own, we are constantly anticipating an attack. Indeed, they may be seen exercising, and it lies with them to take the initiative; and not having to maintain a blockade, they have greater facilities for drying their ships.

'This we should scarcely be able to do, even if we had plenty of ships to spare, and were freed from our present necessity of exhausting all our strength upon the blockade. For it is already difficult to carry in supplies past Syracuse; and were we to relax our vigilance in the slightest degree it would become impossible. The losses which our crews have suffered and still continue to suffer arise from the following causes. Expeditions for fuel and for forage, and the distance from which water has to be fetched, cause our sailors to be cut off by the Syracusan cavalry; the loss of our previous superiority emboldens our slaves to desert; our foreign seamen are impressed by the unexpected appearance of a navy against us, and the strength of the enemy's resistance; such of them as were pressed into the service take the first opportunity of departing to their respective cities; such as were originally seduced by the temptation of high pay, and expected little fighting and large gains, leave us either by desertion to the enemy or by availing themselves of one or other of the various facilities of escape which the magnitude of Sicily affords them. Some even engage in trade themselves and prevail upon the captains to take Hyccaric slaves on board in their place; thus they have ruined the efficiency of our navy.

'Now I need not remind you that the time during which a crew is in its prime is short, and that the number of sailors who can start a ship on her way and keep the rowing in time is small. But by far my greatest trouble is, that holding the post which I do, I am prevented by the natural indocility of the Athenian seaman from putting a stop to these evils; and that meanwhile we have no source from which to recruit our crews, which the enemy can do from many quarters, but are compelled to depend both for supplying the crews in service and for making good our losses upon the men whom we brought with us. For our present confederates, Naxos and Catana, are incapable of supplying us. There is only one thing more wanting to our opponents, I mean the defection of our Italian markets. If they were to see you neglect to relieve us from our present condition, and were to go over to the enemy, famine would compel us to evacuate, and Syracuse would finish the war without a blow.

'I might, it is true, have written to you something different and more agreeable than this, but nothing certainly more useful, if it is desirable for you to know the real state of things here before taking your measures. Besides I know that it is your nature to love to be told the best side of things, and then to blame the teller if the expectations which he has raised in your minds are not answered by the result; and I therefore thought it safest to declare to you the truth.

'Now you are not to think that either your generals or your soldiers have ceased to be a match for the forces originally opposed to them. But you are to reflect that a general Sicilian coalition is being formed against us; that a fresh army is expected from Peloponnese, while the force we have here is unable to cope even with our present antagonists; and you must promptly decide either to recall us or to send out to us another fleet and army as numerous again, with a large sum of money, and some one to succeed me, as a disease in the kidneys unfits me for retaining my post. I have, I think, some claim on your indulgence, as while I was in my prime I did you much good service in my commands. But whatever you mean to do, do it at the commencement of spring and without delay, as the enemy will obtain his Sicilian reinforcements shortly, those from Peloponnese after a longer interval; and unless you attend to the matter the former will be here before you, while the latter will elude you as they have done before.'

Such were the contents of Nicias' letter. When the Athenians had heard it they refused to accept his resignation, but chose him two colleagues, naming Menander and Euthydemus, two of the officers at the seat of war, to fill their places until their arrival, that Nicias might not be left alone in his sickness to bear the whole weight of affairs. They also voted to send out another army and navy, drawn partly from the Athenians on the muster-roll, partly from the allies. The colleagues chosen for Nicias were Demosthenes, son of Alcisthenes, and Eurymedon, son of Thucles. Eurymedon was sent off at once, about the time of the winter solstice, with ten ships, a hundred and twenty talents of silver, and instructions to tell the army that reinforcements would arrive, and that care would be taken of them; but Demosthenes stayed behind to organise the expedition, meaning to start as soon as it was spring, and sent for troops to the allies, and meanwhile got together money, ships, and heavy infantry at home.

The Athenians also sent twenty vessels round Peloponnese to prevent any one crossing over to Sicily from Corinth or Peloponnese. For the Corinthians, filled with confidence by the favourable alteration in Sicilian affairs which had been reported by the envoys upon their arrival, and convinced that the fleet which they had before sent out had not been without its use, were now preparing to despatch a force of heavy infantry in merchant vessels to Sicily, while the Lacedæmonians did the like for the rest of Peloponnese. The Corinthians also named a fleet of twenty-five vessels, intending to try the result of a battle with the squadron on guard at Naupactus, and meanwhile to make it less easy for the Athenians there to hinder the departure of their merchantmen, by obliging them to keep an eye upon the galleys thus arrayed against them.

In the meantime the Lacedæmonians prepared for their invasion of Attica, in accordance with their own previous resolve, and at the instigation of the Syracusans and Corinthians, who wished for an invasion to arrest the reinforcements which they heard that Athens was about to send to Sicily. Alcibiades also urgently advised the fortification of Decelea, and a vigorous prosecution of the war. But the Lacedæmonians derived most encouragement from the belief that Athens, with two wars on her hands, against themselves and against the Siceliots, would be more easy to subdue, and from the conviction that she had been the first to infringe the truce. In the former war, they considered, the offence had been more on their own side, both on account of the entrance of the Thebans into Platæa in time of peace, and also of their own refusal to listen to the Athenian offer of arbitration, in spite of the clause in the former treaty that where arbitration should be offered there should be no appeal to arms. For this reason they thought that they deserved their misfortunes, and took to heart seriously the disaster at Pylos and whatever else had befallen them. But when, besides the ravages from Pylos, which went on without any intermission, the thirty Athenian ships came out from Argos and wasted part of Epidaurus, Prasiæ, and other places; when upon every dispute that arose as to the interpretation of any doubtful point in the treaty, their own offers of arbitration were always rejected by the Athenians,—the Lacedæmonians at length decided that Athens had now committed the very same offence as they had before done, and had become the guilty party; and they began to be full of ardour for the war. They spent this winter in sending round to their allies for iron, and in getting ready the other implements for building their fort; and meanwhile began raising at home, and also by forced requisitions in the rest of Peloponnese, a force to be sent out in the merchantmen to their allies in Sicily. Winter thus ended, and with it the eighteenth year of this war of which Thucydides is the historian.

In the first days of the spring following, at an earlier period than usual, the Lacedæmonians and their allies invaded Attica, under the command of Agis, son of Archidamus, king of the Lacedæmonians. They began by devastating the parts bordering upon the plain, and next proceeded to fortify Decelea, dividing the work among the different cities. Decelea is about thirteen or fourteen miles from the city of Athens, and the same distance or not much further from Bœotia; and the fort was meant to annoy the plain and the richest parts of the country, being in sight of Athens. While the Peloponnesians and their allies in Attica were engaged in the work of fortification, their countrymen at home sent off, at about the same time, the heavy infantry in the merchant vessels to Sicily; the Lacedæmonians furnishing a picked force of Helots and Neodamodes (or freedmen), six hundred heavy infantry in all, under the command of Eccritus, a Spartan; and the Bœotians three hundred heavy infantry, commanded by two Thebans, Xenon and Nicon, and by Hegesander, a Thespian. These were among the first to put out into the open sea, starting from Tænarus in Laconia. Not long after their departure the Corinthians sent off a force of five hundred heavy infantry, consisting partly of men from Corinth itself, and partly of Arcadian mercenaries, placed under the command of Alexarchus, a Corinthian. The Sicyonians also sent off two hundred heavy infantry at the same time as the Corinthians, under the command of Sargeus, a Sicyonian. Meantime the five-and-twenty vessels manned by Corinth during the winter, lay confronting the twenty Athenian ships at Naupactus until the heavy infantry in the merchantmen were fairly on their way from Peloponnese; thus fulfilling the object for which they had been manned originally, which was to divert the attention of the Athenians from the merchantmen to the galleys.

During this time the Athenians were not idle. Simultaneously with the fortification of Decelea, at the very beginning of spring, they sent thirty ships round Peloponnese, under Charicles, son of Apollodorus, with instructions to call at Argos and demand a force of their heavy infantry for the fleet, agreeably to the alliance. At the same time they despatched Demosthenes to Sicily, as they had intended, with sixty Athenian and five Chian vessels, twelve hundred Athenian heavy infantry from the muster-roll, and as many of the islanders as could be raised in the different quarters, drawing upon the other subject allies for whatever they could supply that would be of use for the war. Demosthenes was instructed first to sail round with Charicles and to operate with him upon the coasts of Laconia, and accordingly sailed to Ægina and there waited for the remainder of his armament, and for Charicles to fetch the Argive troops.

In Sicily about the same time in this spring, Gylippus came

to Syracuse with as many troops as he could bring from the
cities which he had persuaded to join. Calling the Syracusans
together, he told them that they must man as many ships as
possible, and try their hand at a sea-fight, by which he hoped
to achieve an advantage in the war not unworthy of the risk.
With him Hermocrates actively joined in trying to encourage
his countrymen to attack the Athenians at sea, saying that
the latter had not inherited their naval prowess nor would they
retain it for ever; they had been landsmen even to a greater
degree than the Syracusans, and had only become a maritime
power when obliged by the Mede. Besides, to daring spirits
like the Athenians, a daring adversary would seem the most
formidable; and the Athenian plan of paralysing by the boldness of their attack a neighbour often not their inferior in
strength, could now be used against them with as good effect
by the Syracusans. He was convinced also that the unlooked-
for spectacle of Syracusans daring to face the Athenian navy
would cause a terror to the enemy, the advantages of which
would far outweigh any loss that Athenian science might inflict upon their inexperience. He accordingly urged them to
throw aside their fears and to try their fortune at sea; and the
Syracusans, under the influence of Gylippus and Hermocrates,
and perhaps some others, made up their minds for the sea-fight
and began to man their vessels.

When the fleet was ready, Gylippus led out the whole army
by night; his plan being to assault in person the forts of
Plemmyrium by land, while thirty-five Syracusan galleys
sailed according to appointment against the enemy from the
great harbour, and the forty-five remaining came round from
the lesser harbour, where they had their arsenal, in order to
effect a junction with those inside and simultaneously to attack
Plemmyrium, and thus to distract the Athenians by assaulting them on two sides at once. The Athenians quickly manned
sixty ships, and with twenty-five of these engaged the thirty-
five of the Syracusans in the great harbour, sending the rest
to meet those sailing round from the arsenal; and an action
now ensued directly in front of the mouth of the great harbour,
maintained with equal tenacity on both sides; the one wishing
to force the passage, the other to prevent them.

In the meantime, while the Athenians in Plemmyrium were

down at the sea, attending to the engagement, Gylippus made a sudden attack on the forts in the early morning and took the largest first, and afterwards the two smaller, whose garrisons did not wait for him, seeing the largest so easily taken. At the fall of the first fort, the men from it who succeeded in taking refuge in their boats and merchantmen, found great difficulty in reaching the camp, as the Syracusans were having the best of it in the engagement in the great harbour, and sent a fast-sailing galley to pursue them. But when the two others fell, the Syracusans were now being defeated; and the fugitives from these sailed along shore with more ease. The Syracusan ships fighting off the mouth of the harbour, forced their way through the Athenian vessels and sailing in without any order fell foul of one another, and transferred the victory to the Athenians; who not only routed the squadron in question, but also that by which they were at first being defeated in the harbour, sinking eleven of the Syracusan vessels and killing most of the men, except the crews of three ships whom they made prisoners. Their own loss was confined to three vessels; and after hauling ashore the Syracusan wrecks and setting up a trophy upon the islet in front of Plemmyrium, they retired to their own camp.

Unsuccessful at sea, the Syracusans had nevertheless the forts in Plemmyrium, for which they set up three trophies. One of the two last taken they razed, but put in order and garrisoned the two others. In the capture of the forts a great many men were killed and made prisoners, and a great quantity of property was taken in all. As the Athenians had used them as a magazine, there was a large stock of goods and corn of the merchants inside, and also a large stock belonging to the captains; the masts and other furniture of forty galleys being taken, besides three galleys which had been drawn up on shore. Indeed the first and chiefest cause of the ruin of the Athenian army was the capture of Plemmyrium; even the entrance of the harbour being now no longer safe for carrying in provisions, as the Syracusan vessels were stationed there to prevent it, and nothing could be brought in without fighting; besides the general impression of dismay and discouragement produced upon the army.

After this the Syracusans sent out twelve ships under the

command of Agatharchus, a Syracusan. One of these went to
Peloponnese with ambassadors to describe the hopeful state of
their affairs, and to incite the Peloponnesians to prosecute the
war there even more actively than they were now doing, while
the eleven others sailed to Italy, hearing that vessels laden
with stores were on their way to the Athenians. After falling
in with and destroying most of the vessels in question, and
burning in the Caulonian territory a quantity of timber for
shipbuilding, which had been got ready for the Athenians, the
Syracusan squadron went to Locri, and one of the merchantmen from Peloponnese coming in, while they were at anchor
there, carrying Thespian heavy infantry, took these on board
and sailed along shore towards home. The Athenians were on
the look-out for them with twenty ships at Megara, but were
only able to take one vessel with its crew; the rest getting clear
off to Syracuse. There was also some skirmishing in the harbour about the piles which the Syracusans had driven in the sea
in front of the old docks, to allow their ships to lie at anchor
inside, without being hurt by the Athenians sailing up and
running them down. The Athenians brought up to them a
ship of ten thousand talents' burden furnished with wooden
turrets and screens, and fastened ropes round the piles from
their boats, wrenched them up and broke them, or dived down
and sawed them in two. Meanwhile the Syracusans plied them
with missiles from the docks, to which they replied from their
large vessel; until at last most of the piles were removed by
the Athenians. But the most awkward part of the stockade was
the part out of sight: some of the piles which had been driven
in did not appear above water, so that it was dangerous to sail
up, for fear of running the ships upon them, just as upon a
reef, through not seeing them. However divers went down
and sawed off even these for reward; although the Syracusans
drove in others. Indeed there was no end to the contrivances
to which they resorted against each other, as might be expected
between two hostile armies confronting each other at such a
short distance: and skirmishes and all kinds of other attempts
were of constant occurrence. Meanwhile the Syracusans sent
embassies to the cities composed of Corinthians, Ambraciots,
and Lacedæmonians, to tell them of the capture of Plemmyrium. and that their defeat in the sea-fight was due less to

the strength of the enemy than to their own disorder; and generally, to let them know that they were full of hope, and to desire them to come to their help with ships and troops, as the Athenians were expected with a fresh army, and if the one already there could be destroyed before the other arrived, the war would be at an end.

While the contending parties in Sicily were thus engaged, Demosthenes, having now got together the armament with which he was to go to the island, put out from Ægina, and making sail for Peloponnese, joined Charicles and the thirty ships of the Athenians. Taking on board the heavy infantry from Argos they sailed to Laconia, and after first plundering part of Epidarus Limera, landed on the coast of Laconia, opposite Cythera, where the temple of Apollo stands, and laying waste part of the country, fortified a sort of isthmus, to which the Helots of the Lacedæmonians might desert, and from whence plundering incursions might be made as from Pylos. Demosthenes helped to occupy this place, and then immediately sailed on to Corcyra to take up some of the allies in that island, and so to proceed without delay to Sicily; while Charicles waited until he had completed the fortification of the place, and leaving a garrison there, returned home subsequently with his thirty ships and the Argives also.

This same summer arrived at Athens thirteen hundred targeteers, Thracian swordsmen of the tribe of the Dii, who were to have sailed to Sicily with Demosthenes. Since they had come too late, the Athenians determined to send them back to Thrace, whence they had come; to keep them for the Decelean war appearing too expensive, as the pay of each man was a drachma a day. Indeed since Decelea had been first fortified by the whole Peloponnesian army during this summer, and then occupied for the annoyance of the country by the garrisons from the cities relieving each other at stated intervals, it had been doing great mischief to the Athenians; in fact this occupation, by the destruction of property and loss of men which resulted from it, was one of the principal causes of their ruin. Previously the invasions were short, and did not prevent their enjoying their land during the rest of the time: the enemy was now permanently fixed in Attica; at one time it was an attack in force, at another it was the regular garrison overrunning the country and making forays for its subsistence, and the Lacedæmonian king, Agis, was in the field and diligently prosecuting the war; great mischief was therefore done to the Athenians. They were deprived of their whole country: more than twenty thousand slaves had deserted, a great part of them artisans, and all their sheep and beasts of burden were lost; and as the cavalry rode out daily upon excursions to Decelea and to guard the country, their horses were either lamed by being constantly worked upon rocky ground, or wounded by the enemy.

Besides, the transport of provisions from Eubœa, which had before been carried on so much more quickly over land by Decelea from Oropus, was now effected at great cost by sea round Sunium; everything the city required had to be imported from abroad, and instead of a city it became a fortress. Summer and winter the Athenians were worn out by having to keep guard on the fortifications, during the day by turns, by night all together, the cavalry excepted, at the different military posts or upon the wall. But what most oppressed them was that they had two wars at once, and had thus reached a pitch of frenzy which no one would have believed possible if he had heard of it before it had come to pass. For could any one have imagined that even when besieged by the Peloponnesians entrenched in Attica, they would still, instead of withdrawing from Sicily, stay on there besieging in like manner Syracuse, a town (taken as a town) in no way inferior to Athens, or would so thoroughly upset the Hellenic estimate of their strength and audacity, as to give the spectacle of a people which, at the beginning of the war, some thought might hold out one year, some two, none more than three, if the Peloponnesians invaded their country, now seventeen years after the first invasion, after having already suffered from all the evils of war, going to Sicily and undertaking a new war nothing inferior to that which they already had with the Peloponnesians? These causes, the great losses from Decelea, and the other heavy charges that fell upon them, produced their financial embarrassment; and it was at this time that they imposed upon their subjects, instead of the tribute, the tax of a twentieth upon all imports and exports by sea, which they thought would bring them in more money; their expenditure being now not the same as at first, but having grown with the war while their revenues decayed.

Accordingly, not wishing to incur expense in their present want of money, they sent back at once the Thracians who came too late for Demosthenes, under the conduct of Diitrephes, who was instructed, as they were to pass through the Euripus, to make use of them if possible in the voyage along shore to injure the enemy. Diitrephes first landed them at Tanagra and hastily snatched some booty; he then sailed across the Euripus in the evening from Chalcis in Euboea and disembarking in Boeotia led them against Mycalessus. The night he passed unobserved near the temple of Hermes, not quite two miles from Mycalessus, and at daybreak assaulted and took the town, which is not a large one; the inhabitants being off their guard and not expecting that any one would ever come up so far from the sea to molest them, the wall too being weak, and in some places having tumbled down, while in others it had not been built to any height, and the gates also being left open through their feeling of security. The Thracians bursting into Mycalessus sacked the houses and temples, and butchered the inhabitants, sparing neither youth nor age, but killing all they fell in with, one after the other, children and women, and even beasts of burden, and whatever other living creatures they saw; the Thracian race, like the bloodiest of the barbarians, being ever most so when it has nothing to fear. Everywhere confusion reigned and death in all its shapes; and in particular they attacked a boys' school, the largest that there was in the place, into which the children had just gone, and massacred them all. In short, the disaster falling upon the whole town was unsurpassed in magnitude, and unapproached by any in suddenness and in horror.

Meanwhile the Thebans heard of it and marched to the rescue, and overtaking the Thracians before they had gone far, recovered the plunder and drove them in panic to the Euripus and the sea, where the vessels which brought them were lying. The greatest slaughter took place while they were embarking, as they did not know how to swim, and those in the vessels on seeing what was going on on shore moored them out of bowshot: in the rest of the retreat the Thracians made a very respectable defence against the Theban horse,

by which they were first attacked, dashing out and closing
their ranks according to the tactics of their country, and lost
only a few men in that part of the affair. A good number who
were after plunder were actually caught in the town and put
to death. Altogether the Thracians had two hundred and fifty
killed out of thirteen hundred, the Thebans and the rest who
came to the rescue about twenty, troopers and heavy infantry,
with Scirphondas, one of the Bœtarchs. The Mycalessians lost
a large proportion of their population.

While Mycalessus thus experienced a calamity, for its extent, as lamentable as any that happened in the war, Demosthenes, whom we left sailing to Corcyra, after the building of
the fort in Laconia, found a merchantman lying at Phea in
Elis, in which the Corinthian heavy infantry were to cross to
Sicily. The ship he destroyed, but the men escaped, and subsequently got another in which they pursued their voyage. After
this, arriving at Zacynthus and Cephallenia, he took a body
of heavy infantry on board, and sending for some of the Messenians from Naupactus, crossed over to the opposite coast of
Acarnania, to Alyzia, and to Anactorium which was held by
the Athenians. While he was in these parts he was met by
Eurymedon returning from Sicily, where he had been sent, as
has been mentioned, during the winter, with the money for the
army, who told him the news, and also that he had heard,
while at sea, that the Syracusans had taken Plemmyrium.
Here, also, Conon came to them, the commander at Naupactus,
with news that the twenty-five Corinthian ships stationed
opposite to him, far from giving over the war, were meditating
an engagement; and he therefore begged them to send him
some ships, as his own eighteen were not a match for the
enemy's twenty-five. Demosthenes and Eurymedon, accordingly, sent ten of their best sailers with Conon to reinforce
the squadron at Naupactus, and meanwhile prepared for the
muster of their forces; Eurymedon, who was now the colleague
of Demosthenes, and had turned back in consequence of his
appointment, sailing to Corcyra to tell them to man fifteen
ships and to enlist heavy infantry; while Demosthenes raised
slingers and darters from the parts about Acarnania.

Meanwhile the envoys, already mentioned, who had gone
from Syracuse to the cities after the capture of Plemmyrium,

had succeeded in their mission, and were about to bring the army that they had collected, when Nicias got scent of it, and sent to the Centoripæ and Alicyæans and other of the friendly Sicels, who held the passes, not to let the enemy through, but to combine to prevent their passing, there being no other way by which they could even attempt it, as the Agrigentines would not give them a passage through their country. Agreeably to this request the Sicels laid a triple ambuscade for the Siceliots upon their march, and attacking them suddenly, while off their guard, killed about eight hundred of them and all the envoys, the Corinthian only excepted, by whom fifteen hundred who escaped were conducted to Syracuse.

About the same time the Camarinæans also came to the assistance of Syracuse with five hundred heavy infantry, three hundred darters and as many archers, while the Geloans sent crews for five ships, four hundred darters and two hundred horse. Indeed almost the whole of Sicily, except the Agrigentines, who were neutral, now ceased merely to watch events as it had hitherto done, and actively joined Syracuse against the Athenians.

While the Syracusans after the Sicel disaster put off any immediate attack upon the Athenians, Demosthenes and Eurymedon, whose forces from Corcyra and the continent were now ready, crossed the Ionian gulf with all their armament to the Iapygian promontory, and starting from thence touched at the Chœrades Isles lying off Iapygia, where they took on board a hundred and fifty Iapygian darters of the Messapian tribe, and after renewing an old friendship with Artas the chief, who had furnished them with the darters, arrived at Metapontium in Italy. Here they persuaded their allies the Metapontines, to send with them three hundred darters and two galleys, and with this reinforcement coasted on to Thurii, where they found the party hostile to Athens recently expelled by a revolution, and accordingly remained there to muster and review the whole army, to see if any had been left behind, and to prevail upon the Thurians resolutely to join them in their expedition, and in the circumstances in which they found themselves to conclude a defensive and offensive alliance with the Athenians.

About the same time the Peloponnesians in the twenty-five ships stationed opposite to the squadron at Naupactus to protect the passage of the transports to Sicily, had got ready for engaging, and manning some additional vessels, so as to be numerically little inferior to the Athenians, anchored off Erineus in Achaia in the Rhypic country. The place off which they lay being in the form of a crescent, the land forces furnished by the Corinthians and their allies on the spot, came up and ranged themselves upon the projecting headlands on either side, while the fleet, under the command of Polyanthes, a Corinthian, held the intervening space and blocked up the entrance. The Athenians under Diphilus now sailed out against them with thirty-three ships from Naupactus, and the Corinthians, at first not moving, at length thought they saw their opportunity, raised the signal, and advanced and engaged the Athenians. After an obstinate struggle, the Corinthians lost three ships, and without sinking any altogether, disabled seven of the enemy, which were struck prow to prow and had their foreships stoven in by the Corinthian vessels, whose cheeks had been strengthened for this very purpose. After an action of this even character, in which either party could claim the victory (although the Athenians became masters of the wrecks through the wind driving them out to sea, the Corinthians not putting out again to meet them) the two combatants parted. No pursuit took place, and no prisoners were made on either side; the Corinthians and Peloponnesians who were fighting near the shore escaping with ease, and none of the Athenian vessels having been sunk. The Athenians now sailed back to Naupactus, and the Corinthians immediately set up a trophy as victors, because they had disabled a greater number of the enemy's ships. Moreover they held that they had not been worsted, for the very same reason that their opponent held that he had not been victorious; the Corinthians considering that they were conquerors, if not decidedly conquered, and the Athenians thinking themselves vanquished, because not decidedly victorious. However, when the Peloponnesians sailed off and their land forces had dispersed, the Athenians also set up a trophy as victors in Achaia, about two miles and a quarter from Erineus, the Corinthian station.

This was the termination of the action at Naupactus. To

return to Demosthenes and Eurymedon: the Thurians having now got ready to join in the expedition with seven hundred heavy infantry and three hundred darters, the two generals ordered the ships to sail along the coast to the Crotonian territory, and meanwhile held a review of all the land forces upon the river Sybaris, and then led them through the Thurian country. Arrived at the river Hylias, they here received a message from the Crotonians, saying that they would not allow the army to pass through their country; upon which the Athenians descended towards the shore, and bivouacked near the sea and the mouth of the Hylias, where the fleet also met them, and the next day embarked and sailed along the coast touching at all the cities except Locri, until they came to Petra in the Rhegian territory.

Meanwhile the Syracusans hearing of their approach resolved to make a second attempt with their fleet and their other forces on shore, which they had been collecting for this very purpose in order to do something before their arrival. In addition to other improvements suggested by the former sea-fight which they now adopted in the equipment of their navy, they cut down their prows to a smaller compass to make them more solid and made their cheeks stouter, and from these let stays into the vessel's sides for a length of six cubits within and without, in the same way as the Corinthians had altered their prows before engaging the squadron at Naupactus. The Syracusans thought that they would thus have an advantage over the Athenian vessels, which were not constructed with equal strength, but were slight in the bows, from their being more used to sail round and charge the enemy's side than to meet him prow to prow, and that the battle being in the great harbour, with a great many ships in not much room, was also a fact in their favour. Charging prow to prow, they would stave in the enemy's bows, by striking with solid and stout beaks against hollow and weak ones; and secondly, the Athenians for want of room would be unable to use their favourite manœuvre of breaking the line or of sailing round, as the Syracusans would do their best not to let them do the one, and want of room would prevent their doing the other. This charging prow to prow, which had hitherto been thought want of skill in a helmsman, would be the Syracusans' chief manœuvre, as being that which they should find most useful, since the Athenians, if repulsed, would not be able to back water in any direction except towards the shore, and that only for a little way, and in the little space in front of their own camp. The rest of the harbour would be commanded by the Syracusans; and the Athenians, if hard pressed, by crowding together in a small space and all to the same point, would run foul of one another and fall into disorder, which was, in fact, the thing that did the Athenians most harm in all the sea-fights, they not having, like the Syracusans, the whole harbour to retreat over. As to their sailing round into the open sea, this would be impossible, with the Syracusans in possession of the way out and in, especially as Plemmyrium would be hostile to them, and the mouth of the harbour was not large.

With these contrivances to suit their skill and ability, and now more confident after the previous sea-fight, the Syra-cusans attacked by land and sea at once. The town force Gylippus led out a little the first and brought them up to the wall of the Athenians, where it looked towards the city, while the force from the Olympieum, that is to say, the heavy infantry that were there with the horse and the light troops of the Syracusans, advanced against the wall from the opposite side; the ships of the Syracusans and allies sailing out immediately afterwards. The Athenians at first fancied that they were to be attacked by land only, and it was not without alarm that they saw the fleet suddenly approaching as well; and while some were forming upon the walls and in front of them against the advancing enemy, and some marching out in haste against the numbers of horse and darters coming from the Olympieum and from outside, others manned the ships or rushed down to the beach to oppose the enemy, and when the ships were manned put out with seventy-five sail against about eighty of the Syracusans.

After spending a great part of the day in advancing and retreating and skirmishing with each other, without either being able to gain any advantage worth speaking of, except that the Syracusans sank one or two of the Athenian vessels, they parted, the land force at the same time retiring from the lines. The next day the Syracusans remained quiet, and gave no signs of what they were going to do; but Nicias, seeing that the battle had been a drawn one, and expecting that they would attack again, compelled the captains to refit any of the ships that had suffered, and moored merchant vessels before the stockade which they had driven into the sea in front of their ships, to serve instead of an enclosed harbour, at about two hundred feet from each other, in order that any ship that was hard pressed might be able to retreat in safety and sail out again at leisure. These preparations occupied the Athenians all day until nightfall.

The next day the Syracusans began operations at an earlier hour, but with the same plan of attack by land and sea. A great part of the day the rivals spent as before, confronting and skirmishing with each other; until at last Ariston, son of Pyrrhicus, a Corinthian, the ablest helmsman in the Syracusan service, persuaded their naval commanders to send to the officials in the city, and tell them to move the sale market as quickly as they could down to the sea, and oblige every one to bring whatever eatables he had and sell them there, thus enabling the commanders to land the crews and dine at once close to the ships, and shortly afterwards, the selfsame day, to attack the Athenians again when they were not expecting it.

In compliance with this advice a messenger was sent and the market got ready, upon which the Syracusans suddenly backed water and withdrew to the town, and at once landed and took their dinner upon the spot; while the Athenians, supposing that they had returned to the town because they felt they were beaten, disembarked at their leisure and set about getting their dinners and about their other occupations, under the idea that they had done with fighting for that day. Suddenly the Syracusans manned their ships and again sailed against them; and the Athenians, in great confusion and most of them fasting, got on board, and with great difficulty put out to meet them. For some time both parties remained on the defensive without engaging, until the Athenians at last resolved not to let themselves be worn out by waiting where they were, but to attack without delay, and giving a cheer, went into action. The Syracusans received them, and charging prow to prow as they had intended, stove in a great part of the Athenian foreships by the strength of their beaks; the darters on the decks also did great damage to the Athenians, but still greater damage was done by the Syracusans who went about in small boats, ran in upon the oars of the Athenian galleys, and sailed against their sides, and discharged from thence their darts upon the sailors.

At last, fighting hard in this fashion, the Syracusans gained the victory, and the Athenians turned and fled between the merchantmen to their own station. The Syracusan ships pursued them as far as the merchantmen, where they were stopped by the beams armed with dolphins suspended from those vessels over the passage. Two of the Syracusan vessels went too near in the excitement of victory and were destroyed, one of them being taken with its crew. After sinking seven of the Athenian vessels and disabling many, and taking most of the men prisoners and killing others, the Syracusans retired and set up trophies for both the engagements, being now confident of having a decided superiority by sea, and by no means despairing of equal success by land.

CHAPTER XXII

NINETEENTH YEAR OF THE WAR—ARRIVAL OF DEMOSTHENES
—DEFEAT OF THE ATHENIANS AT EPIPOLÆ—FOLLY AND
OBSTINACY OF NICIAS

B.C. 413: *Demosthenes arrives with new army—Athenians routed— Demosthenes advises retreat, Nicias continuation of siege.*

IN the meantime, while the Syracusans were preparing for a second attack upon both elements, Demosthenes and Eurymedon arrived with the succours from Athens, consisting of about seventy-three ships, including the foreigners; nearly five thousand heavy infantry, Athenian and allied; a large number of darters, Hellenic and barbarian, and slingers and archers and everything else upon a corresponding scale. The Syracusans and their allies were for the moment not a little dismayed at the idea that there was to be no term or ending to their dangers, seeing, in spite of the fortification of Decelea, a new army arrive nearly equal to the former, and the power of Athens proving so great in every quarter. On the other hand, the first Athenian armament regained a certain confidence in the midst of its misfortunes. Demosthenes, seeing how matters stood, felt that he could not drag on and fare as Nicias had

done, who by wintering in Catana instead of at once attacking
Syracuse had allowed the terror of his first arrival to evaporate
in contempt, and had given time to Gylippus to arrive with a
force from Peloponnese, which the Syracusans would never
have sent for if he had attacked immediately; for they fancied
that they were a match for him by themselves, and would not
have discovered their inferiority until they were already invested, and even if they then sent for succours, they would no
longer have been equally able to profit by their arrival. Recol-
lecting this, and well aware that it was now on the first day
after his arrival that he like Nicias was most formidable to
the enemy, Demosthenes determined to lose no time in drawing the utmost profit from the consternation at the moment
inspired by his army; and seeing that the counterwall of the
Syracusans, which hindered the Athenians from investing
them, was a single one, and that he who should become master
of the way up to Epipolæ, and afterwards of the camp there,
would find no difficulty in taking it, as no one would even wait
for his attack, made all haste to attempt the enterprise. This
he took to be the shortest way of ending the war, as he would
either succeed and take Syracuse, or would lead back the
armament instead of frittering away the lives of the Athenians engaged in the expedition and the resources of the
country at large.

First therefore the Athenians went out and laid waste the
lands of the Syracusans about the Anapus and carried all
before them as at first by land and by sea, the Syracusans
not offering to oppose them upon either element, unless it
were with their cavalry and darters from the Olympieum.
Next Demosthenes resolved to attempt the counterwall first
by means of engines. As however the engines that he brought
up were burnt by the enemy fighting from the wall, and the
rest of the forces repulsed after attacking at many different
points, he determined to delay no longer, and having obtained
the consent of Nicias and his fellow-commanders, proceeded
to put in execution his plan of attacking Epipolæ. As by day
it seemed impossible to approach and get up without being
observed, he ordered provisions for five days, took all the
masons and carpenters, and other things, such as arrows, and
everything else that they could want for the work of fortifica-

tion if successful; and after the first watch set out with
Eurymedon and Menander and the whole army for Epipolæ,
Nicias being left behind in the lines. Having come up by the
hill of Euryelus (where the former army had ascended at
first), unobserved by the enemy's guards, they went up to the
fort which the Syracusans had there, and took it, and put to
the sword part of the garrison. The greater number, however, escaped at once and gave the alarm to the camps, of
which there were three upon Epipolæ, defended by outworks,
one of the Syracusans, one of the other Siceliots, and one of
the allies; and also to the six hundred Syracusans forming
the original garrison for this part of Epipolæ. These at once
advanced against the assailants, and falling in with Demosthenes and the Athenians, were routed by them after a sharp
resistance, the victors immediately pushing on, eager to
achieve the objects of the attack without giving time for their
ardour to cool; meanwhile others from the very beginning
were taking the counterwall of the Syracusans, which was
abandoned by its garrison, and pulling down the battlements.
The Syracusans and the allies, and Gylippus with the troops
under his command, advanced to the rescue from the outworks,
but engaged in some consternation (a night attack being a
piece of audacity which they had never expected), and were
at first compelled to retreat. But while the Athenians, flushed
with their victory, now advanced with less order, wishing to
make their way as quickly as possible through the whole force
of the enemy not yet engaged, without relaxing their attack
or giving them time to rally, the Bœotians made the first stand
against them, attacked them, routed them, and put them to
flight.

The Athenians now fell into great disorder and perplexity,
so that it was not easy to get from one side or the other any
detailed account of the affair. By day certainly the combatants
have a clearer notion, though even then by no means of all that
takes place, no one knowing much of anything that does not
go on in his own immediate neighbourhood; but in a night
engagement (and this was the only one that occurred between
great armies during the war) how could any one know anything for certain? Although there was a bright moon they
saw each other only as men do by moonlight, that is to say,

they could distinguish the form of the body, but could not tell for certain whether it was a friend or an enemy. Both had great numbers of heavy infantry moving about in a small space. Some of the Athenians were already defeated, while others were coming up yet unconquered for their first attack. A large part also of the rest of their forces either had only just got up, or were still ascending, so that they did not know which way to march. Owing to the rout that had taken place all in front was now in confusion, and the noise made it difficult to distinguish anything. The victorious Syracusans and allies were cheering each other on with loud cries, by night the only possible means of communication, and meanwhile receiving all who came against them; while the Athenians were seeking for one another, taking all in front of them for enemies, even although they might be some of their now flying friends; and by constantly asking for the watchword, which was their only means of recognition, not only caused great confusion among themselves by asking all at once, but also made it known to the enemy, whose own they did not so readily discover, as the Syracusans were victorious and not scattered, and thus less easily mistaken. The result was that if the Athenians fell in with a party of the enemy that was weaker than they, it escaped them through knowing their watchword; while if they themselves failed to answer they were put to the sword. But what hurt them as much, or indeed more than anything else, was the singing of the Pæan, from the perplexity which it caused by being nearly the same on either side: the Argives and Corcyræans and any other Dorian peoples in the army, struck terror into the Athenians whenever they raised their Pæan, no less than did the enemy. Thus, after being once thrown into disorder, they ended by coming into collision with each other in many parts of the field, friends with friends, and citizens with citizens, and not only terrified one another, but even came to blows and could only be parted with difficulty. In the pursuit many perished by throwing themselves down the cliffs, the way down from Epipolæ being narrow; and of those who got down safely into the plain, although many, especially those who belonged to the first armament, escaped through their better acquaintance with the locality, some of the newcomers lost their way and wandered over the country, and were cut off in the morning by the Syracusan cavalry and killed.

The next day the Syracusans set up two trophies, one upon Epipolæ where the ascent had been made, and the other on the spot where the first check was given by the Bœotians; and the Athenians took back their dead under truce. A great many of the Athenians and allies were killed, although still more arms were taken than could be accounted for by the number of the dead, as some of those who were obliged to leap down from the cliffs without their shields escaped with their lives and did not perish like the rest.

After this the Syracusans, recovering their old confidence at such an unexpected stroke of good fortune, despatched Sicanus with fifteen ships to Agrigentum where there was a revolution, to induce if possible the city to join them; while Gylippus again went by land into the rest of Sicily to bring up reinforcements, being now in hope of taking the Athenian lines by storm, after the result of the affair on Epipolæ.

In the meantime the Athenian generals consulted upon the disaster which had happened, and upon the general weakness of the army. They saw themselves unsuccessful in their enter-prises, and the soldiers disgusted with their stay; disease being rife among them owing to its being the sickly season of the year, and to the marshy and unhealthy nature of the spot in which they were encamped; and the state of their affairs generally being thought desperate. Accordingly, Demosthenes was of opinion that they ought not to stay any longer; but agreeably to his original idea in risking the attempt upon Epipolæ, now that this had failed, he gave his vote for going away without further loss of time, while the sea might yet be crossed, and their late reinforcement might give them the superiority at all events on that element. He also said that it would be more profitable for the state to carry on the war against those who were building fortifications in Attica, than against the Syracusans whom it was no longer easy to sub-due; besides which it was not right to squander large sums of money to no purpose by going on with the siege.

This was the opinion of Demosthenes. Nicias, without deny-ing the bad state of their affairs, was unwilling to avow their weakness, or to have it reported to the enemy that the Athenians in full council were openly voting for retreat; for in that case they would be much less likely to effect it when they wanted without discovery. Moreover, his own particular information still gave him reason to hope that the affairs of the enemy would soon be in a worse state than their own, if the Athenians persevered in the siege; as they would wear out the Syracusans by want of money, especially with the more extensive command of the sea now given them by their present navy. Besides this, there was a party in Syracuse who wished to betray the city to the Athenians, and kept sending him messages and telling him not to raise the siege. Accordingly, knowing this and really waiting because he hesitated between the two courses and wished to see his way more clearly, in his public speech on this occasion he refused to lead off the army, saying he was sure the Athenians would never approve of their returning without a vote of theirs. Those who would vote upon their conduct, instead of judging the facts as eye-witnesses like themselves and not from what they might hear from hostile critics, would simply be guided by the calumnies of the first clever speaker; while many, indeed most, of the soldiers on the spot, who now so loudly proclaimed the danger of their position, when they reached Athens would proclaim just as loudly the opposite, and would say that their generals had been bribed to betray them and return. For himself, therefore, who knew the Athenian temper, sooner than perish under a dishonourable charge and by an unjust sentence at the hands of the Athenians, he would rather take his chance and die, if die he must, a soldier's death at the hand of the enemy. Besides, after all, the Syracusans were in a worse case than themselves. What with paying mercenaries, spending upon fortified posts, and now for a full year maintaining a large navy, they were already at a loss and would soon be at a standstill: they had already spent two thousand talents and incurred heavy debts besides, and could not lose even ever so small a fraction of their present force through not paying it, without ruin to their cause; depending as they did more upon mercenaries than upon soldiers obliged to serve, like their own. He therefore said that they ought to stay and carry on the siege, and not depart defeated in point of money, in which they were much superior.

Nicias spoke positively because he had exact information of the financial distress at Syracuse, and also because of the strength of the Athenian party there which kept sending him messages not to raise the siege; besides which he had more confidence than before in his fleet, and felt sure at least of its success. Demosthenes, however, would not hear for a moment of continuing the siege, but said that if they could not lead off the army without a decree from Athens, and if they were obliged to stay on, they ought to remove to Thapsus or Catana; where their land forces would have a wide extent of country to overrun, and could live by plundering the enemy, and would thus do them damage; while the fleet would have the open sea to fight in, that is to say, instead of a narrow space which was all in the enemy's favour, a wide sea-room where their science would be of use, and where they could retreat or advance without being confined or circumscribed either when they put out or put in. In any case he was altogether opposed to their staying on where they were, and insisted on removing at once, as quickly and with as little delay as possible; and in this judgment Eurymedon agreed. Nicias however still objecting, a certain diffidence and hesitation came over them, with a suspicion that Nicias might have some further information to make him so positive.

CHAPTER XXIII

NINETEENTH YEAR OF THE WAR—BATTLES IN THE GREAT HARBOUR—RETREAT AND ANNIHILATION OF THE ATHE NIAN ARMY

B.C. 413: *Athenians remain at Syracuse—Decisive victory for Syracusan fleet—Despair among Athenians, enthusiasm among Syracusans— List of Athenian allies—Supporters of Syracuse—Athenian decision to risk final sea engagement—Nicias' speech—Gylippus' address— Battle at close range—Athenian defeat—Stratagem of Hermocrates—Plight of retreating Athenians—Nicias tries to encourage his demoralized troops—Panic and disorder—Armies of Demosthenes and Nicias separated—Demosthenes surrenders—Slaughter of Nicias' army—Surrender and execution of Nicias and Demosthenes—Sicilian expedition ends in disaster.*

WHILE the Athenians lingered on in this way without moving from where they were, Gylippus and Sicanus now arrived at Syracuse. Sicanus had failed to gain Agrigentum, the party friendly to the Syracusans having been driven out while he was still at Gela; but Gylippus was accompanied not only by a large number of troops raised in Sicily, but by the heavy infantry sent off in the spring from Peloponnese in the merchantmen, who had arrived at Selinus from Libya. They had been carried to Libya by a storm, and having obtained two galleys and pilots from the Cyrenians, on their voyage along shore had taken sides with the Euesperitæ and had defeated the Libyans who were besieging them, and from thence coasting on to Neapolis, a Carthaginian mart, and the nearest point to Sicily, from which it is only two days' and a night's voyage, there crossed over and came to Selinus. Immediately upon their arrival the Syracusans prepared to attack the Athenians again by land and sea at once. The Athenian generals seeing a fresh army come to the aid of the enemy, and that their own circumstances, far from improving, were becoming daily worse, and above all distressed by the sickness of the soldiers, now began to repent of not having removed before; and Nicias no longer offering the same opposition, except by urging that there should be no open voting, they gave orders as secretly as possible for all to be prepared to sail out from the camp at a given signal. All was at last ready, and they were on the point of sailing away, when an eclipse of the moon, which was then at the full, took place. Most of the Athenians, deeply impressed by this occurrence, now urged the generals to wait; and Nicias, who was somewhat over-addicted to divination and practices of that kind, refused from that moment even to take the question of departure into consideration, until they had waited the thrice nine days prescribed by the soothsayers.

The besiegers were thus condemned to stay in the country; and the Syracusans getting wind of what had happened, became more eager than ever to press the Athenians, who had now themselves acknowledged that they were no longer their superiors either by sea or by land, as otherwise they would never have planned to sail away. Besides which the Syracusans did not wish them to settle in any other part of Sicily, where they would be more difficult to deal with, but desired to force them to fight at sea as quickly as possible, in a position favourable to themselves. Accordingly they manned their

ships and practised for as many days as they though⁴ sufficient. When the moment arrived they assaulted on the first
day the Athenian lines, and upon a small force of heavy infantry and horse sallying out against them by certain gates,
cut off some of the former and routed and pursued them to the
lines, where, as the entrance was narrow, the Athenians lost
seventy horses and some few of the heavy infantry.

Drawing off their troops for this day, on the next the
Syracusans went out with a fleet of seventy-six sail, and at
the same time advanced with their land forces against the
lines. The Athenians put out to meet them with eighty-six
ships, came to close quarters and engaged. The Syracusans and
their allies first defeated the Athenian centre, and then caught
Eurymedon, the commander of the right wing, who was sailing
out from the line more towards the land in order to surround
the enemy, in the hollow and recess of the harbour, and killed
him and destroyed the ships accompanying him; after which
they now chased the whole Athenian fleet before them and
drove them ashore.

Gylippus seeing the enemy's fleet defeated and carried
ashore beyond their stockades and camp, ran down to the
breakwater with some of his troops, in order to cut off the
men as they landed and make it easier for the Syracusans to
tow off the vessels by the shore being friendly ground. The
Tyrrhenians who guarded this point for the Athenians seeing
them come on in disorder, advanced out against them and attacked and routed their van, hurling it into the marsh of
Lysimeleia. Afterwards the Syracusan and allied troops arrived in greater numbers, and the Athenians fearing for their
ships came up also to the rescue and engaged them, and defeated and pursued them to some distance and killed a few
of their heavy infantry. They succeeded in rescuing most of
their ships and brought them down by their camp; eighteen
however were taken by the Syracusans and their allies, and
all the men killed. The rest the enemy tried to burn by means
of an old merchantman which they filled with faggots and
pine-wood. set on fire and let drift down the wind which blew
full on the Athenians. The Athenians, however, alarmed for
their ships, contrived means for stopping it and putting it

out, and checking the flames and the nearer approach of the merchantman, thus escaped the danger.

After this the Syracusans set up a trophy for the sea-fight and for the heavy infantry whom they had cut off up at the lines, where they took the horses; and the Athenians for the rout of the foot driven by the Tyrrhenians into the marsh, and for their own victory with the rest of the army.

The Syracusans had now gained a decisive victory at sea, where until now they had feared the reinforcement brought by Demosthenes, and deep, in consequence, was the despondency of the Athenians, and great their disappointment, and greater still their regret for having come on the expedition. These were the only cities that they had yet encountered, similar to their own in character, under democracies like themselves, which had ships and horses, and were of considerable magnitude. They had been unable to divide and bring them over by holding out the prospect of changes in their governments, or to crush them by their great superiority in force, but had failed in most of their attempts, and being already in perplexity, had now been defeated at sea, where defeat could never have been expected, and were thus plunged deeper in embarrassment than ever.

Meanwhile the Syracusans immediately began to sail freely along the harbour, and determined to close up its mouth, so that the Athenians might not be able to steal out in future, even if they wished. Indeed, the Syracusans no longer thought only of saving themselves, but also how to hinder the escape of the enemy; thinking, and thinking rightly, that they were now much the strongest, and that to conquer the Athenians and their allies by land and sea would win them great glory in Hellas. The rest of the Hellenes would thus immediately be either freed or released from apprehension, as the remaining forces of Athens would be henceforth unable to sustain the war that would be waged against her; while they, the Syracusans, would be regarded as the authors of this deliverance, and would be held in high admiration, not only with all men now living but also with posterity. Nor were these the only considerations that gave dignity to the struggle. They would thus conquer not only the Athenians but also their numerous allies, and conquer not alone, but with their companions-in-

arms, commanding side by side with the Corinthians and Lacedæmonians, having offered their city to stand in the van of
danger, and having been in a great measure the pioneers of
naval success.

Indeed, there were never so many peoples assembled before
a single city, if we except the grand total gathered together
in this war under Athens and Lacedæmon. The following were
the states on either side who came to Syracuse to fight for or
against Sicily, to help to conquer or defend the island. Right
or community of blood was not the bond of union between
them, so much as interest or compulsion as the case might be.
The Athenians themselves being Ionians went against the
Dorians of Syracuse of their own free will; and the peoples
still speaking Attic and using the Athenian laws, the Lemnians,
Imbrians, and Æginetans, that is to say, the then occupants
of Ægina, being their colonists, went with them. To these must
be also added the Hestiæans dwelling at Hestiæa in Eubœa.
Of the rest some joined in the expedition as subjects of the
Athenians, others as independent allies, others as mercenaries.
To the number of the subjects paying tribute belonged the
Eretrians, Chalcidians, Styrians, and Carystians from
Eubœa; the Ceans, Andrians, and Tenians from the islands;
and the Milesians, Samians, and Chians from Ionia. The
Chians, however, joined as independent allies, paying no
tribute, but furnishing ships. Most of these were Ionians and
descended from the Athenians, except the Carystians, who are
Dryopes, and although subjects and obliged to serve, were
still Ionians fighting against Dorians. Besides these there were
men of Æolic race, the Methymnians, subjects who provided
ships, not tribute, and the Tenedians and Ænians who paid
tribute. These Æolians fought against their Æolian founders,
the Bœotians in the Syracusan army, because they were
obliged, while the Platæans, the only native Bœotians opposed to Bœotians, did so upon a just quarrel. Of the Rhodians
and Cytherians, both Dorians, the latter, Lacedæmonian
colonists, fought in the Athenian ranks against their Lacedæmonian countrymen with Gylippus; while the Rhodians,
Argives by race, were compelled to bear arms against the
Dorian Syracusans and their own colonists, the Geloans,
serving with the Syracusans. Of the islanders round Pelopon-

nese, the Cephallenians and Zacynthians accompanied the Athenians as independent allies, although their insular position really left them little choice in the matter, owing to the maritime supremacy of Athens, while the Corcyræans, who were not only Dorians but Corinthians, were openly serving against Corinthians and Syracusans, although colonists of the former and of the same race as the latter, under colour of compulsion, but really out of free will through hatred of Corinth. The Messenians, as they are now called in Naupactus and from Pylos, then held by the Athenians, were taken with them to the war. There were also a few Megarian exiles, whose fate it was to be now fighting against the Megarian Selinuntines.

The engagement of the rest was more of a voluntary nature. It was less the league than hatred of the Lacedæmonians and the immediate private advantage of each individual that persuaded the Dorian Argives to join the Ionian Athenians in a war against Dorians; while the Mantineans and other Arcadian mercenaries, accustomed to go against the enemy pointed out to them at the moment, were led by interest to regard the Arcadians serving with the Corinthians as just as much their enemies as any others. The Cretans and Ætolians also served for hire, and the Cretans who had joined the Rhodians in founding Gela, thus came to consent to fight for pay against, instead of for, their colonists. There were also some Acarnanians paid to serve, although they came chiefly for love of Demosthenes and out of goodwill to the Athenians whose allies they were. These all lived on the Hellenic side of the Ionian gulf. Of the Italiots, there were the Thurians and Metapontines, dragged into the quarrel by the stern necessities of a time of revolution; of the Siceliots, the Naxians and the Catanians; and of the barbarians, the Egestæans, who called in the Athenians, most of the Sicels, and outside Sicily some Tyrrhenian enemies of Syracuse and Iapygian mercenaries.

Such were the peoples serving with the Athenians. Against these the Syracusans had the Camarinæans their neighbours, the Geolans who live next them, and then passing over the neutral Agrigentines, the Selinuntines settled on the farther side of the island. These inhabit the part of Sicily looking

towards Libya; the Himeræans came from the side towards
the Tyrrhenian sea, being the only Hellenic inhabitants in
that quarter, and the only people that came from thence
to the aid of the Syracusans. Of the Hellenes in Sicily the
above peoples joined in the war, all Dorians and independent,
and of the barbarians the Sicels only, that is to say, such
as did not go over to the Athenians. Of the Hellenes outside
Sicily there were the Lacedæmonians, who provided a Spartan
to take the command, and a force of Neodamodes or Freedmen, and of Helots; the Corinthians, who alone joined with
naval and land forces, with their Leucadian and Ambraciot
kinsmen; some mercenaries sent by Corinth from Arcadia;
some Sicyonians forced to serve, and from outside Peloponnese the Bœotians. In comparison, however, with these
foreign auxiliaries, the great Siceliot cities furnished more
in every department—numbers of heavy infantry, ships and
horses, and an immense multitude besides having been
brought together; while in comparison, again, one may say,
with all the rest put together, more was provided by the
Syracusans themselves, both from the greatness of the city
and from the fact that they were in the greatest danger.

Such were the auxiliaries brought together on either side,
all of which had by this time joined, neither party experiencing
any subsequent accession. It was no wonder, therefore, if
the Syracusans and their allies thought that it would win
them great glory if they could follow up their recent victory
in the sea-fight by the capture of the whole Athenian armada,
without letting it escape either by sea or by land. They
began at once to close up the Great Harbour by means of
boats, merchant vessels, and galleys moored broadside across
its mouth, which is nearly a mile wide, and made all their
other arrangements for the event of the Athenians again venturing to fight at sea. There was, in fact, nothing little either
in their plans or their ideas.

The Athenians, seeing them closing up the harbour and
informed of their further designs, called a council of war.
The generals and colonels assembled and discussed the difficulties of the situation; the point which pressed most being
that they no longer had provisions for immediate use (having
sent on to Catana to tell them not to send any, in the belief

that they were going away), and that they would not have any in future unless they could command the sea. They therefore determined to evacuate their upper lines, to enclose with a cross-wall and garrison a small space close to the ships, only just sufficient to hold their stores and sick, and manning all the ships, seaworthy or not, with every man that could be spared from the rest of their land forces, to fight it out at sea, and if victorious, to go to Catana, if not, to burn their vessels, form in close order, and retreat by land for the nearest friendly place they could reach, Hellenic or barbarian. This was no sooner settled than carried into effect: they descended gradually from the upper lines and manned all their vessels, compelling all to go on board who were of age to be in any way of use. They thus succeeded in manning about one hundred and ten ships in all, on board of which they embarked a number of archers and darters taken from the Acarnanians and from the other foreigners, making all other provisions allowed by the nature of their plan and by the necessities which imposed it. All was now nearly ready, and Nicias, seeing the soldiery disheartened by their unprecedented and decided defeat at sea, and by reason of the scarcity of provisions eager to fight it out as soon as possible, called them all together, and first addressed them speaking as follows:—

'Soldiers of the Athenians and of the allies, we have all an equal interest in the coming struggle, in which life and country are at stake for us quite as much as they can be for the enemy; since if our fleet wins the day, each can see his native city again, wherever that city may be. You must not lose heart, or be like men without any experience, who fail in a first essay, and ever afterwards fearfully forebode a future as disastrous. But let the Athenians among you who have already had experience of many wars, and the allies who have joined us in so many expeditions, remember the surprises of war, and with the hope that fortune will not be always against us, prepare to fight again in a manner worthy of the number which you see yourselves to be.

'Now, whatever we thought would be of service against the crush of vessels in such a narrow harbour, and against the force upon the decks of the enemy, from which we suffered before, has all been considered with the helmsmen, and, as far as our means allowed, provided. A number of archers and darters will go on board, and a multitude that we should not have employed in an action in the open sea, where our science would be crippled by the weight of the vessels; but in the present land-fight that we are forced to make from shipboard all this will be useful. We have also discovered the changes in construction that we must make to meet theirs; and against the thickness of their cheeks, which did us the greatest mischief, we have provided grappling-irons, which will prevent an assailant backing water after charging, if the soldiers on deck here do their duty; since we are absolutely compelled to fight a land battle from the fleet, and it seems to be our interest neither to back water ourselves, nor to let the enemy do so, especially as the shore, except so much of it as may be held by our troops, is hostile ground.

'You must remember this and fight on as long as you can, and must not let yourselves be driven ashore, but once alongside must make up your minds not to part company until you have swept the heavy infantry from the enemy's deck. I say this more for the heavy infantry than for the seamen, as it is more the business of the men on deck; and our land forces are even now on the whole the strongest. The sailors I advise, and at the same time implore, not to be too much daunted by their misfortunes, now that we have our decks better armed and a greater number of vessels. Bear in mind how well worth preserving is the pleasure felt by those of you who through your knowledge of our language and imitation of our manners were always considered Athenians, even though not so in reality, and as such were honoured throughout Hellas, and had your full share of the advantages of our empire, and more than your share in the respect of our subjects and in protection from ill treatment. You, therefore, with whom alone we freely share our empire, we now justly require not to betray that empire in its extremity, and in scorn of Corinthians, whom you have often conquered, and of Siceliots, none of whom so much as presumed to stand against us when our navy was in its prime, we ask you to repel them, and to show that even in sickness and disaster your skill is more than a match for the fortune and vigour of any other.

'For the Athenians among you I add once more this reflexion:—you left behind you no more such ships in your docks as these, no more heavy infantry in their flower; if you do aught but conquer, our enemies here will immediately sail thither, and those that are left of us at Athens will become unable to repel their home assailants, reinforced by these new allies. Here you will fall at once into the hands of the Syracusans—I need not remind you of the intentions with which you attacked them—and your countrymen at home will fall into those of the Lacedæmonians. Since the fate of both thus hangs upon this single battle—now, if ever, stand firm, and remember, each and all, that you who are now going on board are the army and navy of the Athenians, and all that is left of the state and the great name of Athens, in whose defence if any man has any advantage in skill or courage, now is the time for him to show it, and thus serve himself and save all.'

After this address Nicias at once gave orders to man the ships. Meanwhile Gylippus and the Syracusans could perceive by the preparations which they saw going on that the Athenians meant to fight at sea. They had also notice of the grappling-irons, against which they specially provided by stretching hides over the prows and much of the upper part of their vessels, in order that the irons when thrown might slip off without taking hold. All being now ready, the generals and Gylippus addressed them in the following terms:—

'Syracusans and allies, the glorious character of our past achievements and the no less glorious results at issue in the coming battle are, we think, understood by most of you, or you would never have thrown yourselves with such ardour into the struggle; and if there be any one not as fully aware of the facts as he ought to be, we will declare them to him. The Athenians came to this country first to effect the conquest of Sicily, and after that, if successful, of Peloponnese and the rest of Hellas, possessing already the greatest empire yet known, of present or former times, among the Hellenes. Here for the first time they found in you men who faced their navy which made them masters everywhere; you have already defeated them in the previous sea-fight, and will in all likelihood defeat them again now. When men are once checked in what they consider their special excellence, their whole opinion of themselves suffers more than if they had not at first believed in their superiority, the unexpected shock to their pride causing them to give way more than their real strength warrants; and this is probably now the case with the Athenians.

'With us it is different. The original estimate of ourselves which gave us courage in the days of our unskilfulness has been strengthened, while the convictions super-added to it that we must be the best seamen of the time, if we have conquered the best, has given a double measure of hope to every man among us; and, for the most part, where there is the greatest hope, there is also the greatest ardour for action. The means to combat us which they have tried to find in copying our armament are familiar to our warfare, and will be met by proper provisions; while they will never be able to have a number of heavy infantry on their decks, contrary to their custom, and a number of darters (born landsmen, one may say, Acarnanians and others, embarked afloat, who will not know how to discharge their weapons when they have to keep still), without hampering their vessels and falling all into confusion among themselves through fighting not according to their own tactics. For they will gain nothing by the number of their ships—I say this to those of you who may be alarmed by having to fight against odds—as a quantity of ships in a confined space will only be slower in executing the movements required, and most exposed to injury from our means of offence. Indeed, if you would know the plain truth, as we are credibly informed, the excess of their sufferings and the necessities of their present distress have made them desperate; they have no confidence in their force, but wish to try their fortune in the only way they can, and either to force their passage and sail out, or after this to retreat by land, it being impossible for them to be worse off than they are.

'The fortune of our greatest enemies having thus betrayed tself, and their disorder being what I have described, let us engage in anger, convinced that, as between adversaries, nothing is more legitimate than to claim to sate the whole wrath of one's soul in punishing the aggressor, and nothing more sweet, as the proverb has it, than the vengeance upon an enemy, which it will now be ours to take. That enemies they are and mortal enemies you all know, since they came here to enslave our country, and if successful had in reserve for our men all that is most dreadful, and for our children and wives all that is most dishonourable, and for the whole city the name which conveys the greatest reproach. None should therefore relent or think it gain if they go away without further danger to us. This they will do just the same, even if they get the victory; while if we succeed, as we may expect, in chastising them, and in handing down to all Sicily her ancient freedom strengthened and confirmed, we shall have achieved no mean triumph. And the rarest dangers are those in which failure brings little loss and success the greatest advantage.'

After the above address to the soldiers on their side, the Syracusan generals and Gylippus now perceived that the Athenians were manning their ships, and immediately proceeded to man their own also. Meanwhile Nicias, appalled by the position of affairs, realising the greatness and the nearness of the danger now that they were on the point of putting out from shore, and thinking, as men are apt to think in great crises, that when all has been done they have still something left to do, and when all has been said that they have not yet said enough, again called on the captains one by one, addressing each by his father's name and by his own, and by that of his tribe, and adjured them not to belie their own personal renown, or to obscure the hereditary virtues for which their ancestors were illustrious; he reminded them of their country, the freest of the free, and of the unfettered discretion allowed in it to all to live as they pleased; and added other arguments such as men would use at such a crisis, and which, with little alteration, are made to serve on all occasions alike—appeals to wives, children, and national gods,—without caring whether they are thought commonplace, but loudly invoking them in the belief that they will be of use in the consternation of the moment. Having thus admonished them, not, he felt, as he would, but as he could, Nicias withdrew and led the troops to the sea, and ranged them in as long a line as he was able, in order to aid as far as possible in sustaining the courage of the men afloat; while Demosthenes, Menander, and Euthydemus, who took the command on board, put out from their own camp and sailed straight to the barrier across the mouth of the harbour and to the passage left open, to try to force their way out.

The Syracusans and their allies had already put out with about the same number of ships as before, a part of which kept guard at the outlet, and the remainder all round the rest of the harbour, in order to attack the Athenians on all sides at once; while the land forces held themselves in readiness at the points at which the vessels might put into the shore. The Syracusan fleet was commanded by Sicanus and Agatharchus, who had each a wing of the whole force, with Pythen and the Corinthians in the centre. When the rest of the Athenians came up to the barrier, with the first shock of their charge they overpowered the ships stationed there, and tried to undo the fastenings; after this, as the Syracusans and allies bore down upon them from all quarters, the action spread from the barrier over the whole harbour, and was more obstinately disputed than any of the preceding ones. On either side the rowers showed great zeal in bringing up their vessels at the boatswains' orders, and the helmsmen great skill in manœuvring, and great emulation one with another; while the ships once alongside, the soldiers on board did their best not to let the service on deck be outdone by the others; in short, every man strove to prove himself the first in his particular department. And as many ships were engaged in a small compass (for these were the largest fleets fighting in the narrowest space ever known, being together little short of two hundred), the regular attacks with the beak were few, there being no opportunity of backing water or of breaking the line; while the collisions caused by one ship chancing to run foul of another, either in flying from or attacking a third, were more frequent. So long as a vessel was coming up to the charge the men on the decks rained darts and arrows and stones upon her; but once alongside, the heavy infantry tried to board each other's vessel, fighting hand to hand.

In many quarters also it happened, by reason of the narrow room, that a vessel was charging an enemy on one side and being charged herself on another, and that two, or sometimes more ships had perforce got entangled round one, obliging the helmsmen to attend to defence here, offence there, not to one thing at once, but to many on all sides; while the huge din caused by the number of ships crashing together not only spread terror, but made the orders of the boatswains inaudible. The boatswains on either side in the discharge of their duty and in the heat of the conflict shouted incessantly orders and appeals to their men; the Athenians they urged to force the passage out, and now if ever to show their mettle and lay hold of a safe return to their country; to the Syracusans and their allies they cried that it would be glorious to prevent the escape of the enemy, and conquering, to exalt the countries that were theirs. The generals, moreover, on either side, if they saw any in any part of the battle backing ashore without being forced to do so, called out to the captain by name and asked him—the Athenians, whether they were retreating because they thought the thrice hostile shore more their own than that sea which had cost them so much labour to win; the Syracusans, whether they were flying from the flying Athenians, whom they well knew to be eager to escape in whatever way they could.

Meanwhile the two armies on shore, while victory hung in the balance, were a prey to the most agonising and conflicting emotions; the natives thirsting for more glory than they had already won, while the invaders feared to find themselves in even worse plight than before. The all of the Athenians being set upon their fleet, their fear for the event was like nothing they had ever felt; while their view of the struggle was necessarily as chequered as the battle itself. Close to the scene of action and not all looking at the same point at once, some saw their friends victorious and took courage, and fell to calling upon heaven not to deprive them of salvation, while others who had their eyes turned upon the losers, wailed and cried aloud, and, although spectators, were more overcome than the actual combatants. Others, again, were gazing at some spot where the battle was evenly disputed; as the strife was protracted without decision, their swaying bodies reflected the agitation of their minds, and they suffered the worst agony of all, ever just within reach of safety or just on the point of destruction. In short, in that one Athenian army as long as the sea-fight remained doubtful there was every sound to be heard at once, shrieks, cheers, 'We win,' 'We lose,' and all the other manifold exclamations that a great host would necessarily utter in great peril; and with the men in the fleet it was nearly the same; until at last the Syracusans and their allies, after the battle had lasted a long while, put the Athenians to flight, and with much shouting and cheering chased them in open rout to the shore. The naval force, one one way, one another, as many as were not taken afloat, now ran ashore and rushed from on board their ships to their camp; while the army, no more divided, but carried away by one impulse, all with shrieks and groans deplored the event, and ran down, some to help the ships, others to guard what was left of their wall, while the remaining and most numerous part already began to consider how they should save themselves. Indeed, the panic of the present moment had never been surpassed. They now suffered very nearly what they had inflicted at Pylos; as then the Lacedæmonians with the loss of their fleet lost also the men who had crossed over to the island, so now the Athenians had no hope of escaping by land, without the help of some extraordinary accident.

The sea-fight having been a severe one, and many ships and lives having been lost on both sides, the victorious Syracusans and their allies now picked up their wrecks and dead, and sailed off to the city and set up a trophy. The Athenians, overwhelmed by their misfortune, never even thought of asking leave to take up their dead or wrecks, but wished to retreat that very night. Demosthenes, however, went to Nicias and gave it as his opinion that they should man the ships they had left and make another effort to force their passage out next morning; saying that they had still left more ships fit for service than the enemy, the Athenians having about sixty remaining as against less than fifty of their opponents. Nicias was quite of his mind; but when they wished to man the vessels, the sailors refused to go on board, being so utterly overcome by their defeat as no longer to believe in the possibility of success.

Accordingly they all now made up their minds to retreat by land. Meanwhile the Syracusan Hermocrates suspecting their intention, and impressed by the danger of allowing a force of that magnitude to retire by land, establish itself in some other part of Sicily, and from thence renew the war, went and stated his views to the authorities, and pointed out to them that they ought not to let the enemy get away by night, but that all the Syracusans and their allies should at once march out and block up the roads and seize and guard the passes. The authorities were entirely of his opinion, and thought that it ought to be done, but on the other hand felt sure that the people, who had given themselves over to rejoicing and were taking their ease after a great battle at sea, would not be easily brought to obey; besides, they were celebrating a festival, having on that day a sacrifice to Heracles, and most of them in their rapture at the victory had fallen to drinking at the festival, and would probably consent to anything sooner than to take up their arms and march out at that moment. For these reasons the thing appeared impracticable to the magistrates; and Hermocrates, finding himself unable to do anything further with them, had now recourse to the following stratagem of his own. What he feared was that the Athenians might quietly get the start of them by passing the most difficult places during the night; and he therefore sent, as soon as it was dusk, some friends of his own to the camp with some horsemen who rode up within earshot and called out to some of the men, as though they were well-wishers of the Athenians, and told them to tell Nicias (who had in fact some correspondence who informed him of what went on inside the town), not to lead off the army by night as the Syracusans were guarding the roads, but to make his preparations at his leisure and to retreat by day. After saying this they departed; and their hearers informed the Athenian generals, who put off going for that night on the strength of this message, not doubting its sincerity.

Since after all they had not set out at once, they now determined to stay also the following day to give time to the soldiers to pack up as well as they could the most useful articles, and, leaving everything else behind, to start only with what was strictly necessary for their personal subsistence. Meanwhile the Syracusans and Gylippus marched out and blocked up the roads through the country by which the Athenians were likely to pass, and kept guard at the fords of the stream and rivers, posting themselves so as to receive them and stop the army where they thought best; while their fleet sailed up to the beach and towed off the ships of the Athenians. Some few were burned by the Athenians themselves as they had intended; the rest the Syracusans lashed on to their own at their leisure as they had been thrown up on shore, without any one trying to stop them, and conveyed to the town.

After this, Nicias and Demosthenes now thinking that enough had been done in the way of preparation, the removal of the army took place upon the second day after the sea-fight. It was a lamentable scene, not merely from the single circumstance that they were retreating after having lost all their ships, their great hopes gone, and themselves and the state in peril; but also in leaving the camp there were things most grievous for every eye and heart to contemplate. The dead lay unburied, and each man as he recognised a friend among them shuddered with grief and horror; while the living whom they were leaving behind, wounded or sick, were to the living far more shocking than the dead, and more to be pitied than those who had perished. These fell to entreating and bewailing until their friends knew not what to do, begging them to take them and loudly calling to each individual comrade or relative whom they could see, hanging upon the necks of their tent-fellows in the act of departure, and following as far as they could, and when their bodily strength failed them, calling again and again upon heaven and shrieking aloud as they were left behind. So that the whole army being filled with tears and distracted after this fashion found it not easy to go, even from an enemy's land, where they had already suffered evils too great for tears and in the unknown future before them feared to suffer more. Dejection and self-condemnation were also rife among them. Indeed they could only be compared to a starved-out town, and that no small one, escaping; the whole multitude upon the march being not less than forty thousand men. All carried anything they could which might be of use, and the heavy infantry and troopers, contrary to their wont, while under arms carried their own victuals, in some cases for want of servants, in others through not trusting them; as they had long been deserting and now did so in greater numbers than ever. Yet even thus they did not carry enough, as there was no longer food in the camp. Moreover their disgrace generally, and the universality of their sufferings, however to a certain extent alleviated by being borne in company, were still felt at the moment a heavy burden, especially when they contrasted the splendour and glory of their setting out with the humiliation in which it had ended. For this was by far the greatest reverse that ever befell an Hellenic army. They had come to enslave others, and were departing in fear of being enslaved themselves: they had sailed out with prayer and pæans, and now started to go back with omens directly contrary; travelling by land instead of by sea, and trusting not in their fleet but in their heavy infantry. Nevertheless the greatness of the danger still impending made all this appear tolerable.

Nicias seeing the army dejected and greatly altered, passed along the ranks and encouraged and comforted them as far as was possible under the circumstances, raising his voice still higher and higher as he went from one company to another in his earnestness, and in his anxiety that the benefit of his words might reach as many as possible:—

'Athenians and allies, even in our present position we must still hope on, since men have ere now been saved from worse straits than this; and you must not condemn yourselves too severely either because of your disasters or because of your present unmerited sufferings. I myself who am not superior to any of you in strength—indeed you see how I am in my sickness—and who in the gifts of fortune am, I think, whether in private life or otherwise, the equal of any, am now exposed to the same danger as the meanest among you; and yet my life has been one of much devotion towards the gods, and of much justice and without offence towards men. I have, therefore, still a strong hope for the future, and our misfortunes do not terrify me as much as they might. Indeed we may hope that they will be lightened: our enemies have had good fortune enough; and if any of the gods was offended at our

expedition, we have been already amply punished. Others
before us have attacked their neighbours and have done what
men will do without suffering more than they could bear;
and we may now justly expect to find the gods more kind,
for we have become fitter objects for their pity than their
jealousy. And then look at yourselves, mark the numbers and
efficiency of the heavy infantry marching in your ranks,
and do not give way too much to despondency, but reflect
that you are yourselves at once a city wherever you sit down,
and that there is no other in Sicily that could easily resist
your attack, or expel you when once established. The safety
and order of the march is for yourselves to look to; the one
thought of each man being that the spot on which he may
be forced to fight must be conquered and held as his country
and stronghold. Meanwhile we shall hasten on our way night
and day alike, as our provisions are scanty; and if we can
reach some friendly place of the Sicels, whom fear of the
Syracusans still keeps true to us, you may forthwith consider
yourselves safe. A message has been sent on to them with
directions to meet us with supplies of food. To sum up, be
convinced, soldiers, that you must be brave, as there is no
place near for your cowardice to take refuge in, and that
if you now escape from the enemy, you may all see again
what your hearts desire, while those of you who are Athenians
will raise up again the great power of the state, fallen though
it be. Men make the city and not walls or ships without men
in them.'

As he made this address, Nicias went along the ranks, and
brought back to their place any of the troops that he saw
straggling out of the line; while Demosthenes did as much
for his part of the army, addressing them in words very similar.
The army marched in a hollow square, the division under
Nicias leading, and that of Demosthenes following, the heavy
infantry being outside and the baggage-carriers and the bulk
of the army in the middle. When they arrived at the ford of
the river Anapus they there found drawn up a body of the
Syracusans and allies, and routing these, made good their
passage and pushed on, harassed by the charges of the Syracusan horse and by the missiles of their light troops. On that
day they advanced about four miles and a half, halting for

the night upon a certain hill. On the next they started early
and got on about two miles further, and descended into a
place in the plain and there encamped, in order to procure
some eatables from the houses, as the place was inhabited,
and to carry on with them water from thence, as for many
furlongs in front, in the direction in which they were going,
it was not plentiful. The Syracusans meanwhile went on and
fortified the pass in front, where there was a steep hill with a
rocky ravine on each side of it, called the Acræan cliff. The
next day the Athenians advancing found themselves impeded
by the missiles and charges of the horse and darters, both
very numerous, of the Syracusans and allies; and after fighting for a long while, at length retired to the same camp, where
they had no longer provisions as before, it being impossible
to leave their position by reason of the cavalry.

Early next morning they started afresh and forced their
way to the hill, which had been fortified, where they found
before them the enemy's infantry drawn up many shields
deep to defend the fortification, the pass being narrow. The
Athenians assaulted the work, but were greeted by a storm
of missiles from the hill, which told with the greater effect
through its being a steep one, and unable to force the passage,
retreated again and rested. Meanwhile occurred some claps of
thunder and rain, as often happens towards autumn, which
still further disheartened the Athenians, who thought all these
things to be omens of their approaching ruin. While they were
resting Gylippus and the Syracusans sent a part of their
army to throw up works in their rear on the way by which
they had advanced; however, the Athenians immediately sent
some of their men and prevented them; after which they
retreated more towards the plain and halted for the night.
When they advanced the next day the Syracusans surrounded
and attacked them on every side, and disabled many of them,
falling back if the Athenians advanced and coming on if they
retired, and in particular assaulting their rear, in the hope
of routing them in detail, and thus striking a panic into the
whole army. For a long while the Athenians persevered in this
fashion, but after advancing for four or five furlongs halted
to rest in the plain, the Syracusans also withdrawing to their
own camp.

During the night Nicias and Demosthenes, seeing the wretched condition of their troops, now in want of every kind of necessary, and numbers of them disabled in the numerous attacks of the enemy, determined to light as many fires as possible, and to lead off the army, no longer by the same route as they had intended, but towards the sea in the opposite direction to that guarded by the Syracusans. The whole of this route was leading the army not to Catana but to the other side of Sicily, towards Camarina, Gela, and the other Hellenic and barbarian towns in that quarter. They accordingly lit a number of fires and set out by night. Now all armies, and the greatest most of all, are liable to fears and alarms, especially when they are marching by night through an enemy's country and with the enemy near; and the Athenians falling into one of these panics, the leading division, that of Nicias, kept together and got on a good way in front, while that of Demosthenes, comprising rather more than half the army, got separated and marched on in some disorder. By morning, however, they reached the sea, and getting into the Helorine Road, pushed on in order to reach the river Cacyparis, and to follow the stream up through the interior, where they hoped to be met by the Sicels whom they had sent for. Arrived at the river, they found there also a Syracusan party engaged in barring the passage of the ford with a wall and a palisade, and forcing this guard, crossed the river and went on to another called the Erineus, according to the advice of their guides.

Meanwhile, when day came and the Syracusans and allies found that the Athenians were gone, most of them accused Gylippus of having let them escape on purpose, and hastily pursuing by the road which they had no difficulty in finding that they had taken, overtook them about dinner-time. They first came up with the troops under Demosthenes, who were behind and marching somewhat slowly and in disorder, owing to the night-panic above referred to, and at once attacked and engaged them, the Syracusan horse surrounding them with more ease now that they were separated from the rest, and hemming them in on one spot. The division of Nicias was five or six miles on in front, as he led them more rapidly, thinking that under the circumstances their safety lay not in staying and fighting, unless obliged, but in retreating as fast as possible, and only fighting when forced to do so. On the other hand, Demosthenes was, generally speaking, harassed more incessantly, as his post in the rear left him the first exposed to the attacks of the enemy; and now, finding that the Syracusans were in pursuit, he omitted to push on, in order to form his men for battle, and so lingered until he was surrounded by his pursuers and himself and the Athenians with him placed in the most distressing position, being huddled into an enclosure with a wall all round it, a road on this side and on that, and olive-trees in great number, where missiles were showered in upon them from every quarter. This mode of attack the Syracusans had with good reason adopted in preference to fighting at close quarters, as to risk a struggle with desperate men was now more for the advantage of the Athenians than for their own; besides, their success had now become so certain that they began to spare themselves a little in order not to be cut off in the moment of victory, thinking too that, as it was, they would be able in this way to subdue and capture the enemy.

In fact, after plying the Athenians and allies all day long from every side with missiles, they at length saw that they were worn out with their wounds and other sufferings; and Gylippus and the Syracusans and their allies made a proclamation, offering their liberty to any of the islanders who chose to come over to them; and some few cities went over. Afterwards a capitulation was agreed upon for all the rest with Demosthenes, to lay down their arms on condition that no one was to be put to death either by violence or imprisonment or want of the necessaries of life. Upon this they surrendered to the number of six thousand in all, laying down all the money in their possession, which filled the hollows of four shields, and were immediately conveyed by the Syracusans to the town.

Meanwhile Nicias with his division arrived that day at the river Erineus, crossed over and posted his army upon some high ground upon the other side. The next day the Syracusans overtook him and told him that the troops under Demosthenes had surrendered, and invited him to follow their example. Incredulous of the fact, Nicias asked for a truce to send a horseman to see, and upon the return of the messenger with the tidings that they had surrendered, sent a herald to Gylippus and the Syracusans, saying that he was ready to agree with them on behalf of the Athenians to repay whatever money the Syracusans had spent upon the war if they would let his army go; and offered until the money was paid to give Athenians as hostages, one for every talent. The Syracusans and Gylippus rejected this proposition, and attacked this division as they had the other, standing all round and plying them with missiles until the evening. Food and necessaries were as miserably wanting to the troops of Nicias as they had been to their comrades; nevertheless they watched for the quiet of the night to resume their march. But as they were taking up their arms the Syracusans perceived it and raised their pæan, upon which the Athenians, finding that they were discovered, laid them down again, except about three hundred men who forced their way through the guards and went on during the night as they were able.

As soon as it was day Nicias put his army in motion, pressed, as before, by the Syracusans and their allies, pelted from every side by their missiles, and struck down by their javelins. The Athenians pushed on for the Assinarus, impelled by the attacks made upon them from every side by a numerous cavalry and the swarm of other arms, fancying that they should breathe more freely if once across the river, and driven on also by their exhaustion and craving for water. Once there they rushed in, and all order was at an end, each man wanting to cross first, and the attacks of the enemy making it difficult to cross at all; forced to huddle together, they fell against and trod down one another, some dying immediately upon the javelins, others getting entangled together and stumbling over the articles of baggage, without being able to rise again. Meanwhile the opposite bank, which was steep, was lined by the Syracusans, who showered missiles down upon the Athenians, most of them drinking greedily and heaped together in disorder in the hollow bed of the river. The Peloponnesians also came down and butchered them, especially those in the water, which was thus immediately spoiled, but which they went on drinking just the same, mud and all, bloody as it was, most even fighting to have it.

At last, when many dead now lay piled one upon another in the stream, and part of the army had been destroyed at the river, and the few that escaped from thence cut off by the cavalry, Nicias surrendered himself to Gylippus, whom he trusted more than he did the Syracusans, and told him and the Lacedæmonians to do what they liked with him, but to stop the slaughter of the soldiers. Gylippus, after this, immediately gave orders to make prisoners; upon which the rest were brought together alive, except a large number secreted by the soldiery, and a party was sent in pursuit of the three hundred who had got through the guard during the night, and who were now taken with the rest. The number of the enemy collected as public property was not considerable; but that secreted was very large, and all Sicily was filled with them, no convention having been made in their case as for those taken with Demosthenes. Besides this, a large portion were killed outright, the carnage being very great, and not exceeded by any in this Sicilian war. In the numerous other encounters upon the march, not a few also had fallen. Nevertheless many escaped, some at the moment, others served as slaves, and then ran away subsequently. These found refuge at Catana.

The Syracusans and their allies now mustered and took up the spoils and as many prisoners as they could, and went back to the city. The rest of their Athenian and allied captives were deposited in the quarries, this seeming the safest way of keeping them; but Nicias and Demosthenes were butchered, against the will of Gylippus, who thought that it would be the crown of his triumph if he could take the enemy's generals to Lacedæmon. One of them, as it happened, Demosthenes, was one of her greatest enemies, on account of the affair of the island and of Pylos; while the other, Nicias, was for the same reasons one of her greatest friends, owing to his exertions to procure the release of the prisoners by persuading the Athenians to make peace. For these reasons the Lacedæmonians felt kindly towards him; and it was in this that Nicias himself mainly confided when he surrendered to Gylippus. But some of the Syracusans who had been in correspondence with him were afraid, it was said, of his being put to the torture and troubling their success by his revelations:

others, especially the Corinthians, of his escaping, as he was wealthy, by means of bribes, and living to do them further mischief; and these persuaded the allies and put him to death. This or the like was the cause of the death of a man who, of all the Hellenes in my time, least deserved such a fate, seeing that the whole course of his life had been regulated with strict attention to virtue.

The prisoners in the quarries were at first hardly treated by the Syracusans. Crowded in a narrow hole, without any roof to cover them, the heat of the sun and the stifling closeness of the air tormented them during the day, and then the nights, which came on autumnal and chilly, made them ill by the violence of the change; besides, as they had to do everything in the same place for want of room, and the bodies of those who died of their wounds or from the variation in the temperature, or from similar causes, were left heaped together one upon another, intolerable stenches arose; while hunger and thirst never ceased to afflict them, each man during eight months having only half a pint of water and a pint of corn given him daily. In short, no single suffering to be apprehended by men thrust into such a place was spared them. For some seventy days they thus lived all together, after which all, except the Athenians and any Siceliots or Italiots who had joined in the expedition, were sold. The total number of prisoners taken it would be difficult to state exactly, but it could not have been less than seven thousand.

This was the greatest Hellenic achievement of any in this war, or, in my opinion, in Hellenic history; at once most glorious to the victors, and most calamitous to the conquered. They were beaten at all points and altogether; all that they suffered was great; they were destroyed, as the saying is, with a total destruction, their fleet, their army—everything was destroyed, and few out of many returned home.

BOOK VIII

CHAPTER XXIV

NINETEENTH AND TWENTIETH YEARS OF THE WAR—REVOLT
OF IONIA—INTERVENTION OF PERSIA—THE WAR IN IONIA

*B.C. 413: Athens learns of disaster—Revolt ascendant—General activity
—Lacedæmonian alliance with Chians and Erythræans—B.C. 412:
Council at Corinth—Peloponnesians sail for Chios—Blockade in
Spiræum—Alcibiades sails for Ionia—Athenian relief to Chios—
Alcibiades stirs Milesian revolt—Terms of Persian-Spartan al-
liance—Samian revolution—Lesbos recovered by Athenians—De-
feat of Chians—Phrynichus persuades Athenians to retreat
—Sacking of Iasus—Pay of Peloponnesian fleet—Astyochus at
Clazomenæ and Miletus—Second treaty with Persia—Siege of
Chios—Defeat of Athenian squadron—Tissaphernes offended.*

SUCH were the events in Sicily. When the news was brought
to Athens, for a long while they disbelieved even the most
respectable of the soldiers who had themselves escaped from
the scene of action and clearly reported the matter, a destruction so complete not being thought credible. When the conviction was forced upon them, they were angry with the
orators who had joined in promoting the expedition, just as if
they had not themselves voted it, and were enraged also with
the reciters of oracles and soothsayers, and all other omen-
mongers of the time who had encouraged them to hope that
they should conquer Sicily. Already distressed at all points
and in all quarters, after what had now happened, they were
seized by a fear and consternation quite without example. It
was grievous enough for the state and for every man in his
proper person to lose so many heavy infantry, cavalry, and
able-bodied troops, and to see none left to replace them; but
when they saw, also, that they had not sufficient ships in their
docks, or money in the treasury, or crews for the ships, they
began to despair of salvation. They thought that their enemies
in Sicily would immediately sail with their fleet against

Piræus, inflamed by so signal a victory; while their adversaries at home, redoubling all their preparations, would vigorously attack them by sea and land at once, aided by their own revolted confederates. Nevertheless, with such means as they had, it was determined to resist to the last, and to provide timber and money, and to equip a fleet as they best could, to take steps to secure their confederates and above all Eubœa, to reform things in the city upon a more economical footing, and to elect a board of elders to advise upon the state of affairs as occasion should arise. In short, as is the way of a democracy, in the panic of the moment they were ready to be as prudent as possible.

These resolves were at once carried into effect. Summer was now over. The winter ensuing saw all Hellas stirring under the impression of the great Athenian disaster in Sicily. Neutrals now felt that even if uninvited they ought no longer to stand aloof from the war, but should volunteer to march against the Athenians, who, as they severally reflected, would probably have come against them if the Sicilian campaign had succeeded. Besides, they considered that the war would now be short, and that it would be creditable for them to take part in it. Meanwhile the allies of the Lacedæmonians felt all more anxious than ever to see a speedy end to their heavy labours. But above all, the subjects of the Athenians showed a readiness to revolt even beyond their ability, judging the circumstances with passion, and refusing even to hear of the Athenians being able to last out the coming summer. Beyond all this, Lacedæmon was encouraged by the near prospect of being joined in great force in the spring by her allies in Sicily, lately forced by events to acquire their navy. With these reasons for confidence in every quarter, the Lacedæmonians now resolved to throw themselves without reserve into the war, considering that, once it was happily terminated, they would be finally delivered from such dangers as that which would have threatened them from Athens, if she had become mistress of Sicily, and that the overthrow of the Athenians would leave them in quiet enjoyment of the supremacy over all Hellas.

Their king, Agis, accordingly set out at once during this winter with some troops from Decelea, and levied from the

allies contributions for the fleet, and turning towards the
Malian gulf exacted a sum of money from the Œtæans by
carrying off most of their cattle in reprisal for their old hostility, and, in spite of the protests and opposition of the
Thessalians, forced the Achæans of Phthiotis and the other
subjects of the Thessalians in those parts to give him money
and hostages, and deposited the hostages at Corinth, and
tried to bring their countrymen into the confederacy. The
Lacedæmonians now issued a requisition to the cities for
building a hundred ships, fixing their own quota and that of
the Bœotians at twenty-five each; that of the Phocians and
Locrians together at fifteen; that of the Corinthians at fifteen;
that of the Arcadians, Pellenians, and Sicyonians together at
ten; and that of the Megarians, Trœzenians, Epidaurians, and
Hermionians together at ten also; and meanwhile made every
other preparation for commencing hostilities by the spring.

In the meantime the Athenians were not idle. During this
same winter, as they had determined, they contributed timber
and pushed on their ship-building, and fortified Sunium to
enable their corn-ships to round it in safety, and evacuated
the fort in Laconia which they had built on their way to
Sicily; while they also, for economy, cut down any other expenses that seemed unnecessary, and above all kept a careful
look-out against the revolt of their confederates.

While both parties were thus engaged, and were as intent
upon preparing for the war as they had been at the outset,
the Eubœans first of all sent envoys during this winter to Agis
to treat of their revolting from Athens. Agis accepted their
proposals, and sent for Alcamenes, son of Sthenelaïdas, and
Melanthus from Lacedæmon, to take the command in Eubœa.
These accordingly arrived with some three hundred Neodamodes, and Agis began to arrange for their crossing over.
But in the meanwhile arrived some Lesbians, who also wished
to revolt; and these being supported by the Bœotians, Agis
was persuaded to defer acting in the matter of Eubœa, and
made arrangements for the revolt of the Lesbians, giving
them Alcamenes, who was to have sailed to Eubœa, as governor, and himself promising them ten ships, and the Bœotians the same number. All this was done without instructions
from home, as Agis while at Decelea with the army that he

commanded had power to send troops to whatever quarter he pleased, and to levy men and money. During this period, one might say, the allies obeyed him much more than they did the Lacedæmonians in the city, as the force he had with him made him feared at once wherever he went. While Agis was engaged with the Lesbians, the Chians and Erythræans, who were also ready to revolt, applied, not to him but at Lacedæmon; where they arrived accompanied by an ambassador from Tissaphernes, the commander of King Darius, son of Artaxerxes, in the maritime districts, who invited the Peloponnesians to come over, and promised to maintain their army. The king had lately called upon him for the tribute from his government, for which he was in arrears, being unable to raise it from the Hellenic towns by reason of the Athenians; and he therefore calculated that by weakening the Athenians he should get the tribute better paid, and should also draw the Lacedæmonians into alliance with the king; and by this means, as the king had commanded him, take alive or dead Amorges, the bastard son of Pissuthnes, who was in rebellion on the coast of Caria.

While the Chians and Tissaphernes thus joined to effect the same object, about the same time Calligeitus, son of Laophon, a Megarian, and Timagoras, son of Athenagoras, a Cyzicene, both of them exiles from their country and living at the court of Pharnabazus, son of Pharnaces, arrived at Lacedæmon upon a mission from Pharnabazus, to procure a fleet for the Hellespont; by means of which, if possible, he might himself effect the object of Tissaphernes' ambition, and cause the cities in his government to revolt from the Athenians, and so get the tribute, and by his own agency obtain for the king the alliance of the Lacedæmonians.

The emissaries of Pharnabazus and Tissaphernes treating apart, a keen competition now ensued at Lacedæmon as to whether a fleet and army should be sent first to Ionia and Chios, or to the Hellespont. The Lacedæmonians, however, decidedly favoured the Chians and Tissaphernes, who were seconded by Alcibiades, the family friend of Endius, one of the Ephors for that year. Indeed, this is how their house got its Laconic name, Alcibiades being the family name of Endius. Nevertheless the Lacedæmonians first sent to Chios Phrynis, one of the Perioeci, to see whether they had as many ships as they said, and whether their city generally was as great as was reported; and upon his bringing word that they had been told the truth, immediately entered into alliance with the Chians and Erythræans, and voted to send them forty ships, there being already, according to the statement of the Chians, not less than sixty in the island. At first the Lacedæmonians meant to send ten of these forty themselves, with Melanchridas their admiral; but afterwards, an earthquake having occurred, they sent Chalcideus instead of Melanchridas, and instead of the ten ships equipped only five in Laconia. And the winter ended, and with it ended also the nineteenth year of this war of which Thucydides is the historian.

At the beginning of the next summer the Chians were urging that the fleet should be sent off, being afraid that the Athenians, from whom all these embassies were kept a secret, might find out what was going on, and the Lacedæmonians at once sent three Spartans to Corinth to haul the ships as quickly as possible across the Isthmus from the other sea to that on the side of Athens, and to order them all to sail to Chios, those which Agis was equipping for Lesbos not excepted. The number of ships from the allied states was thirty-nine in all.

Meanwhile Calligeitus and Timagoras did not join on behalf of Pharnabazus in the expedition to Chios or give the money—twenty-five talents—which they had brought with them to help in despatching a force, but determined to sail afterwards with another force by themselves. Agis, on the other hand, seeing the Lacedæmonians bent upon going to Chios first, himself came in to their views; and the allies assembled at Corinth and held a council, in which they decided to sail first to Chios under the command of Chalcideus, who was equipping the five vessels in Laconia, then to Lesbos, under the command of Alcamenes, the same whom Agis had fixed upon, and lastly to go to the Hellespont, where the command was given to Clearchus, son of Ramphias. Meanwhile they would take only half the ships across the Isthmus first, and let those sail off at once, in order that the Athenians might attend less to the departing squadron than to those to be taken across afterwards, as no care had been taken to keep this voyage secret through contempt of the impotence of the Athenians, who had as yet no fleet of any account upon the sea. Agreeably to this determination twenty-one vessels were at once conveyed across the Isthmus.

They were now impatient to set sail, but the Corinthians were not willing to accompany them until they had celebrated the Isthmian festival, which fell at that time. Upon this Agis proposed to them to save their scruples about breaking the Isthmian truce by taking the expedition upon himself. The Corinthians not consenting to this, a delay ensued, during which the Athenians conceived suspicions of what was preparing at Chios, and sent Aristocrates, one of their generals, and charged them with the fact, and upon the denial of the Chians, ordered them to send with them a contingent of ships, as faithful confederates. Seven were sent accordingly. The reason of the despatch of the ships lay in the fact that the mass of the Chians were not privy to the negotiations, while the few who were in the secret did not wish to break with the multitude until they had something positive to lean upon, and no longer expected the Peloponnesians to arrive by reason of their delay.

In the meantime the Isthmian games took place, and the Athenians, who had been also invited, went to attend them, and now seeing more clearly into the designs of the Chians, as soon as they returned to Athens took measures to prevent the fleet putting out from Cenchreæ without their knowledge. After the festival the Peloponnesians set sail with twenty-one ships for Chios, under the command of Alcamenes. The Athenians first sailed against them with an equal number, drawing off towards the open sea. The enemy, however, turning back before he had followed them far, the Athenians returned also, not trusting the seven Chian ships which formed part of their number, and afterwards manned thirty-seven vessels in all and chased him on his passage along shore into Spiræum, a desert Corinthian port on the edge of the Epidaurian frontier. After losing one ship out at sea, the Peloponnesians got the rest together and brought them to anchor. The Athenians now attacked not only from the sea with their fleet, but also disembarked upon the coast; and a mêlée ensued of the most confused and violent kind, in which the

Athenians disabled most of the enemy's vessels and killed Alcamenes their commander, losing also a few of their own men.

After this they separated, and the Athenians, detaching a sufficient number of ships to blockade those of the enemy, anchored with the rest at the islet adjacent, upon which they proceeded to encamp, and sent to Athens for reinforcements; the Peloponnesians having been joined on the day after the battle by the Corinthians, who came to help the ships, and by the other inhabitants in the vicinity not long afterwards. These saw the difficulty of keeping guard in a desert place, and in their perplexity at first thought of burning the ships, but finally resolved to haul them up on shore and sit down and guard them with their land forces, until a convenient opportunity for escaping should present itself. Agis also, on being informed of the disaster, sent them a Spartan of the name of Thermon. The Lacedæmonians first received the news of the fleet having put out from the Isthmus, Alcamenes having been ordered by the Ephors to send off a horseman when this took place, and immediately resolved to despatch their own five vessels under Chalcideus, and Alcibiades with him. But while they were full of this resolution came the second news of the fleet having taken refuge in Spiræum; and disheartened at their first step in the Ionian war proving a failure, they laid aside the idea of sending the ships from their own country, and even wished to recall some that had already sailed.

Perceiving this, Alcibiades again persuaded Endius and the other Ephors to persevere in the expedition, saying that the voyage would be made before the Chians heard of the fleet's misfortune, and that as soon as he set foot in Ionia, he should, by assuring them of the weakness of the Athenians and the zeal of Lacedæmon, have no difficulty in persuading the cities to revolt, as they would readily believe his testimony. He also represented to Endius himself in private that it would be glorious for him to be the means of making Ionia revolt and the king become the ally of Lacedæmon, instead of that honour being left to Agis (Agis, it must be remembered, was the enemy of Alcibiades) ; and Endius and his colleagues thus persuaded, he put to sea with the five ships and the Lacedæmonian Chalcideus, and made all haste upon the voyage.

About this same time the sixteen Peloponnesian ships from Sicily, which had served through the war with Gylippus, were caught on their return off Leucadia and roughly handled by the twenty-seven Athenian vessels under Hippocles, son of Menippus, on the look-out for the ships from Sicily. After losing one of their number the rest escaped from the Athenians and sailed into Corinth.

Meanwhile Chalcideus and Alcibiades seized all they met with on their voyage, to prevent news of their coming, and let them go at Corycus, the first point which they touched at in the continent. Here they were visited by some of their Chian correspondents, and being urged by them to sail up to the town without announcing their coming, arrived suddenly before Chios. The many were amazed and confounded, while the few had so arranged that the council should be sitting at the time; and after speeches from Chalcideus and Alcibiades stating that many more ships were sailing up, but saying nothing of the fleet being blockaded in Spiræum, the Chians revolted from the Athenians, and the Erythræans immediately afterwards. After this three vessels sailed over to Clazomenæ, and made that city revolt also; and the Clazomenians immediately crossed over to the mainland and began to fortify Polichna, in order to retreat there, in case of necessity, from the island where they dwelt.

While the revolted places were all engaged in fortifying and preparing for the war, news of Chios speedily reached Athens. The Athenians thought the danger by which they were now menaced great and unmistakable, and that the rest of their allies would not consent to keep quiet after the secession of the greatest of their number. In the consternation of the moment they at once took off the penalty attaching to whoever proposed or put to the vote a proposal for using the thousand talents which they had jealously avoided touching throughout the whole war, and voted to employ them to man a large number of ships, and to send off at once under Strombichides, son of Diotimus, the eight vessels, forming part of the blockading fleet at Spiræum, which had left the blockade and had returned after pursuing and failing to overtake the vessels with Chalcideus. These were to be followed shortly afterwards by twelve more under Thrasycles, also taken from the blockade. They also recalled the seven Chian vessels, forming part of their squadron blockading the fleet in Spiræum, and giving the slaves on board their liberty, put the freemen in confinement, and speedily manned and sent out ten fresh ships to blockade the Peloponnesians in the place of all those that had departed, and decided to man thirty more. Zeal was not wanting, and no effort was spared to send relief to Chios.

In the meantime Strombichides with his eight ships arrived at Samos, and taking one Samian vessel, sailed to Teos and required them to remain quiet. Chalcideus also set sail with twenty-three ships for Teos from Chios, the land forces of the Clazomenians and Erythræans moving along shore to support him. Informed of this in time, Strombichides put out from Teos before their arrival, and while out at sea, seeing the number of the ships from Chios, fled towards Samos, chased by the enemy. The Teians at first would not receive the land forces, but upon the flight of the Athenians took them into the town. There they waited for some time for Chalcideus to return from the pursuit, and as time went on without his appearing, began themselves to demolish the wall which the Athenians had built on the land side of the city of the Teians, being assisted by a few of the barbarians who had come up under the command of Stages, the lieutenant of Tissaphernes.

Meanwhile Chalcideus and Alcibiades, after chasing Strombichides into Samos, armed the crews of the ships from Peloponnese and left them at Chios, and filling their places with substitutes from Chios and manning twenty others, sailed off to effect the revolt of Miletus. The wish of Alcibiades, who had friends among the leading men of the Milesians, was to bring over the town before the arrival of the ships from Peloponnese, and thus, by causing the revolt of as many cities as possible with the help of the Chian power and of Chalcideus, to secure the honour for the Chians and himself and Chalcideus, and, as he had promised, for Endius who had sent them out. Not discovered until their voyage was nearly completed, they arrived a little before Strombichides and Thrasycles (who had just come with twelve ships from Athens, and had joined Strombichides in pursuing them), and occasioned the revolt of Miletus. The Athenians sailing up

close on their heels with nineteen ships found Miletus closed
against them, and took up their station at the adjacent island
of Lade. The first alliance between the king and the Lacedæmonians was now concluded immediately upon the revolt of
the Milesians, by Tissaphernes and Chalcideus, and was as
follows:—

The Lacedæmonians and their allies made a treaty with the
king and Tissaphernes upon the terms following:—

1. *Whatever country or cities the king has, or the king's an-*
cestors had, shall be the king's; and whatever came in to the
Athenians from these cities, either money or any other thing,
the king and the Lacedæmonians and their allies shall jointly
hinder the Athenians from receiving either money or any
other thing.

2. *The war with the Athenians shall be carried on jointly*
by the king and by the Lacedæmonians and their allies; and
it shall not be lawful to make peace with the Athenians except
both agree, the king on his side and the Lacedæmonians and
their allies on theirs.

3. *If any revolt from the king they shall be the enemies of*
the Lacedæmonians and their allies. And if any revolt from
the Lacedæmonians and their allies they shall be the enemies
of the king in like manner.

This was the alliance. After this the Chians immediately
manned ten more vessels and sailed for Anaia, in order to
gain intelligence of those in Miletus, and also to make the
cities revolt. A message, however, reaching them from Chalcideus to tell them to go back again, and that Amorges was at
hand with an army by land, they sailed to the temple of Zeus,
and there sighting ten more ships sailing up with which
Diomedon had started from Athens after Thrasycles, fled,
one ship to Ephesus, the rest to Teos. The Athenians took
four of their ships empty, the men finding time to escape
ashore; the rest took refuge in the city of the Teians; after
which the Athenians sailed off to Samos, while the Chians put
to sea with their remaining vessels, accompanied by the land
forces, and caused Lebedos to revolt, and after it Eræ. After
this they both returned home, the fleet and the army.

About the same time the twenty ships of the Peloponnesians
in Spiræum, which we left chased to land and blockaded by

an equal number of Athenians, suddenly sallied out and defeated the blockading squadron, took four of their ships, and sailing back to Cenchreæ, prepared again for the voyage to Chios and Ionia. Here they were joined by Astyochus as high-admiral from Lacedæmon, henceforth invested with the supreme command at sea. The land forces now withdrawing from Teos, Tissaphernes repaired thither in person with an army and completed the demolition of anything that was left of the wall, and so departed. Not long after his departure Diomedon arrived with ten Athenian ships, and having made a convention by which the Teians admitted him as they had the enemy, coasted along to Eræ, and failing in an attempt upon the town, sailed back again.

About this time took place the rising of the commons at Samos against the upper classes, in concert with some Athenians, who were there in three vessels. The Samian commons put to death some two hundred in all of the upper classes, and banished four hundred more, and themselves took their land and houses; after which the Athenians decreed their independence, being now sure of their fidelity, and the commons henceforth governed the city, excluding the landholders from all share in affairs, and forbidding any of the commons to give his daughter in marriage to them or to take a wife from them in future.

After this, during the same summer, the Chians, whose zeal continued as active as ever, and who even without the Peloponnesians found themselves in sufficient force to effect the revolt of the cities and also wished to have as many companions in peril as possible, made an expedition with thirteen ships of their own to Lesbos; the instructions from Lacedæmon being to go to that island next, and from thence to the Hellespont. Meanwhile the land forces of the Peloponnesians who were with the Chians and of the allies on the spot, moved along shore for Clazomenæ and Cuma, under the command of Eualas, a Spartan; while the fleet under Diniades, one of the Periœci, first sailed up to Methymna and caused it to revolt, and, leaving four ships there, with the rest procured the revolt of Mityiene.

In the meantime Astyochus, the Lacedæmonian admiral, set sail from Cenchreæ with four ships, as he had intended, and

arrived at Chios. On the third day after his arrival the Athenian ships, twenty-five in number, sailed to Lesbos under
Diomedon and Leon, who had lately arrived with a reinforcement of ten ships from Athens. Late in the same day
Astyochus put to sea, and taking one Chian vessel with him
sailed to Lesbos to render what assistance he could. Arrived
at Pyrrha, and from thence the next day at Eresus, he there
learned that Mitylene had been taken, almost without a blow,
by the Athenians, who had sailed up and unexpectedly put
into the harbour, had beaten the Chian ships, and landing
and defeating the troops opposed to them, had become masters of the city. Informed of this by the Eresians and the
Chian ships, which had been left with Eubulus at Methymna,
and had fled upon the capture of Mitylene, and three of which
he now fell in with, one having been taken by the Athenians,
Astyochus did not go on to Mitylene, but raised and armed
Eresus, and sending the heavy infantry from his own ships
by land under Eteonicus to Antissa and Methymna, himself
proceeded along shore thither with the ships which he had
with him and with the three Chians, in the hope that the
Methymnians upon seeing them would be encouraged to persevere in their revolt. As, however, everything went against
him in Lesbos, he took up his own force and sailed back to
Chios; the land forces on board, which were to have gone to
the Hellespont, being also conveyed back to their different
cities. After this six of the allied Peloponnesian ships at Cenchreæ joined the forces at Chios. The Athenians, after restoring matters to their old state in Lesbos, set sail from
thence and took Polichna, the place that the Clazomenians
were fortifying on the continent, and carried the inhabitants
back to their town upon the island, except the authors of the
revolt, who withdrew to Daphnus; and thus Clazomenæ became once more Athenian.

The same summer the Athenians in the twenty ships at
Lade blockading Miletus, made a descent at Panormus in the
Milesian territory, and killed Chalcideus the Lacedæmonian
commander, who had come with a few men against them,
and the third day after sailed over and set up a trophy, which
as they were not masters of the country, was however pulled
down by the Milesians. Meanwhile Leon and Diomedon with

the Athenian fleet from Lesbos issuing from the Œnussæ, the isles off Chios, and from their forts of Sidussa and Pteleum in the Erythræid, and from Lesbos, carried on the war against the Chians from the ships, having on board heavy infantry from the rolls pressed to serve as marines. Landing in Cardamyle and in Bolissus they defeated with heavy loss the Chians that took the field against them, and laying desolate the places in that neighbourhood, defeated the Chians again in another battle at Phanæ, and in a third at Leuconium. After this the Chians ceased to meet them in the field, while the Athenians devastated the country, which was beautifully stocked and had remained uninjured ever since the Median wars. Indeed, after the Lacedæmonians, the Chians are the only people that I have known who knew how to be wise in prosperity, and who ordered their city the more securely the greater it grew. Nor was this revolt, in which they might seem to have erred on the side of rashness, ventured upon until they had numerous and gallant allies to share the danger with them, and until they perceived the Athenians after the Sicilian disaster themselves no longer denying the thoroughly desperate state of their affairs. And if they were thrown out by one of the surprises which upset human calculations, they found out their mistake in company with many others who believed, like them, in the speedy collapse of the Athenian power. While they were thus blockaded from the sea and plundered by land, some of the citizens undertook to bring the city over to the Athenians. Appraised of this the authorities took no action themselves, but brought Astyochus, the admiral, from Erythræ, with four ships that he had with him, and considered how they could most quietly, either by taking hostages or by some other means, put an end to the conspiracy.

While the Chians were thus engaged, a thousand Athenian heavy infantry and fifteen hundred Argives (five hundred of whom were light troops furnished with armour by the Athenians), and one thousand of the allies, towards the close of the same summer sailed from Athens in forty-eight ships, some of which were transports, under the command of Phrynichus, Onomacles, and Scironides, and putting in to Samos crossed over and encamped at Miletus. Upon this the Mile-

sians came out to the number of eight hundred heavy infantry, with the Peloponnesians who had come with Chalcideus
and some foreign mercenaries of Tissaphernes, Tissaphernes
himself and his cavalry, and engaged the Athenians and their
allies. While the Argives rushed forward on their own wing
with the careless disdain of men advancing against Ionians
who would never stand their charge, and were defeated by the
Milesians with a loss little short of three hundred men, the
Athenians first defeated the Peloponnesians, and driving before them the barbarians and the ruck of the army, without
engaging the Milesians, who after the rout of the Argives
retreated into the town upon seeing their comrades worsted,
crowned their victory by grounding their arms under the very
walls of Miletus. Thus, in this battle, the Ionians on both
sides overcame the Dorians, the Athenians defeating the
Peloponnesians opposed to them, and the Milesians the Argives. After setting up a trophy, the Athenians prepared to
draw a wall round the place, which stood upon an isthmus;
thinking that if they could gain Miletus, the other towns also
would easily come over to them.

Meanwhile about dusk tidings reached them that the fifty-
five ships from Peloponnese and Sicily might be instantly
expected. Of these the Siceliots, urged principally by the
Syracusan Hermocrates to join in giving the finishing blow to
the power of Athens, furnished twenty-two—twenty from
Syracuse, and two from Selinus; and the ships that we left
preparing in Peloponnese being now ready, both squadrons
had been entrusted to Therimenes, a Lacedæmonian, to take
to Astyochus, the admiral. They now put in first at Leros the
island off Miletus, and from thence, discovering that the
Athenians were before the town, sailed into the Iasic gulf, in
order to learn how matters stood at Miletus. Meanwhile Alcibiades came on horseback to Teichiussa in the Milesian territory, the point of the gulf in which they had put in for the
night, and told them of the battle, in which he had fought in
person by the side of the Milesians and Tissaphernes, and advised them, if they did not wish to sacrifice Ionia and their
cause, to fly to the relief of Miletus and hinder its investment.

Accordingly they resolved to relieve it the next morning.
Meanwhile Phrynichus, the Athenian commander, had re

ceived precise intelligence of the fleet from Leros, and when his colleagues expressed a wish to keep the sea and fight it out, flatly refused either to stay himself or to let them or any one else do so if he could help it. Where they could hereafter contend, after full and undisturbed preparation, with an exact knowledge of the number of the enemy's fleet and of the force which they could oppose to him, he would never allow the reproach of disgrace to drive him into a risk that was unreasonable. It was no disgrace for an Athenian fleet to retreat when it suited them: put it as they would, it would be more disgraceful to be beaten, and to expose the city not only to disgrace, but to the most serious danger. After its late misfortunes it could hardly be justified in voluntarily taking the offensive even with the strongest force, except in a case of absolute necessity: much less then without compulsion could it rush upon peril of its own seeking. He told them to take up their wounded as quickly as they could and the troops and stores which they had brought with them, and leaving behind what they had taken from the enemy's country, in order to lighten the ships, to sail off to Samos, and there concentrating all their ships to attack as opportunity served. As he spoke so he acted; and thus not now more than afterwards, nor in this alone but in all that he had to do with, did Phrynichus show himself a man of sense. In this way that very evening the Athenians broke up from before Miletus, leaving their victory unfinished, and the Argives, mortified at their disaster, promptly sailed off home from Samos.

As soon as it was morning the Peloponnesians weighed from Teichiussa and put into Miletus after the departure of the Athenians; they stayed one day, and on the next took with them the Chian vessels originally chased into port with Chalcideus, and resolved to sail back for the tackle which they had put on shore at Teichiussa. Upon their arrival Tissaphernes came to them with his land forces and induced them to sail to Iasus, which was held by his enemy Amorges. Accordingly they suddenly attacked and took Iasus, whose inhabitants never imagined that the ships could be other than Athenian. The Syracusans distinguished themselves most in the action. Amorges, a bastard of Pissuthnes and a rebel from the king, was taken alive and handed over to Tissaphernes, to carry to the king, if he chose, according to his orders: Iasus was sacked by the army, who found a very great booty there, the place being wealthy from ancient date. The mercenaries serving with Amorges the Peloponnesians received and enrolled in their army without doing them any harm, since most of them came from Peloponnese, and handed over the town to Tissaphernes with all the captives, bond or free, at the stipulated price of one Doric stater a head; after which they returned to Miletus. Pedaritus, son of Leon, who had been sent by the Lacedæmonians to take the command at Chios, they despatched by land as far as Erythræ with the mercenaries taken from Amorges; appointing Philip to remain as governor of Miletus.

Summer was now over. The winter following Tissaphernes put Iasus in a state of defence, and passing on to Miletus distributed a month's pay to all the ships as he had promised at Lacedæmon, at the rate of an Attic drachma a day for each man. In future, however, he was resolved not to give more than three obols, until he had consulted the king; when if the king should so order he would give, he said, the full drachma. However, upon the protest of the Syracusan general Hermocrates (for as Therimenes was not admiral, but only accompanied them in order to hand over the ships to Astyochus, he made little difficulty about the pay), it was agreed that the amount of five ships' pay should be given over and above the three obols a day for each man; Tissaphernes paying thirty talents a month for fifty-five ships, and to the rest, for as many ships as they had beyond that number, at the same rate.

The same winter the Athenians in Samos having been joined by thirty-five more vessels from home under Charminus, Strombichides, and Euctemon, called in their squadron at Chios and all the rest, intending to blockade Miletus with their navy, and to send a fleet and an army against Chios; drawing lots for the respective services. This intention they carried into effect; Strombichides, Onamacles, and Euctemon sailing against Chios, which fell to their lot, with thirty ships and a part of the thousand heavy infantry, who had been to Miletus, in transports; while the rest remained masters of the sea with seventy-four ships at Samos, and advanced upon Miletus.

Meanwhile Astyochus, whom we left at Chios collecting the hostages required in consequence of the conspiracy, stopped upon learning that the fleet with Therimenes had arrived, and that the affairs of the league were in a more flourishing condition, and putting out to sea with ten Peloponnesian and as many Chian vessels, after a futile attack upon Pteleum, coasted on to Clazomenæ, and ordered the Athenian party to remove inland to Daphnus, and to join the Peloponnesians, an order in which also joined Tamos the king's lieutenant in Ionia. This order being disregarded, Astyochus made an attack upon the town, which was unwalled, and having failed to take it was himself carried off by a strong gale to Phocæa and Cuma, while the rest of the ships put in at the islands adjacent to Clazomenæ, Marathussa, Pele, and Drymussa. Here they were detained eight days by the winds, and plundering and consuming all the property of the Clazomenians there deposited, put the rest on shipboard and sailed off to Phocæa and Cuma to join Astyochus.

While he was there, envoys arrived from the Lesbians who wished to revolt again. With Astyochus they were successful; but the Corinthians and the other allies being averse to it by reason of their former failure, he weighed anchor and set sail for Chios, where they eventually arrived from different quarters, the fleet having been scattered by a storm. After this Pedaritus, whom we left marching along the coast from Miletus, arrived at Erythræ, and thence crossed over with his army to Chios, where he found also about five hundred soldiers who had been left there by Chalcideus from the five ships with their arms. Meanwhile some Lesbians making offers to revolt, Astyochus urged upon Pedaritus and the Chians that they ought to go with their ships and effect the revolt of Lesbos, and so increase the number of their allies, or, if not successful, at all events harm the Athenians. The Chians, however, turned a deaf ear to this, and Pedaritus flatly refused to give up to him the Chian vessels.

Upon this Astyochus took five Corinthian and one Megarian vessel, with another from Hermione, and the ships which had come with him from Laconia, and set sail for

Miletus to assume his command as admiral; after telling the Chians with many threats that he would certainly not come and help them if they should be in need. At Corycus in the Erythræid he brought to for the night; the Athenian armament sailing from Samos against Chios being only separated from him by a hill, upon the other side of which it brought to; so that neither perceived the other. But a letter arriving in the night from Pedaritus to say that some liberated Erythræan prisoners had come from Samos to betray Erythræ, Astyochus at once put back to Erythræ, and so just escaped falling in with the Athenians. Here Pedaritus sailed over to join him; and after inquiry into the pretended treachery, finding that the whole story had been made up to procure the escape of the men from Samos, they acquitted them of the charge, and sailed away, Pedaritus to Chios and Astyochus to Miletus, as he had intended.

Meanwhile the Athenian armament sailing round Corycus fell in with three Chian men of war off Arginus, and gave immediate chase. A great storm coming on, the Chians with difficulty took refuge in the harbour; the three Athenian vessels most forward in the pursuit being wrecked and thrown up near the city of Chios, and the crews slain or taken prisoners. The rest of the Athenian fleet took refuge in the harbour called Phœnicus, under Mount Mimas, and from thence afterwards put into Lesbos and prepared for the work of fortification.

The same winter the Lacedæmonian Hippocrates sailed out from Peloponnese with ten Thurian ships under the command of Dorieus, son of Diagoras, and two colleagues, one Laconian and one Syracusan vessel, and arrived at Cnidus, which had already revolted at the instigation of Tissaphernes. When their arrival was known at Miletus, orders came to them to leave half their squadron to guard Cnidus, and with the rest to cruise round Triopium and seize all the merchantmen arriving from Egypt. Triopium is a promontory of Cnidus and sacred to Apollo. This coming to the knowledge of the Athenians, they sailed from Samos and captured the six ships on the watch at Triopium, the crews escaping out of them. After this the Athenians sailed into Cnidus and made an assault upon the town, which was unfortified, and all but took it; and the next day assaulted it again, but with less effect, as the inhabitants had improved their defences during the night, and had been reinforced by the crews escaped from the ships at Triopium. The Athenians now withdrew, and after plundering the Cnidian territory sailed back to Samos.

About the same time Astyochus came to the fleet at Miletus. The Peloponnesian camp was still plentifully supplied, being in receipt of sufficient pay, and the soldiers having still in hand the large booty taken at Iasus. The Milesians also showed great ardour for the war. Nevertheless the Peloponnesians thought the first convention with Tissaphernes, made with Chalcideus, defective, and more advantageous to him than to them, and consequently while Therimenes was still there concluded another, which was as follows:—

The convention of the Lacedæmonians and the allies with King Darius and the sons of the king, and with Tissaphernes for a treaty and friendship, as follows:—

1. *Neither the Lacedæmonians nor the allies of the Lacedæmonians shall make war against or otherwise injure any country or cities that belong to King Darius or did belong to his father or to his ancestors: neither shall the Lacedæmonians nor the allies of the Lacedæmonians exact tribute from such cities. Neither shall King Darius nor any of the subjects of the king make war against or otherwise injure the Lacedæmonians or their allies.*

2. *If the Lacedæmonians or their allies should require any assistance from the king, or the king from the Lacedæmonians or their allies, whatever they both agree upon they shall be right in doing.*

3. *Both shall carry on jointly the war against the Athenians and their allies; and if they make peace, both shall do so jointly.*

4. *The expense of all troops in the king's country, sent for by the king, shall be borne by the king.*

5. *If any of the states comprised in this convention with the king attack the king's country, the rest shall stop them and aid the king to the best of their power. And if any in the king's country or in the countries under the king's rule attack the country of the Lacedæmonians or their allies, the king shall stop it and help them to the best of his power.*

After this convention Therimenes handed over the fleet to Astyochus, sailed off in a small boat, and was lost. The Athenian armament had now crossed over from Lesbos to Chios, and being master by sea and land began to fortify Delphinium, a place naturally strong on the land side, provided with more than one harbour, and also not far from the city of Chios. Meanwhile the Chians remained inactive. Already defeated in so many battles, they were now also at discord among themselves; the execution of the party of Tydeus, son of Ion, by Pedaritus upon the charge of Atticism, followed by the forcible imposition of an oligarchy upon the rest of the city, having made them suspicious of one another; and they therefore thought neither themselves nor the mercenaries under Pedaritus a match for the enemy. They sent, however, to Miletus to beg Astyochus to assist them, which he refused to do, and was accordingly denounced at Lacedæmon by Pedaritus as a traitor. Such was the state of the Athenian affairs at Chios; while their fleet at Samos kept sailing out against the enemy in Miletus, until they found that he would not accept their challenge, and then retired again to Samos and remained quiet.

In the same winter the twenty-seven ships equipped by the Lacedæmonians for Pharnabazus through the agency of the Megarian Calligeitus, and the Cyzicene Timagoras, put out from Peloponnese and sailed for Ionia about the time of the solstice, under the command of Antisthenes, a Spartan. With them the Lacedæmonians also sent eleven Spartans as advisers to Astyochus; Lichas, son of Arcesilaus, being among the number. Arrived at Miletus, their orders were to aid in generally superintending the good conduct of the war; to send off the above ships or a greater or less number to the Hellespont to Pharnabazus, if they thought proper, appointing Clearchus, son of Ramphias, who sailed with them, to the command; and further, if they thought proper, to make Antisthenes admiral, dismissing Astyochus, whom the letters of Pedaritus had caused to be regarded with suspicion. Sailing accordingly from Malea across the open sea, the squadron touched at Melos and there fell in with ten Athenian ships, three of which they took empty and burned. After this, being afraid that the Athenian vessels escaped from Melos might,

as they in fact did, give information of their approach to the
Athenians at Samos, they sailed to Crete, and having lengthened their voyage by way of precaution made land at Caunus
in Asia, from whence considering themselves in safety they
sent a message to the fleet at Miletus for a convoy along
the coast.

Meanwhile the Chians and Pedaritus, undeterred by the
backwardness of Astyochus, went on sending messengers
pressing him to come with all the fleet to assist them against
their besiegers, and not to leave the greatest of the allied
states in Ionia to be shut up by sea and overrun and pillaged
by land. There were more slaves at Chios than in any one
other city except Lacedæmon, and being also by reason of
their numbers punished more rigorously when they offended,
most of them when they saw the Athenian armament firmly
established in the island with a fortified position, immediately
deserted to the enemy, and through their knowledge of the
country did the greatest mischief. The Chians therefore urged
upon Astyochus that it was his duty to assist them, while
there was still a hope and a possibility of stopping the enemy's
progress, while Delphinium was still in process of fortification
and unfinished, and before the completion of a higher rampart
which was being added to protect the camp and fleet of their
besiegers. Astyochus now saw that the allies also wished it and
prepared to go, in spite of his intention to the contrary owing
to the threat already referred to.

In the meantime news came from Caunus of the arrival
of the twenty-seven ships with the Lacedæmonian commissioners; and Astyochus postponing everything to the duty of
convoying a fleet of that importance, in order to be more
able to command the sea, and to the safe conduct of the
Lacedæmonians sent as spies over his behaviour, at once gave
up going to Chios and set sail for Caunus. As he coasted
along he landed at the Meropid Cos and sacked the city, which
was unfortified and had been lately laid in ruins by an earthquake, by far the greatest in living memory, and, as the
inhabitants had fled to the mountains, overran the country
and made booty of all it contained, letting go, however, the
free men. From Cos arriving in the night at Cnidus he was
constrained by the representations of the Cnidians not to dis-

embark the sailors, but to sail as he was straight against the twenty Athenian vessels, which with Charminus, one of the commanders at Samos, were on the watch for the very twenty-seven ships from Peloponnese which Astyochus was himself sailing to join; the Athenians in Samos having heard from Melos of their approach, and Charminus being on the look-out off Syme, Chalce, Rhodes and Lycia, as he now heard that they were at Caunus.

Astyochus accordingly sailed as he was to Syme, before he was heard of, in the hope of catching the enemy somewhere out at sea. Rain, however, and foggy weather encountered him, and caused his ships to straggle and get into disorder in the dark. In the morning his fleet had parted company and was most of it still straggling round the island, and the left wing only in sight of Charminus and the Athenians, who took it for the squadron which they were watching for from Caunus, and hastily put out against it with part only of their twenty vessels, and attacking immediately sank three ships and disabled others, and had the advantage in the action until the main body of the fleet unexpectedly hove in sight, when they were surrounded on every side. Upon this they took to flight, and after losing six ships, with the rest escaped to Teutlussa or Beet Island, and from thence to Halicarnassus. After this the Peloponnesians put into Cnidus, and being joined by the twenty-seven ships from Caunus, sailed all together and set up a trophy in Syme, and then returned to anchor at Cnidus.

As soon as the Athenians knew of the sea-fight they sailed with all the ships at Samos to Syme, and without attacking or being attacked by the fleet at Cnidus, took the ships' tackle left at Syme, and touching at Lorymi on the main land sailed back to Samos. Meanwhile the Peloponnesian ships being now all at Cnidus, underwent such repairs as were needed; while the eleven Lacedæmonian commissioners conferred with Tissaphernes, who had come to meet them, upon the points which did not satisfy them in the past transactions, and upon the best and mutually most advantageous manner of conducting the war in future. The severest critic of the present proceeding was Lichas, who said that neither of the treaties could stand, neither that of Chalcideus, nor that of Therimenes; it being monstrous that the king should at this date pretend

to the possession of all the country formerly ruled by himself
or by his ancestors—a pretension which implicitly put back
under the yoke all the islands, Thessaly, Locris, and everything as far as Bœotia, and made the Lacedæmonians give to
the Hellenes instead of liberty a Median master. He therefore invited Tissaphernes to conclude another and a better
treaty, as they certainly would not recognise those existing
and did not want any of his pay upon such conditions. This
offended Tissaphernes so much that he went away in a rage
without settling anything.

CHAPTER XXV

TWENTIETH AND TWENTY-FIRST YEARS OF THE WAR—IN-
    TRIGUES OF ALCIBIADES—WITHDRAWAL OF THE PERSIAN
    SUBSIDIES—OLIGARCHICAL COUP D'ÉTAT AT ATHENS—
    PATRIOTISM OF THE ARMY AT SAMOS

B.C. 412: *Rhodes goes over to the Peloponnesians—Intrigues of Alci-*
    biades—Oligarchical conspiracy in the army—Phrynichus disap-
    proves—Treachery of Astyochus—Conspiracy at Athens—Defeat
    of the Chians—Athenian mission fails to agree with Tissaphernes—
    *Third Persian-Spartan treaty—Capture of Oropus—*B.C. 411: *Revolt*
    of Abydos—Oligarchical conspiracy—Assassinations at Athens—
    The Four Hundred—The subverters of democracy—Overtures for
    peace with Sparta—Chæreas brings news to the army—Struggle
    between the army and the Four Hundred—Naval manœuvres.

THE Peloponnesians now determined to sail to Rhodes, upon
the invitation of some of the principal men there, hoping to
gain an island powerful by the number of its seamen and
by its land forces, and also thinking that they would be able
to maintain their fleet from their own confederacy, without
having to ask for money from Tissaphernes. They accordingly
at once set sail that same winter from Cnidus, and first put
in with ninety-four ships at Camirus in the Rhodian country,
to the great alarm of the mass of the inhabitants, who were
not privy to the intrigue, and who consequently fled, especially
as the town was unfortified. They were afterwards, however,
assembled by the Lacedæmonians together with the inhabitants of the two other towns of Lindus and Ialysus; and the
Rhodians were persuaded to revolt from the Athenians and
the island went over to the Peloponnesians. Meanwhile

the Athenians had received the alarm and set sail with the
fleet from Samos to forestall them, and came within sight
of the island, but being a little too late sailed off for the
moment to Chalce, and from thence to Samos, and subsequently waged war against Rhodes, issuing from Chalce, Cos,
and Samos.

The Peloponnesians now levied a contribution of thirty-two
talents from the Rhodians, after which they hauled their ships
ashore and for eighty days remained inactive. During this
time, and even earlier, before they removed to Rhodes, the
following intrigues took place. After the death of Chalcideus
and the battle at Miletus, Alcibiades began to be suspected
by the Peloponnesians; and Astyochus received from
Lacedæmon an order from them to put him to death, he being
the personal enemy of Agis, and in other respects thought
unworthy of confidence. Alcibiades in his alarm first withdrew to Tissaphernes, and immediately began to do all he
could with him to injure the Peloponnesian cause. Henceforth
becoming his adviser in everything, he cut down the pay from
an Attic drachma to three obols a day, and even this not paid
too regularly; and told Tissaphernes to say to the Peloponnesians that the Athenians, whose maritime experience was
of an older date than their own, only gave their men three
obols, not so much from poverty as to prevent their seamen
being corrupted by being too well off, and injuring their condition by spending money upon enervating indulgences, and
also paid their crews irregularly in order to have a security
against their deserting in the arrears which they would leave
behind them. He also told Tissaphernes to bribe the captains
and generals of the cities, and so to obtain their connivance—
an expedient which succeeded with all except the Syracusans,
Hermocrates alone opposing him on behalf of the whole confederacy. Meanwhile the cities asking for money Alcibiades
sent off, by roundly telling them in the name of Tissaphernes,
that it was great impudence in the Chians, the richest people in
Hellas, not content with being defended by a foreign force,
to expect others to risk not only their lives but their money
as well in behalf of their freedom; while the other cities, he
said, had had to pay largely to Athens before their rebellion,
and could not justly refuse to contribute as much or even

more now for their own selves. He also pointed out that Tissaphernes was at present carrying on the war at his own charges, and had good cause for economy, but that as soon as he received remittances from the king he would give them their pay in full, and do what was reasonable for the cities.

Alcibiades further advised Tissaphernes not to be in too great a hurry to end the war, or to let himself be persuaded to bring up the Phœnician fleet which he was equipping, or to provide pay for more Hellenes, and thus put the power by land and sea into the same hands; but to leave each of the contending parties in possession of one element, thus enabling the king when he found one troublesome to call in the other. For if the command of the sea and land were united in one hand, he would not know where to turn for help to overthrow the dominant power; unless he at last chose to stand up himself, and go through with the struggle at great expense and hazard. The cheapest plan was to let the Hellenes wear each other out, at a small share of the expense and without risk to himself. Besides, he would find the Athenians the most convenient partners in empire as they did not aim at conquests on shore, and carried on the war upon principles and with a practice most advantageous to the king; being prepared to combine to conquer the sea for Athens, and for the king all the Hellenes inhabiting his country, whom the Peloponnesians, on the contrary, had come to liberate. Now it was not likely that the Lacedæmonians would free the Hellenes from the Hellenic Athenians, without freeing them also from the barbarian Mede, unless overthrown by him in the meanwhile. Alcibiades therefore urged him to wear them both out at first, and after docking the Athenian power as much as he could, forthwith to rid the country of the Peloponnesians. In the main Tissaphernes approved of this policy, so far at least as could be conjectured from his behaviour; since he now gave his confidence to Alcibiades in recognition of his good advice, and kept the Peloponnesians short of money, and would not let them fight at sea, but ruined their cause by pretending that the Phœnician fleet would arrive, and that they would thus be enabled to contend with the odds in their favour, and so made their navy lose its efficiency, which had been very

remarkable, and generally betrayed a coolness in the war
that was too plain to be mistaken.

Alcibiades gave this advice to Tissaphernes and the king,
with whom he then was, not merely because he thought it
really the best, but because he was studying means to effect
his restoration to his country, well knowing that if he did not
destroy it he might one day hope to persuade the Athenians
to recall him, and thinking that his best chance of persuading
them lay in letting them see that he possessed the favour of
Tissaphernes. The event proved him to be right. When the
Athenians at Samos found that he had influence with Tissaphernes, principally of their own motion (though partly also
through Alcibiades himself sending word to their chief men
to tell the best men in the army, that if there were only an
oligarchy in the place of the rascally democracy that had
banished him, he would be glad to return to his country and to
make Tissaphernes their friend), the captains and chief men
in the armament at once embraced the idea of subverting the
democracy.

The design was first mooted in the camp, and afterwards
from thence reached the city. Some persons crossed over from
Samos and had an interview with Alcibiades, who immediately
offered to make first Tissaphernes, and afterwards the king,
their friend, if they would give up the democracy, and make
it possible for the king to trust them. The higher class, who
also suffered most severely from the war, now conceived great
hopes of getting the government into their own hands, and of
triumphing over the enemy. Upon their return to Samos the
emissaries formed their partisans into a club, and openly told
the mass of the armament that the king would be their friend,
and would provide them with money, if Alcibiades were restored, and the democracy abolished. The multitude, if at first
irritated by these intrigues, were nevertheless kept quiet by
the advantageous prospect of the pay from the king; and the
oligarchical conspirators, after making this communication to
the people, now re-examined the proposals of Alcibiades
among themselves, with most of their associates. Unlike the
rest, who thought them advantageous and trustworthy,
Phrynichus, who was still general, by no means approved of
the proposals. Alcibiades, he rightly thought, cared no more

for an oligarchy than for a democracy, and only sought to change the institutions of his country in order to get himself recalled by his associates; while for themselves their one object should be to avoid civil discord. It was not the king's interest, when the Peloponnesians were now their equals at sea, and in possession of some of the chief cities in his empire, to go out of his way to side with the Athenians whom he did not trust, when he might make friends of the Peloponnesians who had never injured him. And as for the allied states to whom oligarchy was now offered, because the democracy was to be put down at Athens, he well knew that this would not make the rebels come in any the sooner, or confirm the loyal in their allegiance; as the allies would never prefer servitude with an oligarchy or democracy to freedom with the constitution which they actually enjoyed, to whichever type it belonged. Besides, the cities thought that the so-called better classes would prove just as oppressive as the commons, as being those who originated, proposed, and for the most part benefited from the acts of the commons injurious to the confederates. Indeed, if it depended on the better classes, the confederates would be put to death without trial and with violence; while the commons were their refuge and the chastiser of these men. This he positively knew that the cities had learned by experience, and that such was their opinion. The propositions of Alcibiades, and the intrigues now in progress, could therefore never meet with his approval.

However, the members of the club assembled, agreeably to their original determination, accepted what was proposed, and prepared to send Pisander and others on an embassy to Athens to treat for the restoration of Alcibiades and the abolition of the democracy in the city, and thus to make Tissaphernes the friend of the Athenians.

Phrynichus now saw that there would be a proposal to restore Alcibiades, and that the Athenians would consent to it; and fearing after what he had said against it that Alcibiades, if restored, would revenge himself upon him for his opposition, had recourse to the following expedient. He sent a secret letter to the Lacedæmonian admiral, Astyochus, who was still in the neighbourhood of Miletus, to tell him that Alcibiades was ruining their cause by making Tissaphernes

the friend of the Athenians, and containing an express revelation of the rest of the intrigue, desiring to be excused if he
sought to harm his enemy even at the expense of the interests
of his country. However, Astyochus, instead of thinking of
punishing Alcibiades, who, besides, no longer ventured within
his reach as formerly, went up to him and Tissaphernes at
Magnesia, communicated to them the letter from Samos, and
turned informer, and if report may be trusted, became the
paid creature of Tissaphernes, undertaking to inform him as
to this and all other matters; which was also the reason why
he did not remonstrate more strongly against the pay not
being given in full. Upon this Alcibiades instantly sent to
the authorities at Samos a letter against Phrynichus, stating
what he had done, and requiring that he should be put to
death. Phrynichus distracted, and placed in the utmost peril
by the denunciation, sent again to Astyochus, reproaching
him with having so ill kept the secret of his previous letter,
and saying that he was now prepared to give them an opportunity of destroying the whole Athenian armament at Samos;
giving a detailed account of the means which he should employ, Samos being unfortified, and pleading that being in
danger of his life on their account, he could not now be blamed
for doing this or anything else to escape being destroyed by
his mortal enemies. This also Astyochus revealed to Alcibiades.

Meanwhile Phrynichus having had timely notice that he
was playing him false, and that a letter on the subject was on
the point of arriving from Alcibiades, himself anticipated
the news, and told the army that the enemy, seeing that Samos
was unfortified and the fleet not all stationed within the
harbour, meant to attack the camp; that he could be certain
of this intelligence, and that they must fortify Samos as
quickly as possible, and generally look to their defences. It
will be remembered that he was general, and had himself
authority to carry out these measures. Accordingly they addressed themselves to the work of fortification, and Samos
was thus fortified sooner than it would otherwise have been.
Not long afterwards came the letter from Alcibiades, saying
that the army was betrayed by Phrynichus, and the enemy
about to attack it. Alcibiades, however, gained no credit, it
being thought that he was in the secret of the enemy's designs,

and had tried to fasten them upon Phrynichus, and to make out that he was their accomplice, out of hatred; and consequently far from hurting him he rather bore witness to what he had said by this intelligence.

After this Alcibiades set to work to persuade Tissaphernes to become the friend of the Athenians. Tissaphernes, although afraid of the Peloponnesians because they had more ships in Asia than the Athenians, was yet disposed to be persuaded if he could, especially after his quarrel with the Peloponnesians at Cnidus about the treaty of Therimenes. The quarrel had already taken place, as the Peloponnesians were by this time actually at Rhodes; and in it the original argument of Alcibiades touching the liberation of all the towns by the Lacedæmonians had been verified by the declaration of Lichas, that it was impossible to submit to a convention which made the king master of all the states at any former time ruled by himself or by his fathers.

While Alcibiades was besieging the favour of Tissaphernes with an earnestness proportioned to the greatness of the issue, the Athenian envoys who had been despatched from Samos with Pisander arrived at Athens, and made a speech before the people, giving a brief summary of their views, and particularly insisting that if Alcibiades were recalled and the democratic constitution changed, they could have the king as their ally, and would be able to overcome the Peloponnesians. A number of speakers opposed them on the question of the democracy, the enemies of Alcibiades cried out against the scandal of a restoration to be effected by a violation of the constitution, and the Eumolpidæ and Ceryces protested in behalf of the mysteries, the cause of his banishment, and called upon the gods to avert his recall; when Pisander, in the midst of much opposition and abuse, came forward, and taking each of his opponents aside asked him the following question: —In the face of the fact that the Peloponnesians had as many ships as their own confronting them at sea, more cities in alliance with them, and the king and Tissaphernes to supply them with money, of which the Athenians had none left, had he any hope of saving the state, unless some one could induce the king to come over to their side? Upon their replying that they had not, he then plainly said to them: 'This we cannot have unless we have a more moderate form of government, and put the offices into fewer hands, and so gain the king's confidence, and forthwith restore Alcibiades, who is the only man living that can bring this about. The safety of the state, not the form of its government, is for the moment the most pressing question, as we can always change afterwards whatever we do not like.'

The people were at first highly irritated at the mention of an oligarchy, but upon understanding clearly from Pisander that this was the only resource left, they took counsel of their fears, and promised themselves some day to change the government again, and gave way. They accordingly voted that Pisander should sail with ten others and make the best arrangement that they could with Tissaphernes and Alcibiades. At the same time the people, upon a false accusation of Pisander, dismissed Phrynichus from his post together with his colleague Scironides, sending Diomedon and Leon to replace them in the command of the fleet. The accusation was that Phrynichus had betrayed Iasus and Amorges; and Pisander brought it because he thought him a man unfit for the business now in hand with Alcibiades. Pisander also went the round of all the clubs already existing in the city for help in lawsuits and elections, and urged them to draw together and to unite their efforts for the overthrow of the democracy; and after taking all other measures required by the circumstances, so that no time might be lost, set off with his ten companions on his voyage to Tissaphernes.

In the same winter Leon and Diomedon, who had by this time joined the fleet, made an attack upon Rhodes. The ships of the Peloponnesians they found hauled up on shore, and after making a descent upon the coast and defeating the Rhodians who appeared in the field against them, withdrew to Chalce and made that place their base of operations instead of Cos, as they could better observe from thence if the Peloponnesian fleet put out to sea. Meanwhile Xenophantes, a Laconian, came to Rhodes from Pedaritus at Chios, with the news that the fortification of the Athenians was now finished, and that, unless the whole Peloponnesian fleet came to the rescue, the cause in Chios must be lost. Upon this they resolved to go to his relief. In the meantime Pedaritus, with the merce naries that he had with him and the whole force of the Chians, made an assault upon the work round the Athenian ships and took a portion of it, and got possession of some vessels that were hauled up on shore, when the Athenians sallied out to the rescue, and first routing the Chians, next defeated the remainder of the force round Pedaritus, who was himself killed, with many of the Chians, a great number of arms being also taken.

After this the Chians were besieged even more straitly than before by land and sea, and the famine in the place was great. Meanwhile the Athenian envoys with Pisander arrived at the court of Tissaphernes, and conferred with him about the proposed agreement. However, Alcibiades, not being altogether sure of Tissaphernes (who feared the Peloponnesians more than the Athenians, and besides wished to wear out both parties, as Alcibiades himself had recommended), had recourse to the following stratagem to make the treaty between the Athenians and Tissaphernes miscarry by reason of the magnitude of his demands. In my opinion Tissaphernes desired this result, fear being his motive; while Alcibiades, who now saw that Tissaphernes was determined not to treat on any terms, wished the Athenians to think, not that he was unable to persuade Tissaphernes, but that after the latter had been persuaded and was willing to join them, they had not conceded enough to him. For the demands of Alcibiades, speaking for Tissaphernes, who was present, were so extravagant that the Athenians, although for a long while they agreed to whatever he asked, yet had to bear the blame of failure: he required the cession of the whole of Ionia, next of the islands adjacent, besides other concessions, and these passed without opposition; at last, in the third interview, Alcibiades, who now feared a complete discovery of his inability, required them to allow the king to build ships and sail along his own coast wherever and with as many as he pleased. Upon this the Athenians would yield no further, and concluding that there was nothing to be done, but that they had been deceived by Alcibiades, went away in a passion and proceeded to Samos.

Tissaphernes immediately after this, in the same winter, proceeded along shore to Caunus, desiring to bring the Peloponnesian fleet back to Miletus, and to supply them with

pay, making a fresh convention upon such terms as he could
get, in order not to bring matters to an absolute breach between them. He was afraid that if many of their ships were
left without pay they would be compelled to engage and be
defeated, or that their vessels being left without hands, the
Athenians would attain their objects without his assistance.
Still more he feared that the Peloponnesians might ravage the
continent in search of supplies. Having calculated and considered all this, agreeably to his plan of keeping the two sides
equal, he now sent for the Peloponnesians and gave them pay,
and concluded with them a third treaty in words following:—

*In the thirteenth year of the reign of Darius, while Alexip-
pidas was Ephor at Lacedæmon, a convention was concluded
in the plain of the Mœander by the Lacedæmonians and their
allies with Tissaphernes, Hieramenes, and the sons of Pharnaces, concerning the affairs of the king and of the Lacedæmonians and their allies.*

1. *The country of the king in Asia shall be the king's, and
the king shall treat his own country as he pleases.*

2. *The Lacedæmonians and their allies shall not invade
or injure the king's country; neither shall the king invade or
injure that of the Lacedæmonians or of their allies. If any
of the Lacedæmonians or of their allies invade or injure the
king's country, the Lacedæmonians and their allies shall prevent it; and if any from the king's country invade or injure
the country of the Lacedæmonians or of their allies, the king
shall prevent it.*

3. *Tissaphernes shall provide pay for the ships now
present, according to the agreement, until the arrival of the
king's vessels; but after the arrival of the king's vessels the
Lacedæmonians and their allies may pay their own ships if
they wish it. If, however, they choose to receive the pay from
Tissaphernes, Tissaphernes shall furnish it; and the Lacedæmonians and their allies shall repay him at the end of the war
such monies as they shall have received.*

4. *After the king's vessels have arrived, the ships of the
Lacedæmonians and of their allies and those of the king shall
carry on the war jointly, according as Tissaphernes and the
Lacedæmonians and their allies shall think best. If they wish*

*to make peace with the Athenians, they shall make peace also
jointly.*

This was the treaty. After this Tissaphernes prepared to
bring up the Phœnician fleet according to agreement, and to
make good his other promises, or at all events wished to make
it appear that he was so preparing.

Winter was now drawing towards its close, when the Bœotians took Oropus by treachery, though held by an Athenian
garrison. Their accomplices in this were some of the Eretrians and of the Oropians themselves, who were plotting the
revolt of Eubœa, as the place was exactly opposite Eretria,
and while in Athenian hands was necessarily a source of great
annoyance to Eretria and the rest of Eubœa. Oropus being
in their hands, the Eretrians now came to Rhodes to invite
the Peloponnesians into Eubœa. The latter, however, were
rather bent on the relief of the distressed Chians, and accordingly put out to sea and sailed with all their ships from
Rhodes. Off Triopium they sighted the Athenian fleet out at
sea sailing from Chalce, and neither attacking the other, arrived, the latter at Samos, the Peloponnesians at Miletus, seeing that it was no longer possible to relieve Chios without a
battle. And this winter ended, and with it ended the twentieth
year of this war of which Thucydides is the historian.

Early in the spring of the summer following Dercyllidas,
a Spartan, was sent with a small force by land to the Hellespont: to effect the revolt of Abydos, which is a Milesian
colony; and the Chians, while Astyochus was at a loss how to
help them, were compelled to fight at sea by the pressure of
the siege. While Astyochus was still at Rhodes they had received from Miletus, as their commander after the death of
Pedaritus, a Spartan named Leon, who had come out with
Antisthenes, and twelve vessels which had been on guard at
Miletus, five of which were Thurian, four Syracusan, one
from Anaia, one Milesian, and one Leon's own. Accordingly
the Chians marched out in mass and took up a strong position,
while thirty-six of their ships put out and engaged thirty-two
of the Athenians; and after a tough fight, in which the Chians
and their allies had rather the best of it, as it was now late,
retired to their city.

Immediately after this Dercyllidas arrived by land from

Miletus; and Abydos in the Hellespont revolted to him and Pharnabazus, and Lampsacus two days later. Upon receipt of this news Strombichides hastily sailed from Chios with twenty-four Athenian ships, some transports carrying heavy infantry being of the number, and defeating the Lampsacenes who came out against him, took Lampsacus, which was un-fortified, at the first assault, and making prize of the slaves and goods, restored the freemen to their homes, and went on to Abydos. The inhabitants, however, refusing to capitulate, and his assaults failing to take the place, he sailed over to the coast opposite, and appointed Sestos, the town in the Cher-sonese held by the Medes at a former period in this history, as the centre for the defence of the whole Hellespont.

In the meantime the Chians commanded the sea more than before; and the Peloponnesians at Miletus and Astyochus, hearing of the sea-fight and of the departure of the squadron with Strombichides, took fresh courage. Coasting along with two vessels to Chios, Astyochus took the ships from that place, and now moved with the whole fleet upon Samos, from whence, however, he sailed back to Miletus, as the Athenians did not put out against him, owing to their suspicions of one another. For it was about this time, or even before, that the democracy was put down at Athens. When Pisander and the envoys returned from Tissaphernes to Samos they at once strengthened still further their interest in the army itself, and instigated the upper class in Samos to join them in establish-ing an oligarchy, the very form of government which a party of them had lately risen to avoid. At the same time the Athe-nians at Samos, after a consultation among themselves, de-termined to let Alcibiades alone, since he refused to join them, and besides was not the man for an oligarchy; and now that they were once embarked, to see for themselves how they could best prevent the ruin of their cause, and meanwhile to sustain the war, and to contribute without stint money and all else that might be required from their own private estates, as they would henceforth labour for themselves alone.

After encouraging each other in these resolutions, they now at once sent off half the envoys and Pisander to do what was necessary at Athens (with instructions to establish oligarchies on their way in all the subject cities which they might touch at), and despatched the other half in different directions to the other dependencies. Diitrephes also, who was in the neighbourhood of Chios, and had been elected to the command of the Thracian towns, was sent off to his government, and arriving at Thasos abolished the democracy there. Two months, however, had not elapsed after his departure before the Thasians began to fortify their town, being already tired of an aristocracy with Athens, and in daily expectation of freedom from Lacedæmon. Indeed there was a party of them (whom the Athenians had banished), with the Peloponnesians, who with their friends in the town were already making every exertion to bring a squadron, and to effect the revolt of Thasos; and this party thus saw exactly what they most wanted done, that is to say, the reformation of the government without risk, and the abolition of the democracy which would have opposed them. Things at Thasos thus turned out just the contrary to what the oligarchical conspirators at Athens expected; and the same in my opinion was the case in many of the other dependencies; as the cities no sooner got a moderate government and liberty of action, than they went on to absolute freedom without being at all seduced by the show of reform offered by the Athenians.

Pisander and his colleagues on their voyage along shore abolished, as had been determined, the democracies in the cities, and also took some heavy infantry from certain places as their allies, and so came to Athens. Here they found most of the work already done by their associates. Some of the younger men had banded together, and secretly assassinated one Androcles, the chief leader of the commons, and mainly responsible for the banishment of Alcibiades; Androcles being singled out both because he was a popular leader, and because they sought by his death to recommend themselves to Alcibiades, who was, as they supposed, to be recalled, and to make Tissaphernes their friend. There were also some other obnoxious persons whom they secretly did away with in the same manner. Meanwhile their cry in public was that no pay should be given except to persons serving in the war, and that not more than five thousand should share in the government, and those such as were most able to serve the state in person and in purse.

But this was a mere catchword for the multitude, as the
authors of the revolution were really to govern. However, the
Assembly and the Council of the Bean still met notwithstanding, although they discussed nothing that was not approved
of by the conspirators, who both supplied the speakers, and
reviewed in advance what they were to say. Fear, and the
sight of the numbers of the conspirators, closed the mouths
of the rest; or if any ventured to rise in opposition, he was
presently put to death in some convenient way, and there
was neither search for the murderers nor justice to be had
against them if suspected; but the people remained motionless, being so thoroughly cowed that men thought themselves
lucky to escape violence, even when they held their tongues.
An exaggerated belief in the numbers of the conspirators also
demoralised the people, rendered helpless by the magnitude
of the city, and by their want of intelligence with each other,
and being without means of finding out what those numbers
really were. For the same reason it was impossible for any
one to open his grief to a neighbour and to concert measures
to defend himself, as he would have had to speak either to one
whom he did not know, or whom he knew but did not trust.
Indeed all the popular party approached each other with suspicion, each thinking his neighbour concerned in what was
going on, the conspirators having in their ranks persons whom
no one could ever have believed capable of joining an oligarchy; and these it was who made the many so suspicious,
and so helped to procure impunity for the few, by confirming
the commons in their mistrust of one another.

At this juncture arrived Pisander and his colleagues, who
lost no time in doing the rest. First they assembled the people, and moved to elect ten commissioners with full powers to
frame a constitution, and that when this was done they should
on an appointed day lay before the people their opinion as
to the best mode of governing the city. Afterwards, when
the day arrived, the conspirators enclosed the assembly in
Colonus, a temple of Poseidon, a little more than a mile outside the city; when the commissioners simply brought forward this single motion, that any Athenian might propose
with impunity whatever measure he pleased, heavy penalties
being imposed upon any who should indict for illegality, or

otherwise molest him for so doing. The way thus cleared, it was now plainly declared, that all tenure of office and receipt of pay under the existing institutions were at an end, and that five men must be elected as presidents, who should in their turn elect one hundred, and each of the hundred three apiece; and that this body thus made up to four hundred should enter the council chamber with full powers and govern as they judged best, and should convene the five thousand whenever they pleased.

The man who moved this resolution was Pisander, who was throughout the chief ostensible agent in putting down the democracy. But he who concerted the whole affair, and prepared the way for the catastrophe, and who had given the greatest thought to the matter, was Antiphon, one of the best men of his day in Athens; who, with a head to contrive measures and a tongue to recommend them, did not willingly come forward in the assembly or upon any public scene, being ill-looked upon by the multitude owing to his reputation for talent; and who yet was the one man best able to aid in the courts, or before the assembly, the suitors who required his opinion. Indeed, when he was afterwards himself tried for his life on the charge of having been concerned in setting up this very government, when the Four Hundred were overthrown and hardly dealt with by the commons, he made what would seem to be the best defence of any known up to my time. Phrynichus also went beyond all others in his zeal for the oligarchy. Afraid of Alcibiades, and assured that he was no stranger to his intrigues with Astyochus at Samos, he held that no oligarchy was ever likely to restore him, and once embarked in the enterprise, proved, where danger was to be faced, by far the staunchest of them all. Theramenes, son of Hagnon, was also one of the foremost of the subverters of the democracy—a man as able in council as in debate. Conducted by so many and by such sagacious heads, the enterprise, great as it was, not unnaturally went forward; although it was no light matter to deprive the Athenian people of its freedom, almost a hundred years after the deposition of the tyrants, when it had been not only not subject to any during the whole of that period, but accustomed during more than half of it to rule over subjects of its own.

The assembly ratified the proposed constitution, without a single opposing voice, and was then dissolved; after which the Four Hundred were brought into the council chamber in the following way. On account of the enemy at Decelea, all the Athenians were constantly on the wall or in the ranks at the various military posts. On that day the persons not in the secret were allowed to go home as usual, while orders were given to the accomplices of the conspirators to hang about, without making any demonstration, at some little distance from the posts, and in case of any opposition to what was being done, to seize the arms and put it down. There were also some Andrians and Tenians, three hundred Carystians, and some of the settlers in Ægina come with their own arms for this very purpose, who had received similar instructions. These dispositions completed, the Four Hundred went, each with a dagger concealed about his person, accompanied by one hundred and twenty Hellenic youths, whom they employed wherever violence was needed, and appeared before the Councillors of the Bean in the council chamber, and told them to take their pay and be gone; themselves bringing it for the whole of the residue of their term of office, and giving it to them as they went out.

Upon the Council withdrawing in this way without venturing any objection, and the rest of the citizens making no movement, the Four Hundred entered the council chamber, and for the present contented themselves with drawing lots for their Prytanes, and making their prayers and sacrifices to the gods upon entering office, but afterwards departed widely from the democratic system of government, and except that on account of Alcibiades they did not recall the exiles, ruled the city by force; putting to death some men, though not many, whom they thought it convenient to remove, and imprisoning and banishing others. They also sent to Agis, the Lacedæ-monian king, at Decelea, to say that they desired to make peace, and that he might reasonably be more disposed to treat now that he had them to deal with instead of the inconstant commons.

Agis, however, did not believe in the tranquillity of the city, or that the commons would thus in a moment give up their ancient liberty, but thought that the sight of a large Lacedæmonian force would be sufficient to excite them if they were not already in commotion, of which he was by no means certain. He accordingly gave to the envoys of the Four Hundred an answer which held out no hopes of an accommodation, and sending for large reinforcements from Peloponnese, not long afterwards, with these and his garrison from Decelea, descended to the very walls of Athens; hoping either that civil disturbances might help to subdue them to his terms, or that, in the confusion to be expected within and without the city, they might even surrender without a blow being struck; at all events he thought he would succeed in seizing the Long Walls, bared of their defenders. However, the Athenians saw him come close up, without making the least disturbance within the city; and sending out their cavalry, and a number of their heavy infantry, light troops, and archers shot down some of his soldiers who approached too near, and got possession of some arms and dead. Upon this Agis, at last convinced, led his army back again, and remaining with his own troops in the old position at Decelea, sent the reinforcement back home, after a few days' stay in Attica. After this the Four Hundred persevering sent another embassy to Agis, and now meeting with a better reception, at his suggestion despatched envoys to Lacedæmon to negotiate a treaty, being desirous of making peace.

They also sent ten men to Samos to reassure the army, and to explain that the oligarchy was not established for the hurt of the city or the citizens, but for the salvation of the country at large; and that there were five thousand, not four hundred only, concerned; although, what with their expeditions and employments abroad, the Athenians had never yet assembled to discuss a question important enough to bring five thousand of them together. The emissaries were also told what to say upon all other points, and were so sent off immediately after the establishment of the new government, which feared, as it turned out justly, that the mass of seamen would not be willing to remain under the oligarchical constitution, and, the evil beginning there, might be the means of their overthrow.

Indeed at Samos the question of the oligarchy had already entered upon a new phase, the following events having taken place just at the time that the Four Hundred were conspiring.

That part of the Samian population which has been mentioned as rising against the upper class, and as being the
democratic party, had now turned round, and yielding to
the solicitations of Pisander during his visit, and of the
Athenians in the conspiracy at Samos, had bound themselves
by oaths to the number of three hundred, and were about to
fall upon the rest of their fellow-citizens, whom they now in
their turn regarded as the democratic party. Meanwhile they
put to death one Hyperbolus, an Athenian, a pestilent fellow
that had been ostracised, not from fear of his influence or
position, but because he was a rascal and a disgrace to the
city; being aided in this by Charminus, one of the generals,
and by some of the Athenians with them, to whom they had
sworn friendship, and with whom they perpetrated other acts
of the kind, and now determined to attack the people. The
latter got wind of what was coming, and told two of the generals, Leon and Diomedon, who, on account of the credit
which they enjoyed with the commons, were unwilling supporters of the oligarchy; and also Thrasybulus and Thrasyllus, the former a captain of a galley, the latter serving with
the heavy infantry, besides certain others who had ever been
thought most opposed to the conspirators, entreating them
not to look on and see them destroyed, and Samos, the sole
remaining stay of their empire, lost to the Athenians. Upon
hearing this, the persons whom they addressed now went
round the soldiers one by one, and urged them to resist, especially the crew of the Paralus, which was made up entirely of
Athenians and freemen, and had from time out of mind been
enemies of oligarchy, even when there was no such thing
existing; and Leon and Diomedon left behind some ships for
their protection in case of their sailing away anywhere themselves. Accordingly, when the Three Hundred attacked the
people, all these came to the rescue, and foremost of all
the crew of the Paralus; and the Samian commons gained the
victory, and putting to death some thirty of the Three Hundred, banishing three others of the ringleaders, accorded an
amnesty to the rest, and lived together under a democratic
government for the future.

The ship Paralus, with Chæreas, son of Archestratus, on
board, an Athenian who had taken an active part in the revo-

lution, was now without loss of time sent off by the Samians and the army to Athens to report what had occurred; the fact that the Four Hundred were in power not being yet known. When they sailed into harbour the Four Hundred immediately arrested two or three of the Parali, and taking the vessel from the rest, shifted them into a troopship and set them to keep guard round Euboea. Chæreas, however, managed to secrete himself as soon as he saw how things stood, and returning to Samos, drew a picture to the soldiers of the horrors enacting at Athens, in which everything was exaggerated; saying that all were punished with stripes, that no one could say a word against the holders of power, that the soldiers' wives and children were outraged, and that it was intended to seize and shut up the relatives of all in the army at Samos who were not of the government's way of thinking, to be put to death in case of their disobedience; besides a host of other injurious inventions.

On hearing this the first thought of the army was to fall upon the chief authors of the oligarchy and upon all the rest concerned. Eventually, however, they desisted from this idea upon the men of moderate views opposing it and warning them against ruining their cause, with the enemy close at hand and ready for battle. After this Thrasybulus, son of Lycus, and Thrasyllus, the chief leaders in the revolution, now wishing in the most public manner to change the government at Samos to a democracy, bound all the soldiers by the most tremendous oaths, and those of the oligarchical party more than any, to accept a democratic government, to be united, to prosecute actively the war with the Peloponnesians, and to be enemies of the Four Hundred, and to hold no communication with them. The same oath was also taken by all the Samians of full age; and the soldiers associated the Samians in all their affairs and in the fruits of their dangers, having the conviction that there was no way of escape for themselves or for them, but that the success of the Four Hundred or of the enemy at Miletus must be their ruin.

The struggle now was between the army trying to force a democracy upon the city, and the Four Hundred an oligarchy upon the camp. Meanwhile the soldiers forthwith held an assembly, in which they deposed the former generals and any of the captains whom they suspected, and chose new captains and generals to replace them, besides Thrasybulus and Thrasyllus, whom they had already. They also stood up and encouraged one another, and among other things urged that they ought not to lose heart because the city had revolted from them, as the party seceding was smaller and in every way poorer in resources than themselves. They had the whole fleet with which to compel the other cities in their empire to give them money just as if they had their base in the capital, having a city in Samos which, so far from wanting strength, had when at war been within an ace of depriving the Athenians of the command of the sea, while as far as the enemy was concerned they had the same base of operations as before. Indeed, with the fleet in their hands, they were better able to provide themselves with supplies than the government at home. It was their advanced position at Samos which had throughout enabled the home authorities to command the entrance into Piræus; and if they refused to give them back the constitution, they would now find that the army was more in a position to exclude them from the sea than they were to exclude the army. Besides, the city was of little or no use towards enabling them to overcome the enemy; and they had lost nothing in losing those who had no longer either money to send them (the soldiers having to find this for themselves), or good counsel, which entitles cities to direct armies. On the contrary, even in this the home government had done wrong in abolishing the institutions of their ancestors, while the army maintained the said institutions, and would try to force the home government to do so likewise. So that even in point of good counsel the camp had as good counsellors as the city. Moreover, they had but to grant him security for his person and his recall, and Alcibiades would be only too glad to procure them the alliance of the king. And above all, if they failed altogether, with the navy which they possessed, they had numbers of places to retire to in which they would find cities and lands.

Debating together and comforting themselves after this manner, they pushed on their war measures as actively as ever; and the ten envoys sent to Samos by the Four Hundred, learning how matters stood while they were still at Delos, stayed quiet there.

About this time a cry arose among the soldiers in the Peloponnesian fleet at Miletus that Astyochus and Tissaphernes were ruining their cause. Astyochus had not been willing to fight at sea—either before, while they were still in full vigour and the fleet of the Athenians small, or now, when the enemy was, as they were informed, in a state of sedition and his ships not yet united—but kept them waiting for the Phœnician fleet from Tissaphernes, which had only a nominal existence, at the risk of wasting away in inactivity. While Tissaphernes not only did not bring up the fleet in question, but was ruining their navy by payments made irregularly, and even then not made in full. They must therefore, they insisted, delay no longer, but fight a decisive naval engagement. The Syracusans were the most urgent of any.

The confederates and Astyochus, aware of these murmurs, had already decided in council to fight a decisive battle; and when the news reached them of the disturbance at Samos, they put to sea with all their ships, one hundred and ten in number, and ordering the Milesians to move by land upon Mycale, set sail thither. The Athenians with the eighty-two ships from Samos were at the moment lying at Glauce in Mycale, a point where Samos approaches near to the continent; and seeing the Peloponnesian fleet sailing against them, retired into Samos, not thinking themselves numerically strong enough to stake their all upon a battle. Besides, they had notice from Miletus of the wish of the enemy to engage, and were expecting to be joined from the Hellespont by Strombichides, to whom a messenger had been already despatched, with the ships that had gone from Chios to Abydos. The Athenians accordingly withdrew to Samos, and the Peloponnesians put in at Mycale, and encamped with the land forces of the Milesians and the people of the neighbourhood. The next day they were about to sail against Samos, when tidings reached them of the arrival of Strombichides with the squadron from the Hellespont, upon which they immediately sailed back to Miletus. The Athenians, thus reinforced, now in their turn sailed against Miletus with a hundred and eight

ships, wishing to fight a decisive battle, but as no one put out
to meet them, sailed back to Samos.

CHAPTER XXVI

TWENTY-FIRST YEAR OF THE WAR—RECALL OF ALCIBIADES TO SAMOS—REVOLT OF EUBŒA AND DOWNFALL OF THE FOUR HUNDRED—BATTLE OF CYNOSSEMA

B.C. 411: *Encounter at Byzantium—Alcibiades elected general—Unpopularity of Tissaphernes—Astyochus recalled to Sparta—Alcibiades' service to Athens—Discontent with the Four Hundred—Treachery in Athens—Phrynichus assassinated—Revolt at Piræus—Peloponnesians at Salamis—Defeat of the Athenian fleet—Panic in Athens—The Four Hundred deposed—Constitution formed—Alcibiades recalled—Betrayal of Œnoe—Peloponnesian fleet at Hellespont—Naval victory for Athenians.*

IN the same summer, immediately after this, the Pelopennesians having refused to fight with their fleet united, through
not thinking themselves a match for the enemy, and being at
a loss where to look for money for such a number of ships,
especially as Tissaphernes proved so bad a paymaster, sent
off Clearchus, son of Ramphias, with forty ships to Pharnabazus, agreeably to the original instructions from Peloponnese; Pharnabazus inviting them and being prepared to
furnish pay, and Byzantium besides sending offers to revolt
to them. These Peloponnesian ships accordingly put out into
the open sea, in order to escape the observation of the
Athenians, and being overtaken by a storm, the majority
with Clearchus got into Delos, and afterwards returned to
Miletus, whence Clearchus proceeded by land to the Hellespont to take the command: ten, however, of their number,
under the Megarian Helixus, made good their passage to the
Hellespont, and effected the revolt of Byzantium. After this,
the commanders at Samos were informed of it, and sent a
squadron against them to guard the Hellespont; and an encounter took place before Byzantium between eight vessels
on either side.

Meanwhile the chiefs at Samos, and especially Thrasybulus, who from the moment that he had changed the government had remained firmly resolved to recall Alcibiades, at last
in an assembly brought over the mass of the soldiery, and

upon their voting for his recall and amnesty, sailed over to Tissaphernes and brought Alcibiades to Samos, being convinced that their only chance of salvation lay in his bringing over Tissaphernes from the Peloponnesians to themselves. An assembly was then held in which Alcibiades complained of and deplored his private misfortune in having been banished, and speaking at great length upon public affairs, highly incited their hopes for the future, and extravagantly magnified his own influence with Tissaphernes. His object in this was to make the oligarchical government at Athens afraid of him, to hasten the dissolution of the clubs, to increase his credit with the army at Samos and heighten their own confidence, and lastly to prejudice the enemy as strongly as possible against Tissaphernes, and blast the hopes which they entertained. Alcibiades accordingly held out to the army such extravagant promises as the following: that Tissaphernes had solemnly assured him that if he could only trust the Athenians they should never want for supplies while he had anything left, no, not even if he should have to coin his own silver couch, and that he would bring the Phœnician fleet now at Aspendus to the Athenians instead of to the Peloponnesians; but that he could only trust the Athenians if Alcibiades were recalled to be his security for them.

Upon hearing this and much more besides, the Athenians at once elected him general together with the former ones, and put all their affairs into his hands. There was now not a man in the army who would have exchanged his present hopes of safety and vengeance upon the Four Hundred for any consideration whatever; and after what they had been told they were now inclined to disdain the enemy before them, and to sail at once for Piræus. To the plan of sailing for Piræus, leaving their more immediate enemies behind them, Alcibiades opposed the most positive refusal, in spite of the numbers that insisted upon it, saying that now that he had been elected general he would first sail to Tissaphernes and concert with him measures for carrying on the war. Accordingly, upon leaving this assembly, he immediately took his departure in order to have it thought that there was an entire confidence between them, and also wishing to increase his consideration with Tissaphernes, and to show that he had now been elected general and was in a position to do him good or evil as he chose; thus managing to frighten the Athenians with Tissaphernes and Tissaphernes with the Athenians.

Meanwhile the Peloponnesians at Miletus heard of the recall of Alcibiades, and already distrustful of Tissaphernes, now became far more disgusted with him than ever. Indeed after their refusal to go out and give battle to the Athenians when they appeared before Miletus, Tissaphernes had grown slacker than ever in his payments; and even before this, on account of Alcibiades, his unpopularity had been on the increase. Gathering together, just as before, the soldiers and some persons of consideration besides the soldiery, began to reckon up how they had never yet received their pay in full; that what they did receive was small in quantity, and even that paid irregularly, and that unless they fought a decisive battle or removed to some station where they could get supplies, the ships' crews would desert; and that it was all the fault of Astyochus, who humoured Tissaphernes for his own private advantage.

The army was engaged in these reflexions, when the following disturbance took place about the person of Astyochus. Most of the Syracusan and Thurian sailors were freemen, and these the freest crews in the armament were likewise the boldest in setting upon Astyochus and demanding their pay. The latter answered somewhat stiffly and threatened them, and when Dorieus spoke up for his own sailors even went so far as to lift his baton against him; upon seeing which the mass of the men, in sailor fashion, rushed in a fury to strike Astyochus. He, however, saw them in time and fled for refuge to an altar; and they were thus parted without his being struck. Meanwhile the fort built by Tissaphernes in Miletus was surprised and taken by the Milesians, and the garrison in it turned out,—an act which met with the approval of the rest of the allies, and in particular of the Syracusans, but which found no favour with Lichas, who said moreover that the Milesians and the rest in the king's country ought to show a reasonable submission to Tissaphernes and to pay him court, until the war should be happily settled. The Milesians were angry with him for this and for other things of the kind, and upon his afterwards dying of sickness, would not allow him to be buried where the Lacedæmonians with the army desired.

The discontent of the army with Astyochus and Tissaphernes had reached this pitch, when Mindarus arrived from Lacedæmon to succeed Astyochus as admiral, and assumed the command. Astyochus now set sail for home; and Tissaphernes sent with him one of his confidants, Gaulites, a Carian, who spoke the two languages, to complain of the Milesians for the affair of the fort, and at the same time to defend himself against the Milesians, who were, as he was aware, on their way to Sparta chiefly to denounce his conduct, and had with them Hermocrates, who was to accuse Tissaphernes of joining with Alcibiades to ruin the Peloponnesian cause and of playing a double game. Indeed Hermocrates had always been at enmity with him about the pay not being restored in full; and eventually when he was banished from Syracuse, and new commanders, Potamis, Myscon, and Demarchus, had come out to Miletus to the ships of the Syracusans, Tissaphernes pressed harder than ever upon him in his exile, and among other charges against him accused him of having once asked him for money, and then given himself out as his enemy because he failed to obtain it.

While Astyochus and the Milesians and Hermocrates made sail for Lacedæmon, Alcibiades had now crossed back from Tissaphernes to Samos. After his return the envoys of the Four Hundred sent, as has been mentioned above, to pacify and explain matters to the forces at Samos, arrived from Delos; and an assembly was held in which they attempted to speak. The soldiers at first would not hear them, and cried out to put to death the subverters of the democracy, but at last, after some difficulty, calmed down and gave them a hearing. Upon this the envoys proceeded to inform them that the recent change had been made to save the city, and not to ruin it or to deliver it over to the enemy, for they had already had an opportunity of doing this when he invaded the country during their government; that all the Five Thousand would have their proper share in the government; and that their hearers' relatives had neither outrage, as Chæreas had slanderously reported, nor other ill-treatment to complain of, but were all in undisturbed enjoyment of their property

just as they had left them. Besides these they made a number
of other statements which had no better success with their
angry auditors; and amid a host of different opinions the one
which found most favour was that of sailing to Piræus. Now
it was that Alcibiades for the first time did the state a service,
and one of the most signal kind. For when the Athenians at
Samos were bent upon sailing against their countrymen, in
which case Ionia and the Hellespont would most certainly at
once have passed into possession of the enemy, Alcibiades
it was who prevented them. At that moment, when no other
man would have been able to hold back the multitude, he put
a stop to the intended expedition, and rebuked and turned
aside the resentment felt, on personal grounds, against the
envoys; he dismissed them with an answer from himself, to
the effect that he did not object to the government of the Five
Thousand, but insisted that the Four Hundred should be
deposed and the Council of Five Hundred reinstated in power:
meanwhile any retrenchments for economy, by which pay
might be better found for the armament, met with his entire
approval. Generally, he bade them hold out and show a bold
face to the enemy, since if the city were saved there was good
hope that the two parties might some day be reconciled,
whereas if either were once destroyed, that at Samos, or that
at Athens, there would no longer be any one to be reconciled
to. Meanwhile arrived envoys from the Argives, with offers of
support to the Athenian commons at Samos: these were
thanked by Alcibiades, and dismissed with a request to come
when called upon. The Argives were accompanied by the crew
of the Paralus, whom we left placed in a troopship by the
Four Hundred with orders to cruise round Eubœa, and who
being employed to carry to Lacedæmon some Athenian envoys
sent by the Four Hundred, Læspodias, Aristophon, and
Melesias, as they sailed by Argos laid hands upon the envoys,
and delivering them over to the Argives as the chief subverters
of the democracy, themselves, instead of returning to Athens,
took the Argive envoys on board, and came to Samos in the
galley which had been confided to them.

The same summer at the time that the return of Alcibiades
coupled with the general conduct of Tissaphernes had carried
to its height the discontent of the Peloponnesians, who no

longer entertained any doubt of his having joined the Athenians, Tissaphernes wishing, it would seem, to clear himself to them of these charges, prepared to go after the Phœnician fleet to Aspendus, and invited Lichas to go with him; saying that he would appoint Tamos as his lieutenant to provide pay for the armament during his own absence. Accounts differ, and it is not easy to ascertain with what intention he went to Aspendus, and did not bring the fleet after all. That one hundred and forty-seven Phœnician ships came as far as Aspendus is certain; but why they did not come on has been variously accounted for. Some think that he went away in pursuance of his plan of wasting the Peloponnesian resources, since at any rate Tamos, his lieutenant, far from being any better, proved a worse paymaster than himself: others that he brought the Phœnicians to Aspendus to exact money from them for their discharge, having never intended to employ them: others again that it was in view of the outcry against him at Lacedæmon, in order that it might be said that he was not in fault, but that the ships were really manned and that he had certainly gone to fetch them. To myself it seems only too evident that he did not bring up the fleet because he wished to wear out and paralyse the Hellenic forces, that is, to waste their strength by the time lost during his journey to Aspendus, and to keep them evenly balanced by not throwing his weight into either scale. Had he wished to finish the war, he could have done so, assuming of course that he made his appearance in a way which left no room for doubt; as by bringing up the fleet he would in all probability have given the victory to the Lacedæmonians, whose navy, even as it was, faced the Athenian more as an equal than as an inferior. But what convicts him most clearly, is the excuse which he put forward for not bringing the ships. He said that the number assembled was less than the king had ordered; but surely it would only have enhanced his credit if he spent little of the king's money and effected the same end at less cost. In any case, whatever was his intention, Tissaphernes went to Aspendus and saw the Phœnicians; and the Peloponnesians at his desire sent a Lacedæmonian called Philip with two galleys to fetch the fleet.

Alcibiades finding that Tissaphernes had gone to Aspendus,

himself sailed thither with thirteen ships, promising to do a great and certain service to the Athenians at Samos, as he would either bring the Phœnician fleet to the Athenians, or at all events prevent its joining the Peloponnesians. In all probability he had long known that Tissaphernes never meant to bring the fleet at all, and wished to compromise him as much as possible in the eyes of the Peloponnesians through his apparent friendship for himself and the Athenians, and thus in a manner to oblige him to join their side.

While Alcibiades weighed anchor and sailed eastward straight for Phaselis and Caunus, the envoys sent by the Four Hundred to Samos arrived at Athens. Upon their delivering the message from Alcibiades, telling them to hold out and to show a firm front to the enemy, and saying that he had great hopes of reconciling them with the army and of overcoming the Peloponnesians, the majority of the members of the oligarchy, who were already discontented and only too much inclined to be quit of the business in any safe way that they could, were at once greatly strengthened in their resolve. These now banded together and strongly criticised the administration, their leaders being some of the principal generals and men in office under the oligarchy, such as Theramenes, son of Hagnon, Aristocrates, son of Scellias, and others; who, although among the most prominent members of the government (being afraid, as they said, of the army at Samos, and most especially of Alcibiades, and also lest the envoys whom they had sent to Lacedæmon, might do the state some harm without the authority of the people), without insisting on objections to the excessive concentration of power in a few hands, yet urged that the Five Thousand must be shown to exist not merely in name but in reality, and the constitution placed upon a fairer basis. But this was merely their political cry; most of them being driven by private ambition into the line of conduct so surely fatal to oligarchies that arise out of democracies. For all at once pretend to be not only equals but each the chief and master of his fellows; while under a democracy a disappointed candidate accepts his defeat more easily, because he has not the humiliation of being beaten by his equals. But what most clearly encouraged the malcontents was the power of Alcibiades at Samos, and their own disbelief in the stability of the oligarchy; and it was now a race be-tween them as to which should first become the leader of the commons.

Meanwhile the leaders and members of the Four Hundred most opposed to a democratic form of government—Phryni-chus who had had the quarrel with Alcibiades during his com-mand at Samos, Aristarchus the bitter and inveterate enemy of the commons, and Pisander and Antiphon and others of the chiefs who already as soon as they entered upon power, and again when the army at Samos seceded from them and declared for a democracy, had sent envoys from their own body to Lacedæmon and made every effort for peace, and had built the wall in Eetionia,—now redoubled their exertions when their envoys returned from Samos, and they saw not only the people but their own most trusted associates turning against them. Alarmed at the state of things at Athens as at Samos, they now sent off in haste Antiphon and Phrynichus and ten others with injunctions to make peace with Lacedæ-mon upon any terms, no matter what, that should be at all tolerable. Meanwhile they pushed on more actively than ever with the wall in Eetionia. Now the meaning of this wall, according to Theramenes and his supporters, was not so much to keep out the army of Samos in case of its trying to force its way into Piræus as to be able to let in, at pleasure, the fleet and army of the enemy. For Eetionia is a mole of Piræus, close alongside of the entrance of the harbour, and was now fortified in connexion with the wall already existing on the land side, so that a few men placed in it might be able to command the entrance; the old wall on the land side and the new one now being built within on the side of the sea, both ending in one of the two towers standing at the narrow mouth of the harbour. They also walled off the largest porch in Piræus which was in immediate connexion with this wall, and kept it in their own hands, compelling all to unload there the corn that came into the harbour, and what they had in stock, and to take it out from thence when they sold it.

These measures had long provoked the murmurs of Thera-menes, and when the envoys returned from Lacedæmon with-out having effected any general pacification, he affirmed that this wall was like to prove the ruin of the state. At this moment

forty-two ships from Peloponnese, including some Siceliot
and Italiot vessels from Locri and Tarentum, had been invited
over by the Eubœans and were already riding off Las in
Laconia preparing for the voyage to Eubœa, under the command of Agesandridas, son of Agesander, a Spartan. Theramenes now affirmed that this squadron was destined not so
much to aid Eubœa as the party fortifying Eetionia, and that
unless precautions were speedily taken the city would be surprised and lost. This was no mere calumny, there being really
some such plan entertained by the accused. Their first wish
was to have the oligarchy without giving up the empire; failing this to keep their ships and walls and be independent;
while, if this also were denied them, sooner than be the first
victims of the restored democracy, they were resolved to call
in the enemy and make peace, give up their walls and ships,
and at all costs retain possession of the government, if their
lives were only assured to them.

For this reason they pushed forward the construction of
their work with posterns and entrances and means of intro-
ducing the enemy, being eager to have it finished in time.
Meanwhile the murmurs against them were at first confined
to a few persons and went on in secret, until Phrynichus, after
his return from the embassy to Lacedæmon, was laid wait for
and stabbed in full market by one of the *Peripoli*, falling down
dead before he had gone far from the council chamber. The
assassin escaped; but his accomplice, an Argive, was taken
and put to the torture by the Four Hundred, without their
being able to extract from him the name of his employer, or
anything further than that he knew of many men who used to
assemble at the house of the commander of the *Peripoli* and
at other houses. Here the matter was allowed to drop. This
so emboldened Theramenes and Aristocrates and the rest of
their partisans in the Four Hundred and out of doors, that
they now resolved to act. For by this time the ships had sailed
round from Las, and anchoring at Epidaurus had overrun
Ægina; and Theramenes asserted that, being bound for
Eubœa, they would never have sailed in to Ægina and come
back to anchor at Epidaurus, unless they had been invited to
come to aid in the designs of which he had always accused the
government. Further inaction had therefore now become im-

possible. In the end, after a great many seditious harangues and suspicions, they set to work in real earnest. The heavy infantry in Piræus building the wall in Eetionia, among whom was Aristocrates, a colonel, with his own tribe, laid hands upon Alexicles, a general under the oligarchy and the devoted adherent of the cabal, and took him into a house and confined him there. In this they were assisted by one Hermon, commander of the *Peripoli* in Munychia, and others, and above all had with them the great bulk of the heavy infantry. As soon as the news reached the Four Hundred, who happened to be sitting in the council chamber, all except the disaffected wished at once to go to the posts where the arms were, and menaced Theramenes and his party. Theramenes defended himself, and said that he was ready immediately to go and help to rescue Alexicles; and taking with him one of the generals belonging to his party, went down to Piræus, followed by Aristarchus and some young men of the cavalry. All was now panic and confusion. Those in the city imagined that Piræus was already taken and the prisoner put to death, while those in Piræus expected every moment to be attacked by the party in the city. The older men, however, stopped the persons running up and down the town and making for the stands of arms; and Thucydides the Pharsalian, *Proxenus* of the city, came forward and threw himself in the way of the rival factions, and appealed to them not to ruin the state, while the enemy was still at hand waiting for his opportunity, and so at length succeeded in quieting them and in keeping their hands off each other. Meanwhile Theramenes came down to Piræus, being himself one of the generals, and raged and stormed against the heavy infantry, while Aristarchus and the adversaries of the people were angry in right earnest. Most of the heavy infantry, however, went on with the business without faltering, and asked Theramenes if he thought the wall had been constructed for any good purpose, and whether it would not be better that it should be pulled down. To this he answered that if they thought it best to pull it down, he for his part agreed with them. Upon this the heavy infantry and a number of the people in Piræus immediately got up on the fortification and began to demolish it. Now their cry to the multitude was that all should join in the work who wished the

Five Thousand to govern instead of the Four Hundred. For instead of saying in so many words 'all who wished the commons to govern,' they still disguised themselves under the name of the Five Thousand; being afraid that these might really exist, and that they might be speaking to one of their number and get into trouble through ignorance. Indeed this was why the Four Hundred neither wished the Five Thousand to exist, nor to have it known that they did not exist; being of opinion that to give themselves so many partners in empire would be downright democracy, while the mystery in question would make the people afraid of one another.

The next day the Four Hundred, although alarmed, nevertheless assembled in the council chamber, while the heavy infantry in Piræus, after having released their prisoner Alexicles and pulled down the fortification, went with their arms to the theatre of Dionysus, close to Munychia, and there held an assembly in which they decided to march into the city, and setting forth accordingly halted in the Anaceum. Here they were joined by some delegates from the Four Hundred, who reasoned with them one by one, and persuaded those whom they saw to be the most moderate to remain quiet themselves, and to keep in the rest; saying that they would make known the Five Thousand, and have the Four Hundred chosen from them in rotation, as should be decided by the Five Thousand, and meanwhile entreated them not to ruin the state or drive it into the arms of the enemy. After a great many had spoken and had been spoken to, the whole body of heavy infantry became calmer than before, absorbed by their fears for the country at large, and now agreed to hold upon an appointed day an assembly in the theatre of Dionysus for the restoration of concord.

When the day came for the assembly in the theatre, and they were upon the point of assembling, news arrived that the forty-two ships under Agesandridas were sailing from Megara along the coast of Salamis. The people to a man now thought that it was just what Theramenes and his party had so often said, that the ships were sailing to the fortification, and concluded that they had done well to demolish it. But though it may possibly have been by appointment that Agesandridas hovered about Epidaurus and the neighbourhood, he would also naturally be kept there by the hope of an opportunity arising out of the troubles in the town. In any case the Athenians, on receipt of the news, immediately ran down in mass to Piræus, seeing themselves threatened by the enemy with a worse war than their war among themselves, not at a distance, but close to the harbour of Athens. Some went on board the ships already afloat, while others launched fresh vessels, or ran to defend the walls and the mouth of the harbour.

Meanwhile the Peloponnesian vessels sailed by, and rounding Sunium anchored between Thoricus and Prasiæ, and afterwards arrived at Oropus. The Athenians, with revolution in the city, and unwilling to lose a moment in going to the relief of their most important possession (for Eubœa was everything to them now that they were shut out from Attica), were compelled to put to sea in haste and with untrained crews, and sent Thymochares with some vessels to Eretria. These upon their arrival, with the ships already in Eubœa, made up a total of thirty-six vessels, and were immediately forced to engage. For Agesandridas, after his crews had dined, put out from Oropus, which is about seven miles from Eretria by sea; and the Athenians, seeing him sailing up, immediately began to man their vessels. The sailors, however, instead of being by their ships, as they supposed, were gone away to purchase provisions for their dinner in the houses in the outskirts of the town; the Eretrians having so arranged that there should be nothing on sale in the market-place, in order that the Athenians might be a long time in manning their ships, and the enemy's attack taking them by surprise, might be compelled to put to sea just as they were. A signal also was raised in Eretria to give them notice in Oropus when to put to sea. The Athenians, forced to put out so poorly prepared, engaged off the harbour of Eretria, and after holding their own for some little while notwithstanding, were at length put to flight and chased to the shore. Such of their number as took refuge in Eretria, which they presumed to be friendly to them, found their fate in that city, being butchered by the inhabitants; while those who fled to the Athenian fort in the Eretrian territory, and the vessels which got to Chalcis, were saved. The Peloponnesians, after taking twenty-two Athenian ships, and killing or making prisoners of the crews, set up a trophy, and not long afterwards effected the revolt of the whole of Eubœa (except Oreus, which was held by the Athenians themselves), and made a general settlement of the affairs of the island.

When the news of what had happened in Eubœa reached Athens a panic ensued such as they had never before known. Neither the disaster in Sicily, great as it seemed at the time, nor any other had ever so much alarmed them. The camp at Samos was in revolt; they had no more ships or men to man them; they were at discord among themselves and might at any moment come to blows; and a disaster of this magnitude coming on the top of all, by which they lost their fleet, and worst of all Eubœa, which was of more value to them than Attica, could not occur without throwing them into the deepest despondency. Meanwhile their greatest and most immediate trouble was the possibility that the enemy, emboldened by his victory, might make straight for them and sail against Piræus, which they had no longer ships to defend; and every moment they expected him to arrive. This, with a little more courage, he might easily have done, in which case he would either have increased the dissensions of the city by his presence, or if he had stayed to besiege it have compelled the fleet from Ionia, although the enemy of the oligarchy, to come to the rescue of their country and of their relatives, and in the meantime would have become master of the Hellespont, Ionia, the islands, and of everything as far as Eubœa, or, to speak roundly, of the whole Athenian empire. But here, as on so many other occasions the Lacedæmonians proved the most convenient people in the world for the Athenians to be at war with. The wide difference between the two characters, the slowness and want of energy of the Lacedæmonians as contrasted with the dash and enterprise of their opponents, proved of the greatest service, especially to a maritime empire like Athens. Indeed this was shown by the Syracusans, who were most like the Athenians in character, and also most successful in combating them.

Nevertheless, upon receipt of the news, the Athenians manned twenty ships and called immediately a first assembly in the Pnyx, where they had been used to meet formerly, and deposed the Four Hundred and voted to hand over the gov-

ernment to the Five Thousand, of which body all who furnished a suit of armour were to be members, decreeing also
that no one should receive pay for the discharge of any office,
or if he did should be held accursed. Many other assemblies
were held afterwards, in which law-makers were elected and
all other measures taken to form a constitution. It was during
the first period of this constitution that the Athenians appear
to have enjoyed the best government that they ever did, at
least in my time. For the fusion of the high and the low was
effected with judgment, and this was what first enabled the
state to raise up her head after her manifold disasters. They
also voted for the recall of Alcibiades and of other exiles, and
sent to him and to the camp at Samos, and urged them to devote themselves vigorously to the war.

Upon this revolution taking place, the party of Pisander
and Alexicles, and the chiefs of the oligarchs immediately
withdrew to Decelea, with the single exception of Aristarchus,
one of the generals, who hastily took some of the most barbarian of the archers and marched to Œnoe. This was a fort
of the Athenians upon the Bœotian border, at that moment
besieged by the Corinthians, irritated by the loss of a party
returning from Decelea, who had been cut off by the garrison.
The Corinthians had volunteered for this service, and had
called upon the Bœotians to assist them. After communicating
with them, Aristarchus deceived the garrison in Œnoe by
telling them that their countrymen in the city had compounded
with the Lacedæmonians, and that one of the terms of the
capitulation was that they must surrender the place to the
Bœotians. The garrison believed him as he was general, and
besides knew nothing of what had occurred owing to the
siege, and so evacuated the fort under truce. In this way the
Bœotians gained possession of Œnoe, and the oligarchy and
the troubles at Athens ended.

To return to the Peloponnesians in Miletus. No pay was
forthcoming from any of the agents deputed by Tissaphernes
for that purpose upon his departure for Aspendus; neither the
Phœnician fleet nor Tissaphernes showed any signs of appearing, and Philip, who had been sent with him, and another
Spartan, Hippocrates, who was at Phaselis, wrote word to
Mindarus, the admiral, that the ships were not coming at all,

and that they were being grossly abused by Tissaphernes.
Meanwhile Pharnabazus was inviting them to come, and making every effort to get the fleet and, like Tissaphernes, to cause
the revolt of the cities in his government still subject to
Athens, founding great hopes on his success; until at length,
at about the period of the summer which we have now reached,
Mindarus yielded to his importunities, and, with great order
and at a moment's notice, in order to elude the enemy at
Samos, weighed anchor with seventy-three ships from Miletus
and set sail for the Hellespont. Thither sixteen vessels had
already preceded him in the same summer, and had overrun
part of the Chersonese. Being caught in a storm, Mindarus
was compelled to run in to Icarus, and after being detained five
or six days there by stress of weather, arrived at Chios.

Meanwhile Thrasyllus had heard of his having put out from
Miletus, and immediately set sail with fifty-five ships from
Samos, in haste to arrive before him in the Hellespont. But
learning that he was at Chios, and expecting that he would
stay there, he posted scouts in Lesbos and on the continent
opposite to prevent the fleet moving without his knowing it,
and himself coasted along to Methymna, and gave orders to
prepare meal and other necessaries, in order to attack them
from Lesbos in the event of their remaining for any length of
time at Chios. Meanwhile he resolved to sail against Eresus,
a town in Lesbos which had revolted, and, if he could, to take
it. For some of the principal Methymnian exiles had carried
over about fifty heavy infantry, their sworn associates, from
Cuma, and hiring others from the continent, so as to make up
three hundred in all, chose Anaxander, a Theban, to command
them, on account of the community of blood existing between
the Thebans and the Lesbians, and first attacked Methymna.
Baulked in this attempt by the advance of the Athenian guards
from Mitylene, and repulsed a second time in a battle outside
the city, they then crossed the mountain and effected the revolt of Eresus. Thrasyllus accordingly determined to go there
with all his ships and to attack the place. Meanwhile Thrasybulus had preceded him thither with five ships from Samos,
as soon as he heard that the exiles had crossed over, and coming too late to save Eresus, went on and anchored before the
town. Here they were joined also by two vessels on their way

home from the Hellespont, and by the ships of the Methymnians, making a grand total of sixty-seven vessels; and the forces on board now made ready with engines and every other means available to do their utmost to storm Eresus.

In the meantime Mindarus and the Peloponnesian fleet at Chios, after taking provisions for two days and receiving three Chian pieces of money for each man from the Chians, on the third day put out in haste from the island; in order to avoid falling in with the ships at Eresus, they did not make for the open sea, but keeping Lesbos on their left, sailed for the continent. After touching at the port of Carteria, in the Phocæid, and dining, they went on along the Cumæan coast and supped at Arginusæ, on the continent over against Mitylene. From thence they continued their voyage along the coast, although it was late in the night, and arriving at Harmatus on the continent opposite Methymna, dined there; and swiftly passing Lectum, Larisa, Hamaxitus, and the neighbouring towns, arrived a little before midnight at Rhœteum. Here they were now in the Hellespont. Some of the ships also put in at Sigeum and at other places in the neighbourhood.

Meanwhile the warnings of the fire-signals and the sudden increase in the number of fires on the enemy's shore informed the eighteen Athenian ships at Sestos of the approach of the Peloponnesian fleet. That very night they set sail in haste just as they were, and hugging the shore of the Chersonese, coasted along to Elæus, in order to sail out into the open sea away from the fleet of the enemy. After passing unobserved the sixteen ships at Abydos, which had nevertheless been warned by their approaching friends to be on the alert to prevent their sailing out, at dawn they sighted the fleet of Mindarus, which immediately gave chase. All had not time to get away; the greater number however escaped to Imbros and Lemnos, while four of the hindmost were overtaken off Elæus. One of these was stranded opposite to the temple of Protesilaus and taken with its crew, two others without their crews; the fourth was abandoned on the shore of Imbros and burned by the enemy.

After this the Peloponnesians were joined by the squadron from Abydos, which made up their fleet to a grand total of eighty-six vessels; they spent the day in unsuccessfully besieging Elæus, and then sailed back to Abydos. Meanwhile the Athenians, deceived by their scouts, and never dreaming of the enemy's fleet getting by undetected, were tranquilly besieging Eresus. As soon as they heard the news they instantly abandoned Eresus, and made with all speed for the Hellespont, and after taking two of the Peloponnesian ships which had been carried out too far into the open sea in the ardour of the pursuit and now fell in their way, the next day dropped anchor at Elæus, and bringing back the ships that had taken refuge at Imbros, during five days prepared for the coming engagement.

After this they engaged in the following way. The Athenians formed in column and sailed close along shore to Sestos; upon perceiving which the Peloponnesians put out from Abydos to meet them. Realising that a battle was now imminent, both combatants extended their flank; the Athenians along the Chersonese from Idacus to Arrhiani with seventy-six ships; the Peloponnesians from Abydos to Dardanus with eighty-six. The Peloponnesian right wing was occupied by the Syracusans, their left by Mindarus in person with the best sailers in the navy; the Athenian left by Thrasyllus, their right by Thrasybulus, the other commanders being in different parts of the fleet. The Peloponnesians hastened to engage first, and outflanking with their left the Athenian right sought to cut them off, if possible, from sailing out of the straits, and to drive their centre upon the shore, which was not far off. The Athenians perceiving their intention extended their own wing and outsailed them, while their left had by this time passed the point of Cynossema. This, however, obliged them to thin and weaken their centre, especially as they had fewer ships than the enemy, and as the coast round Point Cynossema formed a sharp angle which prevented their seeing what was going on on the other side of it.

The Peloponnesians now attacked their centre and drove ashore the ships of the Athenians, and disembarked to follow up their victory. No help could be given to the centre either by the squadron of Thrasybulus on the right, on account of the number of ships attacking him, or by that of Thrasyllus on the left, from whom the point of Cynossema hid what was going on, and who was also hindered by his Syracusan and other opponents, whose numbers were fully equal to his own.

At length, however, the Peloponnesians in the confidence of victory began to scatter in pursuit of the ships of the enemy, and allowed a considerable part of their fleet to get into disorder. On seeing this the squadron of Thrasybulus discontinued their lateral movement and, facing about, attacked and routed the ships opposed to them, and next fell roughly upon the scattered vessels of the victorious Peloponnesian division, and put most of them to flight without a blow. The Syracusans also had by this time given way before the squadron of Thrasyllus, and now openly took to flight upon seeing the flight of their comrades.

The rout was now complete. Most of the Peloponnesians fled for refuge first to the river Midius, and afterwards to Abydos. Only a few ships were taken by the Athenians; as owing to the narrowness of the Hellespont the enemy had not far to go to be in safety. Nevertheless nothing could have been more opportune for them than this victory. Up to this time they had feared the Peloponnesian fleet, owing to a number of petty losses and to the disaster in Sicily; but they now ceased to mistrust themselves or any longer to think their enemies good for anything at sea. Meanwhile they took from the enemy eight Chian vessels, five Corinthian, two Ambraciot, two Bœotian, one Leucadian, Lacedæmonian, Syracusan, and Pellenian, losing fifteen of their own. After setting up a trophy upon Point Cynossema, securing the wrecks, and restoring to the enemy his dead under truce, they sent off a galley to Athens with the news of their victory. The arrival of this vessel with its unhoped-for good news, after the recent disasters of Eubœa, and in the revolution at Athens, gave fresh courage to the Athenians, and caused them to believe that if they put their shoulders to the wheel their cause might yet prevail.

On the fourth day after the sea-fight the Athenians in Sestos having hastily refitted their ships sailed against Cyzicus, which had revolted. Off Harpagium and Priapus they sighted at anchor the eight vessels from Byzantium, and sailing up and routing the troops on shore, took the ships, and then went on and recovered the town of Cyzicus, which was unfortified, and levied money from the citizens. In the meantime the Peloponnesians sailed from Abydos to Elæus, and recovered such of

their captured galleys as were still uninjured, the rest having
been burned by the Elæusians, and sent Hippocrates and
Epicles to Eubœa to fetch the squadron from that island.

About the same time Alcibiades returned with his thirteen
ships from Caunus and Phaselis to Samos, bringing word that
he had prevented the Phœnician fleet from joining the
Peloponnesians, and had made Tissaphernes more friendly to
the Athenians than before. Alcibiades now manned nine more
ships, and levied large sums of money from the Halicarnas-
sians, and fortified Cos. After doing this and placing a governor in Cos, he sailed back to Samos, autumn being now at
hand. Meanwhile Tissaphernes, upon hearing that the
Peloponnesian fleet had sailed from Miletus to the Hellespont,
set off again back from Aspendus, and made all sail for Ionia.
While the Peloponnesians were in the Hellespont, the Antandrians, a people of Æolic extraction, conveyed by land
across Mount Ida some heavy infantry from Abydos, and introduced them into the town; having been ill-treated by
Arsaces, the Persian lieutenant of Tissaphernes. This same
Arsaces had, upon pretence of a secret quarrel, invited the
chief men of the Delians to undertake military service (these
were Delians who had settled at Atramyttium after having
been driven from their homes by the Athenians for the sake
of purifying Delos); and after drawing them out from their
town as his friends and allies, had laid wait for them at dinner,
and surrounded them and caused them to be shot down by his
soldiers. This deed made the Antandrians fear that he might
some day do them some mischief; and as he also laid upon
them burdens too heavy for them to bear, they expelled his
garrison from their citadel.

Tissaphernes upon hearing of this act of the Peloponnesians
in addition to what had occurred at Miletus and Cuidus,
where his garrisons had been also expelled, now saw that the
breach between them was serious; and fearing further injury
from them, and being also vexed to think that Pharnabazus
should receive them, and in less time and at less cost perhaps
succeed better against Athens than he had done, determined
to rejoin them in the Hellespont, in order to complain of the
events at Antandros and excuse himself as best he could in the

matter of the Phœnician fleet and of the other charges against him. Accordingly he went first to Ephesus and offered sacrifice to Artemis.

[When the winter after this summer is over the twenty-first year of this war will be completed.]

THE END

The Best of the World's Best Books
COMPLETE LIST OF TITLES IN
THE MODERN LIBRARY

MISCELLANEOUS

DATE DUE